INDEX TO THE 1820 CENSUS OF TENNESSEE

Compiled by

ELIZABETH PETTY BENTLEY

CLEARFIELD

Reprinted for
Clearfield Company, Inc. by
Genealogical Publishing Co., Inc.
Baltimore, Maryland
1992, 1996, 1999

Library of Congress Catalogue Card Number 81-81537
International Standard Book Number: 0-8063-0946-6

Made in the United States of America

FOREWORD

This index is an alphabetical list of the heads of households in the 1820 Federal Census of Tennessee. First the family name of the head of household is given, followed by his Christian name, then his county of residence (abbreviated), and finally the page number of the census schedule. Table I, in the front matter, contains a list of the counties, the abbreviations used in this index, and the roll number of the National Archives' microfilm copy of the census. Table II lists the counties in the order they appear on the census film, the page numbers covered, and other information essential to the reader.

The researcher will undoubtedly want to consult the original source material because of the additional information it contains. Microfilm copies of the census may be purchased from the Publication Sales Branch (NATS), National Archives (GSA), Washington, D.C. 20408. Their catalogue lists the Tennessee 1820 returns as Microcopy 33, rolls 122-125. The microfilm may also be obtained on interlibrary loan from the Regional Branches of the National Archives. For the address of the branch serving your region, request the National Archives' free pamphlet, GS DC 75-8250. The branch libraries of the Church of Jesus Christ of Latter-day Saints can also order microfilm copies of the census to be viewed at their locations. For the address of the branch nearest you, write to The Genealogical Department, 50 E. North Temple, Salt Lake City, Utah 84150. Photocopies of single pages may be obtained from either of these agencies.

Along with the name of the head of household, in the original census, the following thirty-two columns were filled in with an appropriate entry by the enumerator, left to right: free white males under 10 years of age, of 10 years and under 16, between 16 and 18, of 16 and under 26 (including heads of families), of 26 and under 45 (inc. heads), of 45 and upwards (inc. heads), followed by five age categories for free white females (the same as for males except for the 16-18 category), foreigners not naturalized, number of persons engaged in agriculture, in commerce, in manufacturing, male slaves under 14, of 14 years and under 26, of 26 and under 45, of 45 and upwards, followed by the same four age groups for female slaves and free colored persons (both male and female), and finally all other persons except Indians not taxed. These headings do not always appear at the top of every page.

The Tennessee 1820 films are generally clear and legible. Note, however, that in order to verify those few entries which are not clear it is becoming increasingly difficult to obtain access to the bound photostatic copies available in the Central Search Room of the National Archives in Washington. The photostats may be viewed only if written confirmation of the film's inadequacies is obtained from personnel in charge of the microfilm reading room. It should be noted that the film copies were made from the original returns held by the Industrial and Social Department of the Archives. Some tears in the originals may have occurred between the time the photostats and the films were made. Unfortunately, some indistinct names on the photostats have been written over in ink, presumably by staff members having access to the originals. Some of their interpretations are open to serious question. Also, the page numbers on the film, even the order of the pages, may not be the same in the photostatic volumes.

Every effort has been made, using both the film and the photostatic copies, to interpret illegible names. No visible entry, including names which were crossed out, has been intentionally omitted from this index. When one or more illegible letters has been omitted, the gap is filled with ellipses (...), for example ...*nson*, which appears before names beginning with *A* even though it might be Hanson or Johnson. Totally illegible surnames appear before the partially visible ones, and these are preceded by entries for which no surname was given. The latter are designated by a dash (—).

In the case of questionable interpretations of handwriting I have tried to include cross references to alternative index entries. For example, "Hull see Hall" alerts the reader to possible confusion about the surname. In compiling this index I have intentionally refrained from consulting other published indexes of these same returns in order to preserve the integrity of the work, but I recommend them for other possible interpretations. The reader should further note that since *I* and *J* are practically indistinguishable when written as initials in the old script, they have been consistently indexed as *J*. Abbreviations have been transcribed as they appear except for superscript abbreviations such as $W^{\underline{m}}$ which have been rendered Wm. for ease in typing.

Cross reference notations in this index also refer the reader to various phonetic spellings. The enumerator may have made no attempt whatever to discover the correct spelling of a name, simply spelling it as he heard it pronounced. I have scrupulously avoided any alteration of spellings, so the researcher should try to imagine all possible misinterpretations in sound as well as mistakes in my own transcription.

There are many reasons why a particular individual might not appear in the census. Among others, the reader will note that the returns of several counties are missing (mostly in eastern Tennessee). Then, since the 1820 Federal Census listed only heads of families by name, other family members do not appear in the returns. Also, an individual may be counted among a family of a different surname as a boarder, employee, student, or visitor. He may have avoided enumeration out of fear or superstition, or he may simply have been left out because of his remote residence or temporary absence from home.

Thanks are due to my family, who constantly encourage me in my work, and to Mr. William Leeson, who spent countless hours perfecting the computer program used to compile this list. Again, thanks to Dr. Michael Tepper, editor-in-chief of the Genealogical Publishing Company, for his confidence in me and his seemingly inexhaustible patience.

Elizabeth Petty Bentley

TABLE I

County	Abbreviation	Roll no.
Anderson		missing
Bedford	Bed	122
Bledsoe		missing
Blount		missing
Campbell		missing
Carter		missing
Claiborne		missing
Cocke		missing
Davidson	Dav	122
Dickson	Dic	123
Franklin	Fra	123
Giles	Gil	124
Grainger		missing
Greene		missing
Hamilton		missing
Hardin	Har	122
Hawkins		missing
Hickman	Hic	122
Humphreys	Hum	122
Jackson	Jac	123
Jefferson		missing
Knox		missing
Lawrence	Law	123
Lincoln	Lin	123
Marion		missing
Maury	Mau	124

County	Abbreviation	Roll no.
McMinn		missing
Monroe		missing
Montgomery	Mon	122
Morgan		missing
Overton	Ove	122
Perry	Per	122
Rhea		missing
Roane		missing
Robertson	Rob	125
Rutherford	Rut	124
Sevier		missing
Shelby	She	124
Smith	Smi	125
Stewart	Ste	124
Sullivan		missing
Sumner	Sum	124
Warren	War	122
Washington		missing
Wayne	Way	122
White	Whi	122
Williamson	Wll	125
Wilson	Wil	122

TABLE II

ROLL 122

Bedford Co., pp. 1-54 lower right, double facing pages.

Davidson Co., pp. 57-98 lower right, double facing pages. Corporation or City of Nashville, pp. 75 pt. - 80 pt.; suburbs of Nashville or county outside Nashville, pp. 80 pt. - 89 pt. (may extend to p. 98).

Hardin Co., pp. 1-11 (slightly out of order, 1, 2, 3, 5, 4, 7, 6, 8, 9, 10, 11).

Hickman Co., pp. 1-25 middle left.

Humphreys Co., pp. 1-14 upper left.

Montgomery Co., pp. 1-33 upper left.

Overton Co., pp. 1-20 upper left (underlined). Monroe, p. 20 pt.; Hilham, p. 20 pt.

Perry Co., pp. 1-8 upper left.

Warren Co., pp. 278-320 upper right.

Wayne Co., pp. 1-21 upper left (slightly out of order: 1, 2, 3, 5, 6, 4, 7, 9, 10, 8, 11, 13, 14, 12, 15, 16, 19, 20, 21, 22, 17, 18).

White Co., pp. 340-372 upper right, double facing pages.

Wilson Co., pp. 375-420 upper right (and pp. 111-115 which are a manufacturing schedule which exists only in the photostatic copies, not in the film). Lebanon, p. 391; Statesville, p. 418 pt.

ROLL 123

Dickson Co., pp. 1-17 upper left.

Franklin Co., pp. 1-36 upper left, double facing pages (p. 29 is missing on some copies of the film; pp. 16 and 17 are only single pages; the two double pages between p. 3 and p. 4 are indexed as pp. 35 and 36; and the enumerator on the unnumbered final page is indexed as p. 34).

Jackson Co., pp. 1-28 upper left.

Lawrence Co., pp. 1-14 upper left.

Lincoln Co., pp. 1-48 upper left, double facing pages. Fayetteville, pp. 1-2.

ROLL 124

Giles Co., pp. 2-23 middle right, double facing pages. Pulaski, p. 16 pt., p. 17 pt., and p. 18 pt. (denoted by ditto marks).

Maury Co., pp. 24-70 middle right, double facing pages. Columbia, pp. 58 pt. - 59 pt.; Williamsport, p. 60 pt.

Rutherford Co., pp. 73-105 middle right, double facing pages. Murfreesborough, pp. 73-74.

Shelby Co., pp. 106-107 upper right.

Stewart Co., pp. 109-131 middle right, double facing pages.

Sumner Co., pp. 134-186 middle right, double facing pages. Gallatin, pp. 135-137 pt.

ROLL 125

Robertson Co., pp. 1-36 upper right side (p. 36 is unnumbered and lists manufacturers). Springfield, p. 1.

Smith Co., pp. 1-63 right edge.

Williamson Co., pp. 0-66 upper left. Town of Franklin, pp. 1-3.

INDEX TO THE 1820 CENSUS OF TENNESSEE

——, —— 58 Mau
Andrew 86 Rut
Free Anthony 65 Dav
Free Kelley 8 Jac
Hannah 341 Whi
Scipio 12 Gil
..., ... 24 Mau
... 1 Per
Charles 281 War
...nson, Merrel 2 Bed
...pton, ... 63 Dav
...t, ... M. 61 Dav

--- A ---

Aairhart, Catharine 58 Dav
Aaron, Moses 17 Bed
Aatkison, Polly 88 Dav
Abanatha, Littleton 25 Mau
see Abnatha
Abbetts, George 3 Smi
Abbot, Isaac 27 Mon
Abbott, David 98 Rut
John 23 Lin
Spencer W. 22 Way
Sterlin 33 Lin
William 22 Way
Abbutt, Allumbee 138 Sum
George 138 Sum
James 137 Sum
John 138 Sum
Abel, Alexander 18 Lin
James 18 Lin
John 18 Lin
Joseph 18 Lin
William 7 Lin
Wm. C. 3 Lin
Abell, Jeremiah 26 Lin
Abeney, Elias 11 Dic
Abernathey, Aaron 296 War
Abernathy, Alan 14 Gil
Buckner 22 Gil
Burwell 8 Gil
Charles 89 Dav
Charles C. 2 Gil
David 89 Dav
David 10 Gil
Elisha 10 Gil
Elizabeth 15 Gil
Freeman 89 Dav
Abernathy (cont.)
James 10 Gil
John 4 Gil
John 22 Gil
Joseph 10 Gil
Laban 89 Dav
Labon 91 Dav
Sterling 9 Gil
Thomas E. 8 Gil
William 4 Gil
see Abanatha, Abmatha
Abernethy, Robert 4 Lin
Smith 19 Lin
Able, William 5 Ove
Abmatha, Mark 407 Wil
Abnatha, D. 24 Mau
David 28 Mau
see Abernathy
Abner, George 1 Jac
Isaac 305 War
Abney, John 5 Gil
Nathl. 111 Ste
Rhoda 11 Dic
see Abeney
Abshear, Thomas 49 Mau
Absher, Isaac 361 Whi
Abston, Merry C. 137 Sum
Acarter see Carter
Achley see Ashley
Ackeson, Henry 129 Ste
Acklin, Christopher 1 Fra
Crirstopher 87 Rut
Acles see Aeles 23 Rob
Aclin, Alexander 394 Wil
Acre, Abraham 138 Sum
Dandridge 80 Rut
Hendly 114 Ste
Jesse 114 Ste
Jno. R. 115 Ste
John 114 Ste
Acrers, William 28 Jac
Actkinson, Henry 356 Whi
Martha 347 Whi
Acuff, Elizabeth 14 Dic
Isaac 40 Mau
John 9 Lin
Margaret 9 Lin
Acup, Christopher 344 Whi
Henry 1 Smi
Adair, Jacob 1 Law
James 346 Whi
John 20 Hic

Adair (cont.)		
William	345	Whi
Adams, ...	1	Fra
Aaron	1	Smi
Able	13	Bed
Abraham	2	Smi
Allen	1	Smi
Archibald	37	Bed
Avy	10	Mon
Breaton	24	Wll
Daniel	2	Smi
David	9	Mon
David	51	Wll
Edwin H.	13	Mon
Elijah	2	Smi
Eliza.	81	Dav
Elizabeth	18	Mon
George	14	Bed
George	16	Dic
George	103	Rut
George	311	War
George W.	1	Fra
Henry	1	Smi
Hodge	5	Per
Hugh	6	Gil
Isbel	]	Fra
Jacob	2	Smi
Jacob	56	Wll
James	37	Bed
James	68	Dav
James	4	Law
James	16	Mon
James	90	Rut
James	376	Wil
James	416	Wil
James	49	Wll
Jane	105	Rut
Jesse	1	Smi
John	15	Bed
John	6	Dic
John	2	Fra
John	23	Gil
John	14	Hum
John	5	Mon
John	9	Mon
John	1	Smi
John	137	Sum
John	298	War
John	14	Wll
John, Sen.	2	Fra
Jonathan	23	Gil
Laborn	49	Wll
Lewis	138	Sum
Luke	8	Gil
Margaret	8	Lin
Martha	80	Dav
Martha	15	Lin
Martin	1	Fra
Milley	25	Mon
Moses	76	Dav
Nancy	8	Dic
Nancy	9	Gil
Nathan	5	Rob
Adams (cont.)		
Nathan	4	Wll
Richard	8	Hum
Richd.	29	Mon
Robert	49	Bed
Robert	2	Gil
Robert H.	79	Dav
Samuel	13	Lin
Samuel F.	2	Fra
Sarah	8	Hum
Solomon	1	Smi
Sylvanus	31	Lin
Sylvester, Jr.	8	Hum
Sylvester, Sr.	9	Hum
Thomas	1	Fra
Thomas	49	Wll
Thos.	16	Mon
Wilea	23	Wll
William	2	Fra
William	23	Mon
William	4	Rob
William	103	Rut
William	104	Rut
William	8	Way
William	349	Whi
William	112	Wil
William	384	Wil
William, Jr.	4	Rob
William, Jr.	413	Wil
William, Ser.	413	Wil
Williamson	78	Dav
Wm.	138	Sum
Adcock, Carter	23	Rob
David	304	War
Harmon	88	Rut
Henderson	88	Rut
Henry	23	Rob
Isaac	303	War
Isaac	315	War
James	1	Smi
John	75	Rut
John	310	War
John	315	War
Leonard	290	War
William	27	Bed
William	87	Rut
William	310	War
Willie	88	Rut
Addams, John	43	Mau
Martha	65	Dav
Thomas	43	Mau
Thomas P.	75	Dav
William	43	Mau
Addington, Hardy	30	Lin
Addison, Jesse	412	Wil
Jesse, Sen.	412	Wil
Joseph	412	Wil
Simon	412	Wil
Wells	412	Wil
Addock, John	89	Dav
Adear, Christeeney	50	Mau
Adkins, Drury	9	Dic
Jane	62	Mau

Adkins (cont.)		
John	33	Lin
Joseph	26	Bed
Joseph	32	Lin
William	291	War
Adkinson, Benj.	80	Dav
Jerdan	29	Mau
John	18	Way
John B.	9	Dic
Joseph	18	Way
Adkisn, Jesse	59	Mau
Adkison, William	59	Mau
see Adkisn		
Ady, Walter	22	Gil
Aeirt, Elizabeth	57	Dav
Aeles, Abraham	23	Rob
Aelis, John	376	Wil
Aexander, John	311	War
Rankin	40	Mau
Afflick, John	114	Wil
Agee, Jonathan	2	Smi
Agen, Barnaby	65	Mau
Agent, Celia	104	Rut
Agin, Moses	104	Rut
Ahart, Jacob	2	Fra
James	2	Fra
John	1	Fra
Aidlett, Ann	21	Hic
Joseph	21	Hic
Aikin, Jane	101	Rut
Aims, Hardy	389	Wil
Thomas	389	Wil
Ainsworth, Joseph	138	Sum
Airhart, Abraham	57	Dav
Jacob	57	Dav
Rodney	71	Dav
see Aairhart, Aeirt		
Aken, Burl	55	Mau
Lucracy	57	Mau
Samuel	10	Wll
Samuel	48	Wll
Zekial	54	Mau
Akens, John	1	Smi
John H.	1	Fra
Aker, Peter	11	Hum
Akers, Peter	41	Mau
Uriah	7	Law
Akin, John	33	Mau
John	16	Way
Robbart H.	33	Mau
Saml.	9	Hic
William	35	Mau
Akins, George	101	Rut
Henry	100	Rut
John	5	Gil
Samuel	34	Mau
Thomas	10	Gil
Alagood, Elisha	55	Wll
Alairson, James	137	Sum
Alason, William	70	Mau
William B.	70	Mau
Alaway, Enock	60	Mau
Alberson, Early	20	Way

Albertson, Arthur	8	Lin
Early	17	Ove
John	5	Ove
Solomon	18	Ove
Albright, John	32	Mon
Alcorn, John	406	Wil
Alderson, James	138	Sum
John S.	57	Mau
Simon	127	Ste
Wm.	138	Sum
Aldridge, Clement	111	Ste
John	88	Rut
Nathan	42	Wll
William	32	Mau
Alee, Charles	2	Smi
Aler, John	2	Fra
Aleson, Armsard	61	Mau
John D.	70	Mau
Alesworth, George	346	Whi
Alexander, Abdon	59	Mau
Abner	415	Wil
Allen	311	War
Andrew	65	Mau
Arthur M.	18	Way
Benjamin	385	Wil
Benjmin F.	59	Mau
Cyrus	44	Mau
Dan	44	Mau
Daniel	1	Smi
Daniel	2	Smi
David	137	Sum
Easter	25	Mau
Ebenezar	63	Wll
Edwin	137	Sum
Elias	12	Gil
Elias W.	92	Rut
Eligah	44	Mau
Ezekiel	21	Gil
Ezekiel [2]	414	Wil
Francis	17	Gil
George	397	Wil
George	399	Wil
Gideon	404	Wil
Horatia G.	83	Rut
Hugh	138	Sum
James	34	Bed
James	13	Hum
James	26	Lin
James	53	Mau
James	59	Mau
James	1	Smi
James	121	Ste
James	137	Sum
James	293	War
James A.	2	Smi
James C.	2	Rob
Jawel	68	Mau
Jesse	94	Rut
John	28	Mau
John	62	Mau
John	79	Rut
John	410	Wil
Joseph	47	Bed

Alexander (cont.)		
Joseph	6	Hic
Joseph	53	Wll
Josiah	2	Smi
Mathew	137	Sum
Milton K.	20	Gil
Nathaniel	53	Wll
Obediah	66	Mau
Oswin	77	Rut
Ozni	5	Gil
Polley	18	Gil
Prichett	79	Rut
Reuben	2	Smi
Richard	1	Smi
Richard	2	Smi
Robert	376	Wil
Silas	26	Mau
Silus	24	Mau
Stephen	29	Lin
Thomas	53	Wll
Thomas H.	412	Wil
William	15	Bed
William	21	Gil
William	33	Lin
William	44	Mau
William	68	Mau
William	311	War
Wm.	121	Ste
Wm. L.	138	Sum
Zackius	78	Rut
see Aexander		
Alford, Bailey	8	Law
Burdis	3	Per
Thomas	82	Rut
Thomas	84	Rut
William	68	Dav
William	98	Rut
Alfred, Lee	82	Dav
Richard	317	War
Alin, George	106	She
Alison, James	60	Wll
John	44	Wll
Alkerson, Solomon	2	Way
Allbright, Jacob	20	Lin
John	21	Lin
Allcock, Thos.	21	Mon
Allcorn, James, Jr.	1	Jac
James, Sr.	1	Jac
Robert	1	Jac
Alldridge, John	6	Way
Allen, Abreham	105	Rut
Abreham, Travller	25	Mau
Ananias	1	Jac
Archer	407	Wil
Benjamin	37	Bed
Benjamin	6	Hum
Benjamin	88	Rut
Benjamin	20	Way
Carter	69	Dav
Charles	43	Mau
Charles	1	Smi
Charles	34	Wll
Daniel	17	Gil
Allen (cont.)		
Daniel	138	Sum
David	137	Sum
David	406	Wil
Dempsy	7	Lin
Eli	418	Wil
Felix	7	Mon
Geo.	114	Wil
George	2	Mon
George	370	Whi
George	403	Wil
George	43	Wll
George	61	Wll
George A.	17	Lin
George H.	4	Bed
George S.	91	Dav
Gideon B.	92	Rut
Goshun	1	Jac
Grant	1	Smi
Henry	38	Wll
Hezakiah	2	Smi
Hinry	1	Lin
Hiram	19	Ove
Hugh	319	War
Isaac	81	Dav
Isaac	34	Rob
Isaac	1	Smi
James	34	Mau
James [2]	41	Mau
James	30	Mon
James	100	Rut
James	1	Smi
James	28	Wll
James	33	Wll
Jane	65	Dav
Jane	138	Sum
Jeramiah	65	Dav
Jesse	15	Gil
Jesse	294	War
John	9	Dic
John	91	Rut
John	115	Ste
John	135	Sum
John	137	Sum
John	280	War
John	289	War
John	400	Wil
John	27	Wll
John H.	21	Lin
John L.	81	Dav
Joseph	9	Gil
Joseph	1	Per
Joseph	66	Wll
Lassan	54	Wll
Levi	138	Sum
Lewis B.	6	Mon
Luke	1	Jac
Lytle	135	Sum
Mary	27	Bed
Matthew	71	Dav
Moses	2	Smi
N. H.	4	Mon
Rachel	135	Sum

Allen (cont.)		
Richard	138	Sum
Richd.	24	Mon
Robert	1	Smi
Robert	137	Sum
Robison	95	Rut
Samuel	14	Gil
Samuel	1	Jac
Samuel	33	Wll
Samuel H.	370	Whi
Sarah	2	Smi
Signer	30	Lin
Susan	138	Sum
Terrel	3	Hum
Thomas	94	Dav
Thomas	40	Mau
Thomas	1	Smi
Valentine	32	Bed
Valuntine	22	Mon
William	42	Bed
William	1	Jac
William	40	Lin
William	41	Mau
William	56	Mau
William	25	Mon
William	3	Ove
William	103	Rut
William	1	Smi
William	406	Wil
William	22	Wll
William, Jnr.	103	Rut
William S.	39	Wll
William W.	302	War
Wilson	21	Way
Wm.	137	Sum
Wm.	138	Sum
Zachariah	41	Mau
Allexander, Abner	3	Per
George	386	Wil
James	3	Per
Alley, Benjamin	76	Rut
Peter	98	Dav
Robert	9	Ove
Walter	10	Ove
Allford, John	90	Dav
Surrell	367	Whi
Allgood, James	402	Wil
Allin, Archibald	411	Wil
Charles, Sen.	8	Wll
James	389	Wil
John	66	Dav
Lydia	403	Wil
Allison, Elizabeth	417	Wil
Ezekiel	1	Smi
George	1	Smi
Hugh	93	Dav
Isaac	415	Wil
Joseph	84	Rut
Joseph	3	Smi
Kimbrough	15	Bed
Matilda	1	Smi
Robert	28	Bed
Robert, Senr.	15	Bed
Thomas	2	Smi

Allison (cont.)		
William	14	Bed
see Aleson, Alison		
Allman, Hezekiah	53	Mau
Jeremiah	42	Bed
Nathan	312	War
William	417	Wil
Allmond, Burrel	355	Whi
Alloway, Archilaus	3	Smi
Allred, Francis	18	Ove
John	18	Lin
John	18	Ove
Polly	1	Jac
Allright, Lewis	137	Sum
Allsobrooks, John	3	Lin
John, Jur.	20	Lin
Wesley	20	Lin
Allsup, David	138	Sum
James	4	Lin
John	1	Law
John, Senr.	5	Law
Joseph	4	Lin
Randolph	4	Lin
Robert R.	4	Lin
Thos., Mr.	5	Law
Ally, Herbert	13	Rob
Isaiah	36	Lin
Thomas	14	Lin
Alman, Jacob	11	Gil
Nathaniel	17	Gil
Thomas	36	Bed
Willis	1	Smi
Almon, William	122	Ste
Almond, John	122	Ste
Thomas	87	Rut
Thos.	116	Ste
see Almon		
Alon, George	95	Rut
Alread, John	11	Way
Alred, Jonathan	17	Ove
Solomon	7	Ove
Alsbrook, Henry	11	Rob
Willie	25	Rob
Alsbrooks, Isham	123	Ste
see Allsobrooks		
Alsop, Joseph	2	Gil
Thomas	95	Rut
Alston, Abner	69	Mau
Alexander	401	Wil
James	29	Wll
John	12	Wll
Alsup, Asaph	384	Wil
Elizabth	416	Wil
Joseph	127	Ste
Richard	385	Wil
Samuel	416	Wil
Susannah	384	Wil
Thomas	12	Gil
William	376	Wil
Wm.	130	Ste
Alt, John	2	Fra
Altom, John	3	Law
Altum, Spencer	3	Law
William	3	Law

Alvis, Shadrach	13	Law
Ambrook, Wm.	137	Sum
Ambrooks see Ambrook		
Ambrose, Israel	138	Sum
Amick, Rainy	77	Rut
Amis, John	7	Wll
Ammonds, William	42	Lin
Ammons, Catharine	15	Hic
Eli	2	Hum
Godfrey	13	Hic
Henry	13	Hic
Amos, James	1	Fra
Anders, Eleazer	26	Mau
Anderson, Aaron	12	Law
Allen	5	Dic
Andrew [2]	1	Jac
Archibald	12	Law
Azariah	62	Wll
C.	114	Ste
Caleb	1	Jac
Caleb	73	Rut
Charles	1	Jac
Charles	87	Rut
David	5	Bed
David	25	Mon
David	130	Ste
Edmond R.	52	Bed
Edward	360	Whi
Elisha	1	Fra
Elizabeth	61	Dav
Elizabeth	2	Mon
Francis	1	Jac
Francis	2	Smi
Francis	388	Wil
Garland	1	Jac
George	355	Whi
Hyram	96	Dav
Isaac	47	Bed
Isaac	278	War
Jacob	20	Bed
Jacob	29	Bed
Jacob	50	Bed
Jacob	360	Whi
James	17	Bed
James	37	Bed
James	54	Bed
James	94	Dav
James	67	Mau
James	2	Smi
James	114	Ste
James	137	Sum
James	6	Way
James	352	Whi
James	420	Wil
James D.	12	Bed
Jessee	1	Jac
Jno. G.	24	Hic
Joel	64	Wll
John	94	Dav
John	2	Hum
John	12	Law
John	7	Per
John	357	Whi

Anderson (cont.)		
John	358	Whi
John	372	Whi
John B.	137	Sum
John H.	1	Smi
Johnson	3	Smi
Jonathan	8	Lin
Joseph	11	Ove
Joseph	1	Smi
Joseph	2	Smi
Joseph	350	Whi
Joseph	45	Wll
Joshua [?]	394	Wil
Jubal	1	Jac
Kinnith	52	Bed
Leah	13	Dic
Lurany	2	Fra
Mary	137	Sum
Mathias	341	Whi
Matthew	6	Gil
Matthew	1	Jac
Matthew	2	Smi
Maxwell	119	Ste
Nancy	29	Lin
Nelson	91	Rut
Nelson	99	Rut
Paulden	391	Wil
Payton	1	Jac
Peggy	13	Dic
Peter	1	Fra
Phebe	138	Sum
Philip	24	Lin
Rachel	1	Smi
Richard	12	Hum
Richard	67	Mau
Richard [2]	378	Wil
Richrd.	1	Jac
Robert	8	Gil
Robert	10	Gil
Robert	2	Hum
Robert [2]	1	Jac
Robert	357	Whi
Robert	382	Wil
Robert	38	Wll
Robert	49	Wll
Robt.	17	Hic
Robt., Sr.	19	Hic
Sally	2	Fra
Sally	138	Sum
Saml.	28	Jac
Samuel	35	Bed
Samuel	18	Gil
Samuel	18	Mon
Samuel S.	73	Rut
Sarah	17	Dic
Solomon	96	Dav
Stephen	3	Gil
Thomas	137	Sum
Thomas	45	Wll
Thornsberry	22	Mon
Thos.	16	Hic
Thos.	1	Jac
Tilman	1	Jac

Anderson (cont.)		
Timothy	10	Hum
W. C.	28	Jac
Wiley	3	Per
William	22	Bed
William	93	Dav
William	5	Dic
William	16	Gil
William	1	Jac
William	19	Lin
William	31	Rob
William	84	Rut
William	93	Rut
William	101	Rut
William	2	Smi
William	3	Smi
William	117	Ste
William	341	Whi
William	53	Wll
William A.	96	Dav
Wm. B.	138	Sum
Wm. C.	137	Sum
Wm. H.	137	Sum
Zachariah	356	Whi
see James		
Andres, David	50	Mau
Andress, Addam	48	Mau
Andrew, A.	396	Wil
Ephram	42	Wll
Andrews, ...aniel	12	Ove
A.	118	Ste
Andrew S.	40	Wll
Asy	390	Wil
Benjamin	2	Dic
Benjamin	1	Smi
David	50	Mau
David	82	Rut
David	103	Rut
David	117	Ste
Drewry	1	Smi
Drury	122	Ste
Elizabeth	10	Bed
Ephram	5	Wll
George	10	Wll
Grey	379	Wil
Henry	36	Wll
James	4	Lin
James	117	Ste
James	19	Wll
James	71	Wll
James	65	Wll
James O. K.	138	Sum
Jane	78	Rut
John	22	Gil
John	3	Hic
John	50	Mau
John	129	Ste
John	42	Wll
Knacy	41	Wll
Margaret	89	Rut
Mark, Sn.	42	Wll
Mark L.	33	Wll
Saml.	3	Hic

Andrews (cont.)		
Samuel	1	Smi
Tapley B.	8	Wll
Thomas	9	Hic
William	14	Rob
William	41	Wll
Angel, Andrew	138	Sum
John	5	Hic
John	138	Sum
Lawrence	1	Fra
Martain B.	5	Per
Walthrel	138	Sum
Angle, John	36	Bed
Reuben	19	Bed
Anglin, Aaron	11	Law
Frances	94	Rut
Jessee	6	Law
John	28	Jac
John	2	Way
John	51	Wll
Mary	51	Wll
Nelly	28	Rob
Angling, Cornelius	17	Hic
James	17	Hic
Angus, Alexander	18	Gil
James	17	Gil
Annerton, Edmund	1	Fra
Annes, John R.	17	Rob
Mary	356	Whi
Anold, Thomas	358	Whi
Ansley, Joseph	21	Wll
Anthoney, Zepheniah	97	Rut
Anthony, Elijah	4	Gil
John	8	Law
John	87	Rut
Joseph	8	Gil
Joseph	138	Sum
Phillip	81	Dav
Susan	138	Sum
William	24	Wll
Antony, Phillip	29	Mau
Aperson, Peter	121	Ste
Apple, David	1	Jac
George	1	Jac
Appleton, James	10	Rob
James, Mr.	4	Law
John	10	Rob
John	31	Rob
Thomas	3	Rob
William	14	Rob
Applewhite, Charlet	56	Mau
Arant, William	94	Dav
Arbuckle, Joseph	03	Rut
Archart, Moses	386	Wil
Archer, Daniel	1	Fra
Edward	2	Fra
George	2	Law
Jacob	398	Wil
Thos.	5	Law
see Archart		
Arendell, Benjamin	2	Smi
Arglott, Shadrac	75	Rut
Argo, William	286	War

Argo, William	286	War
Armer, John	1	Jac
Armfield, John	137	Sum
Armonett, Jacob	2	Smi
Armor, Davis	20	Gil
Joseph	20	Gil
Robt.	124	Ste
Armour, Robert	5	Dic
William	5	Dic
Armsfield, Elizabeth	28	Mon
Armstead, Jesse M.	2	Smi
John	2	Smi
Thaddeus	2	Smi
William	2	Smi
William H.	2	Smi
Armsted, Robert	23	Mon
Armstrong, Archibald	137	Sum
Elijah	414	Wil
Elizabeth	43	Bed
Ezekiel	79	Rut
George	20	Ove
Hugh	294	War
Hugh C.	20	Ove
James	12	Bed
James	22	Bed
James	54	Bed
James	10	Gil
James	27	Lin
James	32	Mau
James	44	Mau
James	9	Ove
James	364	Whi
James	415	Wil
James	5	Wll
James, Snr.	32	Mau
James L.	53	Bed
James S.	79	Rut
John	43	Bed
John	54	Bed
John	1	Jac
John	27	Lin
John	29	Mau
John	43	Mau
John	9	Ove
John	17	Wll
John B.	20	Gil
Joseph	44	Mau
Lancelot	6	Law
Landon	20	Ove
Mathew	137	Sum
Nancy	81	Dav
Nancy	14	Ove
Nathanial	51	Mau
Nathaniel	2	Per
Robert	76	Dav
Stephen	42	Mau
Stephen K.	20	Ove
Thomas	22	Bed
Thomas	26	Lin
Thomas	290	War
Thos.	138	Sum
William	54	Bed
William	11	Ove
Armstrong (cont.)		
William	281	War
William	17	Wll
William G.	32	Mau
William L.	32	Rob
Wm.	7	Lin
Arnell, Peter	16	Ove
Arnet, William	1	Smi
Arnett, Andrew	9	Ove
James	11	Gil
James	17	Way
John	3	Gil
John	9	Ove
Samuel	90	Rut
Arney, Adam	14	Ove
Henry	14	Ove
Peter	1	Ove
Arnold, Aaron	1	Hic
Aaron	377	Wil
Ann	1	Hum
Ara	95	Rut
Aron	4	Hum
Burnett	46	Lin
Charles	1	Fra
Darling D.	37	Bed
David [deleted]	46	Mau
Davis	414	Wil
Eleanor	97	Rut
Elijah	2	Fra
Enoch	89	Rut
Ephraim	4	Dic
Francis	45	Bed
Francis	48	Bed
Francis	346	Whi
Hezikiah	22	Hic
Hopson	46	Mau
Israel	131	Ste
Jacob	1	Fra
James	1	Fra
James	13	Hum
James	314	War
James H.	314	War
James L.	50	Mau
John	31	Bed
John	85	Rut
John	96	Rut
John, Jnr.	100	Rut
John H.	49	Mau
Johnson	1	Fra
Joseph	1	Smi
Joshua	2	Fra
Levi	2	Fra
Lindsey	362	Whi
Linza	46	Mau
Mewell	417	Wil
Nancy	415	Wil
Peter	89	Rut
Ralph	42	Lin
Richard	308	War
Richard	358	Whi
Robbert	48	Mau
Smith	37	Bed
Stephen	420	Wil

Arnold (cont.)		
Thomas	37	Mau
Thomas	46	Mau
William	1	Hic
William	50	Mau
William	6	Ove
William	96	Rut
William	2	Smi
William	417	Wil
William K.	34	Rob
Wyatt	12	Hum
Zachariah	41	Lin
Zekial	50	Mau
Zephiniah	75	Rut
see Anold		
Aronhart, George	131	Ste
Arpe, Nancy	32	Lin
Arrey, Henrey	5	Per
Arrington, Benjamin	40	Lin
Higdon	391	Wil
Joel	10	Hic
John	2	Hic
Saml. L.	22	Hic
Thomas	390	Wil
Arron, Samuel	6	Gil
Arterbury, Elijah	1	Jac
Moses	1	Jac
Pricila	1	Jac
Arthur, John	1	Jac
William	77	Dav
Aruss, Archibald	4	Ove
Arvin, Ephraim	38	Mau
Jonas	38	Mau
Ary, Danl.	121	Ste
Asbill, Allen	18	Ove
Christena	18	Ove
Solomon	3	Law
Asbury, John	28	Jac
Asford, Basdale	2	Smi
Ash, Andrew	14	Hum
Ashabraner, John	22	Rob
Ashaw, Benjamin	395	Wil
Ashbourn, Anderson	4	Ove
Jesse	8	Ove
Ashbrooks, Aaron	53	Bed
Ashby, James	406	Wil
John	2	Fra
Travis	23	Lin
Ashford, Butler	106	She
Dempsey	137	Sum
Moses	413	Wil
William	413	Wil
Ashley, James	279	War
Nathaniel	63	Dav
Ashlin, William	32	Wll
Ashlock, Benja.	138	Sum
Isaac	4	Ove
James	138	Sum
Jesse	4	Ove
Philip	138	Sum
Ashmoore, Andrew S.	2	Law
James	3	Law
Ashmore, Calvin	15	Gil
Ashmore (cont.)		
James	15	Gil
Jas. B.	6	Hic
Joshua	10	Law
Ashworth, John	401	Wil
John C.	14	Ove
Joseph	5	Ove
Joseph R.	407	Wil
Moses	2	Smi
Sarah	66	Mau
Askew, Samuel	6	Law
William	1	Smi
Askins, George	93	Rut
Askue, Elisha	125	Ste
Elisha	129	Ste
Josiah	117	Ste
Asky, John	138	Sum
Asley, Miles	26	Mon
Aslon, Edwin	66	Dav
Aspey, Alexander	94	Rut
John	88	Rut
John	92	Rut
William	92	Rut
Aspley, John, Jr.	138	Sum
John, Sr.	138	Sum
Wm.	138	Sum
Astin, Samuel	19	Lin
Atchison, Adam	138	Sum
Nathan	138	Sum
Peter	138	Sum
Wellis	138	Sum
William	127	Ste
Atherly, James	112	Wil
Athill, Nancy	363	Whi
Atkins, Asa	111	Ste
Daniel	4	Law
Ephrm.	118	Ste
George	111	Ste
Henry	111	Ste
Howel	11	Mon
Ica	8	Gil
Isaac	9	Gil
Isham	9	Gil
Jackson	31	Rob
James	9	Gil
James	31	Rob
John	111	Ste
John, Senr.	111	Ste
Lewis	111	Ste
Mary	33	Wll
Richard	4	Gil
Robert	1	Fra
Spencer	19	Gil
Thomas	11	Gil
William	64	Wll
Wm. R.	111	Ste
Wm. S.	111	Ste
Atkinson, A.	8	Wll
Arthur	10	Bed
Charles	12	Ove
David	1	Smi
Elias	2	Smi
Elizabeth	400	Wil

Atkinson (cont.)
Henry 20 Ove
Jesse 63 Wll
John 10 Bed
John 1 Fra
John 120 Ste
John 10 Wll
John 40 Wll
Joshua 279 War
Josiah 62 Wll
Mary 390 Wil
Samuel 9 Wll
Thomas 420 Wil
Thos. 19 Mon
William 8 Ove
William 85 Rut
see Actkinson
Atwood, Edwin 2 Smi
James 411 Wil
William 29 Lin
Auberry, Nolin 79 Rut
Auby, John 123 Ste
Audry, Henery 51 Mau
Aughlin, Alexander D. 289 War
Aurall, Nau [?] 78 Rut
Ausbrook, Polly 37 Bed
see Ambrook
Ausburn, Alexander 46 Mau
Alexander G. 46 Mau
James 44 Mau
John 43 Mau
John 46 Mau
Robbart 46 Mau
Ausler, Helenor 23 Rob
Austain, Richard 2 Ove
Austin, David 10 Dic
Elisha 282 War
Gideon 24 Lin
James 8 Gil
John 8 Way
John 356 Whi
Joseph 92 Rut
Levi 2 Smi
Nathaniel 359 Whi
Samuel 2 Smi
Samuel D. 12 Dic
Sanders 11 Way
Sarah 2 Smi
Stephen 2 Smi
Thos. 138 Sum
William 8 Dic
William 35 Mau
William 15 Way
William 369 Whi
Wm. 137 Sum
Autry, Simeon 91 Rut
Avant, John 110 Ste
Aven, Amos 1 Per
Avens, William 29 Rob
Avent, Abner 2 Smi
James 87 Dav
Mason 135 Sum
Averet, Washington 402 Wil
Averett, David 1 Smi
William 98 Rut
William 16 Way
see Jenkins
Averey see Arney
Averitt, Washington 114 Wil
Avery, Allin 394 Wil
George 394 Wil
Nathan 74 Rut
Nicholas 342 Whi
William 62 Dav
Avetts, Hannah 3 Smi
Joseph 1 Smi
Joseph 1 Smi
Joseph, Senr. 1 Smi
Moses 3 Smi
Wm. 138 Sum
Avis, Robert C. 400 Wil
Avrit, Aquila 10 Mon
John 42 Mau
Awlwood, Eden 411 Wil
Axum, William 2 Smi
Ayers, Arther 65 Mau
Joseph [2] 65 Mau
Ayres, Baker 68 Dav
Gentry 1 Fra
Henry 8 Rob
Henry 25 Rob
Moses 1 Fra
William 1 Fra
William 10 Rob
Ay'rs, James 65 Mau

--- B ---

B..., J... 3 Fra
Babb, Alsa 17 Rob
Bennett 389 Wil
Burwell 4 Rob
James 32 Mau
Jesse 33 Rob
John 377 Wil
Thomas 377 Wil
William 33 Rob
Babbet, Drewry 12 Wll
James 90 Rut
Babbit, Lewis 101 Rut
Bacchus, Minchey 384 Wil
William 384 Wil
Bachamman, William 2 Fra
Bachus, John 73 Dav
Bacon, Benedict 10 Dic
Isaac 7 Per
Badger, Sally 7 Smi
Badgett, Jonathan 145 Sum
Thomas 379 Wil
Baere, Peter 291 War
Bagby, Reddin 13 Hic
Baget, Benton 64 Mau
Bagget, Abraham 29 Mau
Allen 29 Mon

Bagget (cont.)		
Asa	85	Rut
Blake	3	Fra
Granberry	7	Rob
James	20	Mon
James	29	Mon
John	4	Mon
Micajah	3	Mon
Baggit, Grandberry	30	Rob
Bagley, Henry	11	Lin
Bagly, Elisha	11	Lin
Joab	11	Lin
Bagwell, Allen	396	Wil
Drewry	13	Mon
Richd.	8	Mon
Bailess, Burwell	24	Mon
Patience	23	Mon
Thos.	23	Mon
Bailey, Absalom	3	Fra
Andrew	35	Fra
Andrew, Sr.	35	Fra
Charles	1	Mon
Eli	313	War
Enoch	6	Smi
Everet	318	War
Everit	319	War
Haman	35	Fra
Henry	117	Ste
Henry	61	Wll
Henry, Junr.	117	Ste
Jacob	23	Mon
Jeremiah	6	Smi
Jesse	2	Mon
Jno.	139	Sum
John	30	Lin
John W.	32	Mau
Parks	11	Gil
Peter	30	Mau
Richard	18	Gil
Richard T.	11	Law
Sally	128	Ste
Samuel	26	Rob
Shadrack	3	Fra
William	65	Dav
William	4	Lin
William	6	Smi
William	125	Ste
William	139	Sum
Bailley, William	412	Wil
Bails, James	385	Wil
Baily, Elizabeth	90	Dav
George	7	Ove
Henry	385	Wil
Jacob	76	Rut
James	1	Hic
James	89	Rut
John	99	Rut
Bain, Alexander	7	Smi
Archibald	7	Smi
John	87	Rut
Masten Trainalleter [?]		
Landiford Nebucad		
Nezucad Walleter	7	Smi
Baines, Charles	128	Ste
Samuel	5	Smi
Bains see Bows		
Bair, Isaac	48	Mau
John W.	48	Mau
Silas	394	Wil
William	79	Rut
Baird, Benjamin	18	Bed
Bludget	28	Mon
Edwin	18	Hic
Henry	382	Wil
Hugh	3	Bed
James	4	Hum
James	385	Wil
John	77	Dav
John	79	Dav
John, Sen.	386	Wil
Otbert	18	Hic
Saml. M.	18	Hic
Samuel	26	Bed
William	14	Dic
Wm.	396	Wil
Bairden, Eli	30	Bed
Eli	44	Bed
Bairds, John	395	Wil
Baitman, Hozia	52	Mau
Penny	30	Lin
William	32	Lin
Baits, Elizebeth	37	Mau
Jeffery	37	Mau
Robert	72	Dav
Robert [2]	49	Wll
Baity, Arthar	59	Mau
Baize, William	118	Ste
Baker, Abner	312	War
Abraham	11	Ove
Alexander	35	Fra
Alexander	362	Whi
Andrew	89	Dav
Andrew	96	Dav
Andrew	63	Mau
Andrew	2	Way
Baxter	350	Whi
Benjamin	21	Lin
Briant	302	War
Briant	313	War
Christley	15	Ove
Daniel	21	Lin
David	13	Gil
Elizabeth	389	Wil
Esaas	20	Way
Francis	19	Mon
Gabrael	3	Jac
George	4	Smi
Gilbert	97	Dav
Humphrey	11	Wll
Isaac	42	Bed
Isaac	144	Sum
Jacob	100	Rut
James	89	Dav
James	24	Hic
James	29	Mon
James	3	Per

Baker (cont.)		
James	140	Sum
James	404	Wil
James M.	52	Mau
Jane	12	Dic
Jehugh	57	Mau
Jeremiah	411	Wil
Jesse	6	Lin
John	42	Bed
John	44	Bed
John	52	Bed
John	58	Dav
John	9	Dic
John	12	Dic
John	3	Fra
John	23	Hic
John	8	Mon
John	92	Rut
John	3	Smi
John	111	Ste
John	112	Ste
John	127	Ste
John	350	Whi
John	351	Whi
John	357	Whi
John	411	Wil
John	43	Wll
John E.	8	Smi
Joseph	11	Hic
Joshua	13	Gil
Joshua	78	Rut
Larken	6	Law
Larking	3	Per
Martin	141	Sum
Mary	12	Dic
Mathias	356	Whi
Messack	408	Wil
Nathan	93	Rut
Nicholas	2	Dic
Peter	356	Whi
Rachel	15	Hic
Richmond	23	Hic
Robert	4	Mon
Samuel	14	Gil
Samuel	69	Mau
Sarah	3	Jac
Thomas	63	Mau
Thomas	7	Way
Thomas C.	389	Wil
Thos.	19	Mon
Wiley	65	Mau
William	70	Dav
William	14	Gil
William	26	Mon
William	141	Sum
William	346	Whi
William	360	Whi
Balberd, Joseph	78	Rut
Balch, Alfred	47	Bed
Alfred	79	Dav
Amos	47	Bed
George B.	52	Bed
John	7	Gil
Balden, Benjamin	2	Jac
Green	3	Jac
John	25	Rob
William	143	Sum
Baldon, Aaron	52	Wll
Baldridg, Mical	41	Mau
Baldridge, Alexander	8	Gil
Alexander	46	Mau
Andrew	83	Dav
Daniel	8	Smi
Francis	83	Dav
James	40	Mau
John	46	Mau
John	10	Wll
Robert	83	Rut
Wm.	3	Smi
Baldrige, James	82	Dav
Stephen W.	139	Sum
Baldry, William	22	Rob
Baldwin, Jacob	16	Gil
John	15	Rob
Joseph	14	Law
Balentine, Lemuel	96	Dav
William	11	Rob
Baley, Henry	11	Hic
John S.	7	Gil
William	5	Smi
Wyott	5	Smi
Balie, Narvin	3	Jac
Balieu, Micajah	13	Lin
Ball, Isaac	142	Sum
James	139	Sum
James	142	Sum
John	13	Ove
John S.	1	Mon
Lewis	3	Fra
William	17	Gil
Wilson	31	Mau
Ballad, Jawel	46	Mau
Ballan, Gehu	117	Ste
Ballance, Abram	31	Wll
Ballard, Etheldridge	5	Hum
Hawen	21	Bed
Howard	5	Smi
James	6	Smi
John	5	Smi
John	8	Smi
Lewis	29	Wll
William	397	Wil
Willie	79	Rut
Willis	79	Rut
Wyatt	3	Fra
Ballentine, Charles	96	Dav
David	89	Dav
Ballinger, Jacob	61	Dav
Ballow, Ann	18	Wll
James	8	Smi
Leonard	5	Smi
William H.	55	Wll
Balman, Abraham	384	Wil
Balote, Henry	144	Sum
Jeremiah	140	Sum
John	142	Sum

Balt, William	17	Gil
Balthrop, Francis	9	Dic
William	6	Dic
William, Jr.	4	Dic
Willie	6	Dic
Baltzell, Abram	135	Sum
Baly, Champ	50	Bed
Bamhart, John	36	Fra
Bampbell, James	5	Per
Banday, Nathan	398	Wil
Willshire	386	Wil
Bandy, Cara	9	Smi
David	141	Sum
Jameson	141	Sum
Jameson	385	Wil
Joseph	043	Sum
Luke, Jr.	043	Sum
Oratio	143	Sum
Perrin	143	Sum
Richard	141	Sum
Solomoen	139	Sum
Tho.	143	Sum
Thomas	9	Smi
Zadoc	143	Sum
see Bundy		
Bane, Elihu	90	Rut
Banfield, John	398	Wil
John	407	Wil
Banks, David	314	War
John	287	War
Samuel	297	War
Simon	304	War
Solomon	36	Fra
Thomas	3	Smi
Thomas	4	Smi
William	5	Smi
William	2	Wll
Banter, Peter	6	Smi
Banton, John	141	Sum
Barbee, Abimilech	2	Fra
Daniel	411	Wil
John	23	Mon
John	411	Wil
Joseph	4	Mon
Joseph	411	Wil
Barber, Abram	23	Hic
Allen	23	Hic
Edward	9	Smi
George	22	Rob
James	314	War
Joannah	8	Gil
John	10	Gil
John	23	Hic
John	100	Rut
John	9	Wll
John	64	Wll
Lawson	135	Wum
Mary	23	Hic
Samuel	104	Rut
Zeba	23	Hic
Barbour, James	392	Wil
Barby, John	24	Rob
Barckly, Samuel	40	Lin
Barcroft, Nancy	17	Bed
Barefoot, Noah	94	Rut
Baren, Jeremiah	11	Rob
John	23	Rob
Barfield, Frederick	90	Rut
Nancy	20	Wll
Barger, Gasper	342	Whi
Bargo, Jacob	413	Wil
John	6	Smi
Barham, Edwin	62	Dav
Jno.	139	Sum
Josiah	51	Mau
Newsom	93	Dav
William N.	16	Wll
Bark, Fielding	102	Rut
see Burk		
Barker, Alexander	16	Mon
Allen	12	Hum
Ambrose	40	Lin
Brigs	3	Hum
Burrell	15	Ove
George [2]	49	Mau
George W.	10	Wll
Henshey	15	Ove
Israel	141	Sum
James	66	Mau
Jane	8	Hum
John	8	Smi
John W.	17	Mon
Joseph	82	Rut
Josiah	3	Fra
Lewis	3	Hum
Mary Ann	40	Lin
Stephen	419	Wil
Willis	74	Dav
Willis	80	Dav
Barkhart, Sally	7	Smi
Barkley, Benjamin	410	Wil
James	289	War
John	30	Mau
John	4	Smi
John	303	War
Robert	4	Smi
William	304	War
Barkly, John	303	War
Jonathan	2	Lin
Barks, Hilry	3	Jac
Sutton	3	Jac
Barksdale, Alx.	74	Dav
Nathaniel	86	Rut
Randolph	100	Rut
William	3	Ove
William	90	Rut
William	76	Rut
Barley, Robert	312	War
Barlow, Howard	87	Rut
Jessee	15	Mon
John	38	Mau
Wiley	69	Mau
Barnard, David	143	Sum
Elisha	140	Sum
Elisha	143	Sum
Jacob	143	Sum

Barnard (cont.)		
James [2]	143	Sum
James T.	140	Sum
John	14	Lin
Luke, Sr.	143	Sum
William	142	Sum
Barnd, Hiram	115	Wil
Barned, John	115	Wil
Barnes, Abraham	20	Gil
Abraham	20	Lin
Benjamin	57	Dav
Britain	25	Rob
Callum	141	Sum
Charles	1	Hic
Charles	115	Ste
Charles	119	Ste
Dempsey	57	Dav
Dennis	128	Ste
Elijah	286	War
George	11	Gil
George	7	Smi
Jacob	12	Ove
James	43	Lin
James	3	Ove
James	23	Rob
Jeremiah	6	Gil
Joel	91	Dav
John	8	Bed
John	122	Ste
Jordon	5	Lin
Kinchen	30	Mon
Malachi	139	Sum
Nineveh	293	War
Patsey	22	Mon
Pipkin	140	Sum
Rebecca	144	Sum
Reps	20	Mon
Solomon	14p	Sum
William	314	War
Wright	140	Sum
Barnet, Agnis	51	Wll
Elenor	5	Bed
Elijah	9	Rob
James P.	66	Wll
John	2	Fra
John	20	Mon
John	7	Smi
John	121	Ste
Joseph	2	Fra
Nathan	42	Mau
see Basnet		
Barnett, Elijah	368	Whi
Elizabeth	385	Wil
J. W.	5	Way
Jacob	2	Jac
Jarrott	94	Rut
Jarrott	394	Wil
Jeremiah	14	Hic
Jeremiah	81	Rut
John	5	Gil
John	385	Wil
John M.	10	Way
Richard	9	Gil
Barnett (cont.)		
William	18	Lin
William	15	Way
William	385	Wil
William	395	Wil
Barnhart, Adam	141	Sum
Andrew	83	Dav
John	66	Dav
Barnhill, Alexr.	15	Hic
Benjn.	42	Bed
James, Sr.	15	Hic
Jas. M.	15	Hic
Vachel	15	Hic
Barnord, Jacob	142	Sum
Barns, Agatha	26	Wll
Alexander S.	33	Mau
Benjamin, Sr.	57	Dav
Elisabeth	23	Wll
Gabriel	89	Rut
George	4	Wll
Henry	64	Dav
James	82	Dav
James	3	Har
James	14	Law
James	28	Mau
James	57	Mau
James, Sr.	82	Dav
John	66	Mau
Joshua	5	Har
Mary	5	Har
Moses	91	Rut
Peter	26	Wll
Seth	33	Mau
Thomas	91	Rut
Thomas	355	Whi
Wilkeson	38	Mau
William	7	Law
Barnwell, David	67	Dav
Edward	15	Lin
Barons, Charles	5	Per
James	5	Per
William	5	Per
Barr, Alexander	16	Wll
Caleb	3	Fra
Eli	144	Sum
Hezekiah	2	Hic
Hugh	2	Mon
Hugh	144	Sum
Hugh	16	Wll
Hugh, Jr.	144	Sum
Isaac	3	Way
James	2	Hic
James	127	Ste
John	62	Dav
John	139	Sum
John	141	Sum
John	370	Whi
Joseph	36	Fra
Patrick	141	Sum
Samuel [& Gillaspie]	6	Wll
Sarah	144	Sum
William G.	394	Wil
Wm.	139	Sum

Barret, Hayman	303	War
James	5	Smi
see Barrot		
Barrett, James	18	Mon
John	32	Bed
Miles	313	War
Ward	313	War
Barrey, John G.	75	Dav
Barrington, James	86	Rut
Barron, Abraham	19	Gil
Alexander	21	Gil
Dorcas	21	Gil
William [2]	21	Gil
Barrot, Polly	6	Smi
Stephen	5	Smi
see Barret		
Barrott, David [2]	139	Sum
George	139	Sum
Richd.	79	Dav
Tho.	141	Sum
Barrow, Edmund	140	Sum
James	118	Ste
James	125	Ste
Matthew	90	Dav
Wiley	81	Dav
William	18	Lin
Barrum, John	404	Wil
Barry, James	039	Sum
Redmond D.	145	Sum
V. D.	7	Per
William L.	143	Sum
Bartee, Jessee	32	Mon
William B.	73	Rut
Barten, Sarah	354	Whi
Bartie see Bastie		
Bartlet, Mary	398	Wil
Bartlett, Joseph	16	Ove
Joseph	365	Whi
Joshua	365	Whi
Nathan	365	Whi
Bartlette, Thomas	25	Rob
Barton, Ann	407	Wil
Anne	79	Rut
David	85	Rut
Eleazor	6	Smi
Gabriel	407	Wil
Glover W.	93	Rut
Jacob W.	20	Ove
Jesse	90	Rut
Joshua	87	Rut
Lewis	93	Rut
Robert	90	Rut
Seth	9	Smi
Stephen	386	Wil
Swinfield	99	Rut
Tabitha	99	Rut
Tamson	4	Smi
Tamson	4	Jac
Tho.	141	Sum
Thos.	11	Mon
Titus T.	20	Ove
Wade	120	Ste
William	99	Mon
Barton (cont.)		
William	77	Rut
William	140	Sum
Barus, Daniel	96	Rut
Basey, Lewis	69	Dav
Basfield, Williams	74	Rut
Basford, John	17	Rob
Basfort, James	8	Mon
Basham, Archd.	10	Lin
Nathan	4	Law
Samuel	10	Lin
Uriah	4	Jac
Bashaw, Benjamin	68	Dav
Peter	72	Dav
Bashers, Bazel	369	Whi
Berry	369	Whi
John	369	Whi
Middleton	369	Whi
Thomas	369	Whi
Basinger, Solomon	95	Rut
Baskervile, Richard	139	Sum
Basket, William	31	Mau
William	7	Smi
Baskins, Nancy	15	Gil
Robert M.	420	Wil
William	287	War
William	416	Wil
Basnet, William	8	Smi
Bass, Benjamin J.	11	Wll
Cate	385	Wil
Etheldred	409	Wil
Ezekiel	409	Wil
Henry	27	Bed
James	5	Bed
James	80	Rut
Jams	382	Wil
Jethro	126	Ste
John	5	Bed
John	409	Wil
Kinchen	11	Gil
Nathan	11	Gil
Samuel	5	Bed
Sion	381	Wil
Theophelus	416	Wil
Thomas	2	Wll
Zachariah J.	144	Sum
Bassham, John	96	Rut
Richard	7	Gil
Bassie, Murrel	41	Wll
Bastie, Charles	7	Smi
Bastin, Stephen	6	Lin
Batch, John	27	Bed
Batchean, Beniah	18	Wll
Batcheler, Wilson	56	Mau
Bate, Humphrey	139	Sum
Bateman, Edwin	13	Hum
Enoch	20	Wll
Henry	65	Dav
Isaac	20	Wll
Bates, Ambrose	144	Sum
Charles	2	Ove
Fleming	22	Lin
George	29	Mau

Bates (cont.)
Henderson 13 Ove
Isaac 7 Smi
Isaiah 8 Hic
James 316 War
Jane 5 Smi
Jas. 23 Hic
John 6 Smi
Joseph 14 Ove
Martha 23 Bed
Priscilla 30 Bed
Robert, Jr. 7 Wll
Sally 8 Smi
William 36 Fra
William 17 Lin
William 366 Whi
Wm. 24 Hic
Batey, James 6 Smi
Bath, Edward 3 Smi
Batman, Even 16 Wll
Polly 15 Wll
Simon 10 Wll
William 6 Wll
Bato see Bate
Batson, John 278 War
Richard 3 Dic
Richd. 1 Dic
Thos. 5 Mon
Batte, Henry 77 Rut
Thomas 100 Rut
Battle, Benjamin 78 Rut
Oren D. 2 Rob
Battles, Little B. 32 Lin
William 19 Way
Batton, Daniel 6 Smi
Francis 28 Lin
Joel 393 Wil
Maney 75 Rut
Battons, Henry 406 Wil
Batts, Aaron 7 Smi
Benjamin 34 Rob
Frederick 17 Rob
James 382 Wil
William 7 Smi
Baty, Andrew 16 Lin
Henery J. 43 Mau
James 15 Bed
James 33 Mau
John 16 Lin
John 30 Mau
Thomas 48 Mau
William 14 Lin
Bauchman, Daniel 6 Lin
Baugh, James 4 Lin
Martin 4 Lin
Baukum, Cader 42 Wll
Cader 58 Wll
Baulch, William 346 Whi
William 362 Whi
Baum, Adam 18 Wll
Lemuel 77 Rut
Baumgarner, George 9 Gil
Bawers see Bowers 25 Bed
Baxter, David 77 Rut
James 96 Dav
Jane 69 Mau
Jeramiah 94 Dav
Bay, Cannaday 382 Wil
Thomas 378 Wil
Bayer, Hannah 96 Dav
Bayles, William 142 Sum
Bayliss, Britain 118 Ste
Cullen 116 Ste
William 112 Ste
Bayn, Mathew 139 Sum
Williamson N. 139 Sum
Baysinger, George 7 Smi
Henry 32 Lin
Henry 7 Smi
Baytt, Henry 30 Bed
Beace, J. 24 Mau
Beach, Benjamin 14 Lin
John B. 54 Wll
Beacham, Levy 129 Ste
Beadford, James 12 Way
Beady, James 19 Hic
Polly 19 Hic
Beagles, Osburn 416 Wil
William 416 Wil
Beaham, Isaac 128 Ste
Beal, John 9 Smi
Samuel 3 Jac
William 3 Jac
Beale, Benjamin 18 Gil
Micajah 6 Gil
Presley 18 Gil
Beam, Jacob 355 Whi
Beame, Thomas 15 Gil
Bean, Aaron 3 Jac
Conner 3 Fra
Jacob 106 She
John 3 Jac
Leroy 36 Fra
Obediah 35 Fra
Prudy 2 Fra
Russle 107 She
Thomas 4 Har
Walter 7 Smi
Beard, Absolom 21 Lin
Adam 139 Sum
Alexander 40 Lin
Ann 69 Mau
Benjamine 366 Whi
David 143 Sum
Francis A. 4 Lin
George 63 Mau
Isaac 10 Rob
James 37 Mau
Jerimiah 8 Smi
John 76 Rut
John 51 Wll
Josiah 7 Smi
Martin 62 Mau
Mary 139 Sum
Moses 51 Wll
Robbert 49 Mau

Beard (cont.)		
Robert	5	Lin
Robert	45	Lin
Samuel	38	Mau
Samuel	39	Mau
Samuel	96	Rut
Thomas	3	Fra
Thomas	18	Rob
Thos.	139	Sum
William	3	Fra
William D.	82	Rut
Willis	4	Hum
Bearding, John, Jr.	145	Sum
Solo.	145	Sum
William [2]	11	Mon
Beardon, John, Sr.	139	Sum
Beasley, Ann	19	Wll
Ante	55	Wll
Archer	44	Lin
Benjamin	402	Wil
Braddock	9	Smi
Ellis	4	Smi
Emsley	21	Rob
Hannah	21	Mon
Henry	6	Smi
Isham	3	Smi
James	101	Rut
James B.	32	Wll
John	60	Dav
John	94	Dav
John B.	32	Wll
John W.	55	Mau
Johnson	8	Smi
Major	4	Smi
Pitts	96	Rut
Samuel	3	Fra
Sarah	144	Sum
Stephn	140	Sum
Sterling	6	Smi
Thomas	101	Rut
William	3	Fra
William	6	Hum
William	34	Wll
William M.	8	Gil
see Ingram		
Beasly, Burrell	37	Lin
Jesse	8	Gil
Pitts	100	Rut
Sarah	403	Wil
Beason, Benj.	6	Har
Beatie, Joseph	87	Rut
Beaton, Charles	123	Ste
Lochten	123	Ste
Beaty, Andrew	6	Ove
Ann	6	Ove
David	9	Ove
Eleazar	101	Rut
George	17	Ove
James	10	Ove
John	5	Ove
John	15	Ove
John	100	Rut
Robert	15	Ove
Beaty (cont.)		
Thomas	13	Gil
William	5	Ove
William	6	Way
William, Senr.	84	Rut
William F.	85	Rut
Beaver, Jeasse	145	Sum
John	3	Fra
Michael	7	Lin
Patsey	88	Dav
Rigdon	7	Lin
Stephen	29	Lin
William	47	Lin
Beavers, Jesse	6	Rob
John	80	Rut
John	100	Rut
Lewis	103	Rut
Thomas	98	Rut
William	28	Wll
Beazley, Rachel	370	Whi
Beck, Abraham	404	Wil
Devault	39	Lin
Henry	8	Lin
James	68	Mau
John	4	Bed
Levina	62	Dav
Mary	68	Dav
Nathaniel	34	Rob
William	7	Smi
Becket, Charles	11	Lin
Becklow, Asa	64	Dav
Beckly, William	1	Hic
Beckton, Frederick E.	90	Rut
Beckum, Elizabeth	19	Ove
Bedford, Ann	92	Rut
B. W.	78	Dav
Geo. A.	78	Dav
Jonas	1	Jac
Seth	1	Jac
Bedwell, Archibald	6	Bed
Caleb	24	Lin
James	6	Bed
Jesse	294	War
John	299	War
Major W.	24	Lin
Mary	353	Whi
Reuben	6	Bed
Beech, William	12	Ove
Beedels, Bassett A.	363	Whi
John	366	Whi
Beeg, Jerimiah	30	Mau
Beeler, George	12	Gil
Beerbarrow, Adam	280	War
Beesly, Josiah	401	Wil
Solomon	101	Rut
Beetle, John	31	Lin
Beevers, Allen	19	Gil
Spencer	14	Gil
Beggerly, Benjamin	44	Lin
Beggers, Catharine	41	Wll
Belamy, Elisha	5	Rob
Belcher, Andrew	114	Wil
Arthur	310	War

Belcher (cont.)
Bartlett 363 Whi
Isaac 7 Smi
John 417 Wil
John 7 Wll
John 49 Wll
Littleberry 412 Wil
Richard 412 Wil
William 297 War
William 310 War
Belew, Stewart 18 Mon
Belifan, Joseph 54 Wll
Belk, Chamberlain 11 Ove
Bell, Absalom B. 139 Sum
Adam 11 Gil
Ann F. 79 Dav
Benjamin F. 408 Wil
Benjn. 90 Dav
Burrel 3 Hum
Burrel 127 Ste
Charles 139 Sum
David 35 Bed
David 2 Fra
David 8 Smi
David 22 Wll
Elisha 98 Rut
Elisha 417 Wil
Elizabeth 142 Sum
Fulden 409 Wil
George 5 Smi
George 115 Ste
Henry 76 Rut
Henry 126 Ste
Hugh F. 14 Mon
Icim 409 Wil
James 35 Fra
James 27 Mau
James 27 Rob
James 97 Rut
James 376 Wil
James 394 Wil
James 409 Wil
James B. 77 Rut
Jennet 130 Ste
Jeremiah 385 Wil
Jesse 30 Rob
Jesse 8 Smi
Job H. 9 Lin
Joel 18 Lin
John 82 Dav
John 2 Fra
John 51 Mau
John 68 Mau
John 22 Rob
John 73 Rut
John 80 Rut
John 135 Sum
John [2] 403 Wil
John 409 Wil
John 13 Wll
John, Senr. 2 Rob
John, Sr. 61 Dav
John J. 14 Mon
Joseph H. 52 Bed
Joseph M. 139 Sum
Lemuel 117 Ste
Micajah 141 Sum
Montgomery 15 Dic
Nathaniel 83 Dav
Robbert 54 Mau
Robert 89 Rut
Robt. 135 Sum
Samuel 66 Dav
Samuel 83 Dav
Samuel 98 Dav
Samuel G. 86 Rut
Shdrack 11 Dic
Starlin 35 Mau
Thomas 20 Bed
Thomas 83 Dav
Thomas 98 Dav
Thomas H. 9 Lin
Thos. 6 Hic
Thos. [2] 10 Mon
Voluntine 30 Mau
William 68 Mau
William 8 Smi
William 139 Sum
William M. 14 Rob
Wm., Junr. 122 Ste
Wm., Senr. 117 Ste
Zacheriah 101 Rut
see Bill

Bellenfant, John 30 Wll
Bellens, David 405 Wil
Bellihan, Benjamin 417 Wil
Bellow, Samuel 5 Smi
Susannah 5 Smi
Belote, George 8 Smi
Jonas 8 Smi
Smith C. 5 Smi
Below, Battersby 97 Dav
Belsha, Craven 8 Way
Belt, Abijah 15 Lin
Benjn. 31 Bed
Belyen, Isaac 9 Ove
John, Senr. 5 Ove
Oliver 10 Ove
Peter 5 Ove
Benaus, Leonard 92 Rut
Benbrook, Thomas 26 Rob
Bendemans, — 24 Mau
Bender, Briant F. 141 Sum
Daniel 141 Sum
Benderman, William 26 Mau
Benett, Walker 352 Whi
Benge, Richard 2 Fra
Wm. B. 7 Lin
Bengum, William 367 Whi
Benit, Thomas 54 Mau
Benkley, Daniel 5 Rob
Jacob 5 Rob
Jacob 8 Rob
Jacob 16 Rob
Jacob 36 Rob
John 5 Rob
Bennefield, James 92 Dav

Bennefield (cont.)		
John	91	Dav
Bennet, Benjamin	8	Smi
Benjamin, Senr.	8	Smi
Benjamin L.	7	Smi
Drewry	59	Wll
Francis	3	Fra
George	49	Wll
James	7	Smi
John	35	Fra
John	130	Ste
John	20	Wll
John	23	Wll
John	26	Wll
John	40	Wll
John M.	7	Smi
Levi	352	Whi
Levi	353	Whi
Nancy	7	Smi
Nathan	92	Dav
Richard	7	Smi
Risden	123	Ste
Stephen	33	Bed
William [2]	6	Smi
William	7	Smi
William	8	Smi
William J.	341	Whi
Bennett, Etheldred	384	Wil
Griffin	141	Sum
Jacob	420	Wil
Jacob, Jr.	420	Wil
James	36	Lin
James	406	Wil
James R. [?]	25	Mau
Jo...	1	Bed
John	384	Wil
Lydia	3	Lin
Micajah	15	Dic
Polly	385	Wil
Richard	139	Sum
Solomon	3	Lin
Solomon	419	Wil
Thomas	384	Wil
William	74	Rut
William	141	Sum
William K.	395	Wil
Wm. J.	139	Sum
Benningfield, Middleton	4	Lin
Bennit, Alexander	42	Wll
Benodd, C.	24	Mau
Wille	24	Mau
Bensick, Leonard	142	Sum
Benson, Benjamin	11	Gil
Daniel	37	Lin
Early	11	Gil
John	34	Rob
Leven, Jur.	38	Lin
Leven, Ser.	38	Lin
Moses	12	Hum
Richard	16	Rob
Robert	13	Rob
William	4	Rob
William	14	Rob
Benthale, Matthew	15	Gil
Bentley, James	144	Sum
John	8	Gil
John	145	Sum
Richard	14	Gil
Bentol, Mary	408	Wil
Benton, Epaphroditus	7	Rob
James [2]	7	Rob
James	20	Rob
John	6	Rob
Mary	398	Wil
Patsey	5	Smi
Robbert	47	Mau
Samuel	36	Fra
Samuel	12	Hum
Thomas	390	Wil
Williamson	36	Fra
Bentz, Thomas	11	Lin
Berdine, Perry	401	Wil
Bergen, Michael	296	War
Berger, Jacob	311	War
Bergin, Abner	9	Law
James	9	Law
Bergus, Susanah	342	Whi
Berkett, William	140	Sum
Berkley, Nathan	141	Sum
Bermingham, Edward	15	Mon
Bernard, David	143	Sum
John	16	Dic
John	112	Wil
see Barnord		
Bernaw, Mary	1	Bed
Berns, John	33	Mau
Miles	34	Mau
Berrey, John	27	Mau
Berriman, Anderson	35	Wll
Berry, Benjamin	12	Hic
Elizabeth	17	Gil
Elizabeth	8	Smi
Elizabeth	315	War
Enoch	45	Bed
George	10	Rob
Jane	29	Wll
John	93	Dav
John	35	Fra
John	361	Whi
Leonard	13	Way
Leonard	37	Wll
Miles	31	Lin
Nancy	30	Lin
Nathaniel	410	Wil
Olly	3	Har
Rebecca	62	Wll
Right	361	Whi
Sally	36	Fra
Samuel	2	Fra
Samuel	35	Fra
Samuel	3	Har
Sandford	35	Fra
Thomas	21	Lin
Thomas	88	Rut
Thomas	14	Wll
William	17	Lin
William	39	Lin
William	29	Wll

Berry (cont.)		
Wright	17	Rob
see Berrey		
Berryhill, Wm. M.	78	Dav
Berryman, Benjamin	9	Har
Claiborne	18	Hic
Mary	2	Har
Wm.	8	Har
Bert, Richard	378	Wil
Berton, Peter	65	Wll
Beshears, Henry	14	Law
Jesse	14	Law
Lomax	6	Smi
William	2	Jac
William	14	Law
Beson, Henry	143	Sum
Saml.	143	Sum
Best, John	143	Sum
Michael	17	Wll
Beter, Margaret	3	Hic
Nicholas	393	Wil
Bethel, Cantrell	6	Smi
Tilman	6	Smi
Betole see Belote		
Bett, John	99	Rut
Joseph T.	402	Wil
Thomas	390	Wil
William	390	Wil
Bettenton, John	280	War
Bettes, James	106	She
John	106	She
Tilmon	106	She
Wm.	106	She
Betts, John	70	Dav
Samuel	91	Dav
Samuel	389	Wil
William	61	Dav
William	389	Wil
Wyatt	389	Wil
Zachariah	70	Dav
Betty, Henry	33	Wll
Isaac	6	Smi
Bevel, Isham	80	Rut
Bevell, Daniel	12	Mon
Robert	13	Mon
Bever, Kire	5	Per
Beverly, Henry	142	Sum
Bevers, James	5	Bed
Bevill, William	15	Lin
Bewford, Elizabeth	4	Ove
Bianchi, Paul	76	Dav
Biard, David	409	Wil
Bias, Hareld	303	War
Bibb, Benjamin	66	Dav
David	8	Dic
Minor	7	Dic
Sarah	7	Dic
Bickerstaff, Benjamin	3	Jac
John	61	Mau
Wallace	3	Jac
Bickle, Michael	299	War
Biddex, John R.	63	Wll
Biers, James F.	55	Mau
Biers (cont.)		
Moses	4	Jac
Biffel, Jacob	33	Mau
John	9	Way
Nathan	9	Way
Biford, Parker	360	Whi
Bigbee, Archer	2	Rob
George	2	Rob
John	2	Rob
Bigger, Robert	9	Mon
Biggers, John	11	Lin
Joseph	11	Lin
Joshua	141	Sum
Lewis	399	Wil
Biggs, Adam	139	Sum
David	142	Sum
Elijah	19	Rob
Elisha	17	Way
Elisha W.	17	Wll
James W.	110	Ste
John	113	Ste
John	142	Sum
Joseph	142	Sum
Kedar	110	Ste
Luke	130	Ste
Reuben	110	Ste
Ruben P.	91	Dav
Bigham, James	64	Mau
Robert	18	Gil
Robert	76	Rut
Samuel	76	Rut
Thomas	4	Gil
Bigley, Patrick	77	Dav
Bigs, Jane	3	Jac
Peter	63	Mau
Bigum, Andrew	371	Whi
Tildy	371	Whi
Bilberry, John	16	Ove
Larence	9	Ove
Bilbo, William	9	Smi
Bilbus, William	387	Wil
Biles, John	80	Rut
Michael	20	Gil
Obediah	85	Rut
Bill, John	42	Mau
Billings, Peter	366	Whi
Billingsley, Edward	16	Gil
J. A.	1	Jac
Wallis	1	Jac
William	1	Jac
Billingsly, Thomas	16	Gil
Billington, Elias	8	Bed
Ezekiel	5	Bed
James	6	Bed
John	5	Bed
Pennel	8	Bed
Saml.	5	Bed
Billion, William	12	Dic
Bills, Daniel [2]	45	Mau
Daniel	46	Mau
Isaack	27	Mau
Jonathan D.	45	Mau
Thomas	45	Mau

Bimton see Bunton		
Binam, Benjamin	11	Law
Enoch	11	Law
Bingham, Josiah	26	Mau
Martin	124	Ste
Thomas	407	Wil
William	48	Bed
Binghan, William	37	Mau
Bingland, Mary G. [deleted]	48	Mau
Binion, Martin	9	Smi
Binkley, Adam	87	Dav
Catharine	14	Rob
Henrey	87	Dav
Jacob	3	Rob
John	61	Dav
Joseph	87	Dav
Peter	87	Dav
Binron see Binion		
Binum, George	36	Fra
James	3	Fra
John	36	Fra
Rebeckey	62	Mau
Tapley	56	Mau
Birckle, Michael	310	War
Bird, Asa	14	Hic
Briant	120	Ste
David	296	War
Drury	117	Ste
Isham	6	Per
James	126	Ste
John	4	Law
John	126	Ste
John	129	Ste
Mary	420	Wil
Micheal	11	Bed
Nathaniel	7	Hum
Peggy	385	Wil
Sarah	18	Mon
Thomas T.	4	Law
William	14	Hic
William	126	Ste
William	400	Wil
William S. C.	15	Hic
Birdson, Miles	9	Law
Birdsong, Henry	10	Gil
Birdwell, Hugh	100	Rut
Isaac	91	Dav
Jane	61	Dav
John	10	Gil
Margaret	4	Jac
William	2	Jac
Birge, Jeremiah	93	Rut
Birk, Benja.	141	Sum
John B.	145	Sum
Martin	36	Lin
Birks, Andrew	367	Whi
Birmingham, Thos.	5	Law
Birton, Julious	61	Mau
Bishop, Boal	79	Rut
David	317	War
James	4	Smi
Jeremiah	103	Rut
John	99	Rut
Bishop (cont.)		
John	9	Smi
Joseph	3	Smi
Roddy	354	Whi
Sterling	103	Rut
William	90	Rut
William	103	Rut
Bittleman, Lucy	59	Mau
Bivens, John	11	Hum
Bivines, Fielder	80	Rut
Bivins, Anderson	3	Har
Bizzel, Hardy	64	Wll
Black, Alexander	3	Gil
Alexr.	114	Ste
David	31	Mon
David	15	Wll
Elizabeth	3	Smi
George G.	2	Fra
Hugh	8	Smi
Jacob	142	Sum
James	92	Dav
James	58	Mau
James	13	Ove
James	278	War
James	299	War
James A.	77	Rut
John	3	Fra
John	12	Gil
John	3	Jac
John	141	Sum
Josiah B.	3	Fra
Lemuel	2	Fra
Lemuel	36	Fra
Marchus	15	Bed
Matthew	18	Gil
Michael	142	Sum
Nancy	27	Mau
Peggy	8	Ove
Peter	9	Hum
Peter	9	Mon
Rebecca	17	Lin
Robert	72	Dav
Robert	3	Gil
Robert	12	Gil
Robert	4	Hum
Samuel	5	Smi
Susan	13	Hum
Thomas	6	Gil
Thomas	3	Per
Thomas G.	50	Mau
William	15	Bed
William	36	Bed
William	86	Dav
William	5	Gil
William	15	Ove
William	13	Wll
William	30	Wll
Blackamord, Elizabeth	81	Rut
Blackard, Branch	13	Law
Levy	10	Law
Wm.	140	Sum
Blackburn, Benja.	11	Dic
Benjamin	366	Whi

Blackburn (cont.)		
Edward	69	Mau
Elijah	43	Bed
Gidieon [?]	15	Wll
Israel	3	Rob
John	32	Mau
John	69	Mau
John	387	Wil
John	39	Wll
Josiah	21	Hic
Robert	14	Rob
William	21	Mon
William	345	Whi
William	387	Wil
William	39	Wll
Blackerd, Eli	130	Ste
Blacketton, Norman	92	Rut
Blackhard, Jeremiah	36	Fra
Blackley, Nancy	4	Smi
Blacklock, David	42	Lin
Blackman, Alfred	85	Rut
Benet	59	Mau
Elizabeth	85	Rut
John	20	Hic
Blackmore, John	144	Sum
Blackshire, Ezekiel	5	Wll
James	14	Wll
Susan	38	Wll
Blackson, Jesse	79	Dav
Blackston, James	142	Sum
Young	141	Sum
Blackwell, Elizabeth	4	Smi
Gabriel	12	Bed
James	32	Mon
Jesse	14	Hic
Joe	343	Whi
John	53	Bed
John	14	Hic
Joseph	8	Hic
Mical	31	Mau
Nathen	53	Bed
Newell	94	Rut
Pleasant	310	War
Blackwood, James	77	Rut
James	98	Rut
Blades, Benjamin	6	Smi
Bladly, Partrick	385	Wil
Blagg, Mary	143	Sum
Siney	47	Bed
Blain, George	15	Rob
Blair, Andrew	68	Mau
Andrew	294	War
George	13	Lin
George	86	Rut
George D.	57	Mau
Haus	12	Lin
James	23	Hic
James	15	Lin
James, Ser.	15	Lin
John	88	Dav
John	22	Mon
Joseph	17	Gil
Peter	144	Sum
Blair (cont.)		
Ralph	81	Rut
Samuel	97	Dav
Samuel	12	Ove
Solomon	5	Smi
Taylor H.	9	Wll
Thomas	19	Lin
Thomas	19	Wll
William	2	Hum
William	7	Lin
William	24	Mon
William	5	Ove
William	6	Smi
Blaire, Robert	142	Sum
Blake, Abigail	37	Wll
Hugh M.	16	Lin
John	16	Lin
John W.	16	Lin
Joseph	2	Fra
William	9	Dic
Blakefield, David	3	Fra
Blakeley, James	32	Mau
Jennet	32	Mau
Samuel	32	Mau
William	32	Mau
Blakely, James	79	Rut
Phileman	82	Rut
Blakemon, George D.	145	Sum
Blakemore, George	16	Lin
James	13	Lin
James	140	Sum
Tho.	140	Sum
William	98	Rut
Blakeney, Hugh	20	Mon
Thos.	4	Mon
Blakmor, Fielden.	142	Sum
Blalock, David	2	Fra
Miridy	43	Mau
Blan, Samuel	18	Lin
see Blau		
Bland, Arthurd	98	Dav
John	74	Dav
John	96	Rut
Blaney, Rachel	129	Ste
Blankenship, Allen	90	Rut
Barney	8	Smi
Benjamin	73	Rut
Elijah	9	Smi
Gad	13	Rob
Glennis	416	Wil
Rhoda	4	Smi
Sylvester	101	Rut
Blanketen, Norman	81	Rut
Blanketship, William	11	Mon
Blanks, Ingram	82	Rut
John	282	War
William	70	Mau
Blanton, Clabourn	303	War
Elizabeth	74	Rut
John	55	Mau
John	125	Ste
Meredith	93	Rut
Richard	115	Ste

Blanton (cont.)		
Thomas	79	Rut
Vincent	302	War
Blare see Blair, Blau		
Blasingain, Wade	7	Law
Blassengam	13	Gil
Blassingale, Jas.	120	Ste
Blassut, William	1	Har
Blau, Mary	46	Lin
Bledsoe, Agnes	37	Bed
Anthony	12	Bed
Barney L.	9	Dic
Edward	38	Mau
Hawkins	2	Fra
Henry R.	142	Sum
Hezekiah	43	Bed
Isaac	143	Sum
Lewis	19	Lin
Mildred	184	Sum
Pinckney T.	9	Dic
William	19	Lin
William	45	Lin
Wm. L.	141	Sum
Bledsow, Isaac M.	38	Mau
Blenkwell, Henry	93	Rut
Blessing, Jacob	32	Bed
Blevins, Hugh A.	20	Ove
Kitterick	306	War
Blew, Daniel	312	War
Bliach, Dilly	3	Jac
Bligh, William	13	Lin
Blithe, Benjamin	43	Wll
Jacob	5	Law
James	68	Mau
James	42	Wll
John	33	Wll
Joseph	42	Wll
Lemuel	7	Law
William	45	Wll
see Spratt		
Blizard, Thomas	35	Fra
Block, Samuel P.	104	Rut
Blockburn, Samuel	21	Way
Blocker, Eligah	65	Mau
Bloodworth, Edwin	142	Sum
Jesse	99	Rut
John	143	Sum
Josiah	140	Sum
Lemuel	143	Sum
Saml.	143	Sum
Tho.	143	Sum
Webb	140	Sum
William	388	Wil
Wm.	141	Sum
Blount, Benjamin	18	Gil
Isaac	2	Har
Isaac	12	Hum
Margaret	15	Dic
Redin	1	Har
Richd.	16	Mon
Wilie	8	Mon
Young	20	Mon
Bludworth, William	127	Ste

Blue, John	7	Gil
Neal	17	Mon
Bluford, John	4	Jac
Blurton, Edward	382	Wil
Henton	382	Wil
John	380	Wil
John	382	Wil
Blythe, Absolom	33	Lin
Andrew	143	Sum
Champion	32	Lin
Richard	142	Sum
Samul K.	140	Sum
Stephen	416	Wil
Thomas	33	Lin
Thomas, Ser.	33	Lin
William	15	Gil
Boan, Henery	51	Mau
Boatenhammer, Jacob	50	Mau
Boatman, James C.	142	Sum
Boatright, Daniel D.	85	Rut
Jacob	26	Mon
Thomas	2	Hum
William	26	Mon
James	19	Gil
Salley	19	Gil
see Bortwright		
Boaz, Eliphaz	28	Lin
Thomas	66	Dav
Thomas	28	Lin
Boaze, Hardy	5	Smi
John	2	Fra
Bobbet, John	84	Rut
Bobbett, Jubilee	6	Gil
Uriah	21	Lin
Bobbit, Louis	82	Rut
Bobo, Chany	17	Rob
Elijah	39	Bed
Elisha	30	Bed
Hyram	8	Mon
Lucil	44	Bed
William	53	Bed
Willis	44	Mau
Bobs see Bobo, Boles		
Boddie, Elijah	139	Sum
Bodenhammer, Peter	6	Bed
William	13	Gil
see Boatenhammer		
Bodkin, Brettan	61	Mau
Bodkinan, Britten	61	Mau
Boehms, Samuel	1	Wll
Bogan, Henry	35	Fra
John	35	Fra
Bogard, Abraham	20	Gil
Charles	20	Mon
William	20	Mon
Bogas, Polly	4	Hum
Boggis, Briant	67	Mau
Boggs, William R.	32	Mau
Bogle, George	415	Wil
Jane	77	Rut
Peggy	414	Wil
Robert	414	Wil
Sarah	104	Rut

Bogue, Josiah 144 Sum
Bohanna, William 144 Sum
Bohannan, William 2 Fra
Bohannon, Delilah 6 Hum
James 7 Hum
John 7 Hum
Bohanon, Elijah 353 Whi
John 352 Whi
Judah 365 Whi
Lewis 356 Whi
Mary 365 Whi
Boice, Hezikiah 14 Hic
Boid, John 306 War
Boils, Obediah 92 Rut
Boland, James 10 Wll
Bolarjack, James 11 Wll
Bolding, William 8 Per
Bolerson, Thomas 53 Mau
Boles, Able 2 Jac
Charles 6 Dic
J. F. 3 Jac
John 2 Jac
Rolin 2 Jac
Sampson 6 Dic
Sarah 2 Jac
William 2 Jac
Boll, James, Sr. 144 Sum
Susannah 144 Sum
Bollen, Joel 115 Wil
Bolling, Bailey 19 Gil
James 19 Gil
Bolston, George 101 Rut
Bolt see Bott
Bolton, Charles, Junr. 5 Smi
Charles, Senr. 5 Smi
Claburn 63 Dav
Elizabeth 5 Smi
John 25 Hic
Lewis 7 Ove
Moses 8 Smi
Boman, James 3 Jac
James 66 Mau
James H. 48 Mau
Rachel 3 Smi
Bomar, Herod 1 Hic
Reuben 1 Hic
William J. 6 Smi
Bomgarty, Frederick 3 Fra
John 3 Fra
Michael 3 Fra
Bond, Allen 141 Sum
Andrew 387 Wil
Benamin 61 Dav
Elizabeth 114 Ste
Francis 47 Wll
James 86 Dav
James 420 Wil
John 420 Wil
John 7 Wll
John 8 Wll
John B. 142 Sum
Lewis 112 Ste
Lewis 407 Wil
Mary 415 Wil
Bond (cont.)
Morris [& Petway] 1 Wll
Page 36 Wll
William 293 War
William 384 Wil
William 411 Wil
William 8 Wll
William, Sen. 36 Wll
Zebulon 387 Wil
Bonds, Drewry 26 Mon
Margaret 419 Wil
Matthew 384 Wil
Robert 392 Wil
Solomon 384 Wil
William C. 114 Wil
Bone, Abner 28 Mon
Abner 415 Wil
Andrew 415 Wil
Cornelius L. 22 Hic
George E. 66 Mau
Henry 407 Wil
James 26 Mon
James 399 Wil
James 417 Wil
James, Jr. 407 Wil
John 8 Hum
John 140 Sum
John 399 Wil
John, Junr. 1 Per
John, Senr. 1 Per
Robert 417 Wil
Samuel A. 7 Per
Thomas 415 Wil
William 9 Hum
William 417 Wil
Boner, Henry 88 Dav
Bones, James 100 Rut
Bonner, Benjamin 401 Wil
Ezekiel 45 Lin
James 3 Fra
Jesse 19 Lin
John 283 War
John 288 War
John 401 Wil
Thomas 401 Wil
Thomas 408 Wil
William 45 Lin
Williamson 145 Sum
Bonnett, John 7 Hum
Bonns, Lawrence 13 Lin
Nancy 11 Lin
Bonnuck, Rachel 315 War
Booker, John 63 Mau
John 140 Sum
Lavecy 11 Hic
Peter R. 38 Mau
Samuel 392 Wil
Shields 10 Rob
William 411 Wil
Willis 392 Wil
Boon, Benjamin 25 Lin
Bryant 86 Dav
Hiram 11 Har
James 46 Mau

Boon (cont.)
John 16 Lin
John 410 Wil
Mordicai 291 War
Phillip 141 Sum
Reuben H. 26 Lin
Boothe, Benjamin 51 Bed
David 24 Hic
Elizabeth 17 Hic
Henry 51 Bed
Isaac 301 War
James 49 Bed
James 51 Bed
Jeremiah 53 Wll
John 2 Dic
Margret 70 Dav
Mark 2 Mon
Mary 35 Bed
Mary 17 Hic
Nathan 102 Rut
Robert 70 Dav
Stephen 51 Bed
Booton, Elizabeth 10 Mon
Borch, Martha 18 Wll
Boren, Francis 6 Rob
Francis 143 Sum
John 143 Sum
Sarah 143 Sum
see Baren
Borin, James 42 Lin
Boring, Amon 96 Rut
Charles 121 Ste
James 121 Ste
Wm. 121 Ste
Born, Thomas L. 35 Fra
Borrling, William 6 Hum
Borrum, Edmond 398 Wil
Bortwright, Samuel 84 Dav
Bosley, Beal 73 Dav
Charles 62 Dav
James R. 91 Dav
John 74 Dav
Boss, David 281 War
Bossel, Nancy 4 Jac
Polly 25 Wll
Bostic, Floyd 36 Fra
Rice 35 Fra
Bostick, Absolom 9 Lin
John 10 Wll
Bostock, James B. 10 Gil
Boston, Christian 8 Smi
Bostwick, Manoah 18 Mon
Boswell, Andrew 18 Ove
Bomas 1 Per
Hosea 5 Hum
James 53 Bed
James 9 Ove
James 4 Smi
John 32 Bed
John 36 Fra
Samuel 5 Ove
Samuel 18 Ove
Walter 115 Ste
Boswell (cont.)
William 5 Ove
Bosworth, David 77 Dav
William 75 Dav
Bott, John C. 121 Ste
Bottom, William 6 Gil
Bottoms, Merry S. 135 Sum
Botts, Archibald 3 Jac
Boucher, Richard 313 War
Bougard, Joseph 4 Mon
Boughman, Christian 7 Dic
Boulden, Nathan 303 War
Boulton, William 12 Hum
Bounds, John 353 Whi
Bow, Baley 32 Mon
Bowars, David 46 Wll
Bowden, James 37 Mau
John 37 Mau
Thomas 15 Bed
Bowen, Absolam 28 Lin
Allen 11 Dic
Arthur 357 Whi
Charles 355 Whi
Chas. 3 Hic
Elldridge 12 Dic
Jeremiah 3 Smi
John 3 Fra
John 320 War
John H. 135 Sum
Joshua 320 War
Mary H. 144 Sum
Rew 7 Dic
Robt. O. 6 Hic
William 28 Lin
William 380 Wil
Bowers, David 5 Wll
Elizabeth, Mrs. 403 Wil
James 21 Bed
James 24 Mon
Jeremiah 139 Sum
Jesse 406 Wil
John 21 Bed
John 25 Bed
John 3 Fra
John 24 Mon
Joseph 25 Mon
Lemuel 70 Dav
Lemuel S. 24 Mau
Lemul S. 26 Mau
Philemon 3 Lin
William 3 Jac
William P. 69 Dav
Bowgard, Susannah 42 Mau
Bowin, Jesse 12 Way
William 36 Fra
Bowlen, John 46 Lin
Robert 26 Lin
Willoby 26 Lin
Bowles, Anne 11 Hum
John M. 297 War
Robert 11 Hum
Bowlin, James B. 1 Mon
Nathan 306 War

Bowlin (cont.)		
see Bowles		
Bowling, Alexander	140	Sum
Michael	35	Fra
Rodney	5	Smi
Bowls, Anny	131	Ste
Charles	9	Lin
James	7	Ove
James	94	Rut
Thomas	12	Hic
Bowman, Cosby	367	Whi
Daniel	83	Rut
Elijah	22	Bed
James	139	Sum
James	402	Wil
John	22	Bed
John	90	Rut
John	104	Rut
John	145	Sum
John	395	Wil
Josiah	19	Ove
Nathaniel	372	Whi
Samuel	8	Ove
Samuel	101	Rut
William	85	Rut
William	314	War
see Boman		
Bowmon, Benjamine	353	Whi
Bows, William	40	Mau
Box, Abram	10	Hic
Allen	3	Fra
Edward	4	Hum
Jacob	3	Fra
James	10	Hic
John	35	Fra
John	3	Per
Josep	4	Hum
Michael	4	Hum
Moses	5	Hum
Robert	3	Fra
Robert	3	Per
Robert, Senr.	35	Fra
William	3	Hum
Boyce, Alexander	3	Fra
Macklin	36	Fra
Meshech	10	Gil
Boyd, Aaron	2	Bed
Andrew	93	Dav
Andrew	1	Har
Archd.	8	Lin
Elisha	1	Har
George, Junr.	116	Ste
George, Senr.	116	Ste
George W.	86	Dav
Henry	18	Bed
James	7	Har
James	3	Law
James	20	Lin
James	39	Mau
James	30	Mon
James	121	Ste
James	40	Wll
James, Jur.	8	Har
John	3	Bed
Boyd (cont.)		
John	90	Dav
John	3	Fra
John	35	Fra
John	22	Gil
John	7	Har
John	2	Jac
John	104	Rut
John	112	Ste
John, Sr.	144	Sum
Joseph	10	Bed
Mary	32	Wll
Rhody	1	Wll
Richard	85	Dav
Robert	60	Dav
Robert	145	Sum
Robt.	140	Sum
Samuel	3	Fra
Thomas	3	Fra
Thomas	4	Har
William	77	Dav
William	87	Dav
William G.	30	Wll
William J.	4	Wll
see Bond, Boyde, Boyed, Boyt		
Boyde, Andrew	39	Mau
Boyed, John	40	Mau
Boyer, James	2	Fra
Philip	145	Sum
Boyers, Henry	11	Hum
Robt. M.	135	Sum
Boykin, Amelia	143	Sum
Boykin, Hannah Ritter	142	Sum
Polly	142	Sum
Boyle, John	140	Sum
Boyles, Banabas	7	Lin
Charles	1	Lin
Elijah	144	Sum
James	7	Rob
James	141	Sum
James, Jr.	142	Sum
James, Sr.	142	Sum
John	7	Lin
John	411	Wil
Jonathan	297	War
Pleasant	139	Sum
Robt.	144	Sum
William	2	Way
Boyls, Thomas	411	Wil
Boyne, Catharine	144	Sum
John	144	Sum
Boysy, Frances	81	Rut
Boyt, Elijah	115	Ste
James	87	Dav
Thomas	87	Dav
William, Sr.	87	Dav
Bozeman, Caleb	139	Sum
Bozreth, Levi	370	Whi
Bracher, Allen	302	War
Benjamin	290	War
Julialee	284	War
Brachin, John, Jr.	143	Sum
Brack, Derham	143	Sum
William	46	Wll

Brackenridge, John 17 Lin
Brackin, Isaac 141 Sum
James, Jr. 142 Sum
James, Sr. 142 Sum
William 142 Sum
see Brackm
Brackinridge, Joseph 24 Lin
Brackm, John 140 Sum
Bracy, Harrison 16 Rob
Bradberry, James 395 Wil
John 388 Wil
Joshua 396 Wil
Wm. 395 Wil
Bradbury, Edwin 3 Per
George 65 Mau
Jacob 3 Per
Jacob, Junr. 3 Per
Bradby, John 367 Whi
Robert 5 Smi
Bradcut, Susanna 3 Jac
Braddy, Joseph 101 Rut
Joseph, Jr. 101 Rut
Braden, Alexander 407 Wil
Cassandra 4 Lin
Charles 407 Wil
James 407 Wil
John 42 Mau
Joseph 30 Lin
Bradfield, Joseph 48 Bed
Bradford, —, Mrs. 117 Ste
Booker 5 Smi
Christian 124 Ste
Crofford 116 Ste
Darnal 3 Lin
David 3 Jac
David 116 Ste
David, Jr. 3 Jac
Hamilton 25 Bed
Harris 3 Smi
Hugh 8 Hic
James 93 Rut
John 25 Bed
John 65 Dav
Joseph 8 Smi
Kirney 51 Wil
Priestley 140 Sum
Richard 119 Ste
Robert 94 Rut
Simon 79 Dav
Theo F. 37 Bed
Thomas 4 Smi
Thomas 7 Smi
Thomas G. 75 Dav
Thos. 118 Ste
William 142 Sum
William 366 Whi
Bradin, Joseph 20 Gil
Bradley, Anseln 378 Whi
Charles 3 Smi
Danl. 141 Sum
David [2] 141 Sum
David 404 Wil
Elisha 14 Gil
Bradley (cont.)
Elizabeth 10 Gil
Elizabeth 4 Smi
Even B. 413 Wil
George 403 Wil
Henrey 62 Dav
Henry 142 Sum
Hugh 7 Smi
Isaac 6 Smi
James 3 Smi
James 4 Smi
James A. 10 Gil
Jesse 140 Sum
John 82 Rut
John 4 Smi
John 143 Sum
John, Jr. 404 Wil
John, Sen. 404 Wil
Jonas 404 Wil
Joseph 6 Gil
Joseph 404 Wil
Joseph 12 Wil
Joshua 2 Fra
Joshua 140 Sum
Joshua 141 Sum
Motley 400 Wil
Nathaniel 2 Rob
P. 114 Wil
Pleasant 404 Wil
Richard 14 Gil
Richard 140 Sum
Saml. B. 405 Wil
Samuel 6 Gil
Samuel 6 Smi
Samuel 404 Wil
Sherard 7 Smi
Tho., Jr. 143 Sum
Thomas 142 Sum
Thomas 406 Wil
Thomas 20 Wil
William 10 Gil
William 60 Mau
William 140 Sum
Bradly, Edward 145 Sum
Bradon, Samuel 61 Wil
Bradshaw, David 405 Wil
Eli G. 42 Mau
Elias 14 Bed
Field 139 Sum
Henry 35 Fra
Ishmael 379 Wil
James 14 Ove
James 8 Per
James W. 58 Wil
Joe 359 Whi
John 8 Bed
John 37 Bed
John 14 Mon
John 409 Wil
Joseph 16 Mon
Joseph 359 Whi
Richd. 16 Mon
Samuel 3 Fra

Bradshaw (cont.)
Sarah 38 Mau
Soleman 42 Mau
William 35 Fra
William 47 Mau
William 346 Whi
Brady, Ansel 7 Smi
Frederick 95 Rut
Spencer 18 Ove
William 86 Rut
see Beady, Braddy, Braidy
Brafield, Walter 18 Ove
Brag, Henry 114 Ste
Bragg, Dozar 97 Rut
John 97 Rut
John 292 War
John 49 Wll
Richard 279 War
Thomas 98 Rut
Braham, William 2 Fra
Braidy, Sarah 69 Mau
Braine, Melchisedick 37 Bed
see Brame
Brake, Axom 15 Mon
James 124 Ste
John 21 Rob
Levi 7 Smi
Brakefield, George 31 Rob
William 33 Rob
Braley, Walter 304 War
Bramblet, William 12 Law
Brame, Warner 41 Bed
see Braine
Bramley, Ely 62 Mau
Ephraim 43 Mau
William 38 Mau
Bramlitt, John 4 Gil
Lunsford M. 17 Gil
Branch, Henery 53 Mau
James 41 Mau
John 31 Bed
John 3 Fra
John 41 Mau
John N. 3 Smi
Nancy 71 Dav
Nicholas 50 Wll
Pledge 3 Smi
Robert 410 Wil
Brancomb, E. 121 Ste
Brand, Malachi 6 Smi
Brandon, Charles 43 Bed
Cornelius 102 Rut
David 3 Fra
George 103 Rut
Harrison 8 Smi
John S. 11 Gil
Jonathan 5 Smi
Josiah 34 Lin
Lemuel 34 Lin
Richard 11 Gil
Thomas 97 Rut
William D. 5 Smi
see Bradon
Branen, Charles 68 Mau
Branes, Charity 297 War
Branham, William 5 Smi
Brannon, James 3 Fra
Rebecca 4 Har
William 3 Fra
William 4 Smi
Branon, Chrisr. 114 Ste
Bransford, Arthur 4 Smi
John, Junr. 6 Smi
John, Senr. 4 Smi
William 3 Smi
Branston, Jonathan 12 Gil
Brantley, Abram 6 Mon
John 46 Wll
Wilson 17 Mon
Braselton, Hannah 11 Har
Solomon 5 Har
Brashear, Asaph 418 Wil
Jesse 80 Rut
Jesse 89 Rut
Brashears, Betsy 312 War
Jesse 23 Gil
John 5 Gil
John 413 Wil
Meivy 312 War
Robert 4 Law
Samuel 23 Gil
Val A. 312 War
Walter 4 Law
Brashion, Philip 294 War
Brasil, William 145 Sum
Brassel, William 3 Jac
see Brssel
Brasun, William 9 Dic
Brasure, William 48 Mau
Braswell, Sampson 317 War
William 285 War
Bratcher, William 293 War
Bratney, James 144 Sum
James, Sr. 144 Sum
Braton, Enoch 7 Smi
Philip 96 Rut
Bratt, Burwell 35 Wll
Bratton, David 9 Smi
Hugh 9 Gil
James 9 Gil
James 6 Smi
John 3 Fra
Joseph 3 Fra
Joseph 6 Smi
Joshua 6 Smi
Margaret 9 Gil
Paul 37 Wll
Rachel 4 Smi
Robert 4 Smi
Robert 21 Wll
Thomas 9 Gil
Thomas 7 Smi
Thomas 9 Smi
William 7 Smi
William 142 Sum
Braudway, John 6 Lin

Braughton, Thomas	92	Rut
Brawing, Bedah	32	Bed
Brawley, Alfred	307	War
John	98	Rut
Leroy	307	War
Prior	102	Rut
Ruth	102	Rut
Samuel	307	War
Thomas	20	Gil
Thomas C.	21	Gil
Brawner, Dizier	4	Smi
Henry	5	Smi
John	4	Smi
Bray, James	357	Whi
Joseph H.	6	Smi
Kinchen	35	Fra
Stognen	35	Fra
William	35	Fra
William	7	Wll
Brazier, Elijah	3	Fra
James	3	Fra
Brazil, Aaron	7	Smi
Elizabeth	6	Smi
Richard	6	Smi
Robert	6	Smi
Brazill, Archibald	86	Rut
Brazleton, William	36	Fra
Breckenridge, James	7	Gil
see Brackenridge, Brackinridge		
Bredin, Mary	118	Ste
Bredors see Bridges		
Breeding, Briant	9	Ove
Nancy	4	Jac
Breedlove, A. B.	141	Sum
Breidlow, Thomas	401	Wil
Brenfield, Bennard	14	Wll
Brennon, Marth	72	Dav
Brent, Elizabeth	65	Dav
John	5	Smi
Brents, Solomon	311	War
Brerer, Sterling	3	Dic
Breris, William	142	Sum
Bressie, John	142	Sum
Brethett, Edward	1	Wll
Brevard, John	4	Smi
Brewer, Aron	353	Whi
Britton	3	Smi
Cornelius	5	Way
Edward	17	Rob
Edward	18	Rob
Elisha	66	Dav
George	5	Way
H. M.	13	Law
James	64	Dav
Jessee	354	Whi
John	2	Fra
John	35	Lin
John	111	Ste
John H.	17	Lin
Joseph	66	Dav
Julias	13	Law
Lewis	127	Ste
Morriss	395	Wil
Brewer (cont.)		
Nancy	2	Fra
Nicholas	127	Ste
Sarah	417	Wil
Silas	281	War
Solomon	11	Ove
Thomas	127	Ste
William	15	Rob
Willie	13	Law
Brewington, James	2	Jac
Bri...3, James	5	Bed
Brian, Mathew	92	Rut
Briant, Aaron	11	Har
Archilles	12	Hic
Burrel	14	Hum
Elizabeth	25	Lin
Gray	13	Lin
James	93	Rut
Joshua	11	Hic
Mary	11	Hic
Nathaniel	3	Jac
P. O.	2	Jac
Thomas	16	Lin
Thomas	19	Ove
Brice, Stephen	408	Wil
Bridgeforth, David	62	Dav
Bridgemon, Joseph	347	Whi
Thomas	345	Whi
Thomas	347	Whi
Bridgers, Redick	140	Sum
Bridges, Allen J.	4	Smi
Anne	2	Jac
Benjamin	15	Hic
Benjamin	113	Wil
Benjamin	379	Wil
Britain	17	Rob
Daniel	4	Smi
Daniel	381	Wil
David	386	Wil
Deril	54	Mau
Easter	53	Mau
Franck	37	Mau
Henry	21	Gil
Isaac	2	Fra
James B.	4	Smi
Jessy	49	Mau
Jno.	139	Sum
John	21	Gil
John	2	Jac
Joseph	4	Smi
Reuben	21	Gil
Samuel	382	Wil
Samuel B.	37	Wll
Shadrack	2	Jac
Thomas	2	Fra
Thomas	4	Smi
Tyree	8	Smi
William	35	Mau
Willis	2	Fra
Willis	35	Mau
Bridgewater, Isaac	20	Lin
see Brigdwater, Bridgwater(s)		
Bridgwater, Chesley	5	Smi

Bridgwaters, John	15	Ove
Peggy	28	Rob
Brient, James	61	Dav
Brierley, Robt.	80	Dav
Brigams, John	2	Per
William	2	Per
Brigance, Charlotte	144	Sum
Chs. M.	144	Sum
George S.	144	Sum
James	139	Sum
Patsey	144	Sum
Briganer, James	122	Ste
Brigdwater, Richd.	1	Mon
Briggs, George [2]	111	Wil
George	391	Wil
John	69	Mau
John	20	Mon
Nancy	369	Whi
Nathan	6	Smi
Richard	19	Gil
Robt.	80	Dav
Samuel	11	Gil
Wm.	6	Hic
Brigham, David	116	Ste
David, Junr.	128	Ste
James	124	Ste
James, Junr.	128	Ste
James, Senr.	128	Ste
John	128	Ste
Thomas	126	Ste
Wm.	124	Ste
Bright, Benjamin	25	Hic
Caleb	2	Hum
Charles	29	Lin
Jacob	13	Hum
James	2	Lin
Thomas	279	War
William	47	Lin
Brightwell, William	348	Whi
Brignal, George	1	Mon
Briley, Dempsey	5	Hum
James	143	Sum
John	145	Sum
Joshua	1	Way
Saml.	143	Sum
Brim, James	30	Mon
Brimage, Elizabeth	36	Lin
Brimley, John	3	Way
Brimm, John	63	Wll
Raleigh	9	Lin
Brimni see Brimm		
Brinkley, Kindal	141	Sum
William	88	Dav
Timothy	22	Hic
Brinson, Drury	122	Ste
Edward	9	Dic
Zeb	64	Mau
Brintle, Jacob	50	Mau
Brintsfield, James	45	Lin
Brisby, John	61	Wll
Briscoe, George	36	Mau
John	38	Mau
Brisendine, John	140	Sum
Brison, James	20	Wll
Brison (cont.)		
William	414	Wil
see Brasun		
Bristo, James	8	Ove
John	15	Mon
Britain, Cullen	119	Ste
John	115	Ste
William C.	341	Whi
Britchet, John	125	Ste
Britewell, Alexr.	116	Ste
Briton, James	24	Wll
Britston, James	22	Hic
Robt.	22	Hic
Wm.	22	Hic
Britt, Anderson S.	6	Hum
Bartholomew	140	Sum
Bowlen	32	Mon
Jedekiah	27	Mon
Randolph	25	Rob
W. D.	7	Per
Brittain, Jonathan	2	Bed
Joseph	2	Bed
Philip	2	Bed
Thomas	2	Bed
Brittenham, John	91	Rut
Brittle, Milton	411	Wil
Britton, James H.	4	Smi
John	12	Gil
Polly	4	Smi
Samuel	4	Smi
William W.	6	Har
Brixy, John	35	Fra
Thomas	35	Fra
Broadstreet, James	10	Law
Broadway, J.	110	Ste
James	16	Lin
Jesse	28	Lin
John	125	Ste
Joseph	15	Lin
see Braudway, Brodeway		
Brock, Allen	9	Ove
Durham	127	Ste
Elizabeth	6	Ove
George	1	Ove
George A.	35	Fra
James	36	Fra
James	6	Ove
Joel	6	Ove
John	123	Ste
John	342	Whi
Russle	39	Mau
Brocken, John	65	Dav
Brocket, Elisha	8	Smi
Frederick	8	Smi
James	8	Smi
Brockin, Vinson	39	Mau
Brodeway, George	5	Hum
Brodey, Charles	7	Per
Brodie, John	21	Mon
Thos.	23	Mon
Brodley, Abram	140	Sum
Brody, John	4	Per
Brogan, John	415	Wil
Broiles, Isaac	29	Lin

Broiles (cont.)		
Jeremiah	28	Lin
Broils, Abraham	360	Whi
Cornelious	361	Whi
Daniel	362	Whi
John	351	Whi
Mathias	92	Rut
Reubin	351	Whi
Thomas	351	Whi
William	351	Whi
Bromley, Neeley	62	Wll
Broning, Edmund	140	Sum
Brood, Jerry	409	Wil
Brook, David	141	Sum
George	104	Rut
see Brock		
Brooke, Dudly	2	Rob
Brooks, Archibald	2	Fra
Benjmin	27	Mau
Christopher	357	Whi
Elias R.	3	Smi
Emily	10	Har
Francis	13	Lin
George	16	Gil
George	1	Wll
Henrey	67	Mau
Henry	3	Smi
Isaac W.	419	Wil
James	2	Lin
James	14	Lin
James	20	Wll
James, Mr.	7	Law
Jawel	65	Mau
John	2	Jac
John	10	Rob
John	43	Wll
John C.	58	Mau
John D.	286	War
John H.	3	Fra
Joseph	67	Mau
Joseph	8	Ove
Lynch	36	Fra
Mathew	18	Ove
Matthew	2	Jac
Moses S.	85	Dav
Philip	36	Fra
Price	20	Wll
Richard	27	Mau
Robert	3	Fra
Robert	2	Jac
Robert	11	Lin
Samuel	56	Mau
Samuel C.	33	Wll
Samuel C.	43	Wll
Stephen	47	Wll
Tho.	141	Sum
Thomas	10	Har
Thomas	59	Mau
Thomas	64	Mau
William	77	Dav
William	288	War
William B.	10	Gil
Brooksher, E. W.	76	Dav
Brooksher (cont.)		
Tho.	142	Sum
Brookshire, Benjamin	7	Gil
James	78	Rut
Manual	7	Gil
Martha	35	Fra
Thomas	35	Fra
Broom, William	5	Mon
see MBroom		
Broose, Negget	409	Wil
Broslan, William	19	Bed
Brothers, Francis	76	Rut
Francis	89	Rut
John	93	Rut
Thomas	93	Rut
Brotton, John	83	Dav
Brow see Manon		
Brown, Aaron, Sr.	5	Gil
Aaron V.	17	Gil
Abraham	10	Gil
Absalom	291	War
Adam	13	Rob
Aexander	310	War
Alexander	16	Dic
Alexander	299	War
Alexander	319	War
Alexr.	116	Ste
Allen	35	Fra
Anderson	6	Hum
Andrew	10	Law
Andy	65	Mau
Aner	3	Per
Arabia	121	Ste
Asa A.	4	Dic
Augustians	36	Mau
Barnett P.	418	Wil
Bazel	83	Dav
Benjamin	2	Jac
Benjamin	24	Lin
Benjamin	6	Wll
Benjamin G.	27	Wll
Benjn.	127	Ste
Benjn.	129	Ste
Betsey	8	Smi
Beverly	114	Ste
Charles	57	Dav
Charles	401	Wil
Charls. V.	40	Mau
Clabourn	9	Hum
Cornelius	51	Wll
Dance	141	Sum
Daniel	38	Mau
Daniel	58	Mau
Daniel	18	Ove
Daniel	297	War
Daniel	342	Whi
Daniel	55	Wll
David	65	Dav
David	2	Jac
David	9	Smi
David	378	Wil
David	395	Wil
David E.	62	Dav

Brown (cont.)

David G.	94	Rut
Davis	12	Gil
Dempsy	46	Lin
Dudley	89	Rut
Duncan	9	Gil
Duncan	57	Mau
Edward	7	Law
Edward M.	13	Gil
Eli	10	Hic
Elias	4	Way
Elijah	131	Ste
Elizabeth	2	Jac
Ephraim	57	Mau
Ephram	17	Wll
Federick	143	Sum
Francis	8	Smi
George	14	Gil
George	6	Hum
George	2	Jac
George	377	Wil
George G.	24	Rob
George G.	36	Rob
George M.	361	Whi
Gideon	2	Jac
Gordon	9	Ove
Hardy	11	Lin
Henrietta	3	Hum
Henry	43	Mau
Henry	15	Wll
Henry H.	2	Per
Henry W.	14	Hum
Hezekiah	45	Bed
Hiram	2	Jac
Hopy	8	Smi
Hubbard	79	Rut
Hugh	57	Mau
Hugh M.	135	Sum
Isaac	1	Per
Isaac	367	Whi
Isaac W.	39	Mau
Isaiah	20	Lin
Isham	14	Gil
J.	112	Wil
Jackson W.	378	Wil
James	54	Bed
James	84	Dav
James	10	Gil
James	21	Gil
James	5	Hum
James	5	Law
James	11	Lin
James	18	Lin
James	21	Lin
James	31	Lin
James	47	Mau
James	13	Mon
James	16	Mon
James	139	Sum
James	6	Wll
James	34	Wll
James, Junr.	8	Smi
James, Sen.	8	Smi

Brown (cont.)

James C.	13	Hum
James D.	68	Mau
James M.	70	Mau
James R.	30	Lin
James S.	139	Sum
Jane	47	Mau
Jane	77	Rut
Jane	128	Ste
Jane	286	War
Jeremiah	10	Hic
Jeremiah	2	Jac
Jeremiah	13	Mon
Jesse	9	Har
Jesse	3	Jac
Jesse	24	Lin
Jesse	308	War
Jessey	64	Mau
Joel	144	Sum
John	27	Bed
John	50	Bed
John	54	Bed
John	81	Dav
John	17	Gil
John	9	Hic
John	15	Hic
John	6	Hum
John	1	Jac
John [2]	2	Jac
John	13	Law
John	12	Lin
John	34	Lin
John	37	Lin
John	45	Mau
John	54	Mau
John	55	Mau
John	7	Ove
John	88	Rut
John	119	Ste
John [3]	139	Sum
John	290	War
John	300	War
John	315	War
John	351	Whi
John	357	Whi
John	112	Wil
John	388	Wil
John	389	Wil
John B.	7	Dic
John B.	13	Dic
John B.	377	Wil
John H.	316	War
John H.	378	Wil
John S.	4	Ove
Jonathan	4	Dic
Joseph	27	Lin
Joseph	40	Mau
Joseph	7	Per
Joseph	344	Whi
Josiah	35	Fra
Josiah	19	Ove
Lait	86	Rut
Leonard	25	Bed

Brown (cont.)
Leonard 11 Gil
Leonard 143 Sum
Lewis 6 Gil
Lewis 319 War
Lewis H. 9 Gil
Lindsey 350 Whi
Lockey 13 Mon
Luther 5 Wll
Margeret 7 Mon
Matthew 7 Har
McClentic 27 Lin
Michael 35 Fra
Michael 17 Wll
Micheal 12 Bed
Morgan 8 Gil
Morgan 7 Mon
Morris 6 Smi
Nathaniel 19 Lin
Polly 314 War
Rachel 7 Dic
Randolph 27 Mon
Rebecca 143 Sum
Rebecka 354 Whi
Redding 317 War
Reuben 35 Fra
Rewben D. 141 Sum
Richard 91 Dav
Richard 21 Gil
Richard 4 Per
Richard 3 Smi
Richard H. 20 Gil
Richd. 10 Hic
Richd. 13 Mon
Rikard 351 Whi
Robbart L. 35 Mau
Robert 71 Dav
Robert 83 Dav
Robert 78 Rut
Robert 140 Sum
Robert 145 Sum
Robert 378 Wil
Robert 420 Wil
Robert T. 145 Sum
Robt. 10 Hic
Rolley 13 Gil
Ruffin 19 Wll
Sally 6 Smi
Saml. 145 Sum
Samuel 59 Dav
Samuel 349 Whi
Samuel 367 Whi
Samuel 378 Wil
Samuel 393 Wil
Samuel 41 Wll
Sarah 4 Ove
Shadrach 37 Bed
Shedrick 38 Mau
Skelton 140 Sum
Solo. 142 Sum
Spencer 14 Dic
Stephen 5 Law
Sterling 95 Rut

Brown (cont.)
Sylvia 301 War
Thomas 3 Bed
Thomas 8 Bed
Thomas 43 Bed
Thomas 54 Bed
Thomas 65 Dav
Thomas 5 Gil
Thomas 2 Jac
Thomas 47 Mau
Thomas 18 Ove
Thomas 114 Ste
Thomas 289 War
Thomas [2] 296 War
Thomas 303 War
Thomas [2] 310 War
Thomas, Jr. 13 Gil
Thomas A. 24 Lin
Valentine 3 Smi
Walter 5 Ove
Watkins 97 Dav
Wiley 52 Mau
William 59 Dav
William 35 Fra
William 5 Gil
William 17 Gil
William 24 Lin
William 31 Lin
William 32 Lin
William 36 Mau
William 64 Mau
William 4 Mon
William 7 Ove
William 18 Ove
William 77 Rut
William 97 Rut
William 110 Ste
William 141 Sum
William [2] 292 War
William 4 Way
William 363 Whi
William 413 Wil
William 22 Wll
William 55 Wll
William, Jr. 26 Wll
William, Ser. 351 Whi
William F. 35 Mau
Wilson 129 Ste
Wm. 13 Hic
Wm. 4 Lin
Wm. L. 81 Dav
Zacheriah 2 Fra
see Parkerson
Brownfield, John 304 War
Browning, Alfred 20 Rob
Brackston 27 Rob
Charles 7 Gil
David 7 Gil
David 142 Sum
Dorotha 7 Gil
Edmand 6 Rob
Granvill 28 Rob
Jacob 95 Rut

Browning (cont.)
Jacob A. 139 Sum
John 6 Gil
Maben 7 Rob
Martin 7 Gil
Nicholas 7 Gil
Nimrod 4 Rob
Samuel 403 Wil
Spencer 6 Rob
Tho. 144 Sum
Thomas 6 Gil
William 3 Rob
see Broning
Brownlow, Mary 19 Gil
William 19 Gil
Browor see Manon
Brozeal, George 12 Dic
Brssel, John 3 Jac
Bruce, Amos 3 Smi
Anderson 50 Mau
Azariah 379 Wil
Elijah 105 Rut
Henry 14 Bed
James 3 Smi
Jesse 3 Smi
Joel 20 Lin
Joseph 8 Bed
Penelope 7 Smi
Thomas 105 Rut
William 4 Smi
Bruer, William 68 Dav
Bruff, Samuel 2 Jac
Bruice, Benjamin 11 Dic
David 57 Wil
John 13 Dic
John B. 402 Wil
Bruise, Rewben 144 Sum
Robert 144 Sum
Robt. 144 Sum
Thos. 142 Sum
Walker 142 Sum
William 140 Sum
William 145 Sum
Brumbalan, Lewis 11 Rob
Brumbelow, James 98 Rut
Brumble, Isaac 364 Whi
Brumfield, Ann 30 Bed
Elisha 85 Rut
Obediah 2 Mon
Brumhalve, Jesse 99 Rut
Brumley, John 2 Fra
John 8 Law
John 41 Lin
Brumlow, John 3 Fra
Brummet, LeRoy 84 Rut
Brunson, Asbel 23 Mon
David 130 Ste
Isaac 114 Ste
Jesse A. 122 Ste
Moses 114 Ste
Peter 119 Ste
Brush, William 2 Hum
Brussel see Brssel
Brussels, John 368 Whi
Brutan, Samuel 5 Har
Benjamin 8 Smi
George 125 Ste
Bryan, Andrew 367 Whi
Asa 24 Rob
Elisha 18 Bed
Hardy 16 Mon
Hardy 24 Rob
Henry H. 22 Mon
James 37 Bed
James 353 Whi
James H. 4 Rob
Jeremiah 3 Lin
John 18 Bed
John 356 Whi
John 360 Whi
John, Jr. 363 Whi
Needham 88 Rut
Nicholas 23 Mon
Robert 5 Smi
Sarah 362 Whi
Stephen 60 Dav
William 16 Wil
William M. 359 Whi
Bryand, William 31 Mau
Bryant, Archbald 389 Wil
C... ["Clork" written over
in photostats 2 Fra
Elisha 7 Gil
Elisha 405 Wil
Elisha 406 Wil
Elizabeth 143 Sum
Henry 35 Fra
Jacob 19 Gil
James 2 Lin
John 35 Fra
John 5 Hum
John 111 Wil
John 405 Wil
John 418 Wil
John, Jur. 41 Lin
John, Ser. 40 Lin
Josiah 352 Whi
Julia 3 Hum
Moses A. 17 Way
Nelson 414 Wil
Philip 10 Law
Randolph 40 Lin
Richard 418 Wil
Robert 15 Mon
Samuel 382 Wil
Sherad 97 Dav
William 68 Dav
William 84 Dav
William 46 Lin
William 7 Mon
William 19 Ove
William 352 Whi
Bryden, James 27 Rob
Bryder, John 31 Mau
Bryley, John 67 Dav
Bryns, Mathew 140 Sum

Bryon, William S.	30	Wll
Bryson, Elisha	414	Wil
Fielden	144	Sum
John	414	Wil
Joseph	414	Wil
Peter	140	Sum
Samuel	414	Wil
see Byson		
Buchanan, David	15	Lin
Jane	16	Lin
John	14	Gil
John	4	Lin
John	16	Lin
John B.	15	Lin
Nancy	4	Lin
Robert	13	Gil
Robert	16	Lin
Samuel	7	Lin
Samuel	15	Lin
Samuel	47	Lin
Steel	15	Lin
Thomas	7	Lin
W. H., Mr.	1	Law
William	14	Gil
Buchannan, Alexander	91	Dav
James	97	Dav
John, Sr.	63	Dav
Margaret	63	Wll
Margret	97	Dav
Peter	8	Smi
Robt.	78	Dav
Thomas	97	Dav
William	32	Mon
Buchannon, David	5	Smi
Dennis	5	Smi
John	15	Wll
William	5	Smi
Buchner, William	2	Jac
Buck, Cornelius	113	Wil
Cornelius	389	Wil
James	77	Dav
see Beck		
Buckaloo, John	47	Bed
Buckanan, Moses	5	Lin
Buckeen, David	3	Hum
Buckhanan, George	101	Rut
Hugh	6	Rob
William	3	Jac
Buckhannon, John	7	Bed
John	20	Bed
Thomas	21	Bed
Buckhanon, Anny	123	Ste
Danl.	127	Ste
John	124	Ste
Wm.	128	Ste
Buckhanun, C.	122	Ste
Buckingham, Nathl. B.	10	Lin
Thos.	116	Ste
Buckley, James	59	Wll
Joab	10	Lin
John	416	Wil
Payton	5	Mon
Buckner, John	3	Fra
Mary	144	Sum

Buckner (cont.)		
Rice	34	Mau
see Buchner		
Buckton, John	50	Bed
Buey, Edward	120	Ste
Bufford, William	122	Ste
Buford, Charles	9	Gil
Edward	36	Wll
Erasmus	38	Wll
Gabrial	36	Wll
James	9	Gil
Phileman	61	Mau
Spencer	6	Wll
Bugg, Allen	39	Wll
Ephraim M.	7	Lin
Francis	143	Sum
Jesse	61	Wll
Stiles	12	Dic
Buie, Archabald	89	Dav
Daniel	89	Dav
David	88	Dav
Gilbert	25	Mau
William	25	Mau
Buins see Burns		
Bulard, Reubin	26	Mon
Bull, Balem	29	Mon
Richard	141	Sum
Bullard, George H.	399	Wil
John	94	Rut
Buller, Patience	351	Whi
Sterling	398	Wil
William G.	353	Whi
Bullion, Thomas	15	Dic
Bullock, Allen	67	Mau
Amos	14	Wll
John	68	Mau
John	353	Whi
John C.	80	Rut
Jonathan	34	Mau
Nathaniel	33	Wll
Saml., Senr.	14	Bed
Samuel	14	Bed
Bullus, Joseph M.	135	Sum
Bumpas	63	Dav
Bumpass, Gabriel, Mr.	9	Law
Hartwel J., Mr.	9	Law
James, Mr.	1	Law
John	31	Mon
Patcy	3	Law
Robert	30	Mon
Robert	415	Wil
Samuel	31	Mon
William	93	Rut
Bumpus, James	7	Smi
Bun, Jesse	10	Ove
Bunch, Asa	69	Mau
David	8	Gil
David	7	Per
Elijah	107	She
James	8	Gil
Joseph	11	Har
Mary	18	Mon
Nathaniel	13	Ove
Soleman	56	Mau

Bunch (cont.)		
Thos.	2	Mon
Tolton	7	Per
see Burch		
Bundy, Joseph	141	Sum
Robert	145	Sum
William	3	Smi
see Bandy		
Bunge, Peterson	405	Wil
Bunn, Etheldred	13	Gil
John	12	Hic
Bunten, Daniel	114	Ste
Buntin, Wm.	125	Ste
Bunting, David	17	Mon
James	8	Mon
Levina	17	Mon
Bunton, John	141	Sum
Joseph	138	Sum
Tho.	142	Sum
Wm.	139	Sum
Buraw, Peter	10	Gil
Burch, Judith	17	Gil
Larken	30	Wll
see Burck		
Burcham, Isaiah	12	Bed
James	124	Ste
John, Jr.	20	Hic
John, Sr.	20	Hic
Levi	20	Hic
Burchet, Benjamin	5	Smi
Elijah	5	Smi
James	5	Smi
John	129	Ste
Joseph	129	Ste
Burchett, Joseph	128	Ste
Burchfield, Elijah	39	Lin
Burck, John	24	Wll
Burden, Joseph	350	Whi
William	350	Whi
Burderant, Edward	68	Dav
Burdin, John	356	Whi
Burdit, Giles	51	Bed
Burditt, William	32	Bed
William, Junr.	32	Bed
Burdoine, Nathaniel	3	Smi
Burdue, William	354	Whi
see Burdin		
Bures, Enis	2	Jac
Burford, Daniel	14	Wll
John H.	4	Smi
John M.	14	Wll
Solomon	21	Lin
Burfort, Philip T.	54	Bed
Burge, Elisabeth	28	Wll
Richard	102	Rut
Tazwell	28	Wll
Burges, James	59	Wll
Joel	30	Lin
Patsy	30	Lin
Burgess, Auzey	9	Dic
Edward	80	Rut
Edward	83	Rut
Ery	25	Wll
Harrison	5	Gil
Burgess (cont.)		
John	6	Hum
Josiah	3	Jac
Mary	26	Bed
Nathaniel	9	Gil
Richd.	31	Bed
Thomas	292	War
William	35	Fra
William	315	War
Burget, Henry	3	Fra
Burgey, David	75	Dav
Burgies, Peter	343	Whi
Burgus, John	362	Whi
Thomas	368	Whi
see Burgies	343	Whi
Buris, John	2	Jac
John	3	Jac
Burk, Anson	26	Wll
Arnold	102	Rut
Carter	24	Wll
Edward	391	Wil
John R.	42	Wll
Johnson	378	Wil
see Bark		
Burke, Benjamin	8	Gil
Catharine	3	Smi
Samuel	7	Smi
William	15	Hic
William	7	Hum
Burkes, James	8	Smi
Burket, Ephraim	10	Hum
James	35	Mau
Robbert	54	Mau
Thomas	10	Hum
William	35	Mau
Burkett, Burgess	17	Gil
Burkley, Cely	389	Wil
Isaac	22	Way
Burks, George	96	Rut
Isham	19	Lin
James	18	Bed
James	29	Bed
James	95	Rut
John	2	Jac
Leroy	92	Rut
Patience	95	Rut
Riland	287	War
Samuel	3	Lin
Willis	292	War
Burland, Thomas M.	90	Dav
Burlason, John	80	Rut
Joseph	80	Rut
Burleston, David	102	Rut
Burlison, Moses	287	War
William	8	Law
Burmingham, Caleb	19	Lin
James	45	Lin
Burnard, John	112	Wil
Thomas H.	29	Bed
Burner, Isaac	16	Wll
John	7	Ove
Burnes, Laura	6	Dic
Raeson S.	417	Wil
Burnet, Boling C.	5	Wll

Burnet (cont.)			Burrass, Abraham	66	Dav
Daniel	3	Smi	Burres, Sweaney	4	Jac
Dina	67	Dav	Burris, Isaac	2	Ove
John	29	Rob	James	131	Ste
Joseph	97	Dav	John	2	Ove
Joseph	12	Wll	John P.	102	Rut
Statia	25	Rob	Thomas	2	Ove
Thomas	3	Smi	William	10	Law
Thomas R.	8	Smi	Burrow, Bauks M.	28	Bed
Toliver	48	Wll	Elizabeth	32	Bed
Burnett, Brookin	92	Rut	Ephram	28	Bed
George	67	Dav	Freeman	23	Bed
Isham	36	Lin	Ishmeal	35	Bed
Jacob	100	Rut	Jacob	35	Bed
Leonard	95	Dav	Jerrel	32	Bed
Mathew	101	Rut	Peter	40	Lin
Notburn	26	Mau	Peter, Ser.	40	Lin
Obediah	36	Lin	Philip	3	Bed
Reuben	88	Rut	Sterling	3	Bed
Robert	92	Rut	Burrus, Anthoney	35	Fra
Samuel	80	Rut	Edward	35	Fra
Samuel	96	Rut	Elijah	2	Fra
Thomas	89	Rut	Fayette	80	Rut
William	100	Rut	Hutson	35	Fra
Burney, David	31	Mon	Jacob	3	Smi
Mary	32	Rob	John	35	Fra
William	18	Rob	Joseph	91	Rut
Burnham, Joshua	18	Wll	Martin	35	Fra
Newton E.	20	Wll	Samuel	35	Fra
Burningham, William	19	Lin	William	35	Fra
Burnitt, William	46	Bed	Bursby, Stephen	2	Law
Burns, Absolum K.	415	Wil	Burser, James	345	Whi
Amos	2	Fra	Burt, John	35	Fra
Andrew	13	Gil	Burton, Allen	101	Rut
Andrew	50	Mau	Ambrose	4	Dic
Ann	49	Mau	Charles, Jr.	3	Jac
Aquilla, Mr.	8	Law	Charles, Sr.	3	Jac
Brice	2	Jac	David	3	Fra
Charles	10	Way	David	36	Fra
Horatio	98	Rut	David H.	9	Hum
Horatio	56	Wll	David H.	2	Jac
James	29	Mon	Edward D.	93	Rut
James	415	Wil	F. N. W.	99	Rut
James W.	15	Lin	Henry	8	Hum
Jane	37	Mau	Henry	355	Whi
Jesse	58	Dav	Hilory	11	Mon
John	22	Bed	Jacob	2	Jac
John	19	Lin	James	11	Mon
John, Mr.	11	Law	Jesse	2	Jac
Josiah	6	Hic	John	3	Fra
Laid	11	Law	John	11	Mon
Martin	4	Ove	John	14	Mon
Nancy	58	Dav	John	28	Rob
Olly	3	Jac	John	93	Rut
Robert	51	Bed	John	5	Smi
Thomas	415	Wil	John Henry	13	Hum
William	2	Jac	Martha	20	Lin
William	3	Jac	Martin H.	10	Dic
William	4	Ove	Peter	7	Smi
William	10	Way	Polly	4	Smi
see Barns			Rhoda	2	Jac
Burps, Jacob	97	Rut	Samuel H.	5	Hum
Burr see Bun			Thomas	118	Ste

Burton (cont.)
Thos. 123 Ste
William 3 Jac
William 131 Ste
William A. 4 Smi
Wily 392 Wil
Zera 2 Fra
see Bruton
Busby, Dolly 144 Sum
Elijah 140 Sum
Meredith 17 Gil
Micajah 13 Dic
Robert 16 Gil
Robert 13 Hum
Sherwood 17 Gil
William 140 Sum
Bush, Benja. 144 Sum
Jeremiah 4 Jac
John 4 Jac
John 4 Jac
Mary 58 Dav
William 142 Sum
William 143 Sum
Zenas 20 Mon
Buson, Jacob 7 Ove
Bussey, Elliot 9 Bed
John 33 Bed
Lucy 33 Bed
But, Radford 62 Mau
Butcher, Benjamin 102 Rut
Isaac 40 Mau
Butler, Aron 142 Sum
Balie 3 Jac
Benjamin 62 Dav
Benjamin 20 Lin
David 39 Bed
Edward 90 Dav
Edward 7 Smi
Elias 78 Rut
Elizabeth 3 Dic
George 3 Jac
Henry 90 Rut
Isaac 95 Rut
Isaac 100 Rut
James 3 Jac
James 79 Rut
Joel 20 Lin
John 22 Gil
John 3 Jac
John 50 Mau
John 61 Mau
John 17 Wll
Joseph 120 Ste
Joshua [2] 43 Wll
Mary 142 Sum
Price 1 Jac
Samuel 44 Lin
Thomas 3 Jac
Thomas 95 Rut
Thos. 4 Hic
Welcome 3 Jac
William 3 Jac
William 64 Mau
Butler (cont.)
William 78 Rut
William E. 63 Dav
Zachariah 33 Mau
Butrice, Abraham 64 Dav
Butt, Hazle 144 Sum
James 82 Dav
John 144 Sum
Butter, James 32 Bed
Butterworth, Benjamin 70 Dav
Jesse 144 Sum
William 70 Dav
Butteworth, John 140 Sum
Joseph 140 Sum
Buttler, Robert 386 Wil
Buttrey, John 21 Wll
Butts, Christopher 1 Mon
Jeremiah 10 Rob
Lidia 72 Dav
Willie 5 Smi
Wilson 4 Smi
Zachariah 84 Dav
Butz, John 32 Mau
Buyers, William 58 Mau
Buzby, James 36 Bed
Byerd, John 7 Per
Byers, Andrew 25 Lin
David 18 Lin
James 3 Lin
William 79 Rut
William 6 Wll
Byford, Henry 95 Rut
John 35 Fra
William 102 Rut
Byherty, Peter 33 Lin
Byler, Abraham 15 Bed
John 14 Bed
Byles, Charles 21 Gil
Bynum, John 58 Mau
Luke 58 Mau
Mark 58 Mau
Pumphrey 19 Bed
Tapley [2] 58 Mau
Turner 10 Gil
William 58 Mau
William 94 Rut
Byon, Samuel 72 Dav
Byram, Henry 36 Fra
Henry 6 Smi
Ransom 6 Smi
Simon 144 Sum
Byrd, Elizabeth 32 Rob
Francis 12 Gil
Francis 18 Rob
Howel 3 Fra
Byrn, Jno. 139 Wum
John 141 Sum
John W. 135 Sum
Joseph 143 Sum
William P. 60 Dav
Byrne, Charles 70 Dav
Mary Ann 70 Dav
Byrnes, James 10 Rob

Byrnly, Moses 143 Sum
Byrns, Joseph 144 Sum
Byson, Elizabeth 144 Sum
see Bryson
Bysor, John 140 Sum
Bysor, Peter 140 Sum
Byspole, Joseph 78 Rut
Byter, Sarah 27 Lin

--- B ---

Cabe, William 5 Way
Cable, Jacob 24 Bed
Cader, John 5 Fra
Cades, Benjamin 12 Smi
Caffey, Jacob 26 Mau
Jawel 26 Mau
Margrett 26 Mau
Nathan 26 Mau
Cage, Edward 25 Bed
Jesse 146 Sum
John 399 Wil
Leroy 10 Smi
Palimon 13 Smi
Rewben 146 Sum
William 36 Bed
William 147 Sum
Wilson 10 Smi
see Gage
Cagle, Charles 92 Dav
David 14 Hic
Henry 14 Hic
Henry 10 Mon
Simon 25 Hic
Cagles, Henry 418 Wil
Cahal, Edward 73 Dav
Cahea, Perey 49 Mau
Cahoon, Isham 148 Sum
James 403 Wil
John W. 399 Wil
Samuel, Jr. 403 Wil
Samuel, Ser. 403 Wil
Thomas 403 Wil
Cahue, Amos 11 Rob
Cain, Benjamin 285 War
Cornelius 13 Smi
Elijah 401 Wil
George 9 Ove
James 280 War
John 22 Rob
John 280 War
Nancy 136 Sum
Russell 13 Smi
Sarah 70 Dav
William 46 Lin
William 24 Rob
Cairy, Francis 93 Dav
Nancy 53 Wll
Caitton, George W. 97 Dav
Caker, Isaac 406 Wil
Calbreath, Thomas 13 Smi
Calbreath (cont.)
William [2] 13 Smi
Caldwell, Alexander 4 Gil
Alexander 9 Gil
Elizabeth 5 Fra
Henry 10 Smi
Hugh 4 Fra
J. C. 53 Bed
James 49 Bed
James 4 Fra
James 4 Gil
James 147 Sum
James 301 War
John 16 Gil
John 11 Smi
John 307 War
Joseph 49 Bed
Joseph 14 Mon
Robert 81 Dav
Robert 5 Fra
Robert 81 Rut
Samuel 30 Mon
William 29 Bed
William [2] 88 Dav
William 4 Fra
William 301 War
Caleham, Elizebeth 48 Mau
Calehan, Betsey 50 Mau
Caley, Augustin 402 Wil
William 402 Wil
Calhoon, Andrew 19 Bed
Charles 41 Wll
Charles 57 Wll
George 93 Rut
George 42 Wll
Gray 9 Smi
John 21 Bed
John 15 Lin
Warren 14 Lin
William 15 Mon
William 58 Wll
Calhoun, John H. 9 Way
William 1 Way
Call, John 86 Dav
Callahan, John 22 Gil
Milus T. 22 Gil
William 22 Gil
Callaway, William 280 War
William 281 War
Calleham, Samuel 13 Ove
Callen, William 35 Bed
Callet, Nelly 6 Jac
Calley, Signer 46 Mau
Callico, Elizabeth 358 Whi
Callinder, Charles 311 War
Calloway, Gaddah 22 Lin
Joel 19 Gil
Richard 36 Fra
William H. 36 Fra
Calvert, Joseph 6 Gil
Robbert 44 Mau
Willis L. 45 Lin
Cambell, J. D. 96 Dav

Camcron, Daniel 57 Mau
Camden, John W. 5 Fra
Camel, Thomas 5 Jac
Cameron, Ewen 2 Wll
see Camcron, Cammeron, Camron
Cames, John 3 Hum
Cammel, John 4 Jac
John 5 Jac
Moses 5 Jac
Wm. 114 Ste
Cammeron, David 80 Dav
Cammon, John 5 Jac
Camp, Benjamin, Jun. 5 Fra
Benjamin, Sen. 4 Fra
James W. 4 Gil
John H. 8 Gil
John S. 4 Fra
Martha 8 Gil
Nancy 91 Dav
Nathan 5 Fra
Sarah 186 Sum
Saul 5 Fra
Vordy 372 Whi
Campbele, John 2 Law
Campbell, Alexander 64 Dav
Alexander 6 Law
Alexander 33 Wll
Andrew 14 Gil
Ann 3 Lin
Archibald 1 Lin
Argyle 1 Lin
Arthur 27 Bed
Arthur 410 Wil
Collin 12 Lin
Collin 147 Sum
Crockett 15 Gil
Daniel 59 Mau
Daniel 368 Whi
Darnal 10 Mon
David 9 Smi
David 9 Wll
David R. 10 Smi
Doogil 10 Smi
Edward 33 Wll
Edward 49 Wll
Elizabeth 346 Whi
Ellender 41 Mau
Finley 12 Hum
George 34 Bed
George 70 Dav
George 59 Mau
George 405 Wil
Hiram 23 Hic
Hugh 8 Gil
Hugh 27 Mau
Hugh 18 Mon
Hugh 415 Wil
Jacob 91 Rut
James 65 Dav
James 67 Dav
James 18 Gil
James 13 Lin
James 29 Lin
James 43 Mau
Campbell (cont.)
James 68 Mau
James 2 Way
James 415 Wil
James 48 Wll
Jane B. 3 Wll
John 5 Fra
John 43 Lin
John 40 Mau
John 42 Mau
John 11 Smi
John 355 Whi
John 366 Whi
John [2] 410 Wil
John 39 Wll
John B. 6 Gil
John K. 9 Wll
Joseph 4 Lin
Joseph 17 Ove
Joseph 10 Smi
Joseph 12 Smi
Luallen 67 Dav
Lydia 43 Lin
Manning 10 Smi
Margaret 5 Fra
Mary 20 Hic
Metildy 59 Mau
Michael 84 Dav
Michael 7 Gil
Patrick 32 Wll
Phillip 91 Dav
Richard 10 Ove
Richard 53 Wll
Robbert 56 Mau
Robbert 59 Mau
Robert 13 Gil
Robert 12 Law
Robert 343 Whi
Robert 360 Whi
Robert 378 Wil
Robert E. 23 Lin
Samuel 22 Lin
Samuel 81 Rut
Solomon 28 Bed
Washington 57 Dav
Will. 81 Dav
William 63 Dav
William 10 Rob
William 11 Rob
William 12 Smi
William 146 Sum
William 285 War
William 410 Wil
Wm. 21 Hic
see Cambell, Cammel, Compbell
Camper, John 43 Lin
Camron, Elizabeth 6 Ove
Canada, John 74 Rut
Lakes 11 Smi
Robert S. 351 Whi
William 99 Rut
William 12 Smi
William 13 Smi
Canadoy, Andrew 34 Mau

Canady, Evender 37 Mau
Feraby 17 Wll
Francis 48 Mau
Isaack 52 Mau
John 58 Mau
William 44 Mau
see Canada, Caniday, Cannedy,
Canadye, James, Glass Creek 24 Mau
Canalier, Philip 17 Ove
Canan, Howard 40 Mau
Cananda, John 103 Rut
Canberry, Jeremiah 36 Fra
Candis, William 37 Mau
Candle, Tho. 146 Sum
William 35 Mau
Candler, Zedekiah 10 Smi
Candy, Thomas 70 Mau
Cane, Henry 30 Mon
John B. 2 Mon
Caniday, Isaac 390 Wil
Cann, William M. 84 Dav
Cannaday, Enoch 390 Wil
Cannady, Jas. 120 Ste
John 22 Wll
Cannan, Pue 40 Mau
Cannedy, Alfred 389 Wil
Cannekin, see Flannekin
Cannon, Abisha 5 Jac
Andrew 52 Bed
Archibald 3 Hum
Buril 39 Mau
Clement 9 Bed
Dennis 12 Hic
George 408 Wil
Horasha 387 Wil
John 92 Rut
Joseph 92 Rut
Joseph 386 Wil
Jshua 22 Wll
Minas 9 Bed
Minas 56 Wll
Nancy 392 Wil
Newton 56 Wll
Samuel 399 Wil
Theophilus A. 82 Rut
Thomas 9 Ove
William 29 Lin
William 88 Rut
William 369 Whi
see Carmon
Canon, Abner 65 Mau
Canter, Zachariah 4 Jac
Canterberry, Joseph 36 Fra
Joseph, Sr. 36 Fra
Cantrell, Abner 25 Lin
Abraham 297 War
Aron 342 Whi
Elijah 7 Hic
Elijah 302 War
Isaac 302 War
Isaac 315 War
James 63 Dav
James 301 War
Martha 344 Whi
Cantrell (cont.)
Ota 84 Rut
Richard 292 War
Stephen 78 Dav
Steph. 146 Sum
Thomas 310 War
Watson 303 War
Wm. 145 Sum
Canyers, William 31 Mau
Caost see Cavot
Caperton, Archibald 36 Fra
George 4 Fra
Hugh 36 Fra
James 36 Wll
John 36 Fra
John 33 Wll
William 36 Fra
Caplena, Anny 402 Wil
Caplin, David 42 Mau
Capliner, Jacob 114 Wil
Saml. 114 Wil
Caplinger, Enoch 9 Smi
John 9 Smi
Capps, Benjamin 84 Dav
Henry 30 Mau
Shadrack 292 War
Caps, Francis 1 Hum
Ruth 69 Dav
Capshaw, James 289 War
Josiah 297 War
Car, James 4 Jac
James 6 Jac
John 4 Jac
John F. 49 Mau
N. S. William 35 Mau
William 4 Jac
William 2 Way
Cara, William 11 Smi
Caradine, Andrew 26 Mau
Carathers, Andrew 19 Lin
James 5 Lin
Jane 4 Lin
John 20 Lin
John 46 Lin
Mary 29 Lin
William 13 Lin
Carcin, Patsey 398 Wil
Card, William 35 Bed
Cardin, James 5 Fra
Larkin 10 Gil
Leonard 5 Fra
Cardwell, Anderson 11 Smi
Caleb 11 Smi
John 4 Fra
Moses 4 Fra
Nelson 146 Sum
Thomas 147 Sum
Care, David 12 Gil
Carees, Mary 103 Rut
Carey, James 149 Sum
Thomas 149 Sum
Carggall, John H. 7 Har
Cargile, James 6 Ove
James 307 War

Cargile (cont.)		
John	1	Ove
Carheron, Aaron D.	11	Wll
Carier, Nathaniel	386	Wil
Cariger, Nicholas	25	Lin
Carington, Thomas	21	Bed
Carithers, James D.	104	Rut
Mathew C.	98	Rut
Thomas	47	Bed
William	25	Bed
Carl, Jacob	6	Wll
Carland, Joshua	14	Ove
Carlilse, Robert W.	11	Smi
William	34	Bed
Carlin, Hugh	397	Wil
William	408	Wil
Carlise, Simon	5	Jac
Carlisle, James	5	Jac
Peggy	7	Hic
William	5	Jac
Carlock, E.	410	Wil
Isaac	8	Ove
Job	1	Ove
Reuben	1	Ove
Carloss, Benja. W.	145	Sum
Carlton, Henry	5	Jac
Thomas	59	Wll
Carmack, Cornelius	5	Ove
Cornelius	19	Ove
Cornelius	6	Rob
Isaac	13	Ove
James	2	Ove
Jesse	19	Ove
Carman, Archibd.	147	Sum
Larkin	147	Sum
Carmichael, Esther	73	Rut
Carmichal, Archibald	24	Wll
Carmon, Caleb	10	Smi
Elijah	10	Smi
John	9	Smi
Patsy	4	Jac
William, Jun.	10	Smi
William, Sen.	10	Smi
Carmonus, Josiah	102	Rut
Carmouns see Carmonus		
Carnahan, Andrew	78	Rut
Hugh	93	Rut
Carnes, David B.	12	Hum
Joseph	107	She
Sarah	13	Mon
Thomas	8	Hum
Carnett, William	4	Jac
Carney, Elijah	92	Dav
James	31	Bed
James W.	16	Mon
Joshua	149	Sum
Richd.	8	Mon
Stephen W.	5	Mon
Thos. L.	7	Mon
Vincent	74	Dav
Vincent	91	Dav
William	93	Dav
Carnihan, James	88	Rut

Carooth, Alexander	401	Wil
James	114	Wil
James	397	Wil
James	401	Wil
Walter	399	Wil
William	397	Wil
Carothers, Andrew	21	Wll
Ezekiel	148	Sum
Hugh	22	Gil
James	4	Wll
James	65	Wll
John	15	Wll
Robert	21	Wll
Robert	54	Wll
Carpenter, Asa	102	Rut
Benjamin	10	Ove
Ebby	25	Mau
Frederick	84	Dav
George	5	Fra
Harbart	10	Smi
Hensley	17	Gil
James	5	Fra
John	17	Ove
Lewis	10	Ove
Milly	31	Bed
Nancy	2	Gil
Owen	16	Lin
Solomon	39	Bed
Timothy	15	Ove
William	63	Dav
William	17	Gil
Carper, Adam	98	Dav
Carr, Anderson	107	She
Arthur	14	Rob
Benjamin	84	Rut
Ellut	4	Fra
Fanny	8	Ove
George, Jun.	36	Fra
George, Sen.	36	Fra
Guidian	106	She
Henry	4	Jac
James	9	Hic
James	25	Mau
James	7	Mon
James	146	Sum
James	148	Sum
James C.	146	Sum
James D.	148	Sum
John	17	Rob
John	146	Sum
John	148	Sum
John S.	148	Sum
Joseph	351	Whi
King	147	Sum
Overton	107	Shi
Richard	148	Sum
Robert	7	Law
Samuel	103	Rut
Thomas	8	Ove
Thomas	107	She
Walter	25	Hic
William	77	Rut
William	10	Smi

Carr (cont.)		
William	148	Sum
Wm. P.	148	Sum
Carraway, Moses	395	Wil
Willis	396	Wil
Carrel, Daniel	316	War
James	63	Wll
Sarah	46	Wll
Spencer	51	Wll
Carrell, Edmond	347	Whi
Carrington, Eligah	53	Mau
Carrol, James	7	Bed
James	147	Sum
Josiah	385	Wil
Mesheck	385	Wil
Carroll, Daniel	19	Rob
Frank	8	Har
John	22	Hic
John	25	Mon
Joseph	9	Hic
Nathaniel	6	Gil
Sally	9	Dic
Saml.	19	Hic
Solomon S.	84	Rut
William	79	Dav
William	32	Mon
Carroway, Thos.	19	Mon
Carruthers, Robbart	28	Mau
Carsey, Thomas P.	2	Wll
Carsine, Abel	65	Wll
Eli	63	Wll
Carson, David	5	Fra
David	51	Mau
George	4	Jac
Henry	405	Wil
James	149	Sum
James	58	Wll
James	59	Wll
John	18	Wll
John B.	11	Hum
Reuben	40	Lin
Robert	7	Per
Robert	101	Rut
Robert	40	Wll
Thomas	5	Fra
Wade	36	Fra
William	56	Wll
William	58	Wll
Carter, ...e [i ?]	12	Ove
Adam	298	War
Alexander	26	Mau
Alexander	95	Rut
Ammon	12	Smi
Bartlett	314	War
Benj.	6	Jac
Benja.	148	Sum
Benjamin	6	Jac
Bernard	407	Wil
Beverly	10	Smi
Burrell	91	Rut
Charles	5	Jac
Charles	6	Jac
Charles	51	Mau
Carter (cont.)		
Charles	147	Sum
Charlotte	11	Smi
Christopher	97	Dav
Crawford	21	Lin
Daniel	10	Wll
David	24	Hic
David	122	Ste
David	1	Way
David	393	Wil
Elizabeth	358	Whi
Elizebeth	64	Mau
Enoch	6	Jac
Ephraim	111	Ste
Francis	28	Mon
Francis	40	Wll
Frederick	407	Wil
Gideon	147	Sum
Hanson	386	Wil
Harris	147	Sum
Henry	16	Lin
Henry	5	Rob
Jabez	19	Gil
Jacob	45	Bed
Jacob	10	Rob
James	85	Dav
James	5	Jac
James	37	Lin
James	357	Whi
James, Jr.	97	Dav
Jesse	4	Hum
Jesse	296	War
Job	2	Ove
Joel	2	Per
John	26	Bed
John	97	Dav
John	7	Lin
John	31	Mau
John	17	Mon
John	77	Rut
John	81	Rut
John [2]	85	Rut
John	12	Smi
John	13	Smi
John	119	Ste
John	148	Sum
John W.	405	Wil
Johnson	287	War
Joseph	2	Ove
Joseph	148	Sum
Leroy C.	397	Wil
Martin	10	Hum
Matthew	27	Bed
Merry	18	Gil
Nancy	37	Bed
Nancy	148	Sum
Nathan	11	Ste
Nathaniel	12	Smi
Nelson	4	Fra
Nelson	5	Jac
Offey	64	Mau
Peter	359	Whi
Pledge	5	Ove

Carter (cont.)		
Randal	407	Wil
Reuben	6	Jac
Robert	5	Fra
Rubin A.	55	Mau
Sarah	61	Wll
Solomon	24	Hic
Thomas	96	Rut
Travis	3	Lin
Vinson	12	Smi
William [2]	4	Jac
William	5	Jac
William	4	Rob
William	23	Rob
William	10	Smi
William	149	Sum
William	359	Whi
William, Jun.	10	Smi
William L.	60	Dav
William L.	2	Hic
Wren	29	Bed
see Cades		
Cartha, James	103	Rut
Cartmill, John	30	Bed
Martin	113	Wil
Nat.	112	Wil
Nathaniel	112	Wil
Nathaniel	380	Wil
Nathaniel	379	Wil
Cartright, John	16	Wll
Cartrite, Daniel	18	Wll
Cartwright, David	61	Dav
Elizabeth	69	Dav
Elizabeth	13	Smi
Elizabeth	409	Wil
Isaac	5	Fra
Jacob	70	Dav
James	13	Smi
James	146	Sum
Joseph	13	Smi
Joshua	280	War
Robert	407	Wil
Samuel	404	Wil
Thomas	69	Dav
Thomas	70	Dav
Thomas	12	Smi
Thomas	404	Wil
William	408	Wil
Caruthers, Catherine	14	Hic
Saml. M.	6	Hic
Wm.	6	Hic
Carvell, Edmund	19	Gil
William	15	Gil
William	18	Gil
Carver, Cornelieus	6	Jac
Edward	6	Jac
Enoch	19	Mon
Isaac	387	Wil
Jane	6	Jac
John	13	Smi
Thomas	388	Wil
William	387	Wil
Cary, Catharine	148	Sum
Cary (cont.)		
Milford	359	Whi
Robert	15	Lin
Casby, Samuel	66	Mau
Casca, George	69	Mau
Casebolt, Thomas	19	Gil
Caselberry, John	7	Rob
Joseph	3	Rob
Casen, Larkin	305	War
Seth	97	Dav
Casesinger, Jacob	11	Way
Mathias	7	Way
Casey, Abner	20	Way
Abner	21	Way
Charles	41	Bed
Charles	87	Rut
Hiram	10	Smi
James	87	Rut
Jawel	50	Mau
John	28	Mau
John	66	Mau
Samuel	5	Jac
Samuel	12	Smi
William	20	Mon
Cash, Howard	366	Whi
John	3	Way
John	366	Whi
John H.	3	Gil
Simpson	353	Whi
Thomas	36	Wll
William	4	Hic
William	10	Hum
Cashin, David	146	Sum
Martin	146	Sum
Pleasant	145	Sum
Cashorn, Anderson	38	Lin
Archibald	38	Lin
Elizabeth	40	Lin
William	38	Lin
Caskey, Joseph	408	Wil
Thomas	57	Mau
Casky, Robert	403	Wil
Cason, James	5	Jac
John	308	War
Joseph	419	Wil
Steven	96	Dav
William	5	Jac
Casper, John	79	Rut
Joshua	57	Wll
Casselman, David	59	Dav
Cassels, Benjamin	5	Fra
Cassey, Ambrose	22	Wll
Fleming	36	Wll
James	50	Wll
Jeremiah	50	Wll
Thomas	39	Wll
Casshaw, Thos.	25	Hic
Cassilman, Benjamin	395	Wil
Jacob	397	Wil
Cassilmen, Jacob	402	Wil
Cassity, Thomas	13	Smi
Cassleman, Abram	52	Wll
Henry	93	Rut

Castilon, Joseph	13	Smi
Castlan, Edward	32	Mau
Castleman, Andrew	64	Dav
Benjn.	61	Dav
John, Jr.	58	Dav
John, Sr.	58	Dav
Susan	58	Dav
Castler, Daniel	12	Way
Caswell, Jesse	411	Wil
Casy, Benjamin	11	Har
Cate, John T.	405	Wil
Robert	355	Whi
Caten, Jesse	345	Whi
Cates, Charles	6	Gil
Ephraim	5	Fra
Ezra	31	Mau
Isaiah	1	Hic
Josiah	52	Wll
Thomas	5	Fra
Thomas	4	Way
Cathcart, John	4	Fra
Cathel, Jonathan	51	Mau
Josiah W.	51	Mau
Cathey, Alexander	33	Mau
Alexander	68	Mau
George	16	Dic
George	45	Wll
Griffeth	67	Mau
James	67	Mau
John	68	Mau
John R.	13	Dic
Mathew	146	Sum
William	66	May
Cathy, Andrew	118	Ste
George	117	Ste
James	22	Bed
John	129	Ste
Catner, Daniel	43	Bed
Cato, Roland	92	Dav
Catoe, Henry	116	Ste
Rufus	124	Ste
Cator, Levin	18	Wll
Moses E.	17	Wll
Catron, Christly	147	Sum
Cats, John	59	Mau
Cattles, John	113	Wil
John	406	Wil
Cauch, Joseph	29	Bed
Thomas	29	Bed
Thomas	40	Bed
Caudle, James	21	Rob
Jessey	37	Mau
John A.	116	Ste
Caughfield, John	43	Bed
Cauldwell, David	378	Wil
Elizabeth	386	Wil
Cauley, Charles	9	Smi
Nathaniel	12	Smi
Caulfield, John	84	Rut
Caulk, Jacob	80	Rut
Jacob	91	Rut
James	81	Rut
Causeby, William	101	Rut
Cauthen, Ludy	4	Lin
Cavenar, Jarret	16	Hic
Cavenaugh, Andrew	29	Mon
Cavender, Edw.	16	Hic
Nedam [2]	41	Mau
Caveness, Wm.	145	Sum
Cavett, John	400	Wil
Cavey, Roxannah	39	Bed
Cavinnour, James	64	Wll
Cavit, Michaeel	147	Sum
Pggy	31	Mau
Cavitt, Andrew	145	Sum
George	145	Sum
Joseph	146	Sum
Cavot, Mary	85	Rut
Cawell, William	377	Wil
Cawen, William	10	Bed
Cawhorn, James	147	Sum
Cayce, George	55	Mau
Shadrack	20	Wll
Cayton, William	91	Rut
Ceatham, Peter	59	Mau
Cecil, Garrett	3	Mon
Cells, Benjamin	11	Ove
Center, Bird	47	Bed
Certain, Asa	348	Whi
Jobb	348	Whi
Cewell, Samuel	29	Mau
Ceypert, Robert	18	Way
see Cypert		
Chadbourn, John	136	Sum
Chadowin, John	147	Sum
Chadwell, David	27	Wll
George	61	Wll
John	91	Dav
Valentine	25	Wll
Chaffin, Abner	4	Jac
John	2	Law
Joseph, Jr.	4	Jac
Nathen	45	Bed
Phebe	49	Bed
Robert	10	Law
William	5	Jac
William	12	Smi
Chainey, Robert	361	Whi
Chairs, Nathanial	58	Mau
Chamberlane, William	13	Smi
Chamberlin, Samuel	398	Wil
Thomas	398	Wil
Chambers, Alexander	402	Wil
Edward	35	Lin
Eligah P.	70	Mau
Eligah P.	34	Mau
Elizabeth	1	Law
Francis	8	Gil
Green	130	Ste
Hardin	10	Dic
Henry	129	Ste
Henry R.	69	Mau
James	24	Bed
James	11	Hum
James	9	Smi
James	129	Ste

Chambers (cont.)		
John	7	Har
John	9	Smi
John P.	9	Hum
Lewis	114	Wil
Lewis	402	Wil
Moses	34	Lin
Polley	10	Dic
Rebecca	9	Smi
Reubin	4	Per
Richard	9	Smi
Samuel	9	Gil
Thomas	34	Rob
Thomas	394	Wil
Thomas	24	Wll
Thos.	7	Per
Wilis	4	Per
William	9	Smi
Chambley, Daniel	415	Wil
William	415	Wil
Chambliss, Mark	10	Mon
Chamless, James	86	Rut
Champ, Richard	95	Dav
Robbert	47	Mau
Southerland	24	Wll
William	95	Dav
Wiseman	81	Dav
Champion, Daniel	4	Fra
Jane	4	Fra
Jorden	126	Ste
Joseph	4	Fra
Richard	12	Smi
William	4	Fra
Chance, Alexander	396	Wil
George	28	Mon
Thos.	26	Mon
William	28	Mon
William	148	Sum
Chancy, Francis	10	Ove
Chandler, Andrew	394	Wil
Baily	395	Wil
Edings	395	Wil
Gabriel	395	Wil
Henry	400	Wil
Isaac	10	Smi
Jane	18	Ove
John	412	Wil
Jordan	395	Wil
Josiah	395	Wil
Mary	17	Hic
Parker	395	Wil
Ryler	395	Wil
Shedrick	61	May
Thomas	20	Ove
Uncky	388	Wil
William	74	Dav
William	394	Wil
Wm.	24	Hic
Chaney, John	17	Ove
Levi	8	Ove
William	13	Ove
Chanler, John	16	Bed
Sarah	16	Bed
Chapin, Paul	8	Ove
Chapman, Benjaman	34	Wll
Benjamin	6	Gil
Daniel	23	Rob
Daniel	12	Smi
Elijah	12	Smi
Elizabeth	4	Jac
Enoch	5	Fra
Erasmus	47	Lin
George	3	Rob
George	19	Rob
Isaac	12	Smi
James	39	Lin
John	80	Dav
John	10	Gil
John	4	Jac
John	23	Rob
John A.	14	Lin
Martha	147	Sum
Nelson	42	Wll
Peggy	6	Gil
Phillip	148	Sum
Phillip	43	Wll
Samuel	12	Smi
Silas	406	Wil
Thomas	6	Gil
Thomas	20	Gil
Thomas	14	Lin
William	10	Gil
William	34	Lin
William	12	Smi
William	55	Wll
William, Jr.	12	Smi
see Chipman, Crapman		
Chappell, Ann	147	Sum
Saml.	148	Sum
Chappin, Coalman	37	Mau
Moses	39	Mau
Chapple, Richard	394	Wil
William	394	Wil
Charles, Jemima	4	Jac
John	279	War
John	316	War
Melchizadick	315	War
Richard	5	Fra
Stephen K.	357	Whi
Tabitha	344	Whi
Charlton, Abram	145	Sum
Fanny	148	Sum
Jenings	148	Sum
John	146	Sum
see Charton		
Chart, Joseph	68	Mau
Charter, William	19	Hic
Charters, John N.	1	Wll
Chartiers, Tabitha	60	Dav
Chartins, Saml.	75	Dav
Charton, James	146	Sum
Chastain, Royal	35	Lin
Chasted, Elijah	6	Jac
William	6	Jac
Chastain, John	294	War
Chatham, John	10	Smi

Chaves, Jourdan	105	Rut
Cheak, James	12	Smi
William	10	Smi
Cheatam, Leonard P.	81	Dav
Cheatham, Abram	13	Smi
Archer	1	Rob
Anderson	18	Rob
Archibald	11	Smi
Edmund	11	Smi
Joel	11	Smi
John B.	20	Rob
Richard	1	Rob
Samuel	400	Wil
Tho.	145	Sum
Thomas	20	Rob
Thomas	58	Wll
Cheathan, Archer	36	Rob
Cheatom, William	52	Mau
Cheavers, James	27	Bed
Chedicks, Charles	17	Ove
Cheek, Ely	49	Mau
Francis	147	Sum
Jesse	52	Bed
Jessey	51	Mau
Cherey, Jerey	49	Mau
Jerimiah	49	Mau
Cherry, Caleb	96	Dav
Cary	5	Jac
Daniel	406	Wil
Danl.	113	Ste
Eli	74	Dav
Eli	10	Har
Elijah	13	Ove
Ezekiel	2	Bed
Humphrey	113	Ste
Isham	10	Har
James H.	10	Ove
Joel	320	War
John M.	397	Wil
Joshua	2	Bed
Lemuel	5	Jac
Peterson	8	Ove
Rosannah	14	Mon
Wesley	13	Ove
William	83	Dav
William	5	Jac
William	13	Ove
William	117	Ste
Wm.	113	Ste
see Cherey, Chirey		
Chery, James	97	Rut
John	5	Jac
Chesher, Hosia	91	Dav
Cheshire, Benjamin	13	Gil
Chesser, James	3	Bed
James	24	Hic
James	299	War
Tennosson	11	Lin
Chester, David	69	Mau
John	299	Way
John, Jr.	7	Hic
John, Junr.	110	Ste
John, Senr.	7	Hic

Chester (cont.)		
John, Senr.	110	Ste
William	4	Per
Wm.	115	Ste
Chewning, John	21	Rob
John, Senr.	32	Rob
Robert	32	Rob
Chidwood, Joel	5	Fra
Chiffin, Joseph, Sr.	5	Jac
Childers, Joel	1	Law
Childres, Benjamin	6	Per
Jesse	15	Way
John	6	Per
John	18	Way
Moses	6	Per
see Chldres		
Childress, Alexander	35	Wll
Archibald	19	Wll
Asa	19	Lin
David	14	Hum
Elisabeth C.	32	Wll
Elizabeth	75	Dav
Elizabeth	82	Rut
Goin	5	Hum
J. W.	66	Wll
James	19	Lin
James	104	Rut
James W.	0	Wll
Joel	6	Hum
John	9	Hic
Major	96	Rut
Mitchel	37	Wll
Mitchell	5	Hum
Nathaniel G.	69	Dav
Nelson	33	Wll
Perkins	4	Fra
Repps, Ser.	8	Lin
Repps O., Jur.	8	Lin
Robert L.	14	Gil
Stephen	0	Wll
Stephen	4	Wll
Thos.	115	Ste
Vaulton	7	Gil
William	4	Fra
William	87	Rut
William	12	Smi
William G.	4	Wll
Childs, Hezekiah	15	Lin
Thomas	15	Lin
Chiles, John	9	Smi
Lewis	12	Wll
Paul	12	Gil
Chilton, Lemuel	30	Rob
William [2]	18	Ove
Chily, Cuth	303	War
Chinn, Cyrus	4	Fra
Chipman, Hezekiah	5	Rob
John	2	Mon
Chirey, Joel	295	War
Chisam, John	28	Mau
Chisenhall, Reuben	5	Mon
Chisholm, Alexander	22	Gil
Edmund	93	Rut

Chisholm (cont.)		
William	93	Rut
Chishum, John	28	Mau
Chism, Obediah	27	Rob
Taylor	2	Mon
Thomas	27	Rob
William	18	Mon
Chismhall, James	85	Rut
James	96	Rut
Chissum, Nancy	309	War
Chisty, Jonothon	5	Jac
Chisum, John	355	Whi
John	362	Whi
Margaret	351	Whi
William	366	Whi
Chittum, John	55	Mau
Chitwood, Edmond	14	Lin
Joel	7	Lin
Pleasant	13	Smi
Richard	13	Smi
Stephen C.	47	Lin
Chives, Annis	283	War
Chizinhall, Alexander	16	Dic
Chldres, Joel	4	Per
Choat, Aaron, Junr.	9	Law
Aaron, Senr., Mr.	9	Law
Arthur	20	Way
Augustin	12	Rob
Austin	5	Jac
Christopher	17	Ove
Edward	32	Rob
Edward	147	Sum
Gabriel	28	Rob
Gideon	32	Rob
Jno. J.	148	Sum
John	29	Rob
Thomas	9	Law
Volentine	6	Rob
Choate, John	1	Dic
Valentine	12	Gil
Chote, John	8	Har
Nicholas	8	Har
Squir	67	Mau
Chouning, Chatten	9	Ove
Hannah	18	Ove
Chowen, Ann P.	27	Wll
Chrisman, Mary	43	Wll
Sarah	43	Wll
Chrisp, Charles	379	Wil
Christain, George	16	Ove
John	7	Ove
Christian, Barrel	305	War
Christopher	76	Dav
Drury	2	Dic
Drury	297	War
Isam, Mr.	4	Law
James	80	Dav
James W.	2	Dic
Jesse G.	2	Hic
Jno. H.	9	Hic
John	11	Smi
John	305	War
Nathaniel	5	Law
Christie, William	126	Ste
Christman, David	7	Wll
Harvey	4	Fra
Isaac	36	Fra
John	81	Dav
Christmas, Abigail	23	Wll
Christopher, Daniel	41	Wll
John	62	Wll
Thomas	83	Rut
Christy, —, Widow	6	Jac
John	4	Jac
see Chisty		
Chumhall see Chismhall		
Chumney, Joseph	50	Wll
Chun, Silvester	53	Mau
William	50	Mau
see Cun		
Chunn, Lancelot	32	Bed
Church, Abram	50	Wll
John	34	Lin
John	63	Mau
Joshua	35	Lin
Phillip	29	Mau
Robbert	63	Mau
Robert	50	Wll
Thomas	104	Rut
Thomas	50	Wll
Churchwell, John	126	Ste
John	9	Way
Richd.	17	Way
Cile, Hugh	8	Ove
Cirby, Nancy	89	Rut
Clabo, Charles	286	War
Clack, Edmond	27	Bed
John	10	Gil
Martin	4	Jac
Spencer	4	Gil
see Clark	123	Ste
Clackstone, James	149	Sum
Claghorn, John	4	Jac
Robert	12	Dic
Claibourn, Cunard	16	Ove
Claibourne, Thomas	79	Dav
Clairbourn, George R.	83	Dav
Clampet, Ezekiel	386	Wil
James	385	Wil
Jonathan	146	Sum
see Clapet		
Clancy, Cornelieus	6	Jac
Clanton, George	88	Rut
Isaac	12	Lin
John W.	28	Mau
Sarah	95	Rut
Clapet, William	386	Wil
Clarage, John	65	Dav
Clardy, Benjamin	6	Fra
Benjamin	10	Smi
Drewry	9	Smi
James	22	Bed
Joseph	5	Fra
Richard	51	Bed
Claridge, John	57	Dav
Clark, Abraham	4	Jac

Clark (cont.)
Absalom 290 War
Alexander 39 Wll
Andrew 4 Jac
Andrew 6 Jac
Anthony 50 Bed
Barnes 34 Lin
Benjamin 2 Dic
Benjamin 11 Smi
Benjamin 284 War
Bolen 54 Wll
Burgus 345 Whi
Daniel 76 Dav
Daniel 27 Rob
Daniel 307 War
Daniel 367 Whi
Dericus 355 Whi
Elisabeth 18 Wll
Elisha 30 Mon
Elizabeth 8 Hum
George 4 Dic
George 14 Dic
George 410 Wil
Henry 40 Wll
Isaac 6 Jac
Isaac 145 Sum
Isaac 295 War
Isham 285 War
James 12 Lin
James 17 Lin
James 18 Lin
James 32 Lin
James 63 Mau
James 16 Ove
James 9 Smi
James C. 3 Hic
Jesse 6 Jac
Jno. W. 146 Sum
John 8 Law
John 3 Lin
John 6 Lin
John 45 Lin
John 87 Rut
John 98 Rut
John 118 Ste
John 295 War
John E. 6 Hum
Joseph 3 Bed
Joseph 18 Lin
Joseph 145 Sum
Joseph 312 War
Joseph 345 Whi
Joseph 53 Wll
Josiah 118 Ste
Josiah 123 Ste
Leonard 12 Smi
Lewis 36 Fra
Mark 147 Sum
Mathew 46 Lin
Rebecka 27 Rob
Reuben 11 Har
Richard 4 Jac
Richard 5 Jac

Clark (cont.)
Robert 62 Dav
Robert 20 Mon
Robert 9 Smi
Samuel 17 Lin
Samuel 1 Wll
Sarah 5 Ove
Silas 6 Jac
Silas 300 War
Simon B. 120 Ste
Solomon 87 Dav
Stewart 290 War
Thomas 4 Fra
Thomas 8 Lin
Thomas 317 War
Thomas 357 Whi
Thos. 25 Mon
Thos. 32 Mon
Tobias 1 Dic
Vachael 6 Jac
Washington 19 Mon
William 59 Mau
William 29 Mon
William 21 Rob
William 293 War
William 1 Wll
William 49 Wll
Wineford 363 Whi
see Clack, Clarke
Clarke, James 76 Rut
Jesse 84 Rut
John 13 Gil
Joseph 21 Gil
Robert 19 Gil
Robert 82 Rut
Thomas 12 Gil
Clarkson, Joshua 145 Sum
Clary, Daniel 10 Mon
Green 148 Sum
William 12 Hum
Clasby, Lewis 4 Fra
Claton, John 32 Mau
Claxton, Hiram 4 Fra
James 36 Fra
Jonathan 46 Bed
Clay, Archibald 11 Smi
Edward 390 Wil
James L. 47 Wll
John 63 Wll
Jona. 147 Sum
Joshua 84 Rut
Joshua 100 Rut
Mark 29 Wll
Samuel 51 Bed
Woody 29 Wll
Clayton, Alexander 5 Har
Benjamin 392 Wil
John 9 Lin
Morgan 15 Lin
Richard 146 Sum
Robert 8 Har
Stephen 16 Lin
William 79 Rut

Clayton (cont.)		
Wm.	9	Lin
see Claton		
Clear see Cloar		
Cleaton, Henry	22	Hic
Cleaves, John	84	Dav
Micael	84	Dav
Cleek, Micheal	21	Bed
Clegatt, Horatio	19	Hic
Clem, John	368	Whi
Cleman, Jourdan	81	Rut
Clements, Benjamin	3	Lin
Hardy	38	Lin
William	27	Mon
Clemins, Jeptha	395	Wil
Clemm, James S.	2	Wll
Clemments, James	97	Dav
Clemmons, Christopher	5	Jac
Curtis	16	Bed
Dudley	399	Wil
Etheldred	396	Wil
Isaac	85	Dav
J. C.	5	Jac
John	14	Bed
John	6	Jac
Joseph	52	Bed
Samuel	396	Wil
Samuel T., Jr.	419	Wil
William	3	Gil
Clemons, John	394	Wil
Clendennon, James	289	War
Clending, Anthy. B.	146	Sum
Clenny, Jonathan	357	Whi
Saml.	146	Sum
Cleveland, Joseph	11	Smi
William	11	Smi
Clevenger, Reuben	6	Ove
Cliburn, George	146	Sum
James	147	Sum
Joel	147	Sum
Cliburne, John	11	Smi
Cliford, Pierson	49	Wll
Clift, Elizabeth	17	Bed
Henry	21	Lin
Jno.	37	Bed
Margaret	17	Bed
Clifton, Bannon	398	Wil
Benjamin	397	Wil
Edwin	10	Mon
Henry	5	Har
Jesse	397	Wil
John	39	Lin
John	10	Mon
Lemuel K.	10	Mon
Nathan	2	Law
Thomas	55	Mau
Thomas	397	Wil
William	405	Wil
Climer, Thomas	395	Wil
see Climver		
Climver, John	395	Wil
Clinand, Henry	61	Wll
Clinard, John	98	Dav

Clinard (cont.)		
John	3	Rob
Joseph	2	Rob
Lourine	4	Rob
Cline, Adam	147	Sum
John	147	Sum
Martin	147	Sum
Clinton, David	3	Hum
Esther	15	Bed
Henry	9	Bed
John	9	Bed
Richard	83	Dav
Clippet, John	409	Wil
Clitewine, Daniel	13	Smi
Cliton, Bays	21	Hic
Cloar, Ann	148	Sum
Elijah	148	Sum
John, Jr.	148	Sum
John, Sr.	148	Sum
William	148	Sum
Clopton, Anthony	96	Dav
Guy	103	Rut
Walter	419	Wil
Close, Betsy	317	War
Thomas	312	War
Cloud, Edwin	18	Wll
Joseph F.	3	Dic
Clouse, Adam	343	Whi
Elijah	97	Rut
John	345	Whi
Clouston, Edward G.	1	Wll
Clower, Daniel	12	Gil
Cloyd, David	88	Dav
David	385	Wil
Ezekial	385	Wil
John	385	Wil
Joseph	385	Wil
Joshua	38	Wll
Phillip	38	Wll
Clubb, Sarah	11	Smi
Cluck, John	112	Wil
John	384	Wil
see Clack		
Clyer, William	34	Lin
Clymore, Joseph	35	Mau
Coaker, Jonathan	82	Rut
Coal, Edward	27	Mau
Isaiah	349	Whi
Isham	371	Whi
Jacob	350	Whi
James	368	Whi
Richard	371	Whi
Samuel	42	Mau
William F.	57	Mau
Coaldman, Thomas	64	Mau
Coalman, Anney M.	65	Dav
Coalson, John	358	Whi
Coaltart, William	75	Dav
Coalter, Chas.	23	Hic
Esau	23	Lin
James	2	Lin
Coar, Jonathan	39	Wll
Coaram, Eli	89	Rut

Coare, William 35 Wll
Coatman, Winney 80 Dav
Coatney, Ezekiel 5 Law
Jonathan 5 Har
Coats, Barton 30 Rob
Benjamin 409 Wil
John 33 Lin
Mary 302 War
Rott. W. 14 Hic
Sarah 14 Hic
Temperance 33 Lin
Thomas 33 Lin
William 51 Bed
William 32 Lin
William B. 11 Way
Cob, Charles 401 Wil
William 401 Wil
Cobb, Ambrose 9 Gil
Frederick 11 Rob
Hannah 29 Mon
James 113 Ste
Jesse 8 Ove
John 1 Hic
Rice 147 Sum
William 4 Har
see Cob, Coble, Cole
Cobbs, Charles 12 Rob
Jesse 68 Dav
Robert 9 Gil
Thomas 83 Rut
William F. 113 Wil
Cobey, Nathan 402 Wil
Coblar, Francis 14 Wll
Coble, Adam 23 Gil
Adam 5 Lin
Daniel 6 Lin
David 6 Lin
Frederick 30 Lin
Henry 6 Lin
Peter 6 Lin
Cobler, Christian 11 Smi
Christopher 14 Wll
Davis 65 Dav
Frederick 65 Dav
Harry 75 Dav
Henry 11 Smi
Hrris 61 Dav
Precilla 65 Dav
Cobley, George 411 Wil
Cochrain, Edward 65 Mau
William 64 Mau
Cochram, Henry 10 Smi
Cochran, Aaron 45 Wll
Daniel 117 Sum
David 9 Smi
Jacob 42 Mau
James 21 Gil
James 46 Mau
John 21 Bed
John 9 Smi
John 11 Smi
John 25 Wll
John 26 Wll
Cochran (cont.)
Robert 10 Smi
Saml. 145 Sum
Samuel 20 Gil
Thomas C. 4 Law
William 31 Mau
William 42 Mau
Wm. [2] 147 Sum
Zekial 31 Mau
see Cochram, Cockram, Cockrum
Cock, Fleming 380 Wil
John 292 War
John 418 Wil
John, Jr. 419 Wil
Joseph 418 Wil
Thomas J. 376 Wil
William 91 Rut
William 408 Wil
Cockburn, George 59 Mau
Cocke, Charles J. 32 Mon
Mary 1 Mon
Richard 14 Dic
Richard J. 54 Mau
Richd. 19 Mon
Stephen 1 Mon
Cockes, Robert, Doct. 9 Smi
Cocklereas, Jacob 148 Sum
Cocklerees, Nicholas 149 Sum
Cocklins, Henry 145 Sum
Cockram, Danl. 17 Hic
Dicy 17 Hic
Henry 17 Hic
Wilson 26 Lin
Cockran, John 49 Bed
Saml. 21 Hic
Cockrel, James 11 Wll
Cockrell, John 62 Dav
Cockril, John 48 Bed
Cockron, David 5 Ove
Cockrum, James 53 Bed
John 25 Lin
Cocks, Thomas 64 Dav
Cod..., William 1 Per
Coddle, Joshua 50 Mau
Codl, William 61 Mau
Cody, Charles H. 72 Dav
Pierce 361 Whi
Coe, John 398 Wil
Joseph 47 Mau
Joseph 56 Mau
William 405 Wil
Coffe, John 3 Per
Nancy 21 Bed
Coffee, Absolum 28 Bed
David 11 Smi
Jesse 280 War
John 33 Lin
Joshua M. 11 Smi
Pleasant N. 7 Ove
Rice 25 Bed
Coffer, Thomas S. 319 War
Coffey, —, Mr. 24 Mau
Easter 41 Mau

Coffey (cont.)		
Hughey	57	Mau
Jane	62	Mau
N.	24	Mau
Coffeys, J.	24	Mau
Jak.	24	Mau
Coffin, Ezekiel	73	Rut
Coffman, Daniel	41	Lin
Isaac	74	Dav
Jervis	94	Rut
John	19	Lin
Tho.	147	Sum
Cofman, Job	6	Fra
Cogbill, Charles C.	9	Smi
Coger, John	4	Fra
Coggin, Jonathan	11	Smi
Jordon	11	Smi
Coggle, Paul	4	Per
Robert	4	Per
Cohe, John	65	Wll
Cohea, Richd.	22	Hic
Coher, Peter	6	Rob
Coid, William M.	43	Mau
Cokeley, Sarah	14	Mon
Cokely, Griggs	13	Mon
Coker, Austin	370	Whi
George	19	Ove
Jesse	148	Sum
Joseph	13	Smi
Peter	342	Whi
Col...son, Standley	7	Per
Colan, Joseph	4	Fra
Colbert, Cynthia	13	Smi
Colburn, Thomas	38	Mau
Colclough, Benja.	146	Sum
Coldwell, Aberam	6	Dic
Ballard	48	Bed
Joseph	63	Dav
Rahab	146	Sum
Samuel	39	Bed
Cole, Anderson	29	Bed
Andrew	44	Wll
Andrew	65	Wll
David	14	Hum
David	5	Jac
Eli	4	Lin
Elisabeth	55	Wll
Hiram	65	Wll
Isaac	404	Wil
Isham	44	Wll
James	10	Bed
James	4	Fra
James	26	Lin
James	29	Rob
James	146	Sum
James	64	Wll
John	29	Bed
John	46	Bed
John	70	Dav
John	5	Fra
John	5	Jac
John	147	Sum
Jos.	146	Sum
Cole (cont.)		
Joseph	376	Wil
Joseph	33	Wll
Judah	11	Way
Obediah	77	Rut
Peter H.	1	Mon
Robert	5	Jac
S. L.	5	Jac
Samuel	6	Ove
Stephen	4	Lin
Tellmore	70	Dav
Thomas	70	Dav
Thomas	6	Gil
Thomas	4	Jac
Weri	6	Bed
William	21	Rob
William	130	Ste
William	65	Wll
Willis W.	6	Gil
Wm.	148	Sum
Coleman, Abel	84	Rut
Benjamin	13	Hic
Blackman	82	Rut
Daniel	11	Dic
David	18	Hic
Enos	18	Hic
Hardy	145	Sum
John	10	Dic
John	13	Gil
Joseph	83	Rut
Joshua	85	Rut
Joshua	48	Wll
Rice	5	Mon
Rott. S.	116	Ste
Samuel	14	Gil
Stephen	40	Lin
Thos.	2	Mon
Wiatt	102	Rut
Coles, William F.	378	Wil
Coleston, David	19	Way
Coley, Eaton	10	Hum
James	10	Hum
Sally	41	Bed
Sebourn	10	Hum
Wood J. H.	10	Hum
Colgin, Charles	24	Rob
Colier, David	7	Ove
Ingram B.	96	Rut
Robert	283	War
Collens, Joseph	26	Bed
see Collins		
Collia, William	10	Smi
Collie, Charles	18	Lin
James	19	Lin
William	19	Lin
Collier, ...	19	Ove
Amons	4	Per
Charles	24	Lin
Fireby	124	Ste
Frederick	5	Dic
Henry	9	Gil
John C.	15	Dic
Joseph	8	Gil

Collier (cont.)
Robert H. 19 Rob
Salley 16 Gil
Thomas 14 Dic
William 5 Fra
William 8 Gil
Willis 6 Dic
Collininsworth, Allice 67 Dav
Collins, Abner 5 Lin
Absolom 20 Lin
Andrew 110 Ste
Barby 4 Fra
Daniel 313 War
Durham 44 Mau
Elisha Sims 420 Wil
Erastus T. 37 Wll
Frederick 316 War
George 4 Mon
Hadigah 34 Wll
Isaac 36 Fra
James 26 Rob
James 371 Whi
Jerry 394 Wil
John 66 Dav
John 128 Ste
John 311 War
John H. 419 Wil
John R. 15 Mon
Joseph 12 Smi
Lewis 1 Hum
Nancy 341 Whi
Peter 417 Wil
Polly 46 Bed
Stephen 35 Mau
Thomas 67 Dav
Thomas 13 Gil
William 5 Fra
William 36 Fra
William 5 Lin
William 11 Lin
William 128 Ste
William C. 376 Wil
Collum, John 11 Smi
Collums, Barblet 186 Sum
Collville, Josopeh 284 War
Colman, Stephen 147 Sum
Clours, Henry 4 Fra
Colp, John H. 30 Mon
Colquet, John T. 4 Fra
Colquit, John 5 Fra
Reuben 5 Fra
Samuel 5 Fra
Colson, David 293 War
Coltart, Saml. 79 Dav
Coltharp, Norrel 94 Dav
William 88 Dav
Colton see Cotton
Colville, Lush 278 War
Colwell, Amous 63 Mau
Silas 56 Mau
Thomas 56 Mau
William H. 54 Mau
Colyear, Rody 348 Whi
Colyer, Moses 31 Mon
Sarah 17 Mon
Thos. 24 Mon
Comb, Lyps 43 Mau
Comber, Thomas 6 Hum
Combs, ... 24 Mau
David 148 Sum
Henry 71 Dav
John 53 Bed
Labourn 11 Hum
William 27 Mau
Comer, Adam 88 Rut
John 383 Wil
John 406 Wil
Reuben P. 407 Wil
Samuel 5 Jac
William 396 Wil
see Cormer
Comfman, Jacob 84 Dav
Comfort, Danl. T. 80 Dav
Commong, Joel 2 Lin
Joseph 2 Lin
Compbell, Isaac 285 War
Comper, Simon 415 Wil
Comperry, Sampson 14 Hum
Compton, Henry 86 Dav
Philip 70 Mau
Richd., Jr. 19 Hic
Richd., Sr. 19 Hic
William 86 Dav
Wm. 19 Hic
see ...pton
Conaway, James 12 Dic
Conder, Daniel 21 Hic
George 21 Hic
Peter 21 Hic
Condit, Fielding 11 Smi
Condon, James 77 Dav
Condra, George 5 Jac
Condry, Jacob 2 Way
Conely, Thomas 96 Dav
Conger, Isaac 22 Lin
Congo, Eli 11 Smi
James 69 Dav
John 11 Smi
Joshua 11 Smi
Conley, Andrew 13 Hum
John 4 Hum
Neal 34 Bed
Thomas 33 Bed
William 13 Hum
Conn, Jo. H. 146 Sum
John E. 344 Whi
Richard J. 98 Rut
see Corn
Connel, Walter 130 Ste
see McConnel
Connell, Enoch P. 148 Sum
Giles 9 Rob
James 5 Rob
John 28 Rob
Sally 79 Dav
Sally 17 Rob

Connelley, John	305	War
Connelly, George	34	Rob
John	146	Sum
John	307	War
John W.	78	Rut
Connely, Peter	11	Har
Conner, Abraham	360	Whi
Archibald	360	Whi
Elizabeth	148	Sum
James	18	Gil
James	354	Whi
James	17	Wll
John B.	17	Gil
Joseph	14	Ove
William	36	Fra
William	18	Gil
William	43	Wll
Wilson	5	Ove
Conners, Thomas	113	Wil
Connies, Thomas	389	Wil
Connoway, Frederick	36	Fra
Jane	4	Fra
Timothy	12	Smi
Conrod, Philip	9	Rob
William C.	8	Rob
Conway, Charles	353	Whi
Christopher	47	Bed
Henry	47	Bed
Jessee	353	Whi
Lydia	48	Bed
Thomas	369	Whi
William	38	Lin
Cooc see Cox		
Coode, Homer	14	Hic
John	14	Hic
Cook, Abraham	303	War
Augustin	12	Rob
Benjamin	3	Per
Buckner	87	Rut
Charles, Junr.	13	Law
Charles, Sr.	13	Law
Christian	18	Way
Daniel	4	Fra
Daniel	5	Fra
Garrison	10	Smi
George	5	Fra
George W.	102	Rut
Green C.	379	Wil
Henry	379	Wil
Henry, Jur.	5	Fra
Henry, Sen.	5	Fra
Henry, Sn.	7	Wll
Hesekiah G.	100	Rut
Jacob	28	Rob
Jacob C.	146	Sum
James	4	Jac
James	123	Ste
James, Junr.	120	Ste
James W.	4	Fra
Jas.	28	Jac
Jas., Senr.	120	Ste
Joel	145	Sum
John	59	Dav

Cook (cont.)		
John	5	Fra
John	42	Lin
John	70	Mau
John	11	Mon
John	12	Rob
John	131	Ste
John	17	Way
John, Senr.	17	Way
John C.	411	Wil
John D.	81	Rut
John D.	90	Rut
John W.	2	Wll
Jonathan	5	Way
Jones	59	Dav
Joseph	59	Dav
Joseph	33	Mau
Joseph	93	Rut
Joseph	120	Ste
Kirby	102	Rut
Lion	13	Smi
Martin	17	Way
Mercilles	2	Bed
Moses	147	Sum
Nancy	393	Wil
Nicholas	353	Whi
R. F.	4	Jac
Randolph	49	Mau
Richard	419	Wil
Robert	342	Whi
Sarah	3	Ove
Thomas	9	Bed
Thomas	21	Bed
Thomas	4	Lin
Thomas	68	Mau
Thomas	12	Rob
Thomas	102	Rut
Thomas	377	Wil
Thomas	379	Wil
Thomas, Jur.	68	Mau
Uriah	412	Wil
William	44	Bed
William	4	Fra
William	6	Jac
William	9	Law
William	10	Lin
William	53	Mau
William	19	Rob
William	81	Rut
William	18	Way
William	393	Wil
William A.	5	Mon
William P.	52	Mau
Cooke, David	5	Gil
John	32	Bed
John	37	Bed
John	54	Bed
W. H.	8	Per
Cookman, Catharine	5	Law
Cooksey, Jesse	11	Ove
Jessee	14	Mon
Joseph	8	Ove
Phebe	2	Dic

Cooksey (cont.)		
William	16	Ove
Cooksie, Cornelius	295	War
Jesse	301	War
John	9	Smi
John [2]	301	War
Thomas	301	War
Cooksin, Enich	285	War
Cooley, George	131	Ste
Richard	110	Ste
Robert	1	Hum
William	347	Whi
William T.	12	Mon
Wm. M.	110	Ste
Cooly, James	29	Lin
Coon, Conrod	12	Rob
James	93	Dav
William	8	Mon
Coonce, Daniel	26	Lin
George	26	Lin
Philip	15	Lin
Philip	26	Lin
Coonrod, John	409	Wil
Coons, George	9	Ove
John	7	Ove
John	8	Ove
Coonse, Martin	5	Jac
Coop, Horatio	49	Bed
James	49	Bed
John	49	Bed
Richard	49	Bed
Coopar, Isaac	149	Sum
Cooper, —, Mrs.	69	Mau
Alexander	356	Whi
Ambrose	13	Smi
Andrew	11	Ove
Andrew	17	Ove
Augustus	75	Dav
Bennet	13	Smi
Charles	23	Bed
Cornelius	12	Smi
Dabner	13	Smi
David	29	Lin
David	8	Mon
David	15	Rob
David	10	Smi
Edmond	41	Bed
Edmund	78	Dav
George	41	Bed
Henry	84	Rut
Houston	93	Dav
Hugh	51	Wll
Hyram	5	Mon
Jacob	17	Ove
James	23	Bed
James	61	Dav
James	305	War
James	15	Way
James	356	Whi
Job	14	Bed
Joel	41	Bed
John	41	Bed
John	94	Dav
Cooper (cont.)		
John	32	Lin
John	30	Mau
John	48	Mau
John	90	Rut
John	9	Smi
John	15	Way
John	414	Wil
Jonathan	13	Smi
Joseph F.	45	Wll
Kennedy	8	Ove
Mark	129	Ste
Matthew D.	1	Wll
Nancy	146	Sum
Nathan	16	Ove
Polly	32	Lin
Reuben	319	War
Robbart M.	36	Mau
Robert	24	Bed
Robert	115	Ste
Stoofely, Esq.	414	Wil
Tabitha	78	Rut
Thomas	9	Lin
Thomas	15	Ove
Thomas	361	Whi
Wells	87	Rut
Wells	100	Rut
William	63	Mau
William	66	Mau
William	4	Mon
William	7	Ove
William	18	Ove
William	11	Smi
Young	6	Mon
Zacheus	87	Rut
Coot, Jemimah	371	Whi
Cootes, Austin M.	69	Dav
John	65	Dav
Coothus, John	8	Per
Coots, Fredrick	353	Whi
Cope, Andrew	360	Whi
James	286	War
Richard	147	Sum
Wiliam	288	War
Wm.	148	Sum
see Cohe		
Copeland, Jacob	19	Way
James	12	Ove
James	320	War
James G.	94	Rut
Jane	346	Whi
John	20	Mon
John	11	Ove
John	6	Per
John	88	Rut
John	13	Way
Joseph	5	Ove
Josiah	8	Ove
Moses	14	Hic
Rapeley	6	Per
Reubin	6	Per
Richard	5	Ove
Richard	12	Ove

Copeland (cont.)		
Richard	16	Ove
Samuel	402	Wil
Samuel	407	Wil
Singleton	346	Whi
Solomon	11	Ove
Stephen	19	Ove
William	18	Gil
William	19	Ove
William	13	Way
Copen, James	45	Wll
Copher, Jacob	11	Bed
James	7	Bed
Thomas	7	Bed
Willis	7	Bed
Copland, John	53	Wll
Mary	23	Wll
Coplin, Antoney	43	Mau
James	42	Mau
Coppage, Charles	379	Wil
John J.	4	Dic
Copper, Elijah	11	Law
Corbell, William	78	Rut
Corbet, John	65	Dav
Letitia	65	Dav
Meradith	84	Dav
Corbin, Charnel	27	Mon
William	30	Mon
Corbit, Richard	39	Wll
Richard	41	Wll
Corby, Joseph	33	Rob
Corden, Benjamin	410	Wil
Rice	403	Wil
Corder, Darius	364	Whi
Lewis	99	Rut
Cording, Jacob	16	Mon
Cordle, John	34	Rob
Cordy see Thomas		
Coreathers, Robbert	40	Mau
Corey, Leven	27	Mau
William	27	Mau
Corkle, Robert N.	89	Rut
Corkran see Carheron		
Corlew, William	30	Mon
Corley, Larkin	10	Smi
Matthew	10	Smi
Robert	12	Smi
Stephen	12	Smi
Cormack, John	130	Ste
Wm.	123	Ste
Cormer, William	406	Wil
see Comer		
Corn, Benjamin	12	Smi
John	5	Fra
Samuel	5	Fra
William	5	Fra
Cornelison, Jesse	5	Fra
Cornelius, James	89	Dav
Corner, John	145	Sum
William	402	Wil
Cornwell, Charles	13	Smi
Fouchee	12	Smi
Francis	12	Smi
Cornwell (cont.)		
Henry	9	Smi
Samuel C.	12	Smi
Silas C.	12	Smi
Stephen	10	Smi
Thompson	12	Smi
Wm. G.	21	Way
Corothers, Tho.	146	Sum
Correathers, John	5	Jac
see Car(r)uthers, Coreathers, Cruthers		
Corsey, Robert	28	Mon
Thomas	28	Mon
Thos.	28	Mon
Corsine, Enos	63	Wll
Corthan, John	148	Sum
Corthen, Hudson	146	Sum
Corum, Robert	148	Sum
Corzine, Thomas D.	399	Wil
Cosbie, Hans	9	Lin
James	11	Lin
Margaret	11	Lin
William	10	Lin
Cosby, Garland	34	Wll
Thomas W.	9	Smi
Cosebeer, Thomas	4	Way
Cosey, James	6	Hum
Samuel	6	Hum
Cossey, Aaron	118	Ste
John	4	Fra
Cossley, John	7	Bed
Peter	7	Bed
Cossock, John	92	Rut
Cotes, Joshua	104	Rut
Thomas	31	Bed
Cotham, Eligah	2	Per
Richard	27	Lin
Cothey, John	4	Bed
Cothran, John	13	Rob
Lewis	13	Rob
Cotner, Lewis	11	Lin
Cotrel, George	6	Per
Cotrill, Allen	11	Smi
Martin	11	Smi
Cott, Alexander	104	Rut
Cottengim, John	127	Ste
Leven	127	Ste
Levinth	123	Ste
Wm., Junr.	123	Ste
Wm., Senr.	123	Ste
Cotter, Thomas	79	Rut
William	79	Rut
William, Junr.	79	Rut
Cotteril, Wm.	14	Law
Cottingham, Eleventh	3	Hum
John	3	Hum
Cottle, William	1	Law
Cottom, Isaac	13	Hic
Moses	13	Hic
Stephen	13	Hic
Wm.	13	Hic
Cotton, Allen	91	Dav
Arthur	145	Sum

Cotton (cont.)		
Cullen	8	Hum
James	6	Bed
John	6	Bed
John	145	Sum
John	288	War
Lewis	6	Bed
Moore	146	Sum
Peter	26	Lin
Priscilla	148	Sum
William	4	Hum
Young	148	Sum
Couch, Barister	40	Lin
Eli	41	Lin
John	42	Lin
John B.	40	Lin
Jonathan	41	Lin
Joseph	16	Ove
Mellington	41	Lin
Coue, John	19	Lin
Cougill, Martin	147	Sum
Coulsen, Isaac	356	Whi
Coulter, Anderson	97	Rut
Counce, William	11	Law
Council, Dudley	11	Mon
Counsel, Cyrus	10	Smi
David	31	Mon
James	32	Mon
Countess, Peter	288	War
Counts, Adam	36	Fra
Courin, William	320	War
Courts, Jenning H.	81	Rut
Peter	36	Fra
Cousart, John F.	33	Lin
Couse, Daniel	52	Wll
Jacob	52	Wll
Couts, John	12	Rob
Mary	310	War
William	12	Rob
Couwell, Isaac	35	Lin
Jesse	35	Lin
Cov, Wm.	123	Ste
see Care		
Cove see Cov	123	Ste
Covey, James	4	Fra
John	36	Fra
Russle R.	40	Mau
William	49	Mau
Covinger, Walter	306	War
Covington, David	82	Rut
Elisabeth	24	Wll
Jesse	98	Rut
John	98	Rut
William, overseer	40	Wll
Winny	28	Rob
Wm.	146	Sum
Cowan, James	7	Ove
Joseph	8	Gil
William H.	1	Law
Coward, Elisha	14	Ove
Cowardon, Mary	136	Sum
Cowden, John	21	Gil
William	70	Mau
Cowder, James	13	Gil
Cowdon, Josiah	145	Sum
Cowell, Joseph	3	Hum
Joseph	124	Ste
Cowen, Alexander	42	Lin
Andrew	350	Whi
Benjamin	27	Mon
David	2	Hum
David	4	Lin
James	4	Fra
James, Sen.	4	Fra
John	4	Fra
John	5	Fra
Joseph	4	Wll
Matthew	5	Jac
Polly	4	Fra
Robert	4	Fra
Samuel	4	Fra
Stewart	5	Fra
William	36	Fra
William	41	Lin
Cowfield, Willis	403	Wil
Cowgil, Abner	96	Dav
Elishua	59	Dav
Cowgo, Adam	400	Wil
Cowin, David	126	Ste
Stephen	126	Ste
Cowley, Charles	36	Lin
Cowlishaw, John	6	Mon
Cowper, Samuel	4	Fra
Cowthorn, Dolly	387	Wil
James	387	Wil
John	387	Wil
John H.	387	Wil
Lawson	387	Wil
Sarah	386	Wil
Thomas F.	387	Wil
Vincant	387	Wil
Cox, Absalom	12	Smi
Adam	67	Mau
Amon	36	Fra
Archabald	65	Dav
Archibald	15	Hic
Asa	293	War
Benjamin	60	Dav
Benjamin	46	Lin
Caleb	35	Bed
Caleb	36	Bed
Charles	26	Mau
Charles	407	Wil
David	6	Jac
Elijah	83	Rut
Ephraim	99	Rut
Carey	308	War
Geo. P. [?]	4	Jac
Harmon	2	Hum
Isaac	28	Bed
J... [John?]	2	Ove
James	36	Fra
James	3	Hic
James	24	Wll
Jared	7	Ove
Jesse	64	Wll

Cox (cont.)		
John	31	Bed
John	80	Dav
John	19	Lin
John	122	Ste
John [2]	407	Wil
Joseph [2]	39	Bed
Joseph	6	Jac
Joseph	365	Whi
Josiah	283	War
Larkin	13	Ove
Lewis	34	Rob
Lewis	47	Wll
Lorton	7	Dic
Nacy	18	Wll
Polly	41	Lin
Robert	21	Gil
Samuel	8	Gil
Samuel	4	Wll
Temperance	64	Wll
Thomas	39	Bed
Thomas	5	Lin
William	12	Dic
William	44	Lin
William	94	Rut
William	407	Wil
William D.	88	Dav
Coxe, Fowlker	6	Gil
Presley	21	Gil
Samuel, Junr.	7	Gil
Samuel, Senr.	7	Gil
William	21	Gil
Crabb, James	27	Rob
Jno.	148	Sum
Joseph	361	Whi
Ralph	84	Dav
Stephen	372	Whi
Stephn	13	Way
Crabtree, Benjamin	32	Rob
James	28	Jac
James, Jr.	28	Jac
Jobe W.	2	Rob
John	28	Jac
Ransom	4	Fra
Rebecka	385	Wil
Samuel	6	Jac
Samuel	15	Ove
Thomas	15	Ove
Westley	17	Rob
Whitiker	6	Jac
William	6	Jac
Crackling, Mackeing	382	Wil
Craddock, Nathaniel	392	Wil
Pleasent	76	Dav
Richard	416	Wil
William	92	Dav
William C.	419	Wil
Crafford, Alexander	25	Mau
Craig H.	26	Mau
John	52	Mau
Craft, Ezekiel	11	Har
Jessee	26	Mon
John	311	War
Craft (cont.)		
Samuel	26	Mon
Crafton, John B.	45	Mau
Staples	56	Mau
Thomas	34	Wll
Cragg, Richard	59	Mau
Craghead, Peter	12	Smi
Shelton	12	Smi
Cragin, John	10	Smi
Craig, A.	118	Ste
Alexander	19	Wll
Alexander [deleted]	28	Wll
Andrew	63	Wll
Daniel	53	Wll
David	129	Ste
David	63	Wll
Elijah	47	Wll
Elizebeth	70	Mau
George	5	Fra
James	3	Hum
James	9	Hum
James	20	Lin
James	10	Smi
James	127	Ste
James	38	Wll
James	63	Wll
Jane	9	Hum
John	53	Bed
John	10	Smi
John, Jun.	10	Smi
John C.	20	Lin
Johnston	30	Mau
Molly	5	Fra
Robert	5	Fra
Thomas	14	Hum
Thomas	38	Wll
Thomas, Sr.	8	Hum
William	12	Bed
William	31	Mau
William	60	Mau
William	38	Wll
Wm.	4	Hic
Craigan, Saml.	79	Dav
Craige, David	35	Mau
James	43	Mau
James C.	59	Mau
Craighead, David	58	Mau
David	63	Mau
John B.	85	Dav
Thomas B.	71	Dav
Crain, Abrose	51	Bed
Isaac B.	5	Rob
John	126	Ste
Lewis B.	126	Ste
Cramer, Champion	4	Fra
John	4	Fra
Thomas	4	Fra
see Crasner		
Crane, Abijah	354	Whi
Ezekiel	147	Sum
John	10	Dic
Lewis	145	Sum
Nimrod	5	Fra

Crane (cont.)		
Stephen	354	Whi
William	4	Fra
William	29	Mon
Cranford, Arther	53	Mau
Elias	5	Law
Cranister, Philip	10	Law
Cranor, Moses	77	Rut
Crapman, Ben.	406	Wil
see Chapman		
Crapper, William	57	Dav
Crasner, George	378	Wil
Cravan, Wm. P.	149	Sum
Robert	7	Gil
see McCraven		
Cravins, Joseph	7	Ove
Mary	74	Dav
Crawford, Anthony	32	Lin
Benoni	5	Dic
Edward	10	Ove
Elizabeth	87	Rut
George	13	Lin
Hugh	147	Sum
Isaac	24	Lin
James	7	Gil
James	15	Lin
James	45	Lin
John	15	Lin
John	15	Ove
Mary	36	Fra
Raiford	85	Rut
Raiford	98	Rut
Rebecca	85	Rut
Samuel	21	Lin
Thomas	32	Lin
Thomas	281	War
Thomas	9	Way
William	146	Sum
William K.	14	Ove
Wm.	3	Lin
Crawley, Camp P.	5	Hum
Martha	5	Hum
Thomas	358	Whi
Creamor, William	8	Gil
Creath, Samuel	30	Mon
Crecelis, George	12	Ove
Isaac	12	Ove
Creder, George	377	Wil
Credo, James	36	Wll
Creech, Benjamin	91	Rut
George	102	Rut
Joshua	91	Rut
Creecy, Archibald	5	Gil
Bennet	12	Gil
John	22	Gil
John	27	Wll
William [2]	12	Gil
Creed, Colby	4	Ove
Washington	6	Jac
Creek, John	44	Wll
see Crick		
Creel, William	61	Dav
Crenford, Hardy	53	Mau
Crenford (cont.)		
William	53	Mau
Crenshaw, Garland	147	Sum
Joel	149	Sum
John	146	Sum
Joseph	36	Mau
Nancy	58	Mau
Nathl.	149	Sum
Rebekah	16	Gil
Stephen	186	Sum
Wm.	149	Sum
Creps, Jacob	11	Smi
John	11	Smi
Cresiville, William	400	Wil
Creswell, Hallum	377	Wil
Crew, Martha	19	Gil
Crews, Benjamin	1	Dic
John	2	Dic
Pleasant	2	Dic
Plesand	58	Mau
Seburn	1	Dic
Squire	90	Rut
Walter	20	Gil
Crichlon, James	100	Rut
James	82	Rut
Crick, George	56	Wll
Cricket, Samuel	13	Bed
Criddle, John	86	Dav
John	92	Dav
Crider, Amos	4	Jac
Crim, William	368	Whi
Crimm, John	350	Whi
Crinor, George	18	Hic
Crippen, George	39	Mau
Crisman, Abram	23	Wll
Crisp, Mansil	1	Law
Mansil	13	Law
Prescot	117	Ste
Tilman A.	34	Mau
William	32	Mau
Crissle, Andrew	121	Ste
Cristley, Nancy	66	Wll
Criswell, Andrew	44	Wll
Eli	378	Wil
Henry	146	Sum
Robert	147	Sum
Critendon, James	11	Mon
John	11	Wll
Critintun, William	2	Gil
Crittenden, Francis	97	Rut
Wm.	8	Hic
Crittendon, Charles	315	War
William	26	Bed
William	28	Bed
Crocas, John	78	Rut
Crocker, Baily	83	Rut
William	5	Jac
Crocket, George	75	Dav
George	136	Sum
John	5	Fra
John	5	Hum
John	10	Hum
John	25	Lin

Crocket (cont.)		
Joseph	6	Wll
Samuel	5	Fra
Samuel	4	Rob
William	34	Lin
William	4	Rob
William	7	Rob
Wilson	91	Dav
Crockett, Andrew	25	Wll
Andrew, Jr.	25	Wll
Archibald	21	Gil
James	21	Wll
John H.	29	Wll
Patteson	12	Gil
Robert	17	Gil
Robert	21	Gil
Samuel	1	Wll
Samuel	25	Wll
William	16	Ove
Wm.	146	Sum
Crockit, David, Mr.	10	Law
Crody, James	7	Gil
Crof, —	24	Mau
Crofford, Edmond	395	Wil
George	69	Mau
John	57	Mau
Samuel	62	Mau
William	30	Mau
Croft, John	44	Lin
Washington	10	Gil
Croker, Lucy	379	Wil
Crompton, Thomas	9	Lin
Cronan, John	14	Way
Croney, Rhoda	7	Gil
Cronister, Adam	7	Law
Cronk, Jacob	12	Smi
William	12	Smi
Crook, David	10	Gil
James	419	Wil
John	353	Whi
John	368	Whi
Yerby	419	Wil
see Croon		
Croon, Alfred [?]	62	Dav
Crose, Asel	5	Jac
Crosen, John	13	Lin
Cross, Alvin	12	Hic
Asel	45	Bed
Benjamin	4	Gil
Daniel	8	Per
Drewry	26	Mon
Elijah [2]	397	Wil
Henry	11	Gil
Isabela	19	Bed
James	412	Wil
Joel	11	Smi
John	104	Rut
John B.	4	Ove
Samuel	9	Hum
Shadrach	10	Gil
Solomon	281	War
Thomas	46	Wll
William	3	Bed

Cross (cont.)		
William	415	Wil
Crossby, Sarrah, Mrs.	9	Law
Crosser, Leonard	16	Bed
Crossland, James	280	War
William	11	Smi
Crosslane, Samuel	12	Gil
Crossnoe, Henry	21	Way
Crossnow, Thomas	2	Way
Crossway, John N.	70	Dav
Crossweight, John, Mr.	3	Law
Crosthwait, Shelton	85	Rut
Croswell, Nimrod	116	Ste
William	3	Hum
William	127	Ste
Crotzer, George	14	Mon
Jacob	12	Mon
Philip	13	Mon
Crouch, Herder	3	Mon
Isaac	6	Ove
James	15	Ove
Martin	15	Ove
Moses	305	War
Richard	298	War
Crouder, John	17	Wll
Nathaniel	47	Wll
Richard	367	Whi
Robert	64	Dav
Crounel, Jacob	127	Ste
Crous, Daniel	8	Per
Henry	99	Rut
Crouse, John	45	Bed
William	130	Ste
Crouser, Henry	100	Rut
Croutch, Susan	40	Wll
Crow, Brian	45	Wll
James	98	Dav
Samuel	22	Gil
Thomas	12	Law
Crowcer, Dolly	148	Sum
Eliz.	148	Sum
Henry	5	Jac
Ira	14	Gil
Levi	14	Gil
Lucy	11	Smi
Phillip	76	Rut
Thomas	147	Sum
William	13	Smi
Crowell, Joseph	14	Way
Crower, Henry [?]	82	Rut
Crowl, John	5	Fra
Crownover, Joseph	372	Whi
William	361	Whi
Crowson, Abraham	4	Gil
Jacob	4	Gil
Mary	4	Gil
Crozin, Viney	46	Wll
Cruchfield, John	2	Per
Sebern	297	War
Crudson, Reuben	1	Mon
Cruise, Benja.	148	Sum
Jane	148	Sum
Renny	146	Sum

Cruise (cont.)		
William	401	Wil
Crum, Peter	5	Jac
William	47	Lin
Crumb, Peter	319	War
Crumbless, Hugh	6	Law
Crump, Elizabeth	43	Bed
Fendel	48	Wll
George	8	Bed
George	43	Bed
William	8	Bed
Crumpler, Mathew	2	Dic
Rafred	7	Dic
Crumpley, John	146	Sum
Crumpton, Basil	20	Gil
Isaac	20	Gil
John [2]	400	Wil
Matthew	411	Wil
Rebecca	410	Wil
William	400	Wil
Crunk, Felix	12	Lin
George	146	Sum
Ira	12	Lin
John W.	13	Lin
John W.	61	Wll
William	31	Bed
William	13	Lin
William	3	Rob
Crutcher, Edward	391	Wil
Larken	60	Wll
Thomas	80	Dav
William	30	Wll
Crutcherville, John	24	Mon
Crutchfield, Charles	98	Dav
George	10	Smi
Oliver	81	Rut
Samuel B.	10	Smi
Thomas	10	Smi
Cruthers, Sally	10	Smi
Cryder, Henry	146	Sum
Cryer, Hardy M.	147	Sum
John	145	Sum
Mary	147	Sum
Cryner, John	18	Lin
Cryton, Robert	145	Sum
Cuff, Andrew	92	Rut
John	92	Rut
Cuffman, Puwat	147	Sum
Culbern, James [& Vanallen]	1	Wll
Culberson, Jane	23	Mon
William	285	War
Culbert, George	14	Wll
Culbertson, James	5	Rob
Cullum, Jesse	92	Dav
William H.	55	Wll
Cully, Zachariah	4	Fra
Culock, William	319	War
Culp, Adam	33	Bed
Culpeper, B.	119	Ste
Culton, Nancy	4	Har
Culver, John	15	Ove
Culverson, Jesse	124	Ste
Culwell, Hardy	146	Sum
Culwell (cont.)		
James	115	Ste
Cumingham, John	5	Wll
Cumings, Joseph	358	Whi
Cumins, Margaret	145	Sum
Cummerford, Sally	12	Smi
Cummin, William	384	Wil
Cummings, Charles	384	Wil
George	376	Wil
Hugh	418	Wil
John	395	Wil
Cummins, Benjamin	312	War
David	22	Wll
Ellen	26	Rob
Moses	302	War
Samuel	49	Wll
Thomas	17	Lin
Uriah S.	82	Rut
William	94	Dav
Cummons, John	32	Bed
Cumton, Charles	411	Wil
Cun, Bolen	53	Mau
see Chun		
Cunigem, John	123	Ste
see Cottengim		
Cuningham, George	43	Bed
Humphrey	43	Bed
John	23	Bed
John	309	War
Joseph	314	War
Lang.	309	War
Mary	358	Whi
Matthew	44	Bed
Murrel	148	Sum
Richard	30	Bed
Sal.	5	Jac
Cunnghaham, Samuel	48	Mau
Cunniham, Wm.	123	Ste
Cunningham, Alexr.	148	Sum
Andrew [deleted]	67	Mau
Benj.	308	War
Edmond	359	Whi
Enoch	70	Dav
George	4	Fra
George	14	Lin
Griffith	28	Lin
H.	290	War
James	4	Fra
James	99	Rut
James	9	Smi
James W.	40	Lin
Jesse	10	Dic
John	11	Dic
John	48	Mau
John	283	War
John	293	War
John	399	Wil
John T.	21	Lin
Josiah	74	Dav
Moses	399	Wil
Robert	8	Lin
Sally	100	Rut
Samuel	26	Lin

Cunningham (cont.)
Thomas 3 Har
William 22 Lin
William 40 Lin
William 99 Rut
Willie 5 Fra
see Cumingham, Cunigem, Cunnghaham
Cunninghan, Joseph 399 Wil
Cunnings, Garose 377 Wil
Cupp, Anna 14 Law
Cups, Fedricks 65 Mau
Curby, Bennet 27 Mau
John 27 Mau
Malachi 53 Wll
Sarah 388 Wil
Curd, John 387 Wil
John 388 Wil
Curey, James 27 Mau
James 33 Mau
John 26 Mau
Nancy 36 Mau
Silus 69 Mau
William 26 Mau
Wilson 48 Mau
Curl, John 5 Fra
Portland J. 90 Rut
William 6 Hic
William 109 Ste
William 111 Ste
Curlee, Calvin 97 Rut
Cullen 102 Rut
Ewin 111 Ste
Curlon, Isaac 13 Hum
Curray, Elijah 65 Dav
Curren, Robert P. 1 Wll
Currey, Elizabeth 13 Gil
Isaac 3 Per
Currie, William 114 Ste
Currin, John 82 Dav
Jonathan 73 Rut
Curry, David, Jr. 23 Hic
David, Sr. 23 Hic
Elisabeth 26 Wll
James 33 Lin
James W. 19 Wll
John 24 Hic
John 8 Hum
John 13 Lin
John 34 Lin
John 146 Sum
John 393 Wil
Nancy 393 Wil
Robert B. 80 Dav
Samuel 23 Wll
Wm. 2 Mon
Cursiville, Anny 378 Wil
Curtes, James 310 War
Curtice, Marth 76 Dav
William 89 Dav
Curtis, Alsey 37 Wll
Ann 88 Rut
Benager 6 Fra

Curtis (cont.)
Benjamin 10 Wll
Benjamin 37 Wll
David 12 Smi
Eli 13 Hum
Hillery 17 Lin
Jas. W. 6 Jac
Joel 4 Jac
Joshua 6 Hum
Joshua 37 Wll
Josiah 4 Jac
Moses 5 Jac
Nathaniel 86 Dav
Washington 65 Dav
Curtiss, John 320 War
John 10 Way
John, Jr. 8 Way
John, Jur. 320 War
Curtner, John 6 Way
Curtus, Thomas 13 Hum
Curwell, John 96 Dav
Cusenbery, Moses 22 Wll
Custer, Adam 309 War
Michael 36 Fra
Custus, John 343 Whi
Thomas 369 Whi
Cutberson, Lawrance 13 Bed
Cutbirth, Daniel 17 Gil
Daniel 4 Way
Cutchen, Joshua 23 Wll
Cutcheons, Samuel 66 Dav
Thomas 67 Dav
Cutchtons, Henry 65 Dav
Cutler, James 382 Wil
Cutral, Melney 409 Wil
Cypert, Baker 6 Way
Jesse 4 Way
John 6 Way
Lawrence 389 Wil
Sally 12 Way
Thomas 389 Wil
see Ceypert, Sypert
Cyrus, Peggy 17 Gil

--- D ---

Dabbs, Jane 7 Way
Nathaniel 15 Way
Robert 6 Fra
Dabney, Charles A. 8 Wll
John, Sr. 33 Wll
Samuel 19 Mon
William 34 Wll
Dabs, Joel 6 Per
Dacres, Alexander 25 Lin
William 25 Lin
Dacus, Ozd 14 Way
see Dicus
Daff, John 8 Hic
Dagley, John 31 Mau
Dail, Joshuay 65 Mau

Dailey, Benja.	1	Bed
William	3	Ove
Dainwood, Jacob	61	Mau
Dake, John	370	Whi
Dale, Adam	15	Smi
Alexander	13	Smi
Daniel	349	Whi
Edward W.	57	Mau
John	349	Whi
William	3	Ove
William	15	Smi
Dales, Absalom	318	War
Daley, Hezekiah	4	Hum
James	9	Gil
John	8	Gil
Josiah	22	Gil
William	8	Gil
Dallas, Joshua	21	Lin
Dalton, Carter	1	Ove
James	152	Sum
John	12	Law
John	150	Sum
John, Sr.	152	Sum
Robert	150	Sum
Shelton	152	Sum
Tarance	11	Ove
William	151	Sum
William S.	14	Law
Daly, Isaac	43	Bed
Damcol, William	152	Sum
Damewood, George	7	Hum
Damode, Henry	5	Rob
Damrel, Elizabeth	41	Lin
John	41	Lin
Damron, George	121	Ste
John	121	Ste
Rachel	121	Ste
Danaway, Enoch	90	Rut
Danby, Andrew	50	Wll
Nancy	14	Rob
Dance, Mary	419	Wil
Francis	9	Hum
William E.	14	Mon
Dandrdge, Henry	2	Mon
Dandridge see Dandrdge		
Danell, James	103	Rut
Dangle, Joseph	80	Dav
Daniel, Benjamin	122	Ste
Benjn.	124	Ste
David	131	Ste
Delila	15	Mon
Edward	80	Dav
H.	130	Ste
Isaac	6	Fra
James	9	Dic
Jesse	151	Sum
John	13	Dic
John	313	War
John M.	28	Mau
Pompy	316	War
Robert	85	Dav
Robert	115	Ste
Signer	34	Bed
Daniel (cont.)		
Tho.	150	Sum
Throuston	103	Rut
Tilmon R.	14	Gil
Weat	13	Ove
William	3	Hum
William	41	Mau
William	66	Mau
William	20	Mon
William	10	Ove
Wootson	124	Ste
see Dariel		
Dankin, Jonathan	306	War
Dann, Micheal C.	85	Dav
Danna, Isaac	7	Fra
Dannagin, William	15	Dic
Dannell, Edny	399	Wil
Dannely, Wm.	22	Hic
Danner, Joseph	298	War
London C.	302	War
Dansby, Daniel	60	Dav
Dapree, Henry	21	Mon
Darachson, Hessey	15	Smi
William	15	Smi
Daran, William	77	Rut
Darby, William	7	Fra
Darden, Case	28	Rob
Easter	31	Rob
Holland	31	Rob
Joshua, overseer	48	Wll
Dariel, Stephen	88	Rut
Dark, James	413	Wil
Josiah	35	Lin
Rebeckey	60	Mau
Samuel	413	Wil
Sarah	151	Sum
Darke, Joseph	45	Wll
Darkford, John	404	Wil
Darnal, Cornelious	21	Lin
Henry	26	Mon
John	55	Mau
John	23	Mon
Darnall, Nicholas	15	Mon
Nicholas	15	Mon
Samuel	20	Mon
Thos.	15	Mon
Darnel, John	150	Sum
William	6	Jac
Darnell, Littleton	7	Jac
William	86	Rut
Darnol, Jarrett	149	Sum
Darnold, James	6	Fra
Darr, Daniel	87	Dav
Elizabeth	16	Dic
Eve	24	Rob
John	9	Mon
Darrah, William	291	War
Darral, Augustus	7	Fra
John	7	Fra
Philip	7	Fra
Darris, Benjmin	28	Mau
Darton, James	46	Mau
John	47	Mau

Darwin, G. C.	7	Jac
Richman	7	Jac
William	6	Fra
William	7	Jac
Dashazo, Edmund	151	Sum
Datson, Hightour	4	Wil
see Dotson		
Dauby, William	79	Dav
see Danby		
Daugherty, Alexander	4	Ove
John	18	Ove
Robert	17	Bed
Daughtrey, Mary	151	Sum
Tyler	31	Bed
Dauson, Jonathan	37	Mau
Dautry, Thomas	58	Wil
Davadser, William	18	Gil
Davenport, Abraham	13	Gil
George	12	Gil
James	12	Lin
Matthew	9	Gil
Robert	14	Gil
William C.	11	Gil
Davenporte, Abner	6	Gil
Daves, Alexander	24	Lin
Davice, Merredith	400	Wil
Wm. A.	106	She
David, Amos	17	Gil
Daniel	4	Hum
Edward	4	Hum
Isaac	96	Dav
James	63	Dav
John	4	Hum
Susannah	413	Wil
Davidson, Abner	11	Ove
Abraham	8	Dic
Abraham	3	Hum
Alexander	5	Ove
Alexr.	10	Hic
Alliday	300	War
Amy	112	Ste
Andrew	26	Bed
Asa	15	Ove
Benjamin	25	Mon
Blain	288	War
Bracket	42	Mau
Briant	17	Lin
Daniel	8	Bed
Daniel	16	Gil
E. B.	118	Ste
Elizabeth	14	Ove
Ephraim E.	38	Mau
Francis	11	Ove
George	3	Dic
George	6	Fra
George	11	Rob
George	131	Ste
Gilberth F.	42	Mau
Hudson	12	Hum
James	8	Bed
James	131	Ste
Jesse	12	Mon
Jesse	74	Rut
Davidson (cont.)		
Jno.	8	Hic
John	30	Bed
John	17	Lin
John	12	Mon
John	7	Per
John	7	Rob
John	75	Rut
John	112	Ste
John	398	Wil
John	406	Wil
John, Esqr.	114	Ste
John E.	27	Mau
John O.	39	Mau
Joseph	8	Dic
Joseph	17	Hic
Josiah	10	Dic
Mary	12	Hum
Mary	24	Lin
Mary	83	Rut
Reese	30	Bed
Richard	6	Jac
Robert	12	Gil
Rosanna	42	Mau
Sally	115	Ste
Samuel H.	14	Hum
Thomas	7	Bed
Thomas	7	Jac
Thos.	115	Ste
W. H.	7	Jac
William	60	Dav
William	14	Gil
William	308	War
see Davadser		
Davie, Ambrose	21	Mon
John	14	Dic
Davis, Absolom	9	Lin
Alexander	1	Way
Alfred	14	Smi
Allen	15	Lin
Amos	5	Lin
Amos	14	Ove
Anderson	21	Way
Andrew	28	Mon
Andrew	286	War
Andrew P.	286	War
Archd.	149	Sum
Archibald	2	Har
Archibald	31	Lin
Archibald	399	Wil
Arthur	359	Whi
Arthur N.	20	Lin
Augustus	352	Whi
Baba	99	Rut
Barnett	22	Gil
Bartley	87	Rut
Basdell	409	Wil
Benja.	149	Sum
Benja.	152	Sum
Benjamin	13	Gil
Benjamin	74	Rut
Benjamin	102	Rut
Benjamin M.	16	Smi

Davis (cont.)
Benjamine 360 Whi
Benjmin 62 Mau
Benjn. 117 Ste
Charles 103 Rut
Chisholm 150 Sum
Christopher 2 Per
Cloyd 12 Gil
D. W. 79 Dav
Daniel 7 Bed
Daniel 43 Mau
Daniel 8 Ove
Daniel N. 89 Dav
David 28 Mon
David 360 Whi
David S. L. 9 Wll
Edman 42 Mau
Edmond 15 Way
Edward 5 Gil
Eli 6 Fra
Elijah 28 Lin
Elijah 13 Ove
Elijah 11 Ove
Elijah 403 Wil
Elizabeth 15 Smi
Elizabeth 16 Smi
Elizebeth 48 Mau
Enoch 409 Wil
Fielding 387 Wil
Gabriel 26 Mon
Gabril 53 Bed
George 11 Bed
George 299 War
George 20 Wll
Henry 26 Bed
Henry 8 Lin
Henry 89 Rut
Henry 16 Smi
Henry 376 Wil
Henry W. 50 Wll
Hezekiah 15 Smi
Holland 28 Wll
Hugh 53 Bed
Isaac 53 Mau
Isaiah 20 Bed
Israel 103 Rut
James 20 Gil
James 3 Hic
James 7 Jac
James 45 Mau
James 26 Mon
James 22 Way
James 354 Whi
James 362 Whi
James 370 Whi
James 379 Wil
James 50 Wll
James P. 357 Whi
Jane 65 Dav
Jane 10 Hum
Jesse 49 Bed
Jesse 5 Lin
Jesse 6 Rob

Davis (cont.)
Jessee 367 Whi
Jessee 371 Whi
Joab 48 Mau
Joel 92 Rut
John 11 Bed
John 49 Bed
John 76 Dav
John 86 Dav
John 98 Dav
John 6 Fra
John 7 Fra
John 13 Gil
John 21 Gil
John 1 Har
John 20 Hic
John 7 Jac
John 8 Lin
John 14 Lin
John 37 Lin
John 43 Lin
John 44 Lin
John 43 Mau
John [?] 62 Mau
John 18 Ove
John 8 Rob
John 96 Rut
John 15 Smi
John 149 Sum
John 151 Sum
John 284 War
John 360 Whi
John 388 Wil
John 400 Wil
John 43 Wll
John B. 114 Wil
John H. 93 Dav
John L. 114 Wil
John L. 402 Wil
John M. 99 Rut
John P. 103 Rut
Jonathan 6 Fra
Jonathan 2 Ove
Jonathan 150 Sum
Jonathan C. 348 Whi
Joseph 1 Hic
Joseph 5 Hum
Joshua 7 Jac
Joshua 9 Lin
Joshua 24 Rob
Joshua 17 Wll
Josiah 20 Bed
Larkin 15 Gil
Lawson L. 97 Rut
Lemuel 2 Ove
Leonard 3 Ove
Lewis 48 Mau
Lewis 92 Rut
Lewis 111 Ste
Liddy 40 Mau
Lucinda 312 War
Lucket 82 Rut
Margreet 45 Mau

Davis (cont.)
Martin 12 Wll
Martin 31 Wll
Mathew 359 Whi
Matthew 16 Smi
Micajah 5 Gil
Moses 67 Dav
Moses 22 Way
Moses 371 Whi
Moses 21 Wll
Nancy 18 Mon
Nancy 152 Sum
Nathan 9 Gil
Nathaniel 6 Fra
Nathaniel 382 Wil
Nathaniel 393 Wil
Nathaniel 418 Wil
Nathaniel C. 341 Whi
Philip 43 Mau
Porter 29 Mau
Prior 11 Lin
Richard 118 Ste
Richard 121 Ste
Robert 12 Hum
Robert 151 Sum
Robert 2 Wll
Robt. 151 Sum
Ross 15 Smi
Rubin 25 Mau
Saml. 150 Sum
Saml. 151 Sum
Saml. 112 Wil
Samuel 6 Fra
Samuel 12 Gil
Samuel 10 Lin
Samuel 37 Mau
Samuel 20 Mon
Samuel 304 War
Samuel 379 Wil
Sarah 61 Dav
Seth 63 Dav
Shadrach 85 Rut
Solomon 27 Rob
Solomon 152 Sum
Solomon 283 War
Sterlen 35 Wll
Thomas 53 Bed
Thomas 22 Gil
Thomas 3 Ove
Thomas 297 War
Thomas 320 War
Thomas 15 Way
Thomas 113 Wil
Thomas 379 Wil
Thompson 50 Wll
Trudence [?] 27 Wll
Turner 54 Wll
Upsher 21 Rob
Uriah 16 Smi
Wiley J. 15 Wll
William 33 Bed
William 10 Lin
William 25 Mau

Davis (cont.)
William 42 Mau
William 2 Ove
William 295 War
William 1 Way
William 359 Whi
William 400 Wil
William, Jur. 6 Lin
William C. 92 Rut
William E. 60 Mau
William H. 92 Rut
William R. 17 Gil
Willie 9 Dic
Willie O. 6 Fra
Willis 65 Dav
Willis 16 Hic
Wilson 6 Lin
Zachariah 400 Wil
Zacheriah 12 Bed
see Dorris
Davison, George 52 Mau
John 37 Mau
Johnson 2 Lin
Joshua 52 Mau
Davy, John 19 Hic
Joseph 19 Hic
Richd. 19 Hic
Dawden, Rhoda 24 Bed
Dawdy, George 2 Bed
Hawel 52 Bed
John 11 Bed
Rebecca 2 Bed
Daws, Joel 112 Ste
Dawson, Abner 6 Fra
Bradley 25 Lin
David 398 Wil
George 341 Whi
John 60 Dav
John 6 Fra
John 14 Smi
Larkin 12 Dic
Saml. 122 Ste
Willis 31 Mon
Day, Aaron 81 Dav
Elijah 150 Sum
Francis 152 Sum
Henry 151 Sum
Henson 4 Rob
Henson, Mr. 9 Law
Jesse 17 Gil
Jesse 86 Rut
Jesse 100 Rut
Margaret 6 Fra
Martha 152 Sum
Philip 32 Lin
Philip 13 Smi
Samuel 17 Gil
Deacus, Henry 17 Wll
Deadrick, Thomas 76 Dav
Deal, Absalom 304 War
Henry 151 Sum
John 3 Ove
John 15 Smi

Deal (cont.)		
see Dial		
Dean, Abel	24	Hic
Abraham	18	Rob
Aron	93	Dav
Charles	45	Bed
Elizabeth	25	Hic
Francis	282	War
Francis M.	2	Wll
Greenbery	43	Wll
James	94	Dav
James	343	Whi
Jessefy	351	Whi
Job	89	Rut
John	6	Fra
John	44	Lin
Joseph	44	Lin
Joseph	13	Wll
Mary	7	Fra
Michael	296	War
Richard	370	Whi
Thomas	30	Bed
William	28	Mon
William	3	Per
Willis	16	Smi
Dearen, John	43	Mau
John	45	Mau
Dearin, Sims	362	Whi
Dearing, John W.	351	Whi
Dearly, Wm.	149	Sum
Deason, Abraham	23	Bed
Enoch	42	Bed
John	42	Bed
William	15	Bed
William	42	Bed
Deatherage, James	2	Rob
Deaton, Elias	5	Hic
Debow, John A.	14	Smi
Rachel	14	Smi
Solomon	14	Smi
Deckard, Benjamin	6	Fra
Michael	7	Fra
Decker, Frederick	15	Smi
George	16	Ove
Sarah	8	Ove
Deckers, William	282	War
Dedmond, John	15	Smi
Deen, Ellis	57	Mau
Deering, Berry	19	Gil
Laban	8	Gil
William	19	Gil
William	391	Wil
Deery, James	53	Bed
Dees, Jese P.	25	Hic
Jesse	7	Dic
Deeson, William [deleted]	56	Mau
Deets, Frederick W.	1	Hum
Defo, John	15	Gil
Micah [2]	13	Gil
Defrees, James	151	Sum
Degrafenreed, John	61	Wll
William	57	Wll
Degranfenreed, Vincent	61	Wll
Deitz, Fredk.	282	War
Dejarnatt, James	81	Rut
Dejarnett, Bird N.	383	Wil
Delany, Anthony	17	Lin
Jacob	2	Har
Delap, Wm.	150	Sum
Deldine, James	343	Whi
Delhatch, Josiah	7	Fra
Dell, John	413	Wil
Dellis, Dennis	6	Fra
John	6	Fra
Robert	402	Wil
Deloach, Thos.	121	Ste
William	31	Rob
Delock, Jerusha	381	Wil
William	102	Rut
Delong, James	310	War
Delop, Thomas	398	Wil
Delph, Philip	13	Mon
Demambreon, Felix	92	Dav
see Denbreon		
Demanay, Saml.	12	Hic
Demasters, James	98	Rut
Demcut see Denscut		
Dement, Cader	79	Rut
Demery, Allen	98	Rut
Demombrow, Timothy	88	Dav
Demos, Thomas	66	Mau
Thos.	120	Ste
Demoss, Abraham	86	Dav
Henry	60	Dav
James	60	Dav
Lewis	60	Dav
Thomas	63	Dav
Demott, John	74	Dav
Dempsey, George	149	Sum
James	21	Gil
John B.	52	Bed
Dempsy, Lawrence	22	Lin
Demry, David	419	Wil
Demumber, William, overseer	63	Wll
Demumbroe, Timothy	75	Dav
Denbreon, Jno. B.	91	Dav
see Demambreon, Demumbroe		
Denby, Samuel	279	War
Dendly, Peter	101	Rut
Denham, Henry	151	Sum
James	150	Sum
John	150	Sum
Samuel	151	Sum
Tho. [2]	151	Sum
William, Sr.	151	Sum
Wm.	150	Sum
see Durham		
Dening, William	150	Sum
Denis, Andrew	15	Ove
Ezeriah	7	Ove
Isham	18	Ove
James	9	Ove
Levi	9	Ove
William	6	Jac
William	14	Ove
Denison, George	40	Bed

Name	Page	County
Denison (cont.)		
Robert	52	Bed
Dennay, Robert	84	Rut
Dennell, Thomas	93	Rut
Denney, William	94	Dav
Denning, Jno.	151	Sum
see Dinning		
Dennis, Danl.	81	Dav
George W.	39	Lin
James	26	Lin
Jeremiah	26	Lin
Jeremiah	15	Smi
John	1	Ove
Joseph	15	Smi
Samuel	95	Dav
Zebidee	20	Mon
Denny, Benjamin	14	Smi
Claiborne	14	Smi
James	45	Mau
John	14	Smi
William	13	Smi
William	349	Whi
William	403	Wil
Willie	14	Smi
Zachariah	14	Smi
Denscut, Abner	87	Rut
Denson, Asa	344	Whi
George	13	Hic
John, Jun.	6	Fra
John, Sen.	6	Fra
Joseph	6	Fra
William	6	Wll
Denton, Abraham	7	Jac
Abraham	102	Rut
Abram	6	Per
Abroham	6	Per
Absolem	6	Per
Augustine	28	Wll
Benj.	6	Per
Cornelieus	7	Jac
Drewry	14	Smi
Edmund	5	Law
Edward	389	Wil
Elijah	345	Whi
Isaac	12	Ove
Jacob	12	Wll
James	14	Smi
Jeremiah [2]	357	Whi
Jesse	34	Rob
John	7	Ove
Joshua	7	Jac
Samuel [2]	6	Per
Thos.	3	Mon
Depeese, George	366	Whi
Depriest, Green, Mr.	9	Law
Jesse	23	Hic
John	10	Bed
Randolph, Sr. [?]	24	Hic
Samuel	7	Fra
Deprist, Randolph	22	Hic
Derby, Charles	149	Sum
Dereberry, Jacob	51	Mau
John	51	Mau
Derebury, Addam	50	Mau
Derett, Richd.	7	Mon
Derham, Joseph	2	Per
Samuel	12	Rob
Deriberey, Daniel	52	Mau
Derickson, Joseph	81	Rut
Deriney, Mary	8	Hic
Derreberry, Adrew	58	Mau
Derrington, Samuel	20	Rob
Derrit, Francis	18	Rob
Derryberry, Andrew	311	War
Andrew	319	War
Christena	319	War
Daniel	311	War
Daniel	317	War
John	282	War
Michael	299	War
Michael	300	War
Desha, Benja.	152	Sum
Robert	152	Sum
Deshane, Clarisa	1	Wll
Deshazer, Hardy	15	Lin
Deshazo, Clemm B.	32	Wll
Desmakes, Saul	70	Dav
Desmukes, Elisha	420	Wil
Devan, John	14	Lin
William	9	Lin
Devazer see Deshazer		
Devenport, Absolum	414	Wil
Edmond	414	Wil
Hardy	414	Wil
Henry	7	Jac
James	7	Jac
Joseph	7	Jac
Samuel	7	Law
Wm.	150	Sum
Dever, Charles	8	Gil
Devers, Amos	20	Lin
William	36	Mau
Devert, John	15	Smi
Deviney, Jas.	8	Hic
Wm.	9	Hic
Devoir, James	97	Rut
Dew, Arthur	406	Wil
John	377	Wil
Jose. C.	371	Whi
Deweese, Henry	350	Whi
Mogan	361	Whi
William	348	Whi
Dewhitt, Samuel	14	Smi
Dews, Arthur W.	111	Wil
Solomon	52	Bed
Deye, Abraham	3	Hum
Dial, Elizebeth	42	Mau
James	6	Fra
James	6	Wll
Jeremiah	50	Bed
John	51	Bed
John	287	War
Josep	308	War
Joshua	309	War
Samuel	309	War
Shadrack	304	War

Dial (cont.)		
see Deal, Simms		
Dian, Mark	'13	Smi
Dias, Thomas	14	Smi
Dibbrell, Edwin	75	Dav
Dibnan, Thomas R.	66	Dav
Dibrell, Anthony	350	Whi
Charles L.	361	Whi
Dice, Jacob	13	Smi
Dick, ...h	1	Ove
Josiah	11	Bed
Dickason, Benja.	149	Sum
James	150	Sum
James J.	150	Sum
John	149	Sum
John, Jr.	152	Sum
John, Sr.	149	Sum
Robert	7	Hum
Robert	150	Sum
Tho.	152	Sum
Willie	150	Sum
Wm.	149	Sum
Dickens, Jesse	14	Smi
John	15	Smi
Dickerson, Eli	7	Per
John	5	Per
Nathaniel	7	Per
Samuel	102	Rut
Sarah	94	Rut
William	77	Rut
Dickeson	90	Dav
Dickey, Andrew S.	150	Sum
Benoni	32	Mau
David	83	Rut
Ephriam	6	Fra
George	32	Mau
J.	24	Mau
James	15	Gil
James	136	Sum
John	11	Gil
Johnson	8	Bed
William R.	70	Mau
see Dicksy		
Dickie, John	27	Mau
Dickings, James	381	Wil
Lewis D.	413	Wil
Samuel	379	Wil
Dickins, Baxter B.	101	Rut
Henry	7	Jac
Jeremiah	7	Jac
Dickinson, Alben J.	411	Wil
David	84	Rut
Dickison	9	Rob
William G.	57	Mau
Wire	23	Rob
Dicks, William	3	Mon
Dickson, Alexander	5	Dic
Alexr.	121	Ste
Elizabeth	14	Gil
Elizibeth	31	Mau
Enoch	85	Rut
Ephram D.	13	Bed
Esther	4	Hic

Dickson (cont.)		
Hanah	37	Mau
Hugh	4	Dic
Hugh, Jr.	13	Dic
Israel	92	Rut
James	5	Bed
James	44	Bed
James	37	Mau
James	1	Per
John	4	Dic
John	85	Rut
John B.	53	Bed
John M.	60	Dav
Joseph	13	Law
Joseph	1	Per
Joseph	82	Rut
Joseph	93	Rut
Joshep	4	Mon
Margaret	1	Bed
Molton	7	Dic
Robert	4	Dic
Robert	1	Lin
Robert	13	Lin
Robertson	3	Dic
Samuel	11	Mon
Thomas	30	Mau
William	10	Bed
William	33	Bed
William	32	Mau
William	25	Wll
Wm.	1	Lin
see Dickason, Dicke(r)son, Dick-i(n)son, Divichson, Dixon		
Dicksy, George M.	35	Mau
Dicky, James	83	Rut
John	19	Lin
Zacherah	27	Mau
Dicus, Edward	31	Mau
Elijah	14	Way
Joshua	14	Way
Ned	24	Mau
Sally	24	Hic
William	367	Whi
see Dacus		
Dier, George	41	Mau
Dietz, Thomas	4	Gil
Dildine, Keah	347	Whi
Dilehunt, Silas	60	Dav
Dill, Arther [2]	7	Jac
Elijah	7	Jac
Isaac	85	Rut
Isaac, Jur.	77	Rut
Joel	380	Wil
John	15	Smi
John	15	Smi
Joseph	92	Rut
Joseph	15	Smi
Nimrod	15	Smi
Patsy	8	Hic
Philemon C.	15	Smi
Stephen	7	Jac
Thomas	85	Dav
Thomas	28	Rob

Dill (cont.)
William 399 Wil
Dilland, James P. 65 Dav
Dillard, Joel 95 Rut
John 7 Jac
John S. 68 Mau
Josiah 79 Rut
William 403 Wil
Dillehay, Nathan 4 Dic
Dillehay, Sterling 9 Hum
Dillehunty, Will. 74 Dav
Dillen, Hannah 344 Whi
Henry 5 Ove
Henry 6 Ove
Dillenham, William 308 War
Dillian, Isaac 16 Smi
Isaac, Sen. 16 Smi
Jesse 16 Smi
Nathan 14 Smi
William 16 Smi
see Dilliard
Dilliard, Daniel 14 Smi
Elisha 14 Smi
Elly 15 Mon
Jane 26 Mon
Joel 14 Smi
John L. 13 Smi
William 14 Smi
William 16 Smi
Willis 398 Wil
see Dillian
Dillin, Beven 2 Per
John 43 Lin
John 17 Wil
Joshua 7 Jac
Dillinder, Elijah 20 Lin
Dillingham, John 39 Bed
Peter 45 Bed
Dillon, Danl. 149 Sum
James 152 Sum
John 416 Wil
Samuel 19 Ove
Dimerey, John 361 Whi
Dimery, Allen 102 Rut
Stephen 102 Rut
Dimham, Alexander P. 68 Mau
see Durham
Dimond, John 96 Dav
Samuel T. 53 Bed
Dinking, Joshua 110 Ste
John J. 149 Sum
Robert 111 Ste
Dinning, Andrew [2] 151 Sum
William [2] 151 Sum
see Denning
Dinwiddie, James 6 Fra
Dire, Robert H. 8 Per
Dishon, Luke 372 Whi
Dismakes, George 69 Dav
Dismukes, Danl. 151 Sum
John 150 Sum
see Desmukes
Dittle, Elizabeth 381 Wil
Ditto see Gollerthan
Ditty, Abraham 369 Whi
John 367 Whi
Divichson, Joseph 102 Rut
Diving, Robt. 7 Hic
Diviny, Charles 23 Lin
Dix see Dire
Dixon, Addam 38 Mau
Americus 15 Smi
David 7 Jac
Don O. [C. ?] 16 Smi
G. W. 7 Jac
Henry 19 Gil
Jackson 7 Jac
James 20 Ove
Jeremiah 14 Smi
John 10 Bed
John 7 Jac
John 90 Rut
Joseph 14 Gil
Matthew 9 Bed
Matthew L. 6 Fra
Reubin 7 Law
Robert 92 Rut
Samuel 7 Jac
Samuel 5 Ove
William 14 Smi
Dnlap, Samuel 52 Mau
Doak, John 85 Rut
Jonathan 407 Wil
Mary 399 Wil
Robert 38 Mau
Robert 390 Wil
Sarah 6 Lin
Thomas 22 Lin
William 22 Lin
Doatty, James 64 Mau
Dobbin, Alexander 32 Mau
David 31 Mau
David 69 Mau
David [deleted] 25 Mau
James 32 Mau
James 40 Mau
John 54 Mau
Dobbins, Alexr., Sr. 151 Sum
Carson 149 Sum
Hugh 8 Wil
James 7 Fra
James 16 Smi
Jno. 149 Sum
John 10 Har
John 5 Lin
Robt. 151 Sum
Samuel 5 Lin
Dobbs, Ishmail 7 Fra
James 15 Smi
Jeremiah 17 Bed
John 17 Bed
John 31 Rob
Mazy 18 Bed
Polley 18 Gil
Robert 7 Fra
William 17 Bed

Dobbs (cont.)		
William	15	Smi
Dobkins, Reuben	9	Ove
Dobson, Benjamin	393	Wil
Francis	36	Mau
Henry	38	Wll
Hugh	34	Wll
James	393	Wil
John	93	Rut
Robert	19	Way
Thomas	65	Dav
Docking, William	408	Wil
Dockings, Obey	408	Wil
Dockry, Elizabeth	27	Lin
John	10	Lin
Dodd, Allen	61	Mau
Daniel	27	Mon
David	18	Lin
David	22	Lin
Griffin	89	Rut
James	21	Hic
Jesse, Jur.	46	Lin
Jesse, Ser.	46	Lin
Joel	46	Lin
John	34	Wll
Josiah	99	Rut
Mark	2	Bed
Samuel	38	Wll
Thos.	6	Mon
William	152	Sum
Wm.	110	Ste
Dodds, James	411	Wil
Richard	417	Wil
Robert	2	Hum
Saml.	420	Wil
Thomas	17	Lin
Dodson, Abner	60	Mau
Allen	59	Dav
Asa	62	Mau
Beverly	30	Mau
Daniel	358	Whi
David	60	Mau
David	62	Mau
David	65	Mau
Elijah	59	Dav
Elijah	287	War
Elisha	21	Gil
Elisha	283	War
Elizebeth	60	Mau
Fortunate	62	Mau
Greenham	21	Gil
Harvy	59	Dav
Hightower	65	Mau
Jehu	286	War
Jesse	292	War
Jesse	315	War
Jessee	359	Whi
Jessee	372	Whi
Joel	38	Lin
John	18	Mon
John	346	Whi
John	363	Whi
John, Ser.	363	Whi
Dodson (cont.)		
Jordan	19	Gil
Joshua	38	Lin
Martin	279	War
Nimrod	283	War
Sally	342	Whi
Solomon	359	Whi
Timothy	74	Dav
William	6	Jac
William	358	Whi
William, Sr.	358	Whi
William B.	5	Dic
Dodsons, —	24	Mau
Doggatt, Miller	21	Gil
Doggid, Chatin	13	Way
Dogwood, Thomas	18	Way
Doherty, Dennis	18	Mon
James	84	Rut
Mary	47	Wll
Matthew	1	Mon
Susannah	3	Mon
Doleson, Thomas	93	Rut
William	62	Mau
Dollar, William	59	Wll
Dollason, Barnet	2	Hic
Thos.	13	Hic
Dollehite, Cornelius	14	Hum
Willie	14	Hum
Dollence, Tyree	27	Mau
Dollenson, Jacob	121	Ste
Dollins, Joel	27	Lin
Presly	27	Lin
Tolifer	27	Lin
Dolten, Henry	6	Ove
Dolton, John	56	Wll
Timothy	121	Ste
Tolbert	342	Whi
Wm.	121	Ste
Donald, Archibald	40	Bed
Samuel	67	Mau
Donaldson, Andrew	6	Fra
Andrew	4	Mon
Buchness	18	Way
Charaty	71	Dav
Eliza.	74	Dav
James	6	Fra
John	74	Dav
Levin	74	Dav
William	6	Fra
William	3	Ove
Donally, Benjamin	13	Mon
James	73	Dav
James	13	Mon
Donalson, James	18	Mon
Moses	149	Sum
Robert	382	Wil
Umphrey	382	Wil
Donathan, Daniel	6	Fra
James	6	Fra
John	6	Fra
Stephen	6	Fra
Donaway, Drury	104	Rut
Donelson, Lemuel	35	Wll

Donelson (cont.)		
Robert	42	Wll
Robert	50	Wll
Thomas	94	Rut
William	357	Whi
Donley, John	90	Dav
Donnell, Adlia	136	Sum
Eli	376	Wil
George	399	Wil
James	390	Wil
Jesse	409	Wil
John	399	Wil
Joseph	186	Sum
Levi	149	Sum
Martha	407	Wil
Robert	114	Wil
Robert	397	Wil
Samuel	392	Wil
Tho.	149	Sum
Thomas	392	Wil
William	112	Wil
William	399	Wil
William	407	Wil
William, Ser.	399	Wil
Donnelson, Alexander	69	Dav
Mary	6	Gil
Donoho, Anthony	150	Sum
Archd.	151	Sum
Chs.	152	Sum
Edward	78	Rut
Elizabeth	151	Sum
Goldman	152	Sum
Isaac	150	Sum
James	150	Sum
John	150	Sum
John, Jr.	150	Sum
Patrick	14	Smi
Walter	150	Sum
William	15	Smi
Wm.	150	Sum
Donolson, John	16	Lin
Donovan, Thomas	102	Rut
Doogin, Robert	6	Fra
Robert, Sen.	6	Fra
Sharp	6	Fra
Thomas	6	Fra
Dooley, Esum B. [?]	38	Mau
James	38	Mau
James	43	Mau
William	38	Mau
William	355	Whi
Doolin, Nathaniel [& Glasscock]	8	Wll
Rice	7	Way
Dooly, Michael	47	Wll
Doran, James G.	89	Rut
Dore, Richard	7	Fra
Dorherty, James	7	Hum
Robert	120	Ste
Dorhorty, Cornelieus	7	Jac
Dorin, Edward	22	Lin
Doris see Davis		
Dorman, Jesse	22	Bed
William M.	23	Bed
Dorrel, John	150	Sum
Dorris, Elijah	151	Sum
Isaac [2]	12	Rob
Isaac H.	24	Rob
James	5	Rob
John	25	Rob
John	151	Sum
John J.	25	Rob
Joseph	70	Dav
Joseph	26	Rob
Josiah	151	Sum
Nathaniel	12	Rob
Robert	150	Sum
Robert	151	Sum
Saml.	151	Sum
Samuel	6	Rob
Thomas	69	Dav
William	69	Dav
William	24	Rob
William [3]	151	Sum
William B.	5	Rob
Dorriss, John	149	Sum
Wm.	149	Sum
Dorrow, Christopher	87	Dav
Dorset, Ili	13	Lin
Dorsey, Benjamin	23	Lin
John	29	Mau
Dorson, Hutson	45	Wll
John	43	Wll
Dortch, Abel	400	Wil
Isaac	15	Rob
Norfleet	8	Rob
Dorten, Andrew	81	Dav
Dorton, Benjamine	354	Whi
Dosemby, William	83	Dav
Doshier, Enoch	91	Dav
Doss, Azeriah	26	Rob
James	26	Rob
Matthew	26	Rob
Noah	15	Smi
Stewart	15	Smi
Wm.	150	Sum
Dosset, Elizabeth	151	Sum
Nancy	151	Sum
Dossey, Catherine	303	War
Dotson, Alexander	7	Fra
Bird	39	Wll
Caty	151	Sum
Chs.	151	Sum
Elias	93	Dav
Elisha	11	Gil
George	18	Gil
John	16	Smi
Lazrus	9	Wll
Reuben	15	Wll
Reuben	66	Wll
Rolley	10	Wll
Rolly	46	Wll
Samuel	31	Mau
Samuel H.	11	Gil
Thomas	16	Smi
Thomas	48	Wll
William	48	Wll

Dotson (cont.)		
Willis	4	Hic
see Datson		
Doud, Jane	52	Mau
Dougherty, George	14	Smi
John	6	Fra
John	15	Smi
Samuel	30	Wll
William	76	Dav
Doughlas, Berryman	88	Rut
Jonathan	13	Ove
Doughton, Charles	32	Mon
Douglas, Benjamin	6	Jac
Henry	85	Dav
Hugh	33	Mau
John	6	Jac
Thomas	88	Dav
Thomas L.	33	Wll
William M.	298	War
Douglass, A. H.	149	Sum
Alfred M.	149	Sum
Anderson	14	Smi
David	15	Smi
Edward	13	Smi
Edward	149	Sum
Elizabeth	13	Smi
Elizath	385	Wil
Elmore	136	Sum
F. H. W. O.	10	Har
George	14	Smi
Hannah	14	Smi
Harry L.	391	Wil
James	6	Dic
James	20	Gil
James	15	Smi
James	150	Sum
James, Jr.	150	Sum
Jesse	152	Sum
John	7	Wll
Larkin	14	Smi
Mathew	303	War
Nathaniel	19	Gil
Rewben	151	Sum
Richard	402	Wil
Sally	300	War
Susannah	14	Smi
William	95	Dav
William	288	War
Wm. H.	149	Sum
Dougle, John	16	Bed
Dove, Dennis	88	Dav
Dowdy, Allen	52	Wll
Howel	34	Lin
John	45	Wll
Joseph	52	Wll
Micagah	45	Wll
William	122	Ste
William	52	Wll
Dowel, Benjmin F.	63	Mau
John	6	Jac
Ruben	63	Mau
Dower, Amasa	21	Rob
Dowlin, Harris	23	Rob
Downen, James	23	Gil
Josiah	23	Gil
Downey, Jonathan	380	Wil
William	91	Dav
Downing, James	6	Lin
Robert G.	350	Whi
William	6	Lin
William	55	Wll
William	56	Wll
Downs, Blanchy	126	Ste
Patty	128	Ste
Thos. G.	126	Ste
William	131	Ste
Wm.	113	Ste
Wm., Jr.	149	Sum
Wm., Sr.	150	Sum
Dowthart, Evan	6	Fra
Dowthett, Enoch	31	Lin
James	31	Lin
John	31	Lin
John	34	Lin
Doxey, Thomas	151	Sum
Doxy, Jeremiah	150	Sum
Doyel, Joshua [& Hanks]	16	Wll
Doyle, Edward	20	Lin
John L.	3	Rob
Rhodom	349	Whi
Simon	355	Whi
Zachiriah	6	Rob
Dozier, Daniel	316	War
Richard P.	314	War
Timothy	88	Rut
Drake, Ann	6	Fra
Benjamin	92	Dav
Britton	381	Wil
Catherine	49	Bed
Edward	25	Mau
Elijah	304	War
Ely	44	Mau
Isaac	69	Dav
Isaac	302	War
Jacob	288	War
James	6	Fra
Jesse	65	Dav
John, Jr.	92	Dav
Johnathan	63	Dav
Joshua	69	Dav
Mary	10	Dic
Richard	388	Wil
Sally	80	Dav
William J.	92	Dav
Zachariah	5	Wll
Draper, John	7	Jac
Joshua	150	Sum
Matthew	16	Smi
Philip	16	Smi
Saml.	149	Sum
Silas	40	Bed
Thomas	6	Jac
Travis	7	Jac
William [3]	7	Jac
William	151	Sum
William	398	Wil

Draughan, John 30 Rob
Miles 24 Rob
Drefax, John 402 Wil
Drennen, Deffy 393 Wil
James 393 Wil
John 113 Wil
Thomas 393 Wil
see Drinnen
Drennon, Margaret 95 Rut
Margaret 100 Rut
Drenon, David 342 Whi
Drew, Andrew 419 Wil
Benjamin 419 Wil
John 42 Lin
Moses 96 Dav
Drewey, Richard C. 87 Dav
Drewry, George 16 Smi
John 14 Smi
Drinkard, Dance 25 Bed
John 25 Bed
Lancy 25 Bed
Drinnen, John 393 Wil
see Drennen
Driskell, John 20 Rob
Driskill, John 6 Fra
William 6 Fra
Driskle, George 50 Mau
Driver, Abner 60 Dav
Benjamin 33 Lin
Benjamin 16 Smi
Burrell 16 Smi
Daniel 15 Smi
Dempsey 16 Smi
James 379 Wil
James F. 12 Lin
Jesse 14 Smi
Joseph 370 Whi
Pleasant 16 Smi
Redick 319 War
Sally 14 Lin
Thomas 16 Smi
William 13 Lin
William 102 Rut
William 16 Smi
Drum, Frederick 300 War
Drummonds, Thomas 2 Dic
Drummons, John 69 Mau
Drury, John 78 Dav
Richard 90 Dav
Dryden, David 21 Bed
Jonathan 12 Bed
William 12 Bed
Dryer, William 402 Wil
Du..., Thomas 26 Mau
Duboyce, Elisha 29 Mon
Dubusk, Jacob 94 Rut
Peter 93 Rut
Ducan, Thomas 363 Whi
Duckworth, Abel 13 Lin
Abel H. 14 Lin
John 4 Law
Willie T. 11 Har
Dudgeon, John 3 Hum
Dudley, Christopher 14 Smi
Guilford 8 Wll
Hudson 9 Dic
Ransom 37 Wll
Rebeckey 43 Mau
William 405 Wil
Dudly, John 42 Mau
Dudney, Abram 16 Lin
Anne 6 Jac
Arthur 27 Lin
Due, William 391 Wil
Duff, Delilah 16 Mon
Franklin 149 Sum
Hiram 149 Sum
Mary 3 Mon
Sally 7 Jac
Thomas 368 Whi
William 10 Hum
William 14 Smi
Duffel, John 13 Wll
William 13 Wll
Duggan, James 414 Wil
Dugger, Alexander 42 Mau
David 40 Mau
Dread 150 Sum
Flood 149 Sum
James 14 Gil
James 15 Gil
James 150 Sum
John 149 Sum
Joseph 40 Mau
Joseph 2 Wll
Luke 149 Sum
Shedrick 41 Mau
Dugin, Thomas 280 War
William 280 War
Dugless, Daniel 43 Mau
John 43 Mau
Duke, Benjamin 37 Mau
Crenshaw 77 Rut
Gidian 40 Mau
Green 58 Mau
James 150 Sum
John 29 Lin
Josiah G. 1 Mon
Matthew 14 Smi
Micajah 16 Smi
Mordecai 38 Mau
Robert 11 Dic
Saml. 6 Mon
Solomon 23 Lin
Washington 77 Rut
William 39 Mau
William P. 64 Wll
see Decker
Dukes, John 389 Wil
Stephen 359 Whi
Sterling 8 Gil
William 388 Wil
Dulin, George 5 Mon
Dum, William 21 Hic
Dun, Azeriah 14 Rob
Samuel 15 Rob

Dun (cont.)		
William	412	Wil
Dunagan, William	50	Wll
Dunahoo, William	24	Mon
Dunavant, Leonard	3	Wll
Dunaway, Opie	65	Dav
Dunbar, James	112	Ste
William	112	Ste
Dunbarr, Thos.	3	Mon
Duncan, Abner	16	Smi
Abram	23	Hic
Charles	6	Fra
David	15	Hic
David	14	Hum
Elijah	15	Smi
Fleming	14	Smi
Fleming W.	152	Sum
George	150	Sum
James	23	Hic
James	3	Law
James	70	Mau
Jno.	15	Hic
Joel	366	Whi
John	9	Gil
John	50	Mau
John	5	Per
John	7	Rob
John	15	Smi
John	279	War
John, Sr.	23	Hic
Joseph	6	Fra
Joseph	15	Smi
Joseph	127	Ste
Joseph	27	Wll
Josiah	46	Mau
Josiah	15	Smi
Letty	41	Lin
Mark	21	Rob
Marshal	342	Whi
Martin	4	Rob
Melsher	13	Law
Moses	150	Sum
Peter	14	Hum
Robert	41	Lin
Sally	4	Law
Samuel	6	Rob
Tandy P.	152	Sum
Thomas W.	15	Smi
William	31	Bed
William	6	Fra
William	7	Hum
William	45	Mau
William	20	Rob
William	295	War
William H.	70	Mau
Wm.	21	Hic
Wm.	150	Sum
Zacheriah	4	Rob
Dungan, William	29	Wll
Dunge, John	71	Dav
Dungy, Richard	360	Whi
Thomas	84	Dav
Dunham, Daniel A.	63	Dav
Dunham (cont.)		
Joseph	12	Bed
Joseph	43	Bed
see Durham		
Dunhan, William [& Gunter]	8	Wll
Dunigan, Charles	11	Dic
Nancy	151	Sum
Nicholas	10	Ove
Duning, Elizabeth	150	Sum
Lewis	150	Sum
Dunkin, Jeramiah	12	Ove
Joseph	10	Ove
Oen	18	Ove
see Dankin		
Dunlap, Elizabeth	3	Hum
Jesse	293	War
Leroy	9	Hum
Robert	10	Hum
Samuel	10	Hum
Samuel	11	Law
Samuel	52	Mau
William	13	Mon
see Dnlap		
Dunlop, Archibald	33	Rob
Robert	41	Bed
Dunn, Benjamin	16	Mon
Benjamin	87	Rut
Benjamin	111	Ste
Daniel	6	Fra
David	69	Dav
Hugh F.	7	Lin
Jacob	4	Hum
Jane	313	War
John	37	Bed
John	78	Rut
John	111	Ste
Josiah	111	Ste
Levi	8	Rob
Lewis	94	Dav
Samuel	7	Fra
Thomas	85	Rut
Thomas	85	Rut
Thomas	88	Rut
Thos.	127	Ste
Thos., Junr.	131	Ste
see Dum		
Dunnavant, Marth	89	Dav
Dunnaway, James	280	War
Samuel	407	Wil
Dunnevant, Daniel	89	Dav
Dunnigan, John	11	Dic
John	3	Hic
Dunnoway, Eve	6	Fra
Mary	6	Fra
Dupont, Francis	7	Fra
William	7	Fra
Duppin, Elizebeth	40	Mau
Dupree, Nancy	64	Wll
Durant, Edward	6	Ove
Thomas	14	Smi
Duratt, Betsey	93	Dav
Timothy	91	Dav
Durbin, Augustin	5	Law

Durell, John	15	Dic
Duren, George	150	Sum
James	91	Dav
Durgan, John	364	Whi
Durham, Asahel	288	War
Bedford	14	Lin
James	289	War
James	301	War
John	19	Mon
John	136	Sum
John	299	War
Robbert F.	48	Mau
Thomas	15	Smi
Thomas	296	War
William	290	War
Wm.	9	Way
see Denham, Dimham		
Durin, Elias	152	Sum
Durley, John	3	Lin
Durr see Dun		
Durran, Benjamin	24	Rob
Dusinberry, John	30	Lin
Dutton, Aaron	46	Lin
John	15	Smi
Duty, John	14	Smi
Thomas	38	Wll
William	152	Sum
Duval, Alexr. D.	149	Sum
Duvall, Brook	19	Rob
Colman	12	Mon
John	9	Ove
Duvraset, Lewis	371	Wil
Dwier, Daniel	47	Bed
Dwiggins, Daniel	14	Bed
Dwyer, Daniel	1	Wll
Dycus, Edward	5	Mon
Edward, Jr.	6	Jac
Edward, Sr.	6	Jac
James	6	Jac
James	2	Mon
Sarah	17	Mon
Dye, Beckham,	23	Hic
Martin	7	Bed
Martin	23	Hic
Richard	110	Ste
William	3	Lin
Wm.	23	Hic
Dyelle, Moses	3	Ove
Dyer, Abner	39	Lin
Anne	6	Jac
Esther	7	Jac
Ishum	75	Dav
James	6	Jac
James	16	Smi
Joel	73	Rut
Joel	13	Smi
Joel, Sen.	15	Smi
John	7	Jac
John	38	Lin
John	352	Whi
Levina	12	Wll
Mary	77	Dav
Mary	151	Sum
Dyer (cont.)		
Matthw	315	War
Patsey	54	Bed
Samuel	352	Whi
William	6	Jac
William	38	Lin
William	352	Whi
Dykes, Isham	298	War
Dyre, Ahawucras	22	Mon

--- E ---

Eades, Saml.	124	Ste
Eads, Samuel	101	Rut
Solomon	101	Rut
Eagan, Margaret	378	Wil
Hugh	379	Wil
James	379	Wil
Eagle, Philip	57	Mau
Eagles, Phillip	29	Mau
Eaglin, Orsburn	32	Wll
Eagun, Reel	380	Wil
Eakin, Isabellah	75	Dav
John	53	Bed
William	10	Bed
Eakle, Henry	8	Jac
Rosala	8	Jac
Ealam, Dianah	57	Wll
Edward	55	Wll
see Russel		
Ealum, Edward	19	Ove
Ealy, George	19	Ove
Eanes, Daniel	7	Fra
Eaquals, Silas	93	Dav
Earl, R. E. W.	79	Dav
William H.	10	Rob
Earls, Nathan	360	Whi
Pleasent	372	Whi
Early, Nathan	7	Fra
Earnest, Mary	10	Gil
Earnheart, George	33	Bed
Earon, Joseph J.	11	Dic
Earthman, Isaac	88	Dav
Lewis	86	Dav
Earwood, William	100	Rut
Easely, Stephen	11	Law
Easley, Benjamin	7	Hum
Drewrey	7	Per
Drury	3	Rob
Edward	53	Bed
James	4	Mon
John	7	Fra
John	3	Per
John	7	Per
Miller W.	7	Fra
Moses	10	Hic
Pleasant	11	Rob
Robt.	6	Hic
Robt., S. B.	4	Hic
Theodrick	17	Smi
Thos.	7	Hic

Easley (cont.)		
Thos. W.	2	Hic
Tucker	7	Fra
Warham	7	Hic
William	2	Hic
William	16	Rob
Easly, Millington	1	Hic
Millington	152	Sum
Robt.	7	Hic
Eason, Calvin W.	13	Dic
Carter S.	7	Hic
Eleanor	402	Wil
James	13	Dic
Joseph	12	Dic
Robert	406	Wil
East, Anderson	76	Dav
Atha	8	Jac
Edward H.	86	Dav
Joseph	16	Smi
Easter, Moses	16	Smi
Easters, Bartlet	38	Mau
Bethlihem	7	Way
John	38	Mau
Laben	96	Dav
see Eeasters		
Eastham, George W.	348	Whi
Eastis, John C.	97	Dav
Thomas	82	Dav
Eastland, John	29	Rob
Thos.	81	Dav
Easton, Reding	406	Wil
William	1	Wll
Eastridge, Larkin	119	Ste
Peggy	413	Wil
Eastwood, Liddia	53	Mau
Eatherage, Aaron	8	Jac
Eatherley, Jesse	17	Rob
Eaton, Daniel	95	Rut
David	6	Law
David	152	Sum
Elisabeth	1	Wll
James	17	Smi
Jesse	85	Rut
Joel	25	Lin
John	30	Lin
John H.	79	Dav
Jonathan	31	Lin
Joseph	8	Jac
Rebecca	95	Rut
Robert	87	Dav
Thomas	92	Dav
William	17	Ove
Eaves, Davis	7	Gil
Lera G.	7	Fra
Mark	7	Gil
Eblin, Edward	111	Ste
Echoles, Moses	67	Mau
Echols, Joel	377	Wil
Joel, Jr.	389	Wil
John	409	Wil
John	9	Wll
Echridge, David T.	91	Dav
Edde, James	40	Bed

Edding, John	320	War
Joseph	25	Rob
Joseph	390	Wil
Eddings, John	393	Wil
William	390	Wil
William	418	Wil
Eddis	30	Wll
Eddleman, — [& Joston]	8	Jac
John	26	Mau
see Eddlman		
Eddlemon, Margaret	17	Smi
Eddlman, John	8	Jac
Eddy, William	289	War
Edemeson, James D.	29	Mau
Edens, Alexander	361	Whi
Edgar, James	30	Mau
Jesse	18	Gil
John	54	Wll
Edge, Edward	412	Wil
Henry	282	War
Lewis	303	War
Edgin, Nathan	97	Rut
Eding, Isaac	396	Wil
Edman, Robbert	44	Mau
Edmanson, Covington	28	Wll
John	31	Mau
Robert S.	28	Wll
William [2]	30	Mau
Edminson, John	22	Wll
William	63	Wll
Edminston, John, Sn.	22	Wll
Edmison, Samuel	83	Dav
Edmiston, Alexr.	15	Lin
C., General	16	Lin
David	42	Lin
James	42	Lin
John	15	Lin
John	43	Lin
Robert	14	Lin
Samuel	7	Wll
William	8	Lin
William	28	Lin
William	47	Lin
William	7	Wll
Edmonds, Allen	97	Dav
Balam	97	Dav
Edmonds, Judah	343	Whi
Edmondson, Ebenezer	20	Gil
Edmondston, Thos.	75	Dav
Edmonson, John	7	Mon
Robert	5	Mon
Samuel	25	Mon
Edmonston, Thomas	85	Dav
Edmunds, John	17	Smi
Edmundson, John	9	Law
Robert	9	Law
Edney, Edmond	63	Dav
Leven	60	Dav
Newton	63	Dav
Polley	15	Wll
Samuel	8	Wll
Eduards, John	34	Mau
Edwards, Aaron	383	Wil

Edwards (cont.)
Aaron B. 23 Hic
Adiline 37 Wll
Adonijah 2 Dic
Andrew 42 Bed
Benja. 136 Sum
Bradford 419 Wil
Catherine 26 Bed
Charles 15 Gil
Cullin 136 Sum
Daniel 18 Gil
Edward 7 Rob
Edward 33 Rob
Edward 384 Wil
Elendor 12 Way
Eli 112 Wil
Eli 384 Wil
Elizabeth 2 Gil
Elizabeth 97 Rut
Enoch 21 Mon
Eve 23 Hic
Gravit 6 Rob
Henry 118 Ste
Hiram 384 Wil
Howard 384 Wil
J. 131 Ste
James 9 Hic
James 21 Rob
James 343 Whi
James 408 Wil
James 44 Wll
Jesse R. 309 War
John 30 Bed
John [2] 7 Hum
John 8 Jac
John 10 Lin
John 17 Mon
John 15 Rob
John 96 Rut
John 383 Wil
John 384 Wil
John 410 Wil
John 44 Wll
John W. 11 Gil
Jonathan 18 Rob
Joseph 9 Dic
Joseph 4 Ove
Kaleb D. 2 Har
Little B. 152 Sum
M. F. 9 Way
Maria 153 Sum
Mathew 97 Rut
Moreland 95 Rut
Nancy 40 Mau
Nancy 104 Rut
Nancy 383 Wil
Naoma 10 Dic
Nathan 152 Sum
Nicholas 400 Wil
Oliver 15 Rob
Owen 90 Rut
Parka 37 Wll
Rachel 7 Fra

Edwards (cont.)
Ransome 406 Wil
Richardson 16 Hic
Robert 376 Wil
Sampson 15 Gil
Sandford 7 Dic
Selman 10 Dic
Simeon 10 Law
Spier A. 23 Hic
Stephen 43 Mau
Susanah 48 Wll
Tho. F. 152 Sum
Tho. J. 153 Sum
Thomas 3 Bed
Thomas 2 Dic
Thomas 19 Ove
Thomas 85 Rut
Thomas 97 Rut
William 10 Dic
William 7 Hum
William 8 Jac
William 48 Mau
William 55 Mau
William 60 Mau
William 7 Rob
William 7 Rob
William 152 Sum
William 383 Wil
William 400 Wil
William 405 Wil
William, Sr. 153 Sum
Wm. 136 Sum
Eeasters, John H. 47 Mau
Egbert, Solomon 7 Fra
Egnew, John 53 Mau
Eidson, James 152 Sum
Saml. 153 Sum
Einsly, Enoch 67 Dav
Eisan, William 66 Mau
Elam, Daniel 99 Rut
see Ealam
Elder, Eli S. 94 Rut
James 1 Mon
James 100 Rut
James, Jnr. 100 Rut
Mary 8 Gil
Robert 88 Rut
Tilman 8 Gil
William 89 Rut
Eldridge, Elisha 16 Gil
James 2 Ove
John 9 Ove
Nathan 10 Ove
Sampson 9 Ove
William 1 Ove
Zachariah 8 Ove
Eleson, Jane 60 Mau
Robbert 60 Mau
Elgin, Elizabeth 17 Smi
William 17 Smi
Elick, Peter 17 Smi
Eliot, James 29 Mau
Eliott, Barnea 41 Wll

Eliott (cont.)
James 13 Wll
John 61 Wll
Elis, James 28 Lin
Labon 8 Jac
Nathan 8 Jac
Robert 28 Lin
William 8 Jac
Elison, Thos. 3 Per
Elisson, Joseph 8 Jac
Elkins, Absey 119 Ste
Annanias 7 Fra
Gabriel 295 War
M. 130 Ste
Ralph 291 War
Ralph 314 War
Thomas 301 War
William 117 Ste
Ellams, James 59 Mau
Elleat, Elenezar 46 Mau
Elleatt, John 43 Mau
Elledge, Ezekiel 344 Whi
Fielding 313 War
Joseph 296 War
Ellender, E. 119 Ste
Ellenor, Benjamin 15 Mon
Elleoff, John 13 Gil
Ellet, Jonas 8 Jac
William 8 Jac
Ellett, Amos 401 Wil
John P. 34 Mau
Elliatt, Micazer 45 Mau
Samuel 45 Mau
Elliff, Evered 153 Sum
James G. 152 Sum
Ellington, Edward 32 Mon
Stephen 7 Gil
Elliot, Archibald 366 Whi
Jessee 22 Mon
William 18 Mon
Elliott, Benjamin 10 Rob
David 7 Mon
Deborah 100 Rut
Elvira 121 Ste
Foultner 112 Ste
George 6 Mon
George 152 Sum
George, Jr. 152 Sum
Hugh 152 Sum
Isaac 153 Sum
James 34 Lin
James 9 Rob
James 86 Rut
James 152 Sum
James 16 Way
James [2] 29 Wll
John 7 Hic
John 113 Ste
John 30 Wll
John H. 58 Dav
Joseph 101 Rut
Josiah 58 Dav
Lilis 16 Hic

Elliott (cont.)
Mary 10 Gil
Moses 38 Lin
Reuben 7 Hic
Samuel 77 Rut
Simeon 95 Rut
Stephen 7 Fra
T. S. 114 Ste
Thomas 30 Wll
Ellis, Allison 7 Fra
Benjamin 7 Fra
Benjamin, Jr. 7 Fra
Caleb 114 Ste
Dianah 153 Sum
Edmund 10 Gil
Hardy 29 Mon
Hicks 84 Rut
Hicks 99 Rut
Ira 114 Ste
Isaac 153 Sum
James 33 Lin
James 152 Sum
James 397 Wil
Jeramiah 89 Dav
Jessee 25 Lin
John 119 Ste
John 347 Whi
John 386 Wil
John H. 92 Rut
John J. 28 Wll
Joshua 98 Dav
Joshua 96 Rut
Josiah 7 Har
Lewis 99 Rut
Miles 32 Mon
Moses 404 Wil
Moses 408 Wil
Nancy 25 Rob
Nathan 408 Wil
Ranson 152 Sum
Robert 408 Wil
Sally 7 Fra
Saml. 153 Sum
Sarah 33 Lin
Sarah 153 Sum
Sims 14 Rob
Stephen 20 Rob
Thomas W. 55 Mau
Thomas W. 382 Wil
William 17 Lin
William 21 Lin
William 34 Lin
William 16 Smi
William 123 Ste
William 290 War
Willis P. 16 Smi
Wm. 124 Ste
Ellison, Hamblenton 369 Whi
Henry 7 Hum
Hugh H. 74 Rut
James 20 Bed
James 369 Whi
John 20 Bed

Ellison (cont.)
John 41 Lin
John 369 Whi
Joseph 20 Bed
Joseph 41 Lin
Polly 362 Whi
Thomas 19 Bed
Thomas [2] 20 Bed
Thomas 369 Whi
William 19 Bed
Elliss, Ephraim 4 Dic
Francis S. 3 Dic
Jesse 15 Dic
Simelion 152 Sum
Thomas 4 Dic
Ellisson, Joseph 14 Lin
William 17 Lin
Elliston, Henry 93 Dav
Jacob 152 Sum
John 75 Dav
Joseph 17 Smi
Joseph T. 90 Dav
Thomas 7 Fra
Ellmore, Jesse 406 Wil
Ellsberry, Isaac 97 Rut
Ellton, Samuel 19 Gil
Elmal, Thomas 389 Wil
Elmarr, George 28 Rob
Julias 28 Rob
Elmore, Elijah 371 Whi
Henry 20 Rob
Elms, Edward 364 Whi
Elrey, William 7 Fra
Elrod, Giles 368 Whi
Harman 87 Rut
James 8 Jac
James 370 Whi
William 8 Jac
Elston, Allen 13 Lin
Jesse 17 Smi
Emarson, James 11 Har
Embrey, Boaly 7 Fra
Reuben 7 Fra
Embry, Jesse 7 Fra
John [2] 8 Jac
Murray 7 Fra
Thomas 7 Fra
Emerson, John 41 Mau
see Emarson, Emmarson
Emery, Frederick 17 Smi
Meeka 380 Wil
Emeson, James H. 40 Mau
William 46 Mau
Eming see Ewing
Emmarson, Isaac 11 Har
Emmerson, John 7 Fra
Emmit, David 7 Fra
William C. 74 Rut
Emons, Eligah 69 Mau
Sirenus 69 Dav
Empson, Gregory 22 Rob
Enapreet, Benjamin 303 War
Joseph 303 War
Enas, William 311 War
Englan, A. R. 66 Mau
England, Anderson 11 Dic
Aron 352 Whi
Elijah 353 Whi
Isaac 28 Rob
James 20 Rob
James 28 Rob
Jane 352 Whi
Jeremiah 365 Whi
Jesse 284 War
Jessee 342 Whi
John 12 Bed
John 366 Whi
Joseph 127 Ste
Rebeka 32 Rob
Samuel 36 Bed
Titus 28 Rob
William 18 Gil
Engledow, John 282 War
English, Andrew 76 Rut
Hannah 19 Gil
J. 24 Mau
James 7 Fra
James [2] 5 Har
James 8 Har
James 122 Ste
Stephen 130 Ste
Thomas 10 Har
Ennis, James 14 Rob
Vincent 9 Mon
Enochs, Benjamin 16 Smi
David 16 Smi
John 16 Smi
Thompson 34 Lin
William 12 Ove
Enocks, Gabriel 34 Lin
Isaac 34 Lin
John 34 Lin
Enos, Polly 137 Sum
see Enas
Ensey, William 294 War
Eperson, Littlebery 39 Wll
Epperson, Amsel 13 Hic
Anthony 17 Smi
Asa 12 Dic
Benjn. 10 Hic
Jacob 21 Mon
Jesse 12 Dic
Joseph 153 Sum
Samuel 5 Hum
Thomas 10 Hum
Eppeson, Henry 9 Hum
Eppler, John 23 Gil
Epps, Irby 45 Wll
Isham 46 Wll
John 89 Rut
Joshua 46 Wll
Lary 17 Lin
Peterson 30 Mon
Rebecca 95 Rut
Wyott 5 Mon
Erby, Carter 388 Wil

Erby (cont.)		
John	21	Rob
Pleasant	405	Wil
see Kirby		
Ervin, Alexander	348	Whi
David	116	Ste
James	60	Mau
James	29	Rob
James	344	Whi
James	347	Whi
John	13	Gil
Peggy	343	Whi
Rachel	348	Whi
William	44	Mau
William	357	Whi
William	367	Whi
see Erwin, Irvin		
Ervine, Mary, Mrs.	13	Law
Erwim, Bashford	8	Jac
Erwin, Abner	152	Sum
Alexander	67	Mau
Andrew	29	Bed
Charles	403	Wil
David	44	Mau
Elim	153	Sum
George	17	Hic
Hezekiah	33	Lin
James	76	Dav
James	77	Dav
James	68	Mau
John	11	Lin
John	93	Rut
John A.	153	Sum
John P.	76	Dav
John P.	153	Sum
Joseph, Jur.	20	Gil
Joseph, Senr.	20	Gil
Morpass	403	Wil
Nathl.	153	Sum
Peter	85	Dav
Saml.	16	Hic
Samuel	16	Bed
Samuel	6	Har
William	30	Bed
William	68	Mau
Wm.	20	Hic
see Erwim		
Escue, William	152	Sum
Esens, Leonard C.	136	Sum
Eskridge, John	31	Lin
Samuel	93	Rut
Eslick, Isaac B.	37	Lin
William	36	Lin
Esselman, Alexander	22	Lin
Archd. C.	47	Lin
James	22	Lin
Essex, Tho.	152	Sum
Essry, James	292	War
Thomas	297	War
see Eusey		
Ester, John	29	Lin
Estes, Anson L.	98	Rut
Armstead	1	Hic
Asa	15	Gil
Estes (cont.)		
Elisha	38	Mau
Elisha	40	Mau
James D.	5	Lin
Joseph	19	Gil
Matilda	1	Hic
Saml.	14	Hic
Estess, Bartlet	319	War
Bartlett	304	War
Jesse	282	War
Moses	304	War
Moses C.	319	War
Estick, Isaac	35	Lin
Levi	35	Lin
Estill, Isaac	7	Fra
Isaac, Sen.	7	Fra
James	7	Fra
James, Sen.	7	Fra
Jonathan	1	Lin
Wallace, M. D.	7	Fra
Wallace, Sen.	7	Fra
Estis, Ansom L.	87	Rut
Henson	39	Wil
Estridge, Benjamin H.	376	Wil
Etheredge, Bassel	74	Rut
Etheridge, Acheus	6	Dic
Ann	37	Lin
Burwel	16	Dic
Jared	28	Lin
Matthew	418	Wil
Thomas, Mr.	14	Law
Willoughby	14	Dic
Etherington, F.	128	Ste
Etherley, James	381	Wil
John	385	Wil
John, Jr.	383	Wil
John, Sen.	383	Wil
Warran	381	Wil
Etherly, John	381	Wil
Jonathan	387	Wil
see Eatherley		
Ethridge, John	318	War
John, Mr.	14	Law
Rhody	12	Hic
Etter, John	87	Rut
Eubanks, George	7	Fra
John	12	Gil
Lewis	7	Gil
William	12	Gil
Eudaley, David	99	Rut
James	96	Rut
Eull, Jeamiah	86	Dav
Eusey, Dennis	302	War
Eustice, Patsey	102	Rut
Evans, Abraham	289	War
Andrew	30	Bed
Charles	10	Lin
Charles	16	Smi
Charles C.	301	War
Cornelius	152	Sum
Cornelius, Jr.	153	Sum
Dale	17	Smi
Daniel	19	Gil
David	8	Fra

Name	Page	County
Evans (cont.)		
Edward	21	Lin
Eli	22	Lin
Eli	34	Lin
Ephraim	17	Smi
Ezekiel	17	Smi
Ezer	11	Gil
George	11	Dic
Henry	18	Ove
Hugh	136	Sum
Jacob	289	War
James	43	Lin
James	17	Smi
James H.	18	Gil
Jesse	52	Bed
John	30	Bed
John	7	Dic
John	20	Gil
John	11	Ove
John [2]	17	Smi
Joseph	9	Ove
Joseph, Jun.	17	Smi
Joseph, Sen.	17	Smi
Joshua	12	Ove
Lewis	114	Ste
Margaret	13	Dic
Mark	319	War
Nathan	12	Ove
Nathan	17	Smi
Nathaniel	349	Whi
Philip	17	Smi
Reuben	17	Smi
Richard	344	Whi
Snail O.	16	Smi
Stephen	12	Ove
Thomas	43	Lin
Thomas	12	Ove
Thomas	13	Way
Walter	17	Smi
Wathen	13	Bed
William	18	Bed
William	30	Bed
William [2]	95	Dav
William	3	Dic
William	10	Ove
William	12	Ove
William	90	Rut
William	99	Rut
William	17	Smi
William	152	Sum
William D.	17	Smi
William G.	86	Dav
Evens, Ethelrid	10	Wll
George A.	406	Wil
John, Sen.	16	Wll
William R.	93	Dav
Event, John	153	Sum
Everet, James	7	Fra
John	382	Wil
Silas	7	Fra
Simon	84	Dav
Everett, Thos. H.	74	Dav
Everidge, John	103	Rut
Everley, George	2	Wll
Every, Allin	420	Wil
Evetts, Samuel	19	Gil
Evin, John	29	Wll
Evins, Daniel	63	Mau
John	5	Wll
John	54	Wll
John W.	388	Wil
Lawrence G.	13	Wll
Mary	18	Wll
Rebecca	19	Wll
Ewbank, Elijah	19	Rob
James	16	Rob
Martin	26	Rob
Ewbanks, James	153	Sum
see Eubanks		
Ewel, Dulney	19	Bed
Ewen, Alexander	31	Lin
Andrew	20	Wll
Ewin, Jannet	16	Hic
see Erwin		
Ewing, Alexander	90	Dav
Andrew	16	Gil
Andrew F.	37	Mau
James	413	Wil
Joseph P.	35	Mau
Joshua	19	Lin
William	85	Dav
William D.	35	Mau
Exum, Joseph	153	Sum
William	153	Sum
see Oxum		
Eydleott, Thomas	64	Mau
Eyedleott, John	64	Mau
Ezel, Timothy	18	Lin
Ezell, Balam	38	Wll
Fielden	38	Wll
Frederic [?]	32	Wll
Micajah	15	Gil
Timothy	15	Gil
William	15	Gil
Zachus	38	Wll
Fack, Thomas	21	
Fadder, Elisha	77	Rut
Fagan, Robert	94	Rut
Fagans, Philip	46	Lin
Fagg, James	18	Smi
William	18	Smi
William, Sen.	18	Smi
Fahy, Andrew	76	Dav
Fain, Daniel	99	Rut
David	40	Bed
Fair, David D.	46	Wll
Walter	154	Sum
Fairfax, Cecelia	81	Dav
Fairless, Mary	154	Sum
Fakes, John	112	Wil
John	384	Wil
Falkner, Dickinson	11	Har
Francis	8	Fra
John	8	Fra
John	19	Mon
Lewis	11	Har

Falkner (cont.)		
William	19	Mon
Falks, William	89	Rut
Falwell, Elisha	9	Bed
Faman, Sarah	3	Har
Fancee, Henry	8	Fra
Fann, Adams	9	Fra
John	9	Fra
Madison	9	Fra
Fanner see Farmer		
Fanning, Benjamin	28	Lin
John, Mr.	4	Law
Middleton	37	Lin
Thomas	39	Lin
Fanveil, Jeremiah	26	Mau
Fanveille, John	98	Rut
Faquhar, William	18	Smi
Farbus, Robert	10	Har
Farchand, Thomas	19	Wll
Fard, Judah	78	Rut
Farer, Jefferson	5	Har
Faris, Absalom	8	Fra
Absalom G.	9	Fra
Alexander	34	Mau
Calib	68	Mau
Charles	8	Fra
George	8	Fra
Hezekiah	8	Fra
Isaac	68	Mau
James	8	Fra
James [2]	9	Fra
James	33	Mau
James, Jun.	8	Fra
Jeremiah	9	Fra
John	8	Fra
John	67	Mau
Levi	9	Fra
Patience	9	Fra
Richard	8	Fra
Robbart	33	Mau
Samuel B.	33	Mau
Samul	26	Mau
Stephen	9	Fra
Thomas	8	Fra
Thomas	284	War
Thomas C.	36	Mau
William	8	Fra
William [2]	9	Fra
William	33	Mau
Fariss, Bowler	4	Gil
Edward	7	Gil
John	7	Gil
Nimrod	7	Gil
Farless, Robert	8	Rob
Farley, Edward	93	Dav
John	18	Smi
Farlow, Isham	363	Whi
Pleasent	362	Whi
Stephen	361	Whi
Farm see Fann		
Farmar, Thomas	82	Rut
Farmer, Anderson	18	Smi
Benjamin	9	Jac
Farmer (cont.)		
Betey	27	Rob
David	8	Fra
Due	25	Rob
Elisha	15	Rob
Elizabeth	10	Gil
Ezekiel	7	Law
George	106	She
George W.	9	Hum
James	12	Rob
Jetty	127	Ste
John	9	Jac
John	13	Mon
John	19	Smi
John K.	341	Whi
Joseph A.	95	Rut
Josiah	30	Rob
Littleberry	18	Smi
Nancy	65	Dav
Nathan	5	Gil
Rany	12	Rob
Reynard	18	Smi
Samuel	9	Fra
Samuel	22	Gil
Samuel	4	Rob
Samuel, Jr.	9	Fra
Samuel, Sr. [2]	9	Fra
William	13	Mon
William	5	Rob
William	380	Wil
Farney, John	38	Mau
Farr, Ephraim	77	Rut
James	310	War
James	378	Wil
John	387	Wil
Jonathan	19	Smi
Farrar, Cyprian	16	Dic
Jesse C.	11	Lin
John	20	Lin
Landon	94	Dav
William	14	Lin
William	37	Wll
Farras, Field	3	Dic
Farraw, William	57	Mau
Farrier, Mary	7	Mon
Needham	7	Mon
Farrington, Joshua	2	Wll
Farris, Jane	12	Lin
Maury	66	Mau
Farriss, Elisha	6	Gil
Wilford	6	Gil
Farrow, John	9	Fra
Fart see Fort		
Faithing, Solomon	20	Rob
Fasley, William	360	Whi
Faster, Anthony	9	Fra
Cynthia	8	Fra
George	8	Fra
William	8	Fra
Fasthera, Sally	80	Rut
Fate, Samuel	54	Mau
Fatharie, Sally	9	Fra
Fattenberry, Jacob	87	Rut

Fatum, Barnett 378 Wil
Faucet, Allexander 97 Dav
Richard 115 Ste
William 95 Dav
Faulk, William 5 Mon
Faulkner, James W. 136 Sum
William 86 Dav
Faultenbery, David 102 Rut
Fause, Peter 18 Smi
Philip 18 Smi
Fausher, Binam 1 Ove
James 1 Ove
Richard 13 Ove
Favour, John 3 Bed
Fawbush, Jno. 12 Hic
Fawley, John B. 44 Mau
Fawlin, William 66 Mau
Feamster, Eli 8 Fra
Fearrell, John 106 She
Fears, William 87 Rut
Featherston, Burwel 50 Bed
Burwell 32 Rob
Catherine 50 Bed
Charles 80 Rut
Jesse 97 Rut
see Fetherston
Featherton 18 Smi
Feeble, Walter 57 Dav
Feeland, Mary 95 Dav
Thomas W. 95 Dav
Feezor, John 46 Bed
Fegures, Matthew 114 Wil
Feild, Allen 9 Gil
William H. 16 Gil
Feilds, Patience 47 Wll
Felps, Britain 32 Lin
Felps, Derius 17 Wll
Joseph 21 Wll
Felton, John 359 Whi
Thomas 19 Smi
Felts, Drury 9 Rob
George 13 Rob
Hardy 13 Rob
Henry 10 Rob
James 13 Rob
Rowland 12 Rob
William 24 Rob
Felty, Barwell 7 Hic
Fentress, David 9 Dic
James 27 Mon
James 17 Smi
Fergason, James 9 Jac
Fergerson, Alexander 18 Smi
Dixon 18 Smi
James 47 Wll
James C. 19 Smi
Joel 47 Wll
Patrick 19 Smi
William 18 Smi
William 19 Smi
Ferguson, Alexander 28 Lin
Andrew 9 Hic
Berryman 82 Rut
Ferguson (cont.)
Elizabeth 1 Rob
Hugh S. 90 Rut
Joel 26 Lin
Joel 80 Rut
John W. 36 Rob
Robert 19 Bed
Sally 9 Hic
Shadrach 76 Rut
Thomas H. 22 Gil
William 34 Lin
Feril, Eady 37 Mau
John 39 Mau
John David 39 Mau
Levy 37 Mau
Ferrel, Clement 2 Bed
David 4 Bed
George 2 Bed
John 113 Ste
Josiah 93 Dav
Leighton 285 War
William 9 Jac
Ferrell, Anda 9 Jac
Charles 21 Mon
Charles 319 War
Enoch 313 War
Harrison 19 Bed
James 9 Dic
John 313 War
Robert L. 10 Ove
William 7 Ove
Ferriby, Henry 83 Dav
Thomas 83 Dav
Ferrier, John 154 Sum
Ferril, Binow 153 Sum
Burtis 153 Sum
Tho. 154 Sum
Willie 94 Rut
Ferrill, David E. 2 Ove
Francis 9 Fra
John 313 War
Peggy 8 Fra
Theodrick 18 Smi
William 8 Gil
William 17 Smi
Ferrin, Elijah 9 Fra
Smith 9 Fra
Ferrington, Abraham 318 War
Ferris, Josiah 98 Rut
Feser see Fiser
Fetherston, Robert 84 Rut
Fetser, Peggy 14 Ove
Few, James 12 Hic
Fewel, James 63 Wll
Fie, Philip 9 Jac
Fielder, Andrew 47 Bed
John 29 Wll
John L. 4 Wll
William 46 Bed
Fields, Brice 393 Wil
David 3 Mon
David, Jr. 383 Wil
David, Sen. 383 Wil

Fields (cont.)
Denson 291 War
Fielding 4 Bed
Jeremiah 1 Wll
John 4 Bed
John 64 Mau
Nelson 5 Wll
Redding 3 Mon
Richard 89 Rut
Richard 97 Rut
Richard 420 Wil
Stephen 308 War
Thomas 55 Mau
William 56 Mau
William 19 Smi
Fielsey, Robbert G. 34 Mau
Fiers, Susana 38 Lin
Fifer, Bradley 6 Law
Joseph 358 Whi
Peter 46 Mau
Fin, Edward 9 Jac
John 9 Jac
Peter 153 Sum
Richard 9 Jac
William 153 Sum
Finch, Edward 96 Dav
Jarrat 82 Rut
John 91 Rut
Joshua 11 Gil
William 18 Bed
William 28 Bed
Fincher, Francis 40 Lin
Findley, Francis 13 Lin
John 44 Lin
Joseph 44 Lin
Reuben 9 Jac
Findly, Robert 19 Lin
Fine, William 16 Gil
Finger, Henry 81 Rut
Finley, George 16 Ove
Hance 26 Bed
Hezekiah 9 Fra
James 9 Ove
John 8 Fra
Michael 22 Rob
Ob. 111 Wil
Obadiah G. 391 Wil
Reuben 10 Ove
Sarah 363 Whi
Thomas 32 Rob
William 46 Mau
William 32 Rob
see Tinley
Finly, William 38 Mau
Finn, Abednego 7 Hum
Shadrick 11 Hum
Finney, Alexander 33 Lin
Ellender 17 Gil
James 3 Gil
William 92 Rut
Finny, Buck 18 Smi
Mary 98 Rut
Pleasant R. 8 Fra
Fips, Joseph 18 Way
Fips (cont.)
Joshua 9 Fra
Samuel 9 Fra
see Phips
Firger, John 81 Rut
Fiser, Henry 6 Rob
Jacob 4 Rob
Joseph 11 Rob
Michael 4 Rob
Peter 11 Rob
Peter, Senr. 11 Rob
Fish, Nathaniel 19 Ove
Fishburn, Christopher 19 Smi
Frederick 19 Smi
John 19 Smi
Fisher, Bowling 75 Rut
Clement 26 Rob
Edward 74 Rut
Elizabeth 74 Rut
Frederick E. 75 Dav
Fredrick 35 Mau
George 46 Bed
George 35 Mau
George 35 Wll
Jacob 4 Ove
John 292 War
John 296 War
John 376 Wil
Martain 2 Per
Martin 46 Bed
Micheal 46 Bed
Mikieal 3 Per
Nicholas 13 Hic
Peter 153 Sum
Philip 408 Wil
Silvanis 2 Per
Thomas 30 Rob
Thomas 33 Rob
Thomas 19 Smi
William 12 Gil
William 5 Law
William 2 Per
William 8 Rob
William 154 Sum
William 344 Whi
see Fishur, Fosher
Fishur, Anderson 5 Law
Fisk, Alvary 67 Dav
John 13 Wll
Madison 341 Whi
Moses 20 Ove
Fitch, Peter 9 Jac
Samuel 9 Fra
William 25 Bed
Fite, Jacob 19 Smi
John 18 Smi
John 19 Smi
Joseph 412 Wil
Leonard 19 Smi
Leonard 412 Wil
Moses 18 Smi
Fitsgirl, William 36 Mau
Fitts, John 9 Wll
Tabitha 63 Wll

Fittsgarld, Jessey 62 Mau
Fittsgeld, Pleasant 65 Mau
Fittsgerl, Mastan 59 Mau
Fittsgerld, Christpher 64 Mau
James 64 Mau
Nathaniel 64 Mau
Fittsgirld, Edman 62 Mau
John 63 Mau
Fittsgrerld, Jackson 62 Mau
Fittspatrick, John 43 Mau
Morgan 43 Mau
Samuel 43 Mau
Fitz, Ishum 87 Dav
Fitzgerald, John 8 Jac
Langford 9 Gil
Mary 345 Whi
Patrick 8 Jac
Thos. 5 Mon
see Fitsgirl, Fittsgirld, Fitzgeril
Fitzgeril, John 46 Wll
Fitzgerrald, Anderson 9 Fra
Fitzhugh, Ezekeal 66 Dav
John 66 Dav
Samuel 82 Dav
Fitzpatrick, Celia 19 Smi
Edward 11 Ove
John 18 Smi
John 19 Smi
Rachel 306 War
Sally 18 Smi
Fivash, William 15 Rob
Flack, Elijah 154 Sum
Flake, Sampson 10 Gil
Flanery, Daniel A. 10 Law
Flannekin, Robbert 43 Mau
Flannery, Thos. 10 Hic
Flatt, David 18 Way
James 13 Gil
William 13 Gil
Fleatcher, Joshua 107 She
Fleher, David 287 War
Fleming, Beverly 153 Sum
David C. 13 Bed
Elizabeth 86 Rut
Jacob 82 Rut
James 10 Bed
James 11 Bed
John 1 Ove
John 10 Rob
John 74 Rut
John 153 Sum
Josiah 11 Wll
Peter 98 Rut
Rebecca 93 Rut
Robert 153 Sum
Samuel 45 Bed
Samuel 89 Rut
Thomas F. 32 Mau
William 4 Ove
William 154 Sum
William 40 Wll
Flemming, John 302 War
Richard 22 Gil
Flemming (cont.)
Wm. 11 Hic
Flemons, E. 124 Ste
H. 130 Ste
Flennithin, Elias 26 Mau
Samul 26 Mau
Fletcher, E. 113 Ste
Easter 23 Mon
Edmond 122 Ste
Elijah 285 War
James 75 Rut
James 112 Ste
James 313 War
Jane 19 Smi
Jeremiah 81 Rut
John 9 Fra
John 14 Rob
John 75 Rut
John 114 Ste
Lewis 341 Whi
Mary 387 Wil
Moses 112 Ste
Muntford H. 75 Rut
Robert 43 Lin
Robert A. 73 Rut
Thomas H. 94 Dav
Winey 24 Mon
see Fleher
Flewellen, William 9 Rob
Flinchum, Samuel 360 Whi
Flinn, Benjamin 345 Whi
John 356 Whi
Lucy 9 Jac
Luke 360 Whi
Flint, Elizabeth 43 Lin
Richard 21 Lin
T. P. 76 Dav
see Flynt
Flippen, Armstead 17 Smi
Dixon R. 18 Smi
Jacob 5 Wll
William 16 Gil
Flipping, Jesse 154 Sum
Flippo, Garret 20 Rob
Henry 9 Fra
Sarah 9 Fra
Flooty, Ransom 5 Lin
Florada, Partrick 419 Wil
Flournoy, Alfred 16 Gil
Silas 18 Gil
Flowers, Andrew 11 Dic
Anthony 6 Ove
Arthur 6 Ove
Benjamin 1 Ove
Benjamin 94 Rut
David 6 Ove
Green 11 Rob
Hardy 22 Hic
Henery 48 Mau
Henry 22 Hic
James 3 Ove
James 154 Sum
John 48 Mau

Flowers (cont.)
John 94 Rut
Mary 94 Rut
Ralph 18 Smi
Ralph K. 17 Smi
Roland 6 Ove
Valentine 25 Hic
William 17 Smi
William F. 18 Smi
Floyd, Alexander 9 Fra
David 31 Bed
David 39 Bed
David 19 Smi
Drewry 56 Wll
Drury 86 Rut
Elisha 9 Fra
Enoch 39 Bed
George 3 Bed
Jonathan 33 Lin
Jones 81 Rut
Jones 86 Rut
Joseph 7 Wll
Pierce 4 Rob
Richar 78 Rut
William 1 Hic
William, Jr. 9 Fra
William, Sen. 9 Fra
Fly, Elisha 67 Dav
Elisha 25 Wll
Jerimiah 66 Mau
Jesse 7 Bed
John 93 Rut
John 99 Rut
Joshuay 69 Mau
Lawrance 26 Wll
Micaijah 79 Dav
Sally 68 Dav
William 51 Wll
see Isby
Flynt, David 14 Gil
Sandford P. 14 Gil
Foagleman, Michal 51 Mau
Fogg, Francis B. 67 Dav
John 6 Gil
Fogleman, Samuel 51 Mau
see Foagleman
Foley, Caty 21 Wll
Foliver, — 111 Wil
Folkes, Samuel 386 Wil
Folks, Etheldred 122 Ste
Sherrod 125 Ste
Thompson 84 Rut
Wm. 130 Ste
Follis, Mary 19 Gil
William 66 Mau
William 5 Rob
Folts, Alesey 369 Whi
Cady 369 Whi
Fomville, Nancy 66 Dav
Fondrin, Richard 4 Law
Foot, Richard 3 Rob
Forbes, Benjamin 93 Rut
Colin 15 Gil
Mary 18 Ove
Forbes (cont.)
see Farbus, Forbs
Forbis, Collen P. 13 Law
James 13 Law
Nathaniel W. 34 Wll
Forbs, Benjamin 82 Rut
John 8 Rob
William 84 Rut
Forbus, Arthur 390 Wil
Elizabeth 390 Wil
Forbush, Andrew 10 Hum
Samuel 11 Hum
Force, Julius 9 Hum
Ford, Alexr. 154 Sum
Andrew 18 Smi
Boaze 18 Smi
Charles 8 Fra
Daniel 19 Smi
Erasmus 9 Jac
George 20 Lin
George 310 War
Henry 7 Mon
Henry 295 War
Isaac 55 Mau
Jacob 9 Fra
James 23 Gil
James 85 Rut
James 121 Ste
John 111 Ste
John W. 341 Whi
Jonathan 14 Gil
Joshua 99 Rut
Joshua 18 Smi
Lemuel 6 Lin
Lewis 19 Smi
Loyd 9 Jac
Milton 19 Smi
Nathan 99 Rut
Paskal 394 Wil
Peter 19 Smi
Rebecca 154 Sum
Richard 1 Har
Richard 310 War
Rubin 52 Mau
Thomas 16 Gil
Thos. 115 Ste
William 25 Lin
William 362 Whi
Zachary 18 Smi
Fore, William 56 Wll
Forehand, Abner 72 Dav
Foreman, George 8 Fra
Forest, James 10 Hum
James 288 War
John 8 Hum
Richard 297 War
Thomas 2 Per
Forester, Betcy 9 Jac
Charles 19 Smi
James 19 Smi
Lydia 3 Hic
Richd. 13 Hic
Robert 19 Smi
William 280 War

Forga, Andrew	39	Mau
John	39	Mau
Forgason, James	343	Whi
Joshua	343	Whi
Forgerson, Jeremiah	64	Mau
Nathaniel	12	Hum
Rodgle	66	Mau
Forggey, James	70	Mau
Forguson, Isaac	15	Wll
Nancy	401	Wil
Forker, William	19	Smi
Forlong, Samuel	18	Smi
Forrest, Nancy	153	Sum
Nathen	9	Bed
Rewben	153	Sum
Shadrach	3	Bed
Stephn	153	Sum
Stepn, Sr.	153	Sum
Forrester, James	310	War
Mark	297	War
Forrister, Isaac	23	Lin
James	21	Lin
Forsith, Thomas	53	Mau
Forsythe, Jacob	15	Dic
James	41	Lin
John	16	Dic
see Fursith		
Fort, Burwell	7	Mon
Charles	22	Mon
Elias	21	Rob
Elias, Junr.	31	Rob
Jacob H.	17	Rob
Jacob H.	36	Rob
Josiah	3	Rob
Josiah C.	9	Rob
Josiah W.	18	Rob
Lewis B.	2	Rob
Oren B.	9	Rob
Sugg	31	Rob
Whitmel	35	Rob
William	35	Rob
Fortenberry, David	8	Fra
John	8	Fra
Fortner, David	54	Mau
Elizebeth	54	Mau
Jonathan	12	Hum
Keziah	12	Hum
Thos.	8	Hic
Fosher, Richard	4	Ove
Foslin, Lewis	85	Dav
Fosset, John	46	Mau
Fossett, Alexander	50	Mau
David	46	Mau
James	91	Rut
Fossey, Daniel	11	Hic
Foster, Addison	153	Sum
Aexander	294	War
Alexander [2]	9	Jac
Alexander	407	Wil
Ambrose	26	Lin
Celia	17	Smi
David	393	Wil
Edward	17	Smi
Elijah	416	Wil
Foster (cont.)		
Elizabeth	19	Way
Franklin	401	Wil
George	68	Dav
George	18	Hic
Henry	121	Ste
James	24	Bed
James	8	Law
James	57	Mau
James	81	Rut
James	18	Smi
James	121	Ste
James	153	Sum
James	376	Wil
Joel	26	Lin
John	10	Law
John	89	Rut
John	290	War
John	388	Wil
John	407	Wil
Lott	33	Wll
Lucy	96	Rut
Nancy	399	Wil
Richard	29	Mau
Richard	55	Mau
Richard	278	War
Robert	23	Bed
Robert C.	85	Dav
Robert C.	2	Wll
Samuel	91	Rut
Samuel	297	War
Susanah	23	Wll
Thomas	50	Mau
William	67	Dav
William	5	Gil
William	77	Rut
William	88	Rut
William	313	War
William	350	Whi
see Faster		
Foston, Richd.	16	Mon
Fouch, Elijah	18	Smi
William	19	Smi
Fought, William	6	Law
Foulk, Samuel	102	Rut
Foulkes, Gabriel	7	Hic
Foulks, Mary	69	Dav
Founce, Joseph	411	Wil
Foust, Jacob	14	Mon
Foutch, John	418	Wil
Fowler, Benjamin	80	Rut
Benjamin	91	Rut
Enoch	124	Ste
Henry	15	Mon
Holman R.	20	Gil
James	8	Fra
James	8	Mon
John	8	Fra
Joseph	7	Har
Joseph	97	Rut
Mary	73	Dav
Nathl.	124	Ste
Polly	9	Jac
Precilla	61	Dav

Fowler (cont.)		
Rebecca	52	Bed
Robert	8	Fra
Samuel	47	Bed
Sarah	3	Lin
Thomas	97	Rut
William	48	Bed
William	94	Dav
William	67	Mau
William	95	Rut
William	288	War
Fox, Benjamin	9	Jac
Hugh	50	Wll
Jacob	92	Rut
Jacob	298	War
James	46	Bed
James	71	Dav
James	51	Wll
Job	5	Har
John	49	Mau
John	294	War
Joseph	51	Wll
Joshua	362	Whi
Linas	16	Rob
Nathaniel	9	Jac
Peggy	49	Mau
Philip	23	Lin
Samuel	125	Ste
William	49	Mau
Foxhall, Tho.	153	Sum
Foy, James	80	Dav
Fraim, James	34	Lin
William	34	Lin
Fraley, John	153	Sum
Frame, John	8	Fra
Framster, Margaret	8	Fra
Framwell, Shadrach	6	Mon
France, John	9	Jac
William	14	Dic
William	9	Jac
Francis, Henry	13	Ove
James	79	Dav
Joseph	8	Fra
Mays [?]	71	Dav
Nathaniel	8	Fra
Francisco, George	12	Mon
Frank, Charles	344	Whi
Franklin, Agnes	17	Ove
Aron	72	Dav
Benjamin	8	Fra
Elisabeth, Coulard Woman	37	Wll
Elizabeth	348	Whi
Ephraim	9	Har
George	403	Wil
Ice	9	Jac
Isaac	17	Ove
Isham	9	Har
Isham	306	War
James, Jr.	153	Sum
James, Sr.	153	Sum
John	9	Har
John	19	Lin
John	154	Sum
Franklin (cont.)		
John	8	Way
John	353	Whi
John	359	Whi
John A.	46	Mau
Jonathan	35	Lin
Joseph	8	Fra
Laurance	18	Ove
Moses	8	Fra
Owen	9	Jac
Richard	153	Sum
Samuel	8	Fra
Thomas	8	Fra
Thomas	17	Ove
William	34	Lin
Franks, Brereton	21	Gil
Elijah	346	Whi
Henry	344	Whi
Jacob [2]	344	Whi
James	345	Whi
John	19	Smi
John	344	Whi
John	367	Whi
Joseph	355	Whi
Lewis	10	Law
Peter	346	Whi
Robert	12	Law
Thomas	12	Gil
Wesley	21	Gil
Franshire, John	9	Gil
Fraseare, John H.	44	Mau
Fraser, Alexander	354	Whi
Alexander	354	Whi
Thomas	349	Whi
William	359	Whi
Wm.	9	Hic
Frasier, Harman	23	Mon
James	153	Sum
John	11	Mon
Thos.	16	Mon
William	2	Har
William	153	Sum
Frasser, John	39	Wll
Frasure, John	1	Dic
Frazer, James	20	Gil
John	19	Gil
John	46	Mau
Moses B.	69	Dav
Rebeccah	69	Dav
Stephen	27	Wll
Thomas	119	Ste
William	6	Gil
William	122	Sto
Frazier, Aaron	319	War
Charles	8	Fra
Farwick	50	Bed
George	279	War
James	307	War
John	286	War
John [2]	318	War
Joseph	318	War
Levi	318	War
Robert	9	Fra

Frazier (cont.)
Thomas 296 War
Frazzor, James, Dr. 391 Wil
Frealen, John 42 Mau
Frederick see Tedrick
Fredrick, John 9 Jac
Freeland, James 17 Smi
James D. 49 Mau
Mary 33 Bed
Sarah 43 Mau
Tho. 153 Sum
Thomas 48 Mau
Thomas 49 Mau
see Freelard
Freelard, John 48 Mau
Joseph 48 Mau
Freeman, A. R. 77 Dav
Abner 27 Lin
Alexander 50 Bed
Allen 42 Bed
Anderson 84 Rut
Berry 380 Wil
Carney 70 Dav
D. B. 120 Ste
Daniel 95 Rut
Edward 17 Smi
Green 98 Rut
Harris 7 Gil
Henry 15 Rob
Henry 23 Rob
Henry 283 War
Henry 380 Wil
Howell 13 Dic
Isham 22 Hic
James 17 Rob
James 282 War
John 18 Smi
Joseph 33 Bed
Joshua 4 Lin
Lewis 8 Fra
Malone 22 Lin
Matthew 24 Rob
Peter 19 Smi
Reuben 7 Gil
Richard 6 Law
Richard 27 Rob
Robert 94 Rut
Russel 33 Bed
Silas 380 Wil
William 50 Bed
William 8 Fra
William 89 Rut
William 285 War
William R. 13 Dic
see Freman
Freemon, William 345 Whi
Freman, Assa 59 Wll
John 54 Wll
Mary 63 Wll
Saunders 54 Wll
French, Benja. 154 Sum
Daniel 370 Whi
Elizabeth 129 Ste
French (cont.)
Gideon 130 Ste
James 77 Rut
John 21 Mon
Joseph 14 Ove
Marshal 130 Ste
Michael 9 Fra
Nathaniel 9 Fra
Robert 279 War
Saml. 115 Ste
Saml. C. 119 Ste
Samuel 129 Ste
Thomas 9 Ove
Thomas 110 Ste
Fretwell, William 8 Fra
Frey, Bartlett 14 Rob
H. 35 Rob
H. 36 Rob
Henry 1 Rob
Henry 3 Rob
Jacob 6 Rob
John 11 Rob
Joseph 5 Rob
Peter 4 Rob
Peter, Senr. 3 Rob
Friar, Isaac 95 Rut
Friddle, Martin 27 Bed
Mary 45 Bed
Fridy, Elizabeth 76 Rut
Frier, Henry 292 War
Frierson, David 32 Mau
Elizebeth [2] 32 Mau
James M. 32 Mau
John 32 Mau
Mada 32 Mau
Maury J. 35 Mau
Samuel E. 32 Mau
Thomas J. 33 Mau
William 32 Mau
William 70 Mau
Frinsley, William 71 Dav
Frisby, James 348 Whi
Frizzel, Abraham 51 Bed
David 48 Bed
Isaac 36 Bed
Isaac 48 Bed
James 50 Bed
Joseph 48 Bed
Nathen 48 Bed
William 48 Bed
Frogg, Arthur 15 Ove
William 15 Ove
Frost, Ebenezer 23 Mon
Hiram 18 Ove
James 23 Lin
John 8 Fra
John 22 Wll
Robert 32 Lin
William 59 Dav
Wilson 16 Lin
Froupard, William 98 Dav
Frusly, Hansel 381 Wil
Fry, Frederick L. 8 Fra

Fry (cont.)		
John	18	Gil
Michael	19	Gil
Truman	84	Dav
Fryar, Hannah	88	Dav
Fryer, James	125	Ste
John	359	Whi
Fudge, Jacob	85	Dav
James	68	Dav
Fugate, Tournson	89	Rut
Fuget, Moses	17	Bed
Fulgham, Arthur	20	Wll
Fulgum, Anthony	298	War
Edmund	298	War
Elias	306	War
James	20	Lin
John	298	War
Silas	154	Sum
Fulk, John	104	Rut
Fulks, Henry	71	Dav
Fullar, John	65	Wll
Fullcer, Jacob	97	Dav
Fuller, Achimiah [?]	9	Hic
Allen	398	Wil
Elizabeth	23	Lin
Ezekiel	27	Lin
Hosea	42	Wll
Isham	19	Smi
Jesse	19	Smi
John	1	Har
John	154	Sum
John	24	Wll
Polly	37	Bed
Tilman	26	Bed
Fullerton, John	8	Lin
Thomas	8	Lin
Fulliton, Robert	406	Wil
Fulmore, George	36	Bed
Fulton, Daniel	3	Bed
David	136	Sum
G. J.	412	Wil
James	3	Bed
John	101	Rut
Paul	32	Mau
William	6	Rob
Fults, Archibald	18	Smi
Elijah	19	Smi
Fultz, Adam	306	War
Ephraim	307	War
George	307	War
John	289	War
John	307	War
Funderburke, George	16	Gil
Funk, Henry	13	Mon
Funz, J.	24	Mau
Fuqua, Benjamin	9	Jac
F., Doctor	58	Wll
Gabriel	91	Dav
Jesse	96	Dav
Maury	97	Dav
Peter	97	Dav
William	84	Dav
William	9	Jac

Fuqua (cont.)		
William	153	Sum
Fuquay, Aaron	57	Mau
Fuque, James	8	Rob
Furgason, Thomas	76	Rut
Furgerson, Duglas	8	Per
John	153	Sum
Furguson, Edward	154	Sum
John	10	Bed
Lemuel	400	Wil
Mary	36	Bed
Matthew	402	Wil
Polly	154	Sum
Furlong, Hubbard	17	Smi
James	18	Smi
Martin	17	Smi
Furlow, Alexander	51	Mau
Furnatter, Jane	19	Smi
Furner, Ann	70	Mau
Buford	57	Mau
Henry E.	62	Mau
Furrer, Sabina	83	Dav
Fur Sith, John	54	Mau
Fuser, Jess	69	Dav
Fuson, John	18	Smi
Jonathan	19	Smi
Thomas	19	Smi
Fussell, Delilah	13	Dic
Moses	7	Dic
William	16	Dic
Fuston, Elizabeth	413	Wil
Jonathan	413	Wil
Fyke, Nathan	15	Rob
Fykes, Elisha	4	Rob
John	4	Rob
Josiah	8	Rob
Fynch, Daniel	8	Fra
Edward	8	Fra
John	8	Fra
Thomas	8	Fra

--- G ---

Gabbert, David	3	Ove
Gagle, Barna	10	Law
Gadden, Joseph	297	War
Gaddess, William	10	Fra
Gaddis, Isaac	29	Lin
Gaddy, Elijah	412	Wil
Gadess, Susanah	365	Whi
Gafford, Michael	16	Dic
Gage, Aaron	25	Lin
Daniel	371	Whi
Matthew	93	Rut
Samuel	25	Lin
Wm.	22	Hic
Gainer, Rebeckah	11	Hum
Gaines, David	10	Fra
Moses	155	Sum
William	156	Sum
Gains, Benjamin	25	Rob

Gains (cont.)		
Francis	10	Jac
Gideon	387	Wil
Henry	27	Lin
J. V.	10	Jac
John	27	Lin
Polly	10	Jac
Susanna	10	Jac
Thomas	388	Wil
William	83	Dav
Gaither, Martin, Mr.	2	Law
Thomas	16	Lin
Gaiton, Bassil	95	Rut
Edward	97	Rut
Galbrath, John	5	Hum
Galbreth, John J.	5	Hum
Galespie, John	29	Mau
Galladay, Isaac	391	Wil
Gallagley, Sarah	418	Wil
Gallin, John H.	19	Hic
Gallion, Abner	45	Lin
Joshua	45	Lin
Gally, Icim	389	Wil
Galoway, Samuel	83	Dav
Gambell, James	8	Rob
Gambil, Aaron	16	Bed
James	6	Bed
Gambill, Benjn.	34	Bed
James	155	Sum
James H.	8	Way
Jessey	25	Mau
Timothy	13	Way
Gamble, Andrew	348	Whi
Edmond	85	Dav
John	14	Dic
John	40	Mau
John	370	Whi
Martin	10	Jac
Robert	344	Whi
Samuel	13	Gil
Susannah	6	Law
Gambling, James	155	Sum
Gambril, Bradley	99	Rut
John	87	Rut
Susana	82	Rut
Gambrill, Thomas	370	Whi
Gamer, John	12	Dic
Gammel, James	12	Bed
James	28	Bed
William	12	Bed
Gammill, William	15	Dic
Gammon, James	20	Smi
Jeremiah	21	Smi
John	21	Smi
Levi	22	Smi
William	364	Whi
Gan, Thomas	10	Jac
Ganaway, Drucilla	41	Mau
Ganer, James	31	Mon
Jessee	31	Mon
Gann, John	20	Smi
John	345	Whi
Nathan	345	Whi
Gann (cont.)		
William	4	Har
Gannaway, Burrell	91	Rut
James	41	Mau
John	100	Rut
Gannawry, Gregrey	41	Mau
Gans, Lucy	50	Mau
Gant, Elizabeth	16	Hic
Georg H.	63	Mau
George	16	Hic
James	12	Bed
James	34	Lin
Jeremiah	11	Bed
Jesse	17	Bed
Joel	60	Wll
John	10	Bed
John	13	Bed
Lesey	61	Mau
Lewis	17	Bed
Zachariah	10	Lin
Garber, Mathew	315	War
Garden, Jesse	394	Wil
Robert	21	Rob
see Gorden		
Gardener, Saml. G.	53	Bed
Gardenhire, Adam	9	Ove
Jacob	9	Ove
John	12	Ove
Thompson	5	Ove
Gardner, Allen	136	Sum
Cullin	155	Sum
Cully	115	Ste
Demsey	34	Rob
George	15	Mon
George	34	Rob
Henry	18	Rob
Henry	36	Rob
James	31	Rob
Jane	156	Sum
Jesse	34	Rob
Jesse	156	Sum
Joel	50	Wll
John	10	Fra
John	30	Rob
John	131	Ste
John	155	Sum
John	50	Wll
Joshua	9	Rob
Judah	4	Way
Levi	21	Wll
Shadrack	3	Way
Simon	66	Dav
Stephen	67	Dav
Stephen	116	Ste
Thomas	66	Dav
Thomas	48	Wll
William	66	Mau
Garet, Thomas	37	Mau
Gargis, John	25	Mau
Garison, John	41	Mau
Garitt, Ephraim	67	Mau
Garland, Elisha	73	Dav
Elisha	95	Dav

Garland (cont.)		
Jesse	92	Dav
Samuel	23	Lin
Thomas	10	Fra
Garmany, Hugh	417	Wil
Garmon, John	16	Bed
Garner, Adam	17	Ove
Benjamin	299	War
Gree M.	1	Lin
Daniel	9	Fra
Edward	10	Fra
Elisha	291	War
George	10	Jac
Henry	15	Ove
John	4	Law
John	21	Smi
John	411	Wil
Joseph	6	Lin
Nancy	30	Wll
Nathan	95	Dav
Obediah	82	Rut
Obediah	98	Rut
Solomon	18	Way
Thomas	10	Fra
Thomas	83	Rut
Thomas	23	Wll
William	68	Mau
William	80	Rut
Wm.	80	Dav
Garratt, George S.	400	Wil
Garrell, Elijah	22	Smi
Garret, James	49	Mau
Martin	88	Dav
William	22	Mon
Winnefred	61	Dav
Garrett, Caleb	2	Wll
Danl.	22	Hic
Eli	39	Lin
Elisha	3	Lin
Francis	6	Hum
George	12	Gil
Jacob	3	Mon
James	11	Lin
James	43	Lin
James	156	Sum
Jesse	156	Sum
John	155	Sum
John	156	Sum
Levi	5	Hic
Pheby	26	Bed
Polly	39	Bed
Richard	76	Dav
Robt.	156	Sum
Thomas, Jr.	16	Wll
Thomas, Snr.	16	Wll
Timothy	156	Sum
William	394	Wil
Garrison, Azeriah	22	Smi
Catharin	156	Sum
Caty	156	Sum
David	21	Smi
Edmund	22	Smi
Ephraim	21	Smi

Garrison (cont.)		
Isaac	417	Wil
James	10	Bed
Jane	21	Smi
John	8	Law
John	154	Sum
John, Jr.	155	Sum
John F.	403	Wil
Mark	316	War
Mason	12	Gil
Moses	22	Smi
Obadiah	21	Smi
Patsey	22	Smi
Paul	22	Smi
Perkins	404	Wil
Richard	156	Sum
Sally	22	Smi
Samuel	10	Bed
Samuel	21	Smi
William	14	Rob
William	156	Sum
Garrit, Maurice	61	Dav
Garron, James	49	Bed
Garrot, Isaac	19	Mon
Garrott, Abraham	6	Ove
Absalom	12	Ove
David	6	Ove
Elijah	1	Ove
Elisabeth	30	Wll
G. W.	2	Hic
Jacob	10	Ove
Joseph	7	Ove
Joshua	1	Ove
Garsett, John B.	341	Whi
Garton, John	8	Dic
Garven, Archd. D.	2	Lin
John	34	Lin
Gary, Henry	2	Har
Gasset, William	52	Mau
Gassett, John	413	Wil
Gately, Wm.	130	Ste
Gates, James	83	Rut
Jane	413	Wil
Joseph	13	Wll
Joshua	12	Wll
William	22	Smi
Gatewood, Sally	91	Rut
Gatlen, William	40	Wll
Gatlin, Aaron	11	Hic
Edmund	8	Gil
Elener	49	Mau
Ephraim	113	Ste
James	117	Ste
Lazrus	19	Wll
Nathan	62	Dav
Richard	118	Ste
Thomas	3	Per
Gaulding, John	19	Smi
Gault, Hugh C.	8	Lin
James	55	Wll
Thomas	8	Lin
Gausnell, Benjamin	14	Law
Joseph	14	Law

Gawney, John	13	Ove	George (cont.)		
Timothy	5	Ove	William	320	War
Gay, Benjamin	46	Wll	Wm.	78	Dav
Simon	22	Smi	German, Daniel	18	Wll
Zarabable	319	War	Zachariah	14	Wll
Gazers, Simian	37	Mau	Gertin, Joseph	311	War
Gazs, John	10	Jac	Gess, Joseph	291	War
Gealy, Thomas	300	War	Moses	295	War
Gearhart, Volentine	3	Ove	William	291	War
Geay, James	297	War	Geter, John	9	Wll
Gee, David	20	Hic	Gholson, Benjamin	10	Fra
Edmund W.	4	Har	William	41	Mau
James	130	Ste	Ghomley, Michael	41	Lin
James	38	Wll	Ghorkkle, Hannah	29	Mau
John H.	280	War	Ghorkle, Babbart	29	Mau
Thomas	20	Hic	Gibb, John	155	Sum
Thomas	14	Way	Gibbon, Milus	155	Sum
Geer, David	357	Whi	Gibbons, Edmond	19	Ove
Fredrick	361	Whi	Epps	20	Ove
George	127	Ste	Samuel	21	Smi
Moses	11	Gil	Thomas	2	Ove
Gellentin, John	349	Whi	Gibbs, Benjamin	347	Whi
Nicholas	354	Whi	Casen	355	Whi
Gennings, Asaph	416	Wil	Geo. W.	79	Dav
Elijah	416	Wil	Jesse	4	Rob
Jesse	416	Wil	Jesse	292	War
Joel	414	Wil	Jesse	395	Wil
John	416	Wil	John	95	Dav
John	417	Wil	Joshua [2]	20	Smi
Robert [2]	417	Wil	Miles W.	100	Rut
William	414	Wil	Samuel	291	War
William	416	Wil	Shadrach	24	Rob
Gent, Charles	13	Rob	Thomas	112	Ste
Zacheriah	13	Rob	Uriah	347	Whi
Gentry, Charles	2	Ove	William	293	War
Elijah	83	Rut	Gibson, Amos	386	Wil
George	39	Wll	Anna	38	Mau
Jiner	369	Whi	Archibald	407	Wil
Nicholas	58	Wll	Betsey	44	Bed
Thomas	8	Dic	Byrum	7	Bed
Thomas G.	61	Wll	Catherine	40	Wll
William	8	Dic	David [2]	10	Fra
George, Benjamin	35	Lin	David	388	Wil
Daniel	9	Hic	Elijah	52	Wll
David	155	Sum	Faney	156	Sum
Ephrame	350	Whi	George	15	Gil
Henry	412	Wil	George M.	15	Gil
Hizikiah	65	Mau	Gerry	392	Wil
Isaac	155	Sum	Henrey	106	She
James	36	Lin	Henry	70	Mau
James	412	Wil	James	12	Bed
Jesse	46	Lin	James	31	Bed
John	42	Lin	James	53	Bed
Jonathan	61	Mau	James	12	Lin
Leonard	89	Rut	James	26	Lin
Presley	47	Lin	James	17	Way
Reuben	19	Bed	James	7	Wll
Richard	37	Lin	Jeremiah	22	Hic
Solomon	9	Fra	John	33	Bed
Thomas	36	Lin	John	10	Fra
Thomas	32	Rob	John	15	Lin
William	37	Lin	John	24	Lin
William	32	Rob	John	420	Wil

Gibson (cont.)
John B. 10 Wll
John H. 102 Rut
John K. 15 Gil
Joseph 5 Hum
Nancy 392 Wil
Park 7 Lin
Robert 58 Dav
Robert 17 Gil
Robert 79 Rut
Roger 12 Hum
Saml. 156 Sum
Samuel 24 Bed
Thomas 10 Fra
Thomas 12 Lin
Thomas 26 Lin
Trion 39 Lin
William [2] 10 Fra
William 11 Fra
William 9 Hum
William, Jr. 6 Hum
Giddens, Alexander 10 Jac
Asahan 10 Jac
William 11 Gil
Gideon, Francis 34 Wll
Gidion, Reiscilla [Priscilla ?] 46 Wll
Gifferd, William 48 Mau
Giffin, John 3 Dic
William 3 Dic
Gifford, Gideon 21 Smi
Jabus 20 Smi
Joseph 20 Smi
Richard G. 20 Smi
Giger, Sally 11 Rob
Gilbert, Benjamin 8 Dic
Charles 9 Dic
Ebenezar 400 Wil
Jesse 110 Ste
John 10 Gil
John 25 Mau
John 32 Rob
John 155 Sum
Joshua 2 Wll
Mabel 2 Dic
Peter 11 Dic
Ussery 111 Ste
Webster 32 Rob
Wilson 1 Dic
Gilbeys, George 302 War
Gilbirt, Jerimiah 31 Mau
Gilbirth, Hughey 29 Mau
John 36 Mau
John 39 Mau
John 52 Mau
John 60 Mau
Gilbreath, Baston 391 Wil
John 70 Dav
Robert 155 Sum
William 11 Jac
Gilbrith, Andrew 155 Sum
Gilchrist, Daniel 37 Bed
Duncan 25 Mau
John 25 Mau
Gilchrist (cont.)
Malcom 25 Mau
Giles, Eli 154 Sum
Hannah 156 Sum
John 296 War
Josiah E. 155 Sum
Milton 155 Sum
William 40 Wll
Gilfoy, Peter 23 Lin
Gill, Daniel 48 Wll
David 20 Lin
David W. 20 Lin
Elizabeth 22 Smi
Gardean 43 Mau
George 16 Way
James 68 Mau
James 21 Smi
James 14 Way
Jesse 21 Smi
John 33 Mau
John 66 Mau
John 20 Smi
Joseph 41 Mau
Nancy 4 Hic
Richerdson 52 Mau
Terrah 10 Jac
Thomas 41 Mau
Thomas 20 Smi
William 409 Wil
Gillam, Chs. 155 Sum
James 155 Sum
John 155 Sum
John M. 27 Mau
Jawel 50 Mau
Gillaspie, Alexander 15 Lin
Francis 87 Rut
George [& Barr] 6 Wll
John 28 Lin
John 85 Rut
John 8 Wll
Samuel 80 Rut
Thomas 14 Bed
Thomas 50 Mau
William 14 Bed
Gillehan, Thomas 10 Jac
Gilleland, Allen 1 Ove
James 97 Rut
Gillespie, Alexander 43 Mau
George 79 Rut
James 87 Rut
James 156 Sum
John 156 Sum
Mary 156 Sum
Gillcy, Edward 313 War
James M. 25 Mau
Peter 313 War
Gilliam, Anthony 9 Fra
Charles 10 Fra
Charles 418 Wil
Gray 20 Smi
John 10 Fra
John 15 Gil
John, Sen. 10 Fra

Gilliam (cont.)		
Nathaniel	63	Dav
Thomas	60	Dav
Thomas	10	Fra
Thomas	54	Mau
William	49	Mau
William	53	Mau
William	74	Rut
William	21	Smi
Gillis, Alexander	10	Fra
George	308	War
Gillispie, David	44	Wll
George	9	Fra
Isaac	44	Wll
Jacob	155	Sum
Patrick	22	Lin
Thomas	44	Wll
Gillmore, John	27	Lin
Gillum, Anthony	16	Wll
Ezekiel	14	Lin
Jacob	15	Lin
John	26	Lin
Mayvan	40	Bed
Gilmer, Joseph	39	Mau
Joseph	40	Mau
Gilmon, Abner	156	Sum
Gilmore, David	17	Mon
Henry	37	Bed
Huriah	292	War
Jane	156	Sum
Mathew	2	Dic
Samuel	25	Bed
William	51	Bed
William	10	Fra
William	89	Rut
Gilpan, Richard	307	War
Gilpatrick, George	19	Ove
Gilpin, Enoch	10	Ove
Giltiland, Poethiar	50	Mau
Gines, Joseph	34	Mau
Noah	34	Mau
William	34	Mau
Ginger, Henry	38	Mau
Gingerey, Henry	92	Dav
Ginings, George W.	62	Mau
William	62	Mau
Ginkins, Ann	68	Mau
John	56	Mau
Philip	55	Mau
Walter S.	61	Mau
William	61	Mau
William H.	53	Mau
Ginn, Jesse	9	Fra
Ginnings, Clem	382	Wil
James	387	Wil
John	382	Wil
Richard	31	Mau
Samuel	31	Mau
see Gennings, Ginings		
Gion, Good	34	Mau
Gipson, James	81	Rut
James	97	Rut
John	17	Mon
Gipson (cont.)		
John	79	Rut
Samuel	84	Rut
Samuel	102	Rut
Sarah	16	Mon
William	9	Jac
William	28	Mon
William	92	Rut
William R.	16	Mon
Gist, Joseph	1	Law
Joshua	6	Law
Margaret, Mrs.	6	Law
Givans, William	15	Lin
Given, Ransom	304	War
Givens, David	22	Smi
Ephram	11	Wll
James	10	Fra
John	22	Smi
Nancy	21	Smi
William	21	Smi
Givers, William	102	Rut
Givin, Peter	5	Mon
Givins, Robert	11	Jac
Stephen	101	Rut
Givvers, Miles	101	Rut
Givvin, William	85	Dav
Glanton, John	383	Wil
Glascow, Robert	13	Gil
Glasgow, Cornelius	156	Sum
James	20	Smi
Sarah	25	Mau
Glass, Alexander	33	Mau
Daniel	5	Per
David	33	Mau
Elisabeth	30	Mau
Elisha	10	Way
Elizabeth	415	Wil
Josiah	6	Per
Samuel F.	8	Wll
Thomas M.	36	Mau
William	30	Mau
Glasscock, George [& Doolin]	8	Wll
John	50	Mau
Moses H.	101	Rut
Glassgow, Jessey	70	Dav
Glaze, John	95	Rut
Lewis	11	Gil
Glazier, Marnock	21	Lin
Gleason, Edward	367	Whi
Gleave, William	380	Wil
Gleaves, Absolam	57	Dav
John	385	Wil
Martha	69	Dav
Rachael	69	Dav
Thomas	59	Dav
Thomas, Jr.	63	Dav
Gleen, William	156	Sum
Glen, David	35	Lin
James	50	Bed
Jiles	401	Wil
Glenn, Abram	12	Wll
Alexander	10	Fra
Alexander	342	Whi

Glenn (cont.)
Betsey 10 Fra
David 346 Whi
Elizabeth 346 Whi
Isaac 346 Whi
James 35 Lin
Jessee 342 Whi
John L. 347 Whi
Joseph 348 Whi
Mary 21 Gil
Robert 346 Whi
Robert 348 Whi
Robert B. 346 Whi
Robert W. 342 Whi
Samuel G. 348 Whi
Simon 75 Dav
Thomas 10 Jac
William 348 Whi
William 350 Whi
William 362 Whi
William 45 Wll
Glesson, Betey 21 Rob
Easther 21 Rob
Glidewell, Burel 36 Lin
Mark 344 Whi
Robert 35 Lin
Glimph, George 13 Wll
Glins, Thompson 400 Wil
Glov, John 130 Ste
Glove see Glov
Glover, Daniel 20 Smi
Darnel 11 Jac
Edward 20 Smi
Elizabeth 20 Smi
George 10 Fra
Herralson 9 Jac
Jobe 9 Jac
Lancaster 26 Bed
Nathan 10 Jac
Phinehas T. 43 Mau
Polly 22 Smi
Ransom 8 Gil
Richard 20 Smi
William 134 Sum
William 156 Sum
William 8 Wll
Gnage, Matthew 98 Dav
Goacher, Henry 10 Fra
Thomas 10 Fra
Goad, Neill 62 Mau
Peter 62 Mau
Robbert [2] 60 Mau
Ruben 62 Mau
William 10 Ove
Goar, James 10 Fra
Notley 10 Fra
Goard, Aggy 350 Whi
James 354 Whi
John 360 Whi
Joshua 22 Smi
Peggy 21 Smi
Rachel 344 Whi
Reuben 22 Smi
Goard (cont.)
William 14 Ove
William 357 Whi
Goare, Henry 5 Ove
Isaac 9 Ove
Goash, William 34 Rob
Goates, George 14 Gil
Gobble, John 21 Smi
Gocey see Govy
Godard, Moses 358 Whi
Godby, Gabriel 15 Ove
Godd see Goad
Godfrey, James, Jr. 416 Wil
James, Ser. 416 Wil
Godson, Charles 395 Wil
Godwin, George 48 Wll
Jacob 25 Lin
Samuel 37 Mau
Goen, Reuben 21 Rob
Thornton 344 Whi
Goff, Andrew 18 Wll
Asa 118 Ste
Elisha 348 Whi
Felix 19 Gil
Isaac 18 Wll
John 18 Gil
Margaret 18 Wll
Thomas 19 Gil
William 6 Wll
Goforth, Absolom 23 Lin
Andy H. 54 Mau
George 22 Lin
Hiram 54 Mau
Jane 54 Mau
Margaret 366 Whi
Zachariah 4 Lin
Goggin, William 21 Smi
Goin, Federick 186 Sum
Goings, Nathan 409 Wil
Gold, Josiah 402 Wil
Thomas 14 Lin
Zachariah 7 Lin
Golden, Nancy 129 Ste
Goldin, Thomas 94 Rut
Golding, Benjamin 3 Per
Foster 10 Fra
James 21 Hic
Richard 9 Fra
Saml. 20 Hic
William 42 Lin
Goldman, Peggy 155 Sum
Goldsberry, James 22 Gil
Goldsby, Wade 368 Whi
Goldson, Eli 395 Wil
Golesby, John 13 Ove
Golightly, Henry 20 Gil
Shans 19 Gil
Goliksly, Jos. 5 Hic
Gollerthan, John 22 Bed
Martin 22 Bed
William 22 Bed
Gollespea, John 27 Mau
Gollion, Barbary 10 Jac

Golston, John 390 Wil
Gomly, James 155 Sum
John 154 Sum
Margaret 136 Sum
Mary 156 Sum
Gooch, David 81 Rut
David 23 Wll
Nathaniel 81 Rut
Good, Eleanor 5 Ove
Henry 102 Rut
Hugh 88 Rut
Hugh 103 Rut
James 6 Mon
William [2] 31 Mon
Goodall, Charles 20 Smi
David 20 Smi
John 20 Smi
John T. 408 Wil
Jonathan D. 154 Sum
Lucy 20 Smi
Parkes 408 Wil
Parks 406 Wil
William 20 Smi
William 408 Wil
Zachariah 156 Sum
Goodbar, Joseph 20 Ove
Goode, Chales 13 Wll
Joseph 9 Gil
Goodel, Adam 75 Dav
Goodell, A. G. 75 Dav
Jesse 10 Fra
Martha 95 Rut
Goodin, Jesse 4 Har
Joshua 10 Fra
Goodlet, Alexander 11 Fra
Robert 57 Dav
William C. [?] 11 Fra
Goodloe, John 87 Rut
Goodlow, George 390 Wil
Henry 85 Rut
Robert 89 Rut
Goodman, Abreham 39 Mau
Alexander 36 Mau
Boswell 415 Wil
Charles 369 Whi
Clabourn 393 Wil
Edward 415 Wil
Elizebith 33 Mau
Fleming 39 Mau
Henry 6 Per
Henry 358 Whi
Jessey 36 Mau
John 10 Fra
John 11 Jac
John 36 Mau
John 39 Mau
John 45 Wll
Joseph C. 36 Mau
Solomon 10 Fra
Tobias 28 Lin
William 10 Fra
William [3] 36 Mau
William 101 Rut
Goodmon, Robin 395 Wil
Goodner, James 11 Fra
James 22 Smi
John 22 Smi
Goodnight, Henry 14 Gil
John 14 Gil
Goodon, James 300 War
Goodpaster, Arthur 13 Ove
John 18 Ove
Goodram, John 155 Sum
Goodrich, Caleb 67 Dav
Edmund 74 Dav
Henry 11 Dic
James 5 Dic
Rhody 96 Dav
Thomas 38 Mau
Wm. 97 Dav
Goodrick, John 91 Rut
Goodrum, Allen 24 Wll
Daniel 61 Mau
Jane 27 Wll
John 22 Gil
Thomas 41 Mau
Goodsie, James 1 Har
Goodwin, Alexander 72 Dav
Crawford 11 Hic
George 83 Dav
Jesse 120 Ste
Jesse, Junr. 121 Ste
John L. 90 Dav
Joseph 41 Mau
Josiah 11 Hic
Michael 5 Lin
Mills 11 Hic
Peter 16 Dic
Sally 61 Dav
William 77 Dav
Gooldin, Enoch 342 Whi
Goolsly, James 10 Jac
Goore, Elizabeth 8 Ove
Joseph 5 Ove
Goostree, James W. 154 Sum
Watson 154 Sum
Gopage, Edward 155 Sum
Goplin, William 57 Mau
Gordan, William 31 Mau
Gorden, Alexander 33 Rob
John 95 Dav
William S. 95 Dav
Gorder, Richard 10 Jac
William 10 Jac
Gordin, John 11 Hic
Gordon, Alexr. D. 155 Sum
Charles 39 Wll
David 91 Rut
Dolly 19 Hic
Francis 66 Mau
James 30 Mau
Jenney 84 Dav
John 85 Dav
John 5 Gil
John [2] 30 Mau
John 55 Mau
John 69 Mau
John 21 Smi

Gordon (cont.)		
John L.	17	Hic
Josiah	30	Mau
Nicholas	75	Dav
Richmond	54	Mau
Robert	5	Gil
Robert	286	War
Samuel	48	Mau
Thomas K.	18	Gil
Gore, Edward	33	Lin
Mounce	10	Jac
Thomas	20	Hic
Thomas	11	Way
Thos., Jr.	12	Way
Gorham, Thomas	17	Rob
William B.	36	Rob
Gosham, William	7	Rob
Goss, Gideon	32	Mon
John	307	War
Gossage, Daniel	293	War
Jeremiah	156	Sum
Gosset, Elijah	14	Rob
Elisha	37	Wll
John	4	Mon
John	31	Rob
Leroy	15	Rob
Patience	15	Hic
Gossett, Abraham	8	Mon
Abraham	413	Wil
Dandee	57	Mau
Elisha	13	Mon
John	57	Mau
John	413	Wil
William	89	Rut
Got, Joshua	9	Jac
Gothard, Allen	10	Fra
Gouch, Elizabeth	6	Gil
Gouge, John	411	Wil
Thomas	354	Whi
William	12	Law
Gough, Moses F.	154	Sum
William	155	Sum
Gould, Joseph	76	Dav
Goulden, Elizabeth	19	Rob
Gouding see Gaulding		
Gourly see Gomly		
Goven, Gladen	123	Ste
Govers, Abel	315	War
Govy, James	6	Wll
James	65	Wll
Gowdy, John	154	Sum
see Gomly		
Gowen, James B.	33	Lin
John	97	Dav
Joseph	94	Rut
William	90	Rut
William B.	22	Smi
William H.	35	Wll
Gower, Agnus	95	Dav
Eadith	92	Dav
Elisha	91	Dav
Patsey	92	Dav
Russel	92	Dav
Gower (cont.)		
Samuel M.	17	Dic
Gowforth, Cornelious	8	Law
Gowgil, John	74	Dav
Goyne, James	4	Mon
Grace, David	119	Ste
George	365	Whi
James	10	Jac
James	127	Ste
John	106	She
Lelia	365	Whi
Levin	2	Ove
Solomon [2]	17	Mon
Thomas	8	Ove
Thomas	365	Whi
Walker	11	Jac
Zachariah	10	Jac
Gracy, John	32	Wll
Joseph	5	Lin
Newel	19	Hic
William	348	Whi
Grady, John	74	Dav
William	155	Sum
Gragory, John	16	Hic
Graham, Alexr.	154	Sum
Andrew	75	Dav
Andrew	11	Dic
David	7	Har
George	69	Dav
George	317	War
James	10	Bed
James	47	Bed
James	15	Gil
James	7	Har
James	24	Rob
James	155	Sum
James, Mr.	1	Law
Jane	354	Whi
John	3	Bed
John	10	Fra
John	10	Jac
John	6	Ove
John	124	Ste
John	289	War
John	354	Whi
John	5	Wll
John	53	Wll
Joseph	292	War
Lambeth D.	21	Smi
Richard	10	Bed
Richard	8	Wll
Robert	36	Wll
Samuel	6	Har
William	88	Rut
William	315	War
William	320	War
William	354	Whi
William	44	Wll
Wm. P.	80	Dav
Grainger, Benj.	154	Sum
James	156	Sum
Nathan	156	Sum
Tho.	155	Sum

Graives, Nathaniel	70	Mau
Graivs, Thomas	50	Mau
Gramer, Peterson	3	Bed
Granger, William	156	Sum
Grant, Alexander	303	War
Burwell	16	Mon
Charles	15	Mon
David	112	Ste
Duskin	8	Mon
Elizabeth	11	Fra
Ire	10	Jac
Ire	11	Jac
Isaac	112	Ste
James	30	Lin
James	16	Mon
John	10	Jac
John	26	Rob
Joshua	32	Mon
Samuel	16	Mon
Spencer	3	Per
Thomas	44	Mau
Thomas	61	Mau
Ursula	40	Lin
William	10	Jac
William	20	Smi
Wilson	20	Smi
Zechariah	4	Mon
Grantham, Elizebeth	53	Mau
James	359	Whi
Grason, Benjamin	10	Fra
Grass, Adam	9	Fra
Gratcher, Thomas	381	Wil
Grave, Prestgear [?]	46	Mau
Graves, Allen	154	Sum
Anne	21	Gil
Bartlet	377	Wil
Bartlet	407	Wil
Beman	10	Jac
Charles	10	Jac
David	18	Gil
David	19	Rob
Eady	154	Sum
Elizabeth	10	Fra
Esom	9	Jac
Henry	96	Dav
Isaac	19	Rob
Jacob	9	Fra
James	7	Gil
John	72	Dav
John	6	Gil
John [2]	8	Gil
John J.	376	Wil
John O.	9	Gil
John R.	9	Fra
Ralph	4	Gil
Reuben	10	Jac
Rice	11	Jac
Samuel	13	Bed
Sterling	5	Gil
Thomas	12	Dic
Thomas	10	Gil
William	3	Gil
William B.	154	Sum
Graves (cont.)		
William B.	10	Gil
see Graivs, Groves		
Gray, Alexander	7	Hic
Alexr.	3	Lin
Archibald	53	Wll
Auston	47	Bed
Benajah	66	Dav
Colby	36	Lin
Curtis	24	Mon
Daniel	93	Dav
David	8	Dic
David, Senr.	115	Ste
Delila	14	Dic
Ezekiel	8	Hic
Frederick	20	Smi
George	88	Dav
George	11	Fra
George	25	Wll
George H.	21	Smi
Henry	24	Wll
Jacob	29	Mau
Jacob	4	Wll
James	63	Mau
James	65	Mau
James	3	Mon
James	7	Ove
James	115	Ste
James	25	Wll
James	65	Wll
Jeremiah	317	War
John	28	Bed
John	8	Hic
John	36	Lin
John	9	Wll
Joseph	47	Bed
Joseph	68	Mau
Joseph	112	Ste
Martin	13	Lin
Mary	3	Lin
Moses	3	Hum
Permelia	9	Law
Polley	15	Dic
Price	6	Wll
Robert	9	Law
Robert	21	Wll
Saml.	31	Bed
Samuel	88	Rut
Samuel	97	Rut
Samuel	101	Rut
Simon	110	Ste
Sophia	8	Hic
Thomas	9	Dic
Thomas	119	Ste
Thomas	19	Way
William	3	Hum
William	30	Mau
William	101	Rut
Grayar, James M.	154	Sum
Grayham, Richard	67	Mau
William	8	Mon
Gready, John	301	War
Greaves, Lewis	395	Wil

Greegs, Henry	28	Wll
Green, Abner	9	Jac
Abraham	380	Wil
Anderson	15	Rob
Ansell	50	Mau
Aquilla	380	Wil
Arthur	369	Whi
Asa	58	Dav
Asa	7	Rob
Betey	34	Rob
Bethel	315	War
Charity	9	Har
Charles	87	Dav
Daniel J.	61	Wll
David	2	Bed
David	22	Bed
David	310	War
Edmond	37	Bed
Eleanor	14	Hic
Elijah	11	Fra
Elijah	155	Sum
Elisha	6	Bed
Ellephen	19	Bed
Frances	5	Mon
George	36	Mau
Gidion	19	Bed
Green B.	88	Rut
Henry	10	Fra
Hiram	9	Har
Isaac	22	Smi
Isaiha	59	Dav
James	10	Fra
James	24	Rob
James	91	Rut
James	154	Sum
James Y.	29	Mau
Jesse	5	Rob
Jesse	301	War
Joel H.	154	Sum
John	10	Hum
John	4	Law
John	96	Rut
John	125	Ste
John	355	Whi
John	13	Wll
Joseph	48	Bed
Joseph	302	War
Joshua	283	War
Lewis	2	Hic
Lewis	154	Sum
Lewis	23	Wll
Little B.	47	Bed
Martha	10	Fra
Mary	23	Lin
Micheal	45	Bed
Nancy	78	Dav
Nancy	92	Dav
Nancy	42	Lin
Nathan	10	Fra
Needham	156	Sum
Nicholas	75	Rut
Nicholas	88	Rut
Noles	80	Dav
Green (cont.)		
Philmer	22	Gil
Reuben	20	Hic
Robert	6	Rob
Robert S.	1	Mon
Robert W.	75	Dav
Saml. K.	79	Dav
Samuel	78	Rut
Samuel	83	Rut
Samuel	294	War
Samuel	371	Whi
Samuel	384	Wil
Samuel F.	71	Dav
Sherwood	23	Wll
Stephen	13	Law
Thomas	10	Fra
Thomas	396	Wil
Thos.	1	Hic
Wesley	369	Whi
William	11	Jac
William	4	Ove
William	13	Ove
William	85	Rut
William	88	Rut
William	118	Ste
William	127	Ste
William, Jr.	381	Wil
William, Sen.	381	Wil
William D.	288	War
Zach.	154	Sum
Greene, Richard	92	Rut
Greenfield, Gerrard T.	70	Mau
Greenham, Green B.	156	Sum
Greenlee, James	10	Fra
Lewis	10	Fra
Greenwood, George	19	Mon
Yancy	156	Sum
Greer, Alexander	28	Lin
Andrew	10	Jac
Andrew	124	Ste
Aquilla	381	Wil
Asaph	382	Wil
Benj.	73	Dav
Benjamin	18	Hic
Benjamin, Sr.	19	Hic
David	366	Whi
Elijah	382	Wil
George	94	Dav
George	5	Ove
Greenbury	63	Dav
Isaac	73	Dav
Isaac	119	Ste
Jacob	44	Bed
James	12	Lin
James	5	Ove
James	26	Rob
James	417	Wil
James	19	Wll
Jane	13	Bed
John	47	Lin
John	103	Rut
John	20	Smi
John	417	Wil

Greer (cont.)
Joseph 93 Dav
Joseph 23 Lin
Joseph A. 12 Bed
Martin 73 Dav
Moses 94 Dav
Robert 42 Bed
Robert 19 Ove
Sarah 20 Smi
Thomas 13 Bed
Vance 1 Lin
Vincent 16 Wll
Walter 19 Ove
William 93 Dav
William 10 Ove
William 19 Ove
William 380 Wil
Gregard, Jeramiah 97 Dav
Gregory, Abraham 27 Rob
Alexander 99 Rut
Ambrose 22 Smi
Bedford 154 Sum
Boswell 136 Sum
Bry 21 Smi
Byrd 9 Gil
Edward 91 Rut
George 21 Smi
George 155 Sum
Harbard 21 Smi
Henry 21 Smi
Hosea 20 Smi
Humbleton 155 Sum
Isaac 155 Sum
Jacob 155 Sum
Jeremiah 20 Smi
John 76 Rut
John [2] 155 Sum
John 377 Wil
John 409 Wil
Joseph 12 Bed
Labourn 20 Smi
Major 21 Rob
Major 21 Smi
Mary 156 Sum
Mary 379 Wil
Obadiah 10 Jac
Pitts 20 Smi
Rhoena 10 Har
Roper 156 Sum
Stephen 21 Smi
Tapley 20 Smi
Thomas 20 Smi
Thomas 377 Wil
Tulley 62 Wll
Tunstall 37 Lin
William, Jun. 21 Smi
William, Sen. 21 Smi
Grenshaw, Daniel 7 Wll
Sarah 15 Wll
Gresham, Asa 11 Dic
George 2 Law
George 33 Mau
Solomon 2 Law
Grey, Clifford 37 Lin
Grey (cont.)
James 384 Wil
John 379 Wil
Samuel 379 Wil
William 10 Jac
William 379 Wil
see Gray
Gribble, Thomas 299 War
Gribs, Hickerson 402 Wil
Grice, John 287 War
Solomon 128 Ste
Grier, Jesse 300 War
Griffeth, ... 291 War
George 342 Whi
John 299 War
Joseph 299 War
see Cathey
Griffey, Hanah 36 Mau
Griffin, — 24 Mau
Andrew 86 Rut
Andrew 131 Ste
Arthur 114 Ste
Bird 6 Per
Elias 21 Smi
Elizabeth 2 Rob
George 64 Dav
Ira 17 Rob
James 419 Wil
Jemima 10 Fra
Jesse [written over] 10 Jac
John 10 Fra
John 47 Mau
John 93 Rut
John 21 Smi
Joseph 113 Ste
Lewis 410 Wil
Lott 28 Mau
Margaret 20 Rob
Martin 99 Rut
Martin 101 Rut
Matthew 21 Smi
Owel 6 Per
Owen 34 Mau
Polly 21 Hic
Richard 17 Rob
Saul 8 Hic
Seth 8 Hic
Sion 380 Wil
Solomon 22 Gil
Stephen 10 Jac
Thomas 407 Wil
Thomas [written over Jesse] 10 Jac
Wiley 61 Mau
William 69 Mau
Griffis, Ann 18 Lin
Harbert 3 Lin
James 21 Gil
John 17 Lin
Thomas, Junr. 21 Gil
Thomas, Senr. 21 Gil
William 40 Lin
Wm. 124 Ste
Griffith, David 10 Jac
Hiram 120 Ste

Griffith (cont.)
Jacob 367 Whi
Jonas [2] 10 Jac
Jonathan 22 Smi
Nathanl 7 Har
Polly 10 Jac
Robert 348 Whi
Samuel 10 Jac
Samuel 28 Mau
Griffiths, John 20 Hic
Griffy, Bennett 32 Lin
Jonas 21 Smi
Grifin, Elizabeth 156 Sum
Humphrey 156 Sum
Grifun, James 27 Mau
Grig, Right 37 Mau
Grigg, Peter 20 Smi
Richard 410 Wil
Samuel 42 Mau
Shadrick 410 Wil
Griggs, Daniel 22 Way
John 22 Gil
John 19 Way
John 353 Whi
John 13 Wll
Nicholas 22 Gil
Robert 5 Gil
Grigory, John 49 Bed
Thomas 23 Bed
Grigsby, Aaron 18 Gil
Amos 17 Gil
Samuel 17 Gil
William 6 Hum
Grills, William J. 9 Fra
Grim, Abram 155 Sum
Isaac 155 Sum
Grimes, Adam 24 Rob
Alexander 35 Mau
George 121 Ste
Henry 4 Dic
Henry 35 Mau
Henry 8 Way
Isaac G. 16 Way
Jacob 13 Rob
Jacob, Senr. 13 Rob
James 11 Gil
James 33 Mau
James 34 Mau
James 19 Wll
John 7 Dic
John 31 Mau
John 35 Mau
John 67 Mau
John 87 Rut
John 15 Wll
John H. 35 Mau
Loid 36 Mau
Luke 11 Law
Mark 36 Mau
Samuel 36 Mau
William 31 Mau
William 34 Mau
William 35 Mau
Grimmer, Jacob 12 Wll
Grimmet, Benjamin 8 Dic
William 9 Dic
Grimsly, Fielden 155 Sum
Grinage, Edmund 87 Rut
Edmund 101 Rut
Grindel, Benjamin 13 Hic
Grinder, J. 24 Mau
John 22 Way
Joshueay 31 Mau
Robert 22 Way
Robt. 4 Hic
Grinnad, Nancy 22 Smi
Silas 22 Smi
William F. 22 Smi
Grisard, Henry 5 Rob
Grisham, Benjamin 409 Wil
Davis 20 Smi
Harris 20 Smi
James 409 Wil
John 17 Gil
John 22 Smi
Moses 5 Gil
Moses 409 Wil
Peter 21 Smi
Philip 408 Wil
Sally 22 Smi
Thomas 409 Wil
William 20 Smi
Grissard, Hardy 30 Rob
Grissum, Ezekiel 19 Ove
John 17 Ove
Grisum, Benj. 154 Sum
Grizzard, James 81 Dav
William 69 Dav
Grizzarel, Joel 7 Mon
Grizzle, Daniel 311 War
George 285 War
George 311 War
Harod 319 War
Groggen, James 22 Smi
Groom, Molly 10 Fra
Nelly 7 Ove
Conrod 10 Fra
Jacob 25 Lin
John 285 War
Jonathan 9 Lin
Martin 282 War
William 25 Lin
Grove, John 283 War
Grovens, John 156 Sum
Grover, Robert 28 Rob
Groves, Abraham 10 Fra
Abram 17 Hic
Frederick 155 Sum
George 32 Mon
Jacob 155 Sum
John G. [2] 114 Wil
Tho. 155 Sum
Grubbs, Hickerson 9 Gil
John 11 Gil
Thomas 7 Gil
William 63 Dav

Grundey, William 6 Ove
Grundy, Felix 79 Dav
Gubet see Gulet
Guess, Benjamin [2] 10 Jac
Hannah 10 Jac
John 367 Whi
Thomas 357 Whi
Thomas 362 Whi
William 355 Whi
William 360 Whi
Guest, Christopher 22 Smi
Joseph 20 Smi
Joshua 57 Mau
William 11 Hic
Guffey, Ephrame 370 Whi
Thomas 359 Whi
Guibbs, George 106 She
Guider, John 28 Lin
Guin, Christopher 31 Rob
Daniel 28 Rob
Edman 38 Mau
Ruttey 38 Mau
Guinn, Edward 120 Ste
James 40 Bed
John 17 Ove
John [Job?] 4 Hic
Stephen 128 Ste
William 1 Per
William 128 Ste
William 314 War
Gulet, James 49 Mau
Gulladge, William 93 Dav
Gullage, William 9 Rob
Gulledge, William 12 Hic
Gulleford, James 70 Dav
Gullet, George 47 Mau
Solomon 2 Lin
Gulley, William 17 Lin
Gullick, John 21 Smi
Reace 44 Lin
Gully, John 11 Jac
Louis 11 Jac
Thomas 9 Jac
Gulney, William C. 397 Wil
Gum, John 418 Wil
John 418 Wil
Sarah 418 Wil
Gumm, William 73 Rut
Gun, Lawson 9 Hic
Gundstaff, Isaac 411 Wil
Gunn, Alexander 2 Rob
Charles 14 Dic
Daniel 30 Rob
Elisha 14 Dic
Elisha 392 Wil
Graves 2 Rob
James 11 Dic
James 22 Rob
John 15 Dic
John 11 Fra
Joseph 30 Rob
Niles 30 Rob
Samuel 98 Rut
Gunn (cont.)
Sterling 30 Rob
Thomas 31 Rob
William 15 Dic
Gunnells, Joshep 18 Ove
Nicholas 18 Ove
Gunner, Sampson 11 Fra
Guns, J. 24 Mau
Gunson, William 122 Ste
Gunter, Archibald 64 Mau
Charles 54 Wll
Claybourn [2] 313 War
Francis 3 Wll
Hiram 8 Lin
James 21 Smi
Joel 297 War
John 21 Smi
John 282 War
John P. 18 Mon
Joshua 8 Lin
Sterling [& Dunhan] 8 Wll
Walter 302 War
William 8 Lin
Gupton, Abner 13 Mon
Gurdin, John 12 Gil
Gurley, Jesse 3 Bed
Guster, James 11 Fra
Guthery, James C. 32 Lin
John 32 Lin
Guthrey, George 17 Ove
James 392 Wil
Guthrie, David H. 4 Wll
Dudley 10 Fra
Francis 18 Gil
James 11 Fra
James 154 Sum
Robert 18 Gil
Robert 154 Sum
Robert 5 Wll
Westley 156 Sum
William F. 9 Wll
Guthry, Henry 67 Dav
Gutney see Gulney, Guthrey
Gutrey, William 42 Bed
Guwin, Pierce 94 Dav
Guy, John 57 Wll
William 41 Bed
Guyger, Charles 73 Rut
Guyman, Thomas 11 Jac
Gwaltney, Elias 22 Smi
John 22 Smi
Gwin, Alexander 9 Hum
Edwd., Jr. 154 Sum
Ezekiel 155 Sum
James 154 Sum
James, Jr. 154 Sum
John 154 Sum
Joseph 155 Sum
Sally 38 Lin
William 154 Sum
see Given
Gwinn, Champion 41 Lin
Daniel 10 Fra

Gwinn (cont.)		
Daniel	38	Lin
Elias	10	Fra
Isham	41	Lin
Nicholas	20	Hic
William	41	Lin
Gwyn, Ransom	376	Wil
Gwynn, David	62	Dav
Gwynne, Hugh	394	Wil
--- H ---		
Haben, Joshua	309	War
Hableton, David	49	Mau
Habner, Peter	13	Fra
Hackett, John	283	War
Hacking, Benjamin	392	Wil
Hackleman, George	13	Fra
Hackler, George	5	Ove
Jacob	12	Ove
Hackney, Jack M.	15	Gil
Jemimah	69	Dav
Josep	25	Mau
Lott, Mr.	8	Law
Seth	26	Mau
William	69	Dav
Hacomb, H. H.	116	Ste
Hadaway, William W.	60	Dav
Hadden, William B.	1	Dic
Haddor, David	81	Rut
Haden, Jesse	11	Fra
Joseph	26	Smi
Hadley, Ambrous	62	Mau
John	37	Wll
Joshua	157	Sum
Wm.	136	Sum
Hadly, Mark	6	Har
Sherod	6	Har
Hagan, David	111	Ste
Edmond	111	Ste
George	386	Wil
James	125	Ste
John	109	Ste
Micajah	126	Ste
Hagen, Henry	17	Gil
Hager, Jonathan	59	Dav
Steel	414	Wil
Hagerty, Partrick	406	Wil
Hagg, Susanna	158	Sum
Haggard, Alfred	13	Fra
Alfred L.	13	Fra
Edman	48	Mau
James	27	Bed
James	13	Fra
Nathan	341	Whi
Saml.	25	Bed
Saml.	4	Mon
Samuel	36	Bed
William	27	Bed
Wm. H.	110	Ste
Hagler, E. W.	120	Ste
Hagler (cont.)		
John L.	112	Ste
Hagner, James	12	Fra
Hagney, Samuel	11	Bed
Hague, Hiram	99	Rut
James	47	Lin
John	60	Wll
Hagy, Henry	18	Bed
Henry	29	Bed
Hail, George	95	Dav
James E., Mr.	10	Law
John A.	2	Law
Lewis	54	Mau
Linton	98	Dav
Micheck	95	Dav
Powel	54	Mau
Stephen	87	Rut
Stephen	42	Wll
William	95	Dav
Hailes, Jemimah	75	Dav
Hailey, Abraham	341	Whi
Edward	57	Dav
Edward	17	Mon
James	67	Dav
James	72	Dav
John	348	Whi
John	350	Whi
John	40	Wll
Overton	49	Wll
Thomas	60	Mau
Wiatt	38	Wll
Hailly, Tabner	26	Bed
Haily, Barnabas	14	Bed
Robert	82	Rut
Robert	100	Rut
Haims, David T.	96	Dav
Haine, John	85	Rut
Haines, John	100	Rut
Hains, Alexander L.	39	Mau
Hugh	95	Dav
John	38	Mau
John S.	48	Mau
Joseph	48	Mau
Sarah	44	Mau
Haipole, Squire	301	War
Hairgrove, Etheldred	15	Mon
Hairston, Robert	21	Lin
Haisting, Henry	26	Bed
Robert	27	Bed
Haistings, Henry	45	Bed
Joseph	44	Bed
Susannah	45	Bed
Haize, John	25	Smi
Halbert, Daniel	8	Lin
Hannah	4	Lin
James	8	Lin
Jesse	4	Lin
John	8	Lin
Martin	43	Lin
William	9	Lin
Halbrok, John	5	Per
Halbrook, Ezekiel	14	Bed
John	5	Per

Halbrook (cont.)		
William	14	Bed
Halcomb, Kinchen	4	Lin
Hale, Amon	11	Jac
Andrew	31	Mon
Asa	14	Lin
Benjamin	10	Har
Benjamin	25	Smi
Cage	158	Sum
Elizabeth	16	Gil
Ezekiel	24	Smi
Gideon	11	Jac
Guy	96	Rut
James	50	Bed
James	11	Jac
Jane	25	Smi
Joab	26	Smi
Job	7	Hic
Joel	24	Smi
John	15	Bed
John	24	Lin
John	23	Smi
John	26	Smi
John C.	91	Dav
Joshua	121	Ste
Josiah C.	10	Har
Moshack	14	Bed
Nathaniel	23	Smi
Nicholas	11	Jac
Richd.	160	Sum
Ritter	23	Smi
Saml.	14	Hic
Samuel	36	Bed
Sterling	25	Smi
Thomas	23	Smi
William	84	Dav
William	15	Gil
William	31	Mon
William	23	Smi
William	160	Sum
Hales, Isaiah	11	Hic
James	11	Hic
John	11	Hic
Haley, Hartwell	34	Rob
Jessee	357	Whi
John	84	Rut
Nancy	16	Hic
Olive	34	Rob
Richard	32	Wll
Richd.	17	Hic
Walter C.	2	Hic
William	29	Rob
William	361	Whi
Woodson	5	Lin
Halfacre, Jacob	64	Wll
Halfacrer, John	12	Jac
Halfnes, Enoch	48	Mau
Halford, Andy	3	Way
Bradley	1	Law
James	2	Way
Joseph	9	Law
Hall, —	24	Mau
Aaron	88	Rut

Hall (cont.)		
Andrew	75	Rut
Asa	43	Lin
Bennett W.	416	Wil
C. S.	79	Dav
Carter T.	157	Sum
Charles M.	96	Dav
Claiborne	23	Smi
David	79	Rut
Drury	103	Rut
Edward	78	Dav
Eliza.	80	Dav
Elizabeth	8	Bed
Fancis	3	Wll
Francis	10	Hum
Garland	17	Rob
George	159	Sum
Hannah	160	Sum
Henrey	107	She
Henry	7	Bed
Henry	37	Bed
Henry	54	Bed
Henry	14	Dic
Henry	12	Jac
Jacob	103	Rut
James	14	Fra
James	41	Lin
James	53	Mau
Jane	93	Rut
Jedediah	3	Mon
Jno. C.	160	Sum
Joel	37	Bed
John	7	Bed
John	26	Bed
John	28	Bed
John	37	Bed
John	43	Bed
John	57	Dav
John	74	Dav
John	84	Dav
John	7	Dic
John	10	Dic
John	11	Fra
John	4	Hum
John	36	Lin
John	84	Rut
John	90	Rut
John	24	Smi
John	157	Sum
John [2]	159	Sum
John	59	Wll
John B.	90	Dav
John H.	64	Wll
Jonathan	79	Rut
Joseph	5	Bed
Joseph	27	Bed
Joseph	14	Dic
Josiah	26	Smi
Larkin	11	Fra
Levi	159	Sum
Margaret	12	Lin
Marley	159	Sum
Molly	22	Rob

Hall (cont.)
Moses 16 Lin
Nancy 14 Dic
Nathaniel 35 Lin
Pharoah 94 Rut
Phillip 112 Ste
Randolph B. 79 Rut
Richard 23 Smi
Sally 5 Bed
Saml. 158 Sum
Samuel 6 Lin
Samuel 26 Smi
Samuel P. 357 Whi
Thomas 75 Rut
Thomas 23 Smi
William 54 Bed
William 16 Dic
William 13 Fra
William 35 Lin
William 103 Rut
William 159 Sum
William 160 Sum
Williamson 23 Smi
Willis 157 Sum
Winston 42 Lin
see Holt
Hallady, Kelley 55 Mau
Hallaman, William 398 Wil
Halland, Lucy 387 Wil
Hallaway, Levi 396 Wil
Halley, Izah 3 Per
James 3 Per
Susan 43 Bed
Hallon, Harpse 318 War
Halls, Ambrose 44 Lin
Hallum, Cyrus 24 Smi
Henry 24 Smi
Morass 391 Wil
William 24 Smi
William 407 Wil
Hallums, James 406 Wil
William 406 Wil
Halt, William 26 Mau
Haltiman, John 346 Whi
Ham, David 37 Mau
James 95 Rut
Jesse 40 Wll
Joshua 45 Bed
Oring 36 Wll
Samuel 15 Bed
Solomon 30 Wll
William 25 Mon
Young D. 10 Wll
Hamack, Josiah 295 War
Hambeton see Hambleton
Hambey, Isaac 24 Hic
Hamblen, Joseph 19 Wll
Hamblet, Austin 8 Mon
Berry 367 Whi
Bird 29 Wll
James 7 Mon
James 115 Ste
Joshua 112 Ste
Hamblet (cont.)
William 24 Wll
Hambleton, Alexander 394 Wil
David L. 412 Wil
George 393 Wil
James 1 Mon
James 114 Ste
James 128 Ste
John 7 Mon
John 115 Ste
Joseph 393 Wil
Pegy 401 Wil
Robert 128 Ste
Thomas 403 Wil
Thos. 125 Ste
William 131 Ste
William 394 Wil
see Hamblet
Hamblin, John 22 Gil
John 121 Ste
Hamblitt, Elizabeth 19 Gil
John 16 Gil
Hambough, Danl. 157 Sum
Hambrick, Jeremiah 362 Whi
Travis 28 Mau
William 41 Lin
William 363 Whi
Hamby, William 17 Gil
Hamdon, Joseph 386 Wil
Hamel, William 17 Bed
Hamelton, Alexander 37 Mau
David 37 Mau
Francis 8 Bed
Francis 25 Wll
Hance 30 Mau
John C. 65 Mau
Theophilus 5 Bed
William 5 Bed
Hamer, Harriss 22 Wll
John 22 Wll
Hames, Caleb 26 Smi
Reuben 26 Smi
William 54 Mau
Hamett, Nathaniel 22 Gil
Hamilton, Adams 13 Jac
Addams 11 Jac
Alexander 9 Mon
Alexander 3 Ove
Alsey 13 Jac
Andrew 3 Dic
Andrew 37 Lin
Berry 25 Mon
Elijah 0 Wll
Hance 30 Rob
Henry 8 Hum
Jacob 22 Lin
Jacob 32 Lin
James 34 Bed
James 10 Hum
James 45 Lin
James 45 Lin
James 94 Rut
James 158 Sum

Hamilton (cont.)
James 32 Wll
James, Senr. 8 Hum
John 81 Dav
John 11 Fra
John 14 Fra
John 12 Law
John 17 Rob
John 157 Sum
John H., Mr. 1 Law
John T. 5 Wll
John W. 160 Sum
Joseph 5 Bed
Judy 67 Dav
Marc 75 Rut
Martha 8 Lin
Mary 57 Dav
Mary 160 Sum
Midleton 15 Mon
Polly 10 Hum
Robert 9 Hum
Robert 22 Mon
Samuel 28 Wll
Samuel W. 33 Rob
Tho. 157 Sum
Thomas 77 Dav
Thomas 75 Rut
Thomas W. 37 Lin
William 12 Jac
William 31 Lin
William 45 Lin
William 157 Sum
William 17 Wll
William A. 68 Dav
see Hambleton, Ham(e)lton
Hamlet, Thos. 159 Sum
Hamlett, William 2 Per
Hamlin, Sarah 52 Bed
Hamlin, William H. 69 Dav
Hamlton, James 25 Mau
Hammack, Daniel 23 Smi
Lewis 304 War
Lewis 317 War
Hamman, Ezekiel 301 War
Richard 301 War
Hammel, Robert 17 Bed
Hammers, John 411 Wil
Hammil, Andrew 7 Bed
Hammock, Jesse 30 Bed
Peter 12 Gil
William 14 Ove
Hammon, James A. 76 Dav
Hammond, Thomas 16 Lin
Hammonds, Edward 5 Gil
Fredric 20 Mon
James 22 Gil
Thomas 11 Har
William 9 Gil
William 367 Whi
Hammons, Charles 30 Lin
Isaiah 31 Bed
John 312 War
Leroy 290 War
Hammons (cont.)
Nathan 292 War
Nathan 308 War
Willis 4 Law
Woodson 295 War
Hamons, Abreham 67 Mau
Hampton, Adam 160 Sum
Andrew 11 Jac
Anthony 11 Lin
Edith 61 Wll
Edward 33 Rob
James 19 Bed
James 85 Rut
Jeremiah 27 Wll
John 19 Mon
John 32 Mon
John 23 Rob
Joicey 31 Wll
Rhodiah 160 Sum
Richard 97 Rut
Thomas 66 Wll
Thos. 32 Mon
Wade 159 Sum
William 11 Jac
William [2] 64 Wll
Hamton, Jourdon 288 War
William 298 War
Hanah, James [2] 40 Mau
Hanby, John 21 Lin
Hance, Reuben 34 Wll
Hancock, Benjamin 80 Rut
Benjamin 278 War
Clement 12 Jac
Dawson 124 Ste
Elijah 21 Mon
Francis 104 Rut
George 51 Mau
James 13 Jac
John 13 Jac
Joseph 13 Jac
Nancy 13 Jac
Nancy 50 Mau
Hancy, George 7 Hum
Hand, James C. 289 War
John 16 Dic
Samuel 279 War
William 2 Dic
Handcock, Charles 413 Wil
Dossen 396 Wil
James 413 Wil
Lewis 413 Wil
Martin 397 Wil
Richard 413 Wil
Simon 397 Wil
Verlender 396 Wil
Wesly 407 Wil
Handen, Obediah 400 Wil
Handlen, Stephen 20 Mon
William 20 Mon
Handler, Peter 395 Wil
Handlin, William 65 Mau
Handy, William 387 Wil
Hane see Ham

Hanes, James	28	Mon
William	26	Mon
Haney, Elijah	23	Smi
Elijah	157	Sum
James	159	Sum
Jesse	157	Sum
John	71	Dav
Margaret	159	Sum
Samuel	53	Bed
Timothy	12	Jac
William	88	Rut
William	24	Smi
William	160	Sum
Hank, Moses	62	Mau
Hankers, Richard	405	Wil
Hankins, Arthur	408	Wil
David	27	Mau
Richard	111	Wil
William	27	Mon
see Haukins		
Hanks, David	397	Wil
Elijah	62	Mau
Gayden O. [& Doyel]	16	Wll
George	11	Law
Jeremiah	283	War
Richd.	81	Dav
Samuel	86	Rut
Thomas	60	Mau
Hanley, John	11	Fra
Samuel	11	Fra
Hanna, James	15	Gil
James	158	Sum
John	15	Gil
Marthas	158	Sum
William	158	Sum
Hannah, Andrew	40	Lin
Andrew	47	Lin
Elizabeth	95	Dav
Isaac	13	Fra
James S.	95	Rut
John	95	Dav
Samuel	83	Dav
Samuel	11	Jac
William	28	Bed
William	33	Rob
Hannam, Miflen	22	Rob
Hannis, David P.	78	Rut
Enoch	74	Rut
Hannon, William	34	Mau
see Harmon		
Hannons, William	159	Sum
Hannun, Washington L.	78	Dav
Hansberry, Smith	391	Wil
Hansborough, Smith	111	Wil
Hanshrough, William	74	Rut
Hansel, John	118	Ste
Hanson see ...nson		
Haraldson, Burgess	17	Mon
Harben, James	7	Bed
Harber, George	21	Bed
Micajah	95	Rut
Samuel	11	Har
Harbert, David	11	Jac
Harbert (cont.)		
Nathaniel	82	Dav
Harbin, John	54	Bed
Harbour, Elijah	289	War
Harbson, Mathey	29	Mau
Hard, Briant	100	Rut
William C.	10	Ove
Hardaway, Edward	4	Rob
Hardcastle, Alexander	11	Jac
Elisha	12	Fra
Lucy	12	Jac
Susannah	13	Fra
Hardeman, Eleazer	6	Wll
Harden, Jeremiah	10	Wll
John	288	War
John	65	Wll
Presley	65	Wll
William	388	Wil
Harder, Jacob	157	Sum
John	21	Hic
Josiah P.	21	Hic
William	21	Hic
William	6	Wll
Harderster, William	61	Wll
Hardesen, Jawel	53	Mau
Joshua	53	Mau
William	53	Mau
Hardeson, Acy	57	Mau
Edward	52	Mau
James	52	Mau
Joshua	49	Mau
Mark	52	Mau
Hardgrove, Francis	60	Dav
John	84	Dav
Hardican, Joseph	12	Mon
Hardiman, Constant	82	Rut
Susan	35	Wll
Thomas J.	35	Wll
Hardin, Benjamin	10	Way
Edward	33	Lin
Elizabeth	17	Gil
Gibson	5	Har
Giles	85	Dav
Henry	20	Hic
James	1	Har
Jeremiah	17	Gil
John	60	Dav
Joseph	1	Har
Moses	22	Lin
Moses	34	Lin
Silvia	32	Lin
William	17	Gil
William	30	Lin
Harding, David M.	85	Dav
Edward	5	Lin
John	5	Lin
Thomas	85	Dav
Hardison, Daniel	131	Ste
Luke	131	Ste
Hardister, Alfred	12	Jac
Samuel	12	Jac
Hardman, Blaxton	43	Mau
Hardon, Swan	55	Mau

Hardridge, Zachariah 16 Lin
Hardson, Thomas 54 Mau
Hardwick, Leonard 24 Bed
Hardy, Elisha 122 Ste
Elizabeth 77 Dav
Jacob 5 Dic
Nehemiah 4 Dic
Obediah 15 Mon
Samuel 366 Whi
Stephen 84 Rut
William 12 Hum
Hare, Daniel 21 Gil
Sally 11 Jac
William 47 Lin
Hargis, John, (Jur.) 23 Smi
Hargiss, Abner 13 Fra
Abraham 13 Fra
John, Sen. 24 Smi
William 22 Smi
Hargot, Thomas 12 Jac
Hargrove, Amy 158 Sum
Hargus, James J. 353 Whi
William 364 Whi
William A. 356 Whi
Harington, Charles 31 Mau
Whitmell 9 Rob
Haris, Edman 49 Mau
Ezeriel 47 Mau
John 30 Mau
Joseph J. 68 Mau
Richard C. 61 Mau
Harison, George 65 Mau
Henery 39 Mau
John 45 Bed
John 56 Mau
Sarah 56 Mau
William [2] 54 Mau
William 56 Mau
Hariss, George 42 Mau
Harkins, Daniel 46 Lin
Walter 38 Lin
Harkrider, John 16 Rob
Harlemson, Alexander 65 Mau
Harley, John 12 Hic
Harlin, Isaac 39 Lin
Harling, Thomas 84 Dav
Harlock, Mary 36 Lin
Harlow, Obadiah 367 Whi
Robbart 30 Mau
Squire 358 Whi
William 12 Lin
William 69 Mau
Harlson, Hearvidon 51 Bed
Vincent 51 Bed
Harman, Campbell 63 Mau
Hardiman 81 Dav
Henry 5 Bed
John 3 Per
Lewis 37 Bed
Harminer, Elisha 287 War
Harmon, Benjamin 10 Ove
Caleb 11 Ove
George 6 Ove
James 14 Fra
Harmon (cont.)
John 12 Fra
Littleton 7 Hic
Louisa 22 Mon
Nancy 10 Hum
see Hannon
Harness, John 11 Way
Harney, Robert B. 9 Gil
Harp, Burton 9 Ove
Claybour 309 War
Ichabod 13 Ove
Nancy 30 Lin
Sampson 9 Ove
Simon 19 Ove
Solomon 19 Ove
Tery 14 Ove
Thomas 10 Ove
William 16 Ove
William 365 Whi
Willie 13 Fra
Harper, Andw. 158 Sum
Asa 64 Wll
Castleton 157 Sum
David 31 Mon
Edmd. 157 Sum
Elizabeth 160 Sum
George 13 Jac
Henry 8 Har
Henry 158 Sum
Jno. 158 Sum
John [2] 13 Fra
John 22 Smi
John 27 Smi
John 383 Wil
Joseph 97 Rut
Josiah, Jun. 25 Smi
Josiah, Sen. 26 Smi
Matthew 24 Smi
Moses D. 26 Mau
Patsey 26 Smi
Robert 17 Dic
Robert 25 Smi
Robert 27 Smi
Robert 157 Sum
Samuel 2 Lin
Sarah 95 Dav
Summers 159 Sum
T. 24 Mau
Thomas 36 Lin
Thomas 25 Rob
Thomas H. 30 Lin
Whiteman 30 Mon
Wilkins 38 Wll
William 76 Dav
William 13 Fra
William 13 Jac
William 158 Sum
Harpin, Jacob 14 Fra
Harpingding, Andrew 53 Wll
Harpole, Daniel 13 Fra
John 399 Wil
Solomon 312 War
Harpool, Adam, Jr. 401 Wil
Adam, Ser. 401 Wil

Harpool (cont.)		
George	401	Wil
Harrel, Caden	158	Sum
Josiah	25	Mau
Peter	26	Mau
Richard	126	Ste
Harrell, William	11	Fra
Harrelson, John	7	Law
Nancy	5	Law
Harres, Isaac	12	Jac
John	12	Jac
Jorden	11	Jac
Joseph	12	Jac
Reuben	12	Jac
Robert	12	Jac
Silas	11	Jac
Sterling	12	Jac
Totton	12	Jac
Wooton	12	Jac
Harriman see Hamman		
Harrington, Asa	94	Dav
Harris, Abner	9	Mon
Abner	30	Mon
Adam G.	79	Dav
Akilles	27	Smi
Alexander	366	Whi
Alford	396	Wil
Alfred	11	Fra
Alfred M.	16	Gil
Allin	418	Wil
Alsea	97	Rut
Ann	12	Fra
Ansel	1	Hum
Archibald	9	Mon
Archibald	84	Rut
Archibald	89	Rut
Archibald H.	96	Rut
Arthur	419	Wil
Asa	95	Dav
Azel D.	27	Lin
Bartlett	362	Whi
Benjamin	383	Wil
Benjamine	356	Whi
Beverley	60	Wll
Beverly	15	Bed
Blair	160	Sum
Cather	401	Wil
Charles	159	Sum
Claborn	27	Mon
Cornelious	359	Whi
David	20	Bed
David	69	Dav
David	11	Hum
David	6	Ove
David B.	7	Ove
Drewry	54	Bed
Drewry	22	Mon
Drury	12	Lin
Ebby	364	Whi
Edward	376	Wil
Edward, Jun.	12	Fra
Edward, Sen.	12	Fra
Edwin	12	Rob
Harris (cont.)		
Eli	403	Wil
Ephraim G.	93	Rut
Evan	35	Bed
F. S.	114	Wil
Flane	403	Wil
George	12	Fra
George E.	12	Hum
Gideon	92	Dav
Gideon	402	Wil
Hardy	90	Rut
Hawill	13	Rob
Henry	385	Wil
Henry	40	Wll
Howel	7	Lin
Howell G.	282	War
Isaac	95	Dav
Isam V.	1	Hum
Isham	14	Fra
Isra	13	Rob
Jacob C.	32	Wll
James	42	Bed
James	46	Bed
James	86	Dav
James	11	Fra
James	10	Lin
James	4	Per
James	122	Ste
James W.	157	Sum
Jeramiah	3	Ove
Jeremiah	2	Har
Jesse	279	War
John	35	Bed
John	66	Dav
John	13	Fra
John	6	Ove
John	15	Ove
John [2]	23	Smi
John	24	Smi
John	129	Ste
John	158	Sum
John	159	Sum
John	364	Whi
John	402	Wil
Johnson	12	Fra
Jonathan	17	Hic
Jonathan	344	Whi
Joseph	6	Ove
Joseph	20	Ove
Lewis	23	Smi
Mathew H.	158	Sum
Matthew	71	Dav
Matthew	9	Rob
Merridith	5	Lin
Micajah	24	Smi
Michael	13	Fra
Michael	13	Rob
Michael	397	Wil
Mosby	25	Bed
Moses	16	Ove
Nancy	14	Hic
Nathaniel	4	Hum
Nehemiah	12	Fra

Harris (cont.)
Newsom 88 Dav
Polly 87 Rut
Polly 161 Sum
Richard 11 Ove
Robert 81 Rut
Robert 90 Rut
Robert S. 22 Gil
Robt. 160 Sum
Sally 71 Dav
Samuel 11 Fra
Samuel 16 Mon
Samuel A. 11 Fra
Sidon 16 Ove
Simpson 89 Rut
Soleman 51 Mau
Stephen 12 Fra
Susan 23 Mon
Tho. L. 157 Sum
Thomas 12 Fra
Thomas 401 Wil
Thomas 407 Wil
Thomas A. 84 Rut
Thomas A. 97 Rut
Timothy 371 Whi
Toliver 294 War
Turner 24 Smi
Tyre 402 Wil
Wallis, free man of Colour 51 Wll
William 68 Dav
William 95 Dav
William 5 Hic
William 5 Hum
William 8 Per
William 23 Rob
William 26 Smi
William 294 War
William 404 Wil
William 409 Wil
William L. 158 Sum
William L. 160 Sum
Willie 88 Dav
Wily 405 Wil
Wm. 4 Hic
Wm. T. 380 Wil
Wootin 4 Hic
Wyet 27 Mau
Zachariah 14 Hum
Zephaniah 13 Hum
see Mauldin
Harrison, Allen 40 Wll
Ann 40 Wll
Benj. S. 81 Dav
Benjamin 12 Hum
Benjamin 14 Ove
Daniel 6 Law
David 31 Mon
Edly 292 War
Eli 10 Ove
Greenwood 5 Ove
Henry 2 Hum
James 2 Bed
James 13 Ove
Harrison (cont.)
James 18 Ove
James 160 Sum
James 34 Wll
John 35 Bed
John 69 Dav
John 77 Dav
John 8 Per
Joshua 73 Rut
Mary 69 Dav
Michael 115 Ste
Michael 121 Ste
Polly 68 Dav
Polly 12 Fra
Reuben 8 Rob
Richard 25 Rob
Richard 159 Sum
Robert P. 35 Bed
Samuel 297 War
Starling 399 Wil
Stith 403 Wil
Thos. 81 Dav
Thriatt 390 Wil
Walker 361 Whi
William 34 Bed
William 12 Mon
William 25 Rob
William 408 Wil
William 38 Wll
William P. 65 Wll
Zachariah 25 Lin
see Hascolon
Harriss, Bright B. 156 Sum
Daniel 7 Dic
Dorrel Y. 4 Dic
Elmore 157 Sum
John 2 Dic
Randolph R. 4 Dic
Stephen 4 Dic
William 158 Sum
Harrisson, Daniel W. 26 Lin
Harrod, David 80 Rut
Harrol, Lewis 82 Dav
Whitfield 12 Fra
Harroll, George P. 13 Fra
Harroway, Samuel 18 Gil
Harrup, Gilliam 60 Dav
Hart, Barnaby 31 Rob
Elizabeth 160 Sum
George 15 Rob
Hartwell 5 Har
Henry 11 Rob
Henry 25 Smi
Henry 161 Sum
James 99 Rut
John 33 Mau
John 35 Mau
John 23 Mon
John 26 Wll
Joseph 33 Mau
R. W. 65 Dav
Richard [2] 35 Mau
Saml. 160 Sum

Hart (cont.)		
Samuel	81	Dav
Samuel	25	Lin
Sarah	160	Sum
Thomas	6	Hum
Thomas	25	Smi
William	33	Mau
William	25	Smi
Harten, Thomas	12	Gil
Hartgraves, James	4	Wll
Lewis	31	Wll
Hartgroves, Bennet	44	Wll
James	44	Wll
Stephen	45	Wll
Hartin, Jeremiah	19	Hic
John	160	Sum
Harting, Daniel	358	Whi
Hartley, Charles	18	Wll
Dennis	15	Bed
Laben	45	Wll
Hartman, Geo.	97	Dav
Harton, Daniel	4	Rob
Jonathan J.	2	Wll
Harts, —	24	Mau
Hartsfield, Andrew	32	Bed
Jacob	32	Bed
Nathen	41	Bed
William	32	Bed
Hartszoggs, George	17	Hic
Hartta, Joseph C.	9	Gil
Hartwick, John	12	Fra
Harty, Denis	36	Mau
Harvel, Polly	348	Whi
Harvell, George	15	Hic
James	24	Smi
Harvey, Alexander	8	Gil
Bennet	25	Smi
Edward R.	55	Wll
Emanuel	88	Rut
Frederick	62	Dav
John	83	Dav
John	8	Gil
John, Jun.	23	Smi
John, Sen.	26	Smi
Lemuel	7	Hum
Stansell	84	Rut
Stansill	90	Rut
Thos. G.	14	Way
William	24	Smi
William	157	Sum
Harwell, Buckner	18	Gil
Coleman	13	Gil
Featherston	11	Gil
Frederick	22	Gil
Gilliam	22	Gil
Herbert	8	Rob
Hubbard	14	Gil
Jackson	13	Gil
John	18	Hic
Nancy	12	Gil
Rebecca	2	Gil
Richard	22	Gil
Richard	6	Rob
Harwell (cont.)		
Rolley	14	Gil
Samuel [2]	14	Gil
Sarah	6	Gil
Shadrach	22	Gil
Thomas	12	Gil
Thomas	79	Rut
Harwood, Alexander M.	1	Wll
Francis G.	27	Smi
John	73	Dav
Thomas	22	Gil
William	93	Dav
William M.	85	Dav
Hascolon, William	9	Wll
Haser, Volentine V.	388	Wil
Hasey, Jesse	43	Mau
Stephen	43	Mau
Hasford, Richard	41	Wll
Hash, James	301	War
John	308	War
John	368	Whi
Phillip	112	Ste
William	300	War
Hashaw, John	45	Bed
Haskell, Joshua	73	Rut
Haskins, Joseph	27	Lin
Sarah	19	Mon
Haslett, Robert	19	Rob
Haslip, Thomas, Sen.	11	Fra
William	11	Fra
Hass, Abram	26	Smi
Henry	26	Smi
John	26	Smi
Philip	26	Smi
Hassel, Joseph	6	Wll
Hassell, Jennett	157	Sum
Jennot	16	Hic
Jordon	157	Sum
Polly	16	Hic
Silvanus	16	Hic
Zebulon	16	Hic
Hasten, John	23	Smi
Stephen	13	Fra
Hastin see Hartin		
Hasting, David	349	Whi
Isaac	348	Whi
Joseph	344	Whi
Hastley, James	11	Dic
Hasty, Benjamin	12	Fra
Jordon	12	Fra
Hatcher, Amos	3	Mon
Harris	9	Ove
Henry	18	Mon
John	6	Hum
Polley B.	3	Mon
William	41	Wll
Hatchet, Archibald	11	Fra
Edward	24	Smi
Wlisha	23	Smi
Joshua	365	Whi
Parish	24	Smi
Hatchett, Thomas	99	Rut
Hatfield, Ephraim	15	Ove

Hatfield (cont.)		
Valentine, Jr.	15	Ove
Valentine, Senr.	15	Ove
Hathaway, Elizabeth	412	Wil
John	63	Dav
John	412	Wil
William	75	Dav
Hathcock, Howell	316	War
Miles	317	War
Haton, Solomon	410	Wil
Hatsel, Thos.	15	Mon
Vardy	15	Mon
Hatt, James	86	Rut
Hatton, John	411	Wil
Haukins, Daniel	22	Gil
Joel	22	Gil
John	21	Gil
Hauks, Thomas	32	Wll
Hause, Duke	47	Bed
Henry	17	Bed
Joseph	301	War
Robert	81	Rut
Haward, John	29	Mau
Hawe, Joseph	30	Bed
Hawel see Harvel		
Hawerton, Topley	35	Bed
Hawick, Jacob	361	Whi
Hawk, Christopher	309	War
George	309	War
Hawker, Reuben	26	Smi
Hawkings, Samuel	5	Per
Hawkins, Allen	70	Mau
Benjamin	278	War
Benjamin	342	Whi
David	39	Lin
David N.	14	Lin
Edward	39	Lin
Elizabeth	159	Sum
Henrey	29	Mau
James	11	Jac
James L.	420	Wil
John	27	Bed
John	6	Gil
John	12	Jac
John	47	Lin
John	69	Mau
John	313	War
John	317	War
John	346	Whi
Joseph	12	Jac
Joseph	300	War
Larkin	284	War
Mary	70	Mau
Nathan	10	Law
Polly	12	Way
Sally	157	Sum
Samuel	55	Mau
Samuel	30	Rob
Samuel C.	26	Mon
Stephean	69	Mau
Stephen	69	Mau
Susannah	26	Smi
Thomas	66	Dav
Hawkins (cont.)		
Uziel	66	Mau
W.	121	Ste
William	11	Jac
Wilson	1	Law
see Hankins, Haukins		
Hawks see Hanks		
Hawmer, Aaron	288	War
Hawol, Joseph B.	7	Har
Haws, John	11	Fra
Thomas	11	Fra
William	12	Jac
Hay, Andrew	74	Dav
Archer	84	Rut
Balam	43	Wll
James	74	Dav
Jeremiah T.	21	Bed
John	21	Bed
John	4	Wll
Lazarus	17	Bed
William	3	Per
William	11	Wll
William	34	Wll
Hayes, George	34	Mau
Henry	25	Smi
Hugh	25	Smi
James	61	Mau
Rebecca	25	Smi
Reuben	24	Smi
Robert	25	Smi
William	12	Fra
William	25	Smi
William B.	13	Gil
William W.	12	Gil
Haygood, John	14	Mon
John	32	Mon
Hayles, Tho.	157	Sum
Haynard, Philip	6	Mon
Haynes, Abraham	40	Bed
Andrew J.	86	Rut
Benja.	159	Sum
David	24	Smi
Fountain	27	Smi
Gabriel	25	Smi
Henry	35	Bed
James S.	20	Gil
John	20	Gil
John	24	Smi
Joseph	28	Bed
Joseph	20	Gil
Peter	25	Smi
Peter	160	Sum
Rachel	20	Gil
Robt.	157	Sum
Stephen	66	Dav
Thomas	24	Smi
Thomas	5	Wll
Thos.	117	Ste
Wm.	115	Ste
Haynie, Thomas	9	Gil
Hayns, Abran	55	Wll
Anderson	33	Wll
George	11	Wll

Hayns (cont.)		
John	11	Wll
Joseph	42	Wll
Robert	13	Law
Hays, Adam	80	Rut
Alsey	81	Rut
Andrew	79	Dav
Charles	65	Dav
David	97	Dav
Eleanor	6	Lin
Elizabeth	8	Hum
Elizabeth	25	Smi
Emons	12	Jac
Henry	61	Dav
Henry	26	Lin
Hugh	61	Dav
Isaac	12	Jac
Isaac	25	Smi
James	67	Dav
John	4	Dic
John	5	Hic
Joseph	25	Smi
Lewi	87	Rut
Mary	388	Wil
O. B.	79	Dav
Robert	2	Rob
Samuel	54	Mau
Sarah	61	Dav
Sarah	67	Dav
Stockley	87	Dav
Thomas	27	Lin
Thompson	387	Wil
Wallis	5	Hic
William	85	Dav
William	5	Rob
William	291	War
William P.	2	Wll
Hayslip, James	9	Lin
Labon	6	Lin
Haytch, William	30	Bed
Hayter, John J.	11	Fra
Haytor, Abraham	5	Ove
Haywood, John	83	Dav
Hazard, Lewis	23	Smi
Lott	23	Smi
Hazelwood, Thomas	61	Wll
Hazlet, John	157	Sum
Hazlewood, John	417	Wil
Head, Alexr. S.	32	Bed
Benj.	158	Sum
Enoch	86	Rut
George	2	Rob
Robert	9	Rob
William	9	Rob
Headley, Calib	51	Mau
Headon, Luckey	137	Sum
Heady, David	13	Jac
Heald, H. O. T.	282	War
Hearn, Edmond	376	Wil
George	411	Wil
James	408	Wil
James W.	411	Wil
John	391	Wil
Hearn (cont.)		
Milberry	397	Wil
Stephen	407	Wil
Thomas	397	Wil
William	397	Wil
Wilson	408	Wil
Wm., Sr.	397	Wil
Hearne, William R.	73	Rut
Heartfield, William	391	Wil
Heartsfiled, Solomon	397	Wil
Heath, George	12	Fra
Levi	80	Rut
Solomon	91	Rut
Heathman, Joseph	14	Mon
Heaton, Enoch	28	Wll
Hedge, Isaac	3	Per
William	13	Dic
Hedgecock, Moses	8	Hum
Hedgepeth, Jeremiah	20	Lin
Hedger, William	13	Fra
Hedges, Charles	9	Hic
Hedzpeth, Cannsel	30	Mau
Heffington, Henry	7	Law
Heflin, Absalom	7	Mon
James	26	Smi
Joab	26	Smi
Simon	14	Mon
William	26	Smi
William	26	Smi
Hefman, James	8	Mon
Hefner, Marelles	348	Whi
Michael	136	Sum
Hegan, Robert	415	Wil
Heght, John	419	Wil
Height, Jediah	402	Wil
Richard	405	Wil
Robert	418	Wil
Heister, Benjamin	97	Rut
Heistin, Peter	11	Fra
Hellman, James	4	Ove
Hellum, Andrew	24	Smi
Helm, Frederick	15	Ove
George	10	Ove
George	11	Ove
Henry	15	Ove
Jacob	12	Ove
John	32	Mau
Joseph	32	Mau
Malchi	28	Mau
Meridith	59	Mau
Helman, Ewin	1	Ove
Helmantoler, Henry	26	Smi
Jacob	20	Smi
Jacob, Sen.	26	Smi
Helmm see Helmus		
Helms, Jacob	298	War
Jonathin	70	Mau
Joseph	157	Sum
Shadrach	3	Har
Helmus, Fielden	48	Wll
Helsey, George R.	9	Har
Helton, Abraham	13	Bed
Edward	347	Whi

Helton (cont.)
James 3 Law
James 53 Mau
Jesse 9 Law
John 53 Mau
John 344 Whi
Nancy 51 Mau
Rebekeh 13 Law
Susanah 51 Mau
Hemby, Elizabeth 6 Hum
Hemintree, John 12 Fra
Hemphill, James 16 Wll
William 8 Wll
Henby, William 62 Mau
Henderickson, James 25 Smi
Jonathan 26 Smi
Henderson, Abner 15 Rob
Alexander 49 Mau
Andrew 40 Mau
Daniel 7 Hum
David 39 Lin
Davis 364 Whi
Edward 19 Ove
James 34 Bed
James 20 Gil
James 86 Rut
James 388 Wil
James 42 Wll
John 34 Bed
John 5 Gil
John 23 Lin
John 45 Lin
John 46 Lin
John 16 Mon
John 86 Rut
John 90 Rut
John 23 Smi
Joseph 18 Lin
Joseph 2 Ove
Ligan 77 Rut
Margaret 93 Rut
Mary 20 Gil
Nathanal 25 Mau
Palians 25 Mau
Pleasant 293 War
Richard 39 Mau
Robbert 54 Mau
Robert 82 Rut
Robert 290 War
Samuel 23 Lin
Samuel 44 Wll
Tho. 157 Sum
Thomas 15 Gil
Thomas 308 War
William 21 Bed
William 5 Gil
William 2 Law
William 32 Mau
William 3 Mon
William 77 Rut
William S. 39 Mau
Wilson 42 Mau
Hendley, James D. 12 Jac
Hendley (cont.)
Joel 304 War
Ware 36 Wll
Hendly, Abner 12 Jac
Hendman, Sally 6 Hum
Hendon, Berry 11 Fra
Isarell 355 Whi
James 126 Ste
William 13 Fra
Hendren, Adam 9 Ove
Hendrexson, John 4 Ove
Hendrick, Jeremiah 376 Wil
Hendricks, Andrew 128 Ste
Isaac 60 Mau
Isaac, Jur. 31 Lin
Isaac, Ser. 31 Lin
James 13 Jac
Jesse 120 Ste
John 15 Dic
John 2 Hum
John 45 Mau
Maryan 60 Wll
William 3 Dic
Hendrix, Albert 159 Sum
Elijah 8 Hum
Henry 8 Hum
John 14 Gil
William 15 Gil
Hendry, James 13 Gil
William 13 Gil
Heneley, Calib 63 Mau
Henery, Josiah 35 Mau
Heneter, Rewben 158 Sum
Henisee, James 293 War
Thomas 291 War
Henisley, Allen 313 War
Henissee, Patrick 294 War
Henkins, Israe 52 Wll
Henley, George 11 Hum
John 9 Hum
John J. 156 Sum
Margaret 30 Rob
Samuel 25 Rob
William 6 Bed
William 13 Fra
William 10 Rob
Henly, Thomas 9 Lin
William 22 Rob
Hennen, Pennal 390 Wil
Henney, Cypres 19 Mon
Henrickson, John 29 Mon
Henry, Charles 409 Wil
David 12 Rob
Francis 26 Smi
George 364 Whi
Green 23 Lin
Hugh 26 Rob
Hugh 409 Wil
Isaac 13 Fra
James 20 Gil
James 29 Mon
James, Jun. 13 Fra
James, Sen. 13 Fra

Henry (cont.)		
John	1	Law
John	89	Rut
John	299	War
John	364	Whi
Joseph	23	Smi
Joseph	364	Whi
Margaret	160	Sum
Moses	156	Sum
Oney	1	Dic
Samuel	13	Fra
Samuel	409	Wil
Thomas	7	Lin
Thomas	29	Rob
Thomas	399	Wil
Vinet	364	Whi
William	93	Dav
William	26	Smi
William	160	Sum
Henshaw, Benjamin	2	Ove
George	10	Ove
Jacob	14	Ove
Jesse	306	War
Hensley, Charles	372	Whi
Enoch	12	Jac
Gideon	15	Gil
James	7	Way
John	11	Jac
John	22	Way
Larkin	15	Way
Lemuel	2	Way
Lydia	22	Way
Michael	11	Law
Obadiah	9	Ove
Samuel	7	Way
Washington	11	Way
William	31	Mau
Henson, Anne	13	Jac
Henry	1	Ove
Jacob	9	Hum
John L.	6	Law
Joshua	2	Bed
Judah	362	Whi
Philip	396	Wil
Reuben	11	Fra
Samuel [2]	11	Jac
Samuel	12	Jac
Samuel	44	Wll
Henton, Kimbrorugh	22	Mon
William M.	87	Dav
Herald, Eli	418	Wil
Herard, Thomas	70	Dav
Herbert, Richard	22	Wll
Sarah	341	Whi
Herbison, John	93	Dav
Herby, John	113	Wil
John	406	Wil
Herd, James	347	Whi
Joseph	350	Whi
Heren, David	4	Per
Herin, Jane	55	Mau
Herison, Herendon see Henson	78	Rut
Herley, Jno.	111	Wil
Hermans, John	136	Sum
Hermon, Alexander	19	Rob
Hern, John	2	Hum
Herndon, Betsey	13	Fra
Jacob	298	War
Jacob	306	War
Polly	160	Sum
Pomphret, Jr.	13	Fra
Pomphret, Sen.	13	Fra
Heron, Purnell	23	Smi
Herrald, Enos	24	Smi
John	23	Rob
Ruth	26	Smi
Herralson, Sollomon	11	Jac
Herrel, James	14	Fra
Kaader	86	Dav
Andrew	42	Wll
James	6	Wll
Richard	369	Whi
Thomas	42	Wll
William	369	Whi
Herriford, Henry	11	Fra
William	13	Fra
Herrin, Abemelech	70	Dav
Abraham	85	Rut
Benjamin	82	Rut
David	343	Whi
Elisha	14	Fra
Elisha, Jun.	13	Fra
Henry	93	Dav
Isaac	104	Rut
Lemuel	13	Fra
William	94	Dav
Herring, Benjamins	2	Mon
Bright	2	Mon
Henry	115	Ste
Henry	125	Ste
Henry	126	Ste
Jesse	30	Rob
Peyton	6	Gil
Soleman	56	Mau
Spirus	2	Mon
Stephen	20	Rob
Stephen	126	Ste
Herrington, Dempsey	19	Hic
Fanny	19	Hic
Henry	19	Hic
Robt.	19	Hic
Wm.	19	Hic
Herrod, James	24	Smi
Levi	26	Smi
Peter	27	Smi
Rachel	12	Fra
Reuben	19	Bed
Whitmel	19	Bed
William, Sen.	27	Smi
Herron, Beverly	70	Dav
John	10	Hum
William	11	Fra
Hesaw, Andrew	12	Ove
George	5	Ove
James	6	Ove

Hesaw (cont.)		
Robert	5	Ove
Hesket, George	49	Mau
Hesley, William	14	Law
Hess, Margaret D.	50	Bed
W. R.	8	Per
Hessell, John	386	Wil
Hesson, Andrew	27	Smi
Arthur	27	Smi
Hester, Benjamin	82	Rut
Garland	283	War
Graves	3	Gil
Henry	5	Gil
Robert	19	Mon
Stephen	63	Mau
Heth, John	369	Whi
Hethcock, Young	26	Mon
Hethney, George	19	Ove
Hewet, Robert	84	Dav
Hewlett, George	76	Dav
Mary	81	Dav
William	76	Dav
Hews, Archelus, Sn.	61	Wll
James	16	Wll
James	32	Wll
James	62	Wll
Richard	6	Wll
Hewsley, Simeon	5	Gil
Hewston, David	28	Wll
Ross	28	Wll
Heyepeth, Major	20	Lin
Hibbet, Andrew	13	Jac
Hibdon, John	301	War
Hice, Conrod	12	Fra
Jacob	12	Fra
Hick, Susan	4	Wll
Hickason, John	157	Sum
Joshua	282	War
Richd.	160	Sum
Saml.	160	Sum
Saml. D.	156	Sum
Hickerson, David	13	Fra
David, Jun.	13	Fra
Ezekiel	4	Dic
Isaac	27	Smi
John	13	Fra
John	27	Smi
Joseph	13	Fra
William	4	Dic
Hickey, Cornelius	1	Ove
Micheal	1	Ove
Hickinboland, William	2	Har
William G.	2	Har
Hicklin, Hugh	13	Jac
Thomas	13	Jac
Hickman, Elliott	2	Lin
James	34	Mau
James	47	Mau
Nancy	85	Rut
Samuel	15	Ove
Thomas	89	Dav
William	18	Gil
Hickmon, Benjamine	351	Whi
Hickmon (cont.)		
John	396	Wil
Lemuel	396	Wil
Snodon	396	Wil
Stephen	351	Whi
William	406	Wil
Wright	396	Wil
Hicks, Abel	158	Sum
Abraham	365	Whi
Ann	25	Smi
Arthur	13	Gil
Arthur	5	Law
Berry	5	Hic
Caty	26	Smi
Charles	69	Mau
Elias	126	Ste
Elijah	4	Hic
Francis	17	Gil
George	60	Mau
Henry	4	Har
Isaac [2]	365	Whi
James	8	Dic
James	6	Hum
James	1	Rob
James	6	Wll
Jesse	9	Gil
John	9	Gil
John	5	Hic
John	6	Hum
John	51	Mau
John	287	War
John	346	Whi
John C.	8	Rob
Jordan	9	Gil
Joseph	15	Gil
Meshack	304	War
Temple	70	Mau
Thomas	18	Gil
Walker	64	Wll
William	17	Hic
William	8	Ove
William	87	Rut
William	125	Ste
William	298	War
William H.	1	Rob
Wm. R.	122	Ste
Hide, Erwin	12	Bed
Joseph	11	Jac
Higason, David	157	Sum
Saml.	157	Sum
Higden, James	78	Rut
Simeon	2	Hic
Thomas	3	Hic
Higdon, John	15	Gil
William	15	Gil
Higget, James	24	Smi
Higginbotham, Aaron	289	War
Caleb	8	Hic
James	41	Bed
Joseph	1	Bed
Higginbothan, R. A.	77	Dav
see Hickinboland		
Higgings, Isaac	35	Mau

Higgins, Alexander	302	War
Elisha	25	Smi
James	46	Lin
James	75	Rut
James, Jnr.	79	Rut
Jas.	121	Ste
John	414	Wil
Moses	121	Ste
Philemon	4	Lin
Rebecca	22	Way
Westley	414	Wil
William	414	Wil
Higginton, Elijah	105	Rut
Higgs, Edward	11	Law
James	4	Lin
John	10	Bed
Simon	9	Law
High, John	24	Smi
Rebecca	27	Smi
Richard	4	Per
Winston	24	Smi
Highers, George	24	Smi
Martin	27	Smi
Highland, Henry	1	Dic
Highsmith, Susanna	34	Rob
Hight, John	49	Mau
Hightower, George	1	Dic
Hardy	12	Gil
James	32	Mon
Nicholas	18	Rob
Robert	12	Law
Stephen	4	Lin
Sterling	14	Fra
Stilth	380	Wil
William	1	Dic
Higinbotham, Middleton	3	Dic
Higins, Barnard	157	Sum
Highight, John	5	Mon
Hilburn, Richard	53	Wll
William	32	Mau
Hill, Abel	1	Way
Abnatha	44	Mau
Abner	398	Wil
Abram	8	Per
Alexander	290	War
Allen	42	Mau
Allen	46	Wll
Ambrose	5	Per
Amos	400	Wil
Asa	281	War
Bartley	412	Wil
Benjamin	11	Fra
Benjamin	281	War
Caleb	14	Gil
Clanton	47	Mau
Clement	23	Lin
Dan	30	Wll
Daniel	12	Fra
Daniel	13	Fra
David	22	Gil
David	18	Wll
Dolly	5	Law
Drewry	12	Fra
Hill (cont.)		
Edward	13	Fra
Elijah	359	Whi
Elizabeth	347	Whi
Ervin	281	War
Frederick	11	Fra
George	48	Bed
George W.	7	Ove
Gersham	8	Way
Gilliam	12	Lin
Green	67	Mau
Green	23	Smi
Green	6	Wll
Henry	13	Fra
Henry	14	Fra
Henry J. A.	281	War
Henry R. W.	1	Wll
Hugh	17	Hic
Isaac	5	Dic
Isaac	306	War
Isaac	382	Wil
Jacob	46	Wll
James	37	Mau
James	90	Rut
James	8	Way
James	352	Whi
James W.	11	Fra
James W.	37	Mau
Jesse	311	War
John [2]	48	Bed
John	86	Dav
John	4	Hic
John	26	Mau
John	46	Mau
John	15	Mon
John	2	Ove
John	4	Ove
John [2]	91	Rut
John	19	Way
John	55	Wll
John P.	22	Wll
Jonathan	25	Wll
Joseph	15	Bed
Joshua	7	Ove
Joshua C.	6	Wll
Kesiah	86	Rut
Lewis	33	Lin
Luke	17	Wll
Mark	5	Per
Marvill	11	Fra
Mary	98	Rut
Milly	3	Ove
Moses	305	War
Nancy	54	Wll
Penelope	26	Wll
Pleasant	12	Fra
Rachael	77	Rut
Richard	37	Mau
Richard	43	Mau
Richard	44	Mau
Richard	57	Mau
Richard, Mr.	1	Law
Richmond	13	Fra

Hill (cont.)
Robbert 68 Mau
Robert 60 Dav
Robert 15 Wll
Robert 18 Wll
Rubin 65 Mau
Sally 36 Bed
Samuel 416 Wil
Seth 12 Jac
Spencer 35 Bed
Stokseley R. 7 Ove
Theopulas 29 Mau
Thomas 77 Dav
Thomas 12 Jac
Thomas 65 Mau
Thomas 9 Ove
Thomas 81 Rut
Thomas 372 Whi
Thomas 417 Wil
Thomas L. 31 Mau
Walter M. 9 Wll
Whitmill 5 Hic
William 36 Bed
William 48 Bed
William 69 Dav
William 34 Mau
Eilliam 46 Mau
William 49 Mau
William 65 Mau
William 7 Ove
William 5 Per
William 91 Rut
William 352 Whi
William 387 Wil
William 42 Wll
William 60 Wll
William H. 30 Wll
William K. 57 Mau
Winkfield 372 Whi
Hillcum see Hilsclean
Hillhouse, George 8 Gil
John 1 Law
Hilliard, Thomas 32 Wll
Hillis, James 296 War
John 6 Mon
Samuel 45 Mau
Samuel 46 Mau
Hillsclean, Peter 319 War
Hilterbrand, Conrod 31 Rob
Henry 22 Rob
Henry 33 Rob
Hilton, Betsey 25 Smi
Richard 27 Smi
Hinchey, William [2] 11 Fra
Hindeley, Benjamin 26 Smi
Hindman, John 16 Lin
Hinds, Joel 17 Ove
Levi 9 Ove
Simeon 19 Ove
Hinel, Raby 159 Sum
Hines, Catherine 68 Mau
John 12 Jac
Kalib 66 Mau
Hines (cont.)
Ocums [?] 69 Mau
William 12 Jac
William [2] 66 Mau
Hing, James [2] 31 Mau
Hinkle, Anthony 3 Rob
Benjamin 16 Lin
Joseph 16 Lin
Hins, Polley 32 Mau
Hinson, George 52 Mau
Jno. 158 Sum
John 4 Dic
John, Jr. 159 Sum
Josiah 158 Sum
Obediah 3 Mon
Solomon 156 Sum
William 92 Dav
Hinton, Jeramiah 86 Dav
Judith 23 Smi
Saml. 159 Sum
Hire, Elizabeth 28 Mon
Lewis 26 Mon
Hireman, Joseph 301 War
Hirndun, Sarah 54 Mau
Hirt, Bird S. 52 Mau
Elisha 51 Mau
James 50 Mau
Hitchcock, Ezekiel 368 Whi
George 305 War
Isaac 6 Har
Lorenzo 58 Mau
Sarah 368 Whi
William 368 Whi
Hite, Abraham 96 Dav
William 68 Dav
William 51 Mau
Hiter, Thomas H. 2 Wll
Hitford, Thos. 125 Ste
Hitour, Richard 22 Wll
Hitt, James 16 Mon
Hiveley, George W. 41 Bed
Hix, Archibald 301 War
Milly 44 Bed
William 16 Bed
Hoag, George 65 Mau
Hoalt, William 42 Mau
Hoasey, Jessey 29 Mau
Hobbs, Christopher 7 Lin
Colin S. 81 Dav
David 157 Sum
Edward D. 69 Dav
Jacob 7 Lin
James 5 Lin
James 404 Wil
James 28 Wll
Joel 2 Hic
John 14 Hic
Reddick 12 Fra
Rigden 86 Rut
Rigeun [?] 100 Rut
Stephen 73 Dav
Thomas 63 Dav
Thomas 403 Wil

Hobbs (cont.)		
Thomas W.	63	Dav
William	72	Dav
William	3	Hic
William	96	Rut
William	404	Wil
Hobby, Alexander	45	Mau
Hardy	12	Jac
Hobday, John	157	Sum
William	159	Sum
Hobson, John	75	Dav
John	87	Dav
Morning	80	Rut
Nathaniel	80	Rut
Nathaniel	99	Rut
Hockersmith, George	11	Fra
Hodde, Robert	18	Lin
Hodg, Elisabeth	54	Wll
James	56	Wll
Phillip	54	Wll
Hodge, Abner	358	Whi
Caesar	186	Sum
Charles	19	Bed
Edmond [2]	19	Bed
Edmund	14	Fra
Elisha	416	Wil
Ephrame	358	Whi
Francis	9	Bed
Francis	61	Dav
Frazier	31	Lin
George	74	Dav
Henry	17	Wll
James	46	Mau
John	84	Dav
John	11	Ove
Joseph	157	Sum
Joseph	383	Wil
Joseph H.	17	Gil
Nancy	61	Dav
Robert	156	Sum
Robert	5	Wll
Robert	19	Wll
Robert N.	13	Lin
Samuel	388	Wil
Thomas	11	Lin
William C.	26	Lin
Wm.	23	Hic
see Hedge		
Hodgens, John	23	Smi
Hodges, Abel	13	Fra
Aron	159	Sum
Asa, Jr.	157	Sum
Asa, Sr.	159	Sum
David	23	Smi
Hannah	417	Wil
Holly	159	Sum
Isham, Jr.	157	Sum
Isham, Sr.	159	Sum
James	24	Smi
Jesse	417	Wil
John	9	Dic
John	31	Mon
Joseph	29	Lin
Hodges (cont.)		
Josiah	417	Wil
Meredith	157	Sum
Richard	23	Smi
Robert	23	Smi
Robert	24	Smi
Rolen T.	159	Sum
Thomas	23	Smi
Thomas	417	Wil
William	15	Lin
William	23	Smi
Willis	23	Smi
Hodgpeth, John	101	Rut
Hoffman, Christopher	20	Ove
Hoffnagle, Sally	78	Dav
Hoflin, Josiah	34	Bed
Hofman, William	156	Sum
Hogan, Anderson	7	Gil
Anthony	10	Lin
Arthur S.	27	Smi
David	61	Mau
David	6	Per
Edward	12	Jac
Edward	292	War
Ewan	1	Ove
Isaiah	7	Gil
Jane	1	Ove
John	61	Mau
John	100	Rut
John P.	157	Sum
Marcus	279	War
Martha	12	Mon
Orrin	2	Hic
Robert	87	Dav
Wilie	13	Mon
William	41	Bed
William	13	Mon
Hoge, Edward	279	War
Soleman	30	Mau
Hogg, Archiles	14	Law
David	22	Smi
Gibson	14	Law
Gideon	18	Way
John	40	Mau
John B.	79	Rut
Lewis	52	Mau
Pmbethmon	53	Mau
Rebecca	27	Smi
Samuel	76	Dav
see Hagg		
Hoggot, John	74	Dav
Hogh, Gideon	13	Fra
Hogin, John	85	Dav
John	3	Way
William	13	Dic
Hogins, Abraham	13	Dic
William	40	Wll
Hogland, Anthony	7	Lin
James	12	Jac
Hogner, William	14	Fra
Hogue, Miles	12	Fra
Hokum, Samuel	13	Jac
Holan, John	345	Whi

Holand, Peter	62	Mau
Holbert, Enos	285	War
William	1	Har
Holbrooks, Joseph	24	Hic
Maomie	45	Bed
Holcom, Jeptah	311	War
Holcomb, Stephen	302	War
see Hacomb		
Holcombe, Laurence	55	Mau
William	55	Mau
Holcum, Meridith	4	Hum
Nathaniel	1	Hum
Holdaway, John	16	Ove
Holden, Denis	88	Rut
Dennis	84	Rut
George	88	Rut
John E.	18	Gil
Holder, Dempsey	12	Fra
James	12	Fra
James	131	Ste
Jeremiah	12	Fra
John W.	11	Fra
Joseph	11	Fra
Joshua	12	Fra
Moses	12	Fra
Ransom	12	Fra
Solomon	12	Fra
Solomon L.	61	Dav
Spencer	357	Whi
Thomas	12	Fra
Holdmon, Thomas	399	Wil
Hole, Simon	3	Bed
William	3	Bed
Holefield, Elijh.	129	Ste
Holeman, Absolom	3	Ove
Daniel	4	Ove
Daniel	18	Rob
Hardy	19	Ove
Henry	8	Ove
Hud...th	10	Ove
Isaac	19	Ove
James	18	Rob
Jeramiah	8	Ove
Lewis	36	Bed
Reuben	19	Ove
Thomas	14	Rob
William	2	Ove
William	13	Ove
William L.	19	Rob
Holemon, Benjamin	7	Rob
Holford, John	9	Ove
Holiday, Hiram	299	War
Hollace, James	5	Way
James	18	Way
Stephen	7	Way
Hollada, Stephen	11	Jac
Holland, Asa	13	Lin
Benjamin	10	Hic
Benjamin	3	Hum
Britton	24	Smi
Cardy	24	Rob
Charles	8	Har
Daniel	23	Rob
Holland (cont.)		
Daniel	34	Rob
David	5	Mon
David	15	Mon
Eli	27	Smi
Frederic	53	Wll
Gustavus	25	Wll
Hardy	5	Mon
Harrison	372	Whi
Henderson	46	Mau
Jacob	12	Fra
Jacob	13	Gil
James	44	Bed
James	1	Hum
James	49	Mau
James	22	Rob
James	28	Rob
James	346	Whi
Jesse	3	Har
John	3	Har
John	22	Rob
John	129	Ste
John	301	War
Joshua	27	Smi
Josiah	27	Smi
Kemp	6	Wll
Mark	14	Dic
Markus	54	Mau
Martin	27	Smi
Peggy	16	Mon
Peter	13	Lin
Phillip	159	Sum
Richard	14	Hum
Richard A.	397	Wil
Thomas	37	Bed
Thomas	9	Hum
Thomas	7	Rob
Thomas	27	Smi
Thomas, Mr.	7	Law
Tilmon	377	Wil
William	27	Smi
William	414	Wil
Willie	20	Rob
Willie	23	Rob
Willis	27	Smi
see Halland		
Hollandsworth, William	10	Dic
Wm.	383	Wil
Hollaway, E.	129	Ste
Holleman, John	11	Jac
Mark	13	Jac
Thomas	11	Jac
William	11	Jac
Holleway, Sally	5	Hum
Holley, Nicholas [2]	13	Gil
Hollibaugh, George	12	Way
Holligin, Mary	6	Hic
Hollingsworth, Joseph	97	Dav
Lewis	97	Dav
William	98	Dav
Wm.	97	Dav
Hollinsworth, Bengd.	13	Fra
James	13	Fra

Hollis, David 83 Rut
James M. 159 Sum
Jesse 158 Sum
John 33 Mon
John 81 Rut
Micajah 84 Rut
Holliway, John 4 Law
Moses 1 Law
Hollock, William 23 Wll
Holloday, Allen [2] 27 Smi
Ann 27 Smi
Henry 15 Wll
Henry 19 Wll
Holloman, Henry 25 Smi
James 12 Jac
James 13 Jac
Tobias 13 Jac
Hollond, James 3 Lin
Richard 12 Fra
Hollonsworth, Abraham 11 Jac
Samuel 11 Jac
Holloway, Elizabeth 2 Lin
James 11 Fra
Nathan 159 Sum
Robt. 158 Sum
Thos. 3 Hic
William 19 Mon
see Holoway
Hollums see Hallums
Holly, David 24 Lin
James 24 Lin
John 26 Lin
John 25 Smi
Jonathan 158 Sum
Sion 24 Lin
Holm, James 51 Mau
Holman, Daniel 30 Lin
Hardy 30 Lin
Isaac 14 Lin
Isaac 22 Lin
Isaac 47 Lin
James 14 Lin
John 30 Lin
Polly 29 Lin
Yancy 26 Smi
Holmes, Albert 129 Ste
Emanuel 13 Jac
Henry 73 Rut
Isaac 29 Bed
James 23 Bed
James 43 Lin
James 27 Smi
John 11 Jac
John 130 Ste
John 11 Wll
Luke 12 Wll
M. 125 Ste
Mary M. 136 Sum
Nancy 11 Way
Polly 88 Dav
Robert 5 Hum
Robt. 10 Hic
Robt. 158 Sum
Holmes (cont.)
Simon 5 Mon
Solomon 72 Dav
Thomas 5 Hum
William 91 Dav
William 27 Smi
William 389 Wil
Willis 159 Sum
Holms, Sally 23 Rob
Thomas 11 Rob
Hology, Philip 43 Mau
Holoman, Edmond 7 Har
Elizabeth 160 Sum
Josiah 7 Har
Wilson 7 Har
Holoway, George 158 Sum
Nathan, Jr. 159 Sum
Nathl. 160 Sum
Richd. 160 Sum
Holt, Ambrous 25 Mau
Annis 91 Rut
Dempsey 8 Mon
Fielding 88 Rut
Giles 23 Smi
Jacob 14 Fra
James 29 Mon
James 160 Sum
Jesse 24 Smi
Jesse 376 Wil
John 25 Wll
Jorden C. 33 Bed
Joseph 84 Dav
Joshua 1 Bed
Joshua 47 Bed
Micheal 44 Bed
Peter 1 Mon
Peter 3 Mon
Polly 88 Dav
Reubin 8 Mon
Timothy 27 Smi
William 8 Gil
William 3 Mon
William 8 Mon
William 27 Smi
William 160 Sum
Woodley 6 Gil
see Hall, Hatt
Holwell, John 80 Dav
Hombs, Moses 66 Mau
William 66 Mau
Homell, Elisabeth 53 Wll
Homer, Elizabeth 16 Dic
James 17 Dic
John 27 Mau
Homes, Archibald 63 Mau
Horatio 96 Rut
James 6 Per
Robbert 63 Mau
Samuel 28 Mau
William 6 Per
Homsley, John 388 Wil
Honea, James 35 Lin
Honeycut, Adey 160 Sum

Honeycut (cont.)		
Bartlet	160	Sum
Bracy	160	Sum
John	10	Ove
Robert	159	Sum
Hood, Agness	56	Mau
Alexander	7	Gil
Andrew [2]	17	Ove
Charles	21	Mon
Charles	15	Wll
Edward	34	Wll
John	12	Jac
John	14	Ove
Mary	35	Wll
Morgan	13	Dic
Peter	35	Wll
Rolly	12	Jac
Susannah	21	Mon
Thomas	12	Jac
Thomas	359	Whi
Tunis	44	Wll
William	356	Whi
Hoods, Robert	88	Dav
Hooker, James	90	Rut
James	96	Rut
John	37	Bed
Joshua F.	394	Wil
Samuel	5	Law
Thomas	26	Smi
William	96	Rut
Hooks, Charles	111	Ste
Elizabeth	17	Gil
Hooper, Ann	91	Dav
Asa	95	Dav
Baily	8	Hum
Churchwell	91	Dav
Edward	342	Whi
Enoch	1	Per
James	28	Bed
Jeptha	95	Dav
Jesse	92	Dav
John	73	Dav
John	83	Dav
John	8	Hum
Joseph	71	Dav
Joseph	94	Dav
Mary	95	Dav
Nimrod	14	Gil
Thomas	91	Dav
William	39	Bed
William	16	Dic
William	8	Hum
Wm.	1	Mon
Hooser, Jacob	20	Lin
see V. Hooser		
Hooten, Robert	293	War
William	295	War
Hooter, Elijah	310	War
Littleton	298	War
William	310	War
Hooton, Isham	158	Sum
Susanna	159	Sum
Hoover, Ander, Jr.	157	Sum
Hoover (cont.)		
Christopher	95	Rut
Daniel	78	Rut
Henry	6	Ove
Henry	89	Rut
Henry	158	Sum
Jacob	95	Rut
Jacob	121	Ste
John	95	Rut
Martin	49	Bed
Mary	126	Ste
Mathias	89	Rut
Mathias	95	Rut
Mathias, Senr.	95	Rut
Michael	279	War
Philip	315	War
William	25	Bed
Hope, Adam	83	Dav
Eley	30	Mau
Samuel W.	83	Dav
William	8	Wll
Willis	70	Dav
Hopes, John	6	Har
Hopkins, Benjamin	18	Lin
Elizabeth	412	Wil
Jason	10	Gil
John	287	War
Joseph	69	Mau
Neal	62	Dav
Norah	412	Wil
Sarah	23	Smi
Stephen	347	Whi
Thomas	311	War
William	346	Whi
Hopper, Charles	37	Bed
Charles	45	Bed
Charles, Junr.	37	Bed
Gilland	298	War
James	15	Lin
John	6	Gil
Joseph	86	Dav
Lewis	14	Lin
Samuel	22	Gil
Samuel	302	War
Sarah	15	Lin
Thomas	37	Bed
Thomas	65	Dav
Hopson, George B.	32	Mon
John	3	Gil
Lawson	3	Gil
Margret	400	Wil
Youngar	18	Gil
Horace, Isaac	11	Mon
Horcy, Owen	95	Rut
Hord, Standwin	2	Ove
Thomas	2	Ove
Hordway, James	13	Fra
Horn, Charles	406	Wil
Cherry	159	Sum
Edward	15	Gil
Etheldred	389	Wil
Fred.	73	Dav
George	364	Whi

Horn (cont.)
Henry 406 Wil
Howell 405 Wil
Howell 406 Wil
James 14 Gil
James 15 Gil
James 24 Mon
Jane 363 Whi
Joseph 25 Smi
Joshua 14 Gil
Levi 8 Bed
Matthew 377 Wil
Richard 30 Bed
Stephen 7 Ove
Thomas 406 Wil
Willie 8 Gil
see Ham
Hornbarger, Wm. 129 Ste
Hornbeak, Eli B. 1 Hic
James 1 Hic
Hornberger, P. 124 Ste
Horne, George 7 Per
Henry 23 Mon
Josiah 23 Mon
Horner, Jemima 25 Hic
John 4 Per
John, Junr. 5 Per
Russel 4 Per
William 5 Per
Hornhart, George 5 Per
Horning, George 24 Lin
Hornsby, Isaac 88 Rut
John 46 Bed
John 89 Rut
Horse, John 414 Wil
Horsley, James 160 Sum
John 160 Sum
Rolin 160 Sum
William 158 Sum
Horsly, Charles 160 Sum
Horter, Betsey 75 Dav
Horton, Amos 11 Fra
George 160 Sum
James 26 Rob
John 12 Fra
Joseph W. 86 Dav
Josiah 62 Dav
Nelson 88 Rut
William 37 Lin
see Hooton
Hortow see Horton
Hoskins, Jehu 7 Mon
Thomas C. 77 Rut
William, Doct. 418 Wil
Hosley, Stephen 6 Dic
Hoss, George 16 Gil
Joseph D. 48 Bed
Hough, James 36 Wll
Houk, Matthis 377 Wil
Houndskett, Jacob 157 Sum
Housden, Benjamin 13 Wll
House, Ambrose 80 Rut
Claibourn 79 Rut
House (cont.)
David 96 Rut
David 23 Wll
George 118 Ste
Henry 13 Hic
Isaac 24 Wll
Isham 34 Wll
Jacob 16 Lin
Jacob 25 Rob
James 32 Wll
James, Senr. 5 Wll
John 17 Lin
John 118 Ste
John 159 Sum
John 15 Way
John 5 Wll
John C. 95 Dav
Joseph 45 Wll
Robert 23 Wll
William 22 Smi
William [2] 159 Sum
William 35 Wll
see Shouse
Houston, A. C. 2 Law
Aaron 19 Wll
Archibald 8 Gil
Christpher 45 Mau
Edward 3 Dic
James 16 Bed
James 8 Gil
James 45 Mau
James 50 Wll
James B. 77 Dav
John 19 Bed
John 51 Bed
John 291 War
John L. 310 War
Jonathan 31 Lin
Saml. 79 Dav
William 16 Dic
William 11 Fra
William 102 Rut
How, Samuel 92 Dav
William 346 Whi
Howad, G. 24 Mau
Howard, Allen 3 Dic
Allen 95 Rut
Anderson 85 Rut
Barnes 14 Fra
Bradford 383 Wil
Edmund 17 Dic
Elisha 370 Whi
Elizabeth 352 Whi
George D. 359 Whi
Green B. 160 Sum
Henry 12 Fra
Henry 78 Rut
Hierom 16 Gil
Hiram 420 Wil
Isaac 351 Whi
James 12 Fra
James 28 Mau
James 10 Ove

Howard (cont.)
James 111 Ste
James 158 Sum
James 392 Wil
John 9 Lin
John 315 War
John 20 Way
John 27 Wll
Joseph 52 Wll
Joshua 33 Rob
M. 24 Mau
Mace 367 Whi
Meredith 19 Mon
Permenious 28 Mau
Philip 294 War
Philip 315 War
Robert 351 Whi
Samuel 53 Wll
Samuel P. 23 Smi
Sarah 13 Fra
Thomas 14 Fra
Thomas 33 Mau
Thomas 24 Smi
Willeby 38 Mau
William 16 Gil
William 33 Lin
William 352 Whi
Wm. 111 Ste
see Howad
Howe, Jesse 82 Rut
Joseph 7 Hic
Howel, Ambrous 24 Mau
David 38 Lin
Eason 23 Smi
Hiram 37 Lin
Joel 37 Lin
John 84 Rut
John 97 Rut
John 371 Whi
Jonathan 30 Lin
Joseph 1 Way
Josiah 23 Smi
Lydea 12 Jac
Paul 13 Jac
Reas 38 Lin
Samuel 39 Lin
Sterling 160 Sum
Tho. 158 Sum
Willie 27 Smi
see Hawol
Howell, Abner 10 Dic
Charles 127 Ste
Elizabeth 382 Wil
James 98 Dav
Lewis 303 War
Mary 382 Wil
Squire 24 Rob
William 13 Fra
Wm. 24 Hic
Howlett, J. H. 90 Dav
William 65 Dav
Howlin, Francis 89 Rut
Polly 94 Rut
Howrey, George 358 Whi
Howston, David 19 Wll
Hubbard, Benj. 158 Sum
Clark 415 Wil
David 6 Mon
Dempsy 29 Mau
Gootson 36 Wll
James 6 Mon
James 307 War
John 417 Wil
Joseph 43 Wll
Nathaniel 26 Bed
Peter 3 Mon
Robert 24 Smi
Robert 307 War
Robert, Ser. 307 War
Sarah 3 Mon
William 26 Mon
William 17 Rob
Hubberg see Huleberg
Hubbert, Jacob 25 Smi
Richard 25 Smi
Sally 25 Smi
Hubble, Gillead 91 Rut
Hubbles, Bani 96 Dav
Hubboard, Joseph 414 Wil
Reuben 414 Wil
William 414 Wil
Hubbord, John 370 Whi
Hubbs, John 18 Hic
Thomas 6 Hum
William 7 Hum
Wm. 5 Hic
Hubert, William 160 Sum
Huchison, David 93 Rut
Sarah 78 Rut
Huckaby, Bartlett 5 Lin
Elizabeth 5 Lin
John 4 Lin
Samuel S. 21 Gil
Wm. 5 Lin
Huckelue, John 55 Mau
Huddleston, Athony 419 Wil
Benjamin 16 Bed
Benjamin 3 Har
Bennet 11 Rob
Celia 4 Hic
Charles 12 Jac
David 4 Lin
David 29 Rob
David 366 Whi
Field 6 Ove
Henry 26 Smi
James 9 Har
James 4 Lin
James 10 Rob
Jarrott 6 Ove
John 1 Har
John 12 Jac
John 3 Ove
John 10 Rob
John 36 Rob
Jonathan 3 Rob

Huddleston (cont.)
Josiah D. 12 Rob
Lettin 11 Rob
Martha 419 Wil
Milly 6 Ove
Peyton 27 Smi
Simon 5 Ove
William 19 Gil
William 10 Ove
William 11 Rob
William 353 Whi
Willie 6 Ove
Willis 9 Ove
Huddlston, Daniel 11 Way
Hudgings, James 352 Whi
Hudgins, Benjamin 12 Fra
Benjamin 25 Smi
Edward 13 Rob
Gabriel 13 Rob
Holaway 9 Rob
James 13 Rob
Sazuel 26 Rob
Susanna 24 Rob
William 10 Har
William 10 Rob
Hudgon, Farer 10 Har
Hudlow, Barbary 27 Bed
John 33 Rob
Hudnall, Thomas 11 Fra
Hudson, Aaron 20 Rob
Baker 7 Dic
Benjamin 6 Hum
Benjamin 40 Lin
Benjamin 100 Rut
Cutberth 39 Bed
Cuthbert 8 Dic
Damsey P. 12 Hum
David 17 Wll
Edward 9 Hum
Edward 26 Mau
Ezekia 13 Hum
Henry 5 Dic
Henry 76 Rut
Isaac 68 Dav
Isham 13 Gil
James 16 Bed
John 9 Hum
John 158 Sum
Leah 9 Gil
Mary 7 Gil
Moses 26 Rob
Peter 13 Gil
Richard 392 Wil
Thomas 87 Dav
Thomas 5 Dic
Thomas 380 Wil
Thomas W. 4 Hum
William 11 Dic
William 11 Lin
William 420 Wil
Hudspeth, Robert 11 Fra
Seaton 14 Fra
Thomas 64 Mau
Hudspeth (cont.)
William 12 Fra
Hues, James 25 Mau
Huett, Robert 350 Whi
Robert 356 Whi
Huey, Elizabeth 30 Rob
Joseph 30 Rob
Robt. 8 Hic
William 95 Dav
Huf, Lenard 64 Mau
Huff, John 11 Jac
John 15 Ove
Leonard 13 Jac
Susanna 11 Jac
Thomas 10 Wll
Valontine 11 Gil
William 24 Smi
William 367 Whi
Huffman, Balzer 92 Dav
Catharine 24 Rob
Fredrick 28 Bed
George 92 Dav
Henry 28 Bed
John 16 Mon
William 92 Dav
Hufhines, David 23 Smi
Hufman, Michael 4 Rob
Hufmon, Joseph 348 Whi
Huggins, Charles 49 Mau
Jon [Ian?] 93 Rut
Jonathan 74 Rut
Nathaniel 48 Wll
Philip 24 Mon
Polly 26 Lin
Robt. 120 Ste
Vrenar [?] 49 Mau
William 98 Dav
Huggs, Jodiah 114 Wil
Hughbanks, John 3 Per
Hughes, Archilus, Jr. 10 Wll
Edward P. 25 Smi
James A. 12 Fra
John 80 Dav
John 25 Smi
John, Sen. 25 Smi
John B. 25 Smi
Judith 16 Lin
Leander 26 Smi
Littleberry 26 Smi
Robert 62 Dav
Salley 21 Gil
Simeon, Sen. 25 Smi
Simon P. 24 Smi
Thomas 7 Gil
Thomas 22 Lin
William 40 Lin
William 23 Smi
William 24 Smi
William A. 34 Lin
Hughey, Edward 11 Hum
James 56 Mau
John 5 Hic
Hughlette, James 26 Rob

Hughlette (cont.)		
Leroy	17	Rob
Thomas	26	Rob
Toliver	26	Rob
Hughs, Aron	7	Ove
Aron	10	Ove
David	31	Mau
Elijah	16	Rob
Elijah	36	Rob
Harden	315	War
James	14	Law
James	8	Ove
Joel	119	Ste
John	94	Dav
John	26	Mau
John	281	War
John	366	Whi
Josiah	17	Bed
Josiah	365	Whi
Kibble T.	62	Mau
Leander	365	Whi
Nicholas	282	War
Rhody	312	War
Rice	18	Bed
Robert	18	Bed
Robert	401	Wil
Thomas	8	Ove
William	17	Rob
William	158	Sum
Hughston, Joseph	47	Lin
Hughy, Henry, Jur.	9	Lin
Henry, Ser.	9	Lin
Isaac	7	Lin
Hugle, Abraham	388	Wil
Charby	387	Wil
Hukerson, Daniel	10	Dic
Huleberg, Solomon	13	Ove
Hulet, Saml.	118	Ste
Hulett, Silvester	359	Whi
Huling, Fredrick W.	1	Mon
Hullet, William	26	Smi
Hulm, George	33	Wll
Hulme, Robert	17	Wll
Hulmes, John	380	Wil
Hulsy, John	22	Lin
Humble, George	11	Hum
Jacob	1	Hic
Hume, William	98	Dav
Humphreis, John H.	10	Dic
Humphrey, George	19	Rob
John	27	Rob
Sarah	22	Hic
Humphreys, H.	116	Ste
James	59	Dav
John	7	Dic
John	346	Whi
Willie J.	67	Dav
Humphries, George	1	Mon
Parry W.	27	Mon
Uriah	2	Mon
Humtsman, Adam	20	Ove
Hundon, Ann	112	Ste
William	112	Ste
Hundon (cont.)		
Younger	112	Ste
Hunley, John	13	Hic
John	10	Rob
John J.	157	Sum
Josiah	12	Rob
William	158	Sum
Hunnicut, Robert	8	Gil
Hunt, Abel	26	Smi
Andrew	295	War
Archibald	25	Smi
Daniel	12	Law
David	11	Fra
Elijah	32	Lin
Elizabeth	44	Lin
George	19	Gil
George	101	Rut
George W.	44	Lin
Gersham	22	Wll
Harday	113	Wil
Hardy	377	Wil
Henry	13	Fra
Henry	32	Lin
Henry	16	Rob
Henry	101	Rut
Hiram	102	Rut
James	13	Fra
James	5	Rob
James	79	Rut
James	420	Wil
Jeramiah	65	Dav
Jesse	377	Wil
Jno. B.	158	Sum
John	11	Fra
John	25	Rob
John	22	Smi
John	377	Wil
Jorden	16	Rob
Lewis	13	Fra
Martha	158	Sum
Mathew	92	Rut
Matthew	25	Smi
Nathaniel	11	Fra
Pardy	158	Sum
Shadrach	13	Rob
Sion	157	Sum
Sion	4	Wll
Spencer T.	6	Hic
Squier	54	Wll
Thiadoric	158	Sum
Tho.	158	Sum
Tho. W.	158	Sum
Thomas	11	Way
Thomas	377	Wil
William	12	Mon
William	17	Ove
William	16	Rob
Hunter, Aaron	5	Wll
Adam	159	Sum
Alexander	1	Dic
Allen	9	Mon
Andrew	12	Fra
Benjamin	280	War

Hunter (cont.)		
Benjamin	288	War
Burnell	160	Sum
Catherine	49	Wll
Charles	353	Whi
David	86	Dav
Dempsey [2]	9	Mon
Dempsey	157	Sum
Dudley	352	Whi
Elisha	35	Wll
Ephram	21	Bed
Gaskey	11	Dic
Henry	27	Mau
Henry	365	Whi
Isaac	2	Dic
Isaac	401	Wil
James	11	Dic
James A.	401	Wil
John	21	Bed
John	11	Hum
John	29	Mau
John, Jr.	12	Jac
John, Sr.	12	Jac
Josep	314	War
Joseph	366	Whi
Lewis	160	Sum
Lewis	346	Whi
Lydia	159	Sum
Manuel	87	Dav
Needham	159	Sum
Polly	9	Lin
Reuben	46	Lin
Rewben	160	Sum
Sally	12	Jac
Samuel	24	Smi
Samuel	314	War
Thomas	9	Dic
Thomas	13	Rob
Thos.	5	Mon
Washington	1	Dic
William	29	Mau
William	342	Whi
William	365	Whi
see Heneter, Huntey, Hurter		
Huntey, Maury	65	Mau
Huntsman see Humtsman		
Hurbrey, Catharine	22	Bed
Hurd, Armstrong	93	Rut
Charles	92	Rut
Hurley, Amos	9	Lin
John	12	Fra
Josiah	4	Law
Levin	12	Ove
Mary	9	Lin
Telman	12	Ove
Hurly, John C.	7	Bed
William	43	Lin
Hurn, George	10	Ove
Howel	16	Ove
Hurndon, Joseph	53	Mau
Hurst, Elizabeth	91	Dav
Hurt, Harmon	29	Bed
Henry	59	Dav
Hurt (cont.)		
James [2]	51	Mau
Joel	29	Bed
John	29	Bed
Moses	35	Mau
Phillip	87	Dav
Hurter, Cader	159	Sum
Hurtley, Laben	35	Bed
Husbands, John	16	Lin
William	22	Lin
Hush, Thomas	286	War
William	308	War
Husk, Elizabeth	27	Bed
James	34	Lin
James	282	War
James	288	War
Lucy	39	Bed
Mary	293	War
William	30	Bed
see Hanks		
Huson, Richard	56	Mau
Hust, Isaac	319	War
Jesse	4	Way
John	16	Mon
Hustin, John	45	Lin
Huston, Franklin R.	28	Mau
Samuel	62	Mau
Walter	355	Whi
William	9	Rob
Hutceson, James	61	Mau
Hutcheson, James	14	Mon
Jesse	8	Law
John	8	Law
Lewis	19	Mon
William	61	Mau
Hutchings, Eli	2	Har
William	419	Wil
Hutchins, Aron	343	Whi
Benjamin	343	Whi
Charles	343	Whi
John	343	Whi
Moses	343	Whi
Thomas	343	Whi
Webster	343	Whi
Hutchinson, David	93	Rut
Mary	52	Wll
Sarah	52	Wll
Spencer	53	Wll
Thomas	52	Wll
see Huthchison		
Hutchis, William	13	Jac
Hutchison, Ambrose	9	Rob
Coleman	7	Law
Geo.	11	Jac
James	29	Rob
John	13	Jac
John	20	Mon
John	1	Rob
John	158	Sum
John T.	13	Dic
Polly	11	Jac
Sandford	19	Rob
Thomas	11	Jac

Hutchison (cont.)		
William	157	Sum
William, Sr.	159	Sum
William G.	18	Rob
Wilson	12	Rob
see Hutc(h)eson, Hut(h)chi(n)son		
Huthchison, Elizabeth	6	Hic
Huton, Yearley	12	Ove
Hutson, —	24	Mau
Abel	345	Whi
Addam B.	47	Mau
Archibald	353	Whi
Benjamin	357	Whi
Claricy	345	Whi
Creecy	347	Whi
David	348	Whi
George	347	Whi
Isaac	347	Whi
Isaiah	345	Whi
James	364	Whi
John	21	Rob
John	357	Whi
John	45	Wll
John	58	Wll
Mathias	353	Whi
Obadiah	13	Jac
Oby	392	Wil
Patience	364	Whi
Sarah	159	Sum
William	12	Fra
William	13	Jac
William	347	Whi
see Hudson		
Hutton, Henry N.	16	Wll
Isabela	3	Ove
John	12	Fra
John M.	58	Mau
John M.	18	Wll
Samuel	62	Dav
Hyatt, John	37	Lin
Simeon	24	Smi
Hyde, Benjamin	89	Dav
Edmond	88	Dav
Hartwell	11	Wll
Henry	66	Dav
Henry	25	Mau
John	25	Rob
John H.	3	Dic
Rebecca	89	Dav
Richard	86	Dav
Richard W.	11	Wll
see Hide		
Hyder, Jacob	365	Whi
Hylton, Arnold	13	Fra
James	12	Fra
Joseph	11	Fra
Hymes, John	40	Bed
Hynes, Andrew	76	Dav
Isaac	12	Fra
John	27	Smi
Mildred	12	Fra
Willie G. [E. ?]	12	Fra
see Hines, Hins		

--- I ---

Idleit, David	63	Mau
Imes, John	162	Sum
Ince, John	13	Ove
Incur, Mary	91	Rut
Indsly, John	14	Fra
Ing, Joseph	162	Sum
Mathew	162	Sum
Inge, Josiah W.	29	Smi
William	28	Smi
Inglish, Edward	36	Mau
Thomas	33	Mau
Ingram, Beasley	9	Gil
Charles	8	Gil
David	6	Hum
Ira	78	Dav
Job	27	Smi
John	27	Smi
John	22	Way
Marmaduke	161	Sum
Moses	15	Mon
Saml.	18	Bed
Shaderick	381	Wil
Sterling	25	Mon
Susan	64	Wll
William	14	Fra
Inman, Ezekiel	162	Sum
Jehu	14	Fra
John	53	Wll
John, Junr.	12	Law
John, Senr.	12	Law
Kiah	51	Wll
Michael [?]	12	Law
Samuel	6	Per
Innman, John	61	Dav
Lzarus	93	Dav
see Jinnman		
Insley, Littleton	388	Wil
Inwin see Irwin		
Irby, Charles	162	Sum
Gerald	10	Gil
John	401	Wil
Joseph	400	Wil
Iredale, John	71	Dav
William H.	52	Bed
Ireion, George	46	Wll
Ireland, Archd.	47	Lin
Daniel	26	Wll
Henery	59	Mau
Irian, John P.	27	Wll
Irsway, Samuel	62	Wll
Irven, William	18	Rob
William B.	98	Dav
Irvin, Andrew	128	Ste
Charles	9	Gil
Christopher	7	Wll
Robert	44	Wll
William	15	Fra
Irvine, David	21	Gil
Josephus, Mr.	9	Law
Irwin, George H.	17	Hic

Irwin (cont.)		
Jesse	15	Fra
Robert	51	Wll
Vincent	51	Wll
William	107	She
Isaacks, Abraham	45	Lin
John W.	30	Lin
Samuel	30	Lin
Isaacs, Jacob C.	14	Fra
Isam, Arthur	68	Mau
Elizebeth	68	Mau
George, Mr.	3	Law
James	34	Mau
John	68	Mau
Isbel, Thomas	17	Rob
Isbell, Daniel	6	Mon
William	299	War
Zachariah	304	War
Isby, David	30	Mau
John	30	Mau
Isham, Bridges	47	Wll
Charles	350	Whi
Charles	357	Whi
Edmond	47	Lin
Elijah	360	Whi
Elijah	363	Whi
James	47	Lin
James	372	Whi
John	363	Whi
Margaret	27	Smi
Ishmael, Benjamin	11	Gil
Istean, Edward	9	Bed
Ivey, Elijah	12	Dic
Frederic	52	Wll
Lovel	308	War
Ivy, Absolum	13	Bed
Benjamin	103	Rut
Catherine	40	Bed
David	95	Dav
Henry	33	Bed
James	15	Fra
John	72	Dav
John H.	103	Rut
Loven	317	War
Patsey	40	Bed
Thomas	103	Rut
Vardeman	15	Fra
see Jay		
Izbell, Abraham	370	Whi
James	36	Lin
William	37	Lin
Izell, Daniel	13	Law
Izer, Darby	71	Dav
Izzard, Jeremiah	152	Sum

--- J ---

Jack, Andrew	28	Mau
Elisabeth	40	Wll
Milton H.	18	Way
Samuel	65	Mau
Jackson, Abel	122	Ste
Abner	46	Wll
Abraham	386	Wil
Alexander	29	Smi
Ally	46	Lin
Andrew	14	Jac
Andw.	74	Dav
Archibald	26	Mon
Azariah	14	Jac
Ben.	401	Wil
Brice	5	Mon
Burton	6	Hum
Coleman	101	Rut
Colemon	403	Wil
Craven	77	Dav
Daniel	402	Wil
Danl.	127	Ste
David	13	Ove
David	116	Ste
David	127	Ste
David	354	Whi
David	411	Wil
David, Senr.	13	Ove
Dubney	386	Wil
Eli	127	Ste
Elias	14	Jac
Elisha	118	Ste
Elizabeth	93	Dav
Epps	16	Dic
Francis	60	Wll
Graham	349	Whi
Henry	123	Ste
Henry	40-	Wil
Hugh	14	Fra
Hugh	127	Ste
Isam	43	Mau
Isim	402	Wil
James	45	Mau
James	51	Mau
James	10	Ove
James	127	Ste
James	161	Sum
James	162	Sum
James	18	Way
James	364	Whi
James	392	Wil
James	415	Wil
James	56	Wll
Jeremiah	2	Law
Jesse	113	Ste
Jesse	161	Sum
Jesse	401	Wil
Jesse	28	Wll
John	7	Bed
John	3	Hum
John	14	Jac
John	2	Lin
John	2	Ove
John	14	Ove
John	2	Per
John	116	Ste
John	311	War
John	365	Whi

Jackson (cont.)		
John M.	401	Wil
Jordon	80	Dav
Joseph	43	Mau
Joseph	161	Sum
Joshua	9	Way
Josiah	386	Wil
Josiah	62	Wll
Lamuele	14	Jac
Larkin	78	Rut
Larkin	97	Rut
Leroy	96	Rut
Lewis	130	Ste
Lovey	72	Dav
Mark	43	Mau
Mark L.	53	Mau
Matthew	88	Dav
Miles	386	Wil
Mitchel K.	14	Fra
Nelson	51	Mau
Obadiah	58	Dav
Reuben	401	Wil
Richard	1	Dic
Richard	14	Fra
Rilly	54	Mau
Robert	11	Dic
Robert	23	Rob
Robert	28	Smi
Robt.	113	Ste
Sally	94	Rut
Samuel	14	Fra
Samuel	29	Smi
Samuel	311	War
Stephen	161	Sum
Stewart	75	Rut
Thomas	14	Fra
Thomas	28	Smi
Thomas	29	Smi
Thomas	60	Wll
Tishe	124	Ste
William	61	Dav
William	72	Dav
William	15	Fra
William	14	Jac
William	14	Ove
William	120	Ste
William	162	Sum
William	364	Whi
William	386	Wil
William	39	Wll
Willis	15	Dic
Wm.	106	She
Wm.	9	Way
Wm. C.	1	Lin
Jaco, Brooks	305	War
Jeramiah	286	War
Jacob, Perry	31	Bed
Jacobs, Baswell	392	Wil
Caleb	161	Sum
Edward	407	Wil
Edward	410	Wil
Edy	162	Sum
Isaac	186	Sum
Jacobs (cont.)		
Jeremiah	93	Rut
John	94	Rut
Moses	161	Sum
Samuel	96	Rut
William	14	Fra
William	95	Rut
William	291	War
Williams	59	Mau
Jadurn, Josep	308	War
Jakes, John	21	Bed
Jalcob see Johns		
James, Aaron	4	Dic
Abner	46	Lin
Amos	7	Dic
Anderson	85	Rut
Carey	90	Rut
Champ	3	Hum
Champ	127	Ste
Daniel	304	War
David	120	Ste
Edmund	29	Smi
Edmundson, Mr.	9	Law
Enoch	21	Way
Enos	4	Dic
George	31	Rob
Henry	5	Gil
Henry W.	124	Ste
Isaac	15	Fra
Isaac	6	Gil
Jesse	320	War
John	116	Ste
John	162	Sum
John P., Senr.	86	Rut
Joseph	106	She
Joshua	7	Dic
Minzy	29	Smi
Newberry	46	Lin
Noah	303	War
Prianna	123	Ste
Richard	14	Rob
Richard	24	Rob
Robert L.	82	Rut
Samuel	46	Lin
Solomon	26	Rob
Stephen	15	Fra
Thomas	89	Dav
Thomas	5	Har
Thomas	8	Per
Thomas	84	Rut
Thomas	124	Ste
Thos. W.	120	Ste
William	88	Dav
William	22	Gil
William	7	Hum
William	127	Ste
William	360	Whi
William D.	9	Har
Willis	16	Lin
Wm.	404	Wil
Wood	112	Wil
Jameson, Elizabeth	17	Lin
John	59	Mau

Jamison, B.	117	Ste
Henry D.	73	Rut
Hugh B.	76	Rut
James	14	Fra
James	14	Fra
Jeremiah	28	Smi
John	29	Wll
Marshal	28	Wll
Robert	16	Mon
Robert	131	Ste
Thomas	28	Smi
William D.	27	Mon
Wm. C.	1	Mon
see Jimison		
Jane, Gilly	6	Ove
Janes, Philip	283	War
Janigan, Lewis	18	Bed
Lewis	30	Bed
January, Isaac	293	War
Janus, William	96	Dav
Jarman, Amos H.	26	Mau
Hall	25	Mau
John	14	Fra
Robert	419	Wil
Jarmon, Emory	2	Hic
John	15	Fra
Robert	5	Hum
Stephen	5	Hum
Jarrad, Charles	14	Jac
Joseph	14	Jac
Moses	14	Jac
William	14	Jac
William, Jr.	14	Jac
Jarratt, Gideon	95	Rut
Thomas	84	Rut
Jarrell, Charles [2]	7	Har
John	4	Har
John	7	Har
Jarret, John	14	Fra
Vincent	14	Fra
Jarrett, Deverex	396	Wil
John	9	Hic
Susanna	19	Way
Jarrott, Archilous	84	Rut
Jarves, Susana	26	Lin
Jarvis, Abner	298	War
David	6	Mon
Kezia	294	War
Levi	294	War
Nancy	13	Jac
Sally	14	Jac
Jasper, James	14	Fra
Joseph	14	Fra
Nicholas	400	Wil
Jay, David	293	War
John	317	War
William	285	War
William	364	Whi
see Ivy		
Jeanes, Obadiah	15	Fra
Jeans, David	28	Lin
John	28	Lin
Martha	28	Lin
Jefferson, Peter F.	161	Sum
Sarah	162	Sum
Thomas	60	Dav
Jeffreys, James O.	28	Smi
Osborne	28	Smi
Jeffries, John	23	Mon
John	23	Mon
William	24	Mon
Jellet, Jeptha	96	Dav
Jenakin, Alexander	105	Rut
Jenings, Rebeca	363	Whi
Jenkins, Averett	28	Smi
Charles	29	Smi
James	28	Smi
James	36	Wll
James G.	112	Ste
Jehu	15	Fra
Jesse	15	Fra
Jinkey	363	Whi
Jno. N.	22	Hic
Job	22	Hic
John	21	Hic
John	29	Smi
Joseph	14	Fra
Joseph	21	Lin
Littleton	20	Ove
Nathan	418	Wil
Noah	28	Smi
Roderick	29	Smi
Samuel	32	Lin
Samuel	28	Smi
Thomas	92	Dav
Thomas	28	Smi
William	19	Ove
William	28	Smi
Wilson	28	Smi
Wilton F. L.	8	Gil
Jennings, Betsey	28	Smi
Isaac	120	Ste
Jacob	416	Wil
Jesse	5	Lin
Jesse	86	Rut
John	3	Ove
John	11	Ove
Obediah	288	War
Samuel	3	Ove
William	30	Lin
William D.	9	Gil
see Gennings, Jinnings		
Jens, John	29	Smi
Jentry, Claiburn	88	Dav
David	14	Jac
Jesse	13	Jac
Jesse	14	Jac
Robert	13	Jac
Watson	61	Wll
William	17	Ove
Jermon, Josiah	371	Whi
Jerney, James	38	Mau
William	58	Mau
Jernigan, Allen	26	Rob
Braden	20	Rob
David	3	Rob

Jernigan (cont.)		
David	7	Rob
David	114	Ste
Henry	32	Rob
Robert	3	Dic
Silas	40	Wll
Thos.	10	Dic
William	18	Rob
William	21	Rob
Jervas, Samuel	356	Whi
Jervis, Cornelious	347	Whi
Eliphelet	358	Whi
John	361	Whi
Jester, Saml.	396	Wil
Jett, Edward	14	Mon
Ferdinand	14	Fra
Humphrey	99	Rut
John	360	Whi
Jetton, Isaac	80	Rut
Isaac L.	78	Rut
James S.	82	Rut
Joel	14	Fra
John, Sen.	77	Rut
John L.	81	Rut
Robert	74	Rut
Robert	104	Rut
Jewel, George W.	279	War
James	15	Fra
Stephen	14	Fra
Jewell, Joseph	81	Dav
William	73	Dav
William	417	Wil
Jiles, Meadow	14	Jac
Jimerson, Elisabeth	55	Wll
Jimison, William M.	162	Sum
Jinings, John	162	Sum
Jinkens, Obediah	55	Mau
Jinkins, Jacob	13	Jac
James	161	Sum
James P.	162	Sum
Joabmay	18	Way
John	13	Jac
Nimrod	89	Rut
Roderick	161	Sum
Samuel	10	Law
William	408	Wil
William	66	Wll
Wyatt	409	Wil
Jinnings, —, Doctor	7	Per
Jinnman, Ezekiel	93	Dav
see Innman		
Jinsey, William	43	Wll
Jintry, Michael	14	Jac
Jitton, John	14	Jac
Job, Andrew	62	Dav
John	61	Dav
Jobe, Aaron	10	Lin
Abreham	61	Mau
Daniel	36	Mau
Elizebeth	61	Mau
James	63	Mau
John	8	Law
John	12	Lin

Jobe (cont.)		
John	36	Mau
Nathan	14	Law
Samuel	10	Lin
Samuel	61	Mau
John, Palmer	402	Wil
Rice	22	Rob
Johng see Johns		
Johns, Abner	84	Rut
Abraham	91	Rut
Benjamin	28	Smi
Elias	29	Smi
Enoch	28	Smi
Jalcob	103	Rut
Jesse	28	Smi
John	14	Fra
John	100	Rut
John, Jr.	90	Dav
John, Sr.	62	Dav
Joseph	81	Rut
William	63	Dav
William	397	Wil
Johnson, Abnar	38	Mau
Abner	37	Mau
Abner	119	Ste
Alexander	36	Mau
Alexander	56	Wll
Allen	26	Wll
Amey	54	Mau
Amous	66	Mau
Anderson, Mr.	5	Law
Andrew	2	Wll
Andrew M.	14	Wll
Angus	22	Lin
Ann	80	Dav
Archd.	162	Sum
Arthur	12	Rob
Austin	161	Sum
Benja.	161	Sum
Benjamin	14	Fra
Benjamin	15	Fra
Benjamin	99	Rut
Benjamin	28	Smi
Benjamin	26	Wll
Britain	343	Whi
Burel	58	Mau
Carter	29	Smi
Catharine	22	Lin
Charles	384	Wil
Chasita	19	Ove
Daniel	30	Bed
Daniel	23	Wll
Eanl.	161	Sum
David	4	Wll
Duncan	411	Wil
Edmund	15	Fra
Edward	81	Rut
Eleanor	404	Wil
Elizabeth	78	Rut
Elizabeth	413	Wil
Enoch	6	Ove
Francis	4	Hic
Francis	162	Sum

Johnson (cont.)

Fredrick	20	Bed
Garret	29	Smi
Gaun	283	War
General	128	Ste
George H.	161	Sum
Gidian	37	Mau
Gregory	398	Wil
Hardy	279	War
Henry	3	Rob
Henry M.	6	Rob
Hezekiah	11	Hic
Hezekiah	12	Hum
Howel	26	Lin
Hugh	162	Sum
Hutson	3	Dic
Isaac	2	Dic
Isaac	2	Ove
Isaac	397	Wil
Isham	10	Ove
Isim, Jr.	383	Wil
Isim, Sen.	383	Wil
Jacob	128	Ste
James	23	Bed
James	30	Bed
James [2]	14	Fra
James	2	Rob
James	20	Rob
James	31	Rob
James	105	Rut
James	29	Smi
James	161	Sum
James	305	War
James	341	Whi
James	363	Whi
James	376	Wil
James	389	Wil
James	397	Wil
James	404	Wil
James	417	Wil
James F.	27	Lin
James H.	26	Wll
Jeffre	49	Wll
Jermiah	397	Wil
Jesse	161	Sum
Joel	3	Lin
Joel	13	Wll
Joel	50	Wll
John	79	Dav
John	12	Dic
John	15	Fra
John	6	Hum
John	7	Hum
John	10	Hum
John	32	Mau
John	35	Mau
John	38	Mau
John	1	Ove
John	15	Ove
John	2	Rob
John	93	Rut
John [3]	28	Smi
John [4]	29	Smi

Johnson (cont.)

John	311	War
John	19	Way
John	343	Whi
John	383	Wil
John	385	Wil
John	420	Wil
John	48	Wll
John, Sen.	28	Smi
John, Sen.	29	Smi
John A.	29	Smi
John H.	91	Rut
John H.	104	Rut
John O.	15	Fra
John S.	23	Lin
Jonathan	161	Sum
Jonathan	16	Way
Joseph	23	Rob
Larkin	78	Rut
Lemuel	15	Fra
Levy	128	Ste
Lewis	55	Mau
Lewis	161	Sum
Lewis	2	Way
Lewis	396	Wil
Littleton	34	Wll
Lively C.	98	Rut
Martha	24	Wll
Martin	305	War
Mary	80	Dav
Mathew	64	Mau
Matthew	24	Bed
Matthew	405	Wil
Matthew	21	Wll
Meredith	4	Gil
Meredith	4	Hum
Micajah	343	Whi
Moses	19	Hic
Nancy	360	Whi
Neil	22	Lin
Oliver C.	416	Wil
Patsey	54	Wll
Peter	20	Hic
Peter	119	Ste
Peter C.	383	Wil
Philip	398	Wil
Randolph	112	Ste
Reuben	8	Hum
Reuben	28	Smi
Richard	8	Dic
Richard	128	Ste
Richard C.	161	Sum
Richd. [2]	102	Sum
Robert [2]	14	Fra
Robert	5	Law
Robert	100	Rut
Robert	29	Smi
Robert	161	Sum
Robert	384	Wil
Robert	398	Wil
Robert	20	Wll
Saml.	161	Sum
Samuel	14	Fra

Johnson (cont.)		
Samuel	19	Way
Samuel	364	Whi
Samuel	377	Wil
Samuel	401	Wil
Sarah	14	Fra
Sherid	283	War
Silas	14	Fra
Simon	54	Mau
Sion	19	Ove
Solomon	28	Smi
Solomon	400	Wil
Southern H.	18	Rob
Swanson	40	Wll
Tho.	162	Sum
Thomas	15	Fra
Thomas	44	Mau
Thomas [2]	4	Rob
Thomas	20	Rob
Thomas	24	Rob
Thomas	85	Rut
Thomas	29	Smi
Thos.	112	Ste
Turner	19	Ove
Uriah	16	Hic
W. G.	161	Sum
Widie	10	Har
Wilea	2	Wll
Wiley	55	Mau
William	20	Bed
William	23	Bed
William	14	Dic
William	1	Hum
William	29	Mau
William	47	Mau
William	95	Rut
William [2]	29	Smi
William	161	Sum
William	294	War
William	300	War
William	305	War
William	385	Wil
William	386	Wil
William	390	Wil
William	417	Wil
William	2	Wll
William H.	1	Hum
William J.	58	Mau
William W.	417	Wil
Willis	28	Smi
Johnstin, Danl.	161	Sum
Johnston, Abel	24	Mon
Amos A.	67	Dav
Aquila	17	Mon
Benjamin	19	Gil
Cader	36	Bed
Charles	66	Dav
Daniel	24	Bed
Daniel	14	Jac
Dicy	14	Jac
Elisha	5	Gil
Elizabeth	14	Jac
Francis	14	Jac

Johnston (cont.)		
George	25	Mau
Gideon	83	Dav
Henry	103	Rut
Isaac	66	Dav
Isaac	22	Mon
James	24	Bed
James	26	Bed
James	9	Gil
James	30	Mau
James	17	Mon
James B.	84	Dav
Jeffrey	85	Dav
John	60	Dav
John	85	Dav
John	10	Gil
John	22	Gil
John	6	Mon
John	23	Mon
John	105	Rut
John	14	Way
John	54	Wll
John, Senr.	105	Rut
John, Snr.	32	Mau
John S.	16	Mon
Jonathan	14	Mon
Joseph	61	Mau
Josiah	85	Dav
Josiah	13	Mon
Lewis	56	Mau
Lewis [deleted]	57	Mau
Matthew	10	Gil
Nancy	27	Mon
Nimrod	14	Jac
Philip	1	Mon
Randal	67	Dav
Richard	98	Dav
Richard	10	Gil
Robert	61	Dav
Robert	91	Dav
Robert	14	Jac
Robert	22	Mon
Robert G.	19	Mon
Robet	68	Mau
Spirus	39	Bed
Stephen	94	Dav
Thomas	30	Bed
Thomas	66	Dav
Thomas	11	Gil
Thomas	13	Jac
Thomas	43	Mau
Thompson	23	Mon
William	105	Rut
Joice, James	10	Bed
Peter	36	Mau
Pleasant	61	Wll
Robbert	64	Mau
Joiner, Cornelius	381	Wil
Cullen	161	Sum
Icim	382	Wil
Jesse	161	Sum
John	161	Sum
Joseph	298	War

Joiner (cont.)
Joshua 404 Wil
Lott 398 Wil
Micajah 381 Wil
Solomon 14 Fra
Tho. 162 Sum
Thomas 12 Gil
Whitehead 15 Mon
William 13 Jac
William 14 Jac
Joins, John 8 Lin
Jolley, Martha 9 Gil
Jolly, Jesse 113 Ste
Stephen 14 Fra
Thos. 2 Mon
Jones, Abner 12 Lin
Abraham 289 War
Acquilla 279 War
Agnes 14 Jac
Alexander 19 Gil
Allen 14 Fra
Allen 5 Hic
Allen 37 Mau
Alsey 10 Mon
Alston 16 Hic
Amzie 96 Rut
Ann 388 Wil
Anthony 27 Rob
Anthony 32 Rob
Arasmus 415 Wil
Arick 282 War
Augustus L. 22 Lin
Barbary 29 Smi
Benja. 161 Sum
Benjamin 5 Gil
Benjamin 44 Wll
Betsey 29 Smi
Beverel 283 War
Biram 361 Whi
Britton 14 Fra
C. Lewis 1 Per
Charles 1 Bed
Charles 37 Bed
Charles 283 War
Charlotte 19 Gil
Clellin 14 Jac
David 6 Gil
David 18 Lin
David 28 Lin
David 44 Lin
David 10 Mon
David 20 Rob
David 360 Whi
David L. 18 Gil
Davidson 3 Ove
Dempsey 72 Dav
Ebenezer 371 Whi
Edmund 186 Sum
Ednund 99 Rut
Edward 4 Mon
Edward [2] 161 Sum
Edward 314 War
Edward 415 Wil

Jones (cont.)
Edward D. 11 Gil
Edward D. 36 Mau
Eleanor 398 Wil
Elijah 2 Dic
Elijah 1 Per
Elijah 399 Wil
Elijah 403 Wil
Elisha 29 Smi
Elizabeth 87 Rut
Elizabeth 162 Sum
Elizabeth 382 Wil
Elizabeth 416 Wil
Ellis 47 Wll
Enoch 116 Ste
Enoch 282 War
Erasmus 4 Mon
Evan 1 Ove
Ezekiel 6 Mon
Ezra 78 Rut
Francis 8 Hic
Frederick 29 Smi
Gabriel 15 Fra
Gabriel 38 Lin
Gabriel 161 Sum
George 22 Lin
George 57 Wll
George W. 1 Law
Gilis 2 Dic
Glover 19 Mon
Hannah 351 Whi
Hardy 85 Rut
Harrison 29 Smi
Henry 11 Har
Henry 12 Hic
Henry 19 Hic
Henry 13 Jac
Henry 393 Wil
Hezekiah 6 Gil
Hugh 19 Bed
Hugh 21 Hic
Ignatius 394 Wil
Isaac 93 Dav
Isaac 11 Har
Isaac 8 Ove
Isaac 292 War
Isham 127 Ste
J. R. 13 Jac
Jacob 5 Gil
James 11 Bed
James 29 Bed
James 30 Bed
James 2 Dic
James 14 Fra
James 21 Hic
James 14 Jac
James 28 Lin
James 33 Mau
James 36 Mau
James 44 Mau
James 10 Mon
James 17 Mon
James [2] 25 Mon

Jones (cont.)
James 22 Rob
James 29 Rob
James 30 Rob
James 79 Rut
James 84 Rut
James 28 Smi
James [2] 29 Smi
James 120 Ste
James 310 War
James 313 War
James 407 Wil
James 408 Wil
James 409 Wil
James G. 18 Wll
Jarvis 72 Dav
Jarvis 20 Hic
Jedson 26 Wll
Jesse 11 Har
Jesse 44 Lin
Jesse 4 Rob
Jessee 28 Mon
John 11 Bed
John 30 Bed
John 50 Bed
John 62 Dav
John 83 Dav
John 94 Dav
John 7 Dic
John 15 Fra
John 19 Gil
John [2] 14 Jac
John 6 Lin
John 39 Lin
John 34 Mau
John 41 Mau
John 58 Mau
John 19 Mon
John 4 Ove
John 25 Rob
John 74 Rut
John 28 Smi
John 126 Ste
John 129 Ste
John 131 Ste
John [2] 161 Sum
John 398 Wil
John 408 Wil
John, Jur. 21 Gil
John, Sen. 29 Smi
John, Sen. 383 Wil
John B. 79 Rut
John C. 383 Wil
John M. 27 Mau
John W. 96 Dav
John W. 40 Mau
Johnathan 14 Jac
Jonathan 315 War
Jonathan 25 Wll
Jonathan, Jr. 21 Hic
Jonathan, Sr. 21 Hic
Jordan 12 Hic
Jordan 385 Wil

Jones (cont.)
Joseph 7 Gil
Joseph 5 Hic
Joseph 9 Lin
Joseph 28 Smi
Joseph 303 War
Joshua 98 Rut
Joshua T. 286 War
Julius 5 Hum
Laben 29 Bed
Larkin 279 War
Lazrus 354 Whi
Lemuel A. 28 Smi
Lenard [2] 68 Mau
Leonard 28 Smi
Lewis 93 Dav
Lewis 107 She
Lucy 399 Wil
Luton 80 Rut
Margaret 15 Fra
Martin 14 Jac
Martin 25 Rob
Mary [2] 25 Lin
Mary 186 Sum
Mary 356 Whi
Matthew 29 Bed
McClenden 14 Jac
Morton 19 Bed
Moses 93 Rut
Moses 137 Sum
Moses 161 Sum
Mourning 28 Smi
Nancy [2] 14 Jac
Nancy 23 Rob
Nancy 94 Rut
Nancy 162 Sum
Nathaniel 93 Rut
Nathaniel 279 War
Nelson P. 68 Dav
Nicholas 27 Lin
Patey 91 Rut
Patsey 6 Gil
Pleasant 26 Mau
Polly 15 Hic
Protiman 14 Jac
Rachael 18 Ove
Ralph 383 Wil
Redding 383 Wil
Reuben 3 Rob
Richard 14 Fra
Richard 22 Lin
Richard 53 Mau
Richard 68 Mau
Richard 24 Rob
Richard 161 Sum
Richard 384 Wil
Richard 398 Wil
Richd. 20 Mon
Richd. 21 Mon
Robert 14 Jac
Robert 117 Ste
Robertson 385 Wil
Ruth 28 Smi

Jones (cont.)
Sally 72 Dav
Saml. 12 Hic
Saml. 21 Hic
Samuel 3 Lin
Samuel 36 Mau
Samuel 28 Smi
Sarah 36 Mau
Sarah 33 Mon
Solomon 2 Hic
Squire 162 Sum
Susanna 33 Rob
Taylor 48 Wll
Tho. 161 Sum
Thomas 29 Bed
Thomas 45 Bed
Thomas 61 Dav
Thomas 3 Dic
Thomas 21 Hic
Thomas 19 Lin
Thomas 36 Mau
Thomas 7 Rob
Thomas 23 Rob
Thomas 29 Smi
Thomas 283 War
Thomas 308 War
Thomas 315 War
Thomas 318 War
Thomas 343 Whi
Thomas 412 Wil
Thomas [2] 44 Wll
Thomas, Sr. 3 Rob
Thomas A. 9 Wll
Thomas B. 9 Gil
Thornton 8 Rob
Thos. 25 Mon
Vincen 410 Wil
Waddy 6 Rob
Waitman 28 Rob
Westley 14 Jac
Wilea 24 Wll
William [2] 29 Bed
William 74 Dav
William 5 Gil
William 7 Gil
William 22 Gil
William 9 Hic
William 12 Hic
William 14 Jac
William 6 Lin
William 46 Lin
William 5 Ove
William 34 Rob
William 102 Rut
William 29 Smi
William 120 Ste
William [3] 161 Sum
William 315 War
William 371 Whi
William 383 Wil
William 404 Wil
William 419 Wil
William, Jr. 15 Hic

Jones (cont.)
William B. 14 Fra
William F. 410 Wil
Willie 28 Smi
Willie 29 Smi
Willie M. 15 Hic
Willis 14 Fra
Willis 64 Mau
Willis 78 Rut
Wm. 21 Hic
Wood 376 Wil
Zacharia 93 Dav
Zachariah 343 Whi
see Floyd, Imes, Janes
Jonew, James 17 Lin
Jonston, William 63 Mau
Joplin, Elihu 406 Wil
Mark 407 Wil
Robert 407 Wil
Thomas 403 Wil
Jordan, Benjamin 62 Dav
Milley 81 Dav
Jorden, Archibald 55 Wll
Joshua 16 Rob
Richard 14 Rob
Zacheriah 16 Bed
Jordon, Clement 28 Smi
Evins 33 Wll
George 54 Wll
Henry 15 Fra
Henry 27 Wll
Isaac 57 Wll
John 59 Mau
Johnson 7 Wll
Johnson 56 Wll
Reaves 13 Wll
Robert 11 Wll
Stephen 7 Wll
Thomas 56 Wll
Welcher 11 Wll
William 11 Wll
William 54 Wll
Josia, Allen 161 Sum
Patsey 162 Sum
Joslin, Benjamin 60 Dav
Danl. 73 Dav
Gabril 37 Wll
John 14 Dic
Richd. 73 Dav
Samuel 94 Dav
Joston, —— [Eddleman &] 8 Jac
Jouett, Matthew 1 Ove
Tho. 161 Sum
Jourdan, Alexander 103 Rut
John 101 Rut
Samuel 21 Mon
William 18 Mon
see Nancey
Jourdin, Samuel 7 Gil
George J. 9 Gil
Journagin, William 13 Hum
Journy see Jerney
Joy see Ivy

Jucur see Incur
Judah, Hunter 6 Law
Julam, Kelly 300 War
Julan, Willie 305 War
Julian, Benjamine 352 Whi
Benjamine 371 Whi
James 20 Bed
Uban 352 Whi
Jumphres, Daniel 23 Wll
Jurdin, Drury 62 Dav
Jinney 62 Dav
John 68 Dav
Meradith 86 Dav
Justice, Alfred 11 Rob
James 349 Whi
James S. 2 Rob
Julias 2 Rob
Mark 161 Sum
William 8 Mon
Justus, Esther 28 Smi
John 14 Fra

--- K ---

Kabble see Hubble
Kagh see Kagle
Kagle, Charles 314 War
Jacob 281 War
Kalb see Hall
Kalton, Joel 7 Gil
Kanady, Jesse 41 Wll
John M. 56 Mau
Kanannour, William 46 Wll
Kane, Joseph K. 76 Dav
Kannaerd, Philip 17 Way
Kasinger see Basinger
Kaskey, Samuel 21 Gil
Kates, Thos. 24 Mon
Kath, Nancy 30 Smi
Kay, John 32 Mon
William 84 Rut
Kea, Benjamin 16 Ove
Theophilus 11 Ove
Keagle, George 92 Dav
Keagles, Charles 93 Dav
John, Sr. 93 Dav
Kealing, Leonard 63 Dav
Kean, Abner 30 Smi
Currel 163 Sum
Elisha 163 Sum
John 162 Sum
John 163 Sum
John, Sr. 163 Sum
Joseph 81 Dav
Nancy 125 Ste
Keane, Matthias 4 Dic
Kearby, Archibald 15 Jac
Elizabeth 15 Jac
Francis, Jur. 16 Lin
Francis, Ser. 16 Lin
Jacob 15 Jac
Kearby (cont.)
John [3] 15 Jac
William 15 Jac
William 13 Lin
Keath, James 15 Fra
John 15 Fra
John L. 16 Fra
Keaton, John 15 Fra
Keeble, Walter 91 Rut
Keef, Tho. 163 Sum
Keel, John 18 Bed
John 29 Bed
John, Junr. 20 Bed
Philmone 29 Bed
Richard 19 Bed
Samuel 19 Bed
Shelmore 20 Bed
William 95 Rut
William 122 Ste
see Kell
Keeland, Polly 50 Bed
Keeling, Abraham 30 Smi
Ailsey 30 Smi
Edward A. 91 Dav
Leonard 15 Jac
Thomas 15 Jac
Keen, Ashford 162 Sum
see Keer, MKeen
Keenan, John 16 Gil
Keener, John 354 Whi
Keepton, William 413 Wil
see Keeton
Keer, William 162 Sum
Kees, Charles 163 Sum
Keesee, George 162 Sum
George, Sr. 163 Sum
Keesei, George 350 Whi
Keeton, Cornelius 413 Wil
George 31 Mau
Zachariah [2] 413 Wil
see Keepton
Keezee, Leroy 7 Mon
Kegall see Negall
Keith, Andrew 18 Gil
Kelen, Nancy 30 Mau
Keley, Thomas 33 Mau
Keling, James 47 Bed
Kell, Thomas 95 Rut
see Keel
Kellem, Elizabeth 91 Dav
Kellen, William 47 Bed
Keller, Charles M. 4 Lin
Daniel 73 Rut
Francis 29 Bed
John 25 Lin
Joseph 29 Bed
Kelley, Abenezer 11 Dic
Alexander 64 Mau
Allen P. 59 Mau
Cary T. 21 Gil
Edward 49 Mau
Elizebeth 51 Mau
Free 8 Jac

Kelley (cont.)
James 68 Mau
John 12 Dic
John 341 Whi
Joshua 388 Wil
Lavicy 29 Bed
Mordica 68 Dav
William 6 Per
Kellough, John 92 Rut
Samuel 82 Rut
Kellum, Nathanl. 16 Hic
Kelly, Alfred 15 Hic
Andrew 120 Ste
Austin Y. 12 Mon
Beal 26 Rob
Benjamin 25 Rob
Benjn. 125 Ste
Charles 114 Ste
Daniel 416 Wil
Darlin 283 War
Dennis 416 Wil
Durham 15 Fra
Edward 114 Ste
Edward 163 Sum
Elijah 15 Jac
Elisha 9 Hic
Ephraim 3 Har
Gerge W. 298 War
Greenberry 7 Rob
Henry 163 Sum
Henry 285 War
James 16 Fra
James 30 Smi
John 26 Rob
Jonathan 297 War
Joseph 162 Sum
Joshua 11 Lin
Kenady 33 Rob
Mason 7 Ove
Nathan 303 War
Patrick 30 Smi
Richd. 11 Mon
Saml. 125 Ste
Saml. 10 Way
Samuel 412 Wil
Simms 15 Fra
Spencer 30 Smi
Thomas 36 Lin
Thomas 415 Wil
Thos. 23 Hic
William 413 Wil
William S. 15 Fra
see Julam, Skelly
Kelso, James 11 Gil
Joseph D. 56 Mau
Kelsoe, Henry 39 Lin
Keltner, Emanuel 13 Law
George 15 Gil
Henry 17 Gil
Kelton, William 104 Rut
Kem, William 285 War
Kembral, Jesse 7 Law
Kemery, Catharine 34 Lin
Kemp, Burrel 380 Wil
Burrill 381 Wil
Henry 30 Smi
Jesse 7 Wll
Jesse 41 Wll
Jinks 30 Smi
Murfree 30 Smi
Richard 30 Smi
Richard, Sen. 30 Smi
Solomon 18 Ove
Solomon 30 Smi
Solomon 381 Wil
Kenady, Eli 10 Law
John 10 Law
Saml. 112 Ste
William 65 Wll
Kendall, Peter 111 Ste
Kendrick, Austin, Mr. 8 Law
Kenedy, George 3 Way
James 284 War
James 290 War
John 318 War
John 319 War
Keneman, William 27 Mau
Kennady, John 89 Dav
Lemuel 90 Dav
Kennard, John 352 Whi
William 356 Whi
Kenneday, William 12 Gil
William 13 Gil
William B. 414 Wil
Kennedy, Danl. 163 Sum
Esther 48 Lin
Gilbert 15 Lin
James 8 Lin
James 11 Ove
John 84 Dav
John 12 Gil
John 163 Sum
Jonas 16 Fra
Levi 17 Ove
Prudence 163 Sum
Samuel 415 Wil
Thomas 16 Fra
William 93 Dav
William 12 Hic
see Kennerly
Kennerly, John 16 Fra
Thomas 16 Fra
see Kinnerly
Kent, Henry 15 Jac
John 47 Lin
Luke 2 Mon
Nathan 15 Jac
Nathan 30 Smi
William 77 Dav
Keown, Robert 15 Fra
Samuel 16 Fra
Thomas 15 Fra
Kerby, Henry 301 War
James 10 Gil
Jesse 30 Wmi
John [2] 163 Sum

Kerby (cont.)
John 301 War
Leonard 162 Sum
Richard 30 Smi
Robert 287 War
Samuel 30 Smi
Taurance 162 Sum
Wright 36 Wll
see Erby, Kerley
Kercheval, Thomas 2 Lin
Kerdendall, Jesse 120 Ste
Kerley, James 30 Smi
John 30 Smi
Luke 30 Smi
William [2] 30 Smi
William 162 Sum
William, Sen. 31 Smi
William M. 11 Gil
see Kerby
Kerncy, William 93 Rut
Kernel, Hubbard 8 Hum
Kerney, Guston 8 Gil
Kerr, Alexander R. 77 Dav
Andrew M. 29 Mau
David 57 Mau
Elizabeth 46 Lin
Henry 4 Gil
Hugh 12 Gil
James 45 Lin
James 43 Mau
James 357 Whi
John 42 Mau
Richard 400 Wil
Saml. 163 Sum
Thompson 79 Dav
William 371 Whi
Kerry, John 389 Wil
Kersey, David 12 Gil
John 283 War
John 292 War
Thomas 293 War
William 28 Mau
Kesiah, Richard 15 Jac
Kessee, John 26 Mon
Kesterson, Saml. 131 Ste
Ketch, Daniel 63 Mau
Ketcherside, James 356 Whi
Ketchins, James 30 Smi
Ketchum, — 40 Mau
Keth, Alexander 15 Jac
Daniel 15 Jac
Samuel 15 Jac
Kethly, Henry 359 Whi
Jesse 361 Whi
Ketring, Peter 162 Sum
Ketton, Benajah 87 Rut
Elizabeth 77 Rut
James 80 Rut
Key, Bingham 163 Sum
George 35 Wll
Holloway 6 Hum
Jonathan 30 Smi
Logan 30 Smi
Key (cont.)
Macklin 163 Sum
Ruffin 163 Sum
Solomon 30 Smi
Thomas 5 Dic
Thomas 86 Rut
William 66 Dav
William 30 Smi
William 163 Sum
Keys, Elijah 297 War
Kitty 78 Rut
Owen 15 Fra
Thos. 6 Law
Waller 15 Fra
Keyser, John 163 Sum
Phillip 163 Sum
Phillip, Sr. 162 Sum
Keziah, John 4 Hum
Kickade, Thomas 6 Per
Kidd, Benjamin 23 Wll
George 24 Wll
James 23 Wll
William 14 Wll
Kiddy, Jasper 30 Bed
Lewis 31 Bed
Kidmon, Henry 287 War
Kief, Thomas 315 War
Kienary, Mary 15 Fra
Kieth, William 9 Lin
Kiger, George 163 Sum
Kilbourn, Daniel 12 Law
Kilbreath, Robert 42 Lin
Kilburn, Amus, Junr. 3 Law
Amus, Senr. 3 Law
Henry 15 Fra
Kilcrease, Davis 56 Mau
John 56 Mau
William 56 Mau
Kile, Daniel 3 Mon
James 11 Way
Reuben 6 Way
Kiley, John 163 Sum
Kilgare, Charles 18 Rob
Thomas 21 Rob
Kilgore, Isaac 120 Ste
Kilion, Daniel 281 War
John 281 War
Kilketh, Alexander 15 Fra
Killabrew, Edwin D. 19 Mon
Glidwell 19 Mon
Joshua 19 Mon
Killbuck, Robert 163 Sum
Killebrew, Buckner 2 Mon
Edmond 4 Mon
Thomas 26 Mau
Whitfield 4 Mon
William 6 Mon
Killian, Jacob 15 Fra
John 15 Fra
Killibrue, Killian 120 Ste
Killin, Andrew 4 Per
Wm. 16 Hic
Killingsworth, Freeman 45 Mau

Killiogh, James 79 Rut
Killion, William 281 War
Killough, David 16 Hic
Killpatrick, Ebnezer 54 Mau
Joshua W. 55 Mau
Kilpatrick, Andrew 23 Hic
Eleazer 53 Mau
Felix 45 Wll
James 15 Fra
John 16 Fra
Robert 163 Sum
see Gilpatrick
Kilpattrick, James 418 Wil
William 418 Wil
Kimary, John 15 Fra
Kimble, Joseph 4 Dic
William 163 Sum
Kimbro, Joseph 91 Rut
William G. 81 Rut
see Kinbroe
Kimbroe, Azriah 91 Rut
John 81 Rut
William 81 Rut
see Kimbro, Kimbrough, Kinbroe
Kimbrough, George 24 Bed
Henry T. 4 Gil
James 8 Gil
John 98 Rut
Marmaduke 163 Sum
Kimmons, Joseph 35 Bed
Kinbroe, Joseph 81 Rut
see Kimbro, Kimbroe
Kincaid, David 27 Mau
John 95 Rut
Kincanan, David 11 Har
Kincannon, Francis 8 Har
Francis 11 Har
Kinchro see Kimbro
Kindal, Sal. 15 Jac
Sarah 15 Jac
Kindrick, — 24 Mau
John 68 Mau
John, Mr. 3 Law
Obadiah, Mr. 3 Law
Thomas 67 Mau
Thomas 82 Rut
William 26 Mau
Kindue, Thomas 163 Sum
King, Alexander 41 Mau
Alexander 54 Mau
Andrew 29 Lin
Armour 11 Dic
Avery 11 Gil
Baxter 25 Lin
Benja. 163 Sum
Benjamin 11 Gil
Benjamin 24 Rob
Charles [2] 15 Fra
Charles 29 Rob
Charles C. 96 Rut
David 63 Mau
David 163 Sum
Edward 16 Bed
King (cont.)
Edward 407 Wil
Elizabeth 14 Dic
Ephraim 27 Lin
Garrison 21 Gil
George C. 15 Rob
Henry 21 Gil
Henry 118 Ste
Hugh 41 Mau
Isabella 5 Dic
Isaiah 32 Bed
James 115 Ste
James M. 99 Rut
Jesse 15 Fra
John 46 Bed
John 15 Fra
John 11 Hic
John 1 Law
John 36 Lin
John 9 Mon
John 25 Mon
John 27 Mon
John 19 Rob
John 118 Ste
John 163 Sum
John A. 8 Gil
John M. 46 Mau
John W. 30 Smi
Johnson 16 Fra
Jonathan 15 Bed
Jonathan 36 Lin
Joseph 26 Bed
Joseph 7 Dic
Joseph 412 Wil
Joshua 27 Lin
Lewis 29 Smi
Margaret 27 Lin
Martha 5 Dic
Mary 163 Sum
Maury Galord 29 Mau
Miller 15 Fra
Nathaniel 17 Bed
Nathaniel 12 Mon
Needham 53 Bed
Needham 12 Lin
Peter 30 Smi
Pierson 26 Wll
Ransome 401 Wil
Richd. 162 Sum
Robert 413 Wil
Saml. 162 Sum
Samuel [2] 14 Dic
Samuel 11 Gil
Samuel 41 Mau
Samuel 52 Mau
Samuel 31 Smi
Sandford 7 Rob
Sugars 30 Smi
Thomas 15 Fra
Thomas 120 Ste
Thomas S. 5 Wll
Thos. 25 Mon
Timothy 115 Ste

King (cont.)
William 61 Dav
William 15 Fra
William 9 Gil
William 21 Gil
William 43 Lin
William 25 Mon
William 31 Smi
William 118 Ste
William 162 Sum
William 163 Sum
William 392 Wil
William 419 Wil
William 13 Wll
William 30 Wll
William P. 67 Mau
Zachariah 30 Smi
see Hing
Kingeade, Hopson 16 Fra
Joseph 15 Fra
Kingsberry, Joseph P. 79 Dav
Kingsley, Alfa 76 Dav
Kingstown, Thomas 70 Mau
Kinings, John 113 Ste
Kinkaid, Joseph 38 Mau
Kinley, Edward 350 Whi
Rebeccah 306 War
Kinnard, George 8 Wll
Walter 1 Lin
Kinnerly, James 16 Fra
Thomas J. 15 Fra
see Kennerly
Kinney, Alexander 43 Lin
Robt. 6 Hic
Kinningham, James 16 Fra
William 16 Fra
Kinny, Patrick 30 Smi
Kinsbrough, John 11 Gil
Kinston, Richard 90 Dav
Kinzer, George 28 Mau
Kirby, Isaiah 21 Rob
James 21 Rob
Richard 363 Whi
William 19 Rob
William 343 Whi
William 366 Whi
see Cirby, Kerby
Kirk, George 12 Mon
Henry 70 Mau
Hugh 105 Rut
James 13 Dic
Jesse L. 5 Dic
John 41 Mau
John 80 Rut
John 312 War
John, Senr. 78 Rut
John H. 1 Rob
Joshua 15 Jac
Mary 11 Gil
Matthew 30 Smi
Sally 21 Hic
Thomas 79 Rut
William 67 Mau
Kirk (cont.)
William 163 Sum
William 348 Whi
William 35 Wll
Young 8 Dic
Kirkendall see Kerdendall
Kirkindall, Abraham 15 Fra
Abram 16 Fra
Abram, Jr. 16 Fra
John 16 Fra
Jonathan 16 Fra
Matthew 16 Fra
Sally 15 Fra
Simon 16 Fra
Kirkindoll, Jesse 15 Fra
Kirkland, Levi 14 Hum
Moses 20 Bed
Kirklin, Zachariah 15 Jac
Kirkman, Elijah 43 Bed
Thomas 77 Dav
Kirkpartrick, Josiah 393 Wil
Kirkpatrick, Amos 15 Jac
Ann 376 Wil
Edward 15 Jac
Fanny 163 Sum
Henry 65 Wll
Hugh 162 Sum
James 15 Jac
James 162 Sum
Joseph 163 Sum
Robert 15 Jac
Saml. 15 Jac
Samuel 8 Wll
William 15 Jac
Kirkpattrick, Alexander 377 Wil
Joseph 377 Wil
Rebeca 377 Wil
Kirksey, Abraham 15 Rob
John 124 Ste
Mary 31 Mau
Kirkum, Peter 162 Sum
William 162 Sum
Kirkwood, Margret 71 Dav
Kirley see Kerley
Kirnard, Birket 15 Jac
Montgomery 15 Jac
Kirwin, John 29 Smi
Kistail, Henry 403 Wil
Kitchen, Boaz 35 Rob
Samuel 15 Fra
Kithcart, Allen 316 War
Kitrell, Joseph 343 Whi
Nancy 343 Whi
Kitterall, Ann 21 Mon
Kittering, Barbary 163 Sum
Kittrell, George 162 Sum
Kizer, David 27 Mon
Jacob 40 Bed
John 122 Ste
Peter 346 Whi
Valentine 40 Bed
Klyce, Addm [Adam?] 37 Mau
Knight, Absolum 420 Wil

Knight (cont.)		
Allen	87	Dav
Deason	23	Wll
Ellis	30	Smi
James	136	Sum
James	162	Sum
John	77	Dav
John	101	Rut
John	30	Smi
John	414	Wil
Jonathan	162	Sum
Joseph	30	Smi
Moses	61	Dav
Thomas	8	Hum
Thomas	9	Rob
Wade H.	7	Per
William	20	Bed
William	36	Bed
William	37	Bed
William	61	Dav
William	71	Dav
William	15	Fra
William	34	Rob
see Night		
Knott, William	25	Bed
Knowles, Polly	30	Smi
Knox, Benjamin	86	Rut
James	10	Mon
John	49	Mau
Joseph	15	Gil
Joseph	90	Rut
Joseph	94	Rut
Joseph	308	War
Mary	74	Dav
Robert	15	Fra
Thomas	102	Rut
Koener, Martin	344	Whi
Kofer, Joseph	341	Whi
Koher, George	12	Gil
Koonce, Henry	34	Mau
Redding	35	Mau
Koonts, Tobias	103	Rut
Wendel M.	103	Rut
Kosnee, John	40	Bed
Kresil, John	36	Rob
Krisel, John	3	Rob
Kuhn, Christopher	360	Whi
Kyle, Barkley	30	Smi
William	7	Gil
Kymes, Conrad	47	Lin
Henry	15	Lin
Kyzer, Philip	23	Lin
--- L ---		
L..., Abraham	17	Way
Lacefield, Daniel	9	Har
Jesse	9	Har
Nancy	11	Gil
William	9	Har
Lack, Abner	32	Smi
Lack (cont.)		
Moses	32	Smi
Obediah	32	Smi
Lackburn, John	145	Sum
Lackey, Ennis	11	Gil
James	164	Sum
Nancy	17	Fra
Thomas	43	Lin
William	42	Lin
see Lucky		
Lacks, Abraham	17	Fra
Lacky, Andrew M.	28	Mau
George	37	Lin
Sarah	35	Lin
William	35	Lin
Lacy, A. H.	117	Ste
Caleb	43	Lin
Elijah	26	Bed
Jesse	4	Per
John	18	Fra
John	63	Mau
Skilton	24	Wll
Stephen	1	Hic
Susannah	164	Sum
Thomas	18	Fra
Thos.	1	Hic
William	63	Mau
Ladd, Jehosephit	65	Mau
Noble	62	Wll
Laden, Francis	11	Bed
George	17	Bed
William	46	Bed
Lafferty, Andrew	17	Hic
Laffson, Mathew	55	Mau
Lagron, Mary	64	Wll
William	64	Wll
Laid, Lewis	52	Wll
Lain, James	17	Lin
John	26	Lin
Thomas	68	Dav
Thomas	17	Lin
Thomas	62	Wll
William	52	Mau
William	67	Mau
Laird, John	19	Gil
Nathanial	52	Mau
Lake, Allen	31	Smi
Daniel T.	31	Smi
Elijah	73	Dav
Lalier, Frederick C.	18	Fra
Lam, Thomas	1	Rob
Lamascus, James	34	Lin
Lamaster, Joseph	40	Mau
see Lancaster, Laymaster		
Lamb, David	59	Wll
Davis	29	Wll
Equilla	16	Bed
Henry	309	War
James	60	Wll
Jesse	11	Gil
Jessee	1	Lin
Jonathan	60	Wll
Joseph	60	Wll

Lamb (cont.)
Martin 60 Wll
Thomas [2] 60 Wll
William 9 Gil
William 87 Rut
Lambath, William [2] 164 Sum
Lamberson, Conrod 32 Smi
Lawrence, Jun. 32 Smi
Lawrence, Sen. 32 Smi
Leonard 32 Smi
Peter 32 Smi
Lambert, Charles 398 Wil
James 18 Fra
James 64 Mau
Lamberth, Demsey 390 Wil
Lamon, Oran D. 32 Smi
Peyton 33 Smi
Lampley, Joseph 8 Dic
Lams, Warren 4 Ove
Lamus, Samuel 383 Wil
Lancaster, Aaron 17 Gil
Agnes 20 Gil
Benjamin 5 Hic
David 40 Wll
Joseph 8 Law
Levi 24 Hic
Richard 32 Smi
Richd. 18 Hic
Robert, Jun. 32 Smi
Robert A. 32 Smi
Saml. 111 Ste
Samuel 19 Gil
Sarah 4 Hic
Tabitha 117 Ste
Thomas 32 Smi
Thomas A. 32 Smi
William 20 Gil
William 10 Hum
William 32 Smi
William A. 33 Smi
see Lamaster, Lankester
Lance, Henry 287 War
Henry 361 Whi
Rosanah 362 Whi
Samuel 361 Whi
Land, Abram 23 Hic
Benjamin 9 Hic
Endinedge 295 War
Lewis 14 Lin
see Lane
Landers, Joseph 37 Bed
Landis, Abraham 34 Bed
John 34 Bed
Landon, Amous 43 Mau
Amous 45 Mau
John 45 Mau
Joseph 45 Mau
Landress, Henry 31 Lin
Landrom, Thomas 60 Wll
Landrum, Mereman 60 Wll
Randolph 17 Fra
Shepherd 13 Dic
Lane, Amsted 388 Wil
Lane (cont.)
Augustus 420 Wil
Bennett 16 Jac
David 31 Smi
Drury 388 Wil
Elias 20 Hic
Garret 1 Hic
George 293 War
Gishum 420 Wil
Isaac [2] 164 Sum
Ivan, Ser. 388 Wil
Jacob 299 War
Jacob A. 341 Whi
James 21 Gil
James 25 Mon
James 128 Ste
Joel 21 Gil
John 10 Bed
John 37 Bed
John 6 Gil
John 8 Hic
John 13 Hum
John 16 Jac
John 82 Rut
John 165 Sum
Martha 20 Hic
Martin 20 Gil
Oran 388 Wil
Owen 68 Dav
Owen 14 Gil
Richard 304 War
Robert 383 Wil
Robert 65 Wll
Rowland 17 Fra
Rupson 299 War
Samuel 16 Jac
Samuel 341 Whi
Sarah 82 Rut
Thomas 20 Gil
Thos. 128 Ste
Turner 354 Whi
Tyre 388 Wil
Willard, Jr. 388 Wil
William [2] 7 Hum
William 31 Smi
William 293 War
William 65 Wll
William, Jr. 388 Wil
William H. 165 Sum
William K. 65 Wll
Lang, George 66 Wll
Sarah 6 Bed
Langden, William 15 Jac
Langfd., Benjamin 22 Hic
Langford, Henry 63 Dav
Hickman 22 Hic
Jno. 22 Hic
Jordon 165 Sum
see Langfd.
Langham, Robert 17 Fra
Langler, John 16 Jac
Langley, Calib 57 Mau
James 7 Hum

Langley (cont.)		
James	59	Mau
John	410	Wil
John S.	57	Mau
Langly, Lemuel	10	Lin
Langston, Jacob	57	Mau
John	36	Lin
John	98	Rut
Mark	33	Lin
William	33	Lin
Lanier, Buchannan	85	Dav
Edmund	78	Dav
George	4	Ove
Henry	22	Gil
Isaac H.	12	Dic
John	90	Dav
Nicholas	42	Wll
Washington	4	Ove
Lanire, Lemuel	53	Mau
Lankester, Mical	49	Mau
Lankford, Elizabeth	15	Ove
Hyram	11	Mon
James	16	Jac
James	31	Smi
James	33	Smi
Jesse	33	Smi
John	405	Wil
Martin	16	Jac
Parish	32	Smi
Stephen	16	Jac
Thos.	129	Ste
William	32	Smi
Lankston, Henry	110	Ste
Lanning, Benjamin	1	Hum
Lannism, William	101	Rut
Lannum, John	95	Rut
Joseph	100	Rut
Nathan	95	Rut
Tilman	100	Rut
see Lannun		
Lannun, Levi	94	Rut
Lansdon, Thomas	417	Wil
see Lanson		
Lansdown, Margaret	10	Lin
Lansford, Samuel	8	Gil
William	8	Gil
see Samford		
Lanson, James	7	Per
Susan	417	Wil
see Lansdon		
Laphefer, Zacheus	370	Whi
Laprum, Susannah	393	Wil
Laramore, John	17	Fra
Silas	17	Fra
Larance, John	34	Mau
Larb see Lark		
Lard, Alexander	59	Mau
Levan	10	Lin
Nathaniel	6	Bed
William	31	Bed
Largent, John	357	Whi
W.	130	Ste
William	130	Ste
Lark, Dennis	83	Rut
Larkin, David	16	Fra
John	16	Fra
William	16	Fra
Larkins, Hodge	127	Ste
James	7	Dic
John, Jr.	7	Dic
John, Sen.	10	Dic
Joseph	10	Dic
Robert	15	Dic
Roger	31	Smi
William	31	Smi
Larreau, George	17	Fra
Larremore, Elisabeth	15	Wll
Larrimore, Hance	44	Bed
Larue, Isaac B.	49	Bed
Lasater, Absolum	419	Wil
Alexander	419	Wil
Frederick	417	Wil
Hardy	419	Wil
Jacob	419	Wil
Lasenby, Alexander	61	Dav
Robert	61	Dav
Lash, Harmon	408	Wil
Lasiter, Enos	164	Sum
Federick	164	Sum
Willie	164	Sum
Lasley, Thomas	7	Wll
Laslie, George	13	Hum
John	8	Hum
Lassey, Anney	58	Mau
Lassiter, Abner	18	Fra
Hardy	98	Rut
Hezekiah, Jun.	18	Fra
Hezekiah, Sen.	18	Fra
Jas.	19	Hic
John	18	Fra
William	18	Fra
Lassley, William	33	Wll
Lastlie, Burrel	5	Hum
Laswell, Joseph	316	War
Latapie, A.	76	Dav
Laten, Mical	42	Mau
Latham, John	35	Lin
Lathem, Elizabeth	6	Ove
John	165	Sum
Latimer, Danl.	163	Sum
Erastus	165	Sum
George S.	164	Sum
Jonathan	164	Sum
Lucinda	165	Sum
Nicholas	164	Sum
Latimere, Jacob	164	Sum
Latimore, Chs.	164	Sum
Joseph	32	Rob
William	32	Rob
Latiner, Betsy Ann	165	Sum
Laton, Francis	128	Ste
Lydia	6	Per
Latta, John	61	Mau
Martha	72	Dav
Thomas	61	Mau
Lattimer, James	14	Hum

Lattimere, Lyons	8	Hum
Lattimore, Charles	24	Bed
Witheral	24	Bed
Latty, Samuel	65	Mau
William	65	Mau
Lauderdale, David	164	Sum
James	165	Sum
John	12	Lin
John	164	Sum
Robert	165	Sum
Sarah	165	Sum
William	14	Lin
Laughlin, James Y.	82	Rut
Samiel H.	73	Rut
Laughry, Sarah	80	Dav
Lauler, Isaac	16	Fra
see Lawler		
Laurance, Elias	34	Rob
Wm. P.	278	War
Jesse	30	Rob
Martin	296	War
Lauther, George	80	Dav
Lavance, Hiram	31	Smi
see Lorance		
Lavender, Charles	8	Bed
Charles	59	Mau
Lavet, Lancaster	13	Bed
Lavin, Mary	62	Wll
Laviner, Cluff	47	Wll
George	37	Wll
Pickens	47	Wll
William	47	Wll
Law, Edmd.	164	Sum
Henry	164	Sum
James	393	Wil
Jesse	31	Smi
John	31	Smi
Nathl.	164	Sum
Reuben	125	Ste
William	33	Smi
see Lam		
Lawe, William	54	Bed
Lawfield, Samuel	316	War
Lawhorn, Sally	17	Bed
William	165	Sum
Lawing, Samuel	303	War
Lawler, Abner	291	War
Arthur K.	16	Fra
James	294	War
John	288	War
John	368	Whi
Levi	288	War
Thomas	353	Whi
see Lauler		
Lawley, Stephen	32	Smi
Lawlings see Rawlings		
Lawrance, Abraham	50	Bed
Edmun	55	Wll
James	46	Bed
Joel	50	Bed
John	26	Bed
John	46	Bed
Joseph	16	Bed
Lawrance (cont.)		
Samuel	48	Mau
Thomas	46	Bed
Timothey D.	55	Wll
see Llorance		
Lawrence, Alexander	87	Rut
Benjamin	313	War
Charity	32	Smi
David	10	Lin
Edward	32	Smi
Elisabeth	164	Sum
Faris	33	Smi
Isaac	74	Dav
James	67	Dav
James	17	Fra
James	36	Lin
James	77	Rut
Jesse	9	Lin
John	164	Sum
John	409	Wil
John	411	Wil
John	412	Wil
Jonathan	87	Rut
Joseph	411	Wil
Lemuel	163	Sum
Nancy	32	Smi
Samuel	66	Dav
Tho.	163	Sum
Thomas	32	Smi
William	32	Smi
William [2]	411	Wil
see Lawrene		
Lawrene, Mary	165	Sum
Robert	164	Sum
William	165	Sum
Laws, Josiah	16	Ove
see Lams		
Lawsom, Robert	1	Hum
Lawson, James	17	Hic
John	31	Smi
John	348	Whi
Leonard	349	Whi
Moses	31	Smi
Rhoda	18	Fra
Robert	15	Jac
Thomas	33	Smi
Thomas	19	Way
see Lanson		
Lax, Edward	15	Jac
Laxon, James	24	Hic
Jesse	24	Hic
Thomas	24	Hic
Laxton, James	4	Per
John	4	Per
Lay, James	282	War
James	306	War
Jesse	42	Bed
Silvester	164	Sum
William	284	War
Laymaster, Hugh	16	Rob
Lazenby, Henry	14	Lin
Lazewell, Henry	83	Dav
Lea, Edward	136	Sum

Lea (cont.)		
Elisabeth	165	Sum
Garsham	2	Per
Garsham	5	Per
Joseph	5	Per
Richard H.	164	Sum
Thomas S.	20	Ove
Vinxon	164	Sum
William H.	165	Sum
Leach, Daniel	2	Dic
Jacob	10	Dic
James	380	Wil
John H.	300	War
Levi	32	Smi
Thomas	83	Rut
William	32	Lin
Leagan, Joseph	115	Wil
Leagean, Eadith	42	Mau
Leager, Edmund	318	War
League, Hosea H.	116	Ste
Josiah	92	Dav
Leak, Hannah	32	Smi
James	82	Dav
John	73	Dav
Joseph	164	Sum
Leaky, Betsy	317	War
Nancy	316	War
Leamon, John	13	Law
Leasley, Peter	67	Dav
Leatch, Thomas	414	Wil
Leath, Isaac	164	Sum
Richard	26	Wll
Leathe, Peter	392	Wil
Leatherman, Jonas	10	Lin
Leathers, Greenberry D.	10	Hic
James	88	Rut
James	97	Rut
Mary	403	Wil
William	88	Rut
Letherwood, Spencer	20	Lin
Leavy, Thomas	95	Dav
William	74	Dav
Lecoq, Francis	18	Fra
Francis H.	76	Dav
Ledbetter, Aram	8	Ove
Arthur	8	Ove
Buckner	10	Ove
Charles	31	Smi
David	84	Rut
Henry	9	Lin
James	6	Lin
Jesse	6	Lin
John	8	Ove
Jones	7	Ove
Joseph	48	Wll
Middleton	17	Fra
Rollin	6	Lin
Washington	14	Ove
Wesson	6	Lin
Leddon, Sarah	86	Rut
Ledford, John	17	Ove
Samuel	19	Gil
William	14	Lin

Lee, Abner [2]	16	Jac
Anthony	111	Ste
Barnett	16	Jac
Barnett	350	Whi
Benjamin	18	Wll
Benjamin D.	19	Mon
Braxton	85	Dav
Charles	3	Ove
Clement	42	Lin
Curry	16	Jac
Daniel	16	Jac
Daniel	4	Lin
Daniell	9	Gil
Edmund P.	17	Fra
Edward	6	Gil
Elizabeth	6	Gil
Ephraim	16	Jac
George	16	Jac
George	115	Ste
George W.	101	Rut
Gushum	20	Lin
Guy	32	Smi
Guy, Sen.	32	Smi
Henry	87	Dav
Isaac	16	Jac
Jahue	16	Jac
James	75	Dav
James	97	Dav
James [?]	7	Ove
James	32	Smi
Jane	87	Dav
Jas., Junr.	115	Ste
Jas., Senr.	115	Ste
Jeremiah	26	Lin
Jesse	16	Jac
John	51	Bed
John	17	Fra
John	47	Lin
John	53	Mau
John	9	Ove
John	28	Wll
John, Junr.	111	Ste
John, Mt.	110	Ste
John, Sen.	18	Fra
John, Senr.	109	Ste
Matthew	95	Dav
Nancy	42	Lin
Peter	37	Bed
Rolin	16	Jac
Samuel	42	Lin
Samuel	102	Rut
Shadrach	9	Mon
Simpson	4	Har
Thomas D.	396	Wil
Vardemon	3	Ove
Washington	5	Mon
William	18	Fra
William	17	Gil
William	6	Lin
William	31	Mon
see See		
Leech, David	34	Mau
Leek, Randolph	117	Ste

Leek (cont.)		
Susanah	52	Bed
Leeper, James	121	Ste
Lefavar, Thomas O.	61	Mau
Lefever, William	70	Dav
Lefler, John	46	Bed
Leftrich, Jack H.	24	Lin
Jesse	59	Mau
Legan, Elizabeth	30	Mon
Hassen	386	Wil
James	42	Mau
John G.	386	Wil
John H., Sen.	386	Wil
Joseph	15	Mon
Matthew	16	Mon
Peter	120	Ste
see Logan		
Legate, Danl.	114	Ste
James	41	Wll
John	113	Ste
Martin	114	Ste
Michael	21	Wll
Legget, Josiah	17	Lin
Legrand, John O.	31	Smi
Obediah	31	Smi
Peter	82	Rut
Legraves, Wilie	3	Mon
Leigh, John W.	4	Dic
Leitch, James	20	Gil
Leleales, Robert	65	Dav
Lemaster, John W.	57	Mau
Lemasters, James	10	Mon
Lemuel	14	Mon
Lemens, James	71	Dav
Lemley, Philip L.	74	Dav
Lemly, Joseph	18	Hic
Lemmon, John	165	Sum
John	31	Wll
William	165	Sum
Lemmond, David	5	Lin
Thomas	5	Lin
William	19	Lin
Lemmons, John	92	Rut
John	285	War
Lemons, William	7	Bed
Lemount, Cornelius	4	Hum
Lemox, James	25	Hic
Lemuel, Darnell	16	Jac
Lenard, William S.	47	Mau
Lenderman, Henry	63	Mau
Lenox, Samuel	92	Dav
William	17	Rob
Lenton, James	66	Dav
William	72	Dav
Lentz, Benjn.	33	Bed
Jacob	33	Bed
John	47	Bed
Leombley, Edmond	16	Hic
Leomens, Thomas	351	Whi
Leonard, Christian	41	Lin
Collin C.	16	Lin
George	11	Lin
Jacob	41	Lin
Leonard (cont.)		
James	353	Whi
Joshua	16	Jac
Obadiah	352	Whi
Rebecca	317	War
Robert	11	Lin
Robert	165	Sum
Thomas	12	Lin
Wm.	10	Lin
see Lenard		
Leot see Seat		
Leoth, James	163	Sum
Leothers, John	2	Hic
Lephant, Samuel	64	Mau
Leroy, John B.	79	Dav
Leslie see Lastlie		
Lester, Alexander	46	Wll
Fountain	17	Gil
German	17	Gil
Henry	7	Wll
Isham	14	Gil
James	19	Gil
John	294	War
Joshua	416	Wil
Josiah	15	Gil
Mark [& Tomblin]	4	Wll
Sterling H.	76	Dav
William	416	Wil
Letsener, George	405	Wil
Letsinger, Andy	69	Mau
James	69	Mau
Lett, Jesse	17	Fra
Jesse, Sen.	18	Fra
Letts, James	18	Fra
Levan, Benjamin	291	War
Levey, James	92	Dav
Levingston, Robert	16	Dic
Levy, Henry	92	Dav
Lewalen, Josiah	5	Per
Lewallen, Claburn	39	Mau
Lewbo, Polly	320	War
Lewellyn, Myram	6	Hum
Lewis, Aaron	7	Per
Aggy	23	Rob
Amos	5	Dic
Amos	2	Per
Ann	164	Sum
Benjamin	9	Gil
Benjamin	343	Whi
Benjamin	350	Whi
Benjamin F.	77	Dav
Charles	16	Fra
Charles	406	Wil
Danl.	111	Ste
David	18	Fra
Earl	21	Way
Edmund	32	Smi
Elam	83	Rut
Elijah	354	Whi
Elizabeth	7	Rob
Exun	31	Mau
Gabriel	28	Mon
George	12	Dic

Lewis (cont.)		
George	7	Hum
Gravet	12	Wll
Hiram	164	Sum
James	87	Dav
James	18	Fra
James	7	Hic
James	4	Per
James [2]	32	Smi
James W.	16	Fra
Jas. A.	164	Sum
Joel	3	Rob
John	3	Bed
John	95	Dav
John	13	Dic
John	11	Hum
John	32	Smi
John	116	Ste
John	9	Way
John	343	Whi
Levy	7	Law
Lucinda	102	Rut
Malla	123	Ste
Marah	350	Whi
Mary	13	Rob
Micajah	7	Law
Mordecai	16	Ove
Obadiah	17	Hic
Patsy	418	Wil
Richard	70	Mau
Richard	123	Ste
Robert	281	War
Robert	306	War
Samuel	84	Rut
Samuel	412	Wil
Sarah	18	Ove
Thos.	125	Ste
Thos. J.	125	Ste
Walter	9	Way
Washington	24	Rob
William	2	Dic
William	84	Rut
William	86	Rut
William	343	Whi
William	360	Whi
William	413	Wil
William	11	Wll
William B.	60	Dav
see Lews		
Lews, James M.	57	Mau
Lewton, Lemuel	13	Way
Liddon, William A.	76	Rut
Ligate, Charles	58	Wll
Ligett, William	40	Wll
Liggett, William	35	Mau
Light, George	13	Dic
Michael	12	Dic
Right	10	Hic
William	3	Dic
Lightfoot, Henry	115	Ste
John	130	Ste
Wilson	117	Ste
Lightner, Wm. W.	120	Ste
Ligon, Edieth	42	Mau
Evans S.	33	Smi
Henry	31	Smi
James	17	Fra
John	31	Smi
Martin	31	Smi
Tho.	164	Sum
William	18	Fra
William	32	Smi
William	33	Smi
Likiel, John	21	Bed
Liles, Amos	41	Lin
David	31	Mau
John	35	Rob
Samuel	34	Mau
Lillard, James	57	Wll
Mordacai	81	Rut
Lilley, Robert	164	Sum
William	165	Sum
Lilly, Noah	10	Har
Limbock, John	17	Fra
Peter	17	Fra
Linch, James	85	Dav
John	5	Per
Lincoln, Davis	15	Jac
Linder, Jesse	119	Ste
Lindley, Joseph	11	Hum
Lindsay, John	6	Gil
Lindsey, Edward	130	Ste
Hannah, Mrs.	14	Law
James J.	341	Whi
Jesse	4	Law
John	29	Mau
John	130	Ste
John	35	Wll
Moses	26	Wll
Nancy	164	Sum
Robert	16	Jac
Sterlin	14	Law
Taylor	165	Sum
William	126	Ste
Lindsy, Elliott	7	Law
Lingan, William	36	Mau
Lingo, James	39	Lin
Link, Bird	82	Dav
Francis	77	Dav
John	83	Dav
Linley, James	48	Mau
Linn, Allen	16	Jac
Asia	16	Jac
Nathan	8	Hic
Linsey, Carter	65	Mau
Isaac B.	69	Mau
John	65	Mau
Wyatt	408	Wil
Linsley, John	48	Bed
Linthicum, Thomas	22	Lin
William	43	Lin
Linton, Silas	63	Dav
Lintz, George	7	Way
Linville, Henry	32	Smi
William	32	Smi
Linza, John	32	Mau

Linza (cont.)
Silvester B. 32 Mau
Linzey, Catherine 38 Mau
Lions, Andrew 62 Mau
Jeremiah 15 Lin
Lipscomb, Benion P. 33 Smi
John 31 Smi
Thomas 6 Rob
see Comb, Liscomb
Liscomb, John 93 Rut
Lisenberry, Henry 22 Mon
Lisenby, John 22 Mon
Lisk, William 343 Whi
Lister, James 5 Mon
Joseph 6 Mon
Litaker, Peter 6 Mon
Litchford, Austin 31 Smi
Litrell, James 18 Fra
William 18 Fra
Litteral, Rodeham 13 Law
Little, Abram 16 Wll
Anthony 414 Wil
George 11 Bed
Harmon 11 Hum
Harmon 342 Whi
Henry 17 Lin
Isaac 14 Hum
James 15 Jac
James 382 Wil
John 11 Bed
John 24 Bed
John 72 Dav
John 26 Mon
John 382 Wil
John 60 Wll
John M. 356 Whi
Joseph 72 Dav
Neal 20 Wll
Stephen 87 Dav
Thomas 14 Lin
Thomas 369 Whi
William 33 Rob
Littlefield, Edward B. 33 Mau
LittleJohn, Isaac 18 Way
Mercer 18 Way
Littleton, Charles 22 Gil
Mark 22 Gil
Reuben 32 Wll
Savage 28 Rob
William 28 Rob
William 16 Wll
Litton, James 88 Rut
Joseph 77 Dav
Livesay, John 29 Mau
Livesey, Isaac 164 Sum
Livingston, Barnett 4 Lin
Henry 18 Gil
Henry 5 Ove
John 11 Gil
Livsey see Linsey
Lizinley, Hesekiah 16 Jac
Llorance, Michael 81 Rut
Lloyd, George 295 War
Lloyd (cont.)
see Looyd
Loakes, Bejamin 41 Mau
Loaney, Abraham 40 Mau
Lock, Charles 85 Rut
Charles 401 Wil
J. W. 114 Wil
James 68 Mau
James 68 Mau
Joel 85 Rut
John 402 Wil
Joseph 85 Rut
Rebeckah 97 Dav
Richard 401 Wil
William 16 Jac
Lockalier, John 1 Dic
Lovet 1 Dic
Lockard, John, Junr. 2 Law
John, Senr. 10 Law
Lockart, Charles 35 Rob
Joseph 130 Ste
Saml. 116 Ste
Saml. 130 Ste
Shady 100 Rut
Locke, Absolom 18 Lin
Alexander 12 Gil
George 126 Ste
Noah 19 Lin
Walter 19 Gil
William 16 Bed
William 75 Rut
Locked, John 365 Whi
Lockert, Eli 2 Mon
William 7 Mon
Lockett, Wrial 21 Wll
Lockey, Alexander 104 Rut
Lockhart, Betsey 29 Mau
James 76 Dav
James 298 War
John 29 Mau
Joseph 17 Fra
Tho. 164 Sum
Thomas 29 Mau
Lockridge, James 57 Mau
James 60 Mau
Robbert 57 Mau
Robbert 61 Mau
Lodson, Obford 386 Wil
Loftes, Labon 16 Jac
Labon, Sr. 16 Jac
Loftin, Anne 76 Rut
Moses 51 Bed
Thomas [?] 60 Dav
Thomas 63 Dav
Loftis, Martin 9 Hic
William 9 Hic
Lofton, Auguston 54 Wll
Eldridge 75 Rut
Logan, John 17 Fra
John 165 Sum
Joseph 17 Fra
Reuben 25 Lin
Robert 34 Bed

Logan (cont.)		
Thomas	64	Dav
William	42	Lin
William	15	Mon
William	299	War
see Legan		
Loggans, Pricilla	29	Mon
Loggins, Claborn	41	Bed
James	31	Mon
Martin	29	Mon
Nancy	31	Mon
Samuel	22	Way
Login, William	58	Wll
Logue, Carnes	394	Wil
Eloner	69	Dav
Manasseh	28	Mau
Loid, Daniel	32	Mau
Marvell	17	Rob
Owen	32	Mau
William	32	Mau
see Laid		
Loischart, John	67	Dav
Loke, Jesse	283	War
Lokey, George	11	Hic
Loky, Samuel	18	Fra
Lollar, John	280	War
Lomas, Josiah	14	Hic
Lomax, James	5	Per
John	5	Per
Samuel	6	Hic
William	10	Hic
London, John	18	Gil
Martin	33	Smi
Long, Alexander	17	Fra
Anderson	14	Ove
Azariah	21	Wll
Benjamin	7	Gil
Christopher	16	Jac
David	52	Mau
Edward	95	Rut
Elisha	136	Sum
Elizabeth	11	Rob
Francis S.	36	Mau
George	351	Whi
Isaac	18	Wll
Jacob	54	Bed
Jacob	95	Rut
James	62	Dav
James H.	35	Mau
John	17	Fra
John	22	Mon
John	7	Ove
John	19	Rob
John	23	Wll
Joseph	52	Mau
Michael	15	Wll
Nickless	70	Mau
P. W.	78	Dav
Peggy	30	Mau
Robert	6	Rob
Robert	416	Wil
Saml.	13	Mon
Samuel	95	Rut

Long (cont.)		
Thomas	20	Rob
William	17	Fra
William	9	Mon
William	32	Rob
William	418	Wil
William C.	4	Law
William F.	31	Lin
Look, Joseph	16	Jac
Looney, Elisha	31	Smi
Isaac	164	Sum
Michael	163	Sum
Peter	164	Sum
Loony, Daniel	12	Lin
Hugh	12	Lin
James	13	Lin
John C.	13	Lin
Jonathan	31	Lin
Peter	12	Lin
Peter, Ser.	13	Lin
Looper, Magnis	18	Ove
Looter, Wm., Jr.	10	Hic
see Luter		
Looyd, John B.	1	Per
Loplin, Joseph	33	Mau
Lorance, David	31	Smi
Ephraim	81	Rut
William	31	Smi
see Lavance		
Lord, John	79	Dav
Lorence, Martain	8	Per
Lorimier, William	1	Hum
Lossen, Elizabeth	31	Rob
Lotts, John A.	312	War
Lotty, Rachel	11	Hic
Louder, Job	57	Wll
Jobe	60	Wll
Louise, John	80	Rut
Love, Catharine	11	Rob
David	88	Dav
David	37	Mau
Eadan	69	Mau
James	68	Mau
James	164	Sum
James T.	96	Dav
John D.	37	Mau
Joseph	85	Dav
Joseph	10	Wll
Matthew	32	Smi
Robert	16	Lin
William	32	Smi
Loveall, David	16	Jac
Loveing, Gabriel	00	Dav
Lovel, Benjamin	13	Ove
David	13	Ove
James	84	Dav
John	13	Ove
John M.	92	Dav
Lucy	83	Rut
Robert	95	Dav
William	95	Dav
William	23	Wll
Lovelady, Asa	33	Smi

Lovelady (cont.)
James 31 Smi
Jane 13 Dic
Jesse 15 Ove
John 33 Smi
Thomas 46 Lin
Thomas 366 Whi
Loveless, Jesse 19 Lin
Lovell, Colson 165 Sum
Cyrus 164 Sum
Daniel 4 Rob
George 17 Gil
Joshua 165 Sum
Russel 165 Sum
Zacha. 164 Sum
Loven, Lucretia 20 Way
Margaret 39 Lin
Priestly 20 Way
Lovett, John 96 Rut
Joshua 89 Rut
Lancford 54 Bed
Moses 39 Wll
Thomas 281 War
Lovin, John 102 Rut
Loviner see Laviner
Loving, Walter 164 Sum
William 25 Mau
Lovings, Elizabeth 9 Bed
Henry 9 Bed
Low, Danl. 126 Ste
David 10 Hum
David 127 Ste
George 12 Bed
Reuben 126 Ste
Lowder, John 69 Mau
Lowe, Charles 93 Rut
Isaiah 308 War
J. B. 402 Wil
Johan 87 Rut
Martha 14 Hic
Richd. C. 14 Hic
Thomas 94 Rut
Walter 96 Rut
William 12 Bed
William 96 Rut
see Lane
Lower, John 12 Gil
Lowery, James 403 Wil
Joseph 11 Bed
Lowey, Robert E. 360 Whi
Lowise, Robert 100 Rut
Lowmax, Alfred 67 Dav
Lowrance, John 44 Mau
Lowrey, Alexander 363 Whi
Charles A. 79 Rut
Mark 357 Whi
Lowry, Alban 92 Rut
David 279 War
Elijah 123 Ste
Isaac 128 Ste
Isaac 129 Ste
James 123 Ste
John 18 Fra
Lowry (cont.)
John 120 Ste
Michael 364 Whi
Nelson 100 Rut
Rewben 165 Sum
Robert 115 Ste
Shadrach 18 Fra
Turner 101 Rut
Winnifred 128 Ste
Lowther, William 18 Mon
Loyd, Edwd. 6 Hic
Esrom 36 Lin
Henry 11 Gil
James 314 War
Jarrett 398 Wil
Joseph 42 Bed
Joshua 389 Wil
Nicholass 42 Bed
Sarah 12 Lin
Stephen 11 Gil
Talton 16 Jac
William 22 Bed
William 18 Fra
see Lloyd, Loid, Loyed
Loyed, Thomas 165 Sum
Loyons, John B. 79 Dav
Luallen, Birk 344 Whi
Luallin, John 407 Wil
Lucas, Anne 16 Dic
Campbell 164 Sum
Chs. 165 Sum
David 29 Rob
Edward 2 Dic
George A. 136 Sum
Green B. 165 Sum
Hugh 16 Fra
John 55 Mau
John 314 War
Parker 29 Rob
Peter W. 164 Sum
Robert 95 Dav
Samuel 29 Rob
Lucky, David 55 Mau
Hugh 17 Fra
John 31 Smi
Nancy 31 Smi
Lucre, James R. 12 Gil
Lucus, Abraham 64 Dav
Andrew, Sr. 90 Dav
Charles 24 Bed
George, Mr. 1 Law
John 64 Dav
William, Jr. 1 Law
Willis, Mr. 1 Law
Lucy, Edward A. 20 Mon
Ludwell, Edmund 17 Fra
John 17 Fra
Luke, John 28 Mon
Luksay, John, Jr. 3 Dic
John, Sr. 10 Dic
Lum, David 123 Ste
Lumberson, James 32 Mon
Lumbrick, Abraham 5 Lin

Lumford, Eaton 386 Wil
Lumpkin, More 49 Mau
Lumpkins, Anthony 17 Fra
John 17 Fra
John 67 Mau
Obey 387 Wil
Lumsden, Jesse 11 Hum
Luna, Wooton 398 Wil
Lunda, Elijah 11 Ove
Lunden, William 70 Mau
Lundy, Daniel 367 Whi
Lunn, John 34 Wll
Lunsford, Elias 111 Ste
Lunsly, William 316 War
Luois, William D. 84 Dav
Lurtgert, Nancy 62 Dav
Lush, Samuel 280 War
Lusk, Isaac 18 Fra
James 68 Mau
James 290 War
John 18 Fra
John 38 Lin
John 311 War
Robbart 34 Mau
Samuel [2] 68 Mau
Samuel 93 Rut
Thomas 18 Fra
Thomas 38 Lin
William 18 Fra
William 283 War
William, Jun. 18 Fra
William, Sen. 18 Fra
Wilson 18 Fra
Luster, Alexander 85 Dav
Pressley 415 Wil
Susain 88 Dav
Luteis, Henry 12 Hic
Luter, Laurence 8 Rob
Matthew 14 Rob
Wm. 11 Hic
see Looter
Lutman, J. M. 16 Jac
John W. 15 Jac
Luton, Ilson [?] 62 Dav
King, Jr. 163 Sum
King, Sr. 163 Sum
Reed 114 Ste
Lutrell, Delila 312 War
Luttrell, Fielding 40 Lin
Mary 41 Lin
Nathan 40 Lin
Nathaniel 40 Lin
Vincent 40 Lin
Luty, Elisabeth 65 Wll
Lyda, Henry 348 Whi
William 347 Whi
Lyell, Beckworth 68 Mau
Richard 66 Mau
Robbert 69 Mau
Lyelle, John 86 Rut
Lykes see Sykes
Lyle, James 22 Mon
Jourdan 30 Mon
Lyle (cont.)
Sandy 164 Sum
Lyles, Daniel 25 Mon
George N. 292 War
Young 25 Mon
Lyme see Lynn
Lynch, David 30 Mon
David 31 Smi
Edward 40 Lin
James 16 Gil
James 5 Lin
James 25 Mau
Jesse 31 Smi
John 36 Lin
John 29 Mon
John 31 Smi
Lawrence 31 Smi
Polly 41 Lin
Smedley 165 Sum
Stephen 99 Rut
Thomas 32 Smi
William 31 Smi
William 1 Wll
Lynder, Joseph 8 Ove
Lyndsey, Elisha 39 Lin
John 39 Lin
William 36 Lin
Lyner, James S. 349 Whi
Lynes, Samuel 1 Mon
Lynew, Wm. J. 1 Mon
Lynn, Andrew 13 Mon
George 40 Bed
Jacob 306 War
James 300 War
James 306 War
Josep 68 Mau
Thomas 306 War
Lynville, Moses 371 Whi
Lyon, Andrew 28 Mau
Harry 31 Smi
John 31 Smi
John 165 Sum
Nathan 83 Rut
Nelson 81 Dav
Richd. 165 Sum
Lyons, Gutridge 6 Mon
Richard 83 Dav
Richard 14 Gil
Sally 23 Hic
Thomas 355 Whi
see Lions, Loyons, Lynes
Lytle, Archibald 9 Wll
Henry 89 Dav
William 79 Dav
William 84 Rut

--- M ---

Maberry, James 1 Law
Polly 112 Ste
Mabery see Maury

Mabon, John	14	Dic
Mabry, Jacob	5	Ove
James	12	Gil
James	3	Ove
James	168	Sum
Orien	168	Sum
Seth	166	Sum
Mabuary, Mical	28	Mau
Mabury, M.	24	Mau
Macanally, Willis	21	Fra
Macane, John	63	Mau
Mace, Henry	17	Ove
Thompson	37	Smi
Mack, Constantine	39	Mau
James	39	Mau
James H.	39	Mau
John [2]	39	Mau
Lemuel D.	39	Mau
Robbrt	56	Mau
William	25	Mau
William	39	Mau
Macke, John	131	Ste
Thomas	128	Ste
Mackey, Alexander	38	Mau
Benjamin	7	Ove
William	284	War
Macklin, John	167	Sum
Umphrey	395	Wil
Willis	72	Dav
Macks, ...	24	Mau
Macon, John	70	Mau
Mactry, Samuel	97	Dav
Madcalf, Horace	168	Sum
Madden, Alexander	17	Jac
Maddin, John	8	Hum
Samuel	8	Hum
Madding, Champness	33	Smi
Thomas	34	Smi
Violet	37	Smi
Maddison, Norman	35	Smi
Maddox, Mary	15	Lin
William	20	Gil
William	30	Wil
Maddra, William	107	She
Maddux, Elizabeth	112	Ste
Madewell, Charles	364	Whi
James	365	Whi
John	364	Whi
John	364	Whi
Sampson	364	Whi
Mading, Robert	5	Dic
Sarah	50	Mau
Madison, Ambrose	17	Mon
Ann	102	Rut
Jemima	1	Bed
William	16	Bed
Madray, Buckner	10	Gil
Maeen, Nathan	18	Jac
Magby, James	20	Fra
William	20	Fra
Maghan, Pattrick	107	She
Magill, Daniel	19	Gil
Robert	12	Gil

Magness, Lydia	82	Rut
Mago, Jacob	113	Wil
Jacob	377	Wil
William	389	Wil
Magowen, John J.	21	Fra
Maguier, John [deleted]	49	Mau
Maguire, Patrick	57	Mau
see Magwier		
Magwier, Abzaney	55	Mau
Magwire, Holady	55	Mau
Ma Hall, William	20	Fra
Mahan, Bassel	17	Jac
Henry	4	Har
Isaac	99	Rut
Nancy	17	Rob
Thomas	56	Mau
Mahana, Benjamin	17	Jac
Mahew, Aaron	7	Law
Maiben, Alexander	34	Wil
Mainer, William	18	Jac
Mainor, Jethro	20	Rob
Mainord, Drury	344	Whi
John	352	Whi
Maise, Allen	22	Rob
Majeres, S.	24	Mau
Majors, Alexander	21	Fra
Benjamin	21	Fra
Isaac	7	Gil
James	11	Mon
John	11	Mon
John	407	Wil
Noble L.	36	Bed
Robert	51	Bed
Samuel	21	Fra
William	22	Gil
Makerson, Aaron	11	Law
Malengen, James	10	Hum
Malican, William [2]	296	War
Malin, William	12	Hic
Mallard, Eldridge	90	Rut
George	88	Rut
James	23	Lin
Nancy	23	Lin
Thomas	34	Bed
Thornton	34	Bed
Winniford	169	Sum
Mallery, William	416	Wil
Mallory, Frankey	19	Mon
James	9	Mon
James	115	Ste
John	18	Mon
John	33	Wil
Stephen	18	Mon
Willi	115	Ste
William	93	Rut
Malone, Boothe	3	Mon
Charles	31	Lin
George	19	Gil
Hallary	167	Sum
James	36	Smi
Jeremiah	413	Wil
Mark	19	Fra
Nathan	19	Fra

Malone (cont.)		
Nathaniel	9	Hum
Robert	33	Smi
Robert	36	Smi
Samuel	36	Smi
Stephen	19	Fra
Thomas	64	Dav
Vincent	14	Hum
Westley	165	Sum
William	36	Smi
William	166	Sum
William	59	Wll
Maloney, James	9	Hum
Malow, James	390	Wil
Malton, Philip	8	Gil
Mamon, —	24	Mau
Mamor see Mainor		
Manahan, James	95	Rut
Manair, Rhoda	17	Jac
Manaskoe, Joel	10	Law
Mancel, Burrel	17	Jac
Ricd.	17	Jac
Robert	17	Jac
Manchester, Willard	73	Rut
Mandling, Samuel	64	Dav
Mandrell, John	168	Sum
Solo.	168	Sum
William	168	Sum
Mandye, Pretty	48	Mau
Manees, James	98	Rut
Maney, James	87	Rut
Maney, William	84	Rut
Mang, Jane	79	Dav
Mangram, Marthey	62	Mau
Mangrave, Willie	14	Hic
Mangrum, Edwin	48	Mau
Henery	56	Mau
Manier, Agatha	27	Lin
John W.	57	Wll
Phillip	58	Wll
Manifee, Willis	342	Whi
Maning, Bennett	345	Whi
John	113	Ste
John	125	Ste
Matthew	125	Ste
W. M.	125	Ste
Whitdon	14	Wll
William	18	Wll
Willis	113	Ste
Wm.	113	Ste
Mankins, James	95	Rut
John	96	Rut
William	96	Rut
Manley, Caleb	4	Wll
Reuben	48	Bed
Richard	65	Dav
Manlief, Benjmin H.	55	Mau
Manly, David D.	6	Har
Hamblin	111	Ste
John	120	Ste
Joseph	6	Gil
Richard, Senr. [?]	111	Ste
Richard, Senr.	117	Ste
Mann, Able	9	Mon
Andrew	19	Fra
David B.	77	Dav
Joel	9	Mon
Joel	35	Smi
John W.	35	Smi
Mallichi	112	Ste
Robert	21	Mon
Robert	381	Wil
Stephen	35	Smi
Thomas	119	Ste
William	19	Fra
William	21	Mon
Manners, Christly	35	Smi
Manning, John	86	Rut
Thomas	86	Rut
William	86	Rut
Mannon, Charles	16	Bed
William	409	Wil
Manon, Charity Browor [Brow or Manon?]	49	Mau
Manor, Levi W.	14	Ove
Manos, James	35	Smi
Mans, Hugh	384	Wil
Manscell, William	19	Fra
Manscoe, James	58	Mau
Mansker, Casper	169	Sum
William	166	Sum
Mantold, Richd. M.	6	Rob
Manuel, Abraham	97	Dav
Paton	10	Lin
Mar, Alexander	67	Mau
Marable, Benjamin	91	Rut
Branton	90	Rut
Henry H.	9	Dic
Henry H.	92	Rut
John H.	5	Mon
Travers	90	Rut
Maraign, Stephen	37	Smi
Marberry, Isaac	119	Ste
Jacob	127	Ste
John	119	Ste
Marbey, Benjamin	290	War
Marbroad, Daniel	106	She
Marbry, John	293	War
Leonard	282	War
Marchbanks, Joel	4	Hic
Marchent, Mary	36	Bed
Marchett, John	397	Wil
Marcus, J. D.	17	Jac
Mare, James	420	Wil
Mareen, Sophia	30	Wll
Mareign, John	25	Wll
Mares, Alexander	419	Wil
Marham, John	9	Law
Maris, Allen	52	Mau
Mark	320	War
see Moris	52	Mau
Markahm, John	355	Whi
Markan, David	169	Sum
Markery, John	21	Bed
Markes, James	411	Wil
John	411	Wil

Markham, Abner 54 Bed
Arthur 35 Lin
Betsy 313 War
George 167 Sum
Michael 302 War
see Markahm, Markum
Markley, Jacob 320 War
Lawrance 320 War
Marks, Edward 15 Gil
Thomas 15 Gil
Thomas 411 Wil
William 15 Gil
Markum, Abner 345 Whi
Elisha 168 Sum
Nathaniel 345 Whi
Sabrina 169 Sum
William 345 Whi
Markus, Phillip 30 Mau
Marler, Michael 27 Lin
Stephen 37 Smi
Stephen, Sen. 37 Smi
Marley, Adam 35 Smi
Marlin, Archd. 167 Sum
Edward 49 Wll
George 49 Wll
James 16 Wll
Jane 33 Wll
see Mortin
Marlow, Abel 380 Wil
Alfred P. 5 Gil
Allen 364 Whi
Baswell 380 Wil
Charles 9 Gil
Charles 382 Wil
George 31 Mau
Jesse 7 Gil
Nathaniel 348 Whi
Patton 382 Wil
Richard 381 Wil
Thomas 380 Wil
William 348 Whi
see Malow
Marn, Joel 122 Ste
Marper, James 3 Lin
Marquiss, Thomas 166 Sum
Marr, C. H. 2 Mon
G. W. L. 91 Dav
George W. L. 1 Mon
James 54 Bed
James 67 Mau
John 16 Lin
P. N. 1 Mon
Samuel 50 Bed
William 84 Dav
Marrable, George 403 Wil
Marris, Elijah 45 Bed
Hugh 8 Bed
William 10 Bed
see Morris
Marrow, Alexander 30 Mau
David 29 Rob
Marrs, Benjamin 35 Smi
Isaac 14 Wll
Marrs (cont.)
John A. 53 Bed
Marsh, Charles 37 Smi
Daniel 358 Whi
Ezekiel 25 Lin
Gilbert 7 Dic
Jacob 2 Dic
Jacob 3 Hum
James 37 Smi
Joel 13 Dic
John 12 Dic
John 25 Lin
John 372 Whi
Raford 25 Lin
Thomas 25 Lin
Marshal, Benjamin 47 Lin
Elisabeth 48 Wll
Evelen 29 Wll
Francis 169 Sum
Gilbert 28 Wll
Hardaway 169 Sum
James 84 Dav
Jessee 169 Sum
John 19 Fra
William 417 Wil
William 5 Wll
Marshall, Daniel 84 Rut
David 391 Wil
Elihin 80 Dav
Ezekiel 168 Sum
Goodram 22 Mon
John 28 Mon
John 118 Ste
John H. 33 Smi
Josiah 34 Smi
Robert 11 Ove
Robert 415 Wil
Saml. 78 Dav
Thomas 84 Rut
Marshbanks, Josiah 16 Ove
William 11 Ove
Marshell, Francis 32 Bed
John 18 Bed
Leven 37 Bed
Martain, James 1 Per
Martial, Benjamin 18 Jac
William 18 Jac
Martin, Abraham 18 Bed
Abram 169 Sum
Alexander 97 Dav
Alexander 49 Mau
Alexander 2 Mon
Alexander 311 War
Alexander 370 Whi
Ambrose 28 Mon
Ambrose 31 Mon
Ambrose 307 War
Amos 297 War
Amy 37 Smi
Andrew 165 Sum
Ann 3 Ove
Aquilla 7 Gil
Austin 18 Jac

Martin (cont.)		
Barbara	32	Lin
Benjamin	17	Hic
Brice	34	Smi
Brice F.	63	Smi
Brice T.	76	Dav
Cafrey	368	Whi
Campbell	30	Mau
Daniel	18	Fra
Daniel	35	Lin
Danl.	73	Dav
David	57	Mau
David	36	Smi
David	120	Ste
David	369	Whi
David	405	Wil
Edward	21	Fra
Elijah	30	Mon
Federick	169	Sum
Francis	29	Mon
George	3	Hum
George	12	Lin
George	22	Lin
George	29	Lin
George	69	Mau
George	36	Smi
George	403	Wil
George, Jr.	165	Sum
George, Sr.	166	Sum
George M.	47	Mau
George W.	33	Smi
Henry	4	Ove
Henry	166	Sum
Henry	307	War
Holloway	11	Hum
Isaac	26	Lin
Isaac	296	War
J. A.	34	Fra
Jacob	52	Bed
Jacob	291	War
Jacob	419	Wil
James	90	Dav
James	11	Dic
James	19	Fra
James	18	Jac
James	10	Lin
James	25	Lin
James	21	Mon
James	26	Rob
James	100	Rut
James	36	Smi
James	37	Smi
James	126	Ste
James	165	Sum
James	169	Sum
James	283	War
James	285	War
James	299	War
James	4	Way
James	406	Wil
James G.	81	Dav
James L.	166	Sum
Jesse	10	Hum
Job	299	War
Martin (cont.)		
John	19	Fra
John	2	Har
John	19	Lin
John	30	Mon
John	14	Rob
John	90	Rut
John	165	Sum
John	286	War
John	303	War
John	384	Wil
John	405	Wil
John, Jr.	388	Wil
John, Jun.	18	Fra
John, Sen.	388	Wil
John L.	21	Lin
John S.	19	Fra
John T.	21	Fra
Jonathan	19	Fra
Jonathan W.	1	Har
Joseph	2	Ove
Joseph	80	Rut
Joseph A.	18	Fra
Josiah	20	Fra
Josiah	93	Rut
Lewis	39	Bed
Lewis	7	Gil
Lewis	18	Gil
Lewis	169	Sum
Linsey	420	Wil
Lucy	28	Mon
Martha	70	Dav
Matt	18	Bed
Menan M.	7	Ove
Oliver	19	Fra
Patrick	5	Rob
Peter	3	Gil
Peter H.	137	Sum
Pew	405	Wil
Peyton	167	Sum
Polly	66	Dav
Rachel	18	Bed
Rebeca	386	Wil
Richard	8	Gil
Richard	168	Sum
Robert	3	Ove
Robert	97	Rut
Robt.	80	Dav
Saml.	168	Sum
Samuel	61	Mau
Samuel	11	Way
Samuel	23	Wll
Samuel N.	14	Wll
Sarah	36	Smi
Seth	1	Har
Susanah	168	Sum
Tanner	318	War
Thomas	71	Dav
Thomas	16	Gil
Thomas	35	Mau
Thomas	5	Rob
Thomas	37	Smi
Thomas	284	War
Thomas	307	War

Martin (cont.)
Thomas 365 Whi
Thomas 11 Wll
Thos. J. 6 Hic
Tignal 58 Wll
William 39 Bed
William 92 Dav
William 4 Gil
William 21 Gil
William 25 Lin
William 44 Lin
William 31 Mon
William 33 Smi
William 286 War
William 287 War
William 369 Whi
William 385 Wil
Wm. A. 113 Ste
Woody 166 Sum
see Marlin
Martindale, John 10 Ove
Thomas 2 Law
Marton, Hesekiah 81 Rut
Joseph 89 Rut
Martry see Mactry
Marvel, John 17 Jac
Mary, James 12 Rob
Maseley, Archibald 50 Mau
John S. 5 Mon
see Moseley
Masey, Stephen 296 War
Mash, Elizabeth 21 Gil
John 20 Fra
Minor 10 Hic
Obdiah 38 Mau
Robbart 45 Mau
Mashburn, William 19 Fra
Masners, David 302 War
Mason, Abner 95 Rut
Abraham 99 Rut
Asa 31 Rob
Caleb 345 Whi
Charles 47 Wll
Daniel 18 Jac
Daniel 12 Hum
Edmund 91 Rut
Elizabeth 30 Rob
Foster 21 Rob
Isaac 3 Rob
James 99 Rut
Jesse 17 Rob
Jesse 102 Rut
John 34 Smi
John 345 Whi
John 419 Wil
Joseph 99 Rut
Martha 26 Wll
Obediah 102 Rut
Phillip 27 Rob
Robert, Mr. 2 Law
Samuel 33 Rob
Thomas 26 Wll
Warren 9 Law
William 19 Fra
Mason (cont.)
William 18 Rob
see Dollason
Masoner, John 16 Ove
Masse, Allen 69 Mau
Massengill, Blake 14 Hum
Massey, Adam 357 Whi
Daniel 409 Wil
Enoch 14 Dic
Henry 402 Wil
Isaac 5 Hum
James 2 Hum
Jeremiah 7 Hum
John 37 Smi
John 371 Whi
Joshua W. 33 Lin
Martha 7 Hum
Sally 33 Smi
Samuel 34 Smi
Sherwood 34 Smi
Simms 35 Smi
Thomas 97 Rut
William 6 Hum
William 34 Smi
William H. 33 Smi
see Mossey
Massie, Ephraim M. 5 Gil
John 20 Gil
John C. 3 Dic
William A. 9 Gil
Massingale, Mathew 358 Whi
Massingell, George 3 Har
Massy, Sally 76 Rut
Masters, Davis 6 Ove
James 19 Ove
Jesse 9 Ove
Mary 19 Ove
Robert 14 Ove
Thomas 14 Ove
William 5 Ove
Mastin, Sally 25 Rob
Masure see Mosure
Mathas, Abner 28 Mau
John 39 Mau
Robbert 39 Mau
Mathena, Luke 2 Ove
Mathershed, Lucy 73 Dav
Mathew, Simon 169 Sum
Mathews, Daniel, Mr. 1 Law
Elisha 99 Rut
James 78 Rut
Jeramiah 72 Dav
John 82 Rut
Kinchen 291 War
Penelope 169 Sum
Ralph 290 War
Richard 22 Rob
Sampson 3 Rob
Samuel [?] 313 War
Thomas 4 Dic
Thomas B. 9 Rob
Washington 77 Rut
William 97 Rut
William E. 82 Rut

Mathews (cont.)		
Winny	92	Rut
Mathias, Stephen	96	Dav
Mathis, David	34	Mau
James	48	Mau
Joseph	28	Mau
Robbert	25	Mau
Thomas	15	Lin
Matlock, Byrd	7	Per
Elizabeth	14	Ove
George	34	Smi
James	6	Dic
John	6	Gil
John	6	Mon
Moses	24	Lin
Smyth	7	Per
Valentine	20	Ove
William	97	Dav
William	16	Ove
William	351	Whi
Zachariah	19	Fra
see Mattock		
Matlocks, Malley	392	Wil
Matney, Charles	18	Ove
Mattey, B. F.	111	Wil
Matthew, Allon	69	Dav
Elisha	73	Dav
see Mtthew		
Matthews, Archibald	309	War
Chester	294	War
Cornelius	40	Wll
Drewry	31	Mon
Drewry	128	Ste
Elbert	11	Hic
Isaac	58	Wll
Isham	39	Wll
James	128	Ste
Jeremiah	11	Hic
Jesse	14	Hic
John	19	Fra
John	21	Fra
John	16	Hic
John	8	Law
John	29	Mon
John	13	Ove
John	12	Wll
Lemuel	294	War
Martha	35	Smi
Martha	11	Wll
Pricilla	9	Mon
Richard	14	Ove
Wilie	308	War
William	30	Mon
William	14	Ove
William	293	War
William L.	40	Wll
Willis	309	War
Wm.	20	Hic
Matthiet, James	11	Hum
Matthis, Matthew	417	Wil
Nathaniel	413	Wil
Thomas	413	Wil
Matthison, John	123	Ste
Matticks, George	30	Mau
Mattock, Margaret	1	Ove
Moore	2	Ove
William	1	Ove
William	131	Ste
Wm.	19	Hic
see Matlock		
Mattocks, Elijah	400	Wil
Mattox, John	168	Sum
Mauldin, Harris	7	Lin
Hiram	14	Lin
Maultsby, Isabella	15	Gil
Maum, Dennis	167	Sum
Mauntague, Mary	70	Mau
Maupin, Blan	29	Bed
George	29	Wll
Maurr, James	319	War
Maury, Abram	9	Wll
Jobe	36	Wll
Nancy	13	Wll
Phillip P.	35	Wll
Richard	36	Wll
Ryleigh D.	14	Wll
Maus, Joseph	127	Ste
Mawpin, Elizabeth	169	Sum
Mawtry see Mactry		
Maxcy, Nancy	19	Gil
Maxey, John	68	Dav
Survice	103	Rut
William	90	Dav
Maxfield, Robert	20	Ove
William	410	Wil
Maxsey, William	61	Wll
Maxwell, Daniel	14	Bed
David	10	Gil
David	7	Ove
Elizabeth	392	Wil
Henry	7	Ove
James	90	Dav
James	46	Lin
Jesse	90	Dav
Joel	19	Ove
John	11	Har
John W.	100	Rut
Joseph	82	Dav
Robert	40	Lin
Samuel	18	Jac
Samuel	74	Rut
Soleman	40	Mau
Soloman	14	Bed
Thomas	21	Fra
Thomas	9	Gil
Thomas	11	Ove
Thomas, Junr.	14	Bed
Thomas, Senr.	14	Bed
William	39	Mau
William	92	Rut
William	168	Sum
Maxy, Jacob	317	War
James	13	Rob
May, Absolum	8	Bed
Benjamin	11	Law
Daniel	62	Mau
Debericks	22	Mon
Dempsey	12	Hic

May (cont.)		
Dred	291	War
Francis	44	Lin
Hugh	78	Rut
James	294	War
Jesse	6	Dic
John	6	Dic
John	5	Hum
Jonathan	12	Hum
Joseph	67	Dav
Leroy	18	Fra
Moses	40	Mau
Peter	40	Mau
Philip	111	Ste
Phillip	10	Hic
Reynolds	12	Law
Robert	97	Rut
Sterling	9	Dic
Thomas	9	Dic
William	6	Dic
William	9	Gil
William	12	Hic
William	360	Whi
see Moy		
Maybe, William	5	Gil
Mayben, Stephen	41	Bed
William A.	1	Wll
Mayberry, Benja.	165	Sum
Benja.	167	Sum
Benja., Jr.	167	Sum
Daniel	79	Rut
Frederick	16	Hic
Henry, Jr.	4	Hic
Henry, Sr.	20	Hic
Jno.	20	Hic
John	98	Rut
John	167	Sum
Leanner	361	Whi
Robert S.	20	Rob
Samuel	81	Rut
Maybury, Seth	17	Jac
Mayes, Edman	49	Mau
James	66	Mau
James	70	Mau
John	45	Mau
Samuel	32	Mau
Mayfars, Samuel	34	Mau
Mayfeld, Samul	32	Mau
Mayfiel, Isaac	90	Dav
Mayfield, A. Be	39	Mau
Abraham	5	Bed
Archibald	37	Lin
Berry	44	Wll
Elias	40	Wll
Elijah	22	Hic
Elijah	39	Lin
Elijah	44	Wll
Elizabeth	5	Bed
Frances	8	Ove
George	22	Hic
George	21	Wll
Isaac	4	Gil
Isaac	37	Lin
James	21	Hic
Mayfield (cont.)		
James	19	Ove
James	58	Wll
James, Sr.	22	Hic
John	37	Lin
John	1	Ove
John	21	Wll
Larkin	8	Gil
Luke	17	Jac
Nelly	17	Jac
Randolph	39	Lin
Robert	7	Bed
Solomon	287	War
Southerland	66	Wll
Stephen	8	Ove
Stephen	9	Ove
Sulevan	32	Mau
Sutherland	22	Hic
William	10	Gil
William	76	Rut
William	288	War
Wm.	22	Hic
Mayheffer, Robert	377	Wil
Mayo, Wm.	113	Ste
see Mago, Mays		
Mays, Abram	6	Per
Abreham	64	Mau
David	30	Mau
Isaac	30	Mau
James	21	Lin
James	346	Whi
John	90	Dav
John	4	Har
John	355	Whi
Mathew	4	Har
Samuel	94	Dav
Sarah	30	Mau
Thomas	342	Whi
William W.	94	Dav
see Moys		
Mayson, Ramsay L.	166	Sum
Maze, Bozeman	18	Fra
Garner	34	Wll
MBroom, Thomas	86	Rut
McAdams, Amos	31	Bed
Ervin	11	Lin
James	22	Bed
James	11	Lin
Jno.	166	Sum
John	10	Lin
John	4	Ove
John	113	Ste
Joseph	11	Lin
William	10	Mon
McAdin, Henry	169	Sum
McAdo, James	413	Wil
James, Sen.	414	Wil
John	413	Wil
Lilly	18	Jac
Samuel	18	Jac
Stewart	18	Jac
William	413	Wil
McAdoo, Barnett	9	Hic
Barnett A.	16	Hic

McAdoo (cont.)		
David	2	Dic
David C.	12	Dic
Evans	13	Dic
Ezra	6	Dic
John	3	Dic
McAfee, Mills	49	Mau
McAffy, Morgan	21	Fra
McAge, James	7	Hum
William	7	Hum
Mcalee, Andrew	94	Rut
McAlester, Robert	107	She
McAlister, Jno.	15	Hic
John	32	Mon
Joseph	12	Gil
Mcalister, Elisabeth	1	Wll
Nathaniel	85	Rut
McAllelly, Richard	11	Gil
McAllen, James	19	Rob
McAllister, Ann	19	Fra
David	34	Smi
Edward	20	Fra
Garland	34	Smi
James	6	Lin
McAlly, Jesse	21	Fra
McAlpin, Thomas	46	Lin
McAnally, Charles	9	Law
Jesse	10	Gil
John, Junr.	10	Law
John, Senr., Mr.	9	Law
William	9	Law
see Macanally		
McAnaly, Jesse	21	Fra
see McAnnally		
McAnelly, Littleberry	12	Mon
McAninch, Daniel	9	Gil
McAnnally, Jno.	18	Hic
McAnninch, John	9	Gil
Mcartrey, Celia	101	Rut
McAtee, Abednego	11	Law
McAteer, James	45	Mau
McAulay, Danl.	136	Sum
Mcay, David	97	Rut
Henry	79	Rut
McBee, Levi L.	341	Whi
McBride, Abraham	408	Wil
Andrew	351	Whi
Charles	87	Rut
Daniel	408	Wil
David	67	Mau
Edward	40	Lin
Francis	20	Way
Hugh	41	Bed
Hugh	166	Sum
James	97	Dav
John	41	Bed
John	11	Lin
John	35	Mau
John	67	Mau
Moses	18	Jac
Nathaniel	20	Fra
Samuel	1	Way
William	14	Lin

McBride (cont.)		
William	358	Whi
Mcbride, Mary	5	Law
McBroom, Henry D.	297	War
Jas. J.	17	Jac
see MBroom		
McBroon, James	17	Jac
McCabb, James, Sr.	18	Hic
Jas., Jr.	18	Hic
John, Jr.	18	Hic
McCabe, Charles	31	Wll
James H.	33	Smi
Starky	19	Wll
William	16	Gil
see McCale		
McCafferty, James	27	Mau
McCagg, John	289	War
McCain, Elizabeth	383	Wil
Elizebeth	55	Mau
Hugh	7	Law
John	66	Dav
John	5	Law
John	59	Mau
William	7	Law
McCale, Hugh	6	Hic
McCall, Catherine	41	Wll
James	286	War
Robert	300	War
Samuel	4	Bed
Thomas	6	Bed
Wilia	41	Wll
William	17	Jac
William	166	Sum
McCallen, Robert	4	Wll
McCalley, Denis	19	Jac
McCallister, Barnabas	15	Bed
McCallum, Daniel	10	Gil
Margaret	21	Gil
Thomas	21	Gil
see McCollum		
McCalpen, William	21	Wll
McCammon, Joseph	34	Bed
McCan, James	18	Jac
James	362	Whi
McCanel, Francis	124	Ste
McCanless, David	5	Gil
James	5	Gil
John	22	Gil
Samuel	12	Gil
Thomas F.	22	Gil
William	22	Wll
McCann, James	5	Hic
Jno.	5	Hic
John	11	Law
John	166	Sum
Joseph	5	Hic
Sarah	5	Hic
William	9	Law
McCannal, Walter	26	Mau
McCannon, Elizabth.	33	Mau
William	38	Wll
McCants, Maxfield	27	Lin
McCard, Eleson	51	Mau

McCarley, Abraham	28	Mau
Abraham, Jr.	28	Mau
James	25	Rob
John	6	Rob
Moses	20	Rob
Zekial	56	Mau
McCarmon, Matthew	6	Hum
McCarrahan, Charles	19	Wll
McCarrell, Izeal	6	Wll
Jas.	128	Ste
John	412	Wil
McCarrol, Abner	1	Hum
James	18	Mon
McCarter, Andrew	26	Mau
Robbert	53	Mau
Zadock	116	Ste
McCartie, Amos G.	168	Sum
James	169	Sum
Mary	169	Sum
McCartney, Andrew	38	Lin
John	167	Sum
Lewis	396	Wil
see Mcartrey	101	Rut
McCarty, Patrick	20	Fra
McCarver, John	359	Whi
Nathaniel	359	Whi
McCary, Franklin	55	Wll
McCaslin, Harmon	15	Hic
Isaac	70	Dav
James	49	Wll
John	70	Dav
John	94	Dav
John	49	Wll
Younger	3	Hic
McCasling, Andrew	37	Mau
McCaughlin, Rebecca	16	Wll
McCaul, Alexander	33	Smi
Alexr.	124	Ste
McCauley, Catharine	29	Mon
James	9	Dic
John	29	Mon
William	13	Mon
McCaun, Joseph	14	Way
McCawen, John	17	Jac
McCay, Daniel A.	22	Wll
Milly	112	Ste
see Mcay		
McCelroy, George	19	Fra
McChristian, James	20	Fra
McCiernan, John	73	Rut
McClain, Godfrey	33	Mau
Hugh	47	Lin
Jesse	11	Lin
John	24	Wll
Poley	65	Mau
Wm.	2	Lin
McClamrock, David	23	Lin
McClanahan, James	3	Dic
John	5	Hum
Joseph	114	Ste
see MClanahan		
McClane, John	22	Bed
Mary	17	Dic
McClannahan, Francis	4	Hic
James	3	Hic
Jno.	4	Hic
Wm.	4	Hic
McClaren, Daniel	9	Bed
Daniel	10	Bed
Robert	10	Bed
McClarin, Andrew	7	Law
Daniel	7	Law
John	7	Law
McClary, John	28	Lin
Reuben	13	Bed
Thomas	54	Wll
McClay, Samuel	19	Lin
McCleland, John	6	Ove
McClelen, Hugh	4	Bed
James	4	Bed
McClellan, Samuel	19	Fra
McClelland, Jane	11	Dic
Nelson	16	Dic
William	17	Lin
William B.	67	Dav
McClellen, George	46	Wll
McClenden, George	18	Jac
Jesse	18	Jac
William	4	Per
McClendhan, Samuel	35	Mau
McClendon, Bryant	1	Law
Dennis	98	Dav
McClenehan, Robert	2	Per
McClennahan, William	33	Smi
McClerkin, Saml.	169	Sum
McClery see MClery, Mclery		
McClester see McCarter		
McCletten, John	35	Wll
McCleure, Elizabeth	17	Jac
McClewer, A. S.	8	Way
McCleyea, Humphrey	9	Hic
McClintic, Alexander	1	Har
McClintock, John	33	Bed
Robert	7	Hum
Saml.	33	Bed
McClish, James	45	Wll
John	42	Wll
John, Mr.	4	Law
McClosky, George W.	21	Fra
McCloud, Anguish	7	Dic
Danl.	123	Ste
Sollomon	17	Jac
William	19	Fra
see MCloud		
McCluer, Mary	26	Wll
McClung, Jonas	12	Gil
McClure, Alexander	1	Hum
Elijah	19	Fra
Hugh	1	Mon
Huston	43	Wll
James A.	52	Bed
John	50	Bed
John	19	Fra
John	36	Lin
Robert	25	Mon
Saml.	4	Mon

McClure (cont.)
Samuel 22 Gil
William 50 Bed
William 18 Fra
William 22 Gil
William 13 Hum
William 28 Mon
McCollam, Isaac 69 Mau
McCollester, John 3 Way
McCollister, George 9 Dic
James 8 Dic
McCollough, Daniel 363 Whi
John 363 Whi
William 342 Whi
McCollum, Alexander 14 Gil
Cloud 47 Wll
David 46 Mau
David 67 Mau
John 299 War
Levi 24 Hic
Mary 28 Mau
Nancy 42 Lin
Robert 16 Dic
McCombs, Gabrial 85 Dav
James W. 77 Dav
see MCombs
McComell, John 169 Sum
McComick, Andrew 167 Sum
McCommack, William 50 Mau
McConal, D. Samuel 45 Mau
McConell, Fras. 19 Jac
see McCarrell, McComell
McConico, Ganner 6 Wll
McConnal, Archibald 45 Mau
James 63 Mau
John 45 Mau
Manuel 44 Mau
McConnald, David 391 Wil
John 391 Wil
McConnel, Danl. 166 Sum
James 11 Law
James M. 3 Law
John P. 1 Lin
Samuel 31 Mau
McConnell, David 111 Wil
Esther 18 Ove
James 11 Ove
John 111 Wil
Margret 420 Wil
Montgomery 167 Sum
see McComell, Mconnell
McConwell, William 27 Mau
McCord, Agail 18 Fra
David 18 Fra
Elisabeth 62 Wll
James 18 Fra
James 17 Ove
James 37 Wll
James 51 Wll
John 1 Ove
William 3 Ove
William 51 Wll
Wm. 9 Hum
McCord (cont.)
see McOrd
McCorkle, Alexr., Jr. 4 Lin
Alexr., Ser. 3 Lin
Andrew 45 Wll
Archibald 23 Mon
Dinah 186 Sum
James 8 Lin
Lewis 4 Lin
Robert 124 Ste
Saml. M. 166 Sum
see Mcorkle
McCormac, John 15 Dic
John 10 Gil
Masterson C. 17 Gil
McCormack, Charles 7 Gil
George 70 Dav
George 13 Ove
James 8 Lin
Nancy 16 Ove
Richard 70 Dav
William 21 Fra
see McOrmack
McCown, Alexander 371 Whi
Alexander 3 Wll
George 18 Lin
Hannah 397 Wil
Malcolm 18 Lin
McCoy, Daniel 19 Fra
Daniel 21 Fra
Danl. 81 Dav
Francis 72 Dav
James 38 Wll
John 9 Bed
John 18 Fra
John 19 Fra
William 71 Dav
McCrabb, Louisa 24 Mon
McCracken, Elizabeth 23 Lin
James 43 Wll
John 17 Gil
John 8 Hum
Joseph 4 Lin
Robert 1 Wll
Samuel 56 Mau
Thomas 50 Wll
see Mcracken
McCracking, Ephraim 64 Mau
Joseph 63 Mau
McCrady, Alexander 50 Wll
Andrew 39 Wll
David 169 Sum
William 38 Wll
McCraken, Eli 296 War
Samuel 296 War
McCrakin, George 298 War
McCrary, Jos. 14 Hic
Polly 128 Ste
Robert 420 Wil
Samuel 18 Jac
McCraven, James 44 Mau
McCraw, John 19 Fra
Joseph 167 Sum

McCraw (cont.)
Richard 19 Fra
Samuel 18 Ove
William 19 Fra
McCray, Alexander 51 Mau
McCreery, William 19 Gil
McCrory, Hugh, Jr. 23 Hic
Hugh, Sr. 23 Hic
John 48 Bed
Nathaniel 26 Rob
Rachel 21 Wll
Reaze 45 Mau
Thomas 21 Wll
McCue, Charles 4 Per
John 4 Per
McCuistain, Benjn. 18 Bed
James 18 Bed
John 32 Bed
Joseph 8 Bed
Robert 8 Bed
Thomas 18 Bed
McCulla, Poley 70 Mau
McCullah, William 18 Jac
McCuller, James 126 Ste
McCulley, Joseph 8 Mon
McCulloch, David 19 Gil
James 11 Gil
John 19 Gil
Robt. 21 Hic
see MCulloch
McCullough, Alexander 39 Lin
Ambrose 32 Lin
Charles 35 Smi
David 40 Lin
James 19 Bed
James 32 Lin
McCully see Mcully
McCuly, Joseph 74 Dav
McCurda, John H. 3 Lin
McCurdee, Ann H. 44 Lin
Andrew 17 Gil
James 17 Gil
John 23 Wll
Katherine 17 Wll
Robert 17 Wll
McCutcheon, George 21 Fra
James 85 Dav
John 64 Dav
William 64 Dav
Mcdade, Charles 7 Wll
McDanal, Robbert 39 Mau
McDanel, Catherine 37 Mau
McDaniel, Allen 167 Sum
Ann 363 Whi
Charles 20 Fra
Charles 343 Whi
Charles, Sen. 20 Fra
Celmment 63 Dav
Coleman 38 Lin
Collin 20 Wll
Daniel 347 Whi
David 360 Whi
George 129 Ste
H. L. 17 Jac
McDaniel (cont.)
Henry 46 Lin
James 65 Dav
James 69 Dav
James 17 Jac
James 343 Whi
John 30 Bed
John 63 Dav
John 17 Jac
John 167 Sum
John 297 War
John 345 Whi
John 352 Whi
John 19 Wll
Laura 89 Dav
Lucinda 345 Whi
Mathew 169 Sum
Nancy 167 Sum
Neil 124 Ste
Polly 20 Fra
Randolph 370 Whi
Samuel 51 Mau
Stephen C. 69 Dav
Tabitha 12 Hum
William 20 Fra
William 19 Jac
William 10 Mon
Wm. N. T. 73 Dav
McDanil, Martha 169 Sum
McDannel, James 27 Rob
McDannell, Andrew [2] 402 Wil
John 413 Wil
Stephen 402 Wil
McDanniel, Danl. 73 Dav
Joseph 14 Gil
McDavid, James 43 Lin
Nancy 43 Lin
Samuel 18 Fra
McDeerman, Bryant 387 Wil
McDole, Alx. 81 Dav
Andrew 369 Whi
Andrew 370 Whi
McDonald, Alexander 14 Gil
Alexander 78 Rut
Alexander W. 16 Gil
Archibald 20 Gil
Henry B. 35 Smi
James 30 Mau
John 6 Gil
John 14 Gil
John 35 Smi
John, Mr. 1 Law
Joseph 14 Gil
Robert 14 Gil
McDonnald, James 403 Wil
McDonnell, James 417 Wil
see McDannell
McDonnold, Alley 7 Ove
Elizabeth 18 Ove
Hugh 16 Ove
John, Jr. 1 Ove
John, Senr. 5 Ove
Redmond 10 Ove
McDoogle, Archibald 35 Smi

McDowel, John 66 Mau
Joseph C. 5 Wll
Luke 36 Smi
Samuel 59 Mau
McDowell, James 33 Rob
James 74 Rut
Joseph 33 Rob
Moremon 415 Wil
McDowl, Shadrack 5 Way
McDowleod, Samuel 77 Rut
McDowrell, Jacob 380 Wil
McDuff, John 21 Fra
McDuffee, Angus 2 Law
McDuffy, Duncan 9 Law
McDuffy, Neel 35 Smi
McDugal, Duncan 136 Sum
McDugle, Robt. 126 Ste
McEhern, Mary 33 Smi
McElhaney, Henry 349 Whi
John 354 Whi
McElhatton, Mary 103 Rut
McElhenney, Joseph 29 Wll
McElherring, John 19 Fra
McElroy, Andrew 308 War
John 92 Dav
John T. 16 Gil
William 47 Lin
see McCelroy, Mcler(o)y, Muckleroy
McElvy, Hugh 5 Hum
McElwain, Henry 73 Dav
John 73 Dav
McElwrath, John 166 Sum
Joseph 165 Sum
William 166 Sum
McElyea, John 27 Mon
Patrick 27 Mon
McEwen, Alexander 86 Rut
Alexander 46 Wll
Christopher E. 6 Wll
David 18 Wll
Ebenezer 46 Lin
James 278 War
James, Sn. 6 Wll
John 65 Dav
John 20 Fra
John 87 Rut
Robert M. 1 Lin
Sarah 20 Wll
MCewen, Josiah 86 Rut
Mcewin, James 80 Rut
McFadden, James 53 Mau
Robert 17 Wll
see McShadden
Mcfadden, Candour 12 Wll
Mcfaddin, Samuel 98 Rut
McFadin, David 15 Mon
McFall, Daniel 19 Fra
Henry 26 Mon
Henry 27 Mon
John 60 Mau
Saml. 2 Mon
Samuel 7 Hum
Samuel P. 13 Hum
Mcfall, John 33 Smi
McFarlan, Joseph 22 Lin
McFarland, James 37 Mau
James 17 Ove
John 66 Dav
John 41 Lin
John 60 Mau
John 385 Wil
Joseph 294 War
Robt. P. 78 Dav
Mcfarland, Lewis 33 Smi
McFarlane, Robert 297 War
William 303 War
McFarlen, Mary 350 Whi
McFarlin, James 389 Wll
John 388 Wil
Mcfarlin, Alexr. 167 Sum
Benjamin 94 Rut
Benjamin, Sen. 94 Rut
John 76 Rut
John 91 Rut
Thomas 89 Rut
William 94 Rut
McFarling, Robert 44 Bed
McFashon, Cornelius 72 Dav
McFatter, Niven 10 Gil
McFawls, George 69 Mau
John 49 Mau
Thomas Mc. 70 Mau
McFearson, James 17 Jac
Reuben 17 Jac
McFedden, Edward 34 Mau
McFee, Ezariah 26 Lin
McFerrin, James 20 Lin
Thomas 3 Lin
Mcferrin, Burton L. 97 Rut
James 86 Rut
Martin 101 Rut
Samuel 37 Smi
William 94 Rut
McGaha, James 51 Wll
McGahee, David 11 Lin
Elijah 37 Lin
Joseph 11 Lin
Margaret 11 Lin
McGahey, Mary 21 Gil
McGamen, Robbert B. 53 Mau
McGamery, James 64 Mau
McGann, Eli 2 Wll
McGaugh, Mathew 44 Lin
Thomas 15 Lin
McGavock, David 71 Dav
Jacob 76 Dav
James 87 Dav
James 14 Wll
Joseph 13 Wll
Randal 60 Dav
Randol 33 Wll
see McGerros
McGee, Abraham 3 Per
Asa 7 Gil
Chiles 29 Mau
Clendenon 283 War

McGee (cont.)		
George	34	Smi
John	37	Smi
John	351	Whi
John	46	Wll
Micajah	2	Dic
Nathan	36	Smi
Richard	19	Gil
Solomon	34	Smi
William	1	Wll
William	51	Wll
William H.	17	Ove
Williams	34	Smi
see Megee		
McGeeka, Josiah	401	Wil
McGehee, Green	297	War
Jame	23	Mon
James [2]	24	Mon
Pyatt	24	Mon
Thos.	22	Mon
Thos.	24	Mon
William	41	Lin
William	296	War
McGerros, Anna	371	Wil
McGill, David	101	Rut
James	37	Bed
John	3	Hum
John	67	Mau
Joseph	19	Bed
Sarah	21	Gil
Thomas	21	Gil
Thos.	123	Ste
see Megill, MGill		
McGilniry, William	2	Wll
McGimsey, John W.	51	Bed
McGinnis, Alexander, Jr.	36	Smi
Alexander, Sr.	36	Smi
Polly	26	Bed
Richard	35	Smi
William	20	Lin
William	36	Smi
McGipson, Gorge	17	Jac
McGlathery, Martha	43	Lin
McGloflin, Daniel	18	Jac
McGlothlin, John	169	Sum
Joseph [2]	168	Sum
William	168	Sum
Mcgonagle, Eli	102	Rut
McGowan, William	4	Mon
McGowen, Andrew	20	Fra
Betsey	20	Fra
David	20	Fra
Ebenezer	101	Rut
James	20	Lin
Samuel	20	Fra
McGowin, Saml.	121	Ste
McGown, Amos	345	Whi
James	345	Whi
McGraw, Cornelius	8	Rob
Jenne	88	Dav
Matthew	17	Gil
Reuben	131	Ste
Winey	9	Mon
McGreger, Ezekiel	284	War
Harris	110	Ste
Richmond	282	War
William	46	Mau
William	290	War
Willis	289	War
McGregor, William	114	Wil
McGrew, William	50	Bed
William, Senr.	50	Bed
McGriger, Bartlet	110	Ste
McGrite, John	49	Mau
McGrughey, James	42	Mau
McGuffin, Joseph	53	Bed
McGuffy, Edmund	35	Smi
McGuier, James	62	Wll
McGuire, Aleganey	66	Mau
Charles	350	Whi
Danl. J.	2	Hic
David	12	Gil
Elias	8	Per
Elijah	23	Bed
Elijah	2	Hic
George	168	Sum
John	7	Mon
John	27	Rob
Merryman	2	Hic
Neely	22	Bed
Neely	45	Bed
Thomas [2]	22	Bed
Thomas	24	Bed
Vincent	289	War
Vincent	304	War
William [2]	22	Bed
William	25	Bed
McHany, Andrew	417	Wil
William	417	Wil
McHenry, Jesse	393	Wil
John, Senr.	83	Rut
Mcherson, William	3	Per
McHughs, Charles	6	Law
McIlberry, George H.	167	Sum
Robt.	166	Sum
McIntire, Archibald	36	Smi
Duncan	57	Mau
John	28	Mau
Leonard	72	Dav
McIntosh, Benj.	18	Jac
Charles	34	Rob
Danl.	80	Dav
James	3	Rob
John	7	Rob
John	22	Rob
Mary Ann	1	Rob
Nimrod	19	Hic
Nimrod	6	Rob
William	16	Bed
Mcintosh, Jesse	126	Ste
McInturf, Andrew	35	Smi
McIntush, William	67	Mau
McIntyer, Malcome, Mr.	8	Law
McIntyre, Daniel, Mr.	10	Law
Duncan, Mr.	2	Law
John	6	Law

McIntyre (cont.)		
John	107	She
McInvale, John C.	20	Fra
McKada, John C.	2	Lin
McKagg, James	293	War
McKaimie, Francis	44	Bed
James	44	Bed
John	44	Bed
McKain, Matthew	72	Dav
Robert	72	Dav
Saml.	165	Sum
McKane, James	59	Wll
McKaughan, Forester	16	Gil
Hue	17	Jac
McKay, Henry	22	Gil
James	13	Lin
McKean, John	112	Ste
Lewis	93	Rut
McKee, Alexander	39	Mau
Alexander	48	Mau
Ambrose	86	Rut
Ambrose	104	Rut
Archibald	39	Lin
Isaac	395	Wil
James	5	Lin
James	104	Rut
John	104	Rut
Robobert	16	Wll
William	61	Mau
William	289	War
see McKle, Meckie		
McKeen see MKeen		
McKees, Thomas	46	Mau
McKeller see Keller		
McKeloy, William	19	Fra
McKemie, James	4	Per
Joseph	5	Per
Samuel L.	5	Per
McKendree, Dudley E.	166	Sum
James	166	Sum
McKenney, Henry	7	Ove
William		
McKenny, Ewing	113	Ste
Isaac	113	Ste
Joseph	113	Ste
Rebecka	114	Ste
Saml.	113	Ste
McKerley, Moses	21	Fra
Samuel	21	Fra
McKernan, Bernard	60	Dav
McKever, Duncan	1	Per
McKewin, Joseph H.	67	Mau
McKey, Hezekiah	18	Fra
Hugh	36	Smi
James	15	Dic
John	15	Mon
John	47	Wll
Robert	27	Wll
William	9	Wll
McKimie, William	34	Smi
McKindley, James	17	Jac
Robert	17	Jac
McKiney, Archibald	168	Sum
McKinley, Daniel	4	Lin
John	17	Lin
Mckinly, John	73	Rut
McKinney, Alexander	22	Gil
Charles	2	Lin
John B.	17	Gil
John V.	2	Lin
Reuben	23	Gil
Robert	22	Gil
Rowland	23	Gil
Thomas	6	Gil
Thomas	314	War
William	6	Gil
Willie	33	Smi
McKinnie, Jordon	33	Smi
Thomas	20	Fra
see McKimie		
McKinnis, Alexander	37	Smi
Daniel	37	Smi
James	37	Smi
John	33	Smi
see McKinnie		
McKinny, John	356	Whi
Samuel	13	Law
McKinsey, Daniel	51	Wll
Malcomb	124	Ste
Thomas	51	Wll
McKinzey, William	26	Lin
McKinzy, John	70	Mau
Neel	19	Fra
McKircle, Abram	2	Mon
McKisick, David	52	Bed
James	1	Bed
Jane	1	Bed
Joseph	1	Bed
Joseph	48	Bed
Robert	165	Sum
McKissack, Archibald	3	Gil
Thomas	8	Gil
McKissick, John	25	Mau
McKle, George	29	Mon
McKnab, John	49	Wll
McKnight, Abigal	102	Rut
Alexander	87	Rut
Eleanor	77	Rut
Elisabeth	30	Wll
James	13	Gil
James	78	Rut
James	87	Rut
James	102	Rut
James	30	Wll
John	6	Gil
John	13	Gil
John	81	Rut
John	86	Rut
John M.	78	Rut
Joseph	89	Rut
Lewis	99	Rut
Samuel	13	Gil
Samuel B.	47	Wll
Thomas P.	39	Mau
William	84	Rut
William	97	Rut

McKnight (cont.)
William 419 Wil
see Mcnigh
McKorkle, Samuel 7 Har
McLain, Absalom 8 Hic
Colemon 20 Fra
Elisha 21 Fra
Matthew 35 Smi
William 21 Fra
William 35 Smi
McLair, James 131 Ste
MClanahan, Mathew 90 Rut
McLane, Archibald 18 Jac
Archibald, Jr. 18 Jac
George 34 Bed
John 34 Bed
John 42 Bed
McLauchlin, James 365 Whi
McLaughlin, Elijah 37 Lin
James 78 Dav
Joseph 16 Hic
Samuel 37 Lin
Wm. H. 97 Dav
see McGlothlin, Mglaughlin
McLaurin, Robert 8 Gil
William 86 Dav
Willis S. 11 Gil
McLean, Allen 90 Dav
Betsey 307 War
James 309 War
John 81 Dav
Sarah 86 Dav
MClean, Charles 88 Rut
McLellan, David 33 Smi
Hugh 36 Smi
Samuel 20 Fra
Samuel 34 Smi
Samuel 36 Smi
McLelland, Silus 9 Lin
McLemman, Richard 29 Mau
McLemore, Burwell 9 Gil
Joel 30 Lin
John 14 Gil
Nathaniel 83 Dav
Robert 10 Wll
Sterling C. 14 Lin
Young 4 Wll
McLeod, Alexander 12 Hum
Roderick 5 Hum
McLeroy, Adam 78 Rut
Mcleroy, James S. 169 Sum
MClery, John 87 Rut
Mclery, Samuel 93 Rut
McLewis, Andrew 168 Sum
McLimore, John C. 81 Dav
McLin, William A. 77 Rut
Mclin, Robert 418 Wil
McLinn, Alexr. 22 Lin
John 22 Gil
McLoud, Roderic 12 Hic
MCloud, Argus 85 Rut
McLure, Thomas 18 Fra
MClure, James 81 Rut
MClure (cont.)
James 92 Rut
Mclure, William 78 Rut
McMackin, Andrew 35 Mau
McMaes, James 26 Mau
McMahan, Daniel 5 Wll
David 89 Rut
Joseph 8 Har
Thomas 18 Ove
William 285 War
McMahon, Jonathan 287 War
McMannus, Samuel 76 Dav
McManus, Aaron 25 Mau
Jonathin 45 Mau
Larance 46 Mau
McMasters, Jesse 7 Bed
John 7 Bed
Jonathan 5 Bed
Nancy 11 Gil
McMellon, James 8 Law
McMilion, Hanner 8 Per
G. W. 123 Ste
Hugh 123 Ste
John 123 Ste
Malcolm 10 Hic
Mcmillan, Elizabeth 94 Rut
McMillen, Elizabeth 100 Rut
John 7 Rob
Theophilus 16 Ove
McMillian, Ablert 8 Per
Peter 45 Lin
McMillin, James 8 Lin
John 22 Lin
Joseph 2 Lin
Joseph 17 Lin
McMillion, Jesse 5 Gil
John 5 Gil
K...am 5 Gil
Stephen 5 Gil
McMillon, Edward 18 Fra
Jane 37 Smi
Malcom 36 Smi
McMin, Daniel 415 Wil
Elihu 420 Wil
Jahu [John?] 415 Wil
Jodiah 415 Wil
Mcminemay, John 93 Rut
McMinn, Betsey 97 Dav
James 41 Bed
Robert 79 Dav
McMinson, David 20 Mon
McMintry, John 167 Sum
Mcmullen, Thomas 27 Wll
William 54 Wll
McMullin, Elizabeth 26 Bed
John 9 Lin
McMulling, John 412 Wil
McMullins, Wm. 9 Lin
McMurray, Alexander 290 War
David 404 Wil
James 165 Sum
James 279 War
James 288 War

McMurray (cont.)
John 304 War
Saml. 166 Sum
Samuel 67 Dav
McMurry, Betsy 313 War
Charles 34 Smi
David 32 Rob
Elizabeth 168 Sum
Hosea 33 Smi
John 33 Smi
Samuel 29 Rob
Samuel D. 35 Smi
Samuel W. 37 Smi
William 14 Dic
Mcmurry, Robert 78 Rut
Samuel 78 Rut
William 105 Rut
McMurtrey, James 6 Hum
Thomas 14 Hum
McMurtry, Matthew 21 Fra
William 20 Fra
McNab, Babtist 3 Per
McNabb, John 363 Whi
McNailey, Hugh 16 Dic
McNairey, Boyd 76 Dav
John 89 Dav
McNairy, Nathan 90 Dav
Robert 2 Gil
Robert 13 Gil
Robert 15 Gil
McNalge, William 21 Fra
McNatt, Benjn. 114 Ste
Charles 23 Lin
David 114 Ste
John 24 Lin
Levan 24 Lin
Richard 24 Lin
Solomon 114 Ste
McNeal, Archa. 76 Dav
Mcneal, John 99 Rut
McNeally, Jas. 13 Hic
McNeelly, John 405 Wil
McNeely, Ezekiel 19 Bed
Jas. 120 Ste
Margaret 405 Wil
Mcneely, Alexander 91 Rut
McNees, James 101 Gil
Mcneese, Allem 86 Rut
McNeice, H. M. 57 Dav
McNeil, Call 17 Rob
Elizabeth 167 Sum
Joseph 30 Rob
McNeill, Geo. 76 Dav
Henry 65 Mau
John 21 Fra
John 61 Mau
John 65 Mau
Thomas 61 Mau
William 59 Mau
McNichols, Samuel 18 Mon
McNier, Samuel 11 Lin
Mcnigh, Moses 78 Rut
McNight, David 103 Rut
McNight (cont.)
John 10 Lin
see McWright
McNut, William B. 31 Bed
McNutt, George W. 21 Hic
Joel 350 Whi
Robbart 44 Mau
Thomas 349 Whi
MCoid see Coid
MCombs, Robert 89 Rut
MConell, John 11 Har
Mconnell, Moses 93 Rut
McOrd, Allen H. 18 Fra
see McCord
Mcorkle, Jane 100 Rut
McOrmack, David 20 Fra
James 36 Smi
James 37 Smi
William 35 Smi
Mcoy, Amos 104 Rut
Bradley 75 Rut
Ezekiel 79 Rut
Robert 79 Rut
McPeak, Esther 100 Rut
Henry 100 Rut
Mcpeak, John 81 Rut
McPeck, Danl. 9 Hic
John 19 Hic
McPeek, James 355 Whi
William 360 Whi
see McPeck
McPeters, David 29 Rob
McPhaddon, Ralph S. 68 Dav
McPhadon, George 68 Dav
McPhail, Angus 4 Wll
McPherson, Joseph 18 Wll
see McFearson, Mcherson
McQuary, Micajah 95 Dav
Pleasant 37 Mau
see Mcquay
Mcquay, William 167 Sum
McQueen, John 20 Fra
McQuerter, Georg 420 Wil
McQuistian, Hanah 46 Mau
McQuorter, Hugh 381 Wil
Mcracken, John 79 Rut
Joseph R. 79 Rut
Sally 79 Rut
McRae, John L. 5 Dic
McRaferty, Edward 26 Mon
Mcrary, Arthur 84 Rut
McRee, David W. 57 Mau
Mcree, William E. 28 Mau
Mcrery, John 94 Rut
McReynolds, James 289 War
John 289 War
Joseph 42 Lin
Joseph 166 Sum
Joseph [2] 167 Sum
Samuel 286 War
McRobberts see Robberts
McRoberts, James 19 Jac
McShadden, Samuel 307 War

McSpading, Thomas 404 Wil
see McSprading
McSprading, John 404 Wil
Wm. 404 Wil
see McSpading
McSwine, John 10 Hum
MCulloch, Alexander 85 Rut
Alexander 92 Rut
Benjamin 89 Rut
Mcully, William 100 Rut
McVay, Claiborne W. 21 Gil
Kinson 2 Gil
John C. 36 Lin
McWarter, Jeremiah 379 Wil
McWerter, James 11 Lin
McWharton, George 390 Wil
George B. 381 Wil
McWhirter, Aexander 317 War
Hugh B. 166 Sum
Moses 51 Mau
Wiley 35 Mau
McWhorter, Francis 13 Bed
Henry 35 Smi
Moses 316 War
McWilliams, Henry 74 Rut
John 19 Fra
William 48 Mau
McWright, Margret 49 Mau
McYea, Samuel 32 Mon
Mead, Stith H. 28 Lin
Meador, Bennet 167 Sum
Isham 167 Sum
Job 166 Sum
John 167 Sum
see Meadow, Medor
Meadow, Asa 168 Sum
Deaton 37 Smi
Eli 168 Sum
Ephraim 35 Smi
Fleming 168 Sum
Ira 35 Smi
Ira, Sen. 37 Smi
Isham 37 Smi
James 35 Smi
Jehu 34 Smi
Job 37 Smi
Joel 37 Smi
Joel 168 Sum
Joel, Sen. 37 Smi
John 37 Smi
Jonas 37 Smi
Pleasant 37 Smi
Ramey 168 Sum
Richard 34 Smi
Thomas 168 Sum
Thomas W. 37 Smi
William 100 Rut
William 37 Smi
see Meador
Meadowes, Daniel 299 War
Meadows, Celia 19 Gil
Elijah 20 Gil
Ephraim 75 Rut
Meadows (cont.)
Hierom 21 Gil
Jane 25 Bed
Jason 19 Jac
Job 18 Jac
Joseph 17 Jac
Polley 21 Gil
Rebekah 21 Gil
Thomas 295 War
William 25 Bed
Means, Clemons 1 Ove
Mears, William 303 War
Mease, Catherine 60 Mau
Mary 46 Mau
Measles, Hezekiah 14 Rob
Isaac 169 Sum
Levi 56 Wll
William 35 Smi
Mechency, Hezekiah 409 Wil
Meck, Elizabeth 406 Wil
John 12 Bed
Meckie, James 413 Wil
Mecks see Meiks
Medders, Levy 130 Ste
Meddows, Jonas 40 Wll
Joseph 8 Wll
Medearis, B. W. H. 12 Bed
Washington D. 8 Bed
Meder, Jepthew 168 Sum
Mediate, Jesse 119 Ste
Medkiff, Calaway 351 Whi
Medley, John 355 Whi
John, Ser. 354 Whi
Joseph 358 Whi
Richard 358 Whi
Samuel 358 Whi
Medlin, Alphard 54 Mau
Robert 11 Bed
Medling, Bradley 382 Wil
Jesse 83 Rut
John 419 Wil
Medlock, Luke 10 Dic
Medor, Ambrose 166 Sum
Meek, Alexander 39 Lin
Charles 5 Lin
David 20 Fra
George B. 3 Wll
James 14 Lin
John 18 Lin
Josiah 16 Dic
Robert 18 Lin
Thomas 360 Whi
William 13 Bed
William 21 Lin
see Mick
Meeke, James 420 Wil
Meelray, Jonathan 70 Mau
Samuel 70 Mau
Meesles, Henry 27 Mon
Megagon, Flower 387 Wil
Megee, Adam 122 Ste
James 117 Ste
Thos. 117 Ste

Megee (cont.)		
Wm.	116	Ste
Megehe, John	118	Ste
Megill, John	127	Ste
Megomery, Robbert B.	55	Mau
Megumery, Jacob	41	Mau
Meiks, Joseph	15	Way
Nacy	43	Bed
Meilly, Elisha	67	Mau
Meller, Sarah	78	Dav
Mellon, Jacob	420	Wil
Meloin see Melvin		
Melone, Daniel	17	Jac
Robbert	68	Mau
Thomas	68	Mau
Thomas T.	67	Mau
Melson, Peter, Jur.	24	Lin
Peter, Ser.	27	Lin
William	27	Lin
Melton, Anse	303	War
David	8	Per
Elijah	6	Law
Henry	9	Gil
James	10	Hic
James	302	War
John	302	War
John	316	War
Joseph	1	Hum
Mary	168	Sum
Mathew	285	War
Matthew	14	Hum
Mildred	6	Mon
Nathaniel	53	Wll
Philip	13	Bed
Plewry	5	Gil
Richard	3	Ove
Sion	12	Hum
Thomas	34	Lin
Thomas	401	Wil
William	168	Sum
Wm.	116	Ste
Melugin, Wm.	20	Hic
Melugon, James	10	Dic
Jonathan	9	Dic
Joseph	10	Dic
Melvin, Aaron	168	Sum
Edmond	61	Dav
Edward	58	Dav
James	122	Ste
Thomas	168	Sum
William	58	Dav
William	367	Whi
Memeck, Nelly	6	Ove
Mendy, David	4	Per
Menefee, James N.	85	Dav
Menfree, Hutchinson, Sr.	20	Fra
James	20	Fra
Mennefee, James	83	Dav
Mennifee, Elizabeth	6	Gil
John	7	Gil
William	6	Gil
Menter, Margaret	168	Sum
Mercer, Edward	17	Jac
Mercer (cont.)		
Levi	11	Hum
Mary	5	Hum
Thomas	17	Jac
Thomas	34	Smi
Merchant, Edward	10	Bed
John	10	Bed
Meredith, Frederick	9	Way
James	21	Fra
James	6	Har
James	102	Rut
John	10	Way
John, Sr.	21	Fra
Saml.	420	Wil
Samuel	101	Rut
Thomas H.	4	Gil
Wm.	3	Hic
Merewither, Douglass	19	Mon
Meridith, James	24	Hic
John	24	Hic
Moses	24	Hic
see Merith		
Meriman, James	27	Mau
Robert	68	Dav
Merith, John	21	Fra
Meriwether, Richard T.	5	Mon
Merkson, Meredick	1	Per
Merpan, Brice	78	Dav
Merrell, Amos	33	Lin
Jonathan, Jur.	33	Lin
Jonathan, Ser.	33	Lin
William	33	Lin
Merreman, Judy	90	Dav
Merret, James	16	Wll
Samuel	7	Wll
Shimi	65	Wll
Thomas	66	Wll
Merrett, James	384	Wil
John	407	Wil
Obadiah	384	Wil
Silas	420	Wil
Merrick, Griffith	4	Hum
Moulton	7	Hum
Rachel	6	Hum
William	4	Hum
Merrill, Benjamin	19	Lin
John	7	Gil
Merrimon, Abednego	11	Law
Merrimson, Isham	125	Ste
Lewis	125	Ste
Merrit, Benjamin	19	Wll
Merritt, James	93	Rut
John	384	Wil
Mark	419	Wil
Merryman, Jeremiah	290	War
Littlebury	62	Dav
William	279	War
William	291	War
Messacar, Ruben	88	Dav
Messack, John	21	Fra
Messer, Asa	38	Lin
Christiana	14	Gil
Messuck, Thomas	396	Wil

Metcalf, Ilia	34	Rob
Metheney, Simms	13	Gil
Metheny, Charles	111	Ste
Cullen	111	Ste
Job	111	Ste
John	111	Ste
Wm.	115	Ste
Metlock, Benjamin	12	Hum
Caswell	7	Hum
Metthews see Matthews		
Metton see Melton		
Mewhorter, George F.	389	Wil
Aaron	377	Wil
Henry	377	Wil
Meyers, Charles, Junr.	12	Gil
MGill, David	81	Rut
James	102	Rut
Mglaughlin, Absalom	75	Rut
Alexander	98	Rut
Saml.	75	Rut
Micham, William	48	Wll
Mick, John	11	Bed
Micks see Meiks		
Micky, George, Mr.	11	Law
Midcalf, William	37	Mau
Middleton, Alfred	34	Mau
Drury	4	Har
Jackson	317	War
James	302	War
John	19	Fra
Nelly	19	Hic
Thomas	20	Lin
Thomas	303	War
Thomas	316	War
Watson G.	12	Law
William [2]	316	War
William [2]	317	War
Midkiff, William	353	Whi
Midleton, John	67	Mau
John, Sr.	67	Mau
Midlin, Robert	54	Bed
Miers, Danl.	167	Sum
Elisha	166	Sum
Humphrey	166	Sum
Miles	136	Sum
Rebecca	167	Sum
Mifflin, Armstrong	168	Sum
Mifford, George	8	Rob
Migget, George	409	Wil
Neel	409	Wil
Milam, Adam	124	Ste
Gideon	124	Ste
John	5	Hic
John [2]	124	Ste
Ransom	124	Ste
Rowland	124	Ste
Saml.	5	Hic
Thomas	13	Lin
William	6	Mon
see Milan		
Milan, Jordan	5	Hic
see Milam		
Milburn, Kinchen	50	Bed
Milegin, James, Jr.	414	Wil
James, Sen.	414	Wil
Miles, Alexander	30	Rob
Cartwell	83	Dav
Charles	2	Per
Charles	10	Rob
Elisha	95	Dav
George L.	73	Rut
Hardy D.	87	Dav
Jacob	2	Rob
Jacob, Senr.	34	Rob
Jesse	17	Jac
John	45	Bed
Richard	126	Ste
Saml.	114	Ste
Saml.	126	Ste
Samuel	87	Dav
Samuel	95	Dav
Samuel	18	Rob
Thomas	9	Rob
William	19	Fra
William	317	War
see Hathcock		
Milford, Wm.	129	Ste
Milican, William	27	Rob
Miligan, William	48	Mau
Miligard, William	2	Har
Millanner, Jesse	8	Per
Millar, Nathaniel	91	Rut
Mille, Joseph	60	Mau
Miller, —, Mrs.	67	Mau
Abraham	284	War
Abraham	299	War
Abram	34	Smi
Adam	42	Bed
Alexander	10	Law
Anderson	56	Mau
Andrew	86	Rut
Catharine	347	Whi
Charles	6	Hum
Charles	350	Whi
Chrisly	25	Lin
Daniel	347	Whi
Daniel B.	55	Mau
Darcas	2	Mon
Dianah	8	Hic
Edmond	128	Ste
Elizabeth	17	Lin
Esther	348	Whi
Ezekiel	292	War
Federick	166	Sum
Fredrick	65	Mau
Fredrick	355	Whi
Garland B.	18	Fra
George	20	Mon
George	92	Rut
George	356	Whi
Harman	55	Mau
Henry	52	Bed
Henry	14	Gil
Henry	55	Mau
Henry	100	Rut
Henry	34	Smi

Miller (cont.)
Hugh 9 Ove
Isaac 21 Lin
Isaac 76 Rut
Jacob 9 Gil
Jacob 10 Gil
Jacob 12 Hum
Jacob 362 Whi
Jacob, Jun. 19 Fra
Jacob, Sen. 19 Fra
Jain 300 War
James 44 Lin
James 25 Mon
James 34 Smi
James 124 Ste
James 346 Whi
James 347 Whi
James D. 77 Dav
James R. 1 Har
James R. 82 Rut
James R. 131 Ste
John 19 Fra
John 4 Law
John 67 Mau
John 20 Mon
John 5 Ove
John 9 Rob
John 169 Sum
John 281 War
John 284 War
John 315 War
John 363 Whi
John 377 Wil
Joseph 87 Dav
Joseph 18 Fra
Joseph 114 Ste
Julius 19 Fra
Keder 124 Ste
M. 120 Ste
Margaret 91 Rut
Mark 18 Gil
Marton 34 Smi
Maury 38 Mau
Mildred 88 Rut
Nathaniel 3 Lin
Pearson 15 Ove
Peter 347 Whi
Robert 76 Rut
Robert G. 18 Fra
Ruthey 300 War
S...uel 7 Ove
Saml. 8 Hic
Samuel 349 Whi
Samuel 406 Wil
Stephen 68 Mau
Thomas 9 Wil
Vinson 56 Mau
William 86 Dav
William 7 Dic
William 12 Hum
William 55 Mau
William 8 Ove
William 78 Rut

Miller (cont.)
William 91 Rut
William B. 298 War
William S. 86 Dav
Willie 7 Ove
Millian, Alexander 25 Mau
Milligan, James 31 Bed
Milligin, Amos 121 Ste
Millikan, John 5 Lin
Milliken, Samuel D. 5 Lin
Millis, William D. 81 Dav
Millner, Devina 401 Wil
Mills, Andrew 54 Mau
Ann 368 Whi
David 13 Hum
Ellis 26 Lin
Gibson 29 Mon
Griffin 29 Mon
Guilford 25 Mon
James 23 Lin
James 54 Mau
John 25 Lin
John 54 Mau
John 35 Smi
John 169 Sum
John 355 Whi
Kairy 2 Har
Leonard 29 Lin
Mary Ann 13 Hum
Molly 20 Fra
Nancy 6 Lin
Patterson 393 Wil
Sanders 40 Mau
T. 24 Mau
Thomas 28 Mau
Thomas, Jr. 393 Wil
Thomas, Sen. 393 Wil
William 8 Hum
William 353 Whi
Millstead, James 34 Smi
Milstead, Eli 48 Lin
James 48 Lin
Peter 289 War
Zeal 48 Lin
Milton see Melton
Milugeon, Saml. 16 Hic
Mims, Duiguid 280 War
Minaway, Alexander W. 94 Rut
Mincer, John 68 Dav
Minche, Benjamin 18 Jac
Richard 18 Jac
Mindock, Alexander 19 Fra
Miner, William 56 Mau
William 66 Mau
Mink, Strahan 59 Dav
Minnick, John 37 Smi
Joseph P. 136 Sum
Minor, Ann 17 Mon
Thomas 3 Ove
Minrell see Murrell
Minter, Jeremiah 26 Rob
John T. 169 Sum
Minton, Simon 35 Smi

Minum, John 25 Mau
Minus, Ann 25 Rob
James 5 Rob
Nancy 31 Rob
Miracle, George 33 Smi
Mires, Adam 383 Wil
Charles 5 Law
Simon 7 Dic
Mitcham, James 22 Mon
Spencer 18 Mon
Mitchel, Benj. 74 Dav
Charles 34 Smi
Dicy 18 Jac
Elizebeth S. 29 Mau
Frederic 39 Wil
George 29 Mau
George, Jr. 8 Dic
Isaiah 18 Jac
James 33 Mau
James 38 Mau
James 56 Mau
James 65 Mau
John 29 Mau
John 64 Mau
John 65 Mau
John 22 Rob
John 136 Sum
John 53 Wil
Mary 63 Mau
Peter 186 Sum
Robert 46 Lin
Solomon 166 Sum
Thomas 43 Mau
William 13 Rob
Mitchell, Allen 37 Smi
Allen 280 War
Allen 291 War
Andrew 281 War
Archd. 169 Sum
Benjamin 13 Hum
Betsey 70 Dav
David 37 Smi
David 360 Whi
Delpha 18 Mon
Elizabeth 401 Wil
Everet 401 Wil
George 5 Dic
George 34 Mau
Hardy 93 Dav
Henry 379 Wil
Hiram 168 Sum
Isaac 13 Hum
Isbel 15 Bed
Jacob 349 Whi
James 20 Gil
James 2 Rob
James 98 Rut
James 103 Rut
James 369 Whi
Jeremiah 5 Hum
Jesse [?] 10 Gil
Jesse 90 Rut
John 37 Bed
Mitchell (cont.)
John 24 Hic
John 24 Mon
John 167 Sum
John 168 Sum
John 169 Sum
John 292 War
John 22 Way
John 342 Whi
John 346 Whi
John 394 Wil
John, Jr. 409 Wil
John, Sen. 409 Wil
Joshua 104 Rut
Lewis 77 Dav
M. D. 52 Bed
Marcus 2 Gil
Mark 81 Rut
Mark 291 War
Missnier 12 Mon
Ransom 86 Rut
Robert 21 Fra
Robert 10 Ove
Robert 89 Rut
Robert 379 Wil
Robt. I. 73 Dav
Samuel 9 Dic
Samuel 415 Wil
Spencer 349 Whi
Stephen 289 War
Stephen 320 War
Thomas 15 Dic
Thomas 18 Gil
Thomas 8 Law
Thomas 300 War
Thomas 379 Wil
Thos. 73 Dav
William 84 Rut
William 280 War
William 341 Whi
William C. 417 Wil
Winny 36 Smi
Zadock 379 Wil
Mitchum, William 169 Sum
Mith, Eli 71 Dav
Mitheny, Peter 21 Mon
Mixon, Charles 15 Dic
John 15 Lin
Samuel 15 Lin
Thomas 318 War
Mize, Jesse 17 Bed
MKeen, Alexander M. 81 Rut
Moak, Jacob 13 Rob
Moasley, Jeptha 84 Dav
Mobley, Edward 73 Dav
Susan 38 Mau
Mobly, Allen 37 Lin
Mockley, Joseph 390 Wil
Moderal, James 408 Wil
Modeville, Emily 30 Lin
Modgalin, Maryann 398 Wil
William 398 Wil
Moffet, Robert 166 Sum

Moffett, Hamilton	39	Lin
Henry	296	War
William	39	Lin
Moffitt, Kennedy	47	Lin
Mogelin, James	390	Wil
Mois, Drury	53	Mau
Molberry, John	402	Wil
Molder, Daniel	3	Per
Molley, Benjamin	405	Wil
Molloy, Daniel	4	Lin
Moncrief, Samuel	11	Gil
Monday, J. G.	17	Jac
Money, James	387	Wil
John	381	Wil
Nancy	52	Bed
see Movey		
Mongold, John	20	Ove
Mongomery, Alexander	19	Jac
Monks, Eli	40	Lin
James	44	Lin
Monnahon, Daniel	20	Fra
Monnyham, John	360	Whi
Monroe, David P.	13	Lin
William	7	Lin
Montague, Abreham	70	Mau
see Mauntague		
Montgomery, Alexander	63	Wll
Charity	8	Gil
David	93	Dav
David	21	Fra
Elisabeth	44	Wll
Hamilton	18	Jac
Hamilton	8	Wll
Hanah	17	Jac
Hugh	19	Fra
Hugh	32	Lin
Hugh	78	Rut
James	19	Fra
James	20	Gil
James	92	Rut
James	35	Smi
James	371	Whi
James, Senr.	104	Rut
John	21	Fra
John	20	Gil
John	19	Hic
John	13	Hum
John	11	Law
John	45	Lin
John	42	Mau
John	8	Per
John F.	106	She
Phares	19	Jac
Robert	18	Jac
Robert	32	Lin
Robert	92	Rut
Samuel	20	Gil
Stephen	35	Smi
William	19	Fra
William	44	Lin
William [2]	166	Sum
William	53	Wll
William	64	Wll
Montgomery (cont.)		
see Lee (Mt.), Megomery, Megumery, Mongomery		
Moody, Andrew	2	Har
Anna	27	Wll
Fredrick	21	Mon
Gilliam	85	Rut
Henry	4	Law
James	4	Law
James	14	Rob
John	168	Sum
Jonathan	15	Gil
Joseph	4	Law
Marshall	2	Gil
Moses	4	Law
Nathaniel	16	Gil
Patsey	14	Mon
Philip	13	Hum
Thomas	18	Gil
Thomas	122	Ste
William	15	Bed
Moon, Armstreet	33	Smi
Elizabeth	10	Gil
Thomas	318	War
William	33	Smi
William	319	War
Mooney, David	302	War
Jacob	302	War
James	302	War
Sampson	349	Whi
William	349	Whi
Mooningham, Matthew	33	Smi
Moony, Joseph	1	Lin
Moonyham, Joel	354	Whi
Shadrack	358	Whi
Moor, Benjamin	64	Wll
Elijah [& Stallings]	13	Wll
Hartwell	5	Hic
Hugh	28	Wll
Hugh	66	Wll
James	21	Wll
John	39	Wll
Moses	3	Hic
Nathanuel W.	21	Wll
Samuel	32	Wll
Thomas	88	Rut
Thomas L.	62	Wll
William	4	Hic
William	4	Wll
Moore, Aaron	33	Lin
Abednego	12	Gil
Abner	35	Smi
Abner	415	Wil
Abraham	33	Rob
Alexander	43	Lin
Alexr.	10	Lin
Alfred	73	Rut
Alfred	168	Sum
Amos	33	Rob
Aramento	83	Dav
Archibald	10	Gil
Arthur	10	Gil
Arthur	39	Lin

Moore (cont.)
Asa 6 Gil
Benjamin 65 Dav
Benjamin 11 Ove
Benjamin 5 Rob
Benjamin 36 Smi
Brittian 311 War
Daniel 4 Dic
Daniel F. 6 Lin
David 78 Dav
David [2] 20 Fra
David 84 Rut
David 93 Rut
David 110 Ste
David 305 War
Debby 3 Per
Dempsey 1 Ove
Edward 411 Wil
Edwin 69 Dav
Elisha 20 Fra
Elizabeth 396 Wil
Enoch 36 Smi
Francis 34 Smi
Francis 110 Ste
Francis 167 Sum
Francis 169 Sum
Francis 364 Whi
George 19 Fra
George 20 Fra
George 19 Gil
George 16 Ove
George 6 Per
George 88 Rut
George 408 Wil
George 411 Wil
George L. 90 Rut
George W. 107 She
Gulley 28 Mon
Haynes 34 Smi
Henry 43 Bed
Henry 27 Lin
Isaac 409 Wil
Israel 165 Sum
Israel, Jr. 378 Wil
Israel, Sen. 378 Wil
James 54 Bed
James 67 Dav
James 77 Dav
James 78 Dav
James 20 Fra
James 11 Gil
James 12 Law
James 78 Rut
James 96 Rut
James 35 Smi
James 36 Smi
James 169 Sum
James 350 Whi
James 367 Whi
James [2] 411 Wil
James B. 71 Dav
James C. 90 Rut
Jesse 9 Hum

Moore (cont.)
Jesse 12 Lin
Jesse C. 97 Rut
Jno. 168 Sum
Joel 33 Rob
John 22 Bed
John 54 Bed
John 13 Dic
John [2] 20 Fra
John 20 Gil
John 16 Lin
John 18 Lin
John 22 Lin
John 1 Mon
John 5 Mon
John 7 Ove
John 26 Rob
John 96 Rut
John 34 Smi
John 36 Smi
John, Jun. 36 Smi
John, Sen. [2] 36 Smi
John H. 27 Lin
John R. 8 Lin
John S. 110 Ste
Jonathan 1 Ove
Joseph 66 Dav
Joseph 27 Lin
Joseph 167 Sum
Joseph 169 Sum
Joseph 309 War
Joshua 420 Wil
Josiah 23 Lin
Lemuel 412 Wil
Lewis 85 Rut
Liza 166 Sum
Lodwick 21 Gil
Martha 16 Ove
Mary 107 She
Mason 36 Smi
Mathew 351 Whi
Micajah 14 Hum
Micheal 11 Bed
Milley 28 Mon
Milton 76 Rut
More 20 Fra
Morgan 4 Mon
Nancy 6 Gil
Nimrod 48 Bed
Patrick 36 Smi
Peter 80 Rut
Rachel 10 Gil
Reuben 47 Lin
Richard 9 Ove
Richard 166 Sum
Richard T. 165 Sum
Risdon 168 Sum
Robert 11 Hum
Robert 9 Lin
Robert 10 Lin
Robert 30 Lin
Robert 167 Sum
Robert C. 34 Smi

Moore (cont.)		
Saml.	167	Sum
Samuel	5	Lin
Samuel	370	Whi
Samuel A.	342	Whi
Shadrick	403	Wil
Shadrick	404	Wil
Solom	402	Wil
Stephen H.	11	Law
Susanah	167	Sum
Thomas	36	Smi
Thomas	349	Whi
Thomas C.	53	Bed
Thos.	5	Mon
Travis	117	Ste
Whartan	390	Wil
William	19	Fra
William	8	Gil
William	12	Lin
William	46	Lin
William	18	Rob
William	91	Rut
William	92	Rut
William	36	Smi
William	124	Ste
William	131	Ste
William	378	Wil
William	388	Wil
William	389	Wil
William	418	Wil
William	16	Wll
William H.	36	Smi
Wiseman	19	Fra
Wm.	115	Ste
see Moon, Moor, More		
Moores, Daniel R.	39	Lin
Isaac	36	Smi
Isaac, Sen.	36	Smi
William	34	Smi
Moorhead, John	36	Lin
William	36	Lin
Mooris, Joshua	3	Lin
Moors, John	77	Dav
Moran, Charles	3	Wll
Delila	34	Smi
Uriah	33	Smi
More, Benet W.	61	Mau
Bury	44	Mau
Denton	18	Jac
Francis	2	Ove
Garratt	18	Jac
Isaac	44	Mau
James	27	Mau
John	18	Jac
John	19	Jac
John	27	Mau
John T.	59	Mau
Jonathan	44	Mau
Joseph	52	Mau
Luke	55	Mau
Mathiew	51	Mau
Moses	54	Mau
Nathanial	47	Mau

More (cont.)		
Richard	17	Jac
Robbart	32	Mau
Robbert	27	Mau
Samuel	43	Mau
Samuel	44	Mau
Thomas	41	Mau
Moredock, Tobias	2	Ove
Morefield, Green	122	Ste
Green	123	Ste
Thos.	81	Dav
Morehead, Joseph	51	Mau
Moreland, Edward	85	Rut
John	18	Jac
John	112	Ste
Vincent	282	War
Vinson	37	Smi
William	66	Dav
Morell, John	314	War
Moreman, Charley	37	Mau
Morgain, Anderson	384	Wil
William	410	Wil
Morgan, Abraham	317	War
Betey	33	Rob
Cairy	86	Rut
Catharine	17	Jac
Charles	166	Sum
Daniel	44	Bed
Daniel	79	Rut
Edward	168	Sum
Elizabeth	33	Lin
Henry	7	Gil
Henry	24	Lin
Hiram S.	1	Lin
Isaac	6	Hum
Isaac	21	Lin
James	11	Hic
James	169	Sum
James, Mr.	3	Law
Jobe	18	Jac
John	46	Bed
John	88	Dav
John	7	Hic
John	11	Hum
John	17	Jac
John	10	Rob
John	90	Rut
John	36	Smi
John	113	Ste
John	320	War
Jonathan	8	Law
Joseph	45	Bed
Joseph	35	Smi
Joseph	117	Ste
Lewis	24	Lin
Mary	48	Lin
Mary	358	Whi
Mathew	90	Rut
Matthew	118	Ste
Micajah	3	Law
Nancy	45	Bed
Peter	4	Hic
Reuben	16	Rob

Morgan (cont.)
Riddy 46 Bed
Rolly 87 Rut
Saml. 167 Sum
Samuel 75 Rut
Theophilus 10 Rob
Theophilus 33 Rob
Thomas 11 Rob
William 6 Hum
William 11 Rob
William 90 Rut
William 316 War
Willis 11 Mon
Willis 58 Wll
Wm. 389 Wil
Moris, James 52 Mau
Joseph 169 Sum
Meshach 52 Mau
Rubin 52 Mau
see Maris
Morison, Francis 13 Hum
Mathew 67 Mau
William 97 Rut
Morlin see Martin
Morning, Joshua 403 Wil
Morningham, Elijah 403 Wil
Morras, Silas M. 18 Wll
Morrass, Benjamin 392 Wil
Edward 377 Wil
Icim 398 Wil
Morrel, Rece 18 Jac
William 18 Jac
William, Sr. 18 Jac
Morres see Moores
Morrice, Polly 70 Dav
Thomas 88 Dav
Morris, Amos 24 Lin
Asa 114 Ste
Christiana 169 Sum
Claburn 167 Sum
Daniel 20 Fra
Dempsey 34 Smi
Edmund 43 Wll
Eleanor 24 Lin
Ennis 15 Gil
George 98 Rut
George C. 7 Rob
George P. 14 Way
Groves 20 Fra
Henry 16 Hic
Henry S. 167 Sum
Hesakiah 96 Dav
Hirum 51 Bed
Isaac, Junr. 14 Gil
Isaac, Senr. 14 Gil
Jeptha 124 Ste
Jeremiah 13 Rob
Jesse 8 Har
Jesse 113 Ste
Joel 62 Wll
John 21 Fra
John 3 Hum
John 25 Mau

Morris (cont.)
John 19 Ove
John 2 Rob
John 14 Rob
John 34 Smi
John 35 Smi
John 37 Smi
John 13 Way
John 368 Whi
John G. 6 Gil
John H. 21 Fra
Jordan 13 Way
Joseph 35 Bed
Lemuel 24 Rob
Lester 22 Gil
Micajah 8 Mon
Michey 77 Dav
Millerson 37 Smi
Moses 19 Fra
Nancy [2] 34 Smi
Nathan 24 Mon
Newman 25 Mau
Nimrod 3 Per
Rebecca 413 Wil
Samuel 27 Bed
Samuel 4 Hum
Sarah 52 Mau
Spencer 409 Wil
Thomas 8 Har
Thomas 12 Hic
Thomas 25 Rob
Thomas 34 Smi
William 5 Hic
William 8 Ove
William 120 Ste
William 8 Way
William 16 Wll
William 55 Wll
see Marris
Morriset, William 7 Dic
Morrison, Andrew 12 Bed
Andrew 78 Dav
Andrew 415 Wil
Daniel 30 Mon
David 415 Wil
James 42 Bed
James 16 Mon
James 283 War
John 42 Bed
John 6 Har
John 297 War
Joseph 15 Mon
Joshua 14 Ove
Josiah 30 Mon
Lovett 31 Mon
Miles 3 Way
Robert 33 Bed
Robert 417 Wil
Samuel 290 War
Sly 23 Bed
Stephen 23 Bed
William 9 Dic
William 15 Mon

Morrison (cont.)
Wm. 5 Hic
Morriss, Grisum 395 Wil
Holloway 12 Dic
Jessee 169 Sum
John 169 Sum
William 8 Dic
William 169 Sum
William 392 Wil
Morrisson, Hugh 407 Wil
Morrow, Benjamin, Mr. 1 Law
David 284 War
Eleanor 37 Smi
Hugh 285 War
James 3 Hic
James 7 Mon
James 23 Mon
John [2] 20 Fra
John 21 Fra
John 3 Hic
John 97 Rut
Leonard 3 Way
Polley 16 Gil
Robert 286 War
Robert 298 War
Thomas 16 Gil
Thos. 3 Hic
William 13 Mon
William 285 War
William 20 Way
William B. 9 Hum
Morten, James 128 Ste
Mortin, Boston 167 Sum
Geo., Jr. 167 Sum
James 167 Sum
William 167 Sum
see Morlin
Morton, A. B. 52 Bed
Abner W. 43 Wll
Alexander 7 Lin
Catharine 82 Rut
Elisabeth 48 Wll
Elisha 45 Wll
Jacob 13 Wll
James 7 Lin
James 85 Rut
Jesse 12 Wll
Jessey 44 Mau
John 84 Rut
John 58 Wll
Joshua 346 Whi
Samuel 84 Rut
Samuel 12 Wll
Silas 86 Dav
Step 51 Wll
William 388 Wil
William 13 Wll
Zachariah 37 Mau
see Orton
Mosby, Obeddiah 4 Per
Moseley, Caleb 6 Bed
Drury 403 Wil
John 50 Mau
Moseley (cont.)
John 11 Mon
John 101 Rut
Peter 112 Wil
Peter 383 Wil
Samuel 380 Wil
William 35 Smi
see Maseley
Mosely, Daniel 403 Wil
Fanney 388 Wil
George 18 Fra
Green 43 Lin
James 8 Bed
Samuel 400 Wil
Moser, William 315 War
Moses, Abram 22 Wll
James 94 Dav
Josiah 35 Smi
Z. 24 Mau
Mosley, Isaac B. 26 Mau
Tart 286 War
Mosrren, John 41 Bed
Moss, Cate 166 Sum
David 93 Dav
David 3 Har
Edward 40 Lin
Isannah 23 Gil
James 8 Hum
James B. 36 Smi
John 387 Wil
Mathew 7 Har
Mathew 10 Lin
Obediah 120 Ste
Samuel 20 Fra
Sarah 103 Rut
Solomon 8 Gil
Spencer 29 Rob
Thomas 390 Wil
William 29 Rob
Mossey, John 5 Hum
see Massey
Mosure, Daniel 400 Wil
Henry 407 Wil
Peter 402 Wil
Motherel, John 378 Wil
Robert 378 Wil
Samuel 378 Wil
Mothral, John 17 Wll
Motlow, Zadock 32 Lin
Moton, John 67 Dav
Moulton, John M. 21 Rob
Mounds, Michael 34 Smi
Mount, Richard 384 Wil
Thompson 44 Lin
William 383 Wil
Movey, Josep 316 War
Moy, Cradick H. 166 Sum
James 166 Sum
James 167 Sum
Thomas 166 Sum
William 166 Sum
William [2] 167 Wum
see May

Moyalin, Benton	391	Wil
Moyer, Gooden	66	Mau
Moyers, George	2	Lin
Henry	2	Lin
Peter	2	Lin
Peter, Ser.	2	Lin
Samuel	1	Lin
Moyrs, Nicholas	14	Mon
Peter	14	Mon
Moys, Federick	168	Sum
William	168	Sum
Mt. see Lee		
Mtthew, John	17	Jac
Muckelwe, Thomas	52	Mau
Muckkleroy, Charles	396	Wil
Muckle, Elijah	20	Fra
Isaac	20	Fra
Muckleherrin, John	19	Fra
Mucklerath, Wm.	124	Ste
Muckleroth, Joseph	23	Bed
Muckleroy, John	34	Smi
Samuel	19	Fra
William	33	Lin
see McElroy, Muckkleroy		
Mucklevaney, Esther	24	Bed
Muirhead, Chas.	6	Hic
Henry, Jr.	4	Hic
Henry, Senr.	3	Hic
Jacob	3	Hic
Jno.	4	Hic
Wm.	4	Hic
Mulbian, John	284	War
Mulcaster, Celia	28	Mon
Christopher	28	Mon
Mulherren, Charles	97	Dav
Mulherrin, James	84	Dav
Mulky, Philip	18	Jac
Mullen, Henry	25	Wll
Jane	96	Dav
John	386	Wil
Mary	25	Wll
Mullens, William	354	Whi
Mullian, Allen	35	Smi
Mulligan, James	20	Fra
John	20	Fra
Mullin, Bud	17	Jac
John	98	Rut
Josiah	65	Dav
Patcy	18	Jac
Mullinax, Eli	17	Ove
Nathaniel	7	Ove
Richard	17	Ove
Mulling, Daniel C.	313	War
Mullingnax, Joseph	412	Wil
Nancy	412	Wil
William	416	Wil
Zadock	412	Wil
Mullings, James	46	Lin
Stephen	3	Lin
Mullins, ...	6	Ove
Andrew	45	Lin
Anthony	45	Lin
Anthony W.	20	Fra
Mullins (cont.)		
Clemm	20	Gil
Ezekiel	304	War
Patrick	2	Ove
Samuel	44	Lin
William	102	Rut
Muloy, Daniel	19	Rob
Daniel	36	Rob
Mumford, Marshall B.	98	Rut
Muncrief, Martha	10	Gil
Samuel	11	Gil
William	10	Gil
Munday, Thomas	104	Rut
Walker	169	Sum
Mungrel, Isaac	6	Rob
John	6	Rob
Munn, Duncan	10	Law
James	2	Way
Murder, Saml.	126	Ste
Murdoch, John	6	Lin
Murdock, Thomas	3	Bed
Murel, John	49	Mau
Murf, Fredrick	9	Mon
Murfree, Danl.	13	Hic
Hutchinson	19	Fra
John	34	Smi
Mathias B.	84	Rut
Muricle, Peter	296	War
Murkerson, Keneth	22	Way
Murphee, Enoch	9	Ove
Joseph	18	Ove
Murphey, Charles	25	Mau
Ezekiel	98	Rut
George	2	Rob
George	4	Rob
John	36	Lin
John	2	Rob
Lucy	32	Rob
Mark	128	Ste
Mark	381	Wil
Nathanial	53	Mau
Robertson	9	Rob
William	81	Dav
William	64	Mau
Murphree, John	9	Hic
Nimrod	1	Hic
Rodger	22	Hic
Sarah	9	Hic
Murphrey, Bartholomew	2	Per
Daniel	2	Per
Daniel	4	Per
John G.	78	Rut
Murphrie, Elijah	49	Bed
Enos	4	Hic
Stephen	49	Bed
William	49	Bed
Murphy, Alexander	2	Law
Aron	67	Dav
Bassel	166	Sum
Ezekiel	86	Rut
Ezekiel	95	Rut
Jeremiah	166	Sum
Joseph	86	Rut

Murphy (cont.)		
Stephen	318	War
William	95	Rut
Murray, Elizabeth	282	War
James	5	Hic
Jane	5	Hum
John	24	Hic
John M.	72	Dav
Jonthan	169	Sum
Joseph	5	Hic
Joseph D.	79	Dav
Robt.	3	Hic
Rosanna	72	Dav
Thomas	19	Jac
Thomas	90	Rut
Thomas	166	Sum
William	12	Hum
Wm. M.	97	Dav
Murrel, Enus	63	Wll
Jeffre	42	Wll
Thomas, Jr.	7	Dic
Murrell, Andrew	7	Gil
Richard	15	Dic
Thomas, Senr.	15	Dic
William	8	Gil
William	168	Sum
William S.	5	Dic
Murren, Henry	44	Bed
John	44	Bed
see Mosrren		
Murrie, William	11	Hum
Murry, Abel V.	46	Lin
James	128	Ste
John	18	Jac
John	33	Smi
Miles	27	Lin
Samuel	20	Fra
William	21	Fra
William	27	Lin
William	31	Rob
William	394	Wil
Muse, Daniel	21	Fra
Isaac	16	Bed
John	21	Fra
John	17	Gil
Nancy	21	Fra
Musgrave, Thomas	1	Law
Mustin, William	5	Way
Myatt, Kindrick	14	Dic
Willie	12	Dic
Myers, Abigail	307	War
Abraham	17	Jac
Ashar	13	Gil
Charles, Senr.	12	Gil
Elizabeth	35	Lin
John	94	Rut
Marmaduke	14	Gil
Orim [?]	80	Dav
Philip	18	Jac
Thomas	14	Gil
Thomas	166	Sum
Thomas	307	War
Myrach, Harrison	95	Rut
Myrack, Lemuel	115	Ste
M.	128	Ste
Myreck, Geo.	114	Wil
Myrich, William	80	Rut
Myrick, John	27	Mau
Sterling	22	Mon
Mytheny, Amos	24	Mon
Lewis	24	Mon

--- N ---

Nabors, John	11	Hic
Naceo see Nave		
Nail, Archer	1	Law
Saml.	420	Wil
Nailer, James	344	Whi
Nailler, James	42	Bed
Nall, John	37	Wll
William	52	Wll
Nally, Richard	23	Lin
Naman, Barton	22	Fra
Namur, John	103	Rut
Nance, Allen	3	Har
Allen	92	Rut
Drury	81	Rut
Harwood	38	Smi
Henry	83	Rut
Isham	83	Rut
John	82	Rut
Reuben	23	Bed
Stephen	61	Wll
William	67	Dav
William	82	Rut
William	100	Rut
William H.	63	Wll
Nancey, Jourdan	6	Har
Nanna, Polly	19	Jac
Nanny, Nicholas	366	Whi
William	5	Hic
Nanor, Preston	11	Hic
Nantz, Joseph	5	Gil
William H.	67	Dav
Napier, Elias W.	5	Dic
George F.	14	Dic
Henry A. C.	3	Dic
Isaac	12	Ove
James R.	72	Dav
James R.	16	Dic
John W.	3	Dic
R. C.	16	Dic
Richard, Sr.	15	Dic
Thos.	2	Mon
Napper see Nopper		
Nash, Charles	17	Wll
Denicy	17	Wll
George R.	74	Rut
Jonathan	22	Gil
Thomas	88	Rut
Thomas	94	Rut
Thomas	97	Rut
Thomas	38	Smi

Nash (cont.)		
Travers	88	Rut
William	22	Gil
William	89	Rut
see Read		
Nasom, William	72	Dav
Nations, Eli	11	Gil
Thomas	92	Rut
Naughters see Vaughters		
Nave, Daniel	9	Rob
Joseph	4	Rob
Naylor, Dixon	290	War
Neal, Brooks	169	Sum
Charles	289	War
Gilbert	379	Wil
James	7	Gil
James	11	Hum
James	379	Wil
Jeremiah	3	Per
Jesse	282	War
Joseph	381	Wil
Ralph	91	Rut
Saml.	169	Sum
Samuel	379	Wil
Stephen	2	Hic
Thomas	92	Rut
Turner	91	Rut
William	18	Gil
William	3	Wll
Neald, William	286	War
Neale, Andrew	5	Gil
Henry	4	Gil
Jane	170	Sum
Mathew	137	Sum
Nealey, Jane	68	Dav
Samuel	63	Dav
Samuel	71	Dav
William	68	Dav
William	69	Dav
Nealy, John	93	Rut
William	90	Rut
Nearen, Equila	354	Whi
Nearing, Benjamin	22	Fra
Nearn, Benjamin	22	Fra
Nease, John	23	Lin
Needam, Enock	27	Mau
Needham, Lewis	26	Mau
Luis	24	Mau
Thomas	38	Smi
William	37	Smi
Needy, Ned	81	Dav
Neel, Elizabeth	411	Wil
James	48	Wll
James	57	Wll
Lydia	38	Smi
Pallis	411	Wil
William	38	Smi
William	412	Wil
see Veel		
Neeley, Robert	10	Ove
Thomas	51	Mau
Neelie, James	19	Jac
Neely, Andrew	21	Hic
Neely (cont.)		
George	8	Wll
Henry	21	Fra
Isaac	43	Bed
Isaac	14	Wll
James	21	Hic
James	73	Rut
James	78	Rut
James	15	Wll
James	65	Wll
John	98	Rut
John	29	Wll
Joseph	350	Whi
Robt.	21	Hic
Samuel	96	Rut
Samuel	110	Ste
Thos. C.	21	Hic
William	38	Smi
William	16	Wll
Nees, George	341	Whi
Neesbet, Nathan	12	Hum
Negall, Jesse	89	Rut
Neidham, James	21	Fra
Thomas	22	Fra
Neighbors, Charles	22	Fra
Fleet	22	Fra
Greenberry	22	Fra
John	302	War
Nathan	22	Fra
Richard	371	Whi
Thomas	285	War
Warren	22	Fra
William	347	Whi
Neil, Elizabeth	21	Lin
Joseph	20	Bed
Robert	23	Rob
Neill, Alexander	54	Bed
Charles	22	Fra
John	24	Bed
Nicholas	24	Bed
William	63	Mau
Neilly, ...	24	Mau
Andrew	38	Mau
Isaac M.	57	Mau
James	28	Mau
James	36	Mau
John	65	Mau
John S.	65	Mau
Margrett	68	Mau
Robbert	29	Mau
Samul	28	Mau
Thomas L.	35	Mau
William	33	Mau
Neiper, John	22	Fra
Nellems, William	92	Dav
Nellums, John	22	Fra
Nelly, Simpson	69	Mau
Nelmes, James	389	Wil
Nelms, James	22	Fra
Samuel	22	Fra
Nelson, Bazel	4	Mon
Beverly	97	Rut
Charles B.	1	Har

Nelson (cont.)
Daniel 98 Rut
David 33 Mau
Elijah 361 Whi
George 170 Sum
Henry 21 Fra
James 22 Fra
James 21 Mon
Jarret 86 Dav
John 4 Gil
John 19 Gil
John 13 Law
John 83 Rut
John W. 42 Mau
Joseph 19 Jac
Joshua 343 Whi
Lewis 4 Gil
Lydia 18 Gil
Moses 53 Bed
Nathl. 170 Sum
Pleson 59 Mau
Prudance 59 Mau
Rachel 21 Fra
Robert 11 Hum
Samuel 47 Bed
Susannah 21 Mon
Taylor 121 Ste
Thomas 93 Rut
Thomas 26 Wll
William 14 Ove
William 19 Ove
William D. 42 Mau
Wm. 121 Ste
Wm. B. 1 Mon
Nelums, James 114 Wil
Nemor see Nanor
Nepper, William 14 Rob
Nesbitt, James 3 Dic
Jeremiah 6 Dic
John 10 Dic
John, Jr. 6 Dic
John, Sr. 10 Dic
Joseph 15 Dic
Nathan 3 Dic
Robert 15 Dic
Robert, Sr. 6 Dic
Samuel 1 Dic
see Neesbet
Netherley, Robert 53 Bed
Netherton, James 362 Whi
Netles, Shadrick 11 Way
Nettles, James 7 Way
Jesse 12 Way
Joseph 19 Jac
Shadrick 12 Way
William 10 Way
Zacheriah 5 Bed
Nettly, William 410 Wil
Neuman, Joshua 70 Mau
Neumery, Rebecca 13 Hic
Nevans, Isaac 98 Rut
Robert 3 Ove
William 3 Ove
Nevel, Joseph 19 Jac
Joseph 353 Whi
Nevell, George W. 6 Mon
John 7 Mon
Solomon 7 Mon
Nevels, Benjamin 22 Fra
Yealvelton 19 Jac
Nevill, Charles 10 Gil
Neville, Joseph B. 113 Ste
Nevils, Wiley 61 Mau
Nevins, Josep 312 War
New, John 15 Gil
John 399 Wil
Pleasant 13 Gil
Spencer 399 Wil
William 13 Gil
William 401 Wil
William 407 Wil
Newbel, William 38 Smi
Newberry, James 19 Jac
Newby, Henry 38 Smi
James 295 War
Jeremiah 285 War
Jeremiah 306 War
John 397 Wil
Thomas 296 War
William 38 Smi
Newcomb, Polly 18 Hic
Newcome, John 12 Hic
Newel, William 4 Mon
Newell, John 62 Dav
Newgent, John 91 Rut
John D. 73 Rut
William 91 Rut
Newhouse, William 38 Smi
Newland, Isaac 88 Dav
Jesse 62 Dav
Thomas 22 Fra
Newlin, Henry M. 20 Gil
Newman, Conrod 38 Smi
James 104 Rut
Jane 410 Wil
John 76 Rut
Joseph 96 Rut
Joseph, Sen. 99 Rut
Nancy 22 Fra
Nathaniel 22 Fra
William 22 Fra
Newmon, Daniel 355 Whi
Peggy 346 Whi
Newnon, John 79 Dav
Newsom, Balam 73 Dav
Charles S. 6 Gil
Debenport 38 Smi
Eldridge 85 Dav
Greenberry 4 Hum
Rebecca 24 Wll
Robert 29 Wll
Solomon 83 Rut
Newsome, Harmon 51 Bed
Starling 51 Bed
William 37 Bed
Newson, Francis 85 Dav

Newtion, John 7 Per
Newton, Bing 281 War
Edward 284 War
George 29 Bed
George 61 Mau
Henry 5 Rob
Isam 7 Hum
James 22 Fra
James 11 Rob
Jesse 4 Per
John 9 Bed
John 14 Gil
John 10 Rob
John 280 War
Nicholas 39 Bed
Rachel 53 Bed
Robert 5 Law
Robert 10 Rob
William 26 Bed
William 4 Hum
William 10 Way
see Newtion
Niblett, Edward 30 Mon
John 25 Mon
John 26 Mon
Stephen 26 Mon
Sterling 30 Mon
William 32 Mon
Nichals, Robbart 35 Mau
Nichels, Griffey 25 Mau
Nichelson, William 27 Mau
Nichol, John 78 Dav
Josiah 79 Dav
Nicholas, Cairy 79 Dav
Daniel 80 Rut
Isaac 12 Hic
John 22 Fra
Joseph 87 Rut
Thomas 19 Jac
Thomas 5 Per
William 16 Ove
William 80 Rut
Nicholasson, Nicholson 19 Jac
Nicholds, Benjn. 48 Bed
Jesse 49 Bed
John 32 Bed
Joseph 6 Way
Nicholls, Ephraim 18 Gil
Joshua 21 Gil
Nichols, Allen 65 Wll
Arthur 89 Rut
Briton 9 Mon
Byrd 38 Smi
Daniel M. 400 Wil
David 22 Fra
Elemelech 10 Hum
Elias 319 War
George 22 Fra
Henry 26 Lin
Henry C. 397 Wil
Isaac 123 Ste
James 22 Fra
James [2] 129 Ste
Jesse 38 Smi
Nichols (cont.)
John 60 Dav
John 13 Dic
John 12 Lin
John 14 Lin
John 6 Wll
John, Jun. 22 Fra
John, Sen. 22 Fra
John W. 397 Wil
Joshua 9 Lin
Jourdan 10 Hum
Lawrence 12 Lin
Lucy 38 Smi
Matthew 38 Smi
Matthias 11 Lin
Moses 26 Lin
Nathan 89 Rut
Robert 396 Wil
Sarah 71 Dav
Stephen 2 Hum
William 22 Fra
William 26 Lin
William 38 Smi
Nicholson, Atkins 8 Wll
Charles 396 Wil
Cordey 34 Wll
Elishua 62 Dav
Griffin 12 Mon
John 62 Dav
Maica 36 Wll
Walace 12 Mon
William 88 Dav
see Nicholasson
Nick, Charles 413 Wil
Nickerson, George 59 Mau
Nicking, Pescot 398 Wil
Nickins, William 170 Sum
Nicklas, Gilbert 64 Mau
Nickles, Benjamin 394 Wil
William 67 Mau
Nickolds see Nuckolds
Nicks, Absalom 6 Hic
Doks 16 Hic
George 6 Hic
John 6 Hic
John 20 Way
Milley 50 Mau
Robbert 50 Mau
Thomas 44 Mau
William 6 Hic
William 50 Mau
William 13 Way
Nickson, John 34 Mau
Niel, John 101 Rut
Nield, Elias 20 Lin
William 2 Lin
Niell, Andrew 17 Bed
John 7 Law
Philip 6 Law
Nielson, Thomas 4 Wll
Night, Absalum 414 Wil
Samson 420 Wil
Thomas 413 Wil
Niles, Charles 74 Rut

Niles (cont.)		
John	21	Fra
Nillums, John A.	170	Sum
Nimmoe, Henry	170	Sum
William	170	Sum
Nimms, Allen C.	2	Dic
Nimrod, Samuel	22	Fra
Nip, John	12	Ove
Nipper, Hughston	12	Ove
Jordan	4	Law
Pan	95	Rut
Nisbet, Alexander	80	Rut
Joseph	104	Rut
Niton, James	6	Per
Nivaces, James	81	Rut
Nivens, Robert	392	Wil
Nix, Anderson	17	Hic
Isaac	17	Hic
Jno., Sr.	16	Hic
Jonathan	11	Hum
Lelman	46	Mau
Moses	13	Hic
Robert	39	Lin
Nixon, Absalum	84	Rut
Charles	38	Smi
Frederick	82	Rut
George	25	Mon
Hanah	83	Rut
Henry	2	Hic
John	82	Rut
Robert	38	Smi
William	93	Dav
William	45	Lin
Noble, Gilbert	12	Gil
Nobles, Drewry	50	Wll
John	50	Wll
Noblet, David	371	Whi
John	51	Bed
William	51	Bed
Noblitt, William	22	Gil
Noe, Abraham	21	Fra
Joseph	21	Fra
Peter, Jun.	21	Fra
Peter, Sen.	21	Fra
Noel, Elijah	170	Sum
Nancy	170	Sum
Ruben	70	Dav
William	8	Gil
Noland, Elijah	6	Ove
Lewis	85	Rut
Marge	342	Whi
Phillip B.	2	Dic
Samuel	348	Whi
Thomas	2	Dic
Wm.	116	Ste
Nolds, James	345	Whi
John, Jr.	345	Whi
John, Sr.	345	Whi
Nolen, Berry	14	Wll
Charles, Jun.	38	Smi
David	25	Wll
James	11	Hum
Joseph	25	Wll
Nolen (cont.)		
Paskens	406	Wil
Stephen	38	Smi
Stephen	24	Wll
William	24	Wll
William, Jr.	14	Wll
Noles, Butler	26	Mau
Carbin	81	Dav
see Knowles		
Nolin, David	406	Wil
Lee, Generall	86	Rut
Thomas	16	Wll
see Noulin		
Noll, Nathan	11	Dic
Richard	8	Dic
Nopper, Ashford	170	Sum
John	170	Sum
Susanah	170	Sum
Norfleet, James	31	Rob
James	36	Rob
Norflet, Cordell	7	Mon
Filicia	23	Mon
James	8	Mon
Norman, Absalom	21	Fra
Alexander	19	Way
Betsey	22	Fra
Hannah	79	Rut
Henry	79	Rut
James	37	Bed
John	16	Gil
Jonathan	37	Bed
Joseph	33	Mau
Mary	61	Dav
Mary	33	Lin
Phebe	26	Rob
Robert	39	Bed
Samuel	31	Mau
Samuel	36	Mau
Thomas	60	Dav
William	5	Ove
William	384	Wil
Normans, —	24	Mau
Normon, Moses	341	Whi
Wilee	341	Whi
Norred, William	117	Ste
Norrel, Robt.	170	Sum
Norrell, John	13	Gil
Norrels, Anne	6	Hum
Norris, Abner	365	Whi
Absolom	365	Whi
Elisabeth	51	Wll
Ephraim	18	Hic
Ezekiel	2	Lin
George	38	Smi
James	38	Smi
Jean	11	Rob
Joel	361	Whi
Joseph	75	Rut
Samuel	385	Wil
Simon	356	Whi
Stephen	15	Mon
Norriss, Hugh	16	Dic
Jane	13	Dic

Norriss (cont.)
Susanna 4 Dic
William 170 Sum
Norrod, Benjamin 38 Smi
Norsworthy, Thomas 16 Bed
Willis 5 Dic
see Nosworthey
North, Abram 39 Wll
Elisha 42 Wll
William 81 Rut
William 283 War
Northcoal, Archibald 9 Har
Northcott, Hozea 81 Rut
Northcross, Thomas 299 War
Northcut, Abraham 306 War
Isaac 6 Way
Linchy 306 War
Richard 6 Lin
Northcutt, Ruhama 78 Rut
William 91 Rut
Northen, Samuel 57 Mau
Northern, John 3 Dic
Martha 48 Wll
Northington, David 1 Yum
David 7 Mon
Henry 7 Mon
Samuel 7 Mon
Norton, Jacob 48 Bed
John 45 Lin
John W. 19 Lin
Thomas 57 Mau
Norvall, Moses 77 Dav
Norvell, William 170 Sum
Zachariah 90 Dav
Norvill, David 49 Bed
James 49 Bed
James, Junr. 49 Bed
John 49 Bed
John, Junr. 49 Bed
Nathaniel 49 Bed
William 25 Bed
Norwood, Charles 18 Lin
John 22 Fra
Samuel 21 Fra
William 17 Gil
Nosworthey, James 16 Bed
Nial 16 Bed
see Norsworthy
Not, William 38 Mau
Notgrass, James 59 Mau
Notlow, Agnes 31 Lin
Notts, Levi 38 Smi
Noulin, James 44 Wll
Novothy, Francis 303 War
Nowhen, Birol 170 Sum
Nowlan, Robert 27 Mon
Nowland, Stephen 15 Way
Nowlen, Micager 36 Mau
Nox, John 416 Wil
Nuckolds, Richard 30 Rob
Nucom, Nelson 45 Wll
Nugent, John 22 Fra
Null, Jacob 170 Sum
Null (cont.)
John 13 Gil
Nunley, Archibald 303 War
John 280 War
John W. 2 Way
Manuel 306 War
William 306 War
Nunm, Zephaniah 53 Mau
Nunn, John 8 Way
Mary 58 Wll
William R. 58 Wll
Nunnally, Branch 38 Smi
John 38 Smi
Nunneley, William 22 Way
Nunnely, Anderson 7 Hic
Edwd. 25 Hic
Nutt, Kedar 21 Gil
William 44 Bed
Nye, Shadrach 16 Gil
Shadrach 170 Sum

--- O ---

Oakes, Joseph 52 Bed
Oakless, William 24 Mau
Oakley, Alexander 66 Mau
George 39 Smi
Henery 30 Mau
James [2] 66 Mau
John 39 Smi
Thomas B. 39 Smi
William 30 Mau
William 64 Mau
Oaks, Isaac 32 Wll
Oar, Joshua 41 Mau
Oatan, Isham 84 Dav
Oaton, John 77 Rut
Oatton, James 75 Rut
Obanon, James 23 Fra
Samuel 23 Fra
Obar, Benjamin 23 Fra
Constant 279 War
Robert 41 Lin
Obarr, Nancy 27 Mon
Obford, Willy 286 Wil
Obryan, John 22 Fra
Obryant, Cheatham 58 Dav
William 58 Dav
Ocley, George 411 Wil
Oconner, Robert 22 Fra
Ocuff, Carter 5 Per
Odam, John 31 Mau
O'Dannel, Henry 4 Hum
Odel, James 78 Rut
John 46 Wll
Odell, Josiah 310 War
Reanell 307 War
Odem, John 106 She
Oden, Hezekiah 17 Wll
Solomon 4 Wll
Thomas A. 77 Rut

Odil, John	56	Mau
Odle, Anderson	3	Per
Enoch	368	Whi
James	10	Har
James	2	Ove
John	8	Ove
John	4	Per
Margarett	12	Ove
Uriah	2	Ove
William	19	Jac
Odom, Absalom	29	Mon
Odom, Jacob	24	Lin
James	170	Sum
Lewis	28	Lin
Littleberey	54	Mau
Seaborn	369	Whi
Simeon	370	Whi
Odonally, Henry	12	Mon
Odonel, Matthew	46	Wll
Odum, James	414	Wil
Sarah	38	Smi
William	415	Wil
Odun, Britton	411	Wil
Oenby, Daivus	27	Rob
see Overby		
Oens, Bailey	17	Ove
George	17	Ove
Sarah	17	Ove
Wesley	14	Ove
Willis	13	Ove
Offenshine, John	300	War
Officer, Henrietta	13	Ove
James	364	Whi
Ogburn, Joseph	23	Mon
Matthew	23	Mon
Ogden, Lucinda	39	Smi
William	170	Sum
Ogdon, Frances	62	Dav
Ogee, John, Jun.	23	Fra
John, Sen.	23	Fra
Samuel	22	Fra
Ogelvie, Elizebeth P.	36	Mau
Oggalsvie, John	41	Wll
Ogilsvie, Richard	60	Wll
Ogle, Dennis	309	War
Heretus, Ser.	354	Whi
John	354	Whi
Wiett	354	Whi
Ogleby, Archibald	6	Bed
Asa	3	Bed
Joseph	6	Bed
Kimbro	20	Bed
William	6	Bed
Oglesby, Daniel	8	Mon
Daniel	170	Sum
Elisha	38	Smi
Harris	82	Dav
William	82	Dav
William	3	Lin
Ogletree, Edmond	41	Lin
Martin	22	Fra
Pleasant	8	Ove
Turner	41	Lin
Ogletree (cont.)		
William	22	Fra
Oglevie, William	15	Bed
Ogue, Joseph P.	64	Mau
O'Guinn, Hardy	7	Hum
OKindrick, Nathaniel	17	Lin
Old, Thomas	9	Wll
William	26	Lin
Oldham, Bishop	14	Wll
Elias	23	Fra
Elisha R.	5	Mon
George	39	Smi
George	8	Wll
Isaac	20	Mon
Jesse	23	Fra
Jessee	19	Mon
Richard	86	Dav
Washington	3	Mon
Oldum, Charlotte	110	Ste
Olephant, Lambert C.	68	Mau
Oleson, Josiah	49	Mau
Olfon, James	126	Ste
Olivant, James	80	Rut
Samuel	99	Rut
Olive, Robbart	43	Mau
William	126	Ste
Oliver, Acy	56	Mau
Andrew	23	Fra
Asa	22	Fra
Catharine	19	Mon
Drewry	28	Mon
George	14	Gil
George	13	Ove
George W.	73	Rut
James	28	Mau
James	45	Wll
John	22	Fra
John	31	Lin
John	112	Ste
Levi	341	Whi
Moses	115	Ste
Patsey	38	Smi
Peter	13	Wll
Rebecca	13	Gil
Reece	130	Ste
Robert	13	Gil
Rosanna	9	Lin
Samuel	42	Lin
Samuel	96	Rut
Simpson	22	Fra
Thomas	103	Rut
William	31	Lin
William	96	Rut
Zebulon	14	Gil
see Olves		
Olley, William	411	Wil
Olliver, Ahijah	305	War
Olves, Abram	38	Smi
Edmund	38	Smi
Omaddin, John	22	Fra
Omahundro, Mary	23	Bed
Omley see Oenby		
Onails, Samuel	355	Whi

Oneal, Alphred 62 Mau
Benja. 170 Sum
Brian 125 Ste
Henry 37 Bed
Isham 21 Bed
James 37 Bed
James 22 Fra
James 56 Mau
James 405 Wil
John 20 Bed
John 37 Bed
John F. 64 Dav
Mary 125 Ste
Nancy 62 Mau
Patrick 170 Sum
Polly 37 Bed
O'Neal, Barney 12 Hum
O. Neal, John 4 Per
ONeal, Charles 312 War
Peter 6 Mon
Thos. H. 4 Mon
Oneel, Custus 408 Wil
John 408 Wil
Robert 409 Wil
Oneill, William 2 Bed
Onstott, William 7 Per
Ony, Hezekiah 22 Lin
Ooton, Daniel 88 Dav
Thomas 88 Dav
see Oatan, Oat(t)on
Orange, Byrd 39 Smi
John 39 Smi
Yerby 39 Smi
Zepheniah 39 Smi
Orear, William 22 Fra
OReilly, James C. 55 Mau
Orenduff, Aaron 21 Rob
Orgain, Bennet 405 Wil
Cornelius 405 Wil
Emy 405 Wil
Enoch 390 Wil
James 416 Wil
Rolley 405 Wil
Sarah 405 Wil
Simpson 405 Wil
Sterling 74 Rut
Organ, Benjamin 30 Mon
Orick, Joel 7 Lin
John 7 Lin
Samuel 7 Lin
Thomas 22 Lin
Oring see Ham
Orman, Allen 37 Wll
David 170 Sum
Ormes, Even 21 Wll
Ormon, William 4 Way
Ormsby, Robert 123 Ste
Ornen, John 413 Wil
Thomas 413 Wil
Orr, Alexander 46 Mau
Alexander 103 Rut
David 22 Bed
George 4 Har
Orr (cont.)
Green B. 170 Sum
James 44 Mau
Jehur [Ishur?] 64 Mau
John 68 Dav
Robert 57 Dav
William 32 Wll
see Ott
Ors, William 55 Mau
Orsbon, Bartholomew 170 Sum
Orsborn, Robert A. 170 Sum
Orsburn, John W. 30 Wll
Nathan 6 Har
Noble 5 Wll
Noble 29 Wll
Robert 30 Wll
William 19 Jac
Orten, Joseph 19 Wll
Ortmen, Phebe 41 Bed
Orton, Jane 23 Wll
Rebecca 26 Wll
Richard 2 Wll
Samuel 16 Wll
Orwood see Ottwood
Osborn, Nathan 22 Fra
William 22 Fra
Osborne, Claiborne 22 Fra
David 22 Fra
John 97 Dav
John 39 Smi
William 22 Fra
Zachariah 22 Fra
Zedikiah 23 Fra
Osbourn, Alfred M. 77 Dav
William 29 Mau
Osbourne, Fany 17 Gil
Osbrook, Dolly 7 Bed
Osburn, Abner 26 Mau
Alexander 26 Mau
George 44 Bed
James 14 Hic
James 27 Mau
Maury 27 Mau
Thomas 26 Mau
Thompson 60 Dav
W. 24 Mau
Oslin, Mathew 42 Wll
Osmore, William 84 Dav
Osteain, Hilery 34 Mau
Ostean, John 120 Ste
see Istean
Osteen, David 6 Way
Ott, John 100 Rut
Malachi 73 Rut
Ottwood, James 60 Wll
Ounsby, Neddy 170 Sum
Outan, Lewis 44 Mau
Outland, Enos 126 Ste
Joseph 126 Ste
Outlaw, David 26 Mon
George 26 Mon
Jno. C. 170 Sum
Prudence 26 Mon

Outlaw (cont.)		
Seth	129	Ste
Ovelby, Amy	170	Sum
Nicholas	170	Sum
Oventine, William	350	Whi
Overall, Abram	39	Smi
Elizabeth	39	Smi
Isaac	89	Rut
Jacob	39	Smi
John	98	Rut
John	103	Rut
Nathaniel	98	Rut
Robert	78	Rut
Overby, Anderson	26	Rob
Danl.	17	Hic
Owenby	27	Rob
Overstreet, Henry	170	Sum
James	39	Mau
Jesse	38	Smi
John	2	Ove
William	4	Ove
Overton, Archibald	38	Smi
Arthur	12	Way
David	292	War
Elias	18	Wll
George	38	Smi
James	78	Dav
James	22	Fra
James	15	Ove
Jessey	56	Mau
John	113	Ste
John W.	76	Dav
Richard	22	Mon
Samuel	22	Fra
Samuel	38	Smi
Thomas	86	Dav
Westberry	39	Smi
Owen, Andrew	63	Mau
Bedford	64	Wll
Benjamin	66	Dav
David	90	Rut
Edmond	67	Dav
Edward	86	Dav
Everett	66	Dav
Frederick	66	Dav
Fredrick	21	Wll
Henry	83	Dav
Isaac E.	47	Wll
James	66	Dav
James	64	Mau
James	3	Rob
John	70	Mau
John [2]	38	Smi
Josua	285	War
Michael	10	Lin
Moses	103	Rut
Nathan	25	Wll
Peter	90	Dav
Peter	30	Mau
Phillip	26	Wll
Polley	67	Dav
Polly	66	Dav
Samuel	39	Smi
Owen (cont.)		
Sterlin	26	Wll
Thomas	81	Rut
Thomas	19	Way
William	8	Gil
William	70	Mau
William	38	Smi
William	170	Sum
William E.	3	Wll
Owenby, James	20	Rob
Walter	18	Rob
see Oenby, Ounsby, Owensby		
Owens, Abraham	22	Gil
Baxter	13	Ove
Belitha	4	Hum
Christopher	20	Mon
David	5	Lin
David	69	Mau
Demsey	93	Rut
Elijah	93	Rut
Francis	295	War
Henry	347	Whi
Jabez	22	Wll
James	347	Whi
Jeremiah	405	Wil
John	22	Gil
John	405	Wil
John, Jur.	5	Lin
John, Ser.	5	Lin
Joshua	20	Lin
Joshua	308	War
Josiah	415	Wil
Peter	400	Wil
Rabin	29	Mau
Robert	61	Wll
Samuel	3	Hum
Shadrack	400	Wil
Smallwood	8	Gil
Susanah	365	Whi
Thomas	25	Bed
Thomas	82	Rut
Thomas	363	Whi
William	11	Bed
William	10	Gil
William	39	Lin
William	404	Wil
see Oens, Owings		
Owensby, Thomas	19	Jac
see Owenby		
Owin, Nathan	78	Dav
see Owen		
Owings, Samuel	119	Ste
see Owens		
Oxendine, Archibald	19	Ove
David	19	Jac
Oxford, Abel	16	Gil
John	7	Gil
Samuel	28	Rob
Oxum, John	73	Dav
Sally	73	Dav
Ozment, James	395	Wil
John	395	Wil
Jonathan	396	Wil

--- P ---

Pablett see Pallett		
Pace, Demsey	16	Rob
Drury	12	Hic
Edmund	295	War
Gideon	11	Mon
Hardy	11	Mon
Hennon	409	Wil
Jeremiah	11	Hic
John	11	Mon
John	301	War
Kinchen	5	Hic
Marian	85	Rut
Richmond	24	Fra
William	5	Hic
William [2]	16	Ro
Wilson	5	Hic
Pack, Bartemius	15	Rob
Benj. D.	95	Dav
Elisha	25	Rob
Jane	96	Dav
Smith	171	Sum
Packwood, Larkin	39	Smi
Padget, Nehemiah	23	Fra
Padgett, John O.	170	Sum
Reuben	5	Ove
Padley, Robert	403	Wil
Paffon, Thomas	318	War
Pafford, James	318	War
Page, Barney	42	Smi
David	23	Bed
David D.	29	Wll
Giles	84	Dav
Jacob	42	Smi
John	3	Per
John	40	Smi
John M.	89	Dav
John W.	91	Dav
Jonathan	3	Way
Joseph	91	Dav
Katy	64	Dav
Michael	14	Dic
Robert	61	Dav
Samuel	6	Way
Samuel	56	Wll
Thomas	42	Smi
William	64	Dav
William	14	Hum
William	79	Rut
William	42	Smi
Pagget, Henry G.	45	Wll
John	2	Hum
Mary	45	Wll
Pain, Daniel	62	Mau
Dudley	26	Rob
Gideon	22	Rob
Hardin, Mr.	9	Law
Henry	415	Wil
James	32	Mau
James	19	Rob
James	415	Wil
Pain (cont.)		
John	19	Rob
Micoger	62	Mau
Robbert	62	Mau
Thomas	20	Rob
Warren	19	Rob
Paine, Charles [2]	305	War
Daniel	289	War
Gidean	36	Rob
James	10	Gil
Larkin	308	War
Robert	10	Gil
Rosanna	7	Gil
Solomon	36	Rob
Wilson	7	Gil
Painer, Dinah	25	Bed
Edward	32	Bed
Joseph	25	Bed
Painter, Mary	413	Wil
Samuel	22	Lin
Pair see Parr		
Paise, Rachel	42	Mau
Paisley, James N.	85	Dav
Thomas	33	Rob
Palding, Washington	42	Bed
Palett, William	283	War
Paley, Elijah	6	Har
Pallett, Stewart	297	War
see Pollett		
Palmer, Benjamin	2	Hum
Elisha	22	Gil
Francis	405	Wil
Henry	22	Gil
John	23	Fra
John	24	Fra
John	11	Hic
John	42	Smi
Jonathan	11	Hum
Philip, Jun.	42	Smi
Philip, Sen.	42	Smi
Robert	88	Rut
Sarah	41	Smi
Thomas	75	Rut
Ths. W.	106	She
William	112	Ste
William	319	War
William	384	Wil
William P.	41	Smi
see John		
Palmore, Branch	12	Wll
Woodson	41	Smi
Pampin, William	22	Lin
Pan see Parr		
Pandy, Lewis	4	Hum
Pane, Gaven	14	Dic
John	354	Whi
Pryor	15	Dic
Pankey, Lewis	171	Sum
Panky, Uzzi	41	Smi
Pannel, Jediah	96	Rut
Pannell, Thomas	3	Dic
Panter, John	95	Rut
Pape see Pope		

Paradice, John	87	Dav
William	87	Dav
Paradise, Parker	15	Lin
Paratt, Isaac	5	Hum
Parchman, James	2	Law
Philip, Mr.	2	Law
Parchment, John	122	Ste
Parham, Ephraim	4	Gil
Ephraim	22	Lin
George	4	Wll
Leonard	98	Rut
Thomas	401	Wil
Thomas	48	Wll
William	4	Wll
Parish, Jas.	120	Ste
John	20	Jac
John	40	Smi
Shared	47	Lin
William	39	Smi
William	380	Wil
Willis	39	Smi
Pariss, James	39	Smi
Obediah	39	Smi
Park, J. G.	19	Jac
James	3	Wll
John	9	Lin
Joseph	78	Dav
Moses	10	Lin
Samuel	48	Mau
William	318	War
see Pack		
Parkenson, Manuel	353	Whi
Parker, Aaron	37	Lin
Abraham	41	Smi
Alexander	23	Fra
Allen	4	Rob
Arthur	349	Whi
Catharine	90	Rut
Cincinnatus	172	Sum
Daniel	21	Way
David	71	Dav
David D.	18	Lin
Dempsey	172	Sum
Edmond D.	18	Lin
Edward	20	Jac
Edward	43	Smi
Edward	389	Wil
Elisha	6	Law
Elizabeth	11	Mon
Elizabeth	80	Rut
Elizabeth	40	Smi
Francis	41	Smi
Gilliard	92	Rut
Green B.	20	Bed
Isaac	100	Rut
Isaac	171	Sum
Isam A.	68	Dav
James	8	Rob
James	40	Smi
James	41	Smi
James M.	14	Hum
Jeremiah	16	Gil
Jess	71	Dav
Parker (cont.)		
Jesse	9	Hum
Jessee	348	Whi
Joel	90	Rut
John	9	Hum
John [2]	9	Mon
John	42	Smi
John [2]	171	Sum
John	172	Sum
John B.	30	Rob
John C.	90	Dav
Jonathan	78	Rut
Joseph	41	Smi
Joseph	352	Whi
Joshua	8	Hum
Judah	171	Sum
King	171	Sum
Lewis	6	Law
Lewis	42	Smi
Lidia	5	Hum
Lotty	3	Ove
Lydia	40	Smi
Matthew	43	Smi
Matthew, Sen.	43	Smi
Micajah	19	Lin
Moses	8	Dic
Nathan	19	Ove
Nathan	110	Ste
Nathaniel	19	Rob
Nathl.	125	Ste
Nathl.	171	Sum
Noah	22	Lin
Patsey	40	Smi
Piety	58	Wll
Polly	43	Smi
Rebecca	20	Hic
Richard	40	Smi
Richard	305	War
Robert	171	Sum
Robert	287	War
Samuel	349	Whi
Seth	23	Fra
Stephen	5	Hum
Stephen	110	Ste
Sterling C.	21	Gil
Susana	110	Ste
Susanna	37	Bed
Thomas	87	Dav
Thomas	24	Fra
Thomas	8	Hum
Thomas	26	Lin
Thomas	171	Sum
Wilie	8	Mon
William	60	Dav
William	71	Dav
William	8	Gil
William	8	Hum
William	28	Mon
William	4	Ove
William	80	Rut
William	95	Rut
William [2]	39	Smi
William	40	Smi

Parker (cont.)		
William, Jr., 2nd	40	Smi
Zechariah	13	Gil
Parkerson, Brown	23	Lin
George	42	Smi
George W.	39	Smi
George W.	42	Smi
Hugh	44	Lin
John	40	Bed
John	44	Lin
Richard	42	Smi
Parkes, James	403	Wil
Parkhurst, Charles	41	Smi
Daniel	302	War
David	40	Smi
Parkman, David	84	Dav
William	84	Dav
Parks, Bartlemas	318	War
Benjamin	66	Wll
Charles	99	Rut
Davis	4	Ove
Francis	53	Mau
George	23	Fra
Hugh	403	Wil
Jacob	171	Sum
James	7	Wll
John	7	Bed
John	16	Lin
John	28	Mau
John	31	Mau
John	32	Rob
John	80	Rut
John	285	War
John	65	Wll
John, Jr.	65	Wll
Joshua	47	Bed
Joshua	43	Mau
Linsfield W.	17	Lin
Malinda	45	Wll
Martin L.	32	Lin
Ony	22	Lin
Reuben	16	Lin
Richard	171	Sum
Robert	28	Lin
Robert	171	Sum
Samuel	23	Fra
Samuel	24	Fra
Theophilus	22	Hic
Thomas	28	Lin
Thomas	45	Mau
Thomas L. D.	21	Lin
Parkwood see Packwood		
Parky see Panky		
Parman, William	407	Wil
Parmer, Icim	408	Wil
John	398	Wil
Stephen	371	Whi
William	370	Whi
Parmerly, Samuel	6	Har
Parnol, John, Jr.	172	Sum
John, Sr.	172	Sum
Parr, Berry T.	19	Lin
Elizabeth	171	Sum
Parr (cont.)		
John	9	Mon
John, Jur.	45	Lin
John, Ser.	45	Lin
Mary	39	Bed
Mary	23	Lin
Sally	79	Rut
William	6	Gil
William	97	Rut
Parris, Joel	1	Ove
Thomas	283	War
William	17	Ove
Parrish, Benja.	171	Sum
Calham	15	Gil
David W.	171	Sum
Eleanor	4	Dic
Fountain	39	Wll
Hannah	60	Dav
Hewell	11	Dic
Joel	171	Sum
Joel	1	Wll
Johnson	397	Wil
Johnson	411	Wil
Susanah	46	Wll
Thomas	171	Sum
William	400	Wil
Wyatt	4	Dic
Parrot, Benjamin	40	Smi
Harp	41	Smi
John	6	Dic
Parrott, Benjamin	20	Ove
Danl.	18	Hic
Isaac	15	Gil
Parsens, Samuel	2	Har
Parsley, Anthony	299	War
John	82	Rut
Stephen	88	Rut
William	22	Rob
see Pasley		
Parson, Jane	5	Per
Parsons, Edmund	42	Smi
Geo. W.	46	Bed
James	34	Rob
Joseph	412	Wil
Thomas	56	Wll
Thomas S.	31	Bed
Thos.	46	Bed
William	39	Smi
William	412	Wil
Partam, Charles	24	Fra
Partee, Abner	63	Mau
Benjamin	40	Smi
Charles	64	Mau
Partlow, Thomas	394	Wil
Parton, Nancy	37	Mau
Pascal, John, Jun.	41	Smi
John, Sen.	41	Smi
John H.	41	Smi
Silas	41	Smi
Paschal, Eli	14	Law
Icim	382	Wil
Pase, Thomas	48	Mau
William	47	Mau

Pasey, James	83	Rut
Paskal, Asa	128	Ste
Dennis	383	Wil
Pasker, Felix	98	Rut
Pasley, Moses	23	Rob
Moses	82	Rut
Moses	101	Rut
William	20	Jac
see Parsley		
Pass, James H.	351	Whi
Thomas	351	Whi
Passby, Nancy	394	Wil
Passens, Majer	372	Whi
Passmore, David	8	Dic
Richard B.	63	Mau
Pastan, James	4	Law
Pasteley, James	6	Gil
Pate, Edward	405	Wil
Elisha	19	Jac
Esabah	20	Jac
Isaac	11	Ove
Jemima	24	Hic
Jesse	303	War
Jesse	56	Wll
John	11	Har
John, Junr.	20	Gil
John, Senr.	19	Gil
Kinchen	59	Wll
Leah	398	Wil
Lewis	2	Hic
Stephen	39	Smi
Thomas	56	Wll
Willeroy	19	Jac
William	32	Rob
Patey, Charles	41	Smi
Eli	41	Smi
Elizabeth	41	Smi
Patrick, Allen	86	Rut
Elias	39	Lin
Ephraim	5	Gil
Jerimiah	102	Rut
John	6	Ove
John	42	Smi
Joseph	34	Lin
Levi	302	War
Levi	313	War
Samuel	5	Gil
Wilie	313	War
see Petrick		
Patt, Nancy	91	Rut
Patterson, Alexander [2]	85	Rut
Alexander	97	Rut
Allen L.	1	Rob
Alxander	39	Smi
Baily	100	Rut
Burrell	418	Wil
David	18	Mon
Drurey	107	She
Edward	96	Rut
Ellen	71	Dav
George	43	Smi
Gideon	84	Dav
Hillary	61	Wll
Patterson, Hugh	40	Smi
Icim	419	Wil
James	6	Bed
James	7	Bed
James	37	Mau
James	16	Ove
James	19	Ove
James	40	Smi
James	128	Ste
James	170	Sum
James	59	Wll
John	11	Lin
John	100	Rut
John	40	Smi
John [2]	41	Smi
John	43	Smi
John	415	Wil
John	59	Wll
John, Sen.	40	Smi
John T.	9	Hum
Malcolm	11	Lin
Malcolm	43	Lin
Margarett	59	Wll
Mark	16	Rob
Martin	91	Dav
Nancy	9	Bed
Nelson	79	Dav
Patrick	18	Rob
Peggy	418	Wil
Peters	376	Wil
Rebecca	18	Hic
Robert	9	Bed
Robert	11	Dic
Robert	11	Ove
Robt.	15	Hic
Sarah	286	War
Thomas	107	She
William	1	Per
William	40	Smi
William	41	Smi
William [2]	410	Wil
William	418	Wil
Patteson, Bernard M.	17	Gil
James	16	Gil
Nelson	17	Gil
Robert	93	Rut
Patton, Alexander	382	Wil
Alx.	73	Dav
Andrew	411	Wil
David	94	Rut
Edward	24	Fra
George	28	Mau
Isaac	46	Wll
James	1	Bed
James	2	Bed
James	28	Bed
James	41	Bed
James	24	Fra
James	93	Rut
James	38	Wll
James	62	Wll
James E.	28	Bed
Jason	62	Wll

Patton (cont.)		
John	1	Bed
John	2	Bed
John	41	Bed
John [2]	24	Fra
John	1	Hic
John	14	Hic
John	1	Mon
John	17	Ove
John	309	War
John [2]	411	Wil
Joseph	17	Ove
Joseph	410	Wil
Mary	172	Sum
Matthew	73	Dav
Matthew	101	Rut
Nathaniel	382	Wil
Neely S.	18	Bed
Peru	37	Lin
Richard T.	3	Har
Robert	17	Ove
Robert [2]	172	Sum
Sally	172	Sum
Samuel	26	Bed
Samuel	96	Rut
Samuel	62	Wll
Thomas	32	Rob
Thos.	8	Hic
Tristram	5	Wll
William	26	Bed
William	40	Bed
William	76	Dav
William	97	Dav
William	24	Fra
William	97	Rut
William	171	Sum
William C.	319	War
William S.	172	Sum
see Marlow		
Paty, Rachael	19	Jac
Paul, Andrew	24	Fra
Elias	172	Sum
John	22	Gil
John	17	Lin
William	19	Lin
Paulding, William V.	23	Fra
Pauley, Valuntine	66	Mau
Paully, William	27	Bed
Pawell see Powell		
Pawin, William	15	Bed
Paxton, Samuel	18	Gil
Thompson	42	Mau
Payn, Reuben	86	Dav
Payne, Amy	41	Smi
Charity	36	Lin
Daniel	291	War
Demariss	42	Smi
Greenwood	85	Dav
Hamilton	7	Hum
Haynes	23	Fra
Isaac	40	Smi
Jacob	87	Rut
James	54	Bed
Payne (cont.)		
James	84	Rut
James	42	Smi
Jesse	31	Lin
John	12	Bed
John	43	Bed
John	14	Hum
John	39	Smi
John	170	Sum
John	171	Sum
Joseph	172	Sum
Joseph, Jun.	40	Smi
Joseph, Sen.	40	Smi
Lawrence	39	Smi
Ledford	43	Smi
Levy	6	Ove
Linsey	6	Ove
Mary	22	Mon
Mary	39	Smi
Milly	23	Fra
Nehemiah	43	Smi
Poindexter	23	Fra
Ransom T.	293	War
Reuben	25	Bed
Robert	171	Sum
Sarah	40	Smi
Solomon	1	Rob
Solomon	41	Smi
Sylvister	24	Fra
Thomas	23	Fra
William	54	Bed
William [2]	40	Smi
William	293	War
William	318	War
Payton, Cravar	320	War
Elias	39	Mau
Eligah	39	Mau
John W.	399	Wil
Joseph	68	Mau
Margret	39	Mau
Robbert	31	Mau
Pea, Elias	66	Dav
George	67	Dav
William	30	Mon
Peace, Abner	42	Wll
William H.	400	Wil
Peach, Archibald	49	Wll
John	38	Wll
Peacock, Jno.	4	Hic
John	18	Bed
John	23	Fra
Peak, Ann	172	Sum
Jeffery	93	Rut
Jesse	83	Rut
Joseph	89	Rut
Simmons	87	Rut
Pearce, Aaron	131	Ste
Abner	125	Ste
Elizabeth	4	Per
John	92	Dav
John	12	Gil
John	119	Ste
John	123	Ste

Pearce (cont.)		
Moses	127	Ste
Polly	110	Ste
Stokely D. P.	88	Rut
William	128	Ste
Pearcy, Boswell	419	Wil
John R.	59	Wll
Robert	20	Mon
Shearwood	419	Wil
Simon	24	Fra
Thomas	104	Rut
Pearl, Dycie	78	Dav
Pearmon, Jacob	414	Wil
see Perryman		
Pearre, Joshua, Sn.	4	Wll
Pearsall, Benjamin	6	Dic
Pearse, Arthur	19	Wll
Robbart	28	Mau
Pearson, Daniel	101	Rut
David	78	Rut
Ellis	24	Fra
Henry	172	Sum
Isham	97	Dav
John	23	Bed
John	18	Gil
John	18	Rob
John B.	77	Rut
Kindred	39	Bed
Margaret	83	Rut
Margaret	89	Rut
Samuel	16	Gil
Thomas	37	Bed
Thomas	77	Rut
Thomas	102	Rut
William	39	Bed
William	2	Dic
Wm.	24	Hic
Peay, Mary	27	Wll
Thomas	12	Wll
see Ray		
Pebles, Howel	9	Wll
William	1	Wll
Peck, Cariline	78	Dav
Garret	295	War
James	2	Ove
James	362	Whi
Jane	16	Ove
Zachariah	388	Wil
Pecock, Abraham	393	Wil
Micajah	392	Wil
Pedago, William	24	Fra
Pedego, Joshua	414	Wil
Pee, Joseph	24	Fra
Peebles, Jesse	16	Gil
Peel, George	412	Wil
Richard	12	Wll
Peeler, George A.	17	Hic
Jacob	20	Hic
Jacob	51	Mau
Jesse	16	Hic
Lavina	16	Hic
Peeples, Nathan	9	Hum
Nathan	27	Mon
Peery, Benjamin	306	War
George	21	Hic
James, Jr.	20	Hic
James, L. C.	19	Hic
James, Sr.	21	Hic
John	20	Hic
John	1	Way
Robt.	19	Hic
Saml.	20	Hic
William	13	Gil
see Perry		
Pegg, James	89	Dav
Stephen	50	Wll
Pegram, Lucy	124	Ste
Pegrim, William	367	Whi
Peke, Judith	19	Jac
Pellam, William	311	War
Pellet, Thomas	354	Whi
Pembleton, Jesse	405	Wil
John	417	Wil
Richard	415	Wil
Pendergrass, Fanny	6	Ove
Jesse	394	Wil
Richard	186	Sum
Sarah	6	Ove
Thornton	3	Ove
Pendexter, George	42	Wll
Pendland, Noble	31	Lin
Pendleton, Benjamin	295	War
James	42	Smi
John	23	Fra
John	290	War
John C.	24	Fra
Thomas	82	Rut
Penick, Edward	23	Bed
Peningcuff, John	17	Ove
Penington, Clemantes	40	Wll
Henry	111	Ste
Joshua	20	Jac
Reuben	20	Jac
Robert	31	Rob
Saml.	20	Jac
Penn, Benjn.	17	Bed
Edmund	88	Rut
George	90	Rut
James	23	Fra
Jesse	4	Gil
Joseph	7	Lin
Penney, James	395	Wil
Pennington, Abraham	8	Law
Asa	37	Lin
Charles	353	Whi
David	8	Law
Graves	87	Dav
Isaac	8	Law
Jacob	46	Lin
Jacob, Jr.	8	Law
John	8	Bed
John	366	Whi
Joshua	354	Whi
Levi	8	Bed
Moses	8	Law
William	8	Law

Penny, Richardson 382 Wil
Thomas 386 Wil
Pennywell, Lucy 416 Wil
Penrice, Francis 5 Mon
Sarah 30 Mon
Pentecost, Mary 397 Wil
Penticost, Morgan R. 172 Sum
Penticuff, Jacob 6 Law
see Peningcuff
Peoples, Cordy C. 92 Dav
Joel 8 Law
John 15 Lin
Mary 97 Dav
Pepper, Elisha 293 War
Hilley 297 War
Nathan 3 Rob
Richard 3 Rob
William 21 Jac
William 6 Rob
William B. 2 Gil
Perdue, Asa 172 Sum
Danl. 171 Sum
Howel 14 Mon
Jarret 8 Mon
Luke 172 Sum
Perin, Elizabeth 20 Jac
Perkins, Charles 16 Gil
Charles 11 Mon
Charles, a man of Colour 15 Wll
Daniel 14 Wll
Elisabeth 52 Wll
Eliza 15 Wll
Elizabeth 93 Rut
Gabriel 42 Smi
Jesse 23 Fra
John 23 Fra
John B. 292 War
Joshua 91 Rut
Lemuel 172 Sum
Nicholas 15 Wll
Nicholas 32 Wll
Nicholas P. 2 Wll
Nicholas T. 10 Wll
Reuben 20 Jac
Robert 100 Rut
Robert B. 366 Whi
Sally 41 Smi
Samuel 5 Gil
Samuel 54 Wll
Sophia 78 Dav
Thomas H. 15 Wll
Uty 366 Whi
William 63 Dav
William 383 Wil
Wright 20 Hic
Permenton, Malachi 18 Gil
Pernal, Levi 414 Wil
Perrey, Curtis 6 Gil
Perrigen, Samuel 369 Whi
Perrin, Elizabeth 370 Whi
Phillip 28 Mau
Perry, Allen 9 Bed
Asa 172 Sum
Perry (cont.)
Benjamin 40 Smi
Benjamin 296 War
Benjamin 309 War
Burrell 92 Rut
Burton 13 Hic
Charles 69 Dav
Georg 391 Wil
George 69 Dav
Hannibal 24 Fra
Jacob 413 Wil
James 18 Gil
James 170 Sum
John 23 Fra
John 18 Gil
John 21 Mon
John 172 Sum
John, Jr. 173 Sum
John, Sr. 173 Sum
Joseph 7 Bed
Joseph 15 Rob
Kinchen 13 Hic
Littleton 84 Dav
Martin 9 Bed
Nathaniel 78 Rut
Olbert 42 Smi
Polly 170 Sum
Ralls 171 Sum
Robert 8 Rob
Roundtree 173 Sum
Simeon 25 Mau
Simpson 40 Mau
Thornton 49 Wll
Tilman 8 Dic
Turner 94 Rut
William 40 Mau
William 172 Sum
William J. 13 Rob
see Peery, Perrey, Pery
Perryman, Alexander 414 Wil
Isaac 411 Wil
John 296 War
Joseph 416 Wil
Joshua 49 Wll
Samuel 416 Wil
Vincent 281 War
see Pearmon, Perrymon
Perrymon, John 415 Wil
Perrymore, James 8 Gil
Persines, James 173 Sum
Persise, John B. 3 Rob
Person, Howell 402 Wil
Simon 8 Gil
Thomas H. 107 She
Persons see Persines
Perteat, Mark 172 Sum
Pertite, James 414 Wil
Perviand, Thomas 405 Wil
Pervius, Peter 20 Hic
Pery, Francis S. 64 Mau
Petaway, William 401 Wil
Peter, James P. 56 Mau
Peterman, George 3 Ove

Peterman (cont.)		
Jacob	3	Ove
William	3	Ove
Peters, Andrew M.	4	Gil
James	24	Fra
James	58	Mau
Peterson, Andrew	14	Mon
Babel	17	Dic
Elizabeth	16	Mon
Isaac	3	Mon
Johan	39	Smi
Roland	2	Mon
Susan	7	Mon
Petree, Peter	20	Jac
Petrey, John	14	Ove
Petrick, James D.	91	Rut
Pettice, Stephen	2	Mon
Pettigon, Wm.	120	Ste
Pettus, Henry	64	Wll
Petty, Alexander	320	War
Alfred	23	Fra
Ambros	8	Hic
Ambrose	87	Rut
Andrew	320	War
Ebenezer	16	Dic
Gabriel	8	Hic
George	117	Ste
Henry	406	Wil
Henry	66	Wll
Hubbard	16	Way
Isaac	6	Way
James	23	Fra
James	20	Jac
John	23	Hic
John	19	Jac
John	320	War
Joseph	42	Lin
Micajah	320	War
Solomon	8	Hic
Thomas	11	Lin
Thos., Jr.	8	Hic
Thos., Senr.	8	Hic
William	41	Smi
Wm.	23	Hic
Pettypool, John	70	Mau
see Pool		
Petway, Henchey	33	Wll
Henchey [& Bond]	1	Wll
William	30	Wll
Pew, David	15	Hic
Fletcher	40	Smi
Gilbert	75	Dav
Joel	16	Hic
Samuel	42	Smi
William	7	Way
Pewet, Joel	53	Wll
Pewit, James	53	Wll
Pewitt, Thomas	6	Per
Peyton, Ephraim	171	Sum
G. E.	14	Way
Jno., Sr.	171	Sum
John, Jr.	172	Sum
Jonathan C.	172	Sum
Peyton (cont.)		
William	171	Sum
Phares, Catharine	19	Jac
Dilly	19	Jac
Pharis, Davidson	300	War
James	19	Jac
Lewis	352	Whi
see Faris, Phares		
Phea, Moses	291	War
Phelps, Daniel	68	Dav
David	13	Gil
Elisha	92	Rut
Ephram	68	Dav
Henry	170	Sum
John	405	Wil
Joshua	96	Rut
Josiah	11	Gil
Kelin	9	Lin
Marian	92	Rut
Richard	408	Wil
Silas	92	Rut
Phelts, Cary	97	Dav
Phenix, Henry, Mr.	10	Law
Phesmire, William	35	Lin
Phibs, Mathew	172	Sum
Philip, James	41	Smi
Philips, Benjamin	410	Wil
Charles	20	Jac
Elijah	38	Lin
Ezekiel	23	Fra
George	24	Fra
Hiram	318	War
Isaac	14	Bed
James	23	Fra
James	39	Lin
James	45	Lin
John	11	Bed
John	20	Jac
John	4	Law
John	40	Smi
John	42	Smi
John	115	Ste
John	410	Wil
John, Junr.	5	Law
John, Senr.	5	Law
Johnson	24	Fra
Josep	296	War
Joseph	24	Fra
Joseph	410	Wil
Joshua	24	Fra
Leah	3	Ove
Martha	8	Lin
Martin	301	War
Matthew	23	Bed
Nancy	82	Rut
Richard	76	Rut
Samuel	24	Bed
Samuel	25	Lin
Samuel [2]	88	Rut
Shadrick	304	War
Stephen	38	Lin
Sterlin	295	War
Susan	412	Wil

Philips (cont.)
Thomas 78 Rut
Thompson 24 Fra
Trithina 27 Mon
Washington 8 Har
William 19 Jac
William 18 Ove
William 408 Wil
William 410 Wil
Williams 7 Law
Phillip, Lewis 355 Whi
Phillipps, Susanah 56 Mau
Abraham 118 Ste
Bennett 76 Rut
Burrel 121 Ste
Burrell 171 Sum
David 83 Dav
David 76 Rut
David 353 Whi
Elijah 385 Wil
Elizabeth 90 Dav
Elizabeth Anne 9 Gil
Elum 171 Sum
Eve 56 Wll
Ezekiel 172 Sum
Henry 57 Wll
Henry 58 Wll
James 172 Sum
James 10 Wll
James N. 5 Gil
John 11 Gil
John 352 Whi
John M. 170 Sum
Joseph 94 Dav
Joseph 27 Wll
Leonard 172 Sum
Mann 124 Ste
Moses 127 Ste
Richard 172 Sum
Samuel 83 Dav
Thomas 7 Gil
Thomas 353 Whi
William 74 Dav
William [2] 1 Hic
William 170 Sum
William 56 Wll
see Philps
Philpot, James 23 Fra
James 24 Fra
John 23 Fra
Samuel 24 Fra
Warren 289 War
Philpott, Samuel 3 Ove
Philps, Elisha 21 Rob
Jesse 17 Wll
Thomas 172 Sum
Phipps, Benjamin 11 Lin
Berthena 13 Gil
Phips, C. N. 61 Dav
Isaac 29 Rob
Jordon 52 Wll
Lewellen 7 Rob
Peter 137 Sum
Phips (cont.)
Richardson 63 Dav
Phoebus, George T. 4 Hum
Leonard 4 Hum
Lewis 4 Hum
Phoenix see Phenix
Pholks, Edwin 31 Mon
Pibus, John 26 Lin
Picey, Nathaniel 13 Wll
Pickard, Henry 30 Mau
Isaac 30 Mau
Isaac 31 Mau
John 33 Mau
William 30 Mau
Pickens, James H. 18 Gil
John 20 Way
John G. 44 Mau
Mathew Z. 44 Mau
William 44 Mau
Pickering, Joseph 8 Mon
Picket, Henry 17 Hic
Pickett, Andrew 43 Smi
David 13 Way
Ebenezer 23 Fra
Edward 16 Dic
Edward 7 Hum
James 23 Fra
John 12 Dic
Jonathan 41 Smi
Samuel 23 Fra
Pickings, Elizebeth 54 Mau
William 46 Mau
Pickins, Gabriel 2 Har
Jonathan 2 Har
Jonathan R. 2 Har
William 12 Bed
William H. 44 Mau
Pickle, Henry 20 Bed
Polly 82 Dav
William 82 Dav
Pickrell, Polley 405 Wil
Pieister, Richmond 23 Fra
Pierce, Ambrose 13 Lin
Arthur 81 Rut
Arthur 89 Rut
Chs. 172 Sum
Daniel 5 Law
Daniel 17 Way
Edmund 171 Sum
George 72 Dav
George 171 Sum
Isaac [2] 172 Sum
Jeramiah 91 Dav
John 69 Dav
Keron 172 Sum
Martin 70 Dav
Nathan 370 Whi
Samuel 13 Lin
Spencer 6 Law
Thomas 92 Dav
Thomas 78 Rut
Thomas 370 Whi
Washington 365 Whi

Pierce (cont.)		
Willie	103	Rut
Piercue, Mary	362	Whi
Sarah	362	Whi
Pierson see Cliford		
Pigg, Claiborne	41	Smi
George	41	Smi
James	17	Hic
James	361	Whi
John	7	Lin
John	42	Smi
John J.	42	Smi
Nather	286	War
Paul	300	War
William	286	War
Piggott, Simon	36	Wll
Pike, James	12	Rob
Job	172	Sum
John	6	Rob
John	29	Rob
Joshua	2	Mon
Thomas	24	Fra
William	8	Rob
William	171	Sum
Piker, John	23	Fra
Pilant, Elisha	9	Rob
Pile, Conrod	7	Ove
Piles, Newton	6	Rob
Pilkton, Larking	39	Mau
Pillo, Abner	37	Mau
Clabern	61	Mau
John	64	Mau
Josep	64	Mau
Joseph	64	Mau
Vinson	63	Mau
William	61	Mau
Pillow, Gideon	11	Gil
John	63	Wll
John J.	42	Smi
Martin	43	Smi
Mordica	83	Dav
William	38	Mau
Pimager, Matthias	42	Smi
Pinckston, Michac	63	Dav
Pindarvis, William	40	Smi
Pinedexter, David	20	Jac
Francis	20	Jac
John	20	Jac
Saml.	20	Jac
Pinegar, Mathias	360	Whi
Piner, Charles M.	25	Wll
David	22	Wll
James	8	Hum
James	24	Wll
John	22	Wll
Pinkerton, David	60	Dav
James	63	Dav
John	44	Lin
Joseph	64	Dav
Joseph	94	Dav
William	15	Bed
Pinkley, Charles H.	83	Dav
Frederick	59	Dav
Pinkley (cont.)		
Silas	20	Jac
Pinkston, David	6	Wll
Hugh	27	Wll
James	73	Dav
Matthew	19	Wll
Peter	5	Wll
Turner	41	Bed
Turner	5	Wll
William	40	Bed
Pinner, John	113	Ste
Pinnigar, James	363	Whi
Peter	363	Whi
Pinsel, Hetty	19	Jac
Pinson, Duke	11	Mon
Harrison	30	Bed
Joel	46	Lin
Larkin	11	Mon
Moses	40	Smi
Nathan G.	8	Per
Polly	35	Bed
see ...nson		
Piper, Abram	40	Smi
Benjamin	41	Smi
John	41	Smi
Samuel	172	Sum
Pipkin, Clemency	43	Smi
Enos	29	Mau
Hughes	43	Smi
Lewis	43	Smi
Mark	66	Mau
Stewart	8	Dic
Phillip	64	Dav
William	23	Fra
Pippin, Joseph	19	Jac
Kinchin	20	Jac
Willis	19	Jac
Pirant, Isaiah	21	Jac
Pirkard, Baily	86	Rut
Pirkins, Absolom	369	Whi
Henry	28	Mau
Joseph	27	Mau
Levi	369	Whi
Nickles	66	Mau
Piron, Charles	44	Wll
Pirtillar, John	62	Mau
Purtle, George	346	Whi
Pistole, Charles	67	Mau
Charles	9	Wll
David	64	Mau
James	42	Smi
John	351	Whi
Thomas	42	Smi
William	39	Smi
William	42	Smi
Pitchford, John	8	Law
Pitcock, Stephen	41	Lin
William	41	Lin
Pitman, Lewis	2	Hic
Lewis	4	Hum
Whinney	303	War
Pitner, Michael	382	Wil
Pitt, Arthur	21	Rob

Pitt (cont.)		
Davis	131	Ste
Henry	171	Sum
James	172	Sum
John G.	26	Rob
Robt.	172	Sum
Sterling	128	Ste
Thomas	11	Rob
William	171	Sum
Winiford	171	Sum
see Pitts		
Pittman, William	94	Dav
William	172	Sum
Pitts, Allen	10	Gil
Bartley	30	Rob
Burwell	30	Rob
Esther	45	Bed
Ezekiel	59	Wll
James	42	Lin
John	170	Sum
Mark	42	Lin
Patsy	21	Rob
Sarah	23	Fra
see Beasl(e)y, Pitt		
Plain, Godfrey	98	Dav
Plasters, Thomas	25	Rob
Platt, Roswell	2	Mon
Plock, Lucy	24	Wll
Plowman, J.	24	Mau
Jacob	317	War
John	26	Mau
Plumbley, Isaac	355	Whi
Plumer, James R.	57	Mau
Plumler, Solomon	7	Wll
Plumley, Archibald	20	Jac
John [2]	20	Jac
Rachel	15	Bed
William	20	Jac
Plummer, Rebecca	94	Rut
Plunket, James	13	Hum
Reuben	42	Smi
Plunkett, Reuben	297	War
Plunt, John	13	Hum
Poarch, Israel	94	Rut
Poe, Hardy	23	Fra
John	24	Fra
Joseph	21	Rob
Judithan	23	Fra
Tabitha	95	Rut
Poerry, Jeremiah	24	Fra
Poesey, William	24	Fra
Pogue, Joshua	17	Ove
Samuel	96	Rut
see Ogue		
Poindexter, Joseph	86	Rut
Poland, Moses	313	War
Polding, Pherebo	42	Bed
Polk, Abigal	34	Rob
Benjmin	61	Mau
Charles	118	Ste
Evin S.	61	Mau
Ezekial	59	Mau
John [2]	23	Bed
Polk (cont.)		
John	61	Mau
John	118	Ste
John, Junr.	23	Bed
Richard	12	Wll
Samuel	57	Mau
Samuel	69	Mau
Shelby	62	Mau
Silas	171	Sum
William	55	Mau
William	118	Ste
William	42	Wll
Pollard, Joseph D.	74	Rut
Polly	23	Bed
Rewbin	2	Mon
Samuel	79	Rut
Pollett, Jane	97	Rut
Polloc, Elizabeth	45	Lin
Pollock, Henry	3	Law
James	40	Bed
John	40	Bed
John	31	Mau
Robert	40	Bed
Saml.	40	Bed
Polly, John	1	Law
Polston, William	17	Lin
Pond, William	171	Sum
William, Sr.	172	Sum
Ponder, Abner	14	Hic
Archibald	9	Hic
Ponds, Benjamin	15	Rob
Pont, Henry	30	Bed
Pool, Aaron	16	Bed
Archibald	97	Rut
Armsted	118	Ste
Ephraim	10	Mon
Ephriam	10	Rob
James	18	Lin
James	10	Mon
Joseph	42	Lin
Mary	74	Rut
Patrick	8	Ove
Peter	44	Bed
Robert	116	Ste
Rozwell	341	Whi
Seth	116	Ste
Thomas P. [Pettypool?]	82	Rut
William	16	Bed
William	21	Rob
William	2	Way
William P. [Pettypool?]	70	Mau
Young A.	19	Jac
Poor, Benjamin	17	Ove
Joseph	7	Ove
Moses	9	Ove
Poore, John	18	Hic
Thomas	20	Hic
Pope, Bennet	4	Law
Cairy W.	10	Way
Charles	12	Rob
Charles	60	Wll
Elijah	20	Way
Ezekiel	99	Rut

Pope (cont.)		
Hardy	81	Rut
Humphrey	101	Rut
James	41	Smi
Jeremiah	10	Wll
John	47	Wll
Martha	41	Smi
Matthias	28	Wll
Micajah	24	Hic
Newet	20	Lin
Newett	40	Lin
Philip	40	Smi
Samuel	30	Mon
Silas	41	Smi
Solomon	80	Rut
Thomas A.	47	Wll
William	17	Rob
William	73	Rut
William	97	Rut
William	41	Smi
Winfield	59	Wll
Poplin, Henry	2	Bed
William	51	Bed
Porch, John	6	Lin
William	6	Lin
Pore, Elijah	23	Fra
John	24	Fra
Porson, John	171	Sum
Port, Henry	18	Bed
John	94	Dav
Portar, William	28	Mau
Porten, Hannah	30	Wll
Porter, Alexander B.	8	Rob
Ambrose	171	Sum
Amos J.	81	Dav
Benjamin	40	Lin
Charles	12	Lin
Charles	63	Mau
Charles M.	63	Mau
David W.	8	Gil
E. H.	78	Dav
Eliza.	78	Dav
George	77	Dav
Hugh	88	Rut
James	63	Mau
James	42	Smi
James	287	War
James B.	11	Gil
Jane	3	Hic
John	3	Gil
John	8	Lin
John	40	Smi
John	41	Smi
John	42	Smi
John	359	Whi
John, Jr.	8	Wll
John, lame	17	Wll
John, N.	73	Rut
Joseph	12	Lin
Joseph	40	Mau
Joseph B.	34	Mau
Joshua	359	Whi
Matthew	85	Dav
Porter (cont.)		
Nimrood	38	Mau
Peter	40	Smi
Rease	37	Mau
Rees	11	Gil
Rees	12	Lin
Samuel	102	Rut
Samuel	354	Whi
Sarah	57	Wll
Stephen	12	Lin
Thomas	6	Bed
Thomas	39	Smi
Thomas D.	11	Wll
William	19	Jac
William	36	Mau
William	37	Mau
William	32	Mon
William	40	Smi
William	32	Wll
William B.	2	Rob
see Partee		
Porterfield, Charles	101	Rut
Francis	2	Lin
James	416	Wil
John	101	Rut
John	418	Wil
Samuel	416	Wil
Susana	20	Jac
Portice, Alex.	80	Dav
Posey, William	85	Rut
William H.	95	Rut
Zacheriah	95	Rut
Poston, John H.	1	Mon
Richard	11	Ove
Poteet, James	35	Wll
John	35	Wll
Pleasant	11	Ove
Samuel A.	2	Law
Squire	11	Ove
Thomas	11	Ove
William	4	Law
Pots, John	38	Mau
Potter, Ann	28	Mon
Donelson	47	Wll
Isaac	49	Wll
James	20	Jac
Samuel	21	Jac
Solomon	2	Hic
Susannah	2	Ove
Thomas [2]	20	Jac
Tilman	304	War
William	2	Hic
William	20	Jac
Zachius	20	Jac
Zedoch	28	Mon
see Patton		
Potts, Abner	90	Rut
Daniel	87	Rut
Drury	8	Hic
George	363	Whi
James	51	Wll
John	87	Rut
John	96	Rut

Potts (cont.)		
John	362	Whi
Mathew	98	Rut
Nathan	284	War
Oswald	99	Rut
Oswell	59	Wll
Patrick	361	Whi
Robert	54	Wll
Stiniger	87	Rut
Thomas	171	Sum
Thomas	59	Wll
William	59	Wll
Pounds, David	21	Gil
John	35	Bed
Leorry	2	Per
Powel, Ambers	64	Mau
Anthony	24	Wll
Charles	24	Wll
Charles M.	43	Smi
Dempsey	42	Smi
Eden	29	Mon
Edmund	39	Smi
El...	27	Lin
Florey	26	Mau
Hampton	25	Mon
Hardin	20	Way
Henry	112	Ste
Hesekiah	8	Har
Isam	64	Mau
Jacob	36	Bed
James	92	Dav
James	8	Har
James	31	Mon
Jesse	42	Smi
John	29	Mau
John	43	Smi
John G.	8	Har
Lewis	20	Way
Mark	64	Mau
Mary	12	Hic
Polly	24	Fra
Rebecca	85	Rut
Sarah	45	Mau
Sarah	170	Sum
Thomas	2	Bed
Thomas	21	Bed
Thomas	79	Rut
Thomas	88	Rut
William	86	Rut
William	20	Wll
William	59	Wll
Williams D.	45	Mau
Willie	92	Dav
Powell, Abram	39	Smi
Alexander	309	War
Allen	419	Wil
Archibald	9	Har
Benjamin	23	Fra
Bennet	16	Gil
Cyrus	16	Gil
Dempsey	69	Dav
George	8	Dic
Isaac	308	War
Powell (cont.)		
John	16	Gil
John	21	Hic
John	308	War
John	389	Wil
Martin	22	Rob
Matthew	8	Rob
Nathan	285	War
Osburn	104	Rut
Peter	16	Gil
Rueben	30	Rob
Samuel	308	War
Samuel	309	War
Seymore R.	74	Rut
Thomas	69	Dav
William	94	Dav
William	5	Rob
William	32	Rob
Power, Edward	7	Gil
Levi	7	Gil
Powers, Arthur	29	Mon
James	6	Mon
James	29	Mon
John	23	Gil
John	370	Whi
Joseph	58	Mau
Lewis B.	11	Hum
Roadham	8	Gil
Samuel	35	Wll
Thomas	63	Mau
Valuntine	12	Mon
William	14	Dic
Poynor, Robert	30	Wll
Poyser, Benj.	76	Dav
Prach, Matthias	19	Rob
Prack, William	24	Rob
Prance, John	32	Mon
Prasser, Jesse	24	Fra
William	24	Fra
Prater, Archilus	312	War
Bazil	284	War
John	312	War
Rebecca	23	Fra
Prator, Brice	21	Way
Holloway	5	Per
Pratt, Bailey	42	Smi
George	40	Bed
James	44	Bed
John	24	Fra
John	4	Hum
John	42	Smi
Samuel	36	Wll
William	44	Bed
William [2]	12	Gil
William	358	Whi
Prauh, Jacob	11	Bed
Preast, Miles	65	Wll
Thomas	64	Mau
Prendergast, John B.	23	Fra
Prescot, Simon	26	Rob
Presgrove, Andrew	27	Bed
Pressgrove, Barnet	48	Mau
Preston, Caleb	42	Smi

Preston (cont.)		
Daniel	38	Lin
John	15	Ove
Lydia	172	Sum
Preweth, Kirk	41	Mau
Prewett, Isaac	38	Lin
Jacob	35	Lin
Richard	35	Lin
Prewit, Geo. H.	16	Way
James	3	Hum
John	67	Mau
Prewith, Lemuel	41	Mau
Prewitt, Abner	41	Mau
Moses	40	Bed
Thomas	22	Gil
Price, Anger	288	War
Ascew	27	Rob
Benjamin	319	War
Cammel	19	Jac
Drury	13	Dic
Edmond	366	Whi
Edwin	20	Jac
George	32	Lin
Henry	23	Fra
Humphrey	45	Mau
James	24	Bed
James	24	Fra
James	314	War
James	15	Wll
James	63	Wll
James J. H.	23	Fra
Jesse	11	Bed
John	77	Dav
John	24	Fra
John	12	Hic
John	12	Hum
John	33	Lin
John	309	War
John S.	16	Lin
Joseph	172	Sum
Joshua	5	Hum
Luke	19	Jac
Mary	4	Gil
Mathew	33	Lin
Michael	20	Jac
Nathan	24	Fra
Nathaniel	17	Ove
Natthaniel	20	Jac
Pleasant H.	21	Lin
Reuben	20	Jac
Richard	371	Whi
Richard	30	Wll
Robert	20	Jac
Sally	3	Hum
Sally	20	Jac
Sampson	346	Whi
Samuel	10	Law
Shadrack	353	Whi
Solomon	24	Lin
Stephen	20	Jac
Thomas	23	Fra
Thomas	20	Jac
Thomas	2	Law

Price (cont.)		
Thomas	5	Rob
Thomas	78	Rut
Thomas L.	366	Whi
Timothy	20	Jac
William	8	Gil
William	12	Hic
William	3	Hum
William	20	Rob
William	309	War
William	367	Whi
William	11	Wll
William, Jun.	24	Fra
William, Sen.	24	Fra
William A.	61	Wll
William V.	298	War
Williamson	30	Wll
Pride, Eleanor	14	Gil
Elizabeth	34	Rob
Francis	41	Smi
John	77	Rut
Shelton	386	Wil
William	13	Gil
Pridgen, Larkin	171	Sum
Prier, Green	61	Mau
James	112	Ste
Peter	56	Mau
Priest, James	1	Wll
Mary	1	Wll
Moses	19	Wll
Priestley, James	96	Dav
John	378	Wil
John T.	1	Rob
Priestville, James	382	Wil
Prim, Abraham	381	Wil
Elizabeth	20	Jac
James	399	Wil
William	399	Wil
Primm, Abraham	84	Rut
Green	22	Wll
Jeremiah W.	22	Wll
Jno. T.	16	Hic
John W.	23	Wll
Primrose, Thomas	35	Bed
Prince, George	18	Lin
Gilbert	11	Law
John	23	Fra
John	42	Smi
Nathaniel	136	Sum
Peter	42	Smi
William	10	Hum
Printice, R. J.	21	Jac
Prior, Allen	95	Rut
Elijah	171	Sum
Jane	20	Jac
Jeremiah	20	Jac
John	43	Lin
Joseph	20	Jac
Pritchard, Benjamin [2]	93	Dav
Benjamin	416	Wil
James	93	Dav
Joseph	72	Dav
Pritchet, David	30	Mon

Pritchet (cont.)		
Enoch	60	Dav
Nathaniel	411	Wil
Thomas	50	Mau
Thomas	8	Ove
Thomas	27	Wll
Thomas J.	17	Wll
Pritchett, David	416	Wil
Edward	416	Wil
Ephraim	79	Dav
Esther	420	Wil
George	410	Wil
John	37	Wll
Prithie, William	74	Dav
Probins, Alexander	404	Wil
Prock, James	170	Sum
Procter, Henry	21	Jac
John	21	Jac
Mary	2	Wll
Samuel	58	Mau
Proctor, Absalom	39	Smi
Benjamin	44	Lin
John	7	Rob
Johnathan	67	Dav
Thomas	15	Rob
William	172	Sum
Proctter, Thomas, Jr.	389	Wil
Procttor, Edward	400	Wil
Procttors, Thomas	389	Wil
Prosser, James	17	Lin
Prowel, Thomas	50	Wll
Prowell, Sampson	96	Dav
Prowty, John W.	29	Lin
Prue, David	83	Rut
Pruet, Danl.	115	Ste
Silas	171	Sum
Pruett, David	5	Hum
John	89	Rut
Martin, Mr.	1	Law
Pruette, Calvin	41	Smi
Joseph	39	Smi
Joshua	39	Smi
Pryer, John	368	Whi
Mary	112	Ste
Thompson	7	Law
John C.	23	Fra
Luke	24	Wll
Nicholas	76	Dav
William	7	Ove
William	352	Whi
Zachariah	69	Dav
Puckeatt, Eligah	30	Mau
Pucket, Acey	62	Mau
Ann	63	Mau
Douglas	89	Dav
Edward	48	Mau
Jarred C.	33	Bed
John	96	Dav
John	369	Whi
Josiah	12	Mon
Nathaniel	63	Mau
Sheppia	394	Wil
Puckett, Arthur	83	Rut
Puckett (cont.)		
Charles	96	Rut
Elam	83	Rut
F.	418	Wil
Francis	419	Wil
Icum	419	Wil
Jacob	8	Dic
James	17	Hic
Leonard	83	Rut
Lodwick	98	Rut
Luke	83	Rut
Thomas	417	Wil
William	416	Wil
William	417	Wil
Pue, —	24	Mau
James	34	Mau
Puffer, Samuel	65	Mau
Pugh, Archbald	33	Mau
Eliza.	73	Dav
Henry	113	Ste
James	48	Wll
Jesse	44	Lin
Martin	43	Lin
Spencer A.	1	Lin
William, Jur.	44	Lin
William, Ser.	44	Lin
Pulear, Elisha	28	Mau
Pullen, Jesse	11	Gil
Moses	19	Gil
Thomas	99	Rut
William	11	Gil
see Pulear		
Pulley, Fredrick	25	Mon
Mary	28	Bed
Pulliam, James	7	Lin
Washington	57	Dav
William	21	Lin
Pullin, Archibald	9	Dic
Pully, David	23	Lin
David	14	Way
Isham	23	Fra
James	39	Smi
Thomas	29	Lin
Pulman, Jahu	418	Wil
Pulse, Nancy	14	Bed
Pumroy, William	11	Wll
Purdam, Elijah	309	War
Samuel	23	Fra
Purdans, John	292	War
Purdie, Seth	23	Fra
Purdy, Robert, General	73	Rut
Purkins, Eben	8	Dic
Edward	8	Dic
Jacob	8	Dic
Prissey	129	Ste
Purnell, Lemuel	39	Smi
William	6	Gil
Pursel, Hardy	20	Jac
James	20	Jac
James	59	Mau
Pursell, Thomas	16	Rob
Pursley, James	56	Wll
Jane	384	Wil

Purtle, George	389	Wil
John	102	Rut
N.	124	Ste
Samuel	38	Lin
William	98	Rut
Purvatt, John	171	Sum
Purvis, Allen	171	Sum
Charles	115	Ste
Cullin	172	Sum
Isaac	13	Gil
Purvyance, Eleazer	9	Gil
Pury see Peery		
Puryear, Daniel	11	Gil
Matildy	36	Wll
Pusley, David	40	Smi
Ephraim	40	Smi
James	40	Smi
Putman, Daniel	60	Wll
Jaben	60	Wll
John	3	Lin
Putts, John	17	Ove
Pyburn, Christopher	15	Way
William	17	Way
Pye, John	24	Fra
Pyland, Robert	419	Wil
Pyle, John	136	Sum
Pyles, Isaac	40	Smi
Pyran, Joshua	40	Smi

--- Q ---

Quales, Elizabeth	376	Wil
Qualls, Abner	15	Rob
Moses	4	Hum
Richard	31	Rob
Quantry, Abraham	24	Fra
Quarles, Ann	16	Ove
Benjamin	24	Fra
Jeremiah	24	Fra
John	13	Ove
Mary	407	Wil
Randal	46	Lin
William	16	Ove
William	307	War
Wm. T.	390	Wil
Quarlis, John	47	Lin
Quarls, William	79	Dav
Quary, William	43	Smi
Queen, Jehu	24	Fra
Querley, Owen	393	Wil
Quigley, John	2	Wll
Quigly, John	300	War
Quill, Bird	386	Wil
Josiah	386	Wil
Quillen, William	7	Law
Quillin, James	24	Fra
Quilton, John	24	Fra
Quimbey, Robert	107	She
Quimby, Burrel, Mr.	3	Law
Quinn, Amos	18	Gil
Enoch	23	Wll
Quinn (cont.)		
Matthew H.	77	Dav
Sarah	23	Wll
William	18	Gil
Quinton, Caleb	121	Ste
Quisenberry, James	384	Wil
John	419	Wil
see Qusomberry		
Quistenberry, Wm. M.	24	Fra
Qusomberry, Henrey	90	Dav

--- R ---

Rabourn, Joseph	8	Lin
Sylvaner	4	Ove
Raburn, James	19	Ove
John	118	Ste
Raby, James	13	Wll
Rachley, James	104	Rut
Rackley, Allen	25	Fra
Fredrick	14	Law
Joshua	45	Smi
Micajah	370	Whi
Silas, Mr.	6	Law
Rackly, Fredrick	18	Way
Shadrack	14	Law
Raddison, William	14	Bed
Radford, Ann	20	Mon
Henry	34	Bed
John	45	Mau
William	63	Wll
Radiken, James	43	Wll
Raebourn, John	4	Ove
Thomas	4	Ove
see Rabourn		
Raffety, William	45	Smi
Ragan, James	22	Gil
Jesse	6	Dic
Nathan	4	Dic
Nathan	10	Hic
Peter	398	Wil
Thomas	70	Dav
William	14	Dic
Ragen, Robert	21	Bed
see Roger, Rozen		
Ragin, James	44	Smi
Lewis	3	Hum
Ragins, Caty	20	Wll
Ragland, Daniel	47	Smi
Jacob	21	Jac
James	26	Fra
John [2]	26	Fra
Otey T.	47	Smi
Reuben	47	Smi
Reubin	355	Whi
Ursula D.	44	Smi
William	47	Smi
Ragsdale, Abel	46	Wll
Abner	10	Wll
Baxter	25	Bed
Benjamin	49	Wll

Ragsdale (cont.)
Claborn J. 18 Bed
Clement 14 Hic
Daniel 49 Wll
Danl. 420 Wil
Edward 18 Bed
Edward 33 Wll
Edward 43 Wll
Elnathan 3 Hic
Henry 33 Wll
Jessee 342 Whi
Joel 5 Rob
John 18 Hic
John 89 Rut
John 99 Rut
John 45 Wll
Lancaster 50 Wll
Nancy 43 Wll
Obadiah 5 Har
Prissilla 419 Wil
Richard 102 Rut
Robert 45 Wll
Samuel 3 Lin
William 10 Rob
William 18 Rob
Wm. 13 Hic
Wm. 18 Hic
Rail, Ritchard 28 Mau
Railsback, Thos. F. 17 Mon
Raily, Samuel 89 Dav
Raimey, Allen 61 Mau
Raimy, Benjamin 22 Lin
John 22 Lin
Raines, Bailey 26 Fra
Henry 311 War
James 284 War
John 284 War
John 297 War
John 303 War
John 317 War
John A. 297 War
Reuben 131 Ste
William 300 War
William 317 War
Rainey, David 31 Mau
David 129 Ste
Elizabeth 136 Sum
Henry G. 5 Gil
Isaac 58 Mau
John 40 Bed
John 55 Wll
Silas 81 Dav
William 78 Rut
Rains, Asahe 284 War
James 66 Mau
John 84 Dav
John, Jr. 90 Dav
Ursula 84 Dav
William M. 25 Fra
Rainwater, R. 129 Ste
William 29 Mon
Rainwaters, Nancy 29 Mon
Raiss, John 113 Wil
Rakins, Samuel 59 Mau
Ralliff, Jesse 7 Hic
Saml. 6 Hic
Thos. H. 21 Mon
Ralph, Alexander 44 Smi
Andreson 46 Smi
John 174 Sum
Lewis 45 Smi
Lewis 174 Sum
Thomas 101 Rut
Thomas 45 Smi
William 46 Smi
Ralston, William 28 Bed
Rambaut, Swann 11 Gil
Ramer, Henry 173 Sum
Philip 13 Hum
Ramey, Elijah 14 Mon
Randolph 1 Mon
see Ramsy
Ramly, Leven 125 Ste
Ramor, Henry 89 Dav
Ramsay, James 25 Fra
Richard 4 Gil
William 21 Gil
Ramsey, Daniel 21 Jac
Daniel 3 Lin
Elijah 22 Jac
George 352 Whi
James 29 Lin
James 41 Mau
James 43 Mau
James 104 Rut
James 366 Whi
James 414 Wil
Jane 304 War
Jerimiah 33 Mau
John 41 Mau
John 16 Ove
John 87 Rut
John 7 Way
John 352 Whi
John 414 Wil
John B. 104 Rut
Joshua 8 Way
Newett 392 Wil
Oby 104 Rut
Randolph 353 Whi
Randolph 366 Whi
Richard 93 Rut
Robbert [2] 41 Mau
Robert 16 Lin
Robert 86 Rut
Robert H. 39 Mau
Stephen 50 Wll
Thomas 42 Mau
Thomas K. 401 Wil
William 66 Dav
William 78 Rut
William 104 Rut
William 304 War
William G. 40 Mau
Wm. 4 Lin
Ramsour, Micheal 7 Ove

Ramsy, John	16	Ove
Richmond B.	401	Wil
Samuel	5	Lin
Samuel	29	Lin
Ran, Thomas	400	Wil
Randal, Joel	46	Smi
John	7	Gil
Thomas	7	Gil
Randall, James	29	Mau
Randle, Ann	115	Ste
George D.	116	Ste
James R.	120	Ste
John	111	Ste
John	116	Ste
John	122	Ste
Wilson	117	Ste
Wm.	116	Ste
Randolph, Chisum	352	Whi
Cloey	50	Wll
Elisha	287	War
George	18	Rob
Henry	282	War
Isham	278	War
James	3	Lin
John	60	Mau
John	287	War
Mary	81	Rut
Nathan	278	War
Pleasent	352	Whi
Robert	2	Rob
Robert	303	War
Thomas	353	Whi
Wm.	2	Rob
Raney, David	22	Gil
James	11	Gil
Johnson	39	Bed
Simon	25	Fra
Zebulun	9	Gil
Rankhorn, Joseph	310	War
Rankin, Catharine	81	Rut
James, Jr.	173	Sum
James, Sr.	175	Sum
John	44	Smi
Mary	7	Hic
Moses	7	Hic
Robert	11	Gil
Robert	28	Lin
Robert	92	Rut
Samuel	78	Rut
Samuel	99	Rut
Rankins, David	54	Mau
David	104	Rut
James	21	Jac
James	61	Mau
Robbert	59	Mau
Rannums, Oran	389	Wil
Ranolds, Thomas	52	Mau
Ransom, Benjamin	80	Rut
John	91	Rut
Joseph	25	Fra
Richard	86	Rut
Rany, Buckner	5	Gil
Rape, Gustavus	96	Dav
Rape (cont.)		
Hery	95	Dav
Rarden, Samuel	64	Mau
Rasberry, Jesse	127	Ste
John	124	Ste
John	130	Ste
Rasbury, William	91	Dav
Rawe, William	44	Smi
Raser, John [deleted]	119	Ste
Rash, John	21	Jac
William	21	Jac
Raspberry, Loveick	1	Way
Raspbery, George	62	Dav
Rassen, Joseph	25	Fra
Rassin, Joseph	2	Bed
Rather, James	404	Wil
Ratliff, Wm.	18	Hic
Ratlith, Aaron	101	Rut
William	101	Rut
Ratree, James	118	Ste
Raw, Philip	11	Bed
Rawland, Elijah	8	Rob
William	23	Bed
Rawles, John	44	Smi
Rawley, Daniel	43	Smi
Rawling, Augustus	49	Bed
Rawlings, Benja.	174	Sum
James	45	Smi
Sarah	165	Sum
Rawlins, Benjamin	25	Fra
Rawls, Benjamin	10	Rob
James	9	Rob
James	129	Ste
Luke	12	Rob
Raworth, Edward	62	Dav
Rawrance, Jacob	44	Mau
Rawson, Charles	10	Gil
Elizabeth	9	Gil
John	23	Gil
Simeon	32	Lin
Rawton, William	98	Rut
Ray, Aba	380	Wil
Acre	414	Wil
Alexanden	29	Wll
Andrew	378	Wil
Andrew	414	Wil
David	311	War
Eleanor	19	Mon
Elizabeth	71	Dav
George	21	Jac
Ginnett	22	Jac
Hicks J.	21	Way
James	12	Bed
James	41	Bed
James	21	Jac
Jesse	408	Wil
John	34	Bed
John	43	Bed
John	2	Law
John	372	Whi
John	380	Wil
John	414	Wil
Joseph	380	Wil

Ray (cont.)
Joseph, Jr. 21 Jac
Joseph, Sr. 21 Jac
Mathias 40 Mau
Milroy 35 Mau
Pleasant 175 Sum
Reuben 13 Gil
Rolston 22 Jac
Sally 5 Bed
Seabord 369 Whi
Solomon 387 Wil
Thomas 311 War
Thomas 380 Wil
Thomas 387 Wil
William 15 Bed
William 33 Bed
William 68 Dav
William 71 Dav
William 22 Jac
William 77 Rut
William 416 Wil
William P. 368 Whi
Willis 380 Wil
see Rhay
Raybon, John 11 Hum
Raybourn see Raebourn
Rayburn, Henry 1 Way
John 1 Way
John 6 Way
Rayburne, James 79 Rut
Rayl, William 17 Gil
Rayley, John 26 Fra
Raynes, Abel 116 Ste
Hugh 116 Ste
Hugh 130 Ste
Raynier, Geoge 87 Dav
Raynolds, Nicholas 10 Law
Raysey, Sally 129 Ste
Rea, Alexander 60 Dav
J. C. 77 Dav
Joseph 15 Gil
Margaret 15 Gil
Samuel 41 Wil
Tabitha 71 Dav
Thomas 15 Gil
William 65 Dav
Reach, Charles 11 Hic
Read, Burel 42 Lin
Daniel 35 Lin
David 21 Lin
David 84 Rut
David 90 Rut
David 103 Rut
Eleonor 174 Sum
Elijah 61 Dav
Elisha 16 Mon
Fanney 76 Dav
Gardiner 284 War
George 4 Har
George 42 Lin
George B. 45 Lin
Henry 3 Per
Hugh 51 Mau
Read (cont.)
Hugh 101 Rut
Isiah 51 Mau
James 49 Mau
James 18 Rob
John 15 Dic
John 31 Mon
John 86 Rut
John H. 80 Rut
John Nash 91 Rut
Jones 90 Dav
Joseph 12 Gil
Joseph 3 Per
Lemuel 85 Rut
Mary 90 Rut
Moses 42 Lin
Nancy 98 Dav
Nancy 174 Sum
Nathaniel 36 Lin
Peter 91 Rut
Robbert 51 Mau
Samuel 12 Gil
Samuel 35 Lin
Samuel 51 Mau
Silas 98 Rut
Sion 82 Rut
Thomas, Senr. 5 Gil
Thos. J. 78 Dav
William 18 Rob
William 173 Sum
see Road
Reader, Benjamin 410 Wil
Edwin 410 Wil
Robert 5 Ove
Reading, Iredell 85 Dav
Ready, Charles 89 Rut
Leonard 73 Dav
Robert 89 Dav
Reagall, Absolem 2 Per
Reagan, Charles 14 Ove
Henery 38 Mau
Henry 5 Ove
Joel 17 Ove
John 9 Ove
Nehemiah 22 Jac
Peter 14 Ove
Peter 15 Ove
Real, James 15 Ove
Reames, Henry 37 Wil
Joshua 37 Wil
Reams, John 37 Wil
Martha 37 Wil
Rease, James H. [deleted] 26 Mau
Reasonover, Joseph, Jr. 46 Smi
Joseph, Sr. 46 Smi
Reasons, James 16 Mon
John 16 Mon
William 6 Mon
Reatherford, James 40 Lin
Reaves, Abner 174 Sum
Benjn. 46 Bed
Daniel 92 Dav
David 11 Bed

Reaves (cont.)		
David	92	Dav
David	17	Lin
Drury	1	Hum
Edmond	90	Dav
Edmund	173	Sum
Elijah	92	Dav
Elisha	92	Dav
Elizabeth	6	Hum
George	72	Dav
George, Jr.	9	Hum
George, Sr.	9	Hum
James	63	Mau
James	6	Mon
James	8	Way
John	84	Rut
John	175	Sum
John H.	310	War
Jordan, Senr.	12	Hum
Malkiah	19	Lin
Osbourn	67	Dav
Peter	2	Way
Robert	66	Dav
Samuel	45	Lin
Solomon	12	Lin
Thomas	3	Way
Timothy	10	Hum
William	72	Dav
William	1	Hum
William	41	Lin
Reavs, Eligah	49	Mau
Hanah	49	Mau
Reay, Hugh	22	Wll
James	22	Wll
Recard, John	45	Mau
Shered	45	Mau
Sion	50	Mau
see Rechord		
Rechord, Mary	45	Mau
Reckman, William	5	Law
Red, Jonathan	27	Fra
see Reed		
Redd, John	37	Mau
Moses	13	Gil
Reddick, John	174	Sum
Reddin, Saml.	13	Hic
Stephen	14	Gil
Redding, Alfred	8	Rob
Alv...ia	43	Mau
Edmund	299	War
Francis	292	War
Hardy	292	War
Nathan	393	Wil
see Redin		
Redditt, Aquilla	173	Sum
Reddock, Reading	24	Lin
Redds, Richard	59	Mau
Redferrin, Elisha	10	Rob
Isaac	22	Rob
John [2]	22	Rob
Redick, Nancy	113	Ste
Redin, Armsted	42	Mau
Henrey [N. Henrey?]	38	Mau
Reding, Augustin	11	Rob
Redit, David	125	Ste
Redith, K.	130	Ste
Reditt, David	122	Ste
Redley, Henry	100	Rut
Samuel J.	85	Dav
Redman, George	12	Wll
Harman	318	War
Soloman	318	War
William	38	Mau
Redmon, Edmund	27	Fra
Redmond, Arthur	60	Dav
Francis	15	Ove
William	46	Smi
Reece, Alsey	381	Wil
John	88	Dav
John	45	Smi
Josiah	18	Hic
Murphey	382	Wil
Thomas B.	408	Wil
William	408	Wil
Yarnel	1	Law
Reed, Adam	12	Ove
Andrew	44	Bed
Andrew	19	Wll
Byrd	43	Smi
David	27	Fra
David C.	43	Smi
Edward	287	War
Elizabeth	4	Way
George C.	49	Bed
Henry	97	Rut
Henry	44	Smi
Henry	397	Wil
Isaac	26	Fra
James	22	Jac
James	46	Smi
James	126	Ste
James	131	Ste
James	173	Sum
James	293	War
James	387	Wil
James	38	Wll
James	41	Wll
James	52	Wll
James, Jr.	41	Wll
Jane	414	Wil
Jesse	9	Ove
Jesse	97	Rut
John	83	Rut
John	44	Smi
John	19	Wll
John C.	387	Wil
Joseph B.	79	Rut
Josiah	59	Wll
Levina	20	Wll
Reuben	287	War
Robert	44	Bed
Robert	58	Wll
Thomas [2]	44	Smi
Thomas	131	Ste
William	27	Bed
William	130	Ste

Reed (cont.)		
William	5	Way
William	396	Wil
William	20	Wll
William B.	14	Way
see Red		
Reeder, Jacob	96	Dav
Reedey, Isaac	28	Mau
Reef, Henry	379	Wil
Reel, Edward	15	Lin
Rees, Charles	15	Lin
John	23	Lin
Jordon	26	Lin
Patrick	36	Wll
Sinah	64	Wll
William	39	Lin
Reese, Asahel W.	136	Sum
Isham	91	Rut
James	124	Ste
James H.	28	Mau
Jeremiah	46	Smi
Jowel	28	Mau
Soleman	37	Mau
Reeser see Raser		
Reeves, Abner	25	Fra
Avery	25	Fra
Edward	25	Fra
George	5	Per
James	15	Hic
Jeremiah	414	Wil
John	5	Per
John	7	Per
John	46	Smi
Jonathan	13	Hic
Malden	25	Fra
Reuben	12	Hic
William	73	Dav
William	18	Hic
William	44	Smi
Reevs, John	100	Rut
see Rews		
Regney, Griffeny	11	Ove
Joab	15	Ove
Regon, Patrick	174	Sum
Reguin, Joel	36	Wll
Rehmond, Levi	173	Sum
Reid, David	3	Gil
Robert	12	Gil
Reif, John	284	War
Reiley, Robert	11	Lin
William	41	Lin
Reily, John	13	Lin
Relingson, Andrew	297	War
Reman, Samuel	19	Ove
Ren, George	30	Mau
Thomas	30	Mau
William	30	Mau
Renegar, George	23	Lin
Henry	29	Lin
Renfrew, John	40	Mau
Renfro, Bartlett	22	Lin
Isaac	56	Mau
Renfrow, Jessey	56	Mau
Renfrow (cont.)		
Moses	54	Mau
William [2]	42	Mau
Reno, Jacob	21	Jac
Johnathan	21	Jac
Renolds, Nancy	14	Ove
Renphro, Peter	16	Way
Renshaw, Esther	89	Rut
Hannah	320	War
John	83	Rut
Rentfro, Elizabeth	22	Hic
John	46	Mau
Samuel	5	Har
Rentfroo, Stephen	5	Har
Rentfrow, William	308	War
Repding, Elisha	39	Mau
Reves, Hambleton	370	Whi
Revis, Allin	27	Fra
William	48	Bed
see Lewis		
Rews, James	92	Rut
Rewton, William D.	87	Rut
Reymon, G. W.	22	Jac
Reynol, Acquilla	69	Dav
Reynolds, Alexander	107	She
Asa B.	174	Sum
Eli	26	Fra
Elijah [2]	25	Fra
Elijah	26	Fra
Elisha	290	War
Ezekiel	21	Bed
Gay	46	Smi
George	73	Dav
Glover	363	Whi
Hamilton	11	Law
Henry	25	Fra
Henry	2	Har
Hosea	26	Fra
Hugh	12	Gil
Isaac	11	Gil
Isaac, Senr.	9	Gil
Jacob, Sen.	27	Fra
James	26	Fra
James	45	Smi
James	112	Ste
James	348	Whi
James B.	5	Mon
Jane	27	Bed
Jesse	26	Fra
John	14	Dic
John	25	Fra
John	11	Har
John	77	Rut
John	46	Smi
Joseph	3	Hum
Joseph	10	Law
Joseph	127	Ste
Josiah	46	Smi
Mark	5	Dic
Michael	174	Sum
Moses	25	Fra
Nancey	107	She
Nancy	6	Har

Reynolds (cont.)
Peggy 307 War
Reuben 44 Wll
Richard 19 Lin
Richard 32 Wll
Richard C. 57 Wll
Samuel 26 Fra
Spencer 58 Wll
Thomas 26 Fra
Thomas 46 Wll
William 8 Hum
William 1 Law
see Ranolds, Renolds, Reyolds, Ruynolds
Rha, Jacob 297 War
Rhay, John 7 Gil
Rhea, Abner 6 Gil
James 45 Smi
John 6 Gil
John 28 Lin
John 35 Mau
John 46 Smi
John 393 Wil
Joseph 19 Lin
Lewis 289 War
Lydia 44 Smi
Robert 45 Smi
Thomas 302 War
William 15 Gil
William 35 Mau
see Rha
Rhemes, Bowling 100 Rut
Rhine, Elias 45 Smi
John 45 Smi
Rhineheart, John 21 Jac
Rhiner, Robert 10 Lin
Rhoades, Abner 47 Smi
Rhoades, Moses 47 Smi
Rhoads, Ephraim 26 Fra
George 26 Fra
Isaac 20 Wll
Israel 26 Fra
John 26 Fra
McCormus 26 Fra
Saml. 7 Mon
Rhoan, Hugh 403 Wil
Rhode, Henry 173 Sum
Rhodes, Abner 62 Dav
Elisha 54 Wll
Hezekiah 419 Wil
James 6 Bed
James 63 Dav
James 21 Hic
Jesse 92 Rut
John 20 Lin
John 173 Sum
Thomas 388 Wil
William 22 Hic
Rhymer, Alexander 26 Fra
Rhyneman, Ferdinand 173 Sum
Riadon, George 173 Sum
Rial, James 44 Smi
Rialy, Moses 90 Rut
Rice, Benjamin 392 Wil
Charity 36 Mau
Colman 24 Wll
David 395 Wil
Ebnezer, Jr. 27 Mau
Eliezar 41 Mau
Francis 64 Wll
Gabriel 25 Fra
George 27 Fra
Henry 394 Wil
Jacob 279 War
James 22 Rob
Jawel 41 Mau
Joel C. 1 Mon
John 11 Hic
John 393 Wil
John, Jr. 392 Wil
John, Senr. 392 Wil
John M. 173 Sum
Joshua 173 Sum
Kenagah 174 Sum
Larken 27 Fra
Nancy 27 Fra
Nancy 174 Sum
Nathaniel 394 Wil
Nathl. 173 Sum
Richard 11 Gil
Theoderick B. 350 Whi
Thomas 394 Wil
William 4 Hum
William 22 Rob
William 174 Sum
William 362 Whi
William 383 Wil
William 386 Wil
William 394 Wil
William 24 Wll
see John, Rise, Rue
Rich, Catharine 15 Ove
Jacob 24 Fra
Jacob 11 Ove
Jesse 4 Ove
John 22 Jac
John 12 Ove
John 349 Whi
Joseph 24 Fra
Nimrod 44 Smi
Thomas 11 Ove
William 12 Ove
William, Sr. 22 Jac
Richard, Alexander 31 Mau
see Rechord
Richards, Ambros R. 19 Hic
Bilby 45 Smi
Daniel 357 Whi
Edmond 27 Rob
Edward 27 Rob
Hiram 66 Mau
Isaac 21 Jac
Isaac 22 Jac
James 79 Rut
James 416 Wil
John 21 Gil

Richards (cont.)		
John	6	Hic
John	91	Rut
John	124	Ste
Jonathan	14	Gil
Josiah	74	Dav
Richard	104	Rut
William	46	Smi
Wm.	15	Hic
Richardson, Alex.	78	Dav
Amos	15	Ove
Austin	7	Dic
Bernard	6	Wll
Booker	63	Dav
Conrad	56	Wll
Daniel	53	Wll
Edward	44	Smi
Eligah	47	Mau
Giles	26	Fra
Giles, Jun.	26	Fra
Harry	63	Dav
Henry	385	Wil
Hopkins	45	Smi
Isham	6	Mon
James	72	Dav
James	26	Fra
James	31	Mon
James	80	Rut
James B.	44	Smi
Jesse	19	Lin
John	62	Dav
John	24	Lin
John	6	Ove
John	21	Rob
John H.	15	Ove
Joseph	314	War
Joseph	387	Wil
Kenedy	62	Dav
Lebeus	12	Dic
Martin	36	Wll
Mary	104	Rut
May	21	Gil
Milly	405	Wil
Montilion	4	Lin
Robert	32	Mon
Robert	15	Ove
Samuel	2	Dic
Samuel	80	Rut
Thomas	35	Lin
Thomas	43	Smi
Walthal D.	15	Wll
Wellea [?]	6	Hic
William	17	Lin
William	47	Lin
William	6	Ove
William	100	Rut
William	416	Wil
William B.	7	Gil
Willie	44	Smi
Willis	378	Wil
Winnefred	3	Dic
Wm.	5	Hic
see Rihardson		
Richason, Saml.	174	Sum
Riche, David	21	Jac
Richerson, Amons	40	Mau
Eaney	62	Mau
Elizebeth	41	Mau
Isiah	63	Mau
Jane	42	Mau
Wiley	41	Mau
William	40	Mau
Richey, Robert	174	Sum
Richison, Benj.	22	Jac
Benj., Jr.	22	Jac
John	22	Jac
Richman, John	21	Jac
Robert	22	Jac
Richmon, Abner	346	Whi
Alexander	392	Wil
James	114	Wil
James	395	Wil
Susannah	396	Wil
Richmond, Barton	76	Dav
Isaac	25	Fra
James	368	Whi
Joel	3	Har
John	368	Whi
Mary	1	Har
see Rehmond		
Rickets, Anthony	342	Whi
Jane	24	Lin
William	35	Mau
Rickett, Robert	278	War
Ricketts, James	7	Per
Thomas	43	Wll
Ricklin, Barbary	35	Lin
Rickman, David	173	Sum
Francis	175	Sum
John	3	Bed
Mary	175	Sum
Paley A.	53	Mau
Robert	173	Sum
see Ricknan		
Rickmon, John	361	Whi
Joshua	11	Gil
Peter	361	Whi
William	359	Whi
Ricknan, Tho.	173	Sum
Riddel, Mary	27	Lin
Riddels, John W.	367	Whi
Thomas	344	Whi
Riddle, Alexander	25	Fra
Benjamin	25	Fra
Charles	6	Har
Elisha	2	Gil
Harmon	25	Fra
John	25	Fra
John	13	Gil
John M.	106	She
Nancy	305	War
Nathaniel	12	Hum
Polley	8	Gil
Randal	25	Fra
Stephen	25	Fra
Thomas, Junr.	2	Gil

Riddle (cont.)		
Thomas, Senr.	4	Gil
Rider, John	174	Sum
Ruben	380	Wil
Thomas	46	Smi
William	174	Sum
Ridge, Thomas	12	Hic
Thomas	6	Hum
Ridgen, William	69	Mau
Ridges, Raichel	69	Mau
see Ridgen		
Ridgeway, John	400	Wil
Ridgway, Elizabeth	88	Rut
James	94	Rut
James	99	Rut
Joseph	85	Rut
Richard	92	Rut
Samuel	98	Rut
Ridings, David	46	Smi
George	14	Hum
Joel	13	Hum
William	129	Ste
Ridley, Beverly	28	Wll
George	84	Dav
James	61	Dav
Orrain	406	Wil
Thomas	3	Wll
Vincent	37	Mau
Ridout, Gordon	95	Rut
Rieff, Joseph	173	Sum
Rieser, Jacob	66	Mau
Rieves, Jourden	2	Hum
Riey, Samuel	287	War
Rife, John	378	Wil
see Rye		
Riff, Henry	112	Wil
Rigan, John	18	Mon
Riggins, Thomas	25	Fra
Riggs, Albert	10	Rob
David	11	Bed
Edward	3	Bed
James	17	Mon
James	44	Smi
Jesse	13	Lin
Joel	3	Bed
John	7	Bed
Reuben	7	Gil
Rhoda	11	Ove
Samuel	61	Mau
Watson	280	War
William	7	Bed
William	7	Gil
Right, Absolum	384	Wil
Aquilla	384	Wil
Benjamin F.	382	Wil
Catherine	36	Mau
Charlotty	387	Wil
Francis	53	Mau
Francis	53	Wll
George	53	Wll
Isaac	377	Wil
Jacob	103	Rut
James	15	Ove

Right (cont.)		
James	32	Wll
Jesse	12	Ove
John	53	Mau
John	383	Wil
Nancy	44	Smi
Reuben, overseer	38	Wll
Robertson	396	Wil
Samuel	387	Wil
Thomas	384	Wil
Thomas	60	Wll
Rigins, John	47	Wll
Rigner, Thomas	361	Whi
Rigs, John	173	Sum
Rigsby, Canada	346	Whi
Daniel	46	Smi
Wright	43	Smi
Rihardson, Barnett	368	Whi
John	368	Whi
Martin	368	Whi
Riley, Armstrong	47	Wll
Edward	173	Sum
John	45	Wll
William	25	Fra
Rilie, William	22	Jac
Rily, John	12	Ove
William	12	Ove
Rimer, Alender	348	Whi
Rineheart, Eleanor	13	Mon
Jacob	13	Mon
John	14	Mon
Rines, John	38	Mau
Ring, Lewis	50	Mau
William	175	Sum
see King		
Ringold, James	27	Fra
Rink, David	306	War
Jacob	280	War
Rion, John	4	Ove
Ripito, John	21	Jac
Rippy, Edmund	173	Sum
James	45	Smi
James	174	Sum
Jessee	174	Sum
Rise, David	41	Mau
Robbin	42	Mau
see Rice		
Riseor, John	12	Gil
William	12	Gil
Risinghoover, Benjamin	318	War
Jacob	318	War
Riston, Bassel	22	Jac
Thomas	22	Jac
Ritch, Benjamin	280	War
Ritche, Polly	2	Ove
Ritcherson, Allen	40	Mau
John	40	Mau
Willis	40	Mau
Ritchie, Daniel	46	Smi
David	25	Fra
David	43	Smi
James	44	Smi
John	25	Fra

Ritter, Tho. 174 Sum
William 174 Sum
see Boykin
Rivers, Edmunds 25 Fra
Robert 9 Gil
Thomas 9 Gil
Thos. 18 Mon
Rizen, Ellery 44 Smi
George 44 Smi
Richard 44 Smi
Rlea, William 1 Har
Roach, Charles 317 War
Edward B. 79 Dav
Edward D. 74 Dav
Elsey 67 Dav
James 9 Mon
James 378 Wil
John 26 Fra
John 9 Mon
John 113 Wil
John [2] 393 Wil
Lemon 51 Wll
Needam 393 Wil
Samuel M. 8 Rob
Sasnett 67 Mau
Stephen 3 Har
Stephen 77 Rut
William 62 Dav
William 74 Dav
William 90 Dav
Roache, James 25 Lin
Lydia 13 Lin
Road, Sarah 80 Rut
see Read
Roades, William 3 Hum
Roads, Kinchean 70 Mau
Thomas W. 96 Rut
Roan, George 50 Mau
Henry 17 Bed
Roark, Asa 46 Smi
Barnet 25 Fra
James 44 Smi
John 45 Smi
John 46 Smi
Josiah 47 Smi
Levi 46 Smi
Mehael 342 Whi
Reuben 46 Smi
Samuel 44 Smi
William 26 Fra
William 46 Smi
Robans, Charles 127 Ste
John, Junr. 117 Ste
John, Senr. 117 Ste
Robb, Ann 67 Mau
James 136 Sum
John 399 Wil
Joseph 173 Sum
William 82 Rut
William 399 Wil
Robberson, Benjmin 33 Mau
James 70 Mau
John 32 Mau
Robberson (cont.)
M. 24 Mau
Moses 33 Mau
see Robbson
Robberts, John B. 55 Mau
Mc. 53 Mau
Poley 55 Mau
William 70 Mau
Robbertson, Edward 63 Mau
James 56 Mau
James S. 68 Mau
John 35 Mau
John 66 Mau
Samuel 70 Mau
William 63 Mau
Robbins, Charles 17 Way
Elizabeth 26 Fra
John 13 Hum
John, Jr. 13 Hum
Mat 26 Fra
Richd. 80 Dav
Samuel 26 Fra
Thomas 96 Rut
William 8 Hum
Robbson, Mathew 32 Mau
Robereson, Andy 393 Wil
Roberson, Charles 48 Wll
David 48 Wll
Edward 22 Jac
Edward 27 Wll
James 56 Wll
John 48 Wll
John 64 Wll
Joseph 41 Wll
Michael 48 Wll
Samuel 9 Hum
Thomas 55 Wll
Thomas L. 2 Wll
Roberts, Aron 9 Hum
Austin 30 Mon
Barton 356 Whi
Benjamin 26 Fra
Benjamin 63 Wll
Cyras 83 Dav
Edmond 21 Jac
Edwin 25 Fra
Eli 8 Hum
Elizabeth 16 Ove
Ephriam 7 Rob
Evans 12 Bed
Franky 344 Whi
George 6 Hum
George 173 Sum
George 420 Wil
Haward 9 Bed
Hosea 8 Hum
Hugh 3 Ove
Humphrey 20 Gil
Humphrey 371 Whi
Isaac 26 Fra
Isaac 281 War
Isaac 305 War
Isaac, Jun. 26 Fra

Roberts (cont.)			Robertson (cont.)		
James	21	Jac	Andrew	404	Wil
James	10	Ove	Asa	45	Smi
James	19	Ove	Augustine	46	Smi
James	299	War	Christopher	3	Dic
James	355	Whi	Christopher	32	Lin
Jeramiah	96	Dav	David	6	Dic
Jesse	22	Bed	David	25	Fra
Jesse	40	Bed	David	44	Smi
Jesse	83	Rut	David	131	Ste
Jesse	98	Rut	David, Sen.	44	Smi
John	11	Bed	Ducan	77	Dav
John	26	Fra	Eldridge B.	17	Gil
John	21	Jac	Elijah	62	Dav
John	46	Smi	Elisha	9	Hum
John	173	Sum	Elizabeth	46	Smi
John	34	Wll	Elizebeth	57	Mau
John	49	Wll	Fanny	46	Smi
John P.	19	Way	Felix	77	Dav
Joseph	342	Whi	Firey	56	Mau
Josiah	7	Per	George	10	Lin
Levi C.	52	Bed	George	14	Ove
Lydia	8	Hum	George	46	Smi
Mark	63	Wll	Henry	24	Rob
Mary	7	Per	Henry	43	Smi
Mary	84	Rut	Henry	405	Wil
Mary	361	Whi	Hezekiah	45	Smi
Moses	1	Way	Hiram	101	Rut
Nancy	83	Rut	Hutson	45	Smi
Nathen	25	Bed	Ira	14	Rob
Peter P.	31	Mon	Isaac	2	Ove
Philip	22	Bed	James	25	Fra
Pleasant	44	Smi	James	9	Gil
Rains	21	Jac	James	14	Gil
Reuben	291	War	James	44	Smi
Richardson	45	Smi	James	130	Ste
Robert	111	Wil	James	315	War
Robert B.	391	Wil	James	21	Way
Saml.	388	Wil	James	412	Wil
Samuel	26	Fra	Jane	68	Dav
Samuel	31	Mon	Jesse	24	Mon
Samuel, Jun.	26	Fra	John	49	Bed
Sarah	7	Ove	John	13	Dic
Sarah	21	Wll	John	25	Fra
Silas	21	Jac	John	16	Gil
Stephen	21	Jac	John	19	Gil
Stephen R.	173	Sum	John	41	Lin
Thomas	12	Hic	John	20	Rob
Thomas	22	Jac	John [2]	44	Smi
Thomas	81	Rut	John	45	Smi
Thomas	115	Ste	John	18	Way
Thomas	47	Wll	John	362	Whi
Watts	22	Jac	John F.	12	Lin
Wille	107	She	John J.	45	Smi
William [2]	26	Fra	Joseph	3	Rob
William	298	War	Joseph	45	Smi
William	299	War	Julius N.	25	Fra
William	308	War	Kiddy	62	Dav
William	367	Whi	Lodwick	31	Lin
Robertson, Abner	30	Lin	Mark	51	Mau
Abraham	4	Dic	Mark	13	Ove
Alexander	70	Mau	Mary [2]	409	Wil
Andrew	43	Smi	Mathew	30	Lin

Robertson (cont.)
Matthew 25 Fra
Matthew 26 Fra
McC. C. 73 Dav
Michael 18 Lin
Michael 30 Lin
Michael 2 Way
Micheal 2 Bed
Moses 46 Smi
Moses M. 28 Bed
Nathaniel [2] 26 Fra
Peggy 26 Fra
Peter 9 Gil
Randal 60 Dav
Richard, Jr. 30 Lin
Richard, Ser. 30 Lin
Robert 79 Rut
Robert A. 12 Bed
Samuel 42 Lin
Samuel 45 Smi
Samuel B. 45 Smi
Samuel N. 45 Smi
Sarah 9 Lin
Sayton 61 Dav
Stephen 45 Smi
Stephen 45 Smi
Susannah 73 Dav
Thomas 24 Bed
Thomas 43 Smi
Thos. 114 Ste
William 13 Dic
William 25 Fra
William 26 Fra
William 31 Lin
William 43 Smi
William 45 Smi
William B. 62 Dav
William G. 27 Fra
William H. 25 Fra
Winny 27 Rob
see Robereson, Shatton
Robeson, Chs. 175 Sum
David 174 Sum
Elijah 173 Sum
Elijah 174 Sum
Jessee 174 Sum
John 174 Sum
Mary 32 Mon
William 174 Sum
William S. 173 Sum
Robeston, Thomas 7 Per
Robins, Isaac 10 Ove
James 16 Ove
John G. 3 Mon
William 17 Mon
Robinson, Daniel 86 Rut
David 5 Har
David J. 82 Rut
David J. 96 Rut
Ezekiel 92 Rut
Hugh 83 Rut
Isaac 362 Whi
Isreal 26 Mon
Robinson (cont.)
Jacob 350 Whi
James G. 355 Whi
Jesse 21 Mon
John 6 Gil
John 6 Hic
John 102 Rut
John 370 Whi
Martha 12 Gil
Mary 94 Rut
Michael 26 Mau
Nigg 12 Gil
Richard 5 Har
Richard 86 Rut
Thomas 4 Har
Thomas 352 Whi
Thomas 357 Whi
William 81 Rut
William G. 98 Rut
William H. 99 Rut
Zacheriah 92 Rut
Robison, David 91 Rut
Futton 80 Rut
John M. 84 Dav
N. H. 90 Dav
Robonett, John 20 Way
Robson, Robert 14 Gil
Roceen, Lavinia 94 Rut
Rochell, James 43 Smi
Rockhold, Loyed 365 Whi
Roddin, Isaac 8 Hic
Rodds, James 32 Mau
Joseph 54 Mau
Newton 54 Mau
Thomas 32 Mau
Roddy, James 22 Jac
Philip 45 Smi
Rodee, Tyree 19 Gil
Roden, Ezekiel 22 Jac
George 22 Jac
Jeremiah [2] 22 Jac
Jesse 305 War
Natthaniel 22 Jac
Rodery, Benjmin 56 Mau
Rodes, Elisha 125 Ste
John 6 Ove
Rodgers, Armstead 173 Sum
Charles 55 Mau
David 46 Mau
Elijah 14 Ove
Evi 285 War
George 15 Hic
George 280 War
Green B. 58 Mau
Isaac 282 War
Jacob 55 Mau
James 52 Mau
James 282 War
Jesse 14 Hic
John 24 Hic
John 90 Rut
John 280 War
John 301 War

Rodgers (cont.)
John 363 Whi
Johnathan 21 Jac
Jonathan 349 Whi
Joseph 46 Mau
Joseph 363 Whi
Josiah 15 Hic
Josiah 282 War
Josiah 288 War
Matt, Sr. 22 Jac
Michael 12 Hic
Peelie 67 Dav
Ralph 21 Jac
Samuel J. 42 Mau
Tavener 314 War
Thomas 46 Mau
William 12 Hic
William 26 Mau
William 56 Mau
William 99 Rut
William 320 War
William 357 Whi
William, Mr. 5 Law
Williamson 26 Mau
Roe, Benjamin 43 Smi
John 44 Smi
Moses 10 Rob
Samuel 23 Lin
Roer, Absolem 2 Per
Roffmer see Romer
Rogen, John 21 Bed
see Ragen
Roger, Anthony 32 Bed
William 32 Bed
see Ragen
Rogers, Abram 30 Wll
Absalam 102 Rut
Absalum 80 Rut
Absolom 44 Lin
Alexander M. 30 Mon
Andrew 85 Rut
Archibald 113 Ste
Brinkley 395 Wil
Britain 174 Sum
Charles 44 Wll
Drewry 49 Bed
Eli 39 Bed
Elias 5 Dic
Euwett 10 Har
George 60 Dav
George 3 Law
Henry 39 Bed
Henry 390 Wil
Isaac 44 Lin
Isaac 365 Whi
James 13 Bed
James 5 Dic
James 25 Fra
James W. 5 Law
Jesse 27 Bed
Jesse 1 Hum
John 13 Bed
John 89 Dav
John 21 Rob

Rogers (cont.)
John 103 Rut
John 365 Whi
John H. 22 Lin
Jonathan 10 Hic
Jones 5 Dic
Jones 44 Lin
Joseph 14 Bed
Joseph 43 Bed
Joseph 6 Dic
Joseph 7 Gil
Joseph 44 Lin
Lemuel 174 Sum
Mary 363 Whi
Mathew 174 Sum
Matthew 25 Fra
Paul 89 Dav
Paul 8 Rob
Peter 389 Wil
Robert 23 Bed
Robert 103 Rut
Ruth 174 Sum
Saml. 174 Sum
Sarah 15 Mon
Sion 11 Hum
Spencer 21 Lin
Stephen 28 Bed
Tabitha 174 Sum
Thomas 409 Wil
William 32 Bed
William 96 Dav
William 29 Lin
William 365 Whi
William 398 Wil
Willie 53 Bed
Wm. 114 Ste
Roggers, Warren 38 Mau
Rogom, Anny 175 Sum
Rolack, Francis 8 Mon
Roland, Birch 6 Mon
David 45 Smi
George 43 Smi
Hugh 78 Dav
James 45 Smi
John 44 Smi
Jordan 74 Dav
Mary 38 Wll
Robert 45 Smi
Stephen 9 Law
Young W. 4 Dic
Roleman, Henry 25 Fra
John 25 Fra
Ruth 43 Smi
Rolin, William 22 Jac
Rollins, Elizabeth 4 Way
John 95 Rut
Rolls, Robert 130 Ste
Rolston, Alexander 56 Wll
David 94 Dav
James 10 Lin
Romer, Thomas 173 Sum
Roney, Benjamin 15 Rob
James, Jr. 173 Sum
James, Sr. 174 Sum

Roney (cont.)		
Phillip	77	Dav
Polly	45	Smi
Saml.	174	Sum
William	173	Sum
Rook, Aaron	299	War
Daniel	4	Mon
Jacob	54	Mau
John	4	Mon
John	32	Mon
Rooker, Caleb	62	Dav
Roon, Hugh	25	Wll
Roper, Charles	111	Ste
David Y.	25	Mau
Joseph	20	Lin
Tennesee	25	Mau
Thomas	13	Hic
William	70	Mau
William	20	Wll
Ropes, John Y.	43	Smi
Roplogle, Frederick	83	Rut
Rorax, David	28	Lin
Rosborough, Samuel	27	Fra
Roscoe, Alexr.	173	Sum
see Ruscoe		
Rose, Alexr.	10	Dic
Bazel	25	Rob
Benjamin [2]	15	Rob
David	22	Jac
Francis	17	Gil
Frederick	3	Way
James	20	Rob
John	22	Jac
John	14	Rob
John	353	Whi
Matthew	7	Rob
Reuben	4	Rob
Sally	128	Ste
Wilie	25	Mon
William	17	Gil
William	14	Way
Roseberry, Thos.	6	Way
Roseborough, James	42	Lin
Margaret	28	Lin
Rosel, Solomon	3	Per
Rosie, Ezekiah	109	Ste
Ross, Abijah	4	Lin
Adam	9	Law
Alexander	4	Hum
Allen	378	Wil
Andrew	47	Smi
Axum	114	Ste
Canny	113	Ste
Charles	112	Ste
Daniel	89	Dav
Ebenezer	19	Hic
Elizabeth	123	Ste
Ezekiel	174	Sum
Federick	129	Ste
Francis	14	Lin
George	10	Dic
George	10	Way
George	379	Wil
Ross (cont.)		
Harman	114	Ste
Henry	2	Law
Hugh	2	Hum
James	33	Bed
James	52	Mau
James	379	Wil
James F.	80	Rut
James M.	4	Dic
Jessey S.	64	Mau
Jno.	113	Ste
John	32	Bed
John	41	Bed
John	12	Gil
John	17	Gil
John	174	Sum
John	298	War
John	378	Wil
John M.	17	Way
Mary	8	Hic
Nathan	113	Ste
Nathaniel	341	Whi
Randolph	293	War
Reubin	6	Mon
Rewben	174	Sum
Robberson	52	Mau
Robert	25	Fra
Robert	7	Gil
Robert	97	Rut
Saml.	113	Ste
Samuel	46	Smi
Samuel	173	Sum
Theodorick	415	Wil
Thomas	46	Bed
Thomas	114	Ste
Vachel	16	Way
William	119	Ste
William B.	3	Way
Wm.	113	Ste
Wm.	126	Ste
Rosseau, Francis	27	Fra
Rossen, John	31	Rob
Joseph	8	Rob
Rossin, Sarah	13	Gil
Rosson, Henry B.	10	Lin
John	10	Lin
William	10	Lin
Rotton, William	356	Whi
Roulet, William	24	Rob
Roulston, Elizabeth	21	Jac
James	21	Jac
Matt	21	Jac
Roulstone, James G.	44	Smi
Roundtree, Polly	43	Smi
Rounsaville, Amos	28	Wll
Rouse, Edmund	77	Rut
John	90	Rut
Rousenbone, Matthias	62	Wll
Rousey, William	173	Sum
Routh, Wm.	393	Wil
Routon, James	297	War
Row, Adam	121	Ste
Ovil	15	Rob

Row (cont.)		
Rhoda	394	Wil
Rowan, John L.	10	Ove
Robert	3	Lin
Rowark, Charles	14	Mon
Rowdon, Jane	79	Rut
Rowe, Anderson	39	Mau
Benjamin	38	Lin
John	32	Lin
Joseph	10	Gil
Rowel, William	18	Lin
Rowen, Samuel	44	Lin
Rowland, Alexander	4	Hum
Charles	26	Fra
Findal	31	Rob
George	27	Fra
Jeremiah	15	Gil
John	175	Sum
Richardson	381	Wil
Robert	26	Fra
William	287	War
Rowler, Ahart	14	Gil
Rowlin, Benjamin	310	War
Rowlins, William	89	Rut
Rowls, Shadrach	9	Rob
Rowntree, Andrew	61	Mau
John	59	Mau
Joseph	59	Mau
Thomas	31	Lin
Rowsey, John	22	Gil
Rowten, Henry	12	Law
Rowton, Green B.	12	Way
John	99	Rut
Roy, Deago	26	Fra
Ephraim L.	13	Dic
John	21	Wll
Royal, John	43	Mau
John, Jr.	22	Jac
John, Sr.	22	Jac
Joseph	59	Mau
William	22	Jac
Royals, Samuel	16	Way
Royalty, Daniel	26	Fra
William	26	Fra
Royley, James	66	Mau
Rozel, Richard R.	43	Mau
Rozen, John	1	Bed
see Rogen		
Rucher, Jerry	85	Rut
Rucker, Benjamin	92	Rut
Benjamin A.	61	Wll
Bennett	83	Rut
Berry	84	Rut
Elliott	35	Bed
Felix	8	Lin
James	83	Rut
Jonathan	83	Rut
Nancy	86	Rut
Ransum	81	Rut
Samuel R.	73	Rut
Thomas [2]	82	Rut
Thomas, Jur.	98	Rut
William R.	73	Rut

Rucker (cont.)		
Williford	85	Rut
Rucks, James	44	Smi
Josiah	43	Smi
Rudd, Benjamin	25	Lin
James	8	Har
William	25	Lin
Rudder, Richard	62	Wll
Rudolph, Elijah	10	Hum
Fredrick	8	Mon
Jacob [2]	12	Mon
Jacob	13	Mon
John	7	Mon
John [2]	14	Mon
Peter	12	Mon
Rue, Lewis	18	Bed
Ruff, Godsend	14	Gil
Henry L.	4	Gil
John	14	Gil
Ruffin, John	22	Jac
Rufty, Mary	112	Ste
Rule, Aaron	412	Wil
Henry	174	Sum
John, Jr.	174	Sum
John, Sr.	174	Sum
Moses	174	Sum
Moses, Jr.	173	Sum
Peter	45	Smi
Rullen, Elisha, F. Creek	24	Mau
Rumbley, James	173	Sum
Ruminer, John	2	Hum
Rumley, Joseph	44	Smi
Stanley	44	Smi
William	174	Sum
Rumly, Thos.	116	Ste
Rummage, Jam	61	Mau
Susanah	61	Mau
Rumzey, Catharine	7	Bed
Runnals, Elizabeth	419	Wil
Runnels, Ile	414	Wil
Rupard, Peter	52	Wll
Ruscoe, James W.	36	Mau
Rush, James	21	Jac
Rushing, A.	128	Ste
Abel	127	Ste
Abraham	96	Rut
Burwel	2	Per
David	123	Ste
Dennes	127	Ste
Elizabeth	127	Ste
Hardy	127	Ste
Jacob	5	Dic
Jaoob	127	Ste
John	35	Bed
John	83	Rut
John P.	126	Ste
Joseph	14	Bed
M.	128	Ste
Mark	21	Hic
Matthew	127	Ste
Peter	48	Bed
Phillip	2	Per
Phillip	127	Ste

Rushing (cont.)		
Reuben	127	Ste
Richard	2	Per
Rowland	8	Hum
Sally	89	Rut
Thomas	48	Bed
Thomas	30	Rob
William	117	Ste
William	127	Ste
Rusk, Joel	126	Ste
Ruske, Gideon	97	Rut
Russel, Benjamin	56	Wll
David	5	Hic
Ealam	62	Wll
Elam	39	Wll
Elizabeth	92	Dav
Hannah	60	Dav
James	30	Wll
James R.	1	Way
Jane	91	Dav
Jas. H.	116	Ste
Jeremiah	57	Wll
John	42	Lin
John	12	Wll
Lewis	4	Per
Matthew	13	Bed
Patsey	12	Gil
Pleasent	4	Wll
Thomas, Jr.	92	Dav
Thomas, Sr.	92	Dav
William	91	Dav
William	308	War
William M.	12	Lin
Russell, Alex.	11	Har
Asa	46	Smi
Edmund	25	Fra
Elam	46	Smi
George	25	Fra
George, Jr.	25	Fra
Henry	46	Smi
Hiram	43	Smi
James	14	Gil
James	10	Ove
James	100	Rut
James	46	Smi
James	355	Whi
Jesse	7	Dic
John	25	Fra
John	26	Fra
John	28	Mon
John	46	Smi
John	368	Whi
John G.	15	Gil
Lemuel	11	Dic
Levi	26	Fra
Lewis	25	Fra
Mitchell	46	Smi
Robert	11	Har
Solomon A.	5	Ove
William	105	Rut
William	395	Wil
Russey, James, Jun.	26	Fra
James, Sen.	26	Fra
Russey (cont.)		
William	26	Fra
Russhin, Peter	48	Bed
Thomas	48	Bed
Russle, David	65	Mau
Richard	42	Mau
Russwanne, John S.	11	Wll
Rust, Beneded	289	War
Enoch	14	Lin
George	287	War
Jeremiah T.	43	Smi
John	43	Smi
Vincent	45	Smi
William	43	Mau
Rusten, Henry	48	Wll
Rutcherford, Archibald	44	Smi
Rutchledge, Thomas	50	Mau
Rutherford, Claiborne	25	Fra
Griffith	43	Smi
Henry	5	Wll
James	1	Hum
James	173	Sum
John	26	Fra
John	173	Sum
John	113	Wil
John	380	Wil
Robert	173	Sum
Thomas	90	Dav
Thomas, Jr.	19	Gil
Thomas, Senr.	19	Gil
William	90	Dav
see Reatherford, Rutcherford		
Rutledge, Allexander	21	Jac
Benjamin	21	Jac
David	90	Rut
Elijah	173	Sum
Elijah	388	Wil
George	97	Rut
Henry	351	Whi
Isaac	21	Jac
James	62	Mau
Joel	18	Gil
John	12	Dic
John	351	Whi
Margaret	43	Bed
Mary	84	Rut
Matilda	21	Jac
Nelly	21	Jac
Rutherford	376	Wil
William	21	Jac
William	33	Mau
William	84	Rut
see Rutchledge		
Rutlidge, Alexander	406	Wil
Henry M.	26	Fra
William	14	Bed
Rutling, Black	387	Wil
Ruynolds, Aaron	41	Mau
Benjmin	41	Mau
Margrett	43	Mau
Ryal, John	14	Lin
Noah	14	Lin
William	34	Lin

Ryan, Berry	30	Lin
James	20	Mon
Joseph	82	Rut
Reuben	82	Rut
Reuben	99	Rut
Ryburn, Matthw	9	Mon
Sarah	12	Ove
William	9	Mon
William	11	Mon
Rye, Benjamin	27	Mon
Henry	404	Wil
Joseph	4	Dic
Solomon	9	Dic
William	16	Dic
Ryherd, Jacob	174	Sum
Rymel, Jacob	21	Way
Ryon, John	5	Rob
John	174	Sum

--- S ---

Sabens, Thomas L.	12	Ove
Sack, John	92	Rut
Sackett, Phillip	7	Hic
Saddler, Thomas	47	Smi
Sadler, Fanny	24	Jac
Henry	23	Jac
James	23	Jac
Jeramiah	87	Dav
John	23	Jac
John	77	Rut
John G.	13	Wll
Thomas	24	Jac
William	23	Jac
William	178	Sum
William	415	Wil
Sadlers, Benja.	179	Sum
Safely, Jesse	280	War
Saffill, Amos	103	Rut
Sage, John	92	Rut
Sagely, John	88	Rut
Joseph	97	Rut
Sail, William	30	Rob
Sailar, Daniel	104	Rut
Sailers, Leonard	368	Whi
Thomas	366	Whi
Sailing, Daniel	34	Bed
Sailors, Michael	23	Jac
Saint, Benjamin	2	Per
Isham	2	Per
Saint John, Abner	317	War
St. John, William	7	Bed
St. Clair, Hugh	10	Law
Sal... see Sul...		
Sale, William	14	Ove
Salis, John	307	War
William	4	Hum
Sallenger, James	23	Mon
Salmon, James	24	Hic
James	5	Per
Salmons, John	28	Fra
Saltom, John	300	War
Salyers, James	7	Hum
Samford, John	10	Gil
Sammins, John	48	Mau
Sammons, John	86	Rut
Newet	11	Wll
Sample, Robert	91	Dav
Sampson, Betsey	48	Smi
Ephram	64	Wll
Francis	47	Smi
Mary	41	Wll
Mary H.	70	Dav
Sarah	64	Wll
Smith	48	Smi
Stephen	48	Smi
Samson, James	58	Dav
Samuel, Anthony	19	Gil
James	32	Rob
John	9	Gil
Stephen	9	Gil
Sandalin, Randal	51	Smi
Sanders, Aaron	28	Fra
Abram	42	Bed
Alfred M.	4	Hic
Andrew	12	Rob
Augustus B.	7	Hic
Benjn.	11	Hic
Britton	66	Mau
Daniel	12	Rob
David	28	Fra
David	29	Fra
Elihu	357	Whi
Elisha	24	Jac
Elisha	96	Rut
Elisha	100	Rut
Eliza	7	Mon
Ethelbert W.	136	Sum
Francis	74	Dav
Francis	51	Smi
Gabreal	87	Dav
George	35	Bed
George	22	Jac
Hubbard	177	Sum
Isaa	94	Rut
Isaac	51	Smi
Isaac, Jur.	94	Rut
Jacob	28	Fra
Jacob	113	Ste
James	95	Dav
James	29	Fra
James	23	Gil
James	13	Lin
James	42	Lin
James	13	Rob
James	52	Smi
James [2]	176	Sum
James	177	Sum
James	350	Whi
James	420	Wil
James, Ser.	43	Lin
Jesse	28	Fra
John [2]	27	Bed
John	27	Fra

Sanders (cont.)		
John	29	Fra
John	43	Lin
John	47	Mau
John	63	Mau
John	24	Rob
John	30	Rob
John	51	Smi
John	420	Wil
John S.	48	Smi
Jordon M.	136	Sum
Joseph	37	Bed
Joseph	38	Mau
Joseph	50	Smi
Julus	420	Wil
Lafayette	136	Sum
Lockey	178	Sum
Moses	43	Lin
Moses	51	Smi
Nathl.	175	Sum
Obediah	47	Smi
Philip	101	Rut
Richard	29	Fra
Richard	420	Wil
Robert	13	Rob
Robert	114	Wil
Robert	401	Wil
Samuel	13	Lin
Silas	50	Smi
Solomon	29	Fra
Sowthy	28	Fra
Stephen	384	Wil
Thomas	27	Bed
Thomas	28	Fra
Thomas	101	Rut
Thomas G.	179	Sum
William	28	Fra
William	10	Rob
William	12	Rob
William	20	Rob
William	52	Smi
William	175	Sum
William L.	52	Smi
Willie	12	Hic
see Sunders		
Sanderson, Edward	29	Lin
Edward	49	Smi
Edward	176	Sum
George	29	Lin
James	1	Mon
Jamime	38	Mau
Jos.	13	Hic
Martha	177	Sum
Milly	383	Wil
Nathaniel	1	Mon
Susannah	49	Smi
Thomas	50	Smi
Sandford, George	28	Fra
Muse	26	Rob
Sarah	178	Sum
Sandlin, James	29	Fra
William	29	Fra
Sandridge, Benjamin	27	Fra
Sandridge (cont.)		
George	28	Fra
Nathan	27	Fra
Stephen	27	Fra
Sands, George	381	Wil
James	40	Mau
Mical	41	Mau
William	381	Wil
Margaret	23	Gil
Sane, Daniel	309	War
Sanford, Augustine	178	Sum
George	12	Wll
James	47	Mau
James	86	Rut
James	12	Wll
James F.	56	Mau
John	72	Dav
Polly	12	Wll
Robert	12	Wll
Sansil, Archibald	10	Dic
Sansom, Peggy	29	Fra
Sansome, Richard D.	13	Dic
Sansum, Samuel D.	10	Lin
William	43	Lin
Santford, George	405	Wil
Sappington, Rebeccah	89	Dav
Roger B.	78	Dav
Sardler, Lemuel	85	Rut
Sargeant, James	28	Fra
Sargent, William	9	Ove
Sarrid, William	290	War
Sarrison, John	412	Wil
Sartin, James	29	Fra
Sarver, George	175	Sum
Jeremiah	176	Sum
John	178	Sum
Sasnett, John	3	Bed
Satinfield, Peter	15	Gil
Satterfield, James	178	Sum
Jerimiah	34	Mau
John	21	Wll
Moses	18	Lin
Reuben	406	Wil
Susan	64	Dav
William	398	Wil
Satterwhite, Paul	29	Fra
Sattsman, Philip	23	Mon
Saul, Abraham	103	Rut
Sauls, Abraham	343	Whi
Barbara	372	Whi
Mary	347	Whi
Saulsbury, James	9	Wll
Saunders, Francis	89	Dav
John	98	Rut
Tierner	2	Wll
William	85	Dav
Savage, Eleven	24	Jac
George	294	War
Jesse	292	War
John	24	Jac
Robert	8	Ove
Sally	342	Whi
Stephen	281	War

Savage (cont.)		
Thomas	29	Rob
William	24	Jac
Savender, Nelson	36	Wll
Savige, Samuel	36	Mau
William	69	Mau
Sawer, Henry	175	Sum
Sawford, Jacob J.	106	She
Sawrey, James	175	Sum
Sawyer, Castin	62	Dav
Sawyers, Baily	25	Lin
Caleb	178	Sum
Demsey	87	Rut
Elizabeth	8	Lin
James	3	Rob
Robert	19	Mon
William	10	Gil
Saxton, John	27	Fra
Samuel	27	Fra
Sayers, Robert	29	Wll
Sampson	23	Wll
Scaggs, Mastin	10	Way
Scales, Absolem	29	Wll
Daniel	58	Wll
Henry	2	Gil
Henry	30	Wll
James	37	Bed
John	29	Wll
John	58	Wll
Joseph	61	Dav
Joseph G.	62	Wll
Joseph H.	62	Wll
Nicholas	30	Wll
Scandland, Benj., Sr.	24	Jac
Robert	24	Jac
Thomas	24	Jac
William	23	Jac
Scarbrough, Alexr.	130	Ste
D.	125	Ste
James	118	Ste
James	130	Ste
James	356	Whi
John	118	Ste
Scats, John H.	52	Mau
William	52	Mau
Scenlock, Patsey	48	Smi
Schasbell, John	175	Sum
Schaslern, Elisha	409	Wil
Schloster, Lewis	176	Sum
Schmier, Frederick	77	Dav
Schooler, John	28	Bed
Nathen	22	Bed
Samuel	3	Bed
Scinnhorn, Matt.	24	Jac
Scipper, Joseph	33	Mau
Scippers, —	24	Mau
Scippin, Hosa	33	Mau
Scisco, Isaac	24	Jac
Sanders	24	Jac
Sclears, David	384	Wil
Scobey, James	404	Wil
John	404	Wil
Joseph	175	Sum
Scoby, John	47	Smi
Scoggin, Benjamin M.	15	Gil
Jessee	360	Whi
John	178	Sum
John	350	Whi
John	366	Whi
Jonathan	367	Whi
Lemuel	360	Whi
William	178	Sum
Scoggins, James	120	Ste
Scoles, Joseph	128	Ste
Nathl.	128	Ste
Scott, Adams	293	War
Alexander W.	17	Gil
Andrew	27	Mau
Andrew D.	13	Wll
Basel	315	War
Berry	16	Way
Betsey	73	Rut
Catherine	17	Lin
Cronich	49	Smi
Edward	4	Ove
Elias	38	Lin
Emanuel	398	Wil
Geo.	73	Dav
George	104	Rut
H.	24	Mau
Hannah	26	Mau
Isaac	46	Wll
Jacob	52	Mau
James [?]	27	Bed
James	2	Law
James	29	Lin
James	48	Mau
James	177	Sum
James	292	War
James	15	Way
James	344	Whi
James	376	Wil
James	399	Wil
James	24	Wll
James	34	Wll
James B.	34	Wll
Jane	50	Mau
Jarett	300	War
Jeremiah	16	Way
Jesse	42	Bed
Jesse	4	Ove
John	28	Bed
John	36	Bed
John	15	Dic
John	28	Fra
John	6	Hic
John	24	Jac
John	51	Smi
John	52	Smi
John	16	Way
John	358	Whi
John	25	Wll
John T.	95	Dav
Joseph	12	Gil
Joseph	12	Way
Lamuel	4	Ove

Scott (cont.)		
Larkin	92	Dav
Martin	51	Smi
Martin	15	Way
Mary	73	Dav
Mary	17	Gil
Moses	48	Smi
Nathaniel	5	Gil
Nehemiah	6	Dic
Richard	54	Mau
Robert	18	Gil
Robert	399	Wil
Sally	306	War
Saml.	80	Dav
Samuel	74	Dav
Samuel	27	Fra
Samuel	12	Gil
Samuel	27	Mau
Samuel	399	Wil
Simeon	79	Dav
Simon	4	Bed
Sinclair	73	Dav
Tabitha	399	Wil
Thomas	11	Gil
Thomas	22	Lin
Thomas	281	War
Thomas	367	Whi
Thos.	73	Dav
Tillman	95	Dav
Wiley	54	Mau
William	96	Dav
William	19	Gil
William	25	Lin
William	34	Mau
William	311	War
William F.	9	Way
Scraggs, Edward	86	Dav
Scrape, James L.	74	Rut
Scribner, John	26	Mau
Jonathan	341	Whi
Pleasant	37	Mau
Scritz, Jacob	34	Wll
Scrius, Littleton	79	Rut
Scrivner, Benjamin	50	Smi
Moses	51	Smi
Thomas	51	Smi
Scroggins, Henry	70	Dav
Scrogins, Richard	6	Per
Scruggs, Allen	8	Gil
Archibald	47	Smi
Cazera	35	Wll
Drury	90	Dav
Edward	15	Wll
Elisha	125	Ste
Fench	66	Wll
Heartwell	344	Whi
John	15	Wll
John B.	35	Wll
Langhorn	71	Dav
Nathan	35	Wll
Thomas	9	Gil
William	67	Dav
Scrugs, Drury	178	Sum
Scrugs (cont.)		
Theophilus	175	Sum
Scudder, Henry	49	Smi
Matthias	50	Smi
Scurlock, Thomas	43	Lin
Sea, John	47	Smi
Seaborn, Christopher	58	Dav
Seal, Anthony	30	Fra
Charles	20	Rob
Charles	48	Smi
James	402	Wil
William	1	Rob
William	49	Smi
Seales, Rhoda	50	Smi
see Scales		
Seals, John	9	Dic
Samuel	60	Wll
Seamore, Alsey	8	Dic
Seamster, John	24	Jac
Searbrough, Robert	356	Whi
William	364	Whi
Searcy, Anderson	92	Rut
James	78	Rut
James	103	Rut
Peter	20	Hic
Reuben	382	Wil
Rewben	175	Sum
Robt.	78	Dav
William	51	Smi
William W.	88	Rut
Searles, Francis	47	Smi
Searlock, Dudley	400	Wil
Sears, David	23	Jac
James	121	Ste
Seat, Anderson	406	Wil
Hartwell	68	Dav
Henry	72	Dav
Herod	406	Wil
James	72	Dav
James	415	Wil
Jarrat	178	Sum
John	23	Rob
Joseph	23	Rob
Joseph	81	Rut
Robert	68	Dav
Willis	23	Rob
see Soat		
Seaton, James	282	War
Seats, Isam	4	Hum
Seaward, James	50	Smi
Zacheriah	51	Smi
Seawell, Benja.	176	Sum
Henry H.	377	Wil
Joseph	28	Fra
Thomas	179	Sum
Seawill, Richard	313	War
Seay, Jane	59	Wll
Samuel	76	Dav
Sebastian, Isaac	29	Lin
Samuel	1	Hic
Joseph	29	Lin
Sebree, Francis	7	Mon
Secrest, Abram	20	Wll

Secrest (cont.)
John 66 Wll
Seddle, Job 30 Rob
Sedwell, John 3 Ove
See, John 22 Lin
John 286 War
Michael 91 Rut
Nicholas 94 Rut
William 4 Lin
Seeds, Wm. 114 Ste
Seely, Edward R., Mr. 13 Law
Segears, William 29 Mau
Segner, Charles 8 Ove
Segraves, Bennet 29 Mau
Isaac 29 Mau
Jacob 29 Mau
see Segears
Sehon, William, Mr. 8 Law
Seith, James 12 Gil
Seitz, Andrew 281 War
Thomas 302 War
Selcocks, Solomon 12 Ove
Selers, James 62 Mau
John 69 Mau
Self, Abner 50 Smi
Abraham 14 Dic
Anne 12 Gil
Jacob 32 Mon
John 50 Smi
Own by [probably the unnamed enumerator] 46 Mau
Samuel 14 Dic
Sell, Andrew 309 War
see Shell
Sellars, Alvis 385 Wil
Lewis 49 Smi
Sellers, Elizebeth 61 Mau
Flin 283 War
Howell 15 Rob
Isaac 62 Mau
Isaac 1 Per
John 8 Law
John 5 Lin
Larken 8 Rob
Richard 2 Per
Robbert 63 Mau
Samuel 16 Dic
Selvage, Micheal 3 Ove
Semble, Isham 4 Ove
Semons, John 6 Ove
Sensibaugh, James 22 Jac
Sensing, John 6 Mon
Sent, Thomas W. 26 Bed
Senter, Freeman 178 Sum
John 177 Sum
Richard 176 Sum
Stephen 20 Ove
Seratt, James 309 War
John 3 Hum
Serrat, Henry H. 76 Dav
Serry, William 409 Wil
Sessions, John 45 Mau
Richard 289 War
Sesson, —, Mr. 67 Mau
Settle, Joel L. 24 Jac
L. B. 24 Jac
Settles, Strother 7 Gil
Seurlock, William 367 Whi
Sevear, Valentine 41 Bed
Sevier, Abraham 14 Ove
George W. 4 Ove
John, Senr. 1 Ove
John F. 4 Ove
Joseph 9 Ove
Samuel 7 Ove
Valentine 11 Ove
William 1 Ove
Sewell, Josep 29 Mau
Joseph 6 Ove
Stephen 6 Ove
see Cewell
Sexton, Allen 117 Ste
B. 118 Ste
Berry 130 Ste
Henry 117 Ste
James 119 Ste
James 130 Ste
Miles 119 Ste
Ransom 28 Mon
William 49 Smi
Shackelford, Thomas 86 Dav
Shadden, Martin 15 Wll
Robert 6 Gil
Robert 33 Wll
Robert 66 Wll
Shaddock, Gabriel 15 Dic
Shaddy, Jacob 43 Bed
Shafer, Andrew 17 Gil
Shafner, Fredrick 24 Bed
John 22 Bed
Shain, Thomas 43 Mau
Shakleford, Roger 27 Mon
Shall, George 77 Dav
Wm. 136 Sum
Shame, John 381 Wil
Shamwell, Joseph 6 Mon
Shanan, Samuel 8 Rob
Shands, William 9 Law
Shane, Andrew 58 Dav
Maivice 59 Dav
Robert 3 Gil
Shankle, George 27 Fra
Jesse 23 Jac
John, Sr. 23 Jac
Thomas 23 Jac
Wilie 23 Jac
Shanklin, Jesse 9 Rob
Shanks, William 392 Wil
Shannan, Finis W. 59 Mau
Harvy 29 Rob
Hugh 32 Rob
James 32 Rob
John 13 Rob
Michael 18 Rob
Shannon, Arthur 395 Wil
David 47 Wll

Shannon (cont.)
George 19 Wll
Henry 395 Wil
James 5 Hum
James 395 Wil
John 1 Har
John D. 13 Wll
Quintin 15 Gil
Robert 3 Har
Robert [2] 395 Wil
Samuel 85 Dav
Sauel H. 8 Per
Thomas 90 Dav
Thos. S. 4 Mon
Shaphard, James 50 Smi
Thomas 47 Smi
Sharan, Matthias 17 Gil
Sharborough, John 59 Wll
Shark, Edwin 98 Rut
Sharp, Daniel 3 Ove
Edwd. 21 Hic
Ezekiel, Jr. 417 Wil
Ezekiel, Sen. 417 Wil
Grove 11 Law
Henry, Mr. 1 Law
James 27 Fra
John 21 Hic
John 29 Wll
Joseph 417 Wil
Joshua 7 Way
M. D. L. F. 179 Sum
Neimiah 32 Mau
Richard 29 Fra
Robert 30 Wll
William 19 Bed
William 31 Mau
William 307 War
Sharpe, Adlai 47 Lin
Alfred 99 Rut
Cyrus 99 Rut
Sharps, James 85 Rut
Sharrock, Stephen, overseer 39 Wll
Shatton, Robertson 24 Rob
Shaver, David 49 Smi
Jacob 351 Whi
Jacob 57 Wll
John 177 Sum
Mary M. 352 Whi
Shaw, Alexander 46 Wll
Basil 48 Smi
Christopher 28 Bed
Daniel 126 Ste
Henry 49 Smi
Hugh 286 War
Jacob 52 Smi
James 52 Smi
James 299 War
Jerry 403 Wil
John 46 Bed
John 47 Smi
John 294 War
John 420 Wil
John L. 50 Smi
Shaw (cont.)
Joseph 23 Jac
Joseph 28 Lin
Joseph 42 Mau
Joseph 114 Ste
Lenord 121 Ste
Levi 33 Mau
Nathaniel 47 Wll
Ralph 9 Hic
Sampson 33 Mau
Sarah 15 Mon
Seebern 136 Sum
Tarrance 18 Wll
Taylor 70 Dav
Thomas 10 Hum
Thomas 16 Rob
Timothey 17 Wll
Washing 36 Mau
William 68 Dav
William 6 Lin
William 28 Lin
William 34 Mau
William 13 Rob
William 29 Rob
William 175 Sum
William 403 Wil
William 420 Wil
Shawl, Benjamin 2 Per
Shaws, Andrews 403 Wil
Sheaf see Skeaf
Shearman, Charls 29 Mau
Shearman, Samuel 6 Har
Shearwood, Thomas 89 Rut
Sheckly, Isaiah 344 Whi
Shed, George 29 Fra
James 29 Fra
Shedrick, John 39 Wll
Sheelar, Abraham 15 Gil
Sheen, Moses 298 War
Sheffield, Nathan 9 Hum
Shegog, Wm. 79 Dav
Shehora, William 44 Mau
Shel, Isaac 1 Ove
Shelburn, John P. 9 Wll
Pettis 34 Wll
Samuel 40 Wll
Sarah 64 Wll
Shelby, Anthy. B. 136 Sum
David 179 Sum
Eleanor 23 Mon
Elizabeth 22 Mon
Evin 69 Mau
George 70 Mau
Isaac 21 Mon
John 79 Dav
Thomas 70 Mau
Vardeman 70 Mau
William 11 Hic
William 67 Mau
Shelent, Thomas 83 Dav
Sheleott, Joshua 125 Ste
Sheleton, Dica 42 Wll
Shell, Christian 289 War

Shell (cont.)		
Frederick	310	War
John	36	Mau
Samuel	300	War
Samuel	305	War
Solomon	291	War
see Sell, Shel, Shull		
Shelly, Thomas	5	Ove
Shelton, Bennet	10	Wll
David	47	Smi
Edmund	9	Gil
Elizabeth	15	Dic
Elizabeth	8	Hic
Enoch	37	Lin
Gilbert	5	Hum
Godfry	67	Dav
Harmon	40	Lin
Isaac	8	Hic
James	10	Dic
James	41	Lin
James [2]	47	Smi
James L.	30	Rob
Jesse	19	Bed
Jesse	20	Bed
Jesse	38	Wll
John	59	Mau
John	63	Mau
John	63	Mau
John	47	Smi
Jonathan	15	Hic
Joseph	8	Hic
Peter	38	Lin
Philemon	7	Lin
Priscilla	41	Lin
Robert	3	Dic
Samuel	63	Mau
Soleman	42	Mau
Stephen	7	Gil
Stephen	8	Gil
William	37	Lin
William	38	Lin
William	99	Rut
William H.	93	Dav
Wm.	8	Hic
see Skelton		
Shepeson, —	24	Mau
Shephard see Shaphard		
Shepherd, Jeremiah	2	Mon
John	177	Sum
John M.	18	Mon
Laban	388	Wil
Samuel	22	Mon
Samuel	386	Wil
Thomas	20	Rob
Thomas	86	Rut
Thomas	103	Rut
William	49	Bed
Shepmon, Isaac	4	Per
Sheppard, Andrew	288	War
Austin	308	War
James	57	Wll
Lewis	51	Wll
Stephen	47	Wll
Sheppard (cont.)		
William	6	Gil
Wm.	74	Dav
Sherad, Arthar	30	Mau
Salathil	23	Mon
William	30	Mau
Sherid, Lemuel	66	Mau
Shermon, John	126	Ste
Sherod, William	31	Rob
Sherran, Sterling	13	Rob
Sherrel, Abraham	368	Whi
George D.	29	Fra
Samuel	29	Fra
Sherrele, —	111	Wil
Sherrell, Aaron	394	Wil
Abel	396	Wil
Archibald	392	Wil
Ephraim	113	Wil
Ephraim	399	Wil
Polly	392	Wil
Saml. W.	391	Wil
Uty	19	Lin
Wilson	390	Wil
Sherren, Jarred	5	Bed
Thomas	31	Bed
Sherrill, Aexander	294	War
John	4	Ove
Levi	12	Gil
Sherwood, Benjamin	77	Rut
Daniel	87	Rut
Howel	90	Rut
Hugh	77	Rut
Jane	48	Smi
John H.	84	Rut
Jonathan	77	Rut
Shetton, Jesse	63	Dav
Shew, Lewis	28	Bed
Shewcroft, Simon	176	Sum
Shewmake, Lithe	176	Sum
Peasey	178	Sum
Shields, Alexander	20	Gil
George	20	Gil
James	41	Mau
James	81	Rut
Leander	20	Gil
Samuel	20	Gil
William	278	War
Shiers, James	8	Lin
Shin, John	13	Ove
Shinall, John	65	Mau
Thomas	65	Mau
Shiner, Hannah	7	Gil
Ship, Binton	47	Smi
Lewis	47	Lin
Makins	47	Smi
Sarah	47	Lin
William	47	Lin
Shipley, Raliegh	288	War
Tolbert	305	War
Shipman, Jacob	7	Per
see Shpmon		
Shipp, Joseph	80	Rut
Lewis	80	Rut

Shipp (cont.)		
Serah	4	Hic
Wm.	4	Hic
Shirer, Christian	53	Mau
Shirkley, Wilson	314	War
Shirley, George, Junr.	10	Law
George, Senr.	10	Law
James	8	Hic
John	351	Whi
Thomas	13	Way
Zekial	43	Mau
Shirly, Champanus	362	Whi
Thomas	353	Whi
Shirrill, William	288	War
Shivers, Luther	2	Rob
Noah	71	Dav
Thomas	70	Dav
Shmith, Rhoda	23	Jac
Shoars, Abiram	27	Fra
Levi	27	Fra
Shoase, Catharine	4	Hic
Shoat, Austain	17	Ove
Nicholas	9	Mon
Shockley, Booker	349	Whi
Ephrame	349	Whi
Isaiah	354	Whi
Samuel	354	Whi
Thomas	349	Whi
William	354	Whi
Wilson	309	War
Shocock, John	177	Sum
Shoemake, Elizabeth	348	Whi
Franks.	22	Jac
John	2	Ove
Michael	49	Smi
Robert	6	Per
Shoemaker, Edmond	3	Hic
Jesse	3	Hic
Shoemate, William J.	7	Wll
Shoffner, Christopher	30	Lin
Sholders, Solomon	175	Sum
Shook, Abraham	32	Bed
Abraham	28	Fra
James	39	Bed
William	32	Bed
William	39	Bed
Shooster, William	347	Whi
Shopshire, John	372	Whi
Shore, Philip	410	Wil
Shores, Nancy	22	Hic
Short, Anderson	102	Rut
Battie	10	Lin
Benjamin	11	Lin
Elizabeth	178	Sum
Isaac	177	Sum
Isaac	36	Wll
Isaiah	3	Hum
James	24	Jac
James	10	Wll
Joab	30	Fra
Joel, Jr.	24	Jac
Joel, Sr.	24	Jac
John	21	Lin
Short (cont.)		
Jonathan	345	Whi
Joshua	24	Jac
Mary	345	Whi
Merrett	10	Lin
Moses, Jun.	30	Fra
Moses, Sen.	30	Fra
Needham	3	Hum
Philip	3	Mon
Samuel	13	Wll
Theophelus	416	Wil
Thomas	11	Lin
Thomas R.	48	Smi
William	42	Bed
William	30	Fra
William	24	Jac
William	178	Sum
Shorter, Berry	405	Wil
James	18	Lin
Shote, Thomas	66	Mau
Shott, Caleb	7	Gil
Daris	6	Per
Shoulders, Malachi	52	Smi
see Sholders		
Shouse, Joseph	10	Hic
Wm.	10	Hic
see House		
Shovin, William	28	Fra
Shpmon, Isaac	6	Per
Shrader, Daniel	290	War
Henry	18	Gil
Shropshire, David	3	Dic
Hutson	5	Dic
James H.	30	Fra
Polley	3	Dic
see Shopshire		
Shuffield, Arther	11	Bed
Arthur	13	Bed
Cordall	3	Lin
Jason	10	Bed
John	11	Bed
John	26	Lin
Shule, Philip	6	Way
Shull, Abraham	10	Lin
David	1	Way
Frederick	294	War
Isaac	57	Wll
Shumate, Willis L.	67	Dav
Shuster see Shooster		
Shute, John	60	Dav
Phillip	75	Dav
William	5	Wll
Shuttle, Philip	22	Jac
Shwin see Shovin		
Shy, Eli	48	Smi
Robert	176	Sum
Sibven, Joseph	400	Wil
Sigman, Abraham	7	Law
Nimrod	49	Smi
Sigon, John W.	15	Gil
Sike, Thomas A.	99	Rut
Sikes, Arthur	116	Ste
Howel	33	Lin

Sikes (cont.)
James 34 Lin
James 346 Whi
Jesse 34 Lin
Jonas 79 Rut
Samson 115 Ste
Silemman, Thomas N. 36 Mau
Siliven see Sibven
Silivin, Elsanah 11 Har
Kaleb 11 Har
Silliman, Thomas 103 Rut
Sillivant, Danl. 131 Ste
Eli 131 Ste
Sills, Isham 126 Ste
Wiat 63 Wll
Silor, John 30 Fra
Sils, Hardy B. 122 Ste
William 122 Ste
Silver, Phillip 27 Rob
Silvertooth, Jacob 31 Lin
John 31 Lin
Mary 31 Lin
Simcock, John 18 Ove
Simington, John, Mr. 2 Law
Simions, Hugh 55 Mau
Simmon, John 418 Wil
Simmonds, Peter 8 Gil
Simmons, Alexander 27 Fra
Allen 78 Rut
Charles 27 Fra
Charles 52 Smi
Chas. 121 Ste
Edward 12 Rob
Elijah 23 Jac
Elisha 9 Hum
James 87 Dav
James 8 Gil
James 27 Lin
James 1 Per
James 130 Ste
James 19 Way
James 344 Whi
James A. 27 Lin
James M. 6 Gil
Jesse 13 Rob
Joel 49 Smi
John 27 Fra
John 11 Hum
John 23 Jac
John 20 Rob
John 95 Rut
John 358 Whi
Joseph 371 Whi
Lemuel 19 Way
Matthew 50 Smi
Matthew D. 6 Mon
Micajah 344 Whi
Nathan 176 Sum
Reuben 27 Fra
Richard 5 Hum
Smith 52 Smi
Solomon 372 Whi
Solomon, Jur. 10 Gil
Simmons (cont.)
Solomon, Sr. 10 Gil
Tho. 176 Sum
Thomas 27 Lin
Thomas 52 Smi
Thomas 11 Way
Thomas 24 Wll
Vincent 50 Smi
Voluntine 28 Rob
William 86 Dav
William 27 Fra
William 60 Wll
William H. 16 Wll
Williams 5 Law
see Sammins
Simms, Absalom 50 Smi
Benjamin 28 Fra
David 22 Gil
Elizabeth 6 Gil
Henry Dial 97 Rut
James 51 Smi
John A. 94 Rut
Micajah 51 Smi
Millenton 3 Wll
Nancy 23 Jac
Parrish 20 Gil
Robert 18 Gil
Robert 51 Smi
Robt. 18 Hic
Swepson 86 Rut
Wythe 7 Gil
see Metheney 13 Gil
Simons, John 52 Smi
Nathaniel 55 Mau
Sally 178 Sum
Simpson, Alexander 97 Dav
Alexander 293 War
Andrew 2 Per
Canada 79 Rut
Charles 8 Gil
David 88 Rut
Elijah 176 Sum
Francis C. 13 Law
Hannah 420 Wil
Isaac 27 Mau
Isaac 287 War
James 50 Smi
James 350 Whi
James 372 Whi
John 16 Gil
John W. 357 Whi
Lawrence 52 Smi
Malachi 28 Fra
Mary 51 Smi
Nathaniel 10 Hic
Peter 315 War
Presley 404 Wil
Rice 28 Fra
Robert 63 Dav
Robert 176 Sum
Roger 22 Gil
Saml. 10 Hic
Sarah 342 Whi

Simpson (cont.)		
Sayer	348	Whi
Thomas	15	Dic
Thomas	5	Gil
Thomas	13	Hum
Thomas	10	Ove
Thomas	96	Rut
Thomas	314	War
Valentine	315	War
Wenney	15	Ove
William	28	Fra
William	16	Gil
William	7	Har
William	7	Per
William	91	Rut
William	49	Smi
William	7	Wil
Wm.	10	Hic
Simrell, James	350	Whi
Sims, Abram	176	Sum
Alexander	3	Mon
Anderson	35	Bed
Anne	4	Law
Chesley	407	Wil
Edwd.	179	Sum
Eli	355	Whi
Elisha	418	Wil
Isham	26	Bed
James	89	Dav
Jeffrey	2	Mon
John	47	Bed
John	34	Mau
John	10	Ove
John	179	Sum
John	309	War
John G.	45	Bed
Judy	36	Mau
Julius C.	28	Fra
Line S.	176	Sum
Martin	20	Bed
Matthew	399	Wil
Matthias	418	Wil
Newton	3	Mon
Polley	11	Dic
Rabeccah	96	Dav
Thomas	67	Mau
Thomas	418	Wil
William	36	Mau
see Collins		
Sinclair, Mark	60	Dav
see St. Clair, Synclair		
Singleton, James	9	Hic
Peter	29	Bed
William	3	Hum
Sington, Sally	178	Sum
William	370	Whi
Sinkler, Benjamin	29	Lin
James	393	Wil
Sinks, Jessee	28	Mon
Sinn, Joseph	1	Hic
Sinnville, Richard	7	Gil
Sisco, John	5	Per
Sisemore, William	27	Fra

Sisemore (cont.)		
William	5	Law
Sisk, Bengess	27	Fra
James	27	Fra
Josiah	4	Way
Rebeca	27	Mon
Sisom, James	95	Rut
Sittler, Isaac	80	Dav
Sivan, Willis	70	Dav
Sively, John	34	Lin
Skeaf, Jesse	50	Smi
William	50	Smi
Skeen, Jessee	175	Sum
John	397	Wil
see Sheen		
Skelly, John	98	Dav
Skelton, Amos	9	Hic
David	8	Gil
Duke	49	Smi
John	17	Dic
Robert	10	Dic
Robert	50	Smi
see Shelton		
Skidmore, Henry	23	Bed
John	6	Bed
Thomas	6	Bed
Skinner, Jesse	23	Rob
Josiah S.	22	Mon
Nathan	114	Ste
Skipper, Archibald	176	Sum
John	67	Mau
Slack, Simeon W.	99	Rut
Slade, John	20	Bed
John	36	Bed
Sladen, William E.	10	Dic
Slagle, John	121	Ste
John, Junr.	121	Ste
Wm.	121	Ste
Slandel, John	114	Ste
Slane, Colemon	391	Wil
Mary	24	Bed
Saml.	52	Bed
Slaon, John	73	Dav
Slarns, John	395	Wil
Moses	395	Wil
Slate, Benjamin	408	Wil
William N.	402	Wil
Slater, Charles	8	Rob
Cornelious	2	Lin
David H.	136	Sum
Henry	28	Rob
Slaton, Daniel	65	Mau
Russell	50	Smi
Slatter, Andrew	53	Mau
Slatton, Archibald	14	Dic
Slaughter, David	8	Mon
Francis	64	Dav
George	53	Mau
Hugh J.	281	War
Tabitha	123	Ste
Z.	123	Ste
Slavens, John	49	Smi
Nancy	98	Dav

Slavins, Henry 52 Smi
Sledge, Henry 40 Wll
Joshua 9 Mon
Sleeder, John 86 Rut
Slicker, William 33 Wll
Sliker, George 10 Wll
Slinkard, William 48 Smi
Sloan, Archibald 52 Smi
Elias 51 Smi
Elizabeth 52 Smi
Hezekiah 176 Sum
Isaac 51 Smi
James G. 179 Sum
John 48 Smi
John 51 Smi
John 179 Sum
John 362 Whi
John, Sen. 51 Smi
Josiah 51 Smi
Samuel 318 War
Thomas 51 Smi
Thomas 361 Whi
William 51 Smi
Slognar, Thomas 88 Dav
Slone, Alexander 11 Har
James [2] 397 Wil
John 11 Har
Thomas 54 Mau
Slonefield, William 314 War
Slons, John 48 Wll
Sloss, Joseph 88 Rut
Sly, Jacob 32 Mon
Small, Amos 14 Lin
George 27 Lin
Henry [2] 1 Mon
Smallman, Grief 358 Whi
John 357 Whi
Smallwood, John 6 Law
Smally, John, Jun. 28 Fra
John, Sen. 28 Fra
Smart, Amy 395 Wil
Bennet 6 Rob
David 20 Rob
John 390 Wil
Philip 395 Wil
Polly 33 Rob
Thomas 12 Rob
William 3 Rob
Smartt, George R. 283 War
Reuben 280 War
Reuben 306 War
William C. 280 War
Smedley, William 20 Rob
Smeedle, William 368 Whi
Smiddy, Robert 24 Jac
Smiley, Allexander 89 Dav
Hugh 47 Bed
Robert 78 Dav
Smily, David 22 Rob
Smiser, John 40 Mau
Smith, Aaron 21 Mon
Abner 13 Ove
Abraham 71 Dav
Smith (cont.)
Abraham 78 Rut
Abram 9 Har
Abram 177 Sum
Absalom 24 Jac
Absalom 99 Rut
Absolum 383 Wil
Adran 34 Mau
Agrippa 105 Rut
Alexander 7 Gil
Alexander 20 Wll
Alfred 48 Smi
Allen 24 Bed
Allen 6 Gil
Allen 21 Gil
Allen 33 Rob
Allen J. 41 Bed
Amon 419 Wil
Amos 290 War
Andrew 71 Dav
Andrew 43 Mau
Andrew 14 Mon
Anthony 49 Wll
Anthony G. 89 Rut
Archibald 13 Gil
Archibald 49 Smi
Arthur 23 Hic
Arthur W. 48 Mau
Austin 15 Gil
Bartholomew 7 Dic
Bazel 20 Mon
Benard 23 Jac
Benjamin 21 Bed
Benjamin 88 Dav
Benjamin 10 Gil
Benjamin 314 War
Benjamin 58 Wll
Benjamin W. 20 Ove
Benjmin 53 Mau
Benjmin B. 47 Mau
Bennett 104 Rut
Bird 415 Wil
Briton 11 Ove
Burrel 123 Ste
Catharine 15 Gil
Charles 31 Mau
Charles 53 Mau
Charles 2 Ove
Charles 1 Way
Charles 360 Whi
Charles 390 Wil
Charles 392 Wil
Charles 34 Wll
Charles A. 53 Mau
Charlotte 34 Rob
Christopher 28 Fra
Cleaton 11 Hic
Coleman 381 Wil
Cornelious 31 Lin
Daniel 11 Har
Daniel 24 Lin
Daniel 9 Ove
Daniel [2] 52 Smi

Smith (cont.)

Name	Page	County
Daniel	411	Wil
David	9	Hic
David	5	Lin
David	7	Ove
David	367	Whi
David	31	Wll
David	47	Wll
Diana	13	Gil
Drewry	381	Wil
Drury	19	Gil
Drury	362	Whi
Drury K.	40	Lin
Duncan	7	Law
Dutten	11	Law
Ebnezer	27	Mau
Edmond	126	Ste
Edward	3	Dic
Edward	6	Gil
Edwin	87	Dav
Edwin, Jr.	60	Dav
Eli	91	Rut
Elias	28	Fra
Elias	29	Fra
Elie	23	Jac
Elijah	71	Dav
Elijah	88	Rut
Eliphus	92	Rut
Elisha	11	Har
Elisha	68	Mau
Elisha	405	Wil
Eliza.	73	Dav
Eliza.	78	Dav
Eliza.	81	Dav
Elizabeth	29	Fra
Elizabeth	4	Gil
Elizabeth	13	Mon
Elizabeth	78	Rut
Eracus	288	War
Evan	97	Rut
Ezekiel	11	Gil
Ezekiel	22	Hic
Francis	29	Fra
Francis	3	Gil
Francis	2	Lin
Francis	122	Ste
Francis C.	52	Mau
Gabiel	61	Dav
Geo.	169	Sum
George	6	Bed
George	9	Bed
George	89	Dav
George	10	Ove
George	2	Rob
George	82	Rut
George	103	Rut
George	50	Smi
George	177	Sum
George	285	War
George	287	War
George	298	War
George	385	Wil
George	390	Wil

Smith (cont.)

Name	Page	County
George	50	Wll
George L.	376	Wil
Guilford	11	Wll
Guy	91	Rut
Guy	17	Wll
Hannah	2	Mon
Hannah	6	Ove
Hannah	110	Ste
Harbert	37	Bed
Harman	24	Lin
Harmer	390	Wil
Harrison	179	Sum
Henery	51	Mau
Henry	9	Hum
Henry	63	Mau
Henry	16	Mon
Henry	22	Mon
Henry	33	Rob
Henry	415	Wil
Henry H.	122	Ste
Ire	1	Ove
Isaac	6	Gil
Isaac	16	Hic
Isaac	14	Lin
Isaac	19	Lin
Isaac	28	Lin
Isaac	27	Rob
Isaac	281	War
Isaac	306	War
Isaac	43	Wll
Jacob	65	Dav
Jacob	23	Rob
Jacob	131	Ste
Jacob	284	War
James	14	Bed
James	82	Dav
James	6	Dic
James	29	Fra
James	6	Gil
James	13	Gil
James	24	Jac
James	12	Law
James	35	Lin
James	37	Lin
James	38	Lin
James	26	Mau
James	51	Mau
James	54	Mau
James	10	Mon
James	23	Mon
James	26	Mon
James	16	Ove
James	18	Ove
James	110	Ste
James	305	War
James	366	Whi
James	378	Wil
James	381	Wil
James	390	Wil
James	397	Wil
James	4	Wll
James C.	31	Lin

Smith (cont.)
James L. 21 Wll
Jane 24 Bed
Jane 52 Mau
Jane 178 Sum
Jarvis 14 Hum
Jas. W. 24 Jac
Jasper 6 Law
Jasper 30 Lin
Jeremiah 27 Fra
Jeremiah 2 Hum
Jeremiah 178 Sum
Jeremiah, Jr. 29 Fra
Jesse 78 Dav
Jesse 89 Dav
Jesse 7 Lin
Jesse 49 Smi
Jesse 50 Smi
Jesse 381 Wil
Jesse K. 115 Wil
Jessee 16 Mon
Jno. 176 Sum
Jno. 390 Wil
Joel 23 Hic
Joel 45 Lin
Joel 95 Rut
Joel 362 Whi
Johanan 120 Ste
John 34 Bed
John 98 Dav
John 27 Fra
John 28 Fra
John 29 Fra
John 9 Gil
John 11 Gil
John 21 Gil
John 11 Har
John 12 Hic
John 19 Hic
John [2] 23 Jac
John 24 Jac
John 11 Law
John 14 Law
John 24 Lin
John 34 Lin
John 35 Lin
John 39 Lin
John 59 Mau
John 63 Mau
John 10 Mon
John 12 Mon
John 14 Mon
John 16 Mon
John 22 Mon
John 2 Ove
John 5 Ove
John 14 Rob
John 19 Rob
John 78 Rut
John 79 Rut
John 80 Rut
John 83 Rut
John 93 Rut

Smith (cont.)
John 94 Rut
John 99 Rut
John 298 War
John 312 War
John 315 War
John 1 Way
John 344 Whi
John 391 Wil
John 393 Wil
John 395 Wil
John 410 Wil
John 21 Wll
John 39 Wll
John 43 Wll
John 46 Wll
John [2] 53 Wll
John, Sen. 29 Fra
John, flathead 14 Wll
John A. 47 Lin
John H. 85 Dav
John H. 53 Mau
John M. 15 Ove
John P. 75 Rut
John P. 32 Wll
John R. 24 Mon
John S. 29 Fra
John W. 2 Hic
John W. 7 Lin
John W. 20 Lin
Joseph 48 Bed
Joseph 98 Dav
Joseph 28 Fra
Joseph 24 Jac
Joseph 6 Law
Joseph 11 Law
Joseph 10 Mon
Joseph 14 Mon
Joseph 34 Rob
Joseph 89 Rut
Joseph 48 Smi
Joseph 125 Ste
Joseph, Junr. 12 Law
Joseph, Senr. 12 Law
Joseph L. D. 9 Hum
Joshua 35 Lin
Joshua 94 Rut
Joshua 177 Sum
Joshua 178 Sum
Josiah 14 Lin
Josiah 25 Mon
Josiah 397 Wil
Larkin 38 Lin
Larkin 51 Smi
Larkin 288 War
Lemuel 45 Lin
Leonard 37 Lin
Levi 177 Sum
Lucy 13 Gil
Malachi 25 Rob
Malcom 49 Smi
Margaret 49 Smi
Martin 86 Dav

Smith (cont.)

Mary	23	Mon
Mary	3	Ove
Mary	78	Rut
Mathias	17	Way
Matthew	22	Mon
Millington	83	Rut
Mitchim	383	Wil
Moses	8	Har
Moses	7	Law
Moses	33	Mau
Moses	23	Mon
Moses	370	Whi
Nancy	21	Mon
Nancy	25	Wll
Nathan	95	Dav
Nathan	287	War
Nathanial	51	Mau
Nedam	54	Mau
Neel	381	Wil
Neel	416	Wil
Nehemiah	34	Mau
Netheldred	11	Rob
Nicholas	32	Wll
Nimrod	96	Rut
Nimrod	316	War
Noah	84	Rut
Nutall	51	Smi
Owen	19	Gil
Penelope	48	Smi
Peter	23	Jac
Peyton	85	Rut
Phebe	366	Whi
Phelps	22	Gil
Phillip	42	Mau
Polly	320	War
Ralph	29	Fra
Ralph	46	Lin
Reazen	43	Bed
Reuben	380	Wil
Rhoda	12	Gil
Richard	97	Dav
Richard	11	Gil
Richard	5	Ove
Richard	5	Way
Richd.	10	Mon
Robbert	62	Mau
Robert	45	Lin
Robert	11	Rob
Robert	73	Rut
Robert	91	Rut
Robert	93	Rut
Robert	49	Smi
Robert [2]	393	Wil
Robert	418	Wil
Robert	15	Wll
Robert, Senr.	93	Rut
Rubin	58	Mau
S. G.	24	Jac
Sally	30	Lin
Sally	177	Sum
Saml.	3	Mon
Saml., Jr.	3	Hic

Smith (cont.)

Saml., Senr.	3	Hic
Samson	376	Wil
Samuel	91	Dav
Samuel	6	Har
Samuel	11	Har
Samuel [2]	52	Mau
Samuel	29	Mon
Samuel	53	Wll
Samuel H.	2	Lin
Samuel H.	31	Mau
Sarah	80	Dav
Sarah	8	Hum
Sarah	14	Law
Sarah	9	Lin
Sarah	28	Mau
Sarah	4	Ove
Sarah	378	Wil
Shadrach	3	Hic
Shadrick	416	Wil
Shelton	177	Sum
Simeon	68	Mau
Solomon	36	Lin
Stephen	36	Mau
Stephen	129	Ste
Stephen	3	Wll
Stepton	47	Mau
Sterling	3	Hic
Sterling	6	Rob
Susanah	386	Wil
Tabitha	34	Rob
Thomas	8	Bed
Thomas	11	Dic
Thomas	28	Fra
Thomas	16	Gil
Thomas	12	Hum
Thomas	18	Lin
Thomas	56	Mau
Thomas	57	Mau
Thomas	3	Ove
Thomas	9	Ove
Thomas	19	Rob
Thomas	79	Rut
Thomas	89	Rut
Thomas	100	Rut
Thomas	49	Smi
Thomas	285	War
Thomas	63	Wll
Thomas, Jun.	50	Smi
Thomas S.	390	Wil
Thos.	1	Mon
Vincent	29	Bed
William	9	Bed
William [2]	29	Fra
William	7	Gil
William [2]	10	Har
William [2]	11	Har
William	6	Law
William	5	Lin
William	16	Lin
William	21	Lin
William	31	Lin
William	36	Lin

Smith (cont.)		
William	45	Lin
William	30	Mau
William	54	Mau
William	7	Mon
William	10	Mon
William	20	Mon
William	4	Ove
William	14	Ove
William	79	Rut
William	85	Rut
William	90	Rut
William	92	Rut
William	98	Rut
William	103	Rut
William	47	Smi
William	49	Smi
William	129	Ste
William	176	Sum
William	178	Sum
William	290	War
William	298	War
William	299	War
William	300	War
William	361	Whi
William	364	Whi
William	366	Whi
William	372	Whi
William	419	Wil
William	1	Wll
William	28	Wll
Williams A.	177	Sum
William C.	21	Lin
William C.	38	Lin
William G.	4	Mon
William H.	90	Rut
William J.	369	Whi
William K.	175	Sum
William L.	177	Sum
William P.	53	Mau
William S.	177	Sum
Willie	48	Smi
Wm.	114	Ste
Wm.	129	Ste
Wm. B.	392	Wil
Zachariah	12	Wll
Zachariah	62	Wll
see Arnold, Shmith, Smiths		
Smithen, Nancy	65	Wll
Smitherman, William	26	Mau
see Smthermen		
Smithron see Smithson		
Smiths, W.	24	Mau
Smithson, Allen	312	War
Baz. C.	290	War
John	283	War
John	62	Wll
Nathaniel	66	Wll
Samuel	66	Wll
Smithwick, Edward	23	Rob
Thomas	47	Smi
Smithy, John	11	Har
Smoot, Charles	16	Hic

Smoot (cont.)		
Saml.	122	Ste
Smotherman, Elijah	88	Rut
Hugh	34	Bed
Hugh	88	Rut
John	88	Rut
Lewis	87	Rut
Saml.	34	Bed
Smothers, Edmund	177	Sum
Eli	178	Sum
Elihu	177	Sum
Elisha	177	Sum
Jacob	176	Sum
John	90	Rut
John	48	Smi
John	176	Sum
Margaret	175	Sum
Thomas	175	Sum
William	176	Sum
William	177	Sum
Smthermen, W.	24	Mau
Smyth, Andrew	4	Per
Andrew	7	Per
Euricus	4	Per
James	4	Per
John	5	Per
Joseph	5	Per
William	1	Per
Snead, Burrel	81	Dav
Isreal	22	Jac
Jane	179	Sum
William	64	Dav
Sned, Muntford	178	Sum
Sneed, Constantine P.	22	Wll
James	414	Wil
John	414	Wil
Thomas P.	29	Fra
William	48	Smi
William	52	Smi
William	414	Wil
Snelgrove, Samuel	314	War
Snell, Charles	100	Rut
Ezekeal	88	Dav
James	30	Lin
James	95	Rut
Roger	47	Bed
Roger	17	Wll
Snelling, Lemuel	37	Bed
Snider, Jacob	23	Jac
Jonas	119	Ste
Peter	119	Ste
Snipes, John	8	Gil
Philip	8	Gil
Snoddy, Adam	177	Sum
Robert	30	Bed
Saml.	16	Hic
Thomas	47	Smi
Snodgrass, Pheobe	23	Jac
Robert	4	Law
Susan	24	Jac
William	4	Law
Snow, David O.	77	Dav
Elizabeth	10	Way

Snow (cont.)		
Henry	35	Lin
James	9	Lin
James	25	Wll
Levi	28	Bed
Mark	9	Lin
William	10	Gil
Snowden, Kizire	50	Mau
Soap, Adam	28	Fra
George	28	Fra
Joseph	28	Fra
Joseph	96	Rut
William	28	Fra
Soary, Michael	47	Smi
Soat, Josiah	57	Dav
Laben	97	Rut
Soathermon, Daniel	11	Gil
Solenson, James	84	Rut
Solomon, Jordon	1	Lin
Oston	16	Bed
Samuel	3	Rob
William	28	Lin
Somers, Alexr.	176	Sum
Joseph	176	Sum
Levi	177	Sum
Mary	7	Gil
Somerset, Joseph	47	Smi
Song see Long		
Sonny, Thomas	176	Sum
Sooter, Alexander	28	Fra
Sootin, Benjamin	6	Hum
Soper, Benoni	176	Sum
John O.	177	Sum
Sorger, George	100	Rut
Sorrels, Edward	33	Bed
Needham	33	Bed
William A.	354	Whi
Sorrver, Henry	175	Sum
Sory, Horatio	14	Rob
Malakiah	24	Mon
Sothen, Boos	408	Wil
Sotherlin, James	40	Mau
Mary	40	Mau
Soto, Anthony	95	Dav
South, John	28	Fra
Joseph	28	Fra
Thomas	28	Fra
William	29	Fra
Southall, James	6	Wll
Southard, Charles	351	Whi
John	28	Mon
McClain	364	Whi
Southerin, Isiah	60	Mau
Southerland, George	15	Dic
James	90	Rut
Southerlin, Thomas	62	Mau
Southerman see Soathermon		
Southern, William	25	Rob
Southorn, John	18	Lin
Soveley, John	175	Sum
Sowel, Charles	69	Mau
George	121	Ste
James	25	Mau
Sowel (cont.)		
John	65	Mau
Jones	86	Rut
Mary	95	Rut
Stephen	99	Rut
Thomas	67	Mau
Thomas	103	Rut
William	21	Lin
Sowell, John	12	Dic
Thomas	84	Rut
Spain, David	41	Wll
James	47	Smi
John D.	47	Lin
Littlebery	82	Rut
Stephen	104	Rut
Thomas B.	37	Wll
Span, Moses	59	Wll
William	84	Rut
William	59	Wll
Willis	9	Bed
Spann, William	98	Rut
Sparey, Thomas	342	Whi
Sparkes, Nathaniel	392	Wil
Sparkman, George	344	Whi
Hugh H.	109	Ste
Jesse	48	Wll
Kinchen	48	Wll
Martha	344	Whi
Umphres W.	29	Mau
William	10	Wll
Sparkmon, Bryant	359	Whi
William	354	Whi
Sparks, Bailey	5	Hum
David	38	Lin
George	307	War
Hardy	11	Hic
Isaac	5	Hum
Jesse	13	Hic
John	94	Dav
John	2	Hum
Joseph	27	Fra
Samuel	6	Dic
William	27	Fra
see Speeks		
Sparlock, Francis	413	Wil
Josiah	413	Wil
Spaulldin, Gideon	355	Whi
Spear, Benjamin	4	Ove
George	14	Ove
Moses	63	Dav
William	3	Law
Spearman, Joshua	26	Rob
Samuel	19	Rob
Spears, Bennett	24	Jac
Dickson	8	Bed
Hastings	13	Law
James	178	Sum
John A.	52	Mau
Joseph	13	Law
Nathan	7	Law
Saml.	8	Bed
William	47	Smi
Speck, George	28	Fra

Speck (cont.)		
John	28	Fra
Micheal	16	Ove
Tobias	28	Fra
Speed, Samuel	377	Wil
Speeks, Mary	9	Hic
Speen, Joseph	304	War
Speers, Rachel	371	Whi
Speir, Hardy	316	War
Spelman, Thomas	177	Sum
Spence, Amos	8	Per
Brent	81	Dav
Brittain	87	Rut
Charles	47	Smi
Charles	51	Smi
Elisha	63	Dav
John D.	129	Ste
Joseph	73	Rut
Jurdin	8	Per
Reusker	87	Rut
Thomas	5	Rob
see Spiner		
Spencer, Ahimdaz	36	Mau
Christopher	347	Whi
Clark	1	Per
Eleanor	27	Fra
Elijah	51	Smi
Elisabeth	30	Wll
Fedrick	33	Mau
Francis	35	Mau
Isaac	51	Smi
Jacob	51	Smi
John	1	Per
John	51	Smi
John	110	Ste
John S.	15	Dic
Moses	51	Smi
Moses, Senr.	6	Law
Nathan	92	Rut
Seamore	384	Wil
Thomas	7	Law
Thomas	34	Lin
William	105	Rut
Spenk, John	395	Wil
Spensers, —	24	Mau
Spever, William	1	Per
Spiceland, Sandford	125	Ste
Sanford [deleted]	125	Ste
Spicer, Clabourn	16	Dic
James, Jr.	11	Hic
James, Sr.	11	Hic
Patrick	11	Hic
Thomas	11	Hic
William	381	Wil
Spickard, Jacob	387	Wil
John	387	Wil
Spied, Nancy	3	Mon
Spiller, Benjamin	22	Rob
Warrington B.	20	Rob
Spillers, John	10	Law
Spiner, David	9	Rob
see Spence		
Spinlock, Byrd	50	Smi
Spinlock (cont.)		
Drewry	50	Smi
Joseph	50	Smi
see Scenlock		
Spires, Sarah	410	Wil
Spirey, Isaac	368	Whi
Spivy, Henery	44	Mau
James [2]	23	Jac
John	50	Smi
William J.	49	Smi
Splann, Isaac	46	Bed
Spooner, Elizabeth	178	Sum
Spraces, George	12	Rob
Spradley, Tavner	410	Wil
Yarine	318	War
Spradlin, David	295	War
James	55	Mau
Obadiah	389	Wil
Spradling, Joseph	175	Sum
Obediah	175	Sum
William	34	Lin
Spradly, Martha	16	Lin
Spraggans, Nancy	45	Bed
Spraggins, Asa	80	Dav
Thomas	82	Rut
Spratt, Andrew	9	Wll
Blithe	43	Wll
Spray, Lewis	306	War
Sprewel, Jessee	16	Wll
Luke	17	Lin
Spring, John	409	Wil
Moses	409	Wil
Springer, George	2	Lin
John	52	Smi
Josiah	23	Bed
Thomas, Senr.	4	Law
William	4	Law
Springfield, Anson	49	Smi
Springkel, Micajah	31	Mau
Springs, Abner	408	Wil
Benjamin	408	Wil
Lavina	52	Smi
Sprinkles, Moses	25	Mau
Sprouce, Aaron	393	Wil
Sprouse, James	24	Rob
John	24	Rob
Spruce, Joseph	21	Gil
Spunlock, Joel	413	Wil
Spurlin, Eli	52	Smi
Spurlock, Joseph	3	Way
Spurr, Isaac	361	Whi
Spyker, Jonathan	28	Fra
Squires, Levi	48	Smi
Robert	116	Ste
Srum, Peter	48	Smi
Stacey, Joseph	384	Wil
Stackard, William	30	Mau
Stacks, Abraham	52	Mau
Adam	8	Mon
Barbary	8	Mon
James	52	Mau
Stacy, Anne	24	Jac
Benjamin	102	Rut

Stacy (cont.)		
Biram	24	Jac
Elisabeth	14	Wll
John	24	Jac
John	14	Wll
Thomas	10	Wll
William	384	Wil
Staesurs, Samuel	75	Dav
Stafferd, Zorabable	11	Ove
Stafford, Adam	31	Bed
Adam	48	Smi
Cain	48	Smi
Ivey	8	Gil
John	8	Dic
John	23	Jac
John	49	Smi
Joseph	23	Jac
Josiah	8	Gil
Labon	23	Jac
Lucy	23	Jac
Polly	48	Smi
Robert	4	Per
Stephen	48	Smi
Thomas	52	Smi
William	23	Jac
William	398	Wil
Staford, William	355	Whi
Stagg, William	34	Bed
Staggs, Abram	5	Way
Felix	37	Wll
Flemen	10	Wll
John	37	Wll
Joseph	5	Way
Martin	5	Way
Nancy	5	Way
Thomas	8	Wll
William	5	Way
Winnie	5	Way
Stagner, B.	129	Ste
Henry	175	Sum
John	23	Mon
N.	129	Ste
Staily, Adam	6	Ove
Staines see Stames		
Stalcup, Barbary	175	Sum
Eli	176	Sum
George	175	Sum
James	8	Per
William	47	Smi
Stales, Constant	1	Lin
Staley, Adam	14	Mon
George	12	Mon
Stalings, Charity	48	Smi
John	48	Smi
Thomas	48	Smi
Stall, Frederick	89	Dav
Stalleons, Sherod	20	Hic
Stallings, David [& Moor]	13	Wll
Stallions, John	21	Bed
Stalls, James	114	Ste
Staly, Eli J.	124	Ste
Stames, John	296	War
Stamfield, William	80	Rut
Stamp, James	29	Fra
John	29	Fra
Joseph	29	Fra
William	29	Fra
William	364	Whi
Stamper, Robert	20	Mon
Stamps, James	364	Whi
John	175	Sum
John	364	Whi
Sandford	364	Whi
Stancil, Nathan	24	Wll
Standerford, William	403	Wil
Standfer, Jessey	25	Mau
Standfield, David	29	Fra
Jacob	67	Mau
James, Jr.	29	Fra
James, Sr.	29	Fra
Jeremiah W.	54	Mau
John	69	Mau
Leah	27	Wll
Neill	29	Fra
Sarah	69	Mau
Thomas	67	Mau
William	67	Mau
Standford, James	50	Smi
Standifer, John	47	Smi
Standley, ...	1	Per
David	114	Wil
John	1	Per
Mark	1	Per
Nathanial	26	Mau
Polly	414	Wil
Samuel	7	Per
Sarah	42	Wll
William	1	Per
Standly, John	413	Wil
Standridge, Richard	94	Rut
Stanfield, Abram	177	Sum
Ashley	136	Sum
George	25	Wll
Marmaduke	25	Wll
Robert G.	25	Wll
Shakspear	27	Wll
Stanfill, Jonathan J.	68	Mau
Stanford, Essex	50	Smi
George	10	Gil
Hugh	18	Mon
James	11	Gil
John	10	Gil
Thomas	10	Gil
Thomas	319	War
William	319	War
Stanhope, James	27	Fra
Stanley, David	398	Wil
Furney	4	Hum
James	29	Fra
James	1	Hum
James	6	Wll
Joseph	23	Rob
Martin	5	Wll
Moses	23	Rob
Noble	23	Rob
Rewben	175	Sum

Stanley (cont.)		
Richard	27	Rob
Thomas	28	Rob
William	177	Sum
Wright	18	Wll
Stanton, Champ	23	Jac
Staples, Charles	29	Fra
John	27	Fra
John	359	Whi
see Stepleton		
Staraly, Peter	177	Sum
Stare, Sarah	30	Wll
Stark, Alexander	177	Sum
Ephriam	10	Rob
James	7	Rob
Jeremiah	22	Rob
Jeremiah	177	Sum
John	176	Sum
Sarah	177	Sum
Thomas	11	Rob
Thornton	177	Sum
Walter	21	Rob
William	11	Rob
William	26	Rob
Starkey, Nathan	341	Whi
Starks, Thomas	175	Sum
Starky, Abraham	18	Mon
Starnes, Adam	175	Sum
David	178	Sum
John	178	Sum
John	60	Wll
Joseph	50	Smi
William	28	Fra
Starnet, Moses	415	Wil
Starns, Samuel S.	63	Wll
see Slarns		
Starret, John	37	Bed
Starrett, Benjamin	24	Bed
Staten, Holeman	33	Bed
Isham	176	Sum
Statham, Charles S.	89	Rut
Statler, Abraham	73	Rut
Stead, Abner	23	Lin
Mark	21	Lin
Steal, William	175	Sum
Stebenson, William	46	Lin
Steed, Moses	279	War
Steel, Aaron	50	Mau
Alexander	89	Dav
Alexander	22	Way
Alexander	357	Whi
Andrew	49	Mau
Andrew	370	Whi
Andrew H.	359	Whi
David, Mr.	4	Law
David C.	122	Ste
George	75	Rut
George	176	Sum
George	400	Wil
Isaac	17	Rob
James	50	Mau
James	110	Ste
James	122	Ste

Steel (cont.)		
John	49	Mau
John	370	Whi
Linenan	122	Ste
Mical	48	Mau
Moses	14	Wll
Nathanial H.	50	Mau
Peter	22	Way
Richard	32	Wll
Robert	175	Sum
Samuel	49	Mau
Sarah	409	Wil
William	399	Wil
William D.	48	Mau
Steele, Henry F.	10	Gil
John	15	Bed
John	25	Mon
Joseph	21	Bed
Nathaniel	4	Gil
Ninnian	1	Har
Thomas	3	Gil
William	19	Gil
Wilson	22	Bed
Steerman, Thomas	299	War
William	287	War
Stegall, Elijah	99	Rut
Nancy	2	Lin
Solomon	21	Gil
William	10	Ove
Stekenson see Stepenson		
Stell, Boaz	355	Whi
James	75	Rut
Stelly, Polly	117	Ste
Stem, Asa	9	Bed
James	9	Bed
James	15	Bed
John	4	Bed
Stembridge, Mary	397	Wil
Stenett, John	30	Lin
Stennet, Benjamin	93	Dav
Stenson, Alexander W.	49	Smi
Step, Colby	52	Smi
Frederick	280	War
Stepenson, Elizebeth	57	Mau
Samuel	57	Mau
Stepeson, Nathaniel	32	Mau
Stephens, Allen	32	Bed
Archelas	19	Ove
Bartholomew	63	Dav
David	17	Ove
E. M.	120	Ste
Edward	27	Fra
Elizabeth	177	Sum
Garrison	49	Smi
Henry	36	Lin
James	2	Bed
James	18	Lin
James	55	Mau
James E.	36	Lin
Jeremiah	27	Fra
Jeremiah	400	Wil
Joel	10	Wll
John	32	Bed

Stephens (cont.)
John 81 Dav
John 23 Jac
John 7 Ove
John 48 Smi
John 64 Wll
John, Sr. 22 Jac
Mark 29 Fra
Nancy 370 Whi
Robert 36 Lin
Robert 312 War
Samuel 28 Fra
Thomas 7 Ove
Vachel 40 Bed
William 178 Sum
Wallace 178 Sum
Zoral 17 Ove
Stephenson, Benjamin 388 Wil
Chiles 66 Mau
Edward 17 Bed
Edward 280 War
Franklin 388 Wil
Hugh B. 48 Smi
James W. 32 Mau
John H. 179 Sum
Josiah 385 Wil
Robert 37 Bed
Rosanah 66 Mau
Sarah 383 Wil
Thomas 32 Mau
William [2] 29 Fra
William 66 Mau
William H. 26 Mau
see Stepenson, Stepeson
Stephins, Henry 13 Hum
William 18 Lin
Stepleton, Jonathan 54 Wll
Stepp, Joshua 9 Gil
Steptoe, Simon 10 Hum
Stergean, John C. 44 Mau
Stern see Stem
Sternes, John 177 Sum
Stevens, Charles 66 Wll
Edward 19 Wll
George 19 Wll
German 19 Wll
Henry 28 Wll
James 5 Per
Jeremiah 41 Wll
Jeremiah 44 Wll
Lovinia 28 Wll
Mary 30 Wll
Reddin 9 Bed
Richard 101 Rut
Silas 4 Wll
Thomas 39 Wll
William 6 Hum
William 29 Wll
Stevenson, Elam 10 Gil
Elizabeth 2 Law
Elizabeth 19 Lin
George 67 Dav
Hugh 19 Lin

Stevenson (cont.)
James 80 Dav
Mary 2 Law
William 56 Wll
see Stebenson
Steverson, Fanny 17 Wll
Moses D. 37 Wll
Samuel 20 Gil
Steveson, John 382 Wil
Steward, Richard 21 Gil
Salley 15 Gil
Stewart, Abner 112 Wil
Abner 379 Wil
Alexander 295 War
Alexander 403 Wil
Alexander 44 Wll
Ame 178 Sum
Andrew 10 Hic
Andrew 16 Rob
Anney 48 Mau
Archibald 19 Bed
Arthur 43 Wll
Barnet 186 Sum
Bart 3 Per
Bartlet 30 Fra
Benj. 22 Jac
Brice 27 Rob
Charles 73 Dav
Charles 27 Rob
Cyrus 380 Wil
Daniel M. 79 Rut
Demsey 4 Rob
Drewry 49 Smi
Elias 12 Hic
Elisha 3 Per
Elisha 360 Whi
Frances 359 Whi
Henry 49 Smi
Henry 16 Wll
Herbert 27 Rob
Hugh 24 Jac
Isaac 51 Smi
James 76 Dav
James 12 Gil
James 10 Mon
James 82 Rut
James 102 Rut
James 49 Smi
James 178 Sum
James 379 Wil
James R. 73 Dav
James W. 83 Rut
Jesse 8 Ove
John 63 Mau
John 10 Mon
John 17 Mon
John 11 Ove
John 17 Ove
John 27 Rob
John 90 Rut
John 116 Ste
John 123 Ste
John 175 Sum

Stewart (cont.)		
John	178	Sum
John	179	Sum
John	401	Wil
Joseph	392	Wil
Judith	10	Hic
Lauzet	10	Law
Marcus	43	Wll
Mary	178	Sum
Memford	186	Sum
Milus	179	Sum
Peyton	186	Sum
Rebecca	12	Mon
Richard	361	Whi
Robert	177	Sum
Robert	66	Wll
Sally	86	Rut
Sally	178	Sum
Samuel	29	Fra
Samuel	176	Sum
Samuel	416	Wil
Samuel P.	10	Ove
Sarah	84	Rut
Thomas	12	Gil
Thomas	21	Gil
Thomas	49	Smi
Thomas	15	Wll
Walter	280	War
William	44	Bed
William	57	Dav
William	4	Har
William	9	Hum
William	10	Mon
William	11	Mon
William	2	Per
William	102	Rut
William	177	Sum
William	352	Whi
William	360	Whi
Wm., Senr.	10	Hic
see Stwarte		
Stewert, Samuel	28	Bed
Stickley, Christopher	349	Whi
Stikes, Enoch	416	Wil
Stiles, John	36	Lin
William	285	War
Zachariah	40	Mau
Still, George	390	Wil
Josiah	82	Rut
Littleberry	98	Rut
Polly	29	Fra
Scinthey	39	Wll
Stinnett, John	270	War
Stinson, Alexander	21	Gil
Alsa	177	Sum
Bendit	52	Smi
James	11	Lin
John	7	Har
John	52	Smi
John L.	176	Sum
Stipe, Jacob	349	Whi
Stobaugh, Andrew	7	Per
Edmun	6	Per
Stobaugh (cont.)		
Henry	14	Hic
John	84	Dav
John	6	Per
William	6	Per
Stobough, A.	9	Way
Stochart, John	92	Rut
Nathan	92	Rut
Stockard, Ellender	34	Mau
James	28	Mau
Joseph	34	Mau
Richard	34	Mau
Stockart, John	120	Ste
Stockdale, Matthew	118	Ste
Stockett, Joseph	17	Wll
Stephen	17	Wll
Stockman, John	66	Wll
John A.	64	Wll
Stocks, Josiah	12	Wll
William	97	Rut
Young	12	Wll
Stockstill, David	286	War
Lebedee	282	War
Warner	288	War
Stocktin, Thomas	8	Har
Stockton, D. H., Mr.	1	Law
Elizabeth, Mrs.	3	Law
John	14	Ove
John	16	Ove
Samuel	2	Ove
Stogdon, David	22	Gil
Stokely, Isaah	284	War
see Vinson		
Stoker, Lewis	287	War
Robert	291	War
Stokes, Abner	112	Ste
James	11	Law
John	23	Jac
John	22	Mon
Jordon G.	50	Smi
Thomas	281	War
William	359	Whi
Stolcup, Rachael	24	Jac
Stone, Asa	28	Fra
Clack	405	Wil
Clark	32	Rob
Corder	352	Whi
Edward	32	Rob
Eusebius	176	Sum
Hendley	10	Wll
Ireby	24	Jac
Jacob	48	Smi
James	29	Fra
James	3	Hic
Jeremiah	51	Smi
Joel	28	Fra
John	9	Gil
John	17	Mon
John	3	Ove
John	4	Rob
John	32	Rob
John B.	301	War
John H.	2	Dic

Stone (cont.)		
Jonathan	294	War
Joseph	7	Rob
Marble	12	Dic
Micajah	26	Lin
Micajah	3	Ove
Moses	24	Lin
Nicholas	20	Rob
Nicholas	175	Sum
Nimrod	300	War
Polly	31	Bed
Prior	18	Lin
Randle	110	Ste
Richard	16	Rob
Roland	22	Wll
Simon	29	Fra
Solomon	9	Law
Stephen	176	Sum
Susana	111	Ste
Thomas	28	Fra
Thomas	23	Jac
Thomas	29	Rob
Thomas	177	Sum
Thomas	179	Sum
Thomas	406	Wil
Thomas C.	19	Gil
Thomas W.	48	Mau
Thos.	20	Mon
Uriah	24	Jac
Uriah	44	Mau
William	7	Dic
William	48	Mau
William	3	Ove
William	176	Sum
William	177	Sum
William	313	War
William	316	War
William	22	Wll
William	53	Wll
William N.	388	Wil
see Slane, Slone		
Stoneman, John	413	Wil
Stonum, George N.	15	Rob
Stores, Richd.	2	Hic
Storey, Archibald	6	Ove
Joshua [2]	12	Ove
Robert	12	Ove
Vinson	26	Mau
Stormond, Thomas	28	Fra
Storn see Stone		
Storr, William	14	Hum
Story, Archibald	17	Gil
Caleb	13	Gil
Daniel, Jr.	7	Hum
Daniel, Sr.	7	Hum
Henry	91	Dav
James	3	Per
James	179	Sum
Robert	35	Lin
Samuel	4	Per
Stothart, Robert	80	Dav
Stott, Rawleigh	47	Smi
Stotts, Joseph	294	War
Stouer, Henry	291	War
Stout, Absalom	91	Rut
Benjamin	316	War
Charles	41	Bed
David	9	Ove
David	19	Ove
Ezekiel	16	Way
Joseph	8	Ove
Robert	17	Way
S. V. D.	79	Dav
Samuel	24	Jac
Samuel	8	Ove
William	18	Ove
Stovall, Bat.	15	Bed
Bat.	179	Sum
Bezard	178	Sum
George	27	Fra
George	179	Sum
George P.	1	Lin
Henry	28	Fra
James	176	Sum
James V.	28	Fra
John	27	Fra
Mary	11	Gil
Thomas	179	Sum
William	179	Sum
Stover, John	342	Whi
Louis	24	Jac
Stow, Hugh	33	Mau
Stowall, Jane	89	Rut
Jesse	96	Rut
Stowe, Nancy	16	Dic
Stowers, Catharine	178	Sum
Thomas	8	Ove
Strader, Henry	179	Sum
Jacob	178	Sum
Strain, David	59	Mau
James	342	Whi
James Q.	42	Lin
John	21	Rob
John	75	Rut
Thomas	42	Lin
Strambler, George	28	Fra
Stramler, Reuben	2	Wll
Strange, Beverly H.	48	Smi
Henry	69	Dav
Stratten, Calvin	8	Bed
Henery	53	Mau
Thomas	63	Dav
William	53	Mau
Stratter, Adam	15	Bed
Stratton, James	175	Sum
William	177	Sum
Straughn, John C.	16	Rob
Strawbridge, William	70	Dav
Strawn, James	10	Law
Jetson	27	Fra
John	61	Dav
Peyton	27	Fra
William	2	Law
Strayhorn, Jane	33	Mau
John	69	Mau
Streaklen, Joseph	15	Wll

Street, Anthony	28	Fra
Asa	14	Lin
Elizabeth	179	Sum
Isaac	25	Lin
John	2	Hum
Lucinda	46	Lin
Moses	13	Dic
Solomon	30	Lin
William	27	Fra
Strice, Anderson	396	Wil
Strickin, Samuel	69	Mau
Strickland, Harmon	48	Smi
James	8	Law
Zechariah	2	Law
Strickler, Warren G.	77	Rut
Stricklin, Campbell	70	Mau
Chloe	36	Lin
Frederick	18	Gil
Gidian	70	Mau
Isham	33	Rob
Stephen	7	Per
Susanna	33	Rob
William	11	Har
Stringer, Edward	12	Hic
Elijah	51	Smi
Gray	17	Rob
James	26	Lin
Reuben	12	Hic
Reuben	7	Hum
Stringfellow, Margaret	81	Dav
William	96	Dav
Striplin, Thomas	53	Mau
Strode, James	177	Sum
John	176	Sum
Strong, Christopher	14	Dic
David	22	Gil
James	50	Smi
John	51	Smi
Samuel	50	Smi
Sherwood	69	Dav
Thomas	90	Rut
Thomas	100	Rut
Thomas	50	Smi
Thomas	177	Sum
William	51	Smi
Stroop, Elizabeth	80	Rut
Strother, Gideon	51	Smi
James	176	Sum
John	15	Rob
Judd	49	Smi
Robert	79	Rut
Susanah	178	Sum
William	28	Fra
Stroud, Allen	103	Rut
Hampton	7	Law
Jesse	7	Dic
Jesse	14	Rob
John	29	Bed
John	31	Rob
Joseph	4	Mon
Marsha	280	War
Oren	320	War
Sherwood	80	Rut
Stroud (cont.)		
Thomas	7	Dic
William	29	Bed
William	12	Mon
William	31	Rob
William	294	War
Stroughn, James L.	17	Rob
Strut, Bird	320	War
Stuard, Elias	29	Mau
Thos.	6	Law
Stuart, James	386	Wil
Jason	11	Hic
Mary	44	Mau
Stubblefield, Clemment	90	Dav
George	176	Sum
Jeremiah	37	Lin
Joel	37	Lin
John	48	Smi
Lemuel	176	Sum
Robert	37	Lin
Stephen	119	Ste
Stephen	11	Way
Tho.	177	Sum
Stubblifield, Geo.	179	Sum
see Sublefield		
Stublefield, Jeremiah	179	Sum
Stublifield, Woodruff	178	Sum
Stubs, Dennis	120	Ste
Stuckland, John	10	Har
Studdart, John	119	Ste
Studevan, Manon	43	Wll
Sylvanus	10	Mon
Stull, Daniel	24	Jac
Nancy	72	Dav
Nicholas	90	Dav
Samuel	58	Dav
Samuel [?]	61	Dav
Stults, George	307	War
Stump, Catharine	88	Dav
Christopher	78	Dav
Harris, of Frederick, Deceased	87	Dav
John	87	Dav
Sturdevant, Benjamin	62	Dav
Henry	68	Dav
Lewis	65	Dav
Sturdivan, John	29	Fra
Sturdivant, Benjamin	5	Dic
Elizabeth	85	Rut
Sturman, William	300	War
Stutts, Solomon	6	Rob
Stwarte, Richard	20	Lin
Sublefield, George	285	War
Sublet, Fields	29	Fra
William	28	Fra
Sublett, A. C.	74	Rut
G. A.	74	Rut
William A.	82	Rut
Sudbury, William D.	14	Wll
Sugg, Harbert	48	Bed
John H.	50	Bed
Josiah	62	Dav
Timothy	50	Bed

Sugg (cont.)		
William	50	Bed
Suggs, Aquilla	26	Lin
Henry	12	Lin
Henry	26	Lin
Rolin	106	She
Solomon	392	Wil
William	318	War
Suiter, Thos.	33	Mon
Suker, Joseph	13	Gil
Sul..., ...ua	96	Dav
Sulavan, Smyth	1	Per
Sulivan, Alexander	301	War
Charles	284	War
Clemma	289	War
Elizabeth	368	Whi
Fletcher	176	Sum
George	369	Whi
John	98	Dav
John	343	Whi
Stephen	58	Dav
Sulivent, John	52	Wil
Peter	396	Wil
Zachariah	94	Dav
Sullavin, Uriah	35	Mau
Sullens, Zachariah	353	Whi
Sullevin, Russel	97	Dav
Sullinger, Thomas	29	Lin
Sullins, Jesse	312	War
Zacheriah	312	War
Sullivan, Abe	387	Wil
Bennet	68	Dav
Caleb	22	Bed
Cornelious	23	Lin
Daniel	52	Bed
Daniel	94	Dav
Daniel	48	Smi
Edmund	177	Sum
Eppsey	23	Lin
George	26	Bed
George	8	Dic
Hollon	394	Wil
Jacob	376	Wil
Jenkins	115	Wil
Jeremiah	23	Lin
Jesse	395	Wil
Jessee	29	Mon
John	26	Lin
Joseph	178	Sum
Lee	49	Smi
Levi	395	Wil
Levin	13	Hic
Lucy	23	Lin
Molly	392	Wil
Nancy	57	Dav
Nancy	8	Dic
Owen	178	Sum
Reuben	394	Wil
Rinkins	394	Wil
Sarah	23	Lin
Simeon	394	Wil
Tabitha	48	Smi
Tabitha	49	Smi
Sullivan (cont.)		
Turner	87	Dav
William	29	Mon
William	32	Mon
William	51	Smi
Willie	49	Smi
Sullivant, Jesse	93	Rut
Jesse	98	Rut
Samuel W.	13	Law
Sumbo, Michael	16	Rob
Sumerville, John	19	Rob
Joseph	176	Sum
Summer, Ezekiel	176	Sum
Summerford, Edward	47	Lin
Summers, Abraham	6	Lin
Anthony	414	Wil
Bassil	96	Rut
Benjamin	96	Rut
Bozeman	175	Sum
Charles	128	Ste
Cornelius	29	Rob
G.	128	Ste
George, Jr.	96	Rut
George, Sen.	96	Rut
George D.	417	Wil
Harden	401	Wil
James	110	Ste
James	395	Wil
James	414	Wil
John	6	Lin
Leven	96	Rut
Matthew	414	Wil
Paul	96	Rut
Thomas	19	Rob
Thomas	96	Rut
Thomas	175	Sum
William	96	Rut
Summons, Thomas	13	Dic
Sumner, Daniel R.	14	Lin
Duke W.	74	Dav
Exum P.	87	Dav
Tartan	36	Bed
Sumners, John	175	Sum
Sumpkin, Edmund	13	Gil
Suter, Edmond	25	Mon
Sutfin, James	103	Rut
Sutherland, Eli	83	Rut
Suthern, Samuel	404	Wil
Sutten, Lemuel	118	Ste
Saml.	113	Ste
Saml.	122	Ste
Sutterfield, Lary	125	Ste
Suttle, John	364	Whi
Pressley	178	Sum
Suttles, Edward	52	Smi
Mark	14	Rob
Sutton, Abner	52	Smi
Colby	47	Smi
Edmund	84	Rut
George	52	Smi
James	52	Smi
James, Sen.	52	Smi
Jasper R.	64	Mau

Sutton (cont.)
John 51 Bed
John [2] 23 Jac
Joseph 50 Smi
Joshua 58 Wll
Levi 406 Wil
Nancy 5 Gil
Richard 65 Dav
Stephen 85 Dav
Thomas 32 Bed
Tollivin 406 Wil
William 31 Bed
William 49 Bed
William 52 Smi
see Sootin
Swafford, Isaac 6 Law
Swaggart, Christian 9 Rob
Swain, John 12 Law
John 21 Wll
William 12 Law
William 55 Wll
William M. 114 Wil
William W. 396 Wil
Wm. 6 Lin
Swaine, William 21 Gil
Swair see Swan
Swallow, Andrew 13 Ove
Jacob 13 Ove
Swan, Alexander 23 Lin
Burch 15 Rob
Edward 16 Rob
Isaac 408 Wil
James 18 Rob
James 408 Wil
John 406 Wil
John 408 Wil
Joseph 18 Rob
Mathew 3 Law
Sarah 44 Lin
Thomas 42 Bed
see Sivin
Swaney, Alexander 11 Har
John L. 176 Sum
Swann, Joseph 28 Fra
Moses 79 Rut
Uriah 12 Rob
Swanner, Joel 3 Lin
John 394 Wil
Swanson, Edward 10 Wll
James 38 Wll
Peter 15 Gil
Richard 39 Wll
William 16 Wll
Swansy, James N. 29 Wll
John 29 Wll
Swar, John 119 Ste
Richard 119 Ste
Robert 119 Ste
Sweany, John 404 Wil
Swearengan, Hugha 15 Ove
Swearingam, James 18 Way
Swearingim, James 23 Jac
Wm. 24 Jac
Sweat, Allen 11 Lin
Anthony 177 Sum
Edward 402 Wil
John 24 Jac
John 13 Lin
Virtue 298 War
William 408 Wil
Sweaton, John 29 Fra
Moses 29 Fra
Sweazea, John 22 Jac
Matthaas 25 Jac
Sweer, Charles 18 Ove
Sweet, James 28 Lin
John 88 Rut
Sweete, John 50 Mau
Moses 50 Mau
Swengle, George 395 Wil
Swenny, William 408 Wil
Sweringim, William 349 Whi
Swett, Caleb 7 Gil
Edward 404 Wil
Jeremiah 369 Whi
Joseph 404 Wil
Levi 369 Whi
Robert 404 Wil
William 404 Wil
Swift, Absalom 26 Mon
Elisha 342 Whi
Flower 31 Bed
P. B. 23 Jac
Richard 6 Lin
Richard 29 Rob
Thos. 25 Mon
William M. 68 Dav
Swim, Levi 347 Whi
William 53 Mau
Swimm, William 27 Fra
Swindel, Asa 344 Whi
Casen 345 Whi
Caswell 345 Whi
George C. 345 Whi
Holawell [Holdwell?] 343 Whi
John 344 Whi
Thomas 355 Whi
Swindle, Christopher 342 Whi
Job 405 Wil
John 2 Hum
Swindler, Joel 404 Wil
Swinea, James 18 Lin
Swink, George 30 Fra
Michael 92 Rut
Swinney, Henry 36 Wll
Janc 353 Whi
Joel 175 Sum
John 1 Bed
John 7 Wll
Joseph 42 Bed
Samuel 286 War
Swintford, Jane 37 Lin
Swisher, Henry 7 Wll
Jas. G. 120 Ste
Swoap, James 30 Fra
Sykes, Benjamin O. 279 War

Sykes (cont.)
Jacob 25 Mon
Joshua 50 Smi
Warren 25 Mon
Syler, Frederick 8 Ove
Synclair, William 10 Ove
Sypert, Stephen 391 Wil
William 398 Wil
see Cypert
Syzley, Rachal 27 Mau

--- T ---

Tabbscott, Albion 30 Fra
Taber, James 5 Per
John 94 Rut
Robert 7 Per
Tabor, James 24 Hic
Russel 24 Hic
Wm. 24 Hic
Tabourn, Gilliam 9 Gil
Tacker, John 19 Gil
Joshua 20 Gil
Seaborn 19 Gil
William 11 Law
Tackett, David 360 Whi
Phillip 369 Whi
William 398 Wil
Tailar, Dempsey 39 Mau
Redan 39 Mau
Tailer, Elizebith 55 Mau
John 63 Mau
Thomas 61 Mau
Tailior, Edward 88 Rut
Tailor, Abner 3 Per
Adair 103 Rut
David 5 Per
George 103 Rut
John 46 Mau
Samuel 8 Per
Tracis 8 Per
Tait, John [2] 58 Dav
John 52 Smi
John, Sen. 52 Smi
John J. 8 Lin
Joseph 59 Dav
Martha 58 Dav
Netherland 38 Wll
William 61 Dav
Zenos 88 Dav
Talbot, Eli 94 Dav
Joseph 78 Dav
Thomas 76 Dav
Tale, Zachariah 383 Wil
Taley, John W. 18 Way
Talkaton, Saml. 121 Ste
Tallent, Thomas 361 Whi
Talley, Abraham 46 Mau
Allen 52 Wll
David 180 Sum
Hopson 6 Per
Talley (cont.)
John 5 Per
Martin 111 Wil
Martin 405 Wil
Nelson 68 Dav
Talliferro, Benjn. 43 Bed
John 43 Bed
Richard 43 Bed
Tallow, Zachariah 391 Wil
Tally, Archibald 76 Rut
Banister 61 Dav
Betsey 31 Fra
Catharine 31 Fra
George 4 Way
Haly 412 Wil
Joshua 53 Smi
Pleasant 104 Rut
Richard 412 Wil
Rubin 180 Sum
William 412 Wil
Zachariah 74 Dav
Tamer, Matthew 305 War
William 305 War
Tamlinggan, Jessey 41 Mau
Tancasley, John 31 Fra
Tankersley, John 36 Bed
John R. 5 Wll
John R. 44 Wll
Rolling 13 Gil
Tankersly, Benjamin 9 Bed
Charles 298 War
Tankesly, Joseph 39 Lin
Tanksby, William 363 Whi
Tannehill, Wilkins 76 Dav
Tanner, Edward 31 Fra
James 110 Ste
John 286 War
Joseph 41 Wll
Richard 39 Wll
Samuel 41 Wll
Wiley 4 Per
Tanver, William 389 Wil
Tanxley, James 25 Jac
Tapley, Henry 411 Wil
Hubbard 179 Sum
Mary 57 Wll
Pleasent 412 Wil
Stearling 401 Wil
Tardall, John 30 Fra
Tare, Richard V. 91 Rut
Tarett, John 7 Per
Tarkenton, Benjamin 18 Wll
John 34 Wll
John [deleted] 38 Wll
Joseph 33 Wll
Joshua 48 Wll
William 18 Wll
Tarket, James 310 War
Tarner see Tamer
Tarpley, Alexander 4 Gil
James 33 Wll
Thomas 11 Gil
Tarrant, Leonard 30 Fra

Tart, James	120	Ste	Taylor (cont.)		
Tarver, Benja.	181	Sum	Alexr.	180	Sum
Benjamin	389	Wil	Also	356	Whi
Edward D.	54	Smi	Anthony	5	Gil
Fanney	389	Wil	Arthur	281	War
Thomas	394	Wil	Barziller	54	Smi
Tarwater, James	31	Fra	Benja.	179	Sum
John	31	Fra	Benjamin	31	Fra
Lewis	31	Fra	Benjamin	54	Smi
Tarwatter, John	31	Fra	Calib	383	Wil
Tassy, John	301	War	Canellium	55	Smi
Tate, Aaron	280	War	Charles	22	Bed
Alexander	286	War	Charlotte	179	Sum
Easther	81	Dav	Daniel	9	Hum
George	29	Mau	Daniel	31	Mon
George	64	Mau	Darman	45	Mau
Henry	78	Dav	David	31	Rob
Henry	303	War	David	53	Smi
James	280	War	David	54	Smi
John	27	Lin	David	55	Smi
John	5	Ove	David	112	Ste
John	18	Ove	David	116	Ste
John	315	War	Drewry	54	Smi
Larkin	12	Dic	Drury	10	Hic
Mackling	386	Wil	Edmond	11	Hum
Robbert	54	Mau	Edmond	37	Lin
Robert	296	War	Edmond	20	Mon
Robert	385	Wil	Edmond	110	Ste
Robert	386	Wil	Edmund	290	War
Samuel	7	Dic	Edward	391	Wil
William	53	Mau	Eli	7	Lin
Zachariah	181	Sum	Elijah	4	Lin
Zachariah	114	Wil	Elisha	385	Wil
Zed	394	Wil	Elizabeth	410	Wil
Tateum, Howel	79	Dav	Eppes	76	Rut
James	11	Dic	Francis	30	Fra
Tatom, John	12	Wll	Frederick	84	Dav
Tatum, Benjamin	8	Rob	Fredrick	2	Bed
Dabney	378	Wil	George	62	Dav
Edward	89	Rut	George	88	Dav
Edward, Jur.	89	Rut	George	5	Gil
Holewell	88	Rut	George	6	Gil
Irey	180	Sum	George P.	181	Sum
Jesse	89	Rut	Goodin	96	Rut
Jisiah [Isaiah?]	62	Mau	Goodwyl	15	Wll
John	8	Lin	Green B.	84	Dav
John, Senr.	11	Dic	Harbord	111	Ste
John C.	8	Lin	Hardin	6	Lin
Jonathan	75	Rut	Henry	8	Lin
Jonathan	89	Rut	Henry	20	Mon
Nathaniel	65	Dav	Henry	54	Smi
Peter	13	Dic	Howel	21	Mon
Stephen	11	Dic	Isaac	371	Whi
William	8	Rob	Jacob	179	Sum
William, Jr.	6	Dic	James	6	Dic
William, Sr.	6	Dic	James [2]	30	Fra
Wm.	24	Hic	James	6	Gil
see Tateum			James	25	Jac
Tayler, Alen	39	Mau	James	9	Mon
Taylor, A.	112	Ste	James	89	Rut
Abraham	6	Gil	James	53	Smi
Abraham	383	Wil	James	119	Ste
Abram	19	Wll	James	181	Sum

Taylor (cont.)
James 316 War
James 357 Whi
James 23 Wll
Jeramiah 18 Ove
Jeremiah 53 Smi
Jesse 51 Bed
John 25 Bed
John 30 Fra
John 19 Rob
John 76 Rut
John 53 Smi
John 179 Sum
John 357 Whi
John 115 Wil
John [2] 410 Wil
John, Jr. 60 Dav
John, Sr. 60 Dav
John C. 50 Bed
John C. 8 Lin
John K. 8 Lin
John L. 180 Sum
John M. 180 Sum
John P. 14 Gil
John S. 7 Hic
John Y. 21 Mon
Jonathan 34 Rob
Joseph 30 Fra
Joseph 5 Hum
Joseph 7 Ove
Joseph 14 Ove
Joseph 53 Smi
Joseph 115 Ste
Joseph 116 Ste
Joseph 181 Sum
Joseph 26 Wll
Joseph, Sen. 31 Fra
Joshua 31 Fra
Joshua 411 Wil
Josiah 22 Rob
Lewis 31 Fra
Lewis C. 20 Mon
Lockey 6 Dic
Manoah 3 Mon
Margaret 181 Sum
Mark N. 82 Dav
Martha 71 Dav
Martha 24 Wll
Matthews 30 Fra
Mekin 362 Whi
Micajah 305 War
Mills 18 Rob
Moses 12 Ove
Nancy 25 Rob
Nancy 54 Smi
Nancy 281 War
Perigran 402 Wil
Pierson 52 Wll
Polley 5 Gil
Polly 12 Ove
Rachel 14 Gil
Rebecka 370 Whi
Reuben 14 Ove

Taylor (cont.)
Richard 53 Smi
Richard 115 Ste
Richd. 21 Mon
Robert 72 Dav
Robert 13 Gil
Robert 180 Sum
Samuel 296 War
Solomon 385 Wil
Stephen 55 Wll
Tabitha 54 Smi
Thean 180 Sum
Tho. 181 Sum
Thomas 31 Fra
Thomas 76 Rut
Thomas 56 Smi
Thomas 357 Whi
Thornton 93 Dav
Timothy 116 Ste
William 60 Dav
William 94 Dav
William 3 Dic
William [2] 30 Fra
William 24 Lin
William 18 Ove
William 30 Rob
William 53 Smi
William 55 Smi
William 124 Ste
William 181 Sum
William 363 Whi
William 367 Whi
William 390 Whi
Willis 281 War
Wilson 54 Smi
Wm. 22 Hic
Wm. 131 Ste
Woody 31 Lin
Young 37 Lin
see Tolar
Tays, Samuel 8 Ove
Teafetilah, Henry 25 Jac
Teague, Abraham 316 War
James C. 420 Wil
John 419 Wil
William 16 Dic
William 419 Wil
Teal, Abraham 97 Rut
John 53 Smi
Tealand, Richard 88 Dav
Teale, Edward 5 Dic
Teas, Joseph 3 Law
Tease, James 14 Hum
William 13 Hum
Teasley, George 13 Rob
George 53 Smi
John 10 Mon
Lucy 10 Mon
Teat, Simon 17 Hic
Tedder, Daniel 55 Smi
John 55 Smi
Tedford, Robert 47 Lin
Thomas 23 Lin

Tedford (cont.)		
William	3	Per
Tedrick, John	2	Wll
Tedwell, Isaiah	9	Dic
Teel, Adam	25	Jac
Alexander	94	Rut
Edward	21	Lin
Henery	31	Mau
Susan	25	Jac
Teisley, Daniel	294	War
Tempest, William B.	7	Har
Temple, Burwell	16	Wll
Jesse	64	Mau
John	25	Jac
Rhodric	31	Wll
William	65	Dav
Zachariah	53	Smi
Temples, John	55	Smi
Templeton, Ann	6	Lin
George	345	Whi
John	367	Whi
Thomas	305	War
Templin, Jacob	17	Gil
Tems, Leonard H.	391	Wil
Tench, John R.	87	Rut
Tendal, Noah B.	71	Dav
Tenison, Matthew	16	Wll
Zechariah	15	Gil
Tenner see Turner		
Tennery, William	9	Gil
Tennesson, Henry	28	Lin
Tennin, William A.	86	Rut
Tennison, Abraham	96	Rut
Joseph	3	Wll
Samuel	94	Dav
Solomon	97	Rut
Tennpenny, Daniel	316	War
see Tenpenny	316	War
Tenpenny, Daniel	96	Rut
Richard	316	War
Tenridges, Brinley	381	Wil
Tensley, Thomas	19	Ove
Ternigan see Jernigan		
Terrel, David	20	Wll
Lewis	15	Mon
William	5	Per
Terrell, James	36	Wll
Joel	13	Wll
Joseph	20	Mon
Tabitha	2	Bed
William	18	Mon
William	396	Wil
see Ferrell		
Terrey, Jeramiah	65	Dav
William	31	Mau
Terril, George	27	Mau
Terrill, James	17	Gil
Terry, Clement	31	Fra
Elizabeth	39	Lin
Francis	25	Jac
George	56	Smi
James	31	Fra
James [2]	25	Jac
Terry (cont.)		
James	54	Smi
Jeremiah	47	Wll
John	17	Bed
John	25	Jac
John	366	Whi
Joseph	25	Jac
Joseph	367	Whi
Ker	25	Jac
Nancy	25	Jac
Nathaniel D.	15	Mon
Peter	53	Smi
Sally	53	Smi
Thomas	55	Smi
Thacher, Elender	10	Har
Thacker, Larkin	96	Rut
Marian	96	Rut
Nathan	27	Mon
Pleasant M.	6	Gil
William	21	Rob
Thackey, Nancy	93	Dav
Tharp, Sally	55	Smi
William	16	Mon
Winney	31	Fra
Tharpe, Goodhope	21	Gil
John	13	Gil
Thaxton, James	8	Mon
John	9	Mon
John	283	War
Paul	25	Jac
William	8	Mon
Z. B.	25	Jac
Thedford, James	13	Dic
Thirman, Flemming	62	Mau
Thistle, Hasna	14	Law
Thmman, Fleming G.	181	Sum
John, Sr.	179	Sum
John G.	181	Sum
see Thurmond		
Thomas, Adam	55	Smi
Allen	80	Rut
Andrew	65	Wll
Ariach	180	Sum
Benjamin	47	Mau
Champion	54	Smi
Charles	312	War
Christian	88	Rut
Cordy	11	Hum
Cornilius	180	Sum
David	55	Smi
David D.	10	Hum
Edward	11	Wll
Elizabeth	38	Mau
Elizebeth	25	Mau
Ephraim	55	Smi
Ezekiah	120	Ste
Franky B.	341	Whi
George	352	Whi
Henry	180	Sum
Henry	181	Sum
Henry	396	Wil
Henry	417	Wil
Hiram	25	Jac

Thomas (cont.)		
Humphrey	55	Smi
Isaac	371	Whi
Isaac J.	39	Mau
Jacob [2]	25	Jac
Jacob	417	Wil
James	27	Mau
James	55	Smi
James	291	War
James	404	Wil
James	415	Wil
James	417	Wil
James J.	16	Wll
James M.	16	Dic
Jesse	14	Gil
Jesse	25	Jac
Job H.	28	Mau
John	79	Dav
John	4	Hum
John	25	Jac
John	38	Mau
John	3	Per
John	8	Per
John	6	Rob
John	27	Rob
John	301	War
John	312	War
John	387	Wil
John	415	Wil
John	15	Wll
John	65	Wll
John P.	418	Wil
Jonathan	31	Fra
Joseph	55	Smi
Joseph	366	Whi
Lewis	26	Mon
Lewis	55	Smi
Lewis G.	89	Rut
Micky	97	Dav
Nancy	71	Dav
Nathan	122	Ste
Nathaniel	65	Wll
Nathaniel H.	7	Wll
Phillip	75	Dav
Phineas	7	Wll
Polly	181	Sum
Richard	30	Fra
Richard	25	Mau
Robert	90	Dav
Robert	180	Sum
Saml.	13	Hic
Samuel	6	Law
Samuel	89	Rut
Samuel	363	Whi
Stephen	29	Mon
Timothy	97	Rut
W.	24	Mau
William	60	Dav
William	12	Dic
William	27	Lin
William	28	Mau
William [2]	77	Rut
William	85	Rut
Thomas (cont.)		
William	55	Smi
William	181	Sum
William	304	War
William	312	War
William	369	Whi
William	396	Wil
William	413	Wil
William	415	Wll
William	19	Wll
William M.	1	Dic
William P.	180	Sum
Willie	88	Rut
Wilson	417	Wil
Young	16	Mon
Zacheriah F.	53	Smi
Zachra	3	Per
Thomason, Edward	121	Ste
Elizabeth	110	Ste
Joseph	110	Ste
Mark	15	Mon
Stephen	116	Ste
Stephen	122	Ste
Thomasson, William	387	Wil
Thomerson, Adam	53	Smi
Elias	56	Smi
George [2]	55	Smi
Joseph	55	Smi
Nathaniel	31	Fra
Samuel	55	Smi
Thomas	55	Smi
Thompson, Alexander	12	Gil
Alexander	30	Mau
Allen	93	Dav
Andrew	7	Rob
Andrew	416	Wil
Archibald	53	Smi
Benjamin	30	Fra
Benjamin	54	Smi
Benjamin	52	Wll
Benwell	31	Fra
Betsey	54	Smi
Charles	6	Dic
Daniel	310	War
David	96	Dav
David	55	Smi
David	306	War
Ebinezer	9	Law
Elijah	16	Ove
Elizabeth	97	Rut
Ephraim	66	Dav
Ezenab	5	Bed
George	25	Bed
George N.	83	Rut
Gideon	91	Rut
Henry	388	Wil
Henry D.	75	Rut
Isaac	29	Mau
Jacob	419	Wil
James	6	Dic
James	20	Gil
James	410	Wil
James	415	Wil

Thompson (cont.)
James 416 Wil
James 14 Wll
James 32 Wll
James 51 Wll
James, Sr. 416 Wil
James B. 8 Wll
James P. 386 Wil
James S. 279 War
Jane 27 Mon
Jason 65 Dav
Jason 8 Wll
Jesse 80 Rut
John 30 Fra
John 1 Hum
John 13 Hum
John 2 Law
John 25 Lin
John 43 Lin
John 41 Mau
John 13 Mon
John 79 Rut
John 90 Rut
John 53 Smi
John 55 Smi
John 386 Wil
John 34 Wll
John P. 91 Dav
Jonathan 30 Mau
Joseph 90 Rut
Joseph 410 Wil
Lawrence 1 Wll
Lemuel 20 Lin
Leonard 370 Whi
Leonard 47 Wll
Levi F. 27 Wll
Mansfield 314 War
Martha 40 Bed
Moses 399 Wil
Nathanal 28 Mau
Neel 409 Wil
Newcom 53 Bed
Nicholas 28 Rob
Osburn 317 War
Owen 97 Rut
Ozburn 388 Wil
Reuben 27 Bed
Richd. 2 Hic
Robert 10 Bed
Robert 10 Hum
Robert 25 Jac
Robert 90 Rut
Saml. 47 Bed
Samuel 66 Dav
Samuel 38 Lin
Samuel 9 Ove
Sarah 53 Smi
Seth 29 Mau
Sherod 8 Dic
Th. 24 Mau
Thomas 14 Bed
Thomas 65 Dav
Thomas 94 Dav

Thompson (cont.)
Thomas 34 Mau
Thomas 35 Wll
Thompson 37 Bed
Thos. 3 Hic
Thos. 9 Way
William 86 Dav
William 91 Dav
William 30 Fra
William 31 Fra
William 6 Hum
William 14 Hum
William [2] 25 Jac
William 20 Lin
William 27 Mau
William 29 Mon
William 53 Smi
William 299 War
William 300 War
William 383 Wil
William 49 Wll
William, Sr. 30 Fra
Wm. 3 Hic
Wm. 7 Lin
Wm. 107 She
Zechariah 6 Way
Thomson, David L. 75 Dav
Hudson 180 Sum
Jacob 179 Sum
James 180 Sum
Jerimiah 26 Mau
Nicholas 181 Sum
Robert 180 Sum
Stephen W. 180 Sum
Thore, Eli 94 Rut
Thorington, Richard 35 Lin
Thorn, Augustine 55 Smi
Eli 118 Ste
Eli 123 Ste
John 27 Mon
Rebecca 29 Mon
Thomas 94 Rut
Wm. 123 Ste
see Thore
Thornberry, Joel 45 Bed
Thos. 80 Dav
Thornhill, Nancy 180 Sum
Thomas 288 War
Thomas 310 War
Thornton, Amelia 118 Ste
Elizabeth 45 Lin
Elizabeth 27 Mon
Felix 54 Smi
Hannah 54 Smi
Henry 411 Wil
James 53 Smi
John 41 Mau
Josiah 2 Hic
Luke 55 Smi
Needham 85 Rut
Nelson 76 Dav
Presley 100 Rut
Richard 27 Mau

Thornton (cont.)		
Richard	28	Mau
Robbert	70	Mau
Ruben	66	Dav
William	8	Gil
William	7	Mon
Thorp, James	61	Mau
John	67	Mau
Thrashed	5	Har
Thrasher, John	95	Rut
Rachael	12	Ove
Threat, Wm. R.	110	Ste
Threet, Howard	40	Wll
Rebecca	46	Wll
Thrift, Isham	320	War
Throgmorton, Wm.	115	Ste
Throop, Francis	12	Bed
Throuston, John	80	Dav
Thrower, Henry	31	Fra
Thomas	286	War
William	377	Wil
Thurman, Berry	104	Rut
see Thmman		
Thurmon, Clarissa	54	Smi
Daniel	30	Fra
Graves	55	Smi
Jesse	19	Gil
Thurmond, John	30	Fra
Tho.	179	Sum
William	30	Fra
Thurston, George W.	316	War
Thweath,	2	Wll
Thweatte, William	55	Smi
Tibbs, Anderson	55	Smi
John	54	Smi
Thomas	55	Smi
William	55	Smi
Tice, George	11	Hum
William	27	Mon
Tickle, William	348	Whi
Tidwell, Edmund, Jr.	8	Dic
Edmund, Sr.	8	Dic
Eli	8	Gil
Isaac	13	Gil
John	25	Mau
John	8	Per
Levi	7	Dic
Mark	317	War
Millington	8	Gil
Reuben	303	War
Rhoad	9	Gil
Richard	42	Mau
Richd.	21	Way
Thomas	42	Mau
Vincent	13	Gil
Tieford, James M.	98	Rut
Nicholas	98	Rut
Tiffany, Walter	32	Wll
Tigart, Elizabeth	23	Mon
John	30	Mon
Tignar, Isaac	35	Wll
Tigner, James	48	Wll
Tilby, Chaity	25	Jac
Tilby (cont.)		
see Tiley		
Tiley, Thomas	25	Jac
see Tilby		
Tilford, Andrew	179	Sum
Hugh	394	Wil
James	25	Jac
John	393	Wil
John	402	Wil
John M.	86	Rut
Saml.	78	Dav
Thomas	394	Wil
William	393	Wil
see Tieford		
Tillet, Sarah	15	Wll
Tilley, John	18	Gil
John	279	War
Tilly, Charity	180	Sum
George	18	Mon
James, Jr.	12	Way
James, Senr.	12	Way
Tilman, George	6	Wll
Jacob	93	Rut
John	18	Bed
Silas	22	Bed
Silas	46	Bed
William M.	350	Whi
Timans, Joseph	57	Mau
Timley, Richard	180	Sum
Timmons, Thomas	4	Per
William	1	Lin
Timms, Jabus	399	Wil
John	30	Fra
John B.	30	Fra
Timons, Williams	58	Mau
Tims, Hiram	31	Fra
Jabis, Jun.	31	Fra
Jabis, Sen.	31	Fra
Jane	31	Fra
John	31	Fra
Thomas	31	Fra
William	31	Fra
Tindel, Jeremiah	368	Whi
Tindle, John	47	Bed
Tiner, Jesse	6	Har
Tiney, John	314	War
Tinker, John	316	War
Tinkle, George W.	17	Lin
Henry	54	Bed
John	54	Bed
Tinley, Archibald	288	War
Archibald	316	War
Daniel	316	War
see Teisley		
Tinnen, James	10	Gil
Robert	10	Gil
Tinnin, Lemuel	70	Dav
Tinnon, Mary	181	Sum
Tinsley, Anderson	18	Gil
Cornelius	181	Sum
Cornelius, Jr.	181	Sum
Elizabeth	25	Jac
Isaac	181	Sum

Tinsley (cont.)		
John	25	Jac
Spencer	66	Mau
Starlin	36	Mau
William	25	Jac
Tipett, Lovel	314	War
Tipper, Kinchen	32	Bed
Tippet, John	296	War
Joseph	409	Wil
William	3	Dic
Tippit, Josiah	3	Law
Tippitt, Erastus	3	Law
Tipps, Barby	30	Fra
George	30	Fra
John	30	Fra
Peter	31	Lin
Tipton, James	379	Wil
James	380	Wil
Joseph	282	War
Joseph	287	War
Rachel	380	Wil
Reece	379	Wil
Stephen	291	War
Tire see Tice		
Tisdale, John	7	Wll
Renerson J.	28	Wll
William	25	Jac
Tittle, Adam	291	War
David	284	War
John	296	War
Samuel	54	Smi
Titus, George	21	Lin
Toatvine, Isaac	32	Mon
Toban, Nathan	13	Lin
Todd, Aaron	80	Rut
Asa	181	Sum
Benjamin	93	Rut
David	415	Wil
Edmund	94	Rut
George	30	Mon
James	102	Rut
Jesse	100	Rut
John	22	Lin
John B.	43	Lin
John S.	20	Gil
Lemuel	181	Sum
Mary	2	Lin
Pleasant	58	Mau
Rheuben	76	Rut
Robert	96	Rut
Samuel	31	Fra
William	93	Rut
William	102	Rut
see Toodd		
Toland, Jacob	11	Hic
Jonathan	10	Hic
Tolar, Bryant	20	Rob
Bryant	34	Rob
Needham	30	Rob
Robert	7	Rob
Tolbert, J. R.	25	Jac
Thomas	25	Jac
Toler, Daniel	5	Dic
Toler (cont.)		
Joel	53	Smi
John	10	Dic
John	53	Smi
Tolley, John	63	Mau
William	63	Mau
Tolly, Jonathan	31	Lin
Zachariah	179	Sum
see Totty		
Tom, Joseph	35	Mau
William	34	Mau
William	69	Mau
Tomberlin, Warren	180	Sum
Tomblen, David	33	Wll
Tomblin, John [& Lester]		
Nancy	38	Wll
Nicholas	67	Dav
Tomblinson, Isaac	34	Mau
Tombs, Edwan	43	Mau
Emanuel	83	Rut
George	181	Sum
John	42	Mau
John	83	Rut
William	83	Rut
see Sumbo		
Tomerson, Edward	55	Smi
Tomkins, John	137	Sum
Tomlin, Gale	345	Whi
Judah	347	Whi
Rebecca	10	Bed
William	347	Whi
Tomlinson, Allen	404	Wil
Ervan	404	Wil
Hugh	101	Rut
Humphrey B.	97	Rut
Jno.	117	Ste
M.	117	Ste
Thos.	125	Ste
Wm. [2]	122	Ste
Tompkins, Harrison	4	Har
Silas	8	Dic
William	3	Ove
Tompson, Jane	69	Mau
Samuel	46	Mau
Toney, Elijah	53	Smi
Elizabeth	25	Jac
John	57	Wll
Tony, Noel	16	Hic
Tood, Owen	54	Smi
Toodd, Edmund	100	Rut
Tool, James	3	Lin
Tooney, Isaac	91	Rut
Topp, John	87	Dav
Tore see Tood		
Torrence, Edward	125	Ste
Torrentine, Daniel	52	Bed
James	40	Bed
Joseph	40	Bed
Torry see Terry		
Tory, James	27	Mau
Tosh, Nancy	25	Jac
Totten, Benjamin	19	Ove
Totty, Barnet	7	Hic

Totty (cont.)
Harrison 18 Hic
Robt. 18 Hic
Thos. H. 18 Hic
William, Sr. 15 Hic
Wm. 13 Hic
Touchstone, Daniel 15 Lin
Toulson, Daniel 26 Mon
Toumbling, Celia 25 Jac
Tounsend, Peter 179 Sum
Tource, P. [O. ?] 114 Wil
Tovends, Elizabeth 180 Sum
Towel, Isaac 179 Sum
Towles, Joseph 278 War
see Tombs
Townes, Edmund 55 Smi
Herbert 67 Dav
Townsand, John 13 Ove
Joseph 13 Ove
Townsend, Eli 41 Lin
John 130 Ste
John 181 Sum
John 367 Whi
Joseph 180 Sum
Joshua 31 Fra
Richard 180 Sum
Robert 345 Whi
Thos. 125 Ste
Thos. 130 Ste
William 30 Fra
William 42 Lin
William 44 Lin
William 121 Ste
Towry, Edward 7 Lin
Isaac 18 Lin
John 18 Lin
Manering 7 Lin
Towson, William 56 Smi
Towsy, Thomas 17 Way
Tracet, Adam 118 Ste
Tracy, Erasmus 9 Law
Evan 410 Wil
Geo. D. 79 Dav
John 7 Per
Michael 180 Sum
Tradewell, Andrew 5 Per
Trail, William 87 Rut
Trainum, Jemiah 54 Mau
William 180 Sum
Tralards, John 386 Wil
Trammel, Daniel 310 War
David 39 Bed
William 54 Smi
Tramsal, Sarah 38 Mau
Trantham, Jesse 15 Wll
Martin, overseer 36 Wll
Trap, James 25 Jac
Jas. 25 Jac
John 25 Jac
Travalin, Edward 400 Wil
Travelstreet, Lucy 180 Sum
Travers, Daniel 103 Rut
John 103 Rut
Travers (cont.)
William 103 Rut
Traverse, Arthur 79 Rut
Travice, Lucey 39 Mau
Beverly 16 Ove
David 16 Ove
George 35 Wll
James 9 Hum
Jeremiah 25 Jac
John 18 Mon
Matthias 16 Rob
Moses 15 Rob
Robert 30 Fra
Thomas 11 Ove
Thos. 3 Mon
Thos. 24 Mon
William 25 Jac
William 11 Ove
William 295 War
Wm. 112 Ste
Traylor, Edward 111 Wil
Hyram 9 Hum
James 62 Dav
Treadaway, Hannah 32 Rob
Tredwell see Triedwell
Trees, John [2] 309 War
Risan 5 Per
Solomon 309 War
Tremble, George 94 Dav
James 90 Dav
Joseph 87 Rut
Tribble, Abram 180 Sum
Absalom 5 Dic
Isaac 415 Wil
James 31 Bed
Jesse 5 Dic
Peter 40 Bed
Shadrack 304 War
Stephen 180 Wum
Trice, Edward 5 Mon
Edward 396 Wil
James 1 Mon
James 19 Mon
John 18 Mon
Lewis 4 Mon
Nace F. 2 Mon
Nelly 34 Bed
Robert 2 Mon
Shepherd 4 Mon
Triedwell, John 54 Smi
Trigg, Abraham 31 Fra
Alanson 419 Wil
Daniel 375 Wil
Daniel 376 Wil
Haden, Jun. 30 Fra
Haden, Sen. 30 Fra
John 74 Rut
Will 181 Sum
William 30 Fra
William 31 Fra
William 17 Mon
Triley, Martin 5 Har
Trimble, John 82 Dav

Trimble (cont.)
John 5 Lin
Trip, Reubin 5 Law
Trollenger, Adam 17 Bed
John 51 Bed
Joseph 17 Bed
Joseph 20 Bed
Troop, Caleb 7 Lin
William 66 Dav
Trott, Benjamin 86 Rut
Benjamin 93 Rut
Henry 91 Rut
Samuel 83 Rut
Trotter, Benjamin 31 Mon
Benjamin 35 Wll
George 31 Mon
Isham 31 Mon
Isham R. 39 Wll
James 1 Mon
James 32 Mon
John 31 Mon
Joseph 17 Gil
Thomas L. 2 Lin
Trousdale, Bryan 1 Rob
Elizabeth 181 Sum
James 24 Mon
John 24 Mon
John [2] 53 Smi
John, Sen. 53 Smi
Polly 53 Smi
William 137 Sum
Wm. 112 Ste
Trout, A... [Acort?] 8 Per
Benjn. 119 Ste
Chesterson 396 Wil
Christopher 398 Wil
John 180 Sum
Joseph 404 Wil
Margaret 180 Sum
Thomas 119 Ste
Thomas 130 Ste
Trowber, Elizabeth 33 Rob
Jacob 22 Rob
Trowt, John 52 Wll
Truet, Elijah 396 Wil
Levi 380 Wil
Truett, Henry M. 18 Hic
Truette, Tabitha 54 Smi
Truit, Abram 15 Wll
Trull, Penelope 44 Wll
Trusdale, Nathan 4 Ove
Trussell, Matthew 7 Way
Trusty, Allen 180 Sum
Hanah 181 Sum
Hansel G. 113 Wil
see Frusly
Tub, John 418 Wil
Tubb, Eli 123 Ste
George 2 Dic
Isaac 2 Dic
James 117 Ste
Nathan 2 Dic
William, Senr. 116 Ste
Tubb (cont.)
Wm. 116 Ste
Tubberville, Willis 3 Hum
Tubbs, Abraham 54 Smi
Carter 14 Hic
Eleanor 78 Rut
Isaac 2 Hum
James 54 Smi
James, Jun. 55 Smi
Jeremiah, Jr. 13 Hic
Jeremiah, Sr. 13 Hic
John 13 Hic
John 54 Smi
Samuel 12 Hic
William 13 Hic
William 2 Hum
William 55 Smi
Tuck, William 54 Bed
Tucker, Aldin 35 Lin
Allen 35 Lin
Anderson 90 Dav
Anderson 13 Gil
Benjamin 4 Rob
Butler 22 Gil
Campbell 15 Way
Curl 31 Mon
Edward 35 Lin
Edward 111 Wil
Edward 391 Wil
Elijah 98 Rut
Elizabeth 29 Rob
Enoch 104 Rut
Enoch, Mr. 12 Law
Frederick 54 Smi
Gabriel 54 Bed
George 6 Gil
George 357 Whi
Green 400 Wil
Hannah 31 Fra
Hendrick 401 Wil
Henry 18 Hic
James [2] 13 Lin
James 57 Mau
James 90 Rut
Jerimiah 51 Mau
Jesse 35 Lin
John 3 Bed
John 8 Dic
John 4 Gil
John 20 Hic
John 12 Rob
John 102 Rut
John 181 Sum
Joseph 5 Per
Lemuel 35 Lin
Lualing 390 Wil
Mary 17 Hic
Matthew 97 Rut
Randolph 61 Dav
Robert 35 Lin
Rodan 23 Wll
Samuel 99 Rut
Samuel C. 100 Rut

Tucker (cont.)
Sarah 30 Mon
Silas 31 Fra
Stephen 6 Per
Thomas 48 Wll
Thomas, Jur. 22 Gil
Thomas, Senr. 22 Gil
Thos. 30 Mon
William 21 Bed
William 20 Gil
William 5 Per
William 44 Wll
William 52 Wll
William, Mr. 12 Law
Wm. 120 Ste
Tuckness, Henery 59 Mau
Tuggle, Harris B. 53 Smi
John 53 Smi
Thomas 53 Smi
Tuley, Charles 15 Lin
Tulgham, Theopholas 63 Dav
Tull, John R. 56 Wll
Tullingim, Henry 7 Hic
Tulloch, David 10 Rob
Tullus, John 63 Wll
Rodham 63 Wll
Tully, Henry 14 Lin
William B. 13 Lin
Tum see Turre
Tumlinson, Peter 32 Mau
Tumter, John 304 War
Tune, James 9 Wll
John 53 Smi
Tungate, Susanna 10 Gil
Tunnage, Isaac 402 Wil
see Turrage
Turbeville, James 10 Bed
William 58 Wll
Turbyfill, William 11 Rob
Turbyville, Benjamin 65 Dav
Willie 83 Dav
Turentine, Nancy 27 Lin
Turkoon, Peter 72 Dav
Turly, John 29 Lin
Turman, Jarret 3 Har
Jiles 3 Har
Turnage, Henry 52 Smi
Isaac 114 Wil
William 16 Wll
Turnboau, Samuel 23 Hic
Turnbough, Hugh 20 Way
Turnbow, Andrew 16 Gil
George 4 Har
Jacob 5 Law
James 16 Gil
Turnbull, William 53 Smi
Turner, Aaron 50 Mau
Adam 180 Sum
Adam, Sr. 180 Sum
Admire 38 Mau
Ann W. 78 Dav
Antoney J. 62 Mau
Bailey 72 Dav

Turner (cont.)
Benjamin 53 Smi
Benjamin 346 Whi
Berryman 52 Smi
Charles 181 Sum
Drury 15 Hic
Dugles 123 Ste
Edmond 180 Sum
Elisha 11 Dic
Elizabeth 69 Dav
Federick 127 Ste
Francis 25 Bed
Francis 30 Fra
Frederick 53 Smi
George 8 Hum
George 37 Wll
Hamner 20 Gil
Hezekiah 55 Smi
Hickman 22 Hic
Howard W. 14 Dic
Jack E. 17 Rob
Jacob 179 Sum
James 10 Ove
James 17 Ove
James 115 Ste
James 365 Whi
James 412 Wil
James 14 Wll
James, Jr. 181 Sum
James, Sen. 179 Sum
Jane 6 Lin
Jeremiah 412 Wil
Jereter [?] 17 Ove
Jesse 22 Hic
Jesse 115 Ste
Jessey 66 Mau
John 30 Fra
John 13 Hum
John 25 Jac
John 23 Lin
John 45 Lin
John 5 Per
John 53 Smi
John 115 Ste
John 179 Sum
John 180 Sum
John, Jr. 9 Dic
John, Jr. 13 Dic
John, Senr. 180 Sum
John C. 30 Fra
Jonas 349 Whi
Joseph 19 Wll
Judith 112 Ste
Keziah 112 Ste
Lewis 56 Smi
Lewis 36 Wll
Martha 98 Dav
Martin 180 Sum
Miles 37 Wll
Milly 181 Sum
Moses 180 Sum
Phillip 180 Sum
Randolph 367 Whi

Turner (cont.)		
Ransom	18	Wll
Robert	54	Smi
Saml.	80	Dav
Saml.	15	Hic
Samuel	16	Dic
Spratley	46	Mau
Susannah	12	Hic
Susannah	53	Smi
Terrisha	180	Sum
Thomas	25	Bed
White	45	Lin
William	2	Dic
William	30	Fra
William	50	Mau
William	2	Ove
William	180	Sum
William D.	11	Dic
William S.	180	Sum
Willie	6	Hum
Willis	7	Rob
Willis	54	Smi
Woodson	18	Lin
Yancy	180	Sum
see Furner, Turrer		
Turney, George	54	Smi
Henrey	69	Mau
Henry [2]	54	Smi
Isaac	54	Smi
Jacob	54	Smi
Peter	54	Smi
Turnhan, Alexander	3	Har
Turnley, Temple	47	Mau
Turpen, Sally	126	Ste
Turpin, Edmond	181	Sum
James	116	Ste
Lebour	131	Ste
Turrage, Thomas	402	Wil
see Tunnage		
Turre, Thomas	396	Wil
Turrentine, Aschalus	9	Bed
Robert	33	Bed
Saml.	31	Bed
Turrer, James	390	Wil
Tursey, Edmund	279	War
Tuten, Obed	23	Gil
Tutin, Abraham	16	Gil
Tutor, Alexander	25	Mon
Tutt, Benjamin	13	Gil
Tuttle, David	42	Mau
Maury	41	Mau
Peter	181	Sum
Solomon	20	Gil
Twaig, Timothy	81	Rut
Twamy, Isaac	82	Rut
Twing, David	25	Lin
Twitty, Sally	25	Jac
Twopence, David	137	Sum
William	137	Sum
Tycer, Elliss	3	Dic
Tygart, Samuel B.	30	Fra
Tyler, John	17	Mon
Richd. K.	17	Mon

Tyler (cont.)		
Thomas	80	Rut
Walter	19	Hic
William, Jr.	20	Hic
William, Sr.	18	Hic
see Syler		
Tyner, Pricilla	10	Mon
Tynes, David	54	Smi
Henry	54	Smi
Tyre, Council	24	Mon
Elizabeth	24	Mon
Tyree, David	53	Smi
Pleasant	179	Sum
Richmond C.	179	Sum
Saml. C.	179	Sum
Thomas	55	Smi
William	54	Smi
William	179	Sum
William, Sen.	55	Smi
Tyson, Richard	31	Fra
Ury	24	Mon
Wright	24	Mon

--- U ---

Uawater see Vawter		
Uhles, Frederick	56	Smi
Jacob, Jun.	56	Smi
Jacob, Sen.	56	Smi
James	31	Fra
Jefferson	56	Smi
John	31	Fra
John	56	Smi
Michael	56	Smi
Richard	56	Smi
Robert	31	Fra
Umphres, David	45	Wll
Michal	37	Wll
see Jumphres		
Underhill, Abraham	410	Wil
Daniel	8	Dic
Underwood, Anderson	56	Mau
David	54	Mau
Henry	412	Wil
Jeremiah	87	Rut
John	181	Sum
Joseph	34	Lin
Joseph	412	Wil
Lucretia	126	Ste
Nathan	181	Sum
Nathaniel	85	Rut
Nathaniel	95	Rut
Percy	376	Wil
Sarah	349	Whi
Thomas	400	Wil
William	87	Rut
Willie	1	Dic
Young	392	Wil
Upchert, Ambrose	119	Ste
David	119	Ste
William	119	Ste

Upchurch, David 13 Ove
Joseph 346 Whi
Stephen 417 Wil
William 26 Jac
Upshaw, Parson 19 Mon
Upton, James 31 Fra
James 56 Smi
Samuel 31 Fra
Stephen 16 Ove
Urkle, Jacob 31 Fra
Winny 31 Fra
Ursry, Lucy 26 Jac
Ury, George 27 Mon
Joseph 1 Hum
Joseph 5 Hum
Nancy 24 Mon
Robert 27 Mon
see Wry
Usra, Maston 94 Dav
Usrery, Hutchens 4 Per
Usry, Zachariah 314 War
Usserey, Richard 356 Whi
Samuel 363 Whi
William 366 Whi
Ussery, John 34 Bed
Peter 22 Gil
Phillip 356 Whi
Thomas 53 Mau
Thomas 368 Whi
William 14 Bed
William 22 Gil
Ussleton, George 95 Rut
Ussry, William 320 War
Utley, Seth 14 Hum
Utzman, Jacob J. [?] 50 Mau
Uzzel, Elisha 57 Mau

--- V ---

Vaden, Peterson 89 Dav
Samuel 79 Rut
Samuel W. 104 Rut
William 2 Bed
Valeir, Isaac W. 4 Mon
Valentine, Benja. 6 Dic
see Voluntine
Vales, Robert 56 Smi
Vanallen, Jacob [& Culbern] 1 Wll
Vanatta, Peter 56 Smi
Samuel 56 Smi
Vance, Charles 32 Fra
David [2] 182 Sum
Elizabeth 32 Fra
James 7 Gil
James 26 Jac
John 7 Gil
John 26 Jac
John 56 Smi
John 181 Sum
Joseph 26 Jac
Louis 26 Jac
Vance (cont.)
Robert 26 Mon
Samuel 1 Mon
Thomas 56 Smi
William 7 Gil
William 20 Lin
William 26 Mon
Vancleave, Ebenezer 42 Bed
Jonathan 42 Bed
William 42 Bed
Vandepool, Elijah 56 Smi
Joseph 56 Smi
Vandever, Arnold 356 Whi
John 356 Whi
Vandiford, Jas. 18 Hic
Vandike, Nebucadnezzer 32 Fra
George 8 Law
Hollandsworth 20 Rob
Vane, Thomas 102 Rut
Van Gillum see Gillum
Vanhook, Aaron 5 Dic
Ashburn 6 Dic
Loyd 56 Smi
Robert 10 Dic
Vanhoose, John 6 Law
Vanhooser, Isaac 26 Jac
V. V. 26 Jac
see Haser, Hooser, V. Hooser
Vanhoozer, Isaac 284 War
Isaac 317 War
Jacob 313 War
Vanhoy, John 56 Smi
Van Iness see Vantruss
Vanleer, A. W., & Co. 15 Dic
Vanpelt, Henry 2 Wll
John C. [?] 32 Fra
William 32 Fra
Vantruss, Jacob 411 Wil
Vanzant, Abraham 32 Fra
George 32 Fra
Isaac 32 Fra
Jacob 32 Fra
Thomas 32 Fra
Vaper see Vasser
Vardell, Mary 90 Rut
Sarah 82 Rut
Vardin, Barnet 72 Dav
Varnell, William 8 Hum
Varner, James 56 Smi
Vasser, George R. 11 Gil
Peter 19 Gil
Vassiur, Joshua 100 Rut
Vat see Not
Vaughan, Abraham 32 Fra
David 32 Fra
Drury 85 Rut
Henrietta 6 Hum
Henry B. 181 Sum
James 80 Rut
James 411 Wil
John 56 Smi
John P. 28 Mon
Johnson 74 Dav

Vaughan (cont.)
Joshua P. 3 Mon
Leticia 57 Smi
Lucy 182 Sum
Mary F. 379 Wil
Melcijah 181 Sum
Peter 39 Lin
Peter 85 Rut
Richard 62 Dav
Richard 83 Rut
Richard B. 83 Rut
Richard C. 182 Sum
Saml. 181 Sum
Samuel 32 Fra
Sarah 104 Rut
Thomas 182 Sum
Thomas 283 War
William 82 Rut
William 182 Sum
Willis 24 Mon
Vaughn, Abner 3 Wll
David 71 Dav
Dixon 9 Wll
Edward 85 Dav
James 358 Whi
James 61 Wll
Joel 83 Dav
Joel 22 Rob
John 62 Wll
John 62 Wll
Paul 71 Dav
Reuben 16 Way
Spencer C. 14 Wll
William 30 Wll
Vaught, Elijah 103 Rut
Sarah 26 Wll
Simeon 79 Rut
Simeon 103 Rut
Vaughters, John 66 Mau
Ludwell 419 Wil
Vaugn, Bevley 358 Whi
Vaulx, Catherine 97 Dav
William 63 Dav
Vaun, David 67 Mau
Sinthey 61 Mau
Vawter, Richard 57 Mau
Veach, James 2 Hum
Vechim, Wm. 115 Ste
Vechine, Wesley 113 Ste
Veel, Charles 411 Wil
Matteson 411 Wil
see Neel
Veil, Gilles 381 Wll
Zephanab 395 Wil
Venable, Andrew 4 Bed
Darcas 58 Wll
Hugh B. 93 Dav
Joseph 29 Wll
Richard 13 Bed
Samuel 6 Bed
Sarah 3 Mon
Thomas 11 Bed
William 8 Law
Venis, Benjamin 306 War
Venters, Sally S. 110 Ste
Ventres, David 57 Smi
see Vantruss, Vontrise
Ventress, James 5 Rob
Loret 56 Smi
Verdell, Thomas 86 Rut
Verhim see Vechim
Vernon, Tinsley 83 Rut
Verplank, Joseph 32 Fra
Vest, Peter 358 Whi
Vesteli, Jay 49 Wll
Vetts, Moses 6 Gil
V. Hooser, Abraham 7 Ove
Isaac 45 Lin
Isaac 5 Ove
John 12 Ove
Squire 7 Ove
see Hooser, Vanhooser
Via, Obediah 99 Rut
Vicars, Jas. 129 Ste
Nathl. 129 Ste
William 46 Lin
Wm. 115 Ste
Wm. 117 Ste
Vick, Azah [?] 1 Per
Charity 33 Rob
Joseph 91 Dav
Joshua, Sen. 56 Smi
Lewis 413 Wil
Pilgrim 56 Smi
Robert 91 Dav
Roland 3 Mon
Samuel 381 Wil
William 91 Dav
William 56 Smi
Vicke, Joel 21 Gil
Joseph 21 Gil
Salley 18 Gil
Vicker, Elizabeth 368 Whi
Harden 368 Whi
Vickers, Joseph 293 War
Vickery, Absolum 36 Bed
John 36 Bed
Richd. 36 Bed
Vicking, Abner 1 Ove
Vickory, John 105 Rut
Vicks, Jonas 18 Gil
Viers, William 17 Lin
Vigrant, James 32 Fra
Vilito, William 26 Jac
Vincent, Aggy 89 Dav
David 411 Wil
Eliab 4 Gil
George 7 Hum
Henry 88 Rut
James 7 Dic
John 32 Fra
Oliver 3 Hic
Ozias 84 Rut
Perry 84 Rut
Richard 303 War
Thomas 32 Fra

Vincent (cont.)
Thomas, Jr. 7 Hum
Thomas, Senr. 11 Hum
Vincin, Moses 371 Whi
Vines, Joseph 38 Lin
see Venis
Vineyard, Frances 34 Lin
Nancy 110 Ste
Uriah 32 Fra
Vinsant, John 26 Jac
Vinson, A. 131 Ste
Benthal 182 Sum
David 31 Mau
David 126 Ste
Elizabeth 126 Ste
Enos 181 Sum
George 182 Sum
Henry [2] 126 Ste
Henry 181 Sum
James 25 Mau
James 44 Mau
James, Jr. 181 Sum
James, Sr. 181 Sum
Jerdan 44 Mau
John 51 Mau
John 56 Smi
Moses 30 Mau
Polly 56 Smi
Richerson 31 Mau
Samuel 56 Smi
Stokely 114 Ste
Thomas [2] 37 Mau
William 31 Mau
William 95 Rut
Willie 181 Sum
Virry, Michael 297 War
Viser, Andrew 4 Mon
Vititoe, Thomas 18 Lin
Viverett, Elizabeth 382 Wil
Vivrett, Lacelot 396 Wil
Voarhies, David 20 Way
Voden, Lodwick 56 Smi
William 56 Smi
Voheirs, Aaron 9 Way
John 2 Law
Volentine, Isaac 182 Sum
Solo. W. 181 Sum
Thomas 181 Sum
Voluntine, Thomas 23 Rob
Vontrise, John 56 Smi
John, Jun. 56 Smi
Valentine 56 Smi
William 56 Smi
see Ventres
Voorhas, Garret L. 59 Mau
Voorhies, William 59 Mau
Voss, James 6 Law
James 18 Way
John 8 Law
William 8 Law
Vow, Lawrance 378 Wil
Vowell, William 399 Wil
William 410 Wil
Vuhine see Vechine

--- W ---

Waddel, George 27 Jac
Waddill, John C. 43 Mau
Noel 70 Mau
Waddle, Allen 45 Bed
James 100 Rut
John S. 38 Mau
S. D. 8 Per
Wade, Abraham 17 Lin
Bartlet 14 Ove
Caleb 81 Rut
Charles 35 Bed
Charles 396 Wil
David 20 Mon
Drury 4 Way
Edward 47 Bed
Enos 107 She
Francis 5 Lin
George 52 Wll
George W. 2 Lin
Henry 87 Dav
Isabel 88 Rut
James 101 Rut
James G. 45 Wll
Jesse 7 Hic
John 81 Rut
John 86 Rut
Nehemiah 59 Smi
Obediah 55 Wll
Peter 20 Mon
Robert 21 Mon
Sarah 103 Rut
Thomas 20 Hic
William 81 Rut
William 103 Rut
William H. 103 Rut
William J. 106 She
Wilson 311 War
Waden see Vaden
Wadkins, John 29 Lin
John 21 Mon
John 309 War
Joseph 66 Dav
Wadley, Daniel 81 Rut
John 100 Rut
Saml. 6 Hic
Samuel 88 Rut
William, Jur. 87 Rut
Wadron, Joseph, Jr. 184 Sum
see Waldron
Wadson, David 5 Lin
Waggoner, Daniel 30 Lin
David 32 Lin
David 184 Sum
Frederick 25 Lin
George 32 Lin
Jacob 30 Lin
Jacob 32 Lin
John 10 Hum
John 32 Lin
John 19 Wll
Joseph 307 War

Waggoner (cont.)		
Lewis	30	Lin
Peter	4	Law
Wagnar, William	34	Mau
Wagner, Cornelius	60	Dav
Phillip	57	Dav
Wagoner, Cornelius	57	Smi
Daniel	57	Smi
Solomon	32	Fra
Wagster, John	51	Bed
Waid, Nancy	56	Mau
Wainright, William	18	Lin
Waits, Allen	286	War
John	287	War
Wakefield, Charles	6	Lin
Hamilton	32	Fra
John	79	Rut
Joseph	50	Wll
Samuel	6	Lin
Thomas	32	Fra
Waker, David	5	Per
Wald, Noah	51	Mau
Walden, Fielding	60	Smi
John	376	Wil
Thomas	96	Dav
William	92	Rut
Waldin, John	81	Rut
Walding, Jesse	60	Smi
Waldon, David	40	Mau
Jesse	59	Dav
Waldridg, Josiah	8	Wll
Waldron, John, Jr.	185	Sum
William	66	Dav
see Wadron		
Waldrop, Abel	12	Law
Michael	4	Way
Robert	33	Fra
Waldrope, John	16	Gil
Walk, Anthony	60	Smi
Westley	413	Wil
Walker, Abram	10	Wll
Alexander	90	Dav
Alexander	311	War
Andrew	21	Mon
Andrew	29	Rob
Andrew W.	31	Lin
Archibald	37	Bed
Archibald	19	Mon
Archibald	312	War
Benjamin	36	Lin
Benjamin	16	Ove
Benjamine	364	Whi
Burrell	87	Rut
Carter	31	Lin
Charles	77	Dav
Charles	9	Har
Charles	3	Law
Charles, Jur.	9	Har
Daniel	26	Jac
David	26	Jac
E.	86	Dav
Eanes	72	Dav
Edmund	1	Wll
Walker (cont.)		
Edward	60	Smi
Elias R.	6	Hic
Elijah	13	Hic
Elijah	18	Hic
Elijah	6	Law
Elisha	64	Wll
Elizabeth	4	Dic
Elizabeth	15	Dic
Elmore	8	Dic
Freeman	28	Wll
Gabriel L.	286	War
Geo. H. M.	21	Way
George	57	Smi
George	382	Wil
Green	47	Lin
Hanbert	394	Wil
Hardridge	12	Rob
Henry	61	Smi
Henry	6	Wll
Henry	65	Wll
Isaac	11	Dic
Isaac	125	Ste
Jacob	2	Dic
James	8	Bed
James	37	Bed
James	63	Dav
James	14	Dic
James	16	Dic
James	33	Fra
James	21	Gil
James	31	Lin
James	35	Mau
James	57	Mau
James	9	Rob
James	182	Sum
James	305	War
James	319	War
James	41	Wll
James, Dr.	17	Dic
James D.	378	Wil
James S.	56	Mau
Jeremiah	46	Lin
Joel	6	Hic
Joel	13	Way
John	3	Dic
John	2	Hic
John	9	Mon
John	30	Mon
John	13	Ove
John	84	Rut
John	57	Smi
John	12	Way
John	363	Whi
John	415	Wil
John	41	Wll
John A.	57	Smi
John B.	4	Dic
John C.	20	Gil
John L.	28	Wll
Julus	387	Wil
Margaret	44	Lin
Martha	26	Jac

Walker (cont.)
Mary 14 Hic
Mary 16 Ove
Mary 92 Rut
Matthew 24 Rob
Matthew P. 68 Dav
Micajah 60 Smi
Nathaniel 35 Bed
Nelson 60 Smi
Nicholas T. 86 Dav
Noah 400 Wil
Noah 50 Wll
Peter 92 Rut
Peter 382 Wil
Philip 13 Bed
Phillip 72 Dav
Pleasent 11 Wll
Polly 131 Ste
Richd. 6 Bed
Robert 7 Bed
Robert 52 Bed
Robert 113 Ste
Robert W. 76 Dav
Saml. 122 Ste
Samuel 27 Jac
Samuel 5 Ove
Samuel 25 Rob
Samuel 95 Rut
Samuel 61 Smi
Samuel 315 War
Samuel, Sen. 60 Smi
Sarah 346 Whi
Silvanus 52 Mau
Simeon, Mr. 12 Law
Simion 25 Hic
Susanna 20 Gil
Tandy 8 Mon
Theodrick 53 Mau
Thomas 5 Gil
Thomas 19 Lin
Thomas 35 Mau
Thomas 67 Mau
Thomas 70 Mau
Thomas 58 Smi
Warren 57 Smi
William 33 Fra
William 2 Hic
William 19 Lin
William 9 Mon
William 5 Ove
William 77 Rut
William 83 Rut
William 57 Smi
William 58 Smi
William 388 Wil
William 396 Wil
William 413 Wil
William 43 Wll
Willis 15 Dic
Wm. B. 15 Way
see Waker, Watker
Walkup, William 98 Rut
Wall, Bengus 33 Fra
Wall (cont.)
Bird 396 Wil
Braxton 21 Mon
Burgess 10 Dic
Clemmt. 7 Wll
David 13 Rob
Drewry 62 Wll
Edmund 66 Wll
Ezekiel 14 Gil
Henry 116 Ste
Hugh 13 Bed
James 13 Mon
John 111 Ste
John, Junr. 14 Gil
John, Senr. 14 Gil
John W. 12 Gil
Johnston 21 Mon
Joshua 10 Lin
Major 10 Lin
Peter 62 Wll
Scogin 62 Wll
William 62 Wll
Wallace, Adam 183 Sum
Archer 183 Sum
Axum 113 Ste
Bennet 11 Law
David 59 Smi
E. 113 Ste
Edmond 113 Ste
Evan 6 Bed
George P. 83 Rut
George W. 87 Dav
Hugh 26 Jac
James 20 Bed
James 54 Bed
James 26 Jac
James 183 Sum
Jesse 32 Fra
John 83 Rut
John 85 Rut
John 101 Rut
John 113 Ste
John 182 Sum
Jonathan 6 Hum
Jonathan M. 83 Rut
Joseph 33 Fra
Joseph 105 Rut
Joseph 185 Sum
Joseph B. 50 Mau
Josiah 11 Law
Matthew 2 Bed
Orem 183 Sum
Peggy 61 Smi
Rebecca 9 Dic
Robert 26 Jac
Ruben 91 Dav
Saml. 184 Sum
Samuel 78 Rut
Samuel 105 Rut
Thomas 3 Law
William 86 Dav
William 33 Fra
William 29 Lin

Wallace (cont.)		
William	83	Rut
William	60	Smi
William, Sr.	184	Sum
Wm.	14	Hic
Wm.	112	Ste
Wallard, Silas	52	Mau
Wallas, Robbert	36	Mau
William	55	Mau
Waller, David	68	Dav
John	5	Mon
Martha	76	Rut
Pleasent	358	Whi
Robert	31	Mon
Thomas	68	Dav
Thomas	85	Dav
William	76	Rut
William	285	War
Wallice, David	11	Hum
Elias	354	Whi
John	349	Whi
Joseph	28	Lin
Richard	342	Whi
Stephen	349	Whi
Walling, Daniel	347	Whi
James	362	Whi
James	362	Whi
Jessee	362	Whi
Joseph	347	Whi
Thomas	347	Whi
Wallis, Alfred	57	Wll
Andrew	5	Gil
Christopher	1	Wll
Daniel	14	Ove
Ezekiel	45	Wll
George	20	Ove
Henry	23	Wll
Hugh	11	Har
Hugh B.	58	Smi
Isaac	11	Law
James	58	Smi
Joseph	16	Gil
Joseph	28	Wll
Robert	23	Gil
Robert	55	Wll
William	4	Per
Walls, Burgus	364	Whi
Daniel	32	Fra
Edmund	316	War
John L.	25	Lin
Millington	183	Sum
Newton	44	Wll
Samuel	44	Wll
see Watts		
Walock, Charles	376	Wil
Walpole, John	81	Rut
Walson, Joseph	27	Jac
Walston, Turner	9	Gil
Walt see Walk		
Walter, Joel	61	Dav
William	51	Mau
Walters, John	182	Sum
Samuel	32	Wll
Walters (cont.)		
Sarah	62	Dav
Walthall, John	9	Gil
Walthrop, ...ph	4	Hum
Ezekiel	4	Hum
Walton, Edward	62	Smi
Edward S.	32	Mon
George	62	Smi
Gracy	184	Sum
Isaac	59	Smi
Isaac	183	Sum
James	184	Sum
Jesse	61	Mau
Jesse	7	Wll
Josiah	182	Sum
Langham T.	6	Wll
Leonard	35	Wll
Mabury	95	Dav
Martin	26	Rob
Meredith	16	Rob
Meredith	184	Sum
Nancy	14	Wll
Sally	61	Smi
Thomas	85	Dav
Thomas	59	Smi
Thomas	35	Wll
Thomas	64	Wll
Thomas G.	57	Smi
Timothy	57	Smi
William	182	Sum
Wamack, Isham	33	Fra
Matthew	70	Dav
Peter	30	Lin
William	70	Dav
Wammach, Thomas	310	War
William	310	War
Wammack, Alexr.	37	Bed
David	37	Bed
Hawkins	39	Bed
Henry	23	Bed
Josiah	39	Bed
Micheal	37	Bed
William	37	Bed
Wamock, Abner	295	War
see Womack		
Wannimaker, Polly	306	War
Wansly, Nathan	29	Lin
Wantler, John	63	Mau
Ward, Anthony	60	Smi
Asa	5	Hic
Benjamin	97	Rut
Bryant	57	Smi
Burrell	80	Rut
Burrell	85	Rut
Dicken	57	Smi
Edward	68	Dav
Eligah	51	Mau
Elijah	185	Sum
Elijah	352	Whi
Eliza	15	Dic
Ezekiel	101	Rut
Ezekiel, Jnr.	80	Rut
Henry [2]	98	Rut

Ward (cont.)		
Henry	403	Wil
Isaac	7	Hum
J. H.	117	Ste
James	47	Bed
James	6	Per
James J.	5	Har
Jeremiah	93	Rut
Jesse	10	Hic
John	10	Dic
John	57	Smi
John	58	Smi
Jonathan	368	Whi
Jordan	414	Wil
Judith	25	Wll
Mary	57	Smi
Matthew	414	Wil
Messer	110	Ste
Michael	129	Ste
Nathan	7	Per
Noah	36	Lin
Pleasant	49	Wll
Rewbin	7	Per
Sally	58	Smi
Samuel	3	Wll
Simeon	110	Ste
Solomon	34	Fra
Susan	12	Lin
Swan	5	Har
Thomas	116	Ste
William	50	Bed
William	74	Dav
William	15	Dic
William	82	Rut
William	61	Smi
William	118	Ste
William	182	Sum
William	414	Wil
Willie	115	Ste
see Wood, Word		
Wardan, James	29	Mau
Warden, John	12	Lin
John	123	Ste
William	118	Ste
Wardlow, Hugh	14	Lin
Ware, Dudly	416	Wil
Henry H.	390	Wil
James	405	Wil
John	3	Per
John	405	Wil
Joseph	405	Wil
Thomas	405	Wil
William	32	Rob
see Mare		
Warfield, Mathius	57	Mau
Warford, John	60	Smi
John, Jun.	60	Smi
Robert	60	Smi
Warker, John H.	2	Per
Warmoth, Thomas	66	Dav
Warnald, Richard	3	Har
Warner, Charles	384	Wil
John	33	Bed
Warner (cont.)		
John	59	Smi
John, Junr.	33	Bed
Richard	51	Bed
William	359	Whi
Warnick, Robert	89	Rut
Warran, Benjamin	402	Wil
Booth	402	Wil
Edwared	51	Mau
Jesse	401	Wil
John	418	Wil
John D.	51	Mau
Joseph	34	Mau
Samuel	30	Mau
William	418	Wil
Warrel, Elisha	8	Per
Warren, Archibald	370	Whi
Benjamin	27	Rob
Bluford	350	Whi
Burris	4	Hic
Burwell	13	Wll
Daniel	6	Har
Daniel	28	Lin
Drury	28	Rob
Drury	78	Rut
Etheldred	59	Smi
Fielden	29	Wll
George	88	Rut
Goodlon	8	Hum
Henry	21	Lin
Henry	313	War
Isaiah	28	Rob
Isham	18	Hic
James	32	Fra
James	12	Lin
James	85	Rut
Jas. S.	7	Hic
Jesse	29	Rob
Jesse	84	Rut
Jesse	98	Rut
Jno. W.	6	Hic
Joel	16	Gil
John	49	Bed
John	11	Gil
John	28	Rob
John	59	Smi
John	130	Ste
John	14	Wll
John	27	Wll
John G.	8	Hum
John H. B. E.	98	Rut
Joshua	19	Rob
Josiah	185	Sum
Julius	32	Fra
Lewis	36	Lin
Lott	28	Rob
Nathan	21	Lin
Nathaniel	54	Wll
Peter	28	Rob
Peter	91	Rut
Reuben	42	Wll
Robert	122	Ste
Robert	130	Ste

Warren (cont.)
Robt. 19 Hic
Sebert 28 Rob
Solomon 80 Rut
Thomas 26 Bed
Thomas 23 Rob
Thos. 5 Hic
William 24 Lin
William 78 Rut
William 83 Rut
William 84 Rut
William 86 Rut
William 29 Wll
William 59 Wll
see Warrens
Warrens, Tabitha 35 Wll
Warrin, Daniel 24 Lin
Edwin W. 83 Rut
Peter 24 Lin
Warrington, Wooley 14 Way
Warters, George 404 Wil
Shelby 404 Wil
Warwick, John 99 Rut
Washburn, Eli 27 Lin
John 43 Lin
Lewis 60 Smi
Reuben 27 Lin
Reuben 43 Lin
Reubin 359 Whi
Thomas 33 Lin
Washer, Peter 111 Ste
Washington, Andrew 7 Rob
Gilbert G. 83 Dav
Joseph 25 Rob
Thos. 78 Dav
Wasson, Able 24 Bed
Abner 418 Wil
John 27 Mau
Josiah 27 Mau
Robert 83 Rut
Samul 27 Mau
Water, Labon 74 Dav
Waters, Andrew 7 Mon
Archibald 123 Ste
Charity 20 Gil
George 408 Wil
James 94 Rut
John 7 Wll
Shelby 409 Wil
Thos. 29 Mon
Turner 408 Wil
William 19 Mon
Watker, William 125 Ste
Watkins, Benjamin 10 Ove
Charles 183 Sum
Frederick 91 Rut
Frederick 102 Rut
Isaac 63 Dav
Isaiah 90 Rut
James 295 War
Jesse 112 Ste
Joel 185 Sum
Joel M. 57 Smi

Watkins (cont.)
John 12 Dic
John 7 Gil
John 9 Rob
John 91 Rut
Joseph 95 Rut
Micajah 89 Dav
Mornin 19 Ove
Noel W. 93 Dav
Owen T. 27 Wll
Pleasant 52 Mau
Reece 412 Wil
Richard 101 Rut
Richard 386 Wil
Robert 183 Sum
S. 119 Ste
Samuel 83 Rut
Silva 57 Smi
Thomas 27 Wll
Thomas 37 Wll
Thomas G. 91 Rut
William 86 Dav
William 28 Wll
Willis 3 Wll
Watley, Warton 305 War
Wats, Babbart 28 Mau
Benjamin 7 Per
Edward 33 Mau
James 49 Mau
Watson, Abram 6 Mon
David 29 Lin
David 127 Ste
David 128 Ste
David 38 Wll
Elizabeth 184 Sum
George 122 Ste
Hardy 184 Sum
Heny 298 War
James 77 Dav
James 83 Dav
James 16 Dic
James 10 Hum
James [2] 26 Jac
James 8 Wll
Jesse 8 Wll
John 31 Bed
John [2] 82 Dav
John 8 Har
John 29 Lin
John 48 Mau
John 342 Whi
John 371 Whi
John 35 Wll
John 36 Wll
Joseph 31 Bed
Joseph 114 Wil
Lewis 68 Dav
Nancy 385 Wil
Peggy 16 Rob
Peter 11 Wll
Rebecca 19 Ove
Robert 11 Gil
Samuel 27 Jac

Watson (cont.)		
Samuel	58	Smi
Samuel	378	Wil
Stewart	26	Jac
Thomas	34	Fra
Thomas	29	Lin
Thomas	385	Wil
Thos.	17	Mon
William	69	Dav
William	10	Gil
William	48	Mau
William	13	Wll
William	64	Wll
William L.	27	Wll
Wm.	74	Dav
Wm. W.	80	Dav
see Walson		
Watt, James N.	12	Mon
John	12	Mon
Samuel	20	Lin
see Wall		
Watters, George	92	Dav
Jesse	57	Smi
Watts, Aura [?]	20	Hic
Bennett	26	Jac
George	26	Jac
George	78	Rut
James	84	Rut
John	15	Ove
John	91	Rut
John	105	Rut
John, Jr.	20	Hic
John, Jur.	15	Ove
John, Sr.	20	Hic
Rachel	418	Wil
Rewben	184	Sum
Richard	32	Lin
Sally	32	Lin
Thomas	85	Dav
William	57	Smi
Watwood, George	182	Sum
William	17	Mon
Waugh, Richard	2	Dic
Waumble, Amous	26	Mau
Way, Nancy	1	Dic
Nicey	1	Dic
Weakfield, Henry	61	Smi
Weakley, Isaac	11	Mon
John	5	Mon
Joshua	27	Mon
Robert	63	Dav
Saml.	8	Mon
Thos.	8	Mon
William	10	Mon
Weaks, Abram	8	Per
Danl.	185	Sum
Henry	22	Mon
Jeptha	32	Fra
John	183	Sum
Joseph	318	War
Joseph	318	War
Samuel	32	Fra
Thomas	318	War
Weaks (cont.)		
William [2]	19	Mon
Wear, Benjamin	32	Fra
Wearley see Webrley		
Weatherford, Archibald	80	Rut
H.	122	Ste
Lewis	61	Wll
William	19	Way
Weatherington, Abram	50	Wll
Joseph	50	Wll
Joshua	50	Wll
Weatherly, Abner	81	Rut
Jeremiah	6	Bed
Levi	392	Wil
William	67	Dav
Weatherred, Francis	186	Sum
Francis M.	183	Sum
John	183	Sum
Weathers, Edmund	66	Wll
Hugh	183	Sum
Thomas	184	Sum
William	6	Hum
Weathersed, Robert	182	Sum
Weatherspoon, David	62	Mau
John	85	Rut
Joseph	87	Rut
Joseph	104	Rut
Westley	62	Mau
Weaver, Abraham	1	Ove
Absolem	52	Wll
Adam	52	Wll
Benjamin	57	Dav
Benjamin	81	Rut
Benjamin	351	Whi
Benjamin	49	Wll
Catharine	33	Fra
Craven	23	Lin
Daniel	33	Fra
George	394	Wil
Hartwell	17	Dic
Henry	33	Fra
Henry	26	Jac
Jacob	296	War
James	125	Ste
John	33	Fra
John	7	Gil
John	19	Hic
John [2]	362	Whi
Mark	13	Law
Orin D.	57	Dav
Peter	19	Hic
Samuel	351	Whi
William	50	Bed
William	26	Mon
William	16	Ove
William, Senr.	50	Bed
Wilson	7	Law
Zebedee	6	Gil
see Wiver	37	Mau
Weaxley, Samuel	71	Dav
Web, Joseph	68	Mau
Webb, Aaron	75	Rut
Abel	75	Rut

Webb (cont.)
Abel 97 Rut
Burrel 126 Ste
Cary 66 Dav
Chisley 311 War
Claiborne 12 Hic
Cornelious 21 Lin
Daniel 28 Rob
Danl. 185 Sum
Elisha 355 Whi
Elizabeth 27 Rob
Ellis 302 War
George 123 Ste
George 415 Wil
George, Senr. 129 Ste
Henry 43 Lin
Hiram 43 Lin
Icim 397 Wil
James 6 Har
James 3 Ove
James 302 War
Jesse 34 Fra
Jesse 279 War
Jessee 344 Whi
John 17 Bed
John 22 Hic
John 16 Ove
John 82 Rut
John 123 Ste
John 184 Sum
John 279 War
John 286 War
John 8 Way
John 377 Wil
John 58 Wll
John B. 304 War
Jordon 184 Sum
Joshua 296 War
Josiah 81 Rut
Julius 130 Ste
Julius 302 War
Kendle 80 Dav
Larkin 11 Gil
Littleberry 15 Gil
Mary 358 Whi
Morris 12 Gil
Moses 26 Jac
Reuben 34 Lin
Richard 379 Wil
Robert 9 Dic
Robert 12 Gil
Robert 1 Hum
Robert 355 Whi
Rutherford 5 Ove
Sally 15 Hic
Samuel 29 Rob
Samuel 129 Ste
Smith 29 Rob
Thomas 15 Gil
Thomas 3 Har
William 4 Dic
William 11 Gil
William 15 Gil

Webb (cont.)
William 58 Mau
William 78 Rut
William 304 War
William 365 Whi
William F. 377 Wil
William S. 56 Wll
Webber, George 66 Mau
John 86 Dav
John 78 Rut
Seth 78 Rut
see Wibber
Webrley, Daniel 75 Dav
Webster, George 48 Mau
John 60 Smi
Jonathan 33 Mau
Katahrine 2 Gil
Landon 48 Mau
Mary 60 Smi
Sally 185 Sum
Thomas 13 Wll
William 110 Ste
Weddle, George 22 Wll
William 21 Wll
Weeb, John 29 Mau
Weeks, Benjn. 125 Ste
Charles 34 Fra
Hughet 119 Ste
John 20 Gil
Stephen 123 Ste
William 370 Whi
Weidemeyer, Lewis 1 Wll
Weight, Elizabeth 7 Hic
Thompson 6 Hic
William 4 Hic
Weights, Eli 64 Dav
Weir, Allen 291 War
George 20 Gil
Hugh 20 Gil
Isham 284 War
Margaret 20 Gil
Roland 284 War
Samuel 20 Gil
Welch, Archibald 359 Whi
George 368 Whi
Isaac 352 Whi
James 12 Law
James 368 Whi
James 397 Wil
John 26 Jac
John 27 Jac
John 11 Law
Jonathan 17 Lin
Lewis 4 Per
Maryan 365 Whi
Mathias 365 Whi
Nicholas 16 Gil
Nicholas 21 Way
Richard 11 Lin
Sarah 2 Law
Thomas 78 Dav
Thomas 9 Law
Thomas 100 Rut

Welch (cont.)		
Thomas	365	Whi
William	11	Har
William	10	Lin
William, Junr.	2	Law
William, Senr.	10	Law
Welden, Jacob	58	Smi
Weldin, Daniel	10	Ove
Welds, Maredth	43	Mau
Welet, John	27	Jac
Well, Wilson	401	Wil
Wellborn, Enoch	137	Sum
Wellet, William	10	Wll
Wellis, George	59	Wll
Wells, Aaron	9	Lin
Abner	40	Lin
Anthony	40	Lin
Brian	46	Wll
David	8	Hum
David	37	Mau
Hayder E.	4	Mon
James	34	Fra
John	34	Fra
John	11	Gil
John	35	Rob
John J.	5	Dic
Lewis	11	Rob
Nancy	13	Dic
Philip	52	Wll
R. W.	114	Ste
Ransom	10	Gil
Roland W.	114	Ste
Samuel	40	Lin
Samuel	9	Wll
Sarah	100	Rut
Thomas	5	Bed
Thomas	10	Gil
Thomas	35	Rob
Thomas	9	Wll
Thomas	36	Wll
William	2	Gil
William	101	Rut
William	36	Wll
William H.	5	Wll
Welsh, Henry	1	Per
Wembs, Mary	43	Mau
Wemms, John	183	Sum
Wendel, David	73	Rut
Wendle, Joseph H.	20	Ove
Wenset, Wiley	55	Wll
Wenton, Robert	2	Ove
Were, John	391	Wil
Wesley, William	36	Wll
Wesmorland, John	14	Ove
Sarah	6	Ove
West, Andrew	185	Sum
Andrew N.	87	Rut
Bassil	84	Rut
Benjamin	59	Smi
David	18	Rob
Eastan	70	Mau
Edward	61	Smi
Elizabeth	13	Dic
West (cont.)		
Erwin	27	Jac
George	19	Lin
George	27	Mon
George	98	Rut
George A.	14	Rob
George A.	36	Rob
Henry	20	Wll
Isaac	12	Dic
Isaac	11	Ove
Isaac	65	Wll
Jacob	183	Sum
James	48	Lin
James	13	Ove
James	80	Rut
James	122	Ste
Jeptha	26	Jac
Jesse	11	Gil
Jesse	61	Smi
John	12	Dic
John	33	Fra
John	35	Lin
John	16	Ove
John	182	Sum
John	185	Sum
John	305	War
John	32	Wll
John	55	Wll
John B.	80	Dav
John F.	60	Smi
John S.	65	Wll
Joseph	18	Gil
Levi	98	Rut
Logan	185	Sum
Margaret	185	Sum
Michael	89	Rut
Miles	58	Smi
Nancy	42	Mau
Nancy	18	Ove
Peter	278	War
Polley	16	Dic
Rhodes	7	Lin
Robert	4	Dic
Robert	183	Sum
Simeon	9	Wll
Stephin	11	Ove
Thomas	19	Rob
Thomas	60	Smi
Thomas S.	20	Wll
William	13	Dic
William	27	Jac
Wm.	106	She
Westall, Thomas	33	Fra
Westbrooks, Thos.	96	Dav
Wheatly	94	Dav
Wester, Hartwell	6	Law
Westerman, Charles	18	Bed
Charles W.	25	Lin
John	16	Bed
Polly	17	Bed
Western, William	17	Ove
Westley, Josiah	17	Mon
Westman, William	67	Mau

Westmoreland, Elizabeth	14	Gil
see Wesmorland		
Weston, Thomas	76	Dav
Wetherspoon, Alexander	414	Wil
Wetson see Wilson		
Wett, Jesse	8	Ove
Wever, John	8	Per
Joshua	1	Per
Whailey, Daniel	33	Fra
Elijah	60	Smi
Thomas	60	Smi
Whaley, Phelin	46	Bed
Thomas	341	Whi
Whaling, John	34	Fra
Whallingworth, Jacob	413	Wil
James	413	Wil
John	413	Wil
Rebecca	413	Wil
Wharry, David	390	Wil
Wharton, George	70	Dav
Jesse	61	Dav
Joshua	12	Law
Sally	12	Law
Samuel J.	86	Dav
Sherod	12	Hic
Wheat, John, Sen.	28	Wll
Wheeler, Benjamin	6	Gil
Benjamine	356	Whi
Edward	403	Wil
Hezekiah	94	Rut
James	35	Bed
James	6	Gil
James T.	9	Gil
James W.	9	Gil
John	26	Jac
John	25	Lin
John, Sr.	26	Jac
Jubal	26	Jac
Margaret	94	Rut
Nancy	410	Wil
Nathen	27	Bed
William	35	Bed
William	26	Jac
William	356	Whi
Wheelis, Aquilla	12	Mon
Harbert	4	Mon
Joseph	12	Mon
Wheeller, Thomas	27	Bed
Wheelor, Drummer	410	Wil
Wheetley, William	3	Hum
Whellow, Henry	417	Wil
Whenry see Wherry		
Wherry, Jackson	103	Rut
Jonathan	102	Rut
William	184	Sum
William T.	182	Sum
Whetington, John	183	Sum
Whetson, Abraham	378	Wil
Jeremiah	366	Whi
see Whilson, Whitson		
Whidby, Polly	18	Wll
Whilley, Pearce	414	Wil
Whilson, John	400	Wil

Whilton, George	284	War
Whinery, Abraham	43	Bed
Abram	1	Bed
Whiny, Sunney	389	Wil
Whipple, Pray H.	5	Mon
William	18	Mon
Whit, William	33	Fra
Whitaker, Benjamin	30	Lin
Benjamin W.	29	Lin
John	29	Lin
John J.	29	Lin
Joseph	29	Lin
Mark	29	Lin
Thomas	30	Lin
see Whiticher		
Whitby, Polly	20	Wll
White, Abrahan	379	Wil
Adam	41	Wll
Alexander	33	Fra
Allen	61	Mau
Amos	103	Rut
Andrew	27	Jac
Anny	61	Smi
Archibald	27	Jac
Bartholomew	59	Smi
Benj.	26	Jac
Benjamin	22	Gil
Benjamin	8	Per
Benjamin	3	Wll
Benjimin	27	Mau
Betsey	35	Bed
Bryant	59	Smi
Caleb	8	Gil
Camm G.	10	Lin
Cato	405	Wil
Chapman	8	Wll
Charles	128	Ste
Charles	379	Wil
Charles	35	Wll
Chs.	183	Sum
Cornelius D.	7	Hic
Daniel	2	Per
Daniel	51	Wll
David	9	Gil
David	2	Per
Demsey	125	Ste
Eli	186	Sum
Elijah	4	Gil
Elisha	18	Gil
Elizabeth	6	Gil
Elizabeth	80	Rut
Epa	26	Wll
Frances	90	Rut
George	403	Wil
George	41	Wll
George	62	Wll
Grinip	8	Per
Hamelton	65	Mau
Hannah	18	Hic
Henry	90	Dav
Henry	3	Gil
Henry	2	Per
Henry	125	Ste

White (cont.)
Henry, Jr. 97 Dav
Hiram M. 31 Lin
Holand L. 3 Wll
Hugh 8 Gil
Isaiah 8 Har
Jabas 72 Dav
Jackson 61 Smi
James 13 Bed
James 10 Hum
James 27 Jac
James 24 Lin
James 62 Mau
James, Jun. 60 Smi
James, Sen. 60 Smi
Jane 20 Wll
Jesse 3 Hic
John 18 Bed
John 86 Dav
John 34 Fra
John 9 Gil
John 1 Har
John 8 Har
John 10 Har
John 11 Hum
John 27 Lin
John 29 Lin
John 131 Ste
John 183 Sum
John 292 War
John 349 Whi
John 361 Whi
John 372 Whi
John 378 Wil
John 404 Wil
John 3 Wll
John 20 Wll
John, Jur. 184 Sum
John, Sen. 19 Wll
John ... 114 Wil
John J. 137 Sum
John L. 396 Wil
Jonathan 32 Wll
Joseph 67 Dav
Joseph 2 Ove
Joshua 3 Bed
Joshua 7 Dic
Josiah 13 Way
Levi 98 Rut
Littleberry 389 Wil
Mary 62 Smi
Meady 65 Mau
Nathan 183 Sum
Noah 65 Mau
Owen 185 Sum
Peter 27 Jac
Peter 40 Mau
Pleasent 356 Whi
Polly 184 Sum
Robert 26 Jac
Robert 2 Per
Robert 183 Sum
Robert 34 Wll

White (cont.)
Robert 42 Wll
Robert, Jur. 184 Sum
Robert M. 5 Lin
Robt. M. 127 Ste
Samuel 33 Bed
Samuel 29 Lin
Samuel 22 Mon
Samuel 50 Wll
Serrel 21 Bed
Sion 21 Bed
Sion 52 Mau
Stephen 90 Rut
Stephen 104 Rut
Stephen 182 Sum
Tho. 185 Sum
Thomas 34 Bed
Thomas 32 Fra
Thomas 7 Gil
Thomas 17 Gil
Thomas 7 Hum
Thomas 59 Mau
Thomas 26 Rob
Thomas 60 Smi
Thomas 182 Sum
Thomas 7 Way
Thomas 26 Wll
Thomas 62 Wll
Thos. 123 Ste
Thos. B. 7 Hic
Thos. B. 22 Mon
Uriah 45 Lin
Whitby 94 Dav
William 85 Dav
William 86 Dav
William 8 Dic
William 6 Gil
William 47 Lin
William 35 Mau
William 91 Rut
William 61 Smi
William 183 Sum
William 185 Sum
William 13 Way
William 388 Wil
William 39 Wll
William 51 Wll
William, Jr. 184 Sum
William, Mr. 1 Law
William H. 68 Dav
William S. 21 Mon
Willie 131 Ste
Willis 89 Dav
Wilson 88 Dav
Woodson P. 340 Whi
Woodson P. 371 Whi
Zacheriah 2 Har
see Whit, Whte
Whiteacre, David 312 War
Whiteaker, Ann 365 Whi
Mark 352 Whi
William 366 Whi
Whitecotton, James 2 Ove

Name	Page	County
Whitehead, A.	117	Ste
Benjamin	30	Mon
Ebenezer	6	Dic
Edmund	57	Smi
Edward	113	Ste
Jacob	41	Wll
John	50	Bed
John	12	Hum
Lazarus	41	Wll
Robert	15	Ove
Robert	14	Rob
William	25	Mon
Whiteit, James	63	Dav
Whiteley, Joseph	96	Rut
Sally	319	War
Whitenbarger, Peter	356	Whi
Whitenbergh, Milly	28	Lin
Whites, Esau	113	Ste
Nelson	66	Dav
William	24	Lin
Whiteside, David	96	Dav
James	20	Ove
Jonathan	20	Ove
William	183	Sum
Whitesides, James	26	Mon
Jenkin	60	Dav
Samuel	68	Mau
Thomas	68	Mau
Whitesids, Abrain	67	Mau
Abreham	59	Mau
Addam	32	Mau
Hugh	65	Mau
John	35	Mau
Jonathan	34	Mau
Robbart	35	Mau
Samuel	34	Mau
William [2]	35	Mau
Whitfield, Bryan	3	Mon
Harison	18	Wll
John	8	Gil
John	88	Rut
John	18	Wll
Lewis	3	Mon
Mathew	94	Rut
Needham	2	Mon
Wilkins	4	Wll
Willis	94	Rut
Wm.	109	Ste
Wm., Junr.	110	Ste
Whitford, William	116	Ste
Whither, John	48	Mau
Whithorn, George	61	Wll
Whiticher, John	10	Ove
Whiticker, Philip	26	Jac
Whitington, Benja.	185	Sum
Beverly	23	Mon
William	27	Mon
Whitis, Joshua	114	Ste
Whitker, Mark	394	Wil
Whitledge, Robert	5	Mon
Whitley, Alexander	45	Lin
Andrew	27	Jac
Charles	127	Ste
Whitley (cont.)		
Exum	58	Smi
James, Jr.	60	Smi
Jonas, Sen.	58	Smi
Jonathan	80	Rut
Macus	45	Lin
Rebecca	80	Rut
Sharp	363	Whi
Taylor	58	Smi
Thomas	55	Mau
Thomas	59	Smi
William	94	Rut
Willie	58	Smi
Whitlock, Bowen	300	War
Charles	38	Wll
Jeremiah	61	Smi
John	417	Wil
Joseph	137	Sum
Thomas	307	War
Whitlow, William	19	Ove
see Whellow		
Whitman, Henrey N.	107	She
Piety	32	Fra
Whitmile, Thornton C.	379	Wil
Whitmill, Thomas	2	Dic
Whitmon, John	13	Gil
Whitmore, Clemment	83	Dav
William	83	Dav
Whitney, Edward	78	Dav
Sally	59	Smi
William O.	52	Bed
Whitsall, Peter	34	Lin
Whitset, William D.	91	Dav
Whitsett, James M.	86	Dav
Joseph	99	Rut
Thomas	91	Rut
Whitsitt, William	26	Mau
Whitson, ...n [Ann?]	62	Mau
Abraham	113	Wil
Allen	6	Per
Ludy	380	Wil
Samuel	62	Mau
William	62	Mau
Whitt, David	45	Lin
Whitted, William	33	Mau
Whittemore, Patsey	101	Rut
William	101	Rut
Whitten, John	298	War
Whittenton, Joseph	58	Smi
Whittey, Britton	382	Wil
Whittington, Azariah	183	Sum
Whittle, Nimon	97	Rut
Whittock, Thomas	415	Wil
Whitton, Ambrose	4	Har
Robert	419	Wil
William	33	Fra
Whitwell, Robert	10	Dic
Thos.	23	Hic
Wm.	23	Hic
Whitworth, Abraham	75	Rut
Clabourn	39	Lin
Edward	10	Bed
Elizabeth	13	Bed

Whitworth (cont.)
Fendal 11 Mon
James 183 Sum
James 397 Wil
John 10 Bed
John 11 Mon
Philomon 14 Mon
Saml. 186 Sum
Thomas 31 Lin
Thomas 39 Lin
Thomas 4 Ove
William 75 Rut
Whorton, Abraham 32 Fra
Abram 33 Fra
Archibald 33 Fra
Whte, Anderson 2 Hum
Joel 2 Per
Whullis, Elijah 379 Wil
Whuston, Edward R. 26 Mau
Whyte, Polly 89 Dav
Robert 79 Dav
Wiatt, Robert 118 Ste
Wibber, Benjamin 87 Rut
Wickham, John 27 Mon
Wickum, Nathan 122 Ste
Wideman, Henery 31 Mau
Wierier, John 50 Mau
Wiggens, John 34 Wll
Wiggin, Harrol 34 Fra
John P. 33 Fra
Thomas D. 33 Fra
Wiggins, Austin 26 Mon
Cary 2 Dic
William 22 Mon
Wigginton, Archelles 183 Sum
George 185 Sum
Nathl. 183 Sum
William 183 Sum
Wiggs, John 33 Wll
Wightman, William 53 Bed
Wigle, Ruth 394 Wil
Wigs, Mathew 46 Mau
Wilberington, Nancy 61 Dav
Wilbourn, Alexander 33 Fra
Elijah 34 Fra
Harris 99 Rut
John 2 Hic
Michael 85 Rut
Robert 62 Smi
Thomas 32 Fra
Thomas 58 Smi
Wilburn, Burrell 6 Hic
Elliott 16 Way
Harris 83 Rut
Wilcher, Thomas 282 War
Wilcox, Charles B. 111 Ste
James 89 Dav
John E. 4 Mon
Mary 84 Dav
Wilcoxon, Aaron 17 Gil
David [2] 17 Gil
Isaac 17 Gil
Wilder, Charles 59 Smi
Wilder (cont.)
Lee 32 Fra
Marth 61 Dav
Nathaniel 33 Fra
Wilebur, Archibald 279 War
Wileman, Benjamin 33 Fra
William 33 Fra
Wiley, Alexander 65 Mau
James 8 Lin
Jane 8 Lin
John 69 Mau
Moses 69 Mau
Moses A. 70 Mau
Robbert 65 Mau
William 9 Hic
Wilhait, Jacob 28 Bed
Lewis 28 Bed
Wilhight, Reubin 351 Whi
Wilhoit, Jacob, Senr. 47 Bed
Sally 47 Bed
Wiliams, Polly 27 Jac
Wilie, John 27 Jac
Wilkas see Willias
Wilkenson, Newton 24 Lin
Wilkerson, Archibald 57 Smi
Brooks 58 Smi
D. B. 21 Bed
Elijah 41 Bed
James 104 Rut
James 46 Wll
John 5 Dic
Rachel 61 Smi
Robert 104 Rut
Turner 58 Smi
William 104 Rut
William [2] 25 Wll
Wilkes, John 44 Mau
Minor 28 Mau
Wilkeson, John 79 Rut
Martha W. 68 Dav
Wilkey, David 8 Ove
Wilkins, Clement, Jr. 13 Hic
Clement, Sr. 13 Hic
James 33 Lin
James 57 Mau
James 66 Wll
Jas. 13 Hic
Richd. 13 Hic
Thomas 33 Fra
Thos. 13 Hic
William 10 Lin
William 103 Rut
Willis 7 Gil
Willis 26 Rob
Wilkinson, Benja. 184 Sum
Benjamin 34 Fra
Daniel 402 Wil
James 391 Wil
John 33 Fra
John 402 Wil
Polly 80 Dav
Stephen 33 Fra
Thomas 18 Gil

Wilkinson (cont.)		
William	95	Dav
Wilkison, Esther	26	Jac
Johnathon	89	Dav
Josep B.	317	War
Mary	33	Rob
Meredith	386	Wil
Thomas	27	Jac
Thos.	27	Jac
Townsend	183	Sum
William	89	Dav
see Withson		
Wilks, Benjamin	10	Hum
Benjmin	27	Mau
Daniel	28	Mau
Daniel	64	Wll
Edman	44	Mau
John	10	Hum
John [2]	44	Mau
John	62	Mau
John	184	Sum
John B.	42	Mau
Miner	44	Mau
Miner	45	Mau
Richard	41	Mau
Richard	44	Mau
Richard S.	184	Sum
Richd., Senr.	186	Sum
Richd. S., Jur.	184	Sum
Thomas	44	Mau
William	44	Mau
William	184	Sum
Wilkson, William	72	Dav
Willard, William	13	Ove
William	10	Ove
Willborn, Wm.	2	Lin
Willcox, Thomas	84	Dav
Willeford, Thos.	22	Mon
William L.	41	Mau
Willis	56	Mau
Willet, Richard	49	Wll
Willett, Edward	26	Lin
Willey, John	12	Dic
John B.	18	Hic
William, Sen.	3	Dic
Willis	6	Dic
Willhouse, Robt.	5	Law
William, John	21	Mon
Williams, Aaron	8	Bed
Abel	87	Dav
Abisha	182	Sum
Absalom	30	Mon
Absolom	353	Whi
Alexr. M.	35	Mau
Allen	7	Gil
Allen	125	Ste
Ambrose	9	Har
Amos	390	Wil
Anderson	36	Mau
Andrew	15	Bed
Ann	6	Lin
Anthony	185	Sum
Arthur	27	Rob
Williams (cont.)		
Barnett	412	Wil
Benjamin	5	Hic
Benjn.	117	Ste
Bennet	61	Smi
Berry	128	Ste
Betsy	308	War
Beverly	381	Wil
Burgess	22	Gil
Caleb	109	Ste
Cely	418	Wil
Charity	67	Dav
Charity	17	Mon
Charles	1	Har
Charles	11	Har
Charles	3	Hum
Charles	20	Lin
Charles	60	Smi
Christopher	62	Dav
Christopher	16	Rob
Dan	27	Mau
Daniel	41	Bed
Daniel	5	Dic
Daniel H.	5	Dic
David	33	Bed
David	10	Gil
David	50	Mau
David	83	Rut
David	59	Smi
David	183	Sum
David	288	War
David	57	Wll
Dickinson	33	Wll
Edith	110	Ste
Edman	36	Mau
Edward	60	Mau
Edward [2]	182	Sum
Elbert	420	Wil
Elijah	44	Bed
Elijah	33	Fra
Elisha	3	Dic
Elisha	113	Ste
Elisha	410	Wil
Elisha	35	Wll
Elishua	89	Dav
Elizabeth	22	Gil
Elizabeth	19	Hic
Elizabeth	34	Rob
Elizabeth	101	Rut
Ephr.	130	Ste
Ephr.	131	Ste
Ethelbert C.	17	Rob
Etheldrod	14	Hum
Evans	58	Smi
Francis	15	Ove
Garland	23	Rob
George	5	Rob
George	77	Rut
George	57	Smi
George W.	344	Whi
Gideon	50	Mau
Gilbert	60	Smi
Giles	60	Smi

Williams (cont.)
Gray 8 Mon
Green 3 Law
Green 379 Wil
Green B. 36 Mau
Griffith 28 Rob
Hannah 33 Fra
Hardin 9 Har
Hardin 311 War
Hector 182 Sum
Henry 16 Bed
Henry 2 Mon
Henry 9 Mon
Henry 58 Smi
Henry 185 Sum
Henry 371 Whi
Henry 23 Wll
Henry 65 Wll
Hickman 3 Law
Humphery 107 She
Isaac 14 Gil
Isaac 22 Gil
Isaac 44 Mau
Isaac 97 Rut
Isaac 284 War
Isaac 416 Wil
Isaac 32 Wll
Isaac, free man of Colour 37 Wll
Isham 61 Smi
Ishmal 51 Mau
Jadock 80 Dav
James 16 Bed
James 26 Jac
James 27 Jac
James 2 Law
James 62 Mau
James 61 Smi
James 109 Ste
James 184 Sum
James 7 Way
James 355 Whi
James 416 Wil
James 13 Wll
James 35 Wll
James 66 Wll
James A. 9 Har
James B. 72 Dav
James S. 26 Wll
Jas. R. 117 Ste
Jason 80 Rut
Jason 86 Rut
Jeptha 416 Wil
Jeremiah 10 Rob
Jeremiah 343 Whi
Jesse 3 Law
Jesse 35 Rob
Jesse 96 Rut
Jesse 101 Rut
Jesse 368 Whi
Jesse 387 Wil
Jesse C. 408 Wil
Jesse E. 54 Wll
Jessee 345 Whi

Williams (cont.)
Jessee 371 Whi
Jessey 26 Mau
John 8 Bed
John 42 Bed
John 33 Fra
John 2 Gil
John 9 Har
John 24 Hic
John 26 Jac
John 17 Lin
John 37 Lin
John 39 Mau
John 52 Mau
John 67 Mau
John 6 Mon
John 24 Mon
John 12 Ove
John 22 Rob
John 27 Rob
John 79 Rut
John 57 Smi
John 59 Smi
John 61 Smi
John 114 Ste
John 184 Sum
John [2] 185 Sum
John 290 War
John 310 War
John 361 Whi
John 403 Wil
John 33 Wll
John 47 Wll
John 56 Wll
John 60 Wll
John B. 7 Gil
John C. 84 Dav
John H. 9 Rob
John H. 83 Rut
John J. 10 Mon
John J. 12 Ove
John P. 60 Smi
John R. 71 Dav
John S. 6 Ove
John W. 33 Fra
Jona. 184 Sum
Jonathan 62 Mau
Jones 95 Dav
Jones 119 Ste
Jones R. [B. ?] 120 Ste
Joseph 6 Dic
Joseph 9 Gil
Joseph 9 Har
Joseph 182 Sum
Joseph 418 Wil
Joseph 59 Wll
Joseph 1 Hum
Joshua 65 Mau
Josiah 74 Dav
Josiah 347 Whi
Julus 419 Wil
Keland 8 Ove
Lacy 24 Hic

Williams (cont.)
Lemy 114 Ste
Lewellen 83 Rut
Lewis 306 War
Lewis 308 War
M. 121 Ste
M. 128 Ste
Margaret 14 Hic
Margaret 410 Wil
Martha 12 Gil
Mary, Mrs. 403 Wil
Matthew 32 Mon
Matthew 28 Rob
Meredith 15 Mon
Milberry 22 Rob
Miles 117 Ste
Morgan 62 Smi
Moses 5 Law
Mosus 416 Wil
Nancy 33 Fra
Nancy 59 Smi
Nancy 185 Sum
Nathan 97 Dav
Nathan 18 Ove
Nathan 81 Rut
Nathaniel 389 Wil
Nathaniel 410 Wil
Nathaniel W. 57 Smi
Newburn 111 Ste
Nicholas 64 Wll
Noris 64 Mau
Oliver 47 Lin
Patience 87 Dav
Paul 32 Fra
Permenas 36 Mau
Peter 59 Smi
Peter 2 Wll
Philip 15 Ove
Polly 313 War
Rachell 92 Dav
Ralph 27 Bed
Rebecca 2 Gil
Richard 66 Dav
Richard 11 Rob
Richard 15 Rob
Richd. F. 9 Mon
Robbert 64 Mau
Robert 65 Dav
Robert 58 Smi
Robert 59 Smi
Robert B. 61 Smi
Rowling 5 Per
Sally 114 Ste
Saml. 118 Ste
Saml. 17 Way
Sampson 26 Jac
Samuel 46 Bed
Samuel 28 Mau
Samuel 1 Ove
Samuel 5 Rob
Samuel 60 Smi
Samuel 54 Wll
Samuel 65 Wll

Williams (cont.)
Samuel H. 35 Mau
Samuel H. 364 Whi
Sarah 71 Dav
Sarah 398 Wil
Sarah M. 23 Gil
Septemus 15 Mon
Sherard 32 Fra
Silas M. 57 Smi
Simon 87 Dav
Simon 33 Fra
Simon 59 Smi
Solomon 398 Wil
Susanah 94 Dav
Synthia 95 Dav
Thomas 39 Bed
Thomas 94 Dav
Thomas 9 Dic
Thomas 9 Gil
Thomas 3 Law
Thomas 9 Lin
Thomas 39 Mau
Thomas 66 Mau
Thomas 9 Rob
Thomas 15 Rob
Thomas 101 Rut
Thomas 57 Smi
Thomas 184 Sum
Thomas 349 Whi
Thomas 362 Whi
Thomas 364 Whi
Thomas, Jr. 397 Wil
Thomas, Ser. 397 Wil
Thomas A. 60 Smi
Thos. 10 Mon
Tobias 61 Smi
Truman 83 Dav
Turner 66 Dav
Vincent 12 Rob
Walker 400 Wil
William 69 Dav
William 71 Dav
William 5 Dic
William 32 Fra
William 15 Gil
William 26 Jac
William 13 Law
William 19 Lin
William 33 Lin
William 31 Mau
William 34 Mau
William 38 Mau
William 52 Mau
William 64 Mau
William 19 Rob
William 34 Rob
William 86 Rut
William 57 Smi
William 60 Smi
William 184 Sum
William 185 Sum
William 301 War
William 320 War

Williams (cont.)		
William	347	Whi
William	11	Wll
William	40	Wll
William, Jun.	60	Smi
William E.	25	Mon
William L.	18	Mon
Williamson	390	Wil
Wilson	71	Dav
Winny	33	Fra
Wm.	113	Ste
Wm.	10	Way
see Wiliams, Willcox		
Williamson, Benjamin	6	Wll
Burwell M.	27	Mon
Charita	343	Whi
David	6	Mon
Edmund	12	Gil
George	83	Dav
George	4	Hic
George	385	Wil
James	69	Dav
James	26	Jac
James	59	Smi
Jesse	4	Hic
John	20	Bed
John	68	Dav
John	6	Lin
John	384	Wil
John	385	Wil
John G.	16	Wll
Joseph	82	Dav
Joseph	26	Jac
Joseph	6	Lin
Lewis	13	Gil
Littleton	98	Rut
Ludy	97	Rut
Martha	20	Wll
Pulliam	58	Smi
Rholand	103	Rut
Sally	26	Jac
Samuel	19	Gil
Seth	12	Gil
Thomas	87	Dav
Thomas	35	Rob
Thomas	385	Wil
William H.	38	Mau
Willians, Richard	33	Mau
Williard, Allegood	398	Wil
Beverly	414	Wil
John	414	Wil
Willias, Francis	33	Mau
Willie, James	19	Gil
Jonathan	9	Hic
William	12	Law
Williford, Britton	18	Gil
Hardy	18	Gil
James	408	Wil
Jeremiah	60	Smi
John	22	Mon
Jourdan	83	Rut
Jourdan	90	Rut
Simeon	76	Rut

Williford (cont.)		
Stephen	34	Fra
Thomas	34	Fra
William L.	40	Mau
Willie	18	Gil
Willims, Richard	60	Wll
Willingham, William	38	Lin
Willis, Able	2	Ove
Anderson	34	Fra
Augustain	36	Mau
Caleb	183	Sum
Cassey	33	Fra
Daniel	185	Sum
David	34	Fra
David	309	War
Edward	387	Wil
Elijah	21	Rob
Elisha	22	Mon
Elisha	21	Rob
Elizebeth	38	Mau
Harvey R.	182	Sum
Isaac	299	War
Jacob	185	Sum
Jarvis	32	Fra
Jeremiah	61	Smi
John	33	Fra
John	27	Jac
John	25	Mon
John	61	Smi
John L.	183	Sum
Joseph	34	Fra
Magar	55	Mau
Meshach	64	Mau
Moses	182	Sum
Nancy	371	Whi
Nathaniel	33	Mau
Peter	34	Fra
Sarah	185	Sum
Sherard	61	Smi
Tho.	185	Sum
Thomas	10	Lin
Vincent	61	Smi
William	46	Bed
William	58	Dav
William	27	Jac
William	32	Lin
William	61	Mau
William	59	Smi
William	61	Smi
William	281	War
Woodson	11	Mon
see Wellis		
Willises, —	24	Mau
Willison, William	405	Wil
Willoby, Sarah	60	Smi
William	59	Smi
Wills, Eliza	5	Law
James	60	Smi
John K.	314	War
William	29	Rob
William	86	Rut
Willson, John	31	Mau
Seley	31	Mau

Willson (cont.)
William C. 74 Dav
Willss, Jessey 28 Mau
Willy, Ezekiel 417 Wil
William 18 Hic
Wilmore, Henry 58 Smi
John 33 Fra
Wilmoth, William 304 War
Wilmouth, Abraham 16 Ove
Wilsford, James 18 Gil
Wilson, Aaron 11 Bed
Aaron 280 War
Aaron J. 13 Bed
Abel 10 Gil
Abel 65 Mau
Abner 19 Rob
Adam 9 Dic
Adam, Jr. 3 Hic
Adam, Senr. 10 Hic
Alexander 47 Wll
Alphonso 27 Jac
Andrew 383 Wil
Archibald 12 Gil
Benja. 183 Sum
Benjamin 19 Hic
Benjamin 38 Lin
Benjamin 1 Mon
Benjamin 17 Rob
Benjamin 90 Rut
Benjamin 102 Rut
Benjamin 412 Wil
Benjn. 127 Ste
Boon 9 Lin
Boyd 19 Gil
Catharine 20 Gil
Cornilious 54 Mau
David 50 Mau
David 60 Smi
David 122 Ste
David 184 Sum
Easther 16 Rob
Ebben 46 Bed
Elijah 58 Smi
Elizabeth 17 Hic
Elizabeth 186 Sum
Elizabeth 346 Whi
Ephraim 27 Jac
Francis 10 Gil
George 76 Dav
Gregory 65 Wll
Heartwell 350 Whi
Henry 102 Rut
Isaac 10 Gil
Israel 33 Fra
Jacob 6 Gil
James [2] 13 Bed
James 88 Dav
James 13 Gil
James 2 Hic
James 3 Hum
James 8 Lin
James 20 Lin
James 39 Lin
Wilson (cont.)
James 9 Mon
James 29 Rob
James 58 Smi
James 122 Ste
James 182 Sum
James 294 War
James 295 War
James 381 Wil
James 11 Wll
James A. 4 Bed
James M. 43 Wll
James S. 182 Sum
Jane 57 Wll
Jason 60 Wll
Jason 61 Wll
Jawel 40 Mau
Jawel 42 Mau
Jerimiah 70 Mau
Jessee 358 Whi
Jno. A. 278 War
Joel 57 Dav
John 11 Bed
John 13 Bed
John 59 Dav
John 9 Dic
John 34 Fra
John 12 Gil
John 15 Gil
John 4 Hum
John 27 Jac
John [2] 8 Lin
John 38 Lin
John 7 Ove
John 16 Ove
John 9 Rob
John 102 Rut
John 182 Sum
John 9 Wll
John 43 Wll
John A. 279 War
Jona. 182 Sum
Jonathan 282 War
Joseph 182 Sum
Joseph [2] 57 Wll
Josiah 41 Wll
Josiah 57 Wll
Juke 182 Sum
Littleberry R. 359 Whi
Lydia 34 Fra
Marcus 9 Bed
Margraret 417 Wil
Mark 9 Wll
Martin 185 Sum
Mary 6 Mon
Mary 183 Sum
Mathew 9 Lin
Mathew 183 Sum
Michael 33 Fra
Montillion W. 182 Sum
Moses 182 Sum
Nancy 5 Bed
Nelly 26 Jac

Wilson (cont.)
Peggy 33 Rob
Phillip 59 Dav
Polly 27 Jac
Randal 61 Smi
Richard 48 Bed
Richard 61 Smi
Robert 88 Dav
Robert 14 Lin
Robert 16 Lin
Robert 17 Ove
Robert 2 Per
Robert 407 Wil
Robert A. 57 Smi
Saml. 184 Sum
Samuel 6 Bed
Samuel 33 Fra
Samuel 18 Gil
Samuel 6 Ove
Samuel 3 Per
Samuel 87 Rut
Samuel 101 Rut
Samuel 347 Whi
Samuel 25 Wll
Samuel 42 Wll
Samuel H. 58 Smi
Sanford 13 Mon
Sarah 356 Whi
Sollomon 26 Jac
Stephen 183 Sum
Thomas 15 Dic
Thomas 46 Mau
Thomas 184 Sum
Thomas 348 Whi
Thomas 371 Whi
Thomas 407 Wil
Thomas 25 Wll
Thomas 39 Wll
Thomas 41 Wll
Thomas 57 Wll
Thos. 26 Jac
W. B. 26 Jac
William 9 Bed
William 31 Bed
William 59 Dav
William 88 Dav
William 32 Fra
William 34 Fra
William 2 Hic
William 13 Hum
William [2] 27 Jac
William 20 Lin
William [2] 17 Ove
William 10 Rob
William 77 Rut
William 103 Rut
William 59 Smi
William 319 War
William 348 Whi
William 42 Wll
William 61 Wll
William H. 34 Mau
William J. 59 Smi

Wilson (cont.)
Zachius 182 Sum
Zachius 183 Sum
Zaecheus 41 Wll
see Whilson, Willson
Wilton, Bartlet 27 Jac
Wily, Hugh 399 Wil
James 392 Wil
Jediah 399 Wil
Josiah 390 Wil
Wimberley, George 34 Rob
Joseph 2 Rob
M. 16 Way
Wimberly, George 112 Ste
Levy 112 Ste
Polly 58 Smi
Wimms, Piney 184 Sum
Thomas 185 Sum
Wims, John 14 Dic
Win, Philip P. 36 Mau
William 65 Mau
Winbourn, Josiah 185 Sum
Winchester, Daniel 37 Mau
Douglas 4 Har
James 186 Sum
Josep 29 Mau
Joseph 42 Mau
Sarah 184 Sum
Thomas 11 Har
Windham, William 285 War
Winfield, Joseph 3 Rob
Winford, John 32 Fra
Joseph 34 Fra
Smith 34 Fra
Winfree, John 26 Jac
Winfrey, Vallentine 71 Dav
Winfry, Mary 63 Wll
Wilson 61 Smi
Winga, Willie 9 Lin
Wingfield, Joseph 54 Mau
Wingo, William 89 Dav
Winham, Stephen 185 Sum
William 182 Sum
Winingham, Mary 54 Bed
Winkler, Ephraim 61 Smi
Jacob 33 Fra
Jacob C. 33 Fra
Winley, Isaac 31 Bed
Winn, Henry 115 Ste
James 17 Hic
James 14 Rob
John 130 Ste
John 131 Ste
Martha 63 Dav
Saml. 122 Ste
Samuel 130 Ste
Samul 33 Mau
Thomas 93 Dav
Thomas 116 Ste
Wadkin W. 14 Lin
Winnett, Norman 294 War
Winningham, David 15 Ove
Winninghand, Abraham 7 Ove

Winninghand (cont.)		
Richard	11	Ove
Winron, John	86	Rut
Winrow, Henry	55	Wll
Winscot, Robert	121	Ste
Winset, Jason	12	Wll
Milley	54	Wll
Winsett, Benjamin	389	Wil
Sela	87	Rut
Winslow, Robert	1	Mon
Winstead, John	11	Wll
Samuel	3	Wll
William	22	Wll
William C.	22	Wll
Winsted, Charles	14	Hum
Johnson	42	Mau
Winston, Anthony	75	Dav
Isaac	419	Wil
John	88	Rut
Nancy	419	Wil
Nathaniel	75	Rut
Tho.	184	Sum
William	376	Wil
Winters, Aaron	126	Ste
Caleb	2	Rob
Hiram	5	Lin
Isaac	4	Rob
James	3	Per
John	25	Mon
Lewis	129	Ste
Saml.	31	Bed
William	64	Dav
Winton, James	293	War
Stephen	307	War
Wire see Wise		
Wisdom, Francis	17	Hic
Francis	3	Way
Francis, Mr.	14	Law
John	14	Gil
John, Mr.	8	Law
Larkin	351	Whi
Pollard	14	Law
Thomas	12	Gil
William	11	Har
William	351	Whi
William, Mr.	14	Law
Wise, Henry	30	Bed
James	9	Law
Joseph	184	Sum
Joseph H.	182	Sum
Step	34	Bed
William	185	Sum
Wiseman, John	21	Lin
John	58	Smi
Nelly	33	Lin
Wisenor, Henry	26	Wll
William	87	Rut
Wisnear, William	90	Rut
Wisner, William	94	Dav
Wisnett, Jarman	101	Rut
Wit, John	58	Mau
Witcher, Asa	58	Smi
Booker	59	Smi
Witcher (cont.)		
Daniel K.	61	Smi
James, Jun.	61	Smi
James, Sen.	61	Smi
T. K.	27	Jac
Witherald, James	83	Dav
Witherly, John	6	Bed
Withers, Jesse	8	Gil
Witherspoon, Henry	304	War
John	4	Wll
Withro, Elizabeth	61	Smi
Withrow, James	279	War
Richard	279	War
Withson, Mary	311	War
see Wilkison		
Witt, Jesse	34	Fra
John	358	Whi
Lucy	34	Fra
Rewben	184	Sum
Thomas	3	Lin
Witts, Silas	300	War
Wiver, John	44	Mau
John	46	Mau
Marthue	46	Mau
Wix, Gamblin	18	Ove
Gideon	8	Ove
Reuben	8	Ove
Wizeman, Jonathan	59	Smi
Wodron, Littleton	183	Sum
Wofferd, Jas.	117	Ste
John	116	Ste
Wm.	125	Ste
Woisor see Worsor		
Woldron, Joseph	183	Sum
see Wodron		
Wolf, George	7	Law
Henry	308	War
John	128	Ste
Peter	24	Lin
Polly	8	Bed
Wolfe, William	21	Wll
Wolfolk, Joseph	15	Mon
Wollard, Churchil	30	Mau
Williba	30	Mau
Wolsey, Jeramiah	17	Ove
Wolvedg, Matthew	405	Wil
Wolverton, James	64	Mau
Womack, Elijah	407	Wil
James	296	War
Lucinda	129	Ste
see Wam(m)ack, Wormack, Wornack		
Wommack, Catharine	57	Smi
James	59	Smi
Womoc, Nathaniel	57	Wll
Wood, A. S.	115	Wil
Ann	185	Sum
Archibald	295	War
Bartholomew	308	War
Christopher	54	Wll
Chs.	185	Sum
Cirtis	29	Mau
Custis	9	Lin
Felix G.	8	Hum

Wood (cont.)
Francis 58 Smi
Icim 402 Wil
Isaac 5 Bed
Isaac 62 Smi
Isham 57 Smi
James 10 Gil
James 102 Rut
James [3] 57 Smi
James 295 War
James 404 Wil
James 409 Wil
Jesse 7 Ove
John 5 Hum
John [2] 57 Smi
John 183 Sum
John 380 Wil
John 54 Wll
John 59 Wll
John H. 25 Lin
John J. 60 Smi
Johnson 11 Wll
Josiah 58 Smi
Josiah 380 Wil
Josiah 7 Wll
Lott 185 Sum
Mahlon 13 Hum
Mason 58 Smi
Nancy 3 Hum
Owen 80 Rut
Owen L. 89 Rut
Polly 12 Hum
Reuben 82 Rut
Reuben 113 Wil
Ribon 393 Wil
Robert 96 Dav
Robert 131 Ste
Squire 59 Smi
Tho. 183 Sum
Thomas 99 Rut
Thomas 57 Smi
Thomas 58 Smi
Thomas 301 War
Thompson 15 Hic
Vincent 59 Smi
Vincent 185 Sum
Water 10 Har
West 1 Per
William 34 Fra
William 12 Hum
William 12 Lin
William 33 Lin
William 295 War
William 318 War
William B. 58 Smi
Zeddock 25 Bed
see James, Ottwood, Ward, Word
Woodall, Christopher 184 Sum
Esther 42 Lin
James 42 Lin
John C. 6 Hum
Joseph 318 War
Martha 44 Lin
Woodall (cont.)
Overton 58 Smi
Suckey 52 Mau
William 182 Sum
William 185 Sum
William 290 War
William, Jr. 182 Sum
Woodard, Asa 17 Rob
Benjamin 94 Dav
Delila 22 Rob
Edward 88 Dav
Elisha 27 Jac
Jeremiah 24 Rob
Jesse 62 Dav
Jules 60 Mau
Micajah 27 Jac
Reuben 16 Lin
Richard 2 Rob
Samuel 47 Lin
Simeon 406 Wil
Thomas 3 Rob
William 12 Lin
William 3 Rob
Woodart, Caleb 16 Rob
Woodbine, Peter 407 Wil
Woodcock, Chesley 61 Smi
Eleanor 62 Smi
Elizabeth 62 Smi
Jesse 114 Wil
John 81 Dav
John, Sen. 62 Smi
Mark 61 Smi
Parish 62 Smi
Thomas 403 Wil
Woodfin, George 20 Gil
James 20 Gil
Nicholas 41 Bed
Nicholas 32 Lin
Samuel 41 Bed
Woodfork, William 26 Jac
Woodley, John 292 War
Woodlie, Jacob 282 War
Woodmore, James 58 Smi
Woodrue, John 402 Wil
Woodruff, Benjamin S. 17 Lin
George 21 Wll
Howel S. 20 Wll
Jesse 37 Lin
Joseph 15 Lin
Richard 75 Rut
William 74 Rut
William R. 17 Lin
Wilson 83 Rut
Wyatt 12 Lin
Woodrum, Jacob 392 Wil
Woods, A. H. 77 Dav
Abaigail 32 Fra
Absalom 27 Jac
Absalom, Sr. 27 Jac
Alexander 27 Wll
Andrew 32 Fra
Archibald 32 Fra
Archibald 307 War

Woods (cont.)		
Charles	32	Fra
Curtis, Sr.	27	Jac
Curtis G.	27	Jac
Daniel T.	11	Gil
Edward	82	Dav
Green	282	War
Hannah	34	Fra
Hugh	82	Dav
Isaac	10	Gil
James	32	Fra
James	409	Wil
James	419	Wil
James	27	Wll
John	88	Rut
John	59	Smi
John	130	Ste
John	289	War
John	27	Wll
Jonathan	36	Wll
Joseph	77	Dav
Kesiah	76	Rut
Leonard	27	Wll
Matilda	41	Lin
Nathan	312	War
Robert	43	Bed
Robert	76	Dav
Saml.	130	Ste
Sarah	27	Wll
Smith	386	Wil
Stephen	305	War
T. J.	27	Jac
Thomas	34	Fra
Thomas	27	Jac
Thomas, Sen.	34	Fra
W. R.	77	Dav
William	32	Fra
William	17	Gil
William [2]	27	Jac
William	59	Mau
William	103	Rut
William	59	Smi
William W.	15	Gil
Woodside, John	59	Smi
Woodsides, John	33	Fra
Woodson, John	60	Smi
Joseph	5	Mon
Obediah	5	Mon
Obediah	61	Smi
Peter	18	Rob
Tucker	60	Smi
Woodward, Edward	94	Dav
Hezekiah	403	Wil
Jeremiah	10	Gil
Pitt	86	Dav
Woodware, John	292	War
Woody, John	8	Lin
Wm. B.	7	Lin
Woolam, Bartly	16	Lin
Woolard, John	406	Wil
Woolbanks, Henry	33	Fra
Owen	34	Fra
Priscilla	33	Fra
Wooldridge, Edmond	13	Hum
James [?]	64	Wll
John	6	Hic
see Wolvedg		
Woolf, Phillip	67	Dav
Woolin, John	59	Dav
Woolkey, Bennet	51	Bed
George S.	48	Bed
Woollard, Nathaniel	49	Mau
Seth	65	Mau
William S.	33	Fra
Woollen, Edward	420	Wil
Joshua	383	Wil
Moses	420	Wil
Woolsey, Samuel	5	Law
Woolvertom, John	60	Mau
William	60	Mau
Woork, Nancy	91	Dav
Woosley, Elijah	3	Bed
Wooten, Stephen	121	Ste
William	6	Law
Wooters, Leven	5	Rob
Wooton, Benjamin	284	War
George	21	Wll
Henry	22	Wll
John	34	Fra
John	57	Smi
Rodom	372	Whi
Saml.	184	Sum
William	20	Mon
William	21	Rob
Wootton, Jesse	304	War
William	307	War
Word, Cutberth	26	Bed
James	417	Wil
John	185	Sum
John	417	Wil
Thomas	281	War
Thomas H.	49	Wll
William	376	Wil
see Ward, Wood		
Work, Andrew	63	Dav
Workin, Henry	184	Sum
Workman, Benjamin	10	Ove
Isaac	19	Ove
John	18	Gil
William	9	Ove
Worley, Elijah	372	Whi
Finch	342	Whi
Francis	17	Hic
Gabriel	60	Wll
George	2	Har
Isaac	36	Bed
James	346	Whi
John	2	Har
John	367	Whi
Joseph	358	Whi
Moses	349	Whi
Moses	60	Wll
William	352	Whi
Wormack, Rachael	407	Wil
Richard	407	Wil
see Womack		

Wormely, John C.	54	Mau
Wormington, Edward	184	Sum
Wornack, David	129	Ste
Worsor, William	412	Wil
Worth, James	417	Wil
Wortham, Alphred H.	52	Mau
Charles	5	Bed
Duke	419	Wil
James L.	5	Bed
John	9	Bed
Robbert	38	Mau
Thomas	39	Mau
William	5	Bed
William	419	Wil
William H.	25	Mau
Worthan, William	8	Ove
William	13	Ove
Worthand, John [Wortham?]	1	Har
Worthley, Isaah	52	Mau
Wosley see Worley		
Wrather, Baker	96	Rut
Wray, John	16	Ove
Leonard	14	Ove
Nelson	19	Ove
Richard	11	Ove
William	17	Ove
Wren, David	73	Dav
James	21	Hic
James	6	Rob
Margaret	82	Rut
William	73	Dav
Wright, Andrew C.	40	Lin
Anna	46	Mau
Anny	381	Wil
Barthmew	5	Per
Bartlet	305	War
Benjamin	70	Dav
Benjamin	12	Hum
Benjamin	30	Lin
Betsey	37	Bed
Cassy	185	Sum
Charles	58	Dav
Charles	49	Dav
David	32	Fra
Dennis	13	Lin
Elijah	17	Lin
Elijah	185	Sum
Elizabeth	102	Rut
Elizabeth	59	Smi
Elizabeth	185	Sum
Fildin	185	Sum
Francis	185	Sum
George	36	Bed
George	61	Smi
Gideon	184	Sum
Gorge	98	Dav
Green	59	Smi
Henry	81	Rut
Henry	82	Rut
Henry	183	Sum
Hollis	57	Dav
Jacob	5	Lin
Jacob	12	Lin
James	37	Bed
Wright (cont.)		
James	85	Dav
James	42	Mau
James	89	Rut
James	94	Rut
James	99	Rut
James	182	Sum
James	384	Wil
James	399	Wil
James A.	94	Rut
Jerry	127	Ste
John	4	Bed
John	20	Bed
John	57	Dav
John	7	Dic
John	11	Gil
John	16	Gil
John	2	Hic
John	15	Ove
John M.	68	Dav
Jonathan	11	Ove
Joseph	86	Dav
Joseph	98	Dav
Joseph	102	Rut
Joseph	58	Smi
Joshua	5	Ove
Lemuel	90	Rut
Margaret	36	Bed
Margaret	79	Rut
Nancy	59	Smi
Newton	83	Dav
Obadiah	5	Ove
Patsey	98	Dav
Rewben	182	Sum
Richard	14	Bed
Richard	10	Gil
Robert	36	Bed
Robert	61	Smi
Robt.	4	Hic
Rodrick	49	Mau
Samuel	281	War
Solomon	16	Lin
Thomas	20	Bed
Thompson	81	Rut
Thompson	58	Smi
William	15	Dic
William	32	Fra
William	182	Sum
William	183	Sum
William F.	94	Rut
William R.	184	Sum
Winkfield	17	Hic
see Weight		
Wriley, Elephus	21	Way
James	21	Way
Wring, Seney	53	Mau
Writ see Avrit		
Wroten, David	31	Lin
Nehemiah	183	Sum
Wry, Absalom [2]	28	Mon
see Ury		
Wyatt, Abraham	2	Per
Francis	21	Lin
Henry	81	Rut

Wyatt (cont.)
James 21 Hic
James 3 Hum
James 2 Lin
James 124 Ste
James 127 Ste
John 2 Per
Martin 12 Hum
Martin 127 Ste
Richard 7 Lin
Samuel 2 Per
Sary 129 Ste
Thos. 30 Mon
Thos. 129 Ste
Vinson 116 Ste
William 127 Ste
William 128 Ste
Wm. 129 Ste
Z. 116 Ste
see Myatt
Wyett, John 4 Mon
Wyley, Thomas 7 Per
Wynee, James T. 183 Sum
Wynn, Elizabeth 185 Sum
Munford 184 Sum
Peter G. 34 Fra
Thomas 7 Hum
Woodson 186 Sum
Wynne, George 390 Wil
James L., Dr. 391 Wil
John 390 Wil
John 393 Wil
Rebecca 393 Wil
Redley 393 Wil
William 405 Wil
Wyott, Christopher 59 Smi
Crystina 59 Smi
Ezekiel 60 Smi

--- Y ---

Yagur, Augustine 43 Lin
Lewis 43 Lin
Samuel 44 Lin
Yaman, Lewis 62 Smi
Yancey, Alfred 11 Gil
Eli7abeth L. 8 Gil
Ezra 34 Fra
James 34 Fra
Tryon M. 17 Gil
William 33 Mau
Yancy, Austin 14 Mon
Richd. 33 Mon
Robert 186 Sum
William 11 Gil
Yandal, David 186 Sum
Saml. 186 Sum
William [2] 186 Sum
Yandell, James 393 Wil
John 86 Rut
Wilson 90 Rut
Yandle, James 70 Mau
Yangblood, A. G. 27 Mau
Yannger, Alexander 2 Bed
Yant, Jacob 27 Jac
Yarber, Rubin 35 Mau
William 2 Per
Yarboro, William 19 Ove
Yarborough, George 25 Mon
Janus 4 Mon
John 309 War
Lee 13 Hic
Moses 6 Mon
William 4 Mon
Yarbraugh, Ambrose 7 Lin
Nelson 39 Lin
Robert 7 Lin
Yarbre, Joel 4 Per
Yarbrough, Ambrose 21 Gil
Davis 111 Ste
Edward 186 Sum
George 112 Ste
James 88 Dav
John 15 Gil
John 119 Ste
Larkin 123 Ste
M. 119 Ste
Mirack 119 Ste
Nathan 118 Ste
Polly 110 Ste
William 88 Dav
William 42 Wll
William L. 74 Rut
Wm. 115 Ste
Wm. 129 Ste
Yardly, Benjamin 105 Rut
Yarrall, Stephen 387 Wil
Yates, Abraham 14 Gil
Benjamine 349 Whi
Benjamine 363 Whi
Charles 18 Rob
Elijah 28 Lin
James 16 Rob
John B. 397 Wil
John P. 18 Rob
Lewis 16 Rob
Marshall 17 Mon
Prier 10 Way
Samuel 7 Gil
Thomas 17 Rob
Thomas 20 Rob
Thomas 348 Whi
William 18 Rob
Yaunt, Abraham 52 Bed
Yoager, Benjamine 351 Whi
James 351 Whi
Joe 363 Whi
Solomon 353 Whi
Yearger, Mical 391 Wil
Yeargin, Bartlet 55 Wll
Yearly, Benjamin 34 Fra
William 34 Fra
Yearwood, James 80 Rut
John 80 Rut
William 79 Rut
Yeates, Henry T. D. 74 Dav

Yeates (cont.)		
Jessey	40	Mau
Yeatman, Thomas	77	Dav
Yeats, Daniel	59	Wll
Elisha	93	Dav
Isa	94	Dav
James [?]	1	Per
John	53	Wll
Joshua	44	Bed
Yeldington, Asa	9	Law
Yell, James	24	Bed
Jane	24	Bed
Percy	24	Bed
Yeomons, Young	8	Law
Yergin, Rebecca	62	Smi
Samuel	62	Smi
Yerkins, Gideon	97	Dav
Yerwood, Isaac	34	Fra
Yoes, James	34	Fra
John	3	Rob
Nathan	9	Rob
Yokeley, Andrew	19	Gil
Yokham, John	18	Way
Yong, Henery	34	Mau
Joseph	49	Mau
Nathanial	65	Mau
Peter	44	Mau
Thomas	56	Mau
Yonger, Thomas	45	Mau
York, James	28	Jac
James	186	Sum
James	382	Wil
John	62	Smi
Levi	34	Fra
Lucy	385	Wil
Rebecca	28	Jac
Richard	62	Smi
Richard	35	Wll
Robert	28	Jac
Samuel	28	Jac
Thomas	28	Jac
Uriah	291	War
William	28	Jac
Yorke, Edward	5	Gil
Yound, David	27	Jac
Hardy	28	Jac
Jacob	27	Jac
Mark	27	Jac
Samuel	27	Jac
Young, Abraham	2	Rob
Abraham	19	Rob
Absalom	6	Hic
Alexander	34	Fra
Alexander	102	Rut
Alexander W.	415	Wil
Ann	17	Ove
Archibald	62	Smi
Archibald	413	Wil
Archibald, Jr.	20	Gil
Archibald, Sr.	20	Gil
Beverley	385	Wil
Clarkes	417	Wil
David	403	Wil
Deborah	20	Hic
Young (cont.)		
Demelrius	383	Wil
Dorrell	26	Mon
Elie	28	Jac
Ellen	90	Dav
Ezekiel	186	Sum
Francis	384	Wil
Henry	317	War
Henry	37	Wll
Isaac	308	War
Jacob	34	Fra
Jacob F.	19	Rob
James	27	Jac
James	28	Jac
James	9	Law
James	1	Per
James	14	Rob
James	77	Rut
James	410	Wil
James T.	8	Way
Jarratt	20	Gil
Jepthah	319	War
Jesse	4	Per
John	28	Bed
John	76	Dav
John	34	Fra
John [2]	13	Gil
John	27	Jac
John	12	Lin
John	42	Lin
John	17	Ove
John	1	Per
John	62	Smi
John	343	Whi
John L.	84	Dav
Jonas	21	Hic
Jones	34	Fra
Joseph	13	Gil
Joseph	94	Rut
Joseph	186	Sum
Joseph	415	Wil
Lawrence	103	Rut
Manson	62	Smi
Mark	77	Dav
Marlin	62	Smi
Mary	5	Lin
Mary	186	Sum
Matthew	17	Ove
Milton	62	Smi
Milton, Jun.	62	Smi
Nathaniel	13	Gil
Parker	17	Ove
Partrick	406	Wil
Perry	314	War
Polly	62	Smi
Robert	27	Jac
Robert	125	Ste
Rufus	13	Gil
Sally	42	Lin
Samuel	36	Lin
Samuel	42	Lin
Samuel	16	Ove
Sepbah	315	War
Silas	34	Fra

Young (cont.)
Stephen 381 Wil
Tandy 62 Smi
Thomas 34 Fra
Thomas 1 Per
Thomas 62 Smi
Thomas D. 94 Rut
Thomas T. 34 Fra
William 44 Bed
William 17 Lin
William 35 Lin
William 92 Rut
William 102 Rut
William 315 War
William 320 War
William 356 Whi
William 381 Wil
William 8 Wll
William 63 Wll
see Youry
Youngblood, Allen 312 War
Henry 302 War
John 312 War
Thomas 79 Rut
William [2] 27 Jac
see Yangblood 27 Mau
Younger, James 53 Bed
James 34 Fra
Thomas 34 Fra
Thomas 51 Wll
Yount, Saley 23 Gil
Yount (cont.)
see Yound
Yource, Francis 78 Rut
Youree, Francis 88 Rut
Francis 186 Sum
William 93 Rut
Yourey, Nancy 186 Sum
Youry, Joseph 83 Rut
Yow, John 62 Smi
Yowel, Allen 13 Lin
Yowell, Joel 12 Lin
Yunt, John 6 Har

--- Z ---

Zablicofer, John J. 37 Mau
Zachary, Polly 62 Smi
Zacherry, James 3 Ove
Zachery, Charles 6 Per
Josiah W. 99 Rut
Zacheus, Joshua 94 Rut
Zackery, Catherine 73 Dav
Zacre, Caleb 66 Dav
Zarecor, John 186 Sum
Zearber, Margret 25 Mau
Zelner, Arnold 11 Gil
Zimmerman, Christin 11 Gil
Zivley, John H. 45 Bed
Zollicofer, George 39 Mau